21ST
CENTURY
ITALIAN-ENGLISH
ENGLISH-ITALIAN
DICTIONARY

LAUREL

Produced by The Philip Lief Group, Inc.

Published by
Dell Publishing
a division of
Bantam Doubleday Dell Publishing Group, Inc.
1540 Broadway
New York, New York 10036

Published by arrangement with
The Philip Lief Group, Inc.
6 West 20th Street
New York, NY 10011

ISBN: 0-440-22090-4

Printed in the United States of America

Published simultaneously in Canada

September 1996

10 9 8 7 6 5 4

OPM

Contents

Introduction

The *21st Century Italian-English/English-Italian Dictionary* is an invaluable reference source for today's students, business people, and travelers. Rather than wasting space on verbose, overly complicated definitions, the *21st Century Italian-English/English-Italian Dictionary* provides essential information in a brief, easy-to-use format.

The dual format of the *21st Century Italian-English/English-Italian Dictionary* eliminates the need to use two dictionaries: one volume for looking up words in Italian; and a separate one for looking up words in English. A student, for example, can use this dictionary to find the English translation to an unfamiliar Italian word—*and* to discover the correct way to express a certain English phrase in Italian. Because each entry is listed in both Italian and English, this dictionary is useful for every situation. Whether you are a business person checking the terms of a contract on an international deal, a foreign exchange student getting settled into an Italian dormitory, or a tourist trying to understand the items on a menu, the *21st Century Italian-English/English-Italian Dictionary* will help you find quick, clear translations from Italian to English—*and* from English to Italian.

Each entry in the *21st Century Italian-English/English-Italian Dictionary* appears in a concise, easy-to-follow format. The headwords are listed in alphabetical order, with a separate A-to-Z section for both the Italian-English and the English-Italian. The pronunciation, complete with syllable markings, appears in brackets after each headword, followed by its part of speech. (See Pronunciation Guide.) Entries for nouns also include an indication of gender, with *M* signifying a masculine word, *F* indicating a feminine word, and *N* representing a neuter word. Verbs are marked either *vt* (verb transitive) or *vi* (verb intransitive). Finally, a clear, succinct translation of each word appears, followed by a list of related forms and common phrases.

Reflecting current attitudes and ever-changing sensitivities in its choice of word list, definitions, translations, and pronunciations, the *21st Century Italian-English/English-Italian Dictionary* provides the most reliable and up-to-date information available. Whether for speaking, writing, or understanding, the *21st Century Italian-English/English-Italian Dictionary* successfully combines a simple, concise format with a contemporary slant, and will serve as an indispensable tool for every occasion.

Pronunciation Guide

This dictionary represents a unique approach to phonetic pronunciation. It relies on plain, or readily understood, symbols and letters. There are no Greek symbols, and most people, whether English-speaking or Italian-speaking should be able to easily sound out the words using this guide.

For English words, the pronunciation is based on conventional (unaccented) American English. The most common pronunciation has been chosen in any instance where there is more than one acceptable pronunciation.

The Italian language is very consistent with the sounds of its vowel groupings as well as consonants. This outline has very few, if any, exceptions. Vowel sounds are generally pure. The groupings in the left column are the Italian language; their English counterparts are in the right hand column.

VOWELS	ENGLISH EQUIVALENT
a = ah	cop, mop
e = eh	eh, hefty, heather
I = ee	seen, keen, mean
o = oh	phone, hope
u = oo	hoop, loop, soup

When the vowel e or o appears in a stressed syllable, its pronunciation is either open or closed. However, such pronunciation is highly regional, and thus is not very important to the user of this dictionary.

CONSONANTS		ENGLISH EQUIVALENT
b	b	*b*at, *b*e, a*b*le
c	c	*c*at
c (in Italian before e or I)	tch	sti*tch*
d	d	*d*ip, see*d*
f	f	*f*all, *ph*ysic, laug*h*
g	g	*g*ap, bi*g*
g (in Italian before e or I)	j	*j*et
gh (in Italian)	g	*g*et
gl̵ (in Italian)	lli	mi*lli*on
gn· (in Italian)	ny	ca*ny*on
h	h	*h*eat
	j	*j*ob, e*dge*
k	k	*c*at, ti*ck*, *k*in, *q*uit
l	l	*l*ip, pu*ll*, he*l*p
m	m	ha*m*, *m*at, li*m*p
n	n	*n*o, ha*n*g, bi*n*
p	p	*p*ut, u*p*
r	r	ta*r*, *r*ipe, pa*r*t
s	s	*s*it, *c*ite, his*s*
sc (in Italian before e or I)	sh	*sh*oe
t	t	ha*t*, *t*in, bu*tt*er
v	v	*v*ine, ha*v*e
w	w	*w*hy, *w*it
y		*y*es
z (English)	z	*z*oo, hi*s*, read*s*
z (Italian)	ts	stet*s*on
	ch	*ch*in, it*ch*
	sh	a*sh*, ac*ti*on
	th	*th*e, *th*at
	zh	vi*si*on
	ng	ba*n*k, a*n*ger

Basic pronunciation in this dictionary

Traditional English phonetics	Becomes	As in
VOWELS		
æ	a	cat, ask
e	ai	gate, they, air
a, a:	ah	hot, father
	au	bought, haunt, war, fall
	e	fell, head
I, I:	ee	see, tea
	I	lid, damage
aï	uy	buy, lie, height, I
o	o	no, foe, road
u	oo	loop, chute, poor
	ou	now, out, town
	oi	boy, void
	uh	but, mother, hunt
	u	bird, aloof, alert, debris book, put, could

This neutral *u* sound is one of the most common vowel sounds in English, and it is use for many unstressed syllables.

Introduzione

Il Dizionario Italiano-Inglese/Inglese-Italiano per il 21° secolo è una preziosa fonte di riferimento per gli studenti, gli uomini d'affari e i viaggiatori d'oggi. Invece di sprecare spazio con definizioni verbose e troppo complicate, *il Dizionario Italiano-Inglese/Inglese-Italiano per il 21° secolo* offre informazioni essenziali in un formato succinto, facile da usare.

Il formato doppio del *Dizionario Italiano-Inglese/Inglese-Italiano per il 21° secolo* elimina la necessità di usare due dizionari: un volume per la ricerca di parole in Italiano, e un altro volume per la ricerca di parole in Inglese. Uno studente, ad esempio, può usare questo dizionario per cercare la traduzione inglese di una parola italiana che non conosce, e scoprire il modo corretto di esprimere una data frase inglese in Italiano. Dato che ogni lemma è elencato sia in Italiano che in Inglese, questo dizionario è utile in ogni situazione: per uomini d'affari che vogliono verificare i termini di un contratto o di una transazione internazionale, per studenti stranieri in un dormitorio italiano, o per un turista che vuole capire un menu, il *Dizionario Italiano-Inglese/Inglese-Italiano per il 21° secolo* aiuterà a trovare rapidamente traduzioni chiare dall'Italiano all'Inglese e viceversa.

Ogni voce del *Dizionario Italiano-Inglese/Inglese-Italiano per il 21° secolo* appare in un formato succinto, facile da seguire. Le voci principali sono elencate in ordine alfabetico, con due sezioni A-Z separate, una per Italiano-Inglese una per Inglese-Italiano. La pronuncia, completa di divisioni in sillabe, appare in parentesi quadre dopo ciascuna voce principale, seguita dalla categoria grammaticale (vedi guida alla pronuncia). Le voci per i sostantivi comprendono anche un'indicazione del genere, con M per genere maschile, F per genere femminile e N per una parola di genere neutro. I verbi sono accompagnati da vt (verbo transitivo) o vi (verbo intransitivo). Per finire, appare una chiara e succinta traduzione di ciascuna parola, seguita da un elenco delle forme d'uso e delle frasi comuni .

Il *Dizionario Italiano-Inglese/Inglese-Italiano per il 21° secolo* riflette le tendenze moderne e una sensibilità al mondo che cambia nella sua scelta di parole, definizioni, traduzioni e pronuncia, offrendo le informazioni più attendibili e aggiornate disponibili. *Il Dizionario Italiano-Inglese/Inglese-Italiano per il 21° secolo* ha un formato semplice e succinto adatto alla vita moderna, e sarà uno strumento indispensabile in qualsiasi occasione, per parlare, scrivere o comprendere.

Guida alla pronuncia

Questo dizionario rappresenta un approccio unico alla pronuncia fonetica. Si basa su simboli e lettere semplici e di facile comprensione. Non include simboli greci, e quasi tutti, Inglesi o Italiani, dovrebbero essere in grado di enunciare facilmente le parole usando questa guida.

Per le parole inglesi, la pronuncia si basa sull'Inglese americano (non accentuato). stata scelta la pronuncia più comune in ogni caso in cui ci sono diversi modi di pronunciare una parola.

La lingua italiana è molto costante nella pronuncia dei gruppi di vocali e consonanti. Le eccezioni a questa guida, se ci sono, sono pochissime. Il suono delle vocali è in genere puro. I raggruppamenti nella colonna di sinistra sono in Italiano, quelli a destra in Inglese.

VOCALI	EQUIVALENTE INGLESE
a = ah	*c*op, m*o*p (piedipiatti, redazza)
e = eh	*e*h, h*e*fty, h*ea*ther (pesante, erica)
I = ee	s*ee*n, k*ee*n, m*ea*n (visto, acuto, mezzo)
o = oh	ph*o*ne, h*o*pe (telefono, speranza)
u = oo	h*oo*p, l*oo*p, s*ou*p (cerchio, occhiello, minestra)

Se la vocale a o e appare in una sillaba accentuata, la pronuncia può essere aperta o chiusa a seconda della regione, e di conseguenza non è molto importante per chi consulta questo dizionario.

CONSONANTI		EQUIVALENTE INGLESE
b	b	*b*at, *b*e, a*b*le (battuta, essere, capace)
c	c	*c*at (gatto)
c (in Italiano prima di e o i)	tch	sti*tch* (punto)
d	d	*d*ip, see*d* (immersione, seme)

f	f	*f*all, *ph*ysic, lau*gh* (caduta, purgante, risata)
g	g	*g*ap, bi*g* (apertura, grande)
g (in Italiano prima di e o i)	J	*J*et (getto)
gh (in Italiano)	g	*g*et (ottenere)
gl (in Italiano)	lli	mi*lli*on (milione)
gn (in Italiano)	ny	ca*ny*on (canyon)
h	h	*h*eat (calore)
j	j	*j*ob, e*dg*e (lavoro, bordo)
k	k	*c*at, ti*ck*, *k*in, *q*uit (gatto, zecca, parente, abbandonare)
l	l	*l*ip, pu*ll*, he*l*p (labbro, tirare, aiutare)
m	m	ha*m*, *m*at, li*m*p (prosciutto, tappetino, floscio)
n	n	*n*o, ha*n*g, bi*n* (no, appendere, contenitore)
p	p	*p*ut, u*p* (mettere, su)
r	r	ta*r*, *r*ipe, pa*r*t (catrame, maturo, parte)
s	s	*s*it, *c*ite, hi*ss* (sedersi, citare, sibilo)
sc (in Italiano prima di e o i)	sh	*sh*oe (scarpa)
t	t	ha*t*, *r*in, bu*tt*er (cappello, lattina, burro)
v	v	*v*ine, ha*v*e (rampicante, avere)
w	w	*w*hy, *w*it (perché, arguzia)
y	y	*y*es (sì)
z (Inglese)	z	*z*oo, hi*s*, read*s* (zoo, suo, legge)
z (Italiano)	ts	ste*ts*on (stetson)
	ch	*ch*in, it*ch* (mento, prurito)
	sh	a*sh*, ac*ti*on (cenere, azione)
	th	*th*e, *th*at (il/lo/la/i/gli/le, quello/quella)
	zh	vi*si*on (visione)
	ng	ba*n*k, a*n*ger (banca, rabbia)

Ortofonia di base in questo dizionario

Fonetica tradizionale
inglese   *Diventa*   *Come in*

VOCALI

æ	a	c*a*t, *a*sk (gatto, domandare)
e	ai	g*a*te, th*ey*, *ai*r (cancello, essi/e, aria)
a, a:	ah	h*o*t, f*a*ther (caldo, padre)
	au	b*ou*ght, h*au*nt, w*a*r, f*a*ll (comprato, ricovero, caduta)
	e	f*e*ll, h*ea*d (caduto/a, testa)
I, I:	ee	s*ee*, t*ea* (vedere, tè)
	I	l*i*d, d*a*mage (coperchio, danno)
aï	uy	b*uy*, l*ie*, h*eig*ht, *I* (comprare, bugia, altezza, io)
o	o	n*o*, f*oe*, r*oa*d (no, avversario, strada)
u	oo	l*oo*p, ch*u*te, p*oo*r (asola, scivolo, povero/a)
	ou	n*ow*, *ou*t, t*ow*n (ora, fuori, città)
	oi	b*oy*, v*oi*d (ragazzo, vuoto)
	uh	b*u*t, m*o*ther, h*u*nt (ma, madre, caccia)
	u	b*i*rd, *a*loof, al*è*rt, d*e*bris, b*oo*k, p*u*t, c*ou*ld (uccello, indifferente, sveglio, rottami, libro, mettere, condizionale di can—potere)

Questo suono neutro della u è uno dei più comuni delle vocali inglesi è viene utilizzato in molte sillabe non accentuate.

A

a [ah] *prep* at; to

abbagliante [ab•ba•LYAHN•te] *adj* glaring

abbaiare [ab•ba•YAH•re] *vi* bark (at)

abbandonare [ab•BAN•do•NAH•re] *vt* abandon

abbandonare [ab•BAN•do•NAH•re] *vt* forsake; quit; relinquish

abbandonato; abbandonata [ab•BAN•do•NAH•to]; [ab•BAN•do•NAH•ta] *adj* forsaken

abbassare [ab•bas•SAH•re] *vt* abase

abbastanza [ab•bas•TAHN•tsa] *adv* enough

abbattere [ab•BAHT•tere] *vt* fell; knock down

abbattersi [ab•BAHT•ter•si] *vi* droop; swoop

abbattuto; abbattuta [ab•bat•TUH•to]; [ab•bat•TUH•ta] *adj* dejected; despondent; downcast

abbazia [ab•BATS•EE•a] *n F* abbey

abbellire [ab•BEL•LEE•re] *vt* embellish

abbonamento [ab•BO•na•MEHN•to] *n M* subscription

abbonare [ab•bo•NAH•re] *vt* subscribe

abbonato; abbonata [ab•BO•NAH•to]; [ab•bon•ah•ta] *n MF* subscriber

abbondante [AB•bon•DAHN•te] *adj* abundant; lavish; plentiful; profuse

abbondanza [AB•bon•DAHN•tsa] *n F* richness; plenty

abbordare [AB•bor•DAH•re] *vt* board (on board); *vt* accost

abborrire [AB•bor•REE•re] *vt* abhor; loathe

abbozzare [AB•bot•SAH•re] *vt* M sketch

abbozzo [ab•BOH•tso] *n M* draft

abbracciare [ab•BRA•TSHYAH•re] *vt* cuddle; embrace

abbraccio [ab•BRAH•tsho] *n M* hug; embrace

abbreviare [ab•bre•VIAH•re] *vt* abbreviate

abbreviazione
[AB•bre•viat•SYOH•ne] *n* F
abbreviation

abbronzatura
[AB•bron•tsa•TUH•ra] *n* F
tan; sun tanned

abbrunato; abbrunata
[ab•bru•nah•to];
[ab•bru•nah•ta] *adj* half-mast

abete [ah•BEH•te] *n* M fir;
spruce; evergreen

abile [ah•BI•le] *adj* skillful;
handy (skilled)

abilitá [ah•BI•li•TAH] *n* F
ability; knack; proficiency;
skill

abilitá tecnica
[ah•BI•li•TAH•TEHK•ni•ka] *n*
F know-how

abisso [ABEES•so] *n* M abyss

abitante di villaggio
[ABI•TAHN•te•dee•vil•LAH
•djo] *n* villager

abitare [ah•bi•TAH•re] *vt*
inhabit

abitazione
[abi•TAT•SYOH•ne] *n* F
dwelling

abiti [ah•BI•ti] *n* M clothes;
clothing

abito [ah•BI•to] *n* M dress;
gown; habit (monastic)

abito da sera
[ah•BITO•da•SEH•ra] *n* M
evening gown

abituare [abi•TUAH•re] *vt*
accustom; get used to

abitudine [abi•TUH•DI•ne] *n* F
habit; routine; wont; custom

abolire [a•BO•LEE•re] *vt*
abolish

abominevole
[abo•mi•neh•VOLE] *adj*
abominable

aborto 1 [ah•BOHR•to] *n* M
abortion

aborto 2 [ah•BOHR•to] *n* M
miscarriage

abrogare [ah•bro•GAH•re] *vt*
repeal

abusare [abu•zah•re] *vt* abuse;
misuse; mistreat

abuso [a•BUH•zo] *n* M abuse

AC [ah•tshi] BC (Before Christ)

accademia [ah•KA•deh•MIA] *n*
F academy; school

accadere [ak•KA•deh•re] *vi*
happen; occur; transpire

accampamento
[ak•KAM•pa•MENHN•to] *n*
M encampment

accappatoio
[ak•KAP•pa•TOH•yo] *n* M
bathrobe

accarezzare [ak•are•TSAH•re]
vt caress

accatastare [ak•ka•ta•STAH•re]
vt stack; pile up

accendere [atsh•ehn•DERE] *vt*
ignite; kindle; light

accendino [a•TSHEN•dee•no] *n*
M lighter

accento [a•TSHEHN•to] *n* M
accent

accesso [a•TSHEHS•so] *n* M
access

accetta [a•TSHEHT•ta] *n* F
hatchet

acchiappare [ak•kyap•PAH•re]
vt catch; grab; trap

acciacco [atsh•AHK•ko] *n* M
infirmity; discomfort; illness

acciaio [atsh•AH•yo] *n* M steel

accidentale [a•tshi•den•TAH•le] *adj* accidental

accidente [a•tshi•DEHN•te] *n* M accident

acciottolato [ah•TSHOT•to•LAH•to] *n* M cobblestones

accludere [ak•KLUH•dere] *vt* enclose; attach

accogliente [ak•ko•LYEHN•te] *adj* inviting

accompagnare [ak•KOM•pan•YAH•re] *vt* accompany

acconsentire [ak•kon•sen•TEE•re] *vi* consent

accorciare [ak•KOR•TSHAH•re] *vt* shorten

accordarsi [ak•KOR•DAHR•see] *vi* agree

accordatura [ak•KOR•da•TUH•ra] *n* F tuning

accordo1 [ak•KOHR•do] *n* M accord; agreement; covenant

accordo 2 [ak•KOHR•do] *n* M chord

accrescere [ak•KREH•she•re] *vt* heighten

accumulare [ak•KUM•ul•AH•re] *vt* accumulate

accurato; accurata [ak•kur•AH•to; ak•ku•RAH•ta] *adj* accurate

accusa [ak•KUH•sa] *n* F prosecution; accusation

accusare [ak•KU•SAH•re] *vt* accuse; impeach; indict; charge

acero [ah•TSHE•ro] *n* M maple

aceto [ah•TSHEH•to] *n* M vinegar

acettare [a•TSHET•TAH•re] *vt* accept

acido [ah•TSHI•do] *n* M acid

acido; acida [ah•TSHI•do; ah•TSHI•da] *adj* acid; acidic

acqua [AH•kwa] *n* F water; d'acqua dolce\ *adj* freshwater

acquarello [akwa•REHL•lo] *n* M watercolor

acquazzone [akwa•TSOH•ne] *n* M downpour

acquisire [ah•kwi•SEE•re] *vt* acquire; get

acquisto [a•kwee•sto] *n* M purchase

acquoso; acquosa [ak•WOH•zo]; [ak•WOH•za] *adj* watery; liquid

acre [AH•kre] *adj* acrid

acro [AH•kro] *n* M acre

aculeo [AKUH•leo] *n* M spike

acutezza d'ingegno [aku•TEH•tsa•din•DJEH•nyo] *n* F wit

acuto; acuta [a•KUH•to]; [a•KUH•ta] *adj* acute; sharp

ad est [ahd•EHST] *adv* eastward

adattare [adat•TAH•re] *vt* accommodate; adapt; adjust

addebitare [AD•de•bit•AH•re] *vt* charge

addio [ad•DEE•o] *n* M farewell

addizionale [ad•DIT•syo•NAH•le] *n* MF plus; bonus

addizione [ad•DIT•SIOH•ne] *n*
F addition

addolcire [ad•dol•TSHEE•re] *vt*
sweeten

addome [ad•DOH•me] *n* M
abdomen

addomesticare
[ad•DOH•me•sti•KAH•re] *vt*
tame

addomesticato;
   addomesticata
[ad•DOH•me•sti•KAH•to];
[ad•DOH•me•sti•KAH•ta] *adj*
tame; domesticated

addormentato;
   addormentata
[ad•DOR•men•TAH•to];
[ad•DOR•men•TAH•ta] *adj*
asleep

addottrinare
[ad•dot•tri•NAH•re] *vt*
indoctrinate

adeguato; adeguata
[a•de•GUAH•to];
[a•de•GUAH•ta] *adj* adequate

adempiere [a•dehm•PYE•re] *vt*
implement

aderire [ah•DEREE•re] *vt*
acquiesce; *vi* comply

adolescenza
[a•DOH•le•SHEHN•tsa] *n* F
adolescence

adombrare [a•dom•BRAH•re]
vt foreshadow; overshadow

adorare [a•doh•RAH•re] *vt*
adore

adottare [a•dot•TAH•re] *vt*
adopt

adozione [a•do•TSIOH•ne] *n* F
adoption

adulazione [adu•la•TSYOH•ne]
n F flattery

adulterio [a•dul•TEH•ryo] *n* M
adultery

adulto; adulta [a•DUHL•to] *n*
adj adult

aerodinamico; aerodinamica
[AE•ro•di•NAH•mi•ko];
[AE•ro•di•NAH•mi•ka] *adj*
streamlined

aeroplano [AH•eroh•PLAH•no]
n M airplane

aeroporto [AH•eroh•POHR•to]
n M airport

affacendarsi
[af•FAT•shen•DAHR•si] *vi*
bustle

affamare [af•fa•MAH•re] *vt*
starve; be hungry

affamato; affamata
[af•fa•MAH•to];
[af•fa•MAH•ta] *adj* hungry

affannoso; affannosa
[AF•fan•NOH•zo];
[AF•fan•NOH•za] *adj* wheezy

affare [af•FAH•re] *n* M deal

affari [af•FAH•ri] *npl* M
business; trade; d'affari *adj* \
business

affascinante
[af•FA•shi•NAHN•te] *adj*
charming; fascinating

affascinare [af•FA•shi•NAH•re]
vt fascinate; charm; entrance

affascinato dal teatro;
   affascinata dal teatro
[af•FAH•tshi•NAH•to dahl
te•AH•tro] *adj* stage-struck

afferrare [AF•fer•RAH•re] *vt*
grab; grasp; clutch; clasp

affettare [AF•fet•TAH•re] *vt* affect; impact

affettuoso; affettuosa [af•fet•touh•so]; [AF•fet•TOUH•sa] *adj* demonstrative

affezione [AF•fe•TSIOH•ne] *n* F affection

affidabile [AF•fi•DAH•bile] *adj* dependable; trustworthy

affidare [AF•fi•DAH•re] *vt* commit (to)

affilare [AF•fi•LAH•re] *vt* whet; sharpen

affittare [AF•fit•TAH•re] *vt* rent

affitto [AF•FEET•to] *n* M rent; in affitto\ *adj* rental

affliggere [af•FLEE•djere] *vt* grieve

affrancatura [af•FRAN•ka•TUH•ra] *n* F postage

affresco [af•FREHS•ko] *n* M mural

affrettare [af•fret•TAH•re] *vt* hasten; *vt* quicken

affrettarsi [af•fret•TAHR•si] *vi* scurry; move quickly; flutter

affrettato; affrettata [af•fret•TAH•to]; [af•fret•TAH•ta] *adj* hurried

Afganistan [AF•gah•NI•stan] *n* M Afghanistan

Africa [AH•fri•ka] *n* F Africa

agente [a•DJEHN•te] *n* MF agent; broker

agente di cambio [a•DJEHN•te dee KAHM•byo] *n* M stockbroker

agenzia [A•gen•TSEE•a] *n* F agency

agenzia di viaggi [AD•jen•TSEE•a dee VYAH•dji] *n* F travel agency

aggettivo [adjet•TEE•vo] *n* M adjective

aggiornare [adjor•NAH•re] *vt* adjourn

aggiudicare [aj•iu•di•KAH•re] *vt* M award; judge; evaluate

aggiungere [a•DJUN•djehre] *vt* add; combine

aggiustare [adj•USTAH•re] *vt* fix; mend

aggravare [AG•gra•VAH•re] *vt* aggravate

aggressivo; aggressiva [AG•gres•SEE•vo] *adj* aggressive

aggrinzare [AG•grin•tsah•re] *vt* shrivel

agile [AH•DJI•le] *adj* nimble

agio [ah•DJO] *n* M ease; leisure

agitarsi 1 [adji•TAHR•si] *vi* fidget

agitarsi 2 [adji•TAHR•si] *vi* tumble

agitazione [AD•ji•ta•TZYOH•ne] *n* F disturbance; agitation; turmoil

aglio [AH•lyo] *n* M garlic

agnello [a•NYEHL•lo] *n* M lamb

ago [AH•go] *n* M needle

ago di sicurezza [AH•go dee SI•ku•REHT•sa] *n* M safety pin

Agosto [a•GOH•sto] *n* M August

agricoltore
[AH•gri•kol•TOH•re] *n* M
farmer

agricoltura
[AH•gri•kol•TUH•ra] *n* F
agriculture; farming

agro; agra [AH•gro]; [AH•gra]
adj sour; tart

aguzzo; aguzza [ah•GUH•tso];
[ah•GUH•tsa] *adj* keen; eager

ahimé [AHEE•me'] *excl* alas

airone [ai•roh•ne] *n* M heron

aiutante [AYU•TAHN•te] *n*
MF helper; aid; assistant

aiuto [a•YUH•to] *n* M aid; help

ala [AH•la] *n* F wing

alato; alata [ah•LAH•to];
[ah•LAH•ta] *adj* winged

alba [AHL•ba] *n* F dawn;
daybreak

Albania [AL•ba•NEE•ah] *n* F
Albania

albergo [AL•BEHR•go] *n* M
hotel; inn; lodging

albero [AHL•be•ro] *n* M tree

albero genealogico
[AHL•bero
DJE•nea•loh•DJI•ko] *n* M tree
(family)

albero maestro
[AHL•bero•ma•ehs•tro] *n* M
mast (of ship)

albicocca [AHL•bi•KOHK•ka] *n*
F apricot

album [AHL•bum] *n* M album

alce [AHL•tshe] *n* M elk

alcolico; alcolica
[AL•koh•LI•ko];
[AL•koh•LI•ka] *adj* alcoholic

alcolista [AL•ko•LEE•sta] *n*
MF alcoholic

alcool [ALKO•ol] *n* alcohol

alfabeto [AL•fa•BEH•to] *n* M
alphabet

algebra [ahl•JEB•rah] *n* F
algebra

Algeria [AL•je•REE•a] *n* F
Algeria

alibi [ah•LI•bi] *n* M alibi

alienato; alienata
[A•lie•NAH•to];
[A•lie•NAH•ta] *adj* estranged

allacciare [AL•la•TSHYAH•re]
vt fasten

allacciare con una fibbia
[ALLA•TSHA•hre kohn uhna
FEEB•bya] *vt* buckle

allarmante [AL•lar•MAHN•te]
adj scary; frightening

allarmare [AHL•LAHR•mah•re]
vt alarm; warn

allarme [AHL•LAHR•me] *n* M
alarm; warning

alle erbe [AHL•le EHR•be] *adj*
herbal

alleanza [AL•le•AHN•tsa] *n* F
alliance

allegare [AL•le•GAH•re] *vt*
attach

alleggerire [AL•le•dje•REE•re]
vt lighten

allegria [al•le•GREE•a] *n* F
glee

allegro; allegra [al•LEH•gro];
[al•LEH•gra] *adj* cheerful;
jolly; sprightly

allenamento
[AL•le•na•MEHN•to] *n* M
training

allenare [AL•le•NAH•re] *vt*
train; coach (sports)

allenatore [AL•le•na•TOH•re] *n* M coach (sports); trainer

allentare [AL•len•TAH•re] *vt* slacken; loosen; ease up

allergia [AL•ler•JEE•a] *n* F allergy

allergico; allergica [AL•lehr•JI•ko];[AL•lehr•JI•ka] *adj* allergic

allettante [AL•let•TAHN•te] *adj* tempting

allevare [AL•le•VAH•re] *vt* breed (animals); nurture

alleviare [AL•le•VYAH•re] *vt* relieve

allodola [AL•loh•DO•la] *n* F lark

alloggio [AL•LOH•djo] *n* M housing; lodgings

allora [al•LOH•ra] *adv* then

alloro [al•LOH•ro] *n* M laurel

allucinazione [al•LU•tshi•na•TSYOH•ne] *n* F hallucination

allungare [AL•lun•GAH•re] *vt* lengthen

allusione [AL•lu•ZIOH•ne] *n* F allusion

alosa [AL•LOH•za] *n* F shad

altalena [AL•ta•LEH•na] *n* F seesaw

altamente [AL•ta•MEHN•te] *adv* highly

altercare [AL•ter•KAH•re] *vi* squabble

alternare [AL•ter•NAH•re] *vi* alternate (with)

altezza [AL•TEH•tsa] *n* F highness; height

altezzoso; aaltezzosa [AL•tet•SOH•zo]; [AL•tet•SHO•za] *adj* haughty

altipiano [AL•ti•PYAH•no] *n* M plateau

alto; alta [AHL•to]; [AHL•ta] *adj* tall; high; il piú ~alto, la piú alta\ *adj* topmost

altoparlante [AL•to•par•LAHN•te] *n* M speaker; loudspeaker

altrettanto [AL•tret•TAHN•to] *adj* likewise

altrimenti [AL•tri•MEHN•tee] *adv* otherwise

altro [AHL•tro] *adv* else; *adj* other

altrove [al•TROH•ve] *adv* elsewhere

alveare [AHL•ve•AH•re] *n* M beehive; hive

alzare [al•TSAH•re] *vt* raise

alzare il cane [al•TSAH•re•il•KAH•ne] *vi* cock (a gun)

amabile [am•AH•bile] *adj* lovable

amaca [a•MAH•ka] *n* F hammock

amante [a•MAHN•te] *n* MF lover; ~ di *adj* fond

amare [a•MAH•re] *vt* cherish

amarezza [a•mah•REHT•za] *n* F bitterness

amaro; amara [a•MAH•ro]; [a•MAH•ra] *adj* bitter

ambasciata [am•ba•TSHYAH•ta] *n* F embassy

ambasciatore [AM•bah•SHIA•toh•re] *n* M ambassador

ambiente [am•BYEHN•te] *n* M
environment; setting

ambiguo; ambigua
[am•BEE•guo]; [am•BEE•gua]
adj ambiguous

ambizioso; ambiziosa
[am•bit•SIOH•so];
[am•bit•SIOH•sa] *adj*
ambitious

America [ah•MER•ika] *n* F
America

America Latina [ah•MER•ika
la•TEE•na] *n* F Latin America

amichevole [A•mi•keh•VOLE]
adj friendly

amicizia [A•mi•TSHEE•tsya] *n*
F friendship

amico [a•MEE•ko] *n* M pal; *n*
MF -o; -a friend

amido [ah•MI•do] *n* M starch

ammaccatura
[AM•mak•ka•TUH•ra] *n* F
dent

ammalarsi [AM•mal•AHR•si]
vi sicken; get ill

ammaliante
[AM•mal•i•AHN•te] *adj*
bewitching; charming;
magnetic

ammazzare [AM•mat•SAH•re]
vt slay; kill

ammettere [AM•meht•TE•re]
vt acknowledge; admit;
concede

ammiccante
[AM•mik•KAHN•te] *adj*
twinkling

ammiccare [AM•mi•KAH•re] *vi*
blink; wink

ammirare [AM•mi•RAH•re] *vt*
admire

ammissione
[AM•mis•SIOH•ne] *n* F
admission

ammobiliare
[AM•mo•BILYAH•re] *vt*
furnish

ammodo [am•MOH•do] *adv*
properly

ammollare [AM•mol•LAH•re]
vt soak

ammonire [AM•mo•NEE•re] *vt*
· admonish

ammorbidire
[AM•mor•bi•DEE•re] *vt* soften

ammuffito; ammuffita
[AM•muf•FEE•to];
[AM•muf•FEE•ta] *adj* musty

ammutinamento
[AM•mu•ti•na•MEHN•to] *n* M
mutiny

amnistia [AM•ni•STEE•ah] *n* F
amnesty

amor proprio [A•mohr
PROH•pryo] *n* M self-respect

amore [AMOH•re] *n* M love;
sake; regard

ampio; ampia [AHM•pyo];
[AHM•pya] *adj* large

analfabeta [A•nal•FA•BEH•ta]
adj illiterate

analfabetismo
[A•nal•fa•be•TEEZ•mo] *n* M
illiteracy

analisi [A•nah•LISI] *n* F
analysis

analizzare [AN•ali•TSAH•re] *vt*
analyze

analogia [ANA•loh•JEEA] *n* F
analogy

ananas [AH•na•nas] *n* M
pineapple

anarchia [AN•ar•kee•ah] *n* F anarchy

anatra [an•AH•tra] *n* F duck

anche [AHN•ke] *adv* also; even; too

ancora [AHN•ko•ra] *n* F anchor

andamento di casa [AN•da•MEHN•to di KAH•za] *n* M housekeeping

andar a prendere [an•DAH•re ah PREHN•dere] *vt* fetch; retreive

andare [an•DAH•re] *vi* go; walk; travel

andare a ruota libera [an•DAH•re ah RUOH•ta•LEEB•era] *vt* coast

andare a tastoni [an•DAH•re ah tas•TOH•ni] *vi* grope

andare con sussiego [an•DAH•re kohn sus•SYEH•go] *vi* strut

andare in bicicletta [an•DAH•re een bi•tSHI•KLEHT•ta] *vi* ride (bicycle)

andare in punta di piedi [an•DAH•re in•PUHN•ta dee PYEH•di] *vi* tiptoe

andare in slitta [an•DAH•re een SLEET•ta] *vi* sled

andare via [an•DAH•re VEE•ah] *vi* take off

andare zig zag [an•DAH•re•ah TSIG•tsahg] *vi* zigzag

andato; andata [an•DAH•to]; [an•DAH•ta] *p.p.* gone (see to go)

andicappato; andicappata [AN•di•kap•PAH•to]; [AN•di•kap•PAH•ta] *adj* handicapped

anello [AN•EHL•lo] *n* M link; ring

angelo [AHN•je•lo] *n* M angel; seraphim

angolo [AHN•go•lo] *n* M angle; corner

angoscia [an•goh•SHIA] *n* F anguish; distress

anguilla [an•GUEEL•la] *n* F eel

anima [ah•NI•ma] *n* F soul

animale [AN•i•MAH•le] *n* M animal

animale di casa [ANI•MAH•le di KAH•za] *n* M pet

animaletti nocivi [ANI•mah•LEHT•ti no•TSHEE•vi] *n* M vermin

animato; animata [AN•i•MAH•to]; [AN•i•MAH•ta] *adj* animated; lively

animella [A•ni•MEHL•la] *n* F sweetbread; sweetbreads

annaspare [AN•na•SPAH•re] *vi* fumble

annegare [AN•ne•GAH•re] *vt* drown

annerire [AN•neh•REE•re] *vt* blacken; tarnish

anni dell'adolescenza [AHN•ni dehl•LADO•le•SHEHN•tsa] *n* M teens

anniversario [AN•ni•ver•SAH•ri•o] *n* M anniversary

anno [AHN•no] *n* M year

anno bisestile [AHN•no bi•zes•TEE•le] *n* M leap year

anno nuovo [AHN•no NUOH•vo] *n* M New Year

annoiare [AN•noy•AH•re] *vt* bore; annoy

annuale [AHN•nu•AH•le] *adj* annual

annullare [AHN•nul•LAH•re] *vt* nullify

annunziare [AN•nun•TSIAH•re] *vt* advertise; announce

anomalo; anomala [AN•oh•MAH•lo]; [AN•oh•MAH•la] *adj* freak

anormale [AH•nor•MAH•le] *adj* abnormal

ansare [an•SAH•re] *vi* pant

ansietá [ahn•SIETA'] *n* F anxiety

ansioso; ansiosa [ahn•SIOH•so]; [ahn•SIOH•sa] *adj* anxious

antenato [an•TEN•AH•to] *n* M ancestor; forefather

anteprima [ahn•te•PREE•ma] *n* F preview

anticamera [AN•ti•KAH•me•ra] *n* F lobby

anticipare [AN•ti•tshi•PAH•re] *vt* advance

antico; antica [an•TEE•ko]; [an•TEE•ka] *adj* ancient; antique

anticonvenzionale [AN•ti•kon•ven•TSYO•nah•le] *adj* unconventional

antimeridiano; antimeridiana [AH•NTI•me•ri•DI•AH•no]; [AH•NTI•me•ri•DI•AH•na] *adj* A.M.

antipasto [AN•ti•PAHS•to] *n* M appetizer

antiquato; antiquata [AN•ti•KWAH•to]; [AN•ti•KWAH•ta] *adj* obsolete; old-fashioned

antisociale [AN•ti•sot•SHIAH•le] *adj* antisocial

antologia [AHN•to•lo•JEE•ah] *n* F anthology

anzianitá [AN•tsya•NI•tah] *n* F seniority

anziano; anziana [an•TSYAH•no]; [an•TSYAH•na] *adj* elderly; aged

ape [AH•pe] *n* F bee

apertamente [A•PER•ta•MEHN•te] *adv* openly; freely

aperto; aperta [a•PEHR•to]; [a•PEHR•ta] *adj* open; all'aperto *adj* outdoor; *adv* outdoors

apertura [aper•TUH•ra] *n* F opening

apice [ah•PIT•she] *n* M heyday

apologia [AH•po•lo•JEE•a] *n* F apology

appalto [ap•PAHL•to] *n* M concession (commercial)

apparecchio [AP•pa•REHK•kyo] *n* M implement

apparente [ap•PAREHN•te] *adj* ostensible; apprarent

apparentemente [AP•pa•REHN•te•MEHN•te] *adv* apparently; ostensibly

apparenza [AP•pa•REHN•za] *n*
F appearance

apparire [AP•pa•REE•ree] *vi*
appear; arrive; show up

appariscente
[AP•pari•SHEHN•te] *adj*
blatant

appartamento
[AP•par•ta•MEHN•to] *n* M
apartment

appartenenza
[AP•par•te•NEHN•tsa] *n* F
membership

appartenere
[AP•par•te•NEH•re] *vi* belong;
appertain; pertain

appassionato; appassionata
[AP•pas•syo•NAH•to];
[AP•pas•syo•NAH•ta] *adj*
passionate

appassire [AP•pas•SEE•re] *vi*
wilt; wither

appena [ap•PEH•na] *adv* barely

appendere [ap•PEHN•DE•re]
vt hang

appetito [AP•pe•TEE•to] *n* M
appetite

appezzamento
[AP•petsa•MEHN•to] *n* M lot

appiattire [AP•pyat•TEE•re] *vt*
flatten

appiccicarsi
[AP•pi•TSHI•KAHR•si] *vt*
stick

applaudire [AP•plau•DEE•re]
vt applaud; clap

applicare [AP•pli•KAH•re] *vt*
apply (to, for)

applicarsi [AP•pli•KAHR•si] *vt*
apply (oneself)

applicazione
[AP•pli•ka•TSIOH•ne] *n* F
application

appoggio [AP•poh•DJO] *n* M
support; hold

appollaiarsi
[AP•pol•LAYAHR•si] *vi*
roost; perch

apprensione
[AP•pren•ZYOH•ne] *npl* F
misgivings

apprezzare [AP•pre•TSA•re] *vt*
appreciate

approccio [AP•proh•TSHO] *n*
M overture

approfondire
[AP•pro•fon•DEE•re] *vt*
deepen

appropriarsi indebitamente
[AP•pro•PRI•AHR•si
in•DE•bi•ta•MEHN•te] *vi*
embezzle

appropriato; appropriata
[AP•pro•PRI•AH•to];
[AP•pro•PRI•AH•ta] *adj*
appropriate; becoming

appropriazione indebita
[AP•pro•PRIA•tsyoh•ne
in•DEH•bi•ta] *n* F
misappropriation

approssimativamente
[AP•pros•si•ma•TEE•va•mehn
•te] *adv* approximately;
roughly

approvare [AP•pro•VAH•re] *vt*
approve; endorse

approvazione
[AP•pro•va•TSIOH•ne] *n* F
approval

approvvigionare
[AP•prov•vi•DJO•nah•re] *vt*
stock

appuntamento
[AP•pun•ta•MEHN•to] *n* M
appointment to have an
appointment w/someone; date
(appointment)

appuntito; appuntita
[AP•pun•TEE•to];
[AP•pun•TEE•ta] *adj* pointed

appunto [AP•PUHN•to] *n* M
memo

Aprile [ah•PREEL•eh] *n* M
April

aquila [ah•KWI•la] *n* F eagle

aquilone [AH•kwi•LOH•ne] *n*
M kite

arachide [AR•ah•KI•de] *n* F
peanut

aragosta [AR•ah•GOHS•ta] *n* F
lobster

araldica [AR•ahl•DI•KA] *n* F
heraldry

araldo [ar•AHL•do] *n* M herald

arancia [ar•AHN•tsha] *n* F
orange

arancio [ar•AHN•tsho] *adj*
orange

arare [AR•AH•re] *vt* till;
cultivate

aratro [a•RAH•tro] *n* M plow

arazzo [a•RAH•tso] *n* M
tapestry

arbitrario; arbitraria
[AHR•bit•RAH•rio];
[AHR•bit•RAH•ria] *adj*
arbitrary

arbitro [ahr•BI•tro] *n* M referee;
umpire

arcaico; arcaica
[AHR•ka•HI•ko];
[AHR•ka•HI•ka] *adj* archaic

archeologia
[AHR•ke•ohl•o•GEE•ah] *n* F
archaeology

architetto [AHR•ki•TET•to] *n*
M architect

architettura
[AHR•ki•tet•TOOR•ah] *n* F
architecture

arco [AHR•ko] *n* M arch; bow
(archery)

arcobaleno
[AHR•ko•ba•LEH•no] *n* M
rainbow

ardesia [AHR•deh•ZIA] *n* F
slate

arenarsi [AHR•e•NAHR•si] *vi*
strand

argano [AHR•ga•no] *n* M
winch

argenteria
[AHR•djen•te•REE•a] *n* F
silverware

argentiere
[AHR•djen•TYEH•re] *n* M
silversmith

argento [ahr•DJEHN•to] *n* M
silver

argine [ahr•DJI•ne] *n*
embankment

argomento
[AHR•go•MEHN•to] *n* M
topic

arguto; arguta [ahr•GUH•to];
[ar•GUH•ta] *adj* witty

aria 1 [AH•rya] *n* F air; a tenuta
d'aria\ *adj* airtight

aria 2 [AH•rya] *n* F song; aria;
tune

aria condizionata [AH•rya
kon•DIT•SION•ah•ta] *n* F
airconditioning

arido; arida [ah•RI•doh] *adj* arid

ariete [ah•RIEH•te] *n* M ram

aringa [AH•REEN•ga] *n* F herring

arma [AHR•mah] *n* F arm; weapon

armadio a muro [AR•mah•DYO ah MUH•ro] *n* M closet

armamentario [AR•ma•men•TAH•ryo] *n* M paraphernalia

armatura [AHR•mah•TUH•ra] *n* F armor

armonia [AHR•mo•NEE•a] *n* F harmony

armonica a bocca [AHR•moh•NI•ka• ah BOHK•ka] *n* F harmonica

armonioso; armoniosa [AR•mon•YOH•zo] [AR•mon•YOH•za] *adj* harmonious

armonizzare [AR•mo•NIT•SAH•re] *vt* harmonize

arnese [ar•NEHSE] *n* M tool

arnesi da pesca [ar•NEH•zi dah PEHS•ka] *n* M tackle (fishing)

aroma [ah•ROH•ma] *n* M aroma

arpa [AHR•pa] *n* F harp

arpione [AR•PYOH•ne] *n* M harpoon

arrampicarsi [AR•ram•pi•KAHR•si] *vi* scramble

arrampicarsi [AR•ram•pik•AHR•si] *vi* climb

arrestare [AHR•re•STAH•re] *vt* arrest; staunch; stem

arricchire [AHR•rik•KEE•re] *vt* enrich

arrivare [AHR•ri•VAH•re] *vi* arrive

arrivo [ahr•REE•vo] *n* M arrival

arrogante [AHR•roh•GAHN•te] *adj* arrogant; overbearing

arrossamento [AHR•ros•sa•MEHN•to] *n* M redness

arrossare [AHR•ros•SAH•re] *vi* redden

arrossire [AHR•ros•SEE•re] *vi* blush

arrostire [AHR•ros•TEE•re] *vt* roast

arruffare [AHR•ruf•FAH•re] *vt* ruffle

arruffato; arruffata [AHR•ruf•FAH•to]; [AHR•ruf•FAH•ta] *adj* dishevelled

arruolare [AHR•ru•o•LAH•re] *vt* enlist

arte [AHRT•e] *n* F art

arteria [AR•teh•RYA] *n* F artery

arteria di grande traffico [AR•teh•RYA dee GRAHN•de TRAHF•fiko] *n* F thoroughfare

articolare [AHR•ti•KOL•ahre] *vt vi* articulate

articolo [ahr•TEE•KO•lo] *n* M article; item

artificiale [AHR•ti•FI•tsha•le] *adj* artificial

artiglio [ar•TEE•lyo] *n* M claw

artista [ahr•TEE•sta] *n* MF
artist

arto [AHR•to] *n* M limb

ascensore [a•shen•SOH•re] *n* M
elevator

ascesa [ah•SHEH•za] *n* F climb

ascia [ah•SHYA] *n* F axe

asciugamano
[ASH•yuh•ga•MAH•no] *n* M
towel

asciugare [AH•shyu•GAH•re]
vt wipe

asciugatore
[AH•shyu•ga•TOH•re] *n* M
dryer

asciutto; asciutta
[a•SHYUHT•to]; [a•shyuht•ta]
adj dry

ascoltare [AS•kol•TAH•re] *vt*
listen

ascoltatore; ascoltatrice
[AS•kol•ta•TOH•re];
[AS•kol•ta•TREE•tshe] *n* MF
listener

asilo infantile [AZEE•lo
in•fan•TEE•le] *n* M
kindergarten

asino [ah•SI•no] *n* M donkey;
dunce

asparago [AS•pah•RA•go] *n* M
asparagus

aspettare [AS•pet•TAH•re] *vt*
expect; wait

aspettativa [AS•pet•ta•TEE•va]
n F expectation

aspetto [as•PEHT•to] *n* M
aspect; guise

aspirina [AH•spir•EE•nah] *n* F
aspirin

assalto [as•SAHL•to] *n* M
onslaught

assassinare
[AS•sas•si•NAH•re] *vt*
assassinate

assassinio [AS•sas•SEEN•yo] *n*
M assassination

assassino [AS•sas•SEE•no] *n* M
murderer; killer

asse [AS•seh] *n* F axis; axle;
board (lumber); plank

assecondare
[AS•se•kon•DAH•re] *vt*
second

assediare [AS•se•DIAH•re] *vt*
besiege

assedio [as•SEH•dyo] *n* M
siege

assegnare [AS•se•NYAH•re] *vt*
assign

assegnare una parte
[AS•se•NYAH•re UH•na
PAHR•te] *vi* cast

assegno [as•SEN•yo] *n* M
check (currency)

assente [as•SEHN•te] *adj*
absent

asservire [AS•ser•VEE•re] *vt*
enslave

asserzione [AS•sert•SIOH•ne]
n F allegation

assicella [AS•si•TSHEHL•la] *n*
F slat

assicurare [AS•siku•RAH•re] *vt*
ensure; insure

assicurazione
[AS•si•kura•TSYOH•ne] *n* F
insurance

assideramento
[AS•side•ra•MEHN•to] *n* M
exposure (cold)

assillare [AS•sil•LAH•re] *vt* nag

associare [AS•sot•SHIAH•rai]
vt associate

associazione
[AS•sot•shia•TSIOH•ne] *n* F
association; fellowship

assodante [AS•sor•DAHN•te]
adj deafening

assoggettamento
[AS•sodjet•ta•MEHN•to] *n* M
subjection

assolutamente
[AS•solu•ta•MEHN•te] *adv*
absolutely

assoluto; assoluta
[AS•so•LUH•to];
[AS•so•LUH•ta] *adj* absolute

assolvere [AS•sohl•VE•re] *vt*
acquit

assomigliare
[AS•so•mil•YAH•re] *vi*
resemble

assorbente [AS•sor•BEHN•te]
n M pad

assorbire [AS•sor•BEE•re] *vt*
absorb; merge

assordare [AS•sor•DAH•re] *vt*
deafen

assumere [AS•suh•ME•re] *vt*
assume

assurdo; assurda
[as•SUHR•do; as•SUHR•da]
adj absurd; preposterous

asta di bandiera [AHS•ta di
ban•DYEH•ra] *n* flagpole

astante [as•TAHN•te] *n* MF
onlooker

astenersi [AS•te•NEHR•si] *vi*
abstain

astrologia [A•stro•lo•GEE•ah]
n F astrology

astronauta [A•stro•NOU•ta] *n*
MF astronaut

astronomia
[AH•stro•noh•MEE•ah] *n* F
astronomy

astuccio [AS•TUH•tsho] *n* M
case

astuto; astuta [as•TUH•to];
[as•TUH•ta] *adj*
crafty

astuto; astuta [a•STUH•to];
[a•STUH•ta] *adj* cunning

astuzia [AS•tuh•TSYA] *n* F
wile

attaccapanni
[AT•tak•ka•PAHN•nee] *n* M
hanger

attaccare [AT•tak•KAH•re] *vt*
attack

attacco [at•TAHK•ko] *n* M bout

attacco cardiaco [at•TAHK•ko
kar•DEE•ako] *n* M heart
attack

attacco isterico [at•TAHK•ko
is•TEH•riko] *n* M hysterics

attendere al varco
[at•TEHN•de•re ahl
VAHR•ko] *vt* waylay

attendibile [AT•ten•DEE•bi•le]
adj reliable

attendibilitá
[AT•ten•di•bi•LI•tah] *n* F
reliability

attento; attenta
[at•TEHN•to];[at•TEHN•ta]
adj attentive; careful

attenuare [AT•te•NUAH•re] *vt*
understate; downplay

attenzione [AT•ten•TSHION•e]
n F attention

atterrire [AT•ter•REE•re] *vt*
horrify; terrify; scare

attesa [AT•teh•za] *n* F waiting;
in attesa\ *prep* expecting

attestare [AT•tes•TAH•re] *vi*
testify; vouch (for)

attico [aht•TI•ko] *n* M
penthouse

attitudine [AT•ti•TUH•di•ne] *n*
F attitude

attivo; attiva [at•TEE•vo];
[a•TEE•vah] *adj* active

attizzare [AT•ti•TSAH•re] *vt*
stoke

attizzatoio [AT•titsa•TOH•yo]
n M poker

atto [AHT•to] *n* M act; deed

atto contrario alla legge
[AHT•to kon•TRAH•ryo
ahl•la LEH•dje] *n* M
misdemeanor

attore [at•TOH•re] *n* M actor

attraente [AT•tra•EHN•te] *adj*
attractive; endearing;
glamorous; engaging

attrarre [at•TRAHR•re] *vt*
attract; engage; endear

attraverso [AT•ra•VEHR•so]
adv across; through

attrazione [AT•tra•TSIOH•ne]
n F attraction

attrezzatura
[AT•tre•tsa•TUH•ra] *n* F
equipment; F rig

attribuire [AT•tri•BUEE•re] *vt*
refer

attrice [AT•TREE•tshe] *n* F
actress

audace [A•u•DAH•tshe] *adj*
bold

audacia [A•u•DAH•tshya] *n* F
boldness

audizione [au•di•TSEE•on] *n* F
audition

aula [AH•ul•a] *n* F classroom

aumento [au•MEHN•to] *n* M
increase

aureola [AU•re•OH•la] *n* F halo

ausiliario; ausiliaria
[AU•zi•LIAH•rio];
[AU•zi•LIAH•ria] *adj n* MF
auxiliary

auspicio [aus•PEE•tsho] *n* M
omen

Australia [au•STRAH•LI•a] *n* F
Australia

Austria [ou•STREE•ah] *n* F
Austria

autentico; autentica
[AU•tehn•TI•ko];
[AU•tehn•TI•ka] *adj* authentic

autista [au•TEES•ta] *n* M
chauffeur; driver

autobiografia
[AU•to•BEE•oh•gra•FEE•ah]
n F autobiography; memoirs

autobus [AH•ut•O•buhs] *n* M
bus

autocontrollo
[AH•uto•kon•TROHL•lo] *n* M
self-control

autodidatta
[AH•uto•di•DAHT•ta] *adj*
self-taught

autografo [AU•toh•GRAF•oh]
n M autograph

automatico; automatica
[AU•to•MAH•ti•ko];
[AU•to•MAH•ti•ka] *adj* MF
automatic

automobile
[AU•to•MOH•bi•le] *n* F car

autore; autrice [au•TOH•re] *n*
MF author

autoritá [AU•to•rree•TAH] *n* F
authority; establishment

autorizzazione
[AU•to•ri•tsa•TSYOH•ne] *n* F
warrant; authorization

autostoppista
[AU•to•stohp•PEE•sta] *n* MF
hitchhiker

autostrada [AU•to•STRAH•da]
n F highway

autunno [AU•tuhn•NO] *n* M
autumn

avambraccio
[A•vam•BRAH•tshyo] *n* M
forearm

avanti [a•VAHN•ti] *adv* forth;
forward; ahead; onward

avanzare [a•VAN•DSAH•re] *vi*
advance

avanzi [a•VAHN•tsi] *npl* M
leftovers

avanzo [a•VAHN•tso] *n* M
scrap

avarizia [AV•a•REE•tsya] *n* F
stinginess

avaro; avara [a•VAH•ro];
[a•VAH•ra] *n* MF miser; *adj*
miserly; stingy

avena [a•VEH•na] *n* F oats

aver diritto [a•VEHR
di•REET•to] *vi* entitled (to be)

avere [a•VEH•re] *vt* (aux) have;
hold; get

avere il raffreddore
[a•VEH•re il
RAF•fred•DOH•re] *vi* snuffle

avere l'intenzione di
[a•VEH•re lin•ten•TSYOH•ne
di] *vi* intend

averla [ah•VEHR•la] *n* F shrike;
shrew

averson [ah•VER•so] *adj*
adverse; opposing

aviditá [AVI•di•TAH] *n* F
greed

avido; avida [a•VEE•do];
[a•VEE•da] *adj* greedy; eager

avorio [A•voh•ryo] *n* M ivory

avvantaggiare
[AV•van•tah•DJIA•re] *vt*
benefit; advantage

avvelenamento
[AV•ve•lena•MEHN•to] *n* M
poisoning

avvenimento
[AV•veni•MEHN•to] *n* M
happening; occurence

avventarsi [AV•ven•TAHR•si]
vi pounce

avventatezza
[AV•ven•ta•TEH•tsa] *n* F
recklessness

avventato; avventata
[AV•ven•TAH•to];
[av•ven•tah•ta] *adj* MF
reckless

Avvento [av•VEHN•to] *n* M
Advent

avventura [AV•ven•TUH•ra] *n*
F adventure

avventura romantica
[AV•ven•TUH•ra
ro•MAHN•ti•ka] *n* F romance

avventurarsi
[AV•ven•tu•RAHR•si] *vi*
venture; risk

avventuroso; avventurosa
[AV•ven•tu•ROH•zo];

[AV•ven•tu•ROH•za] *adj* MF
adventurous

avverbio [av•VEHR•byo] *n* M
adverb

avverità [AV•ve•ri•TAH] *n* F
hardship

avversario; avversaria
[AV•ver•SAH•ryo];
[AV•ver•SAH•rya] *n* MF
opponent

avversione [AV•ver•SYOH•ne]
n F dislike; reluctance
unwillingness; aversion

avversità [AV•ver•si•TAH] *n* F
adversity

avvertimento
[AV•ver•ti•MEHN•to] *n* M
warning

avvertire [AV•ver•TEE•re] *vt*
warn; notice; feel

avvicinare
[AV•vi•tshi•NAH•re] *vt*
approach

avvilirsi [AV•vi•LÈER•si] *vi*
mope

avviluppare
[AV•vilup•PAH•re] *vt* envelop

avviso [av•VEE•zo] *n* M notice;
warning

avvivare [AH•vee•VAHR•eh] *vi*
start; set going; set up; direct

avvocato [AV•voh•KAH•to] *n*
M lawyer; solicitor

avvolgere [AV•vohl•DJE•re] *vt*
coil; wrap

avvoltoio [AV•vol•TOH•yo] *n*
M vulture

azione [at•SYOH•ne] *n* F action

azione legale [a•TSYOH•ne
le•GAH•le] *n* F proceeding
(legal)

azionista [a•TSYO•NEES•ta] *n*
MF stockholder

azoto [AT•zoh•to] *n* M nitrogen

azzardo [ats•AHR•do] *n* M
gamble; bet; risk

azzuffarsi [A•tzuf•FAHR•si] *vi*
wrangle

B

bacca [BAH•ka] *n* F berry

baccello [BA•TSHEHL•lo] *n* M
hull; pod

bacchetta [BA•KEHT•tah] *n* F
baton; wand

bacio [BAH•tsho] *n* M kiss

badare [ba•DAH•re] *vt* tend (a
machine)

baffi [BAHF•fi] *npl* M
mustache; moustache;
whisker

bagaglio [ba•GAH•lyo] *n* M
baggage; luggage

bagnante [bahn•YAHN•te] *n*
MF bather

bagnare [ba•NYAH•re] *vt*
douse; bathe

bagnato; bagnata
[ba•NYAH•to]; [ba•NYAH•ta]
adj wet

bagno [BAH•nyo] *n* M bath;
bathroom

baia [BAH•ya] *n* F bay

baionetta [BAH•yo•NEH•ta] *n* F bayonet

balbettare [BAL•bet•TAH•re] *vt* babble; stammer

balbuzie [BAL•buh•TSIE] *n* F stutter

balcone [BAHL•KOH•ne] *n* M balcony

baldacchino [BAL•dak•KEE•no] *n* M canopy

baldoria [BAL•doh•RYA] *n* F revelry

balena [BA•LEH•na] *n* F whale

baleno [BA•LEH•no] *n* M flash

balla [BAHL•la] *n* F bale

ballata [bal•LAH•ta] *n* F ballad

ballerina [BAL•le•REE•na] *n* F ballerina; -o -a\ MF dancer

balletto [bal•LEHT•to] *n* M ballet

ballonzolare [BAL•lon•tso•LAH•re] *vi* jiggle

balzo [BAHL•tso] *n* M leap

bambinaia [BAM•bi•NAH•ya] *n* F sitter

bambino; bambina [bam•BEE•no]; [bam•BEE•na] *n* MF child

bambola [BAHM•bo•la] *n* F doll

bambù [bam•BU'] *n* M bamboo

banal [ba•NAH•le] *adj* banal; trivial

banana [ba•NAH•na] *n* F banana

banca [BAHN•ka] *n* F bank

bancario [ban•KAH•rio] *n* M banker

bank worker

banchetto [ban•KEHT•to] *n* M banquet; feast

banchina [ban•KEE•na] *n* F dock; pier; quay

banco [BAHN•ko] *n* M counter; M pew (church)

banconota [BAH•ko•NOH•ta] *n* F bank note

banda [BAHN•da] *n* F band

banderuola [BAN•de•RUOH•la] *n* F vane

bandiera [ban•DIEH•ra] *n* F banner; flag

bandire [bahn•DEE•re] *vt* outlaw

bar [bar] *n* M bar; coffee shop

baratro [bah•RA•tro] *n* M chasm

barattolo [BA•raht•TO•lo] *n* M can

barba [BAHR•ba] *n* F beard

barbaro; barbara [BAHR•ba•ro];[BAHR•ba•ra] *adj n* MF barbarian

barbiere [bar•BIEH•re] *n* M barber

barboncino [BAR•bon•TSHEE•no] *n* M poodle

barca [BAHR•ka] *n* F boat

barca a vela [BAHR•ka ah VEH•la] *n* F sailboat

barcollare [BAR•kol•LAH•re] *n* lurch; *vi* stagger; totter

bardatura [BAR•da•TUH•ra] *n* F trappings

barella [BA•REHL•la] *n* F stretcher

barile [BA•REE•le] *n* M cask; keg

barista [BA•HREE•sta] *n* M
bartender

barlume [bar•LUH•me] *n* M
glimmer

Barocco [ba•ROH•ko] *n* M
Baroque

barocco; barocca
[ba•ROH•ko]; [ba•ROH•ka]
adj MF baroque

barometro [BA•róh•ME•tro] *n*
.M barometer

barricata [BAR•ri•KAH•ta] *n* F
barricade

barriera [bar•RIEH•ra] *n* F
barrier

basco [BAHS•ko] *n* M beret

base [BAH•ze] *n* F base; basis;
foundation

baseball [BAIS•bawl] *n* M
baseball

basilare [BAH•zi•LAH•re] *adj*
basic; fundamental

basilico [BAH•zee•LI•ko] *n* M
basil

basso 1 [BAH•so] *n* M bass
(mus)

basso 2; bassa [BAHS•so];
[BAHS•sa] *adj* MF low

bassotto [bas•SOHT•to] *n* M
dachsund

bastardo [ba•STAHR•do] *n* M
bastard; *adj* bastard

bastare [bas•TAH•re] *vi* suffice

bastonare [BAS•to•NAH•re] *vt*
whack; club

bastonatura
[BAS•to•nat•UH•ra] *n* F
hiding

bastone [bas•TOH•ne] *n* M
club; rod; stick; cane (walking
stick)

battaglia [bat•TAHL•ia] *n* F
battle

battaglione [BAT•tal•YOH•ne]
n M battalion

battello [bat•TEHL•lo] *n* M
barge

battente [bat•TEHN•te] *n* M
knocker

battere [baht•TE•re] *vt* beat;
thrash; thump

battere le mani [baht•TE•re
leh MAH•ni] *vi* clap

batteria [BAT•te•REE•ah] *n* F
battery

battesimo [BAT•teh•SI•mo] *n*
M baptism

battezzare [BAT•tet•ZAH•re]
vt baptize; christen

battibecco [BAT•ti•BEHK•ko]
n M squabble

battuta [bat•TUH•ta] *n* F
beating

baule [BA•uhle] *n* M trunk

bavaglino [BA•va•LEE•no] *n*
M bib; gag

bavero [BAH•vero] *n* M lapel

bazar [ba•ZAHR] *n* M bazaar

beagle [BEE•gol] *n* M beagle

beatitudine
[BE•ah•ti•TUH•di•ne] *n* F
bliss

beccata [bek•KAH•ta] *n* F peck

becco [BEH•ko] *n* M beak

beccuccio [bek•KUH•tsho] *n* M
nozzle; spout

beffa [BEHF•fa] *n* F mockery

beige [bezh] *adj* beige; *n* M
beige

bel pezzo [behl•PEH•tso] *n* M
chunk

belga [BEHL•ga] *adj* Belgian

Belgio [BEHL•djo] *n* M
Belgium
bellezza [bel•LEH•tsa] *n* F
beauty
bello; bella
[BEHL•lo];[BEHL•la] *adj* MF
beautiful; fine; good-looking
benché [ben•KE'] *conj*
although; *adv* though
benda [BEHN•da] *n* F blindfold
bene [BEH•ne] *adv* nicely; well
beneamato; beneamata
[BEH•ne•am•AH•to];
[beh•ne•am•ah•ta] *adj* beloved
benedire [BEH•ne•DEE•re] *vt*
bless
benedizione
[BEH•ne•di•TSIOH•ne] *n* F
benediction; blessing
beneducato; beneducata
[behn•edu•KAH•to];
[behn•edu•KAH•ta] *adj*
well-bred; polite
benefattore
[BEH•ne•FAT•TOH•re] *n* M
benefactor
benessere [BE•nehs•se•re] *n* M
welfare; well-being
benestante [BE•nes•TAHN•te]
adj well-to-do
benigno; benigna
[be•NEE•nyo]; [be•NEE•nya]
adj benign
benvenuto; benvenuta
[BEHN•ven•UH•to];
[BEHN•ven•UH•ta] *adj*
welcome
benzina [ben•TSEE•na] *n* F
gasoline
berlina [ber•LEE•na] *n* F sedan

berretto [ber•REHT•to] *n* M
cap
berretto scozzese
[ber•REHT•to skot•SEH•ze] *n*
M tam o' shanter
bersaglio [ber•SAH•lyo] *n* M
target
bestemmiare
[BES•tem•MIAH•re] *vt*
blaspheme
bestia [BEH•sti•a] *n* F beast
bestiale [bes•TI•ah•le] *adj*
beastly
bestiame [bes•TYAH•me] *n* M
cattle; livestock
betulla [be•TUHL•la] *n* F birch
bevanda [be•VAHN•da] *n* F
beverage; drink
biancheria [BYAN•ke•REE•a]
n F underclothes; underwear
bianco; bianca [BYAHN•ko];
[BYAHN•ka] *adj* white; in
bianco\ *adv* blank
biancore [byan•KOH•re] *n* M
whiteness
biasimare [BI•ah•si•MAH•re] *vt*
blame; reprove
biasimo [BI•ah•ZI•mo] *n* M
reproach
Bibbia [BEEB•ya] *n* F Bible
bibita [bee•BITA] *n* F soda
biblioteca [BI•blyo•TEH•ka] *n*
F library
bibliotecario; bibliotecaria
[BI•blyo•te•KAH•ryo];
[BI•blyo•te•KAH•rya] *n* MF
librarian
bicchiere da vino
[bik•KYEH•re dah VEE•no] *n*
M wineglass
bici [BEE•tshi] *n* F bike

bicicletta [BI•tshi•KLEHT•ta] *n* F bicycle

bidello; bidella [bi•DEHL•lo]; [bi•DEHL•la] *n* MF custodian (school)

bidone [bi•DOH•ne] *n* M bin (for garbage)

bietola [BIEH•to•la] *n* F beet

bigamia [BI•ga•MEE•ah] *n* F bigamy

bighellonare [BI•gel•lo•NAH•re] *vi* dawdle; loiter

bigliardo [bil•YAHR•do] *n* M billiards

biglietteria [BI•lyet•te•REE•a] *n* F ticket office

biglietto [bi•LYEHT•to] *n* F ticket

biglietto di San Valentino [bi•LYEHT•to dee SAHN•va•len•TEE•no] *n* M valentine

biglietto in abbonamento [bi•LYEHT•to een AB•bo•na•MEHN•to] *n* M season ticket

bigotto; bigotta [bi•GOHT•to]; [bi•GOHT•ta] *n* MF bigot

bikini [bi•KEE•ni] *n* M bikini

bilancio [bi•LAHN•tshyo] *n* M balance-sheet; budget

bile [BEE•le] *n* F bile; gall

bilingue [bi•LEEN•gwai] *adj* bilingual

bimbetto; bimbetta [bim•BEHT•to]; [bim•BEHT•ta] *n* MF tot

binocolo [bi•NOH•ko•lo] *n* M binoculars

biografia [BEE•o•gra•FEE•ah] *n* F biography

biologia [BI•o•lo•JEE•ah] *n* F biology

biondo; bionda [BIOHN•do]; [BIOHN•da] *adj* blonde

birichinata [BI•ri•kin•AH•ta] *n* F mischief

birra [BEE•rah] *n* F beer

birraio [bir•RAH•yo] *n* M brewer

birreria [BIR•re•REE•ah] *n* F brewery

bis [bees] *n* M encore

bisbetica [BIZ•beh•TI•ka] *n* F shrew

bisbetico; bisbetica [BIZ•beh•TI•ko]; [BIZ•beh•TI•ka] *adj* grumpy

bisboccia [biz•BOH•tsha] *n* F spree

biscottino [BIS•kot•TEE•no] *n* M cookie

bisnonna [biz•NOHN•na] *n* F great-grandmother

bisnonni [biz•NOHN•ni] *n* M great-grandparents

bisnonno [biz•NOHN•no] *n* M great-grandfather

bisogno [bi•ZO•nyo] *n* M need

bisognoso; bisognosa [BI•zo•NYOH•zo]; [BI•zo•NYOH•za] *adj* needy

bistecca [bis•TEHK•ka] *n* F steak

bitume [bi•TUH•me] *n* M pitch

bivio [bee•vyo] *n* M crossroads

bizzarro; bizzarra [bi•TSAHR•ro]; [bi•TSAHR•ra] *adj* MF quaint

blando; blanda [BLAHN•do];
   [BLAHN•da] *adj* MF bland
bleso; blesa [BLEH•zo];
   [BLEH•za] *n* MF tongue-tied
bloccare [blok•AHR•e] *vt* block
blocco [BLOH•ko] *n* M block;
   blockage; blockade; tie-up
blú [blu'] *adj n* MF blue
bluff [bluhff] *n* M bluff
boa [BOH•ah] *n* F buoy
bobina [bo•BEE•na] *n* F coil
   (electrical)
bocca [BOHK•ka] *n* F mouth
boccale [bok•KAH•le] *n* M mug
boccheggiare
   [BOK•ke•DJYAH•re] *vi* gasp
bocciolo [botsh•OH•lo] *n* M
   bud
bocconcino
   [BOK•kon•TSHEE•no] *n* M
   morsel
boccone [bok•KOH•ne] *n* M
   mouthful
boia [BOH•ya] *n* M executioner
boicottare [BOI•cot•TAH•re] *vt*
   boycott
boicotto [boi•COHT•to] *n* M
   boycott
bolla [BOHL•la] *n* F bubble
bollettino [BOL•let•tee•no] *n*
   M bulletin
bollire [bol•LEE•re] *vt* boil
bollitore [BOL•li•TOH•re] *n* M
   teakettle
bollo [BOHL•lo] *n* M stamp
bomba [BOHM•ba] *n* F bomb
bombardamento
   [BOHM•bar•da•MEHN•to] *n*
   M bombing
bombardare
   [BOHM•bar•DAH•re] *vt*
   bombard

bombardiere
   [BOHM•bar•DIEH•re] *n* M
   bomber
boomerang [BUH•me•rang] *n*
   M boomerang
borbottare [BOR•bot•TAH•re]
   vt mumble; mutter
borchia [BOHR•kya] *n* F stud
borsa 1 [BOHR•za] *n* F bag;
   pouch; purse
borsa 2 [BOHR•sa] *n* F Stock
   Exchange
borsa di studio [BOHR•sa dee
   STUH•dyo] *n* F scholarship
borsa valori [BOHR•sa
   •va•LOH•ri] *n* stock market
borsaiolo [BOR•sa•YOH•lo] *n*
   M pickpocket
borsetta [bor•SEHT•ta] *n* F
   handbag; pocketbook
boscaiolo [BOS•ka•YOH•lo] *n*
   M lumberjack
boschetto [bos•KEHT•to] *n* M
   grove
Bosnia [BOHZ•nia] *n* F Bosnia
bosniaco; bosniaca
   [boz•NEEA•ko];
   [boz•NEEA•ka] *adj n* MF
   Bosnian
botanica [BO•tah•NI•ka] *n* F
   botany
botola [boh•TO•la] *n* F
   trap-door
botte [BOHT•te] *n* F barrel; tun
bottegaio; bottegaia
   [BOT•te•GAH•yo];
   [BOT•te•GAH•ya] *n* MF
   storekeeper
botteghino [bot•TEG•eeno] *n*
   M box office

bottiglia [bot•TEE•lya] *n* F
bottle

bottino [bot•TEE•noh] *n* M
booty; loot

botto [BOHT•to] *n* M pop

bottone [bot•TOH•ne] *n* M
button

bovino; bovina
[boh•VEE•no];[boh•VEE•na]
adj MF bovine

bowling [BO•ling] *n* M
bowling

bozzolo [boh•TSO•lo] *n* M
cocoon

braccialetto
[BRA•tshya•LEHT•to] *n* M
bracelet

braccio [BRAH•tshioh] *n* M
arm; fathom

braccio destro [BRAH•tsho
DEHS•tro] *adj* right-hand

braci [BRAH•tshi] *n* F embers

braciola [bra•TSHOH•la] *n* F
chop (of meat)

braille [BRAH•il] *n* M braille

branda [BRAHN•da] *n* F cot

brandello [bran•DEHL•lo] *n* M
shred

brandire [bran•DEE•re] *vt*
wield

brandy [BREHN•di] *n* M
brandy

brano [BRAH•no] *n* M excerpt

bravata [bra•VAH•ta] *n* F stunt

breccia [BREH•tsha] *n* F breach
(in wall); gap

bretella [bre•TEHL•la] *n* F
strap

bretelle [bre•TEHL•le] *npl* F
suspenders

breve [BREH•ve] *adj* brief

brevemente
[BRE•ve•MEHN•te] *adv*
briefly

brevitá [BRE•vi•TA'] *n* F
brevity

brezza [BREH•tsa] *n* F breeze

briciola [bree•TSHO•la] *n* F
crumb

brillante 1 [bril•LAHN•te] *adj*
brilliant

brillante 2 [bril•LAHN•te] *n* M
diamond

brillo; brilla [BREEL•lo];
[BREEL•la] *adj* MF tipsy

brindisi [BREEN•DI•zi] *n* M
toast

briscola [brees•KO•la] *n* F
trump

brivido [bree•VI•do] *n* M
shudder

brocca [BROHK•ka] *n* F jug;
pitcher

broccato [brok•AH•to] *n* M
brocade

broccoli [broh•KO•li] *npl* M
broccoli

brodaglia [bro•DAH•lya] *n* F
slop

brodo [broh•do] *n* M broth

brontolare [BRON•to•LAH•re]
vi grumble; *n* MF grouch

bronzo [BROHN•tso] *n* bronze

bruciacchiare
[BRU•tsha•KYAH•re] *vt*
scorch

bruciare [bru•TSHAH•re] *vt*
burn; sear; singe

bruciatore [BRU•tshia•TOH•re]
n M burner

bruco [BRUH•ko] *n* M
caterpillar

brughiera [bru•GYEH•ra] *n* F
moor

brunetta [bru•NEHT•ta] *n* F
brunette

brusco; brusca [BRUH•sko;
BRUH•ska] *adj* abrupt

brutale [bru•TAH•le] *adj* brutal;
harsh

bruto [BRUH•to] *n* M brute;
slob

bruttezza [brut•TEH•tsa] *n* F
ugliness

brutto; brutta [BRUHT•to];
[BRUHT•ta] *adj* ugly

Bruxelles [BRUS•sehl] *n* M
Brussels

buca [BUH•ka] *n* F hole; pit;
pothole

buca delle lettere [BUH•ka
DEL•le let•TEH•re] *n* F
mailbox

bucare [bu•KAH•re] *vt* pierce;
make a hole in

bucato [bu•KAH•to] *n* M
laundry

buccia [BUH•tsha] *n* F peel;
rind

buco [BUH•ko] *n* M hole

Buddismo [bud•DEEZ•mo] *n* M
Buddhism

budella [bu•DEHL•la] *npl* F
bowels; gut

budino [bu•DEE•no] *n* M
pudding

bue [buhe] *n* M ox; steer

bufalo; bufala
[buh•FA•lo];[buh•FA•la] *n*
MF buffalo

buffet [buf•FE'] *n* M buffet

buffetto [buf•FEHT•to] *n* M
pat

buffo 1 [BUHF•fo] *n* M whiff

buffo 2; buffa [BUHF•fo];
[BUHF•fa] *adj* comic; funny;
hilarious

bugia [bu•DJEE•a] *n* F fib; lie

bugiardo; bugiarda
[bu•DJAHR•do];
[bu•DJAHR•da] *n* MF liar;
adj lying

bulbo [BUHL•bo] *n* M bulb

bulbo oculare [BUHL•bo
oku•LAH•re] *n* M eyeball

Bulgheria [BUL•ge•REE•ah] *n*
F Bulgaria

bulldozer [bul•DOH•zer] *n* M
bulldozer

bullone [bul•LOH•ne] *n* M bolt

buon senso [BU•ohn
SEHN•so] *n* M common sense

buona educazione [BUOH•na
EDU•ka•TSYOH•ne] *n* F
politeness

buona lana [BUOH•na
LAH•na] *n* MF rascal

buona volontá [BUOH•na
vo•lon•TAH] *n* F willingness

buono [BUOH•no] *n* M
voucher; -o -a *adj* good; kind;
right

buono; buona [BUOH•no];
[buoh•na] *adj* good

buono sconto [BUOH•no
SKOHN•to] M coupon

burattino [BU•rat•TEE•no] *n*
M puppet

burbero; burbera
[BUHR•bero]; [BUHR•bera]
adj MF gruff

burla [BUHR•la] *n* F hoax

burlarsi [bur•LAHR•si] *vi* flout;
make fun of

burlone [bur•LOH•ne] *n* M
joker

Burma [BUHR•ma] *n* F
Burma

burmese [bur•MEH•ze] *adj*
Burmese

burocrazia
[BU•ro•kra•TSEE•ah] *n* F
bureaucracy

burrasca [bur•RAHS•ka] *n* F
gale; squall; wind storm

burro [BUHR•ro] *n* M
butter

burro dj arachidi [BUHR•ro
•dee arah•KI•di] *n* M peanut
butter

burrone [bur•ROH•ne] *n* M
ravine; gully

bussare [bus•SAH•re] *n vi* M
knock; rap

bussola [buhs•SO•la] *n* F
compass (nav)

busta [BUH•sta] *n* F envelope

busta paga [BUHS•ta PAH•ga]
n F paycheck

bustarella [BUS•tah•RAIL•la]
n F bribe

busto [BUH•sto] *n* M bust (of
statue)

buttafuori [BUHT•ta•FUOH•ri]
n M bouncer

C

cabina [ka•BEE•nah] *n* F cabin;
stateroom

cabina telefonica [ka•BEE•na
TE•le•FOH•ni•ka] *n* F phone
booth

cacao [ka•KAH•o] *n* M cocoa;
chocolate

caccia [KAH•tsha] *n* F chase;
hunt; da caccia *adj* shooting

cacciare [ka•TSHAH•re] *vt*
chase

cacciatore [KA•tsha•TOH•re] *n*
M hunter

cacciavite [KAH•tsha•VEE•te]
n M screw-driver

cachi [KAH•ki] *adj* khaki

cacto [KAHK•to] *n* M cactus

cadavere [KA•dah•VE•re] *n* M
cadaver; corpse

cadde [KAHD•de] fell

cadetto [ka•DEHT•to] *n* M
cadet

caduta [ka•DUH•ta] *n* F
fall

caffé [KAF•feh] *n* M coffee

caffettiera [KAF•fet•TYEH•ra]
n F coffee pot

cagna [KAH•nya] *n* F bitch

calabrone [KA•la•BROH•ne] *n*
M bumblebee

calamita [KA•la•MEE•ta] *n* F
magnet

calare [ka•LAH•re] *vi* wane;
decrease; lessen

calcio [KAL•tshyo] *n* M
calcium; kick

calcolare [kal•ko•lah•re] *vt*
calculate; reckon

calcolatore
  [KAL•ko•la•TOH•re] *n* M
  calculator

calcolo [kahl•KO•lo] *n* M
  reckoning

caldo; calda [KAHL•do];
  [KAHL•da] *adj* hot; mellow;
  warm

caleidoscopio
  [KA•leh•ydo•SKOH•pyo] *n* M
  kaleidoscope

calendario [KA•len•DAH•rio] *n*
  M calendar

calendula [KA•lehn•DU•la] *n* F
  marigold

calma [KAHL•ma] *n* F
  composure; lull

calmare [kal•MAH•re] *vt* calm
  down; soothe

calmo; calma [KAHL•mo];
  [KAHL•ma] *adj* calm;
  untroubled

calore [ka•LOH•re] *n* M heat;
  warmth

calpestare [KAL•pes•TAH•re]
  vt trample

calunnia [ka•LUHN•nya] *n* F
  slander

calvo; calva
  [KAHL•vo];[KAHL•va] *adj*
  MF bald; hairless

calza [KAHL•tsa] *n* F stocking

calze [KAHL•tse] *npl* F hosiery

calzino [kal•TSEE•no] *n* M
  sock

calzolaio [KAL•tso•LAH•yo] *n*
  M shoemaker

calzoni [kal•TSOH•ni] *n* M
  trousers

camaleonte
  [KA•ma•le•OHN•te] *n* M
  chameleon

cambiare [kam•BIAH•re] *vt*
  change

cambiare direzione
  [kam•BYA•re
  DI•reh•TSYOH•ne] *vi* veer

cambio [KAHM•byo] *n* M
  change; exchange (currency)

Cambogia [kam•BODJ•ah] *n* F
  Cambodia

cambusa [kam•BUH•za] *n* F
  galley

camera [kah•ME•ra] *n* F
  chamber

camera da letto [kah•ME•ra
  dah LEHT•to] *n* F bedroom

camera dei bambini
  [ka•ME•ra dehi bam•BEE•ni]
  n F nursery

cameraman
  [KAH•me•RA•mahn] *n* M
  cameraman

cameriera [KA•me•RYEH•ra] *n*
  F waitress

cameriere [KA•me•RYEH•re] *n*
  M waiter

camerino di prova
  [KA•me•REE•no di
  PROH•va] *n* M fitting room

camicetta [KA•mit•SHEHT•ta]
  n F blouse

camino [ka•MEE•no] *n* M
  chimney; fireplace

camion [KAH•myon] *n* M truck

cammello [kam•MEHL•lo] *n* M
  camel

cammeo [KAM•meho] *n* M
  cameo

camminare [KAM•mi•NAH•re]
  vi walk

camminare faticosamente
  [KAM•mi•NAH•re fa•TI•ko
  za•MEHN•te] *vi* trudge

camminare ondeggiando
[KAM•mi•NAH•re
ON•de•DJAHN•do] *vi* waddle

campagna 1 [kam•PAH•nya] *n*
F campaign

campagna 2 [kam•PAH•nya] *n*
M country

campana [kam•PAH•na] *n* F
bell

campanile [KAM•pa•NEE•le] *n*
M belfry; steeple; carrillon

campata [kam•PAH•ta] *n* F
span

campeggiare
[KAM•pe•DJAH•re] *vi* camp

campeggio [kam•PEHDJ•yo] *n*
M campground

campione [kam•PYOH•ne] *n* M
champion

campo [KAHM•po] *n* M camp;
-o -a MF field

campo giochi [KAHM•po
DJOH•ki] *n* M playground

Canadá [KA•na•DA'] *n* M
Canada

canale [ka•NAH•le] *n* M canal;
channel

canarino [KA•na•REE•no] *n* M
canary

cancellare [KAN•tshel•LAH•re]
vt cancel; call off
(appointment); delete; erase;
obliterate

cancelleria
[KAN•tshel•le•REE•a] *n* F
stationery

cancelletto
[KAN•tshel•LEHT•to] *n* M
wicket

cancelliere
[KAN•tshel•LIEH•re] *n* M
chancellor

cancello [kan•TSHEHL•lo] *n* M
gate

cancro [KAHN•kro] *n* M cancer

candeggina
[KAN•de•DJEE•na] *n* F
bleach

candela 1 [kan•DEH•la] *n* F
candle; tapér

candela 2 [kan•DEH•la] *n* F
spark plug

candeliere [KAN•de•LYE•re] *n*
M sconce

candidato; candidata
[KAN•di•DAH•to];
[KAN•di•DAH•ta] *n* MF
candidate

candido; candida
[kahn•DEE•do];
[kahn•DEE•do] *adj* candid

candore [kan•DOH•re] *n* M
candor

cane [KAH•ne] *n* M dog

cane bastardo [KAH•ne
bas•TAHR•do] *n* M mongrel

cane da caccia [KAH•ne dah
KAH•tsha] *n* M hound

cane da guardia [KAH•ne dah
GUAHR•dya] *n* M watchdog

canestro [kan•EH•stro] *n* M
basket; hamper

canguro [kan•GUH•ro] *n* M
kangaroo

canile [ka•NEE•le] *n* M kennel

canino; canina
[ka•NEE•noh]; [ka•NEE•nah]
adj canine

canna [KAHN•na] *n* F cane;
reed

canna fumaria [KAHN•na
fu•MAH•rya] *n* F flue

cannella [kan•NEHL•la] *n* F
cinnamon

cannibale [KAN•nee•BA•le] *n*
MF cannibal

cannone [kan•NHO•ne] *n* M
cannon

cannuccia [kan•NUH•tsha] *n* F
straw (drinking)

canoa [ka•NOH•ah] *n* F canoe

canottaggio [KA•not•TAH•djo]
n M boating

cantare [kan•TAH•re] *vt* sing

cantare bocca chiusa
[kan•TAH•re ah BOHK•ka
KYUH•za] *vt* hum

cantina [kan•TEE•na] *n* F
cellar; wine cellar

canto [KAHN•to] *n* M chant
(rel)

canyon [KAH•nyon] *n* M
canyon

canzoncina
[KAN•tson•TSHEE•na] *n* F
jingle

canzone [kan•TSOH•ne] *n* F
song

caos [KAH•os] *n* M chaos

capace [ka•PAH•tshe] *adj* able

capacitá [KA•pat•shi•TA'] *n* F
capacity

capanna [ka•PAHN•na] *n* F
hut; shack

caparbio; caparbia
[ka•PAHR•byo];
[ka•PAHR•bya] *adj* willful

capello [ka•PEHL•lo] *n* M hair

capezzolo [ka•PEH•tsolo] *n* M
nipple

capire [ka•PEE•re] *vt* realize;
understand

capire male [ka•PEE•re
MAH•le] *vt* misunderstand

capitale [KA•pi•TAH•le] *n* M
capital

capitalismo
[KA•pi•tal•EEZ•mo] *n* M
capitalism

capitano [KA•pi•TAH•no] *n* M
captain; skipper

capitolo [ka•PEE•to•lo] *n* M
chapter

capo 1 [KAH•po] *n* M chief;
head; leader

capo 2 [KAH•po] *n* M cape
(geog)

capo cuoco [KAH•po
KUOH•ko] *n* M chef

capo operaio [KAH•po
ope•RAH•yo] *n* M foreman

capolavoro
[KA•po•la•VOH•ro] *n* M
masterpiece

caporale [KA•po•RAH•le] *n* M
corporal

cappa del caminetto
[KAHP•pa dehl
KA•mi•NEHT•to] *n* F
mantelpiece

cappella [kap•PEHL•la] *n* M
chapel

cappellano [KAP•pel•LAH•no]
n M chaplain

cappello [kap•PEHL•lo] *n* M
hat

cappero [kahp•PE•ro] *n* M
caper (edible)

cappio [KAHP•pyo] *n* M loop;
noose

cappotto [kap•POHT•to] *n* M
coat; overcoat

cappuccio [kap•PUH•tsho] *n* M
hood

capra [KAH•pra] *n* F goat

capretto [ka•PREHT•to] *n* M
kid (young goat)

capriccio [ka•PREE•tsho] *n* M
tantrum; whim

capriccioso; capricciosa
[KA•prit•SHOH•zo];
[KA•prit•SHOH•za] *adj*
whimsical

capriola [ka•PRYOH•la] *n* F
somersault

capsula [kahp•SU•la] *n* F
capsule

caraffa [ka•RAHF•fa] *n* F
decanter

caramella [KA•ra•MEHL•la] *n*
F candy

carattere [KA•raht•TE•re] *n* M
character; temper; disposition
(attitude)

caratteristica
[KA•rat•te•REE•sti•ka] *n* F
characteristic; feature

caratteristico; caratteristica
[KA•rat•te•REE•sti•ko];
[KA•rat•te•REE• sti•ka] *adj*
characteristic

carbone [kar•BOH•ne] *n* M
carbon; charcoal; coal

carburante
[KAR•bu•RAHN•te] *n* M fuel

carcassa [kar•KAHS•sa] *n* F
carcass

carcere [kahr•TSHE•re] *n* M jail

cardiaco; cardiaca
[KAR•dee•AH•ko];
[KAR•dee•AH•ka] *adj* cardiac

cardinale [KAR•di•NAH•le] *n*
M cardinal

cardine [kahr•DI•ne] *n* M hinge

cardo [KAHR•do] *n* M thistle

carestia [KA•res•TEE•a] *n* F
famine

carezza [ka•REH•tsa] *n* F caress

caricare [KA•ri•KAH•re] *vt*
wind; burden

carico [kah•RI•ko] *n* M cargo;
load

carie [KAH•rie] *n* F cavity
(dental)

carino; carina [ka•REE•no];
[ka•REE•na] *adj* cute; pretty

caritá [ka•ri•TA'] *n* F charity

carlino [kar•lee•no] *n* M pug

carnagione
[KAR•na•DJYOH•ne] *n* F
complexion

carnale [kar•NAH•le] *adj* carnal

carne [KAHR•ne] *n* F flesh;
meat

carne di cervo [KAHR•ne dee
TSHEH•vo] *n* F venison

carnefice [KAR•neh•FI•tshe] *n*
M torturer

carnevale [KAR•ne•VAH•le] *n*
M carnival

carnivoro; carnivora
[KAR•nee•VO•ro];
[KAR•nee•VO•ra] *adj*
carnivorous

carnoso; carnosa
[kar•NOH•zo]; [kar•NOH•za]
adj fleshy

caro; cara [KAH•ro]; [KAH•ra]
adj MF dear

carota [ka•ROH•ta] *n* F carrot

carpa [KAHR•pa] *n* F carp

carreggiata [KAR•re•DJAH•ta]
n F rut; groove; track

carriera [kar•RIEH•ra] *n* F
career

carriola [kar•RYOH•la] *n* F
wheelbarrow

carro [KAHR•ro] *n* M cart

carro funebre [KAHR•ro
fuh•NE•bre] *n* M hearse

carrozza [kar•ROH•tsa] *n* F
carriage; coach

carrucola [KAR•ruh•KO•la] *n* F
pulley

carta [KAHR•ta] *n* F card;
chart; paper

carta da imballaggio
[KAHR•ta dah
IM•bal•LAH•djo] *n* F
wrapping paper

carta da parati [KAHR•ta dah
pa•RAH•ti] *n* F wallpaper

carta di credito [KAHR•ta di
•kreh•DI•to] *n* F credit card

carta geografica [KAHR•ta
DJE•og•rah•FI•ka] *n* F map

carta igienica [KAHR•ta
I•djeh•NI•ka] *n* F toilet paper

cartella [kar•TEHL•la] *n* F
portfolio

cartellino [KAR•tel•LEE•no] *n*
M tag

cartello [kar•TEHL•lo] *n* M
sign (street)

cartilagine
[KAR•ti•lah•DJEE•ne] *n* F
gristle

cartoccio [kar•TOH•tsho] *n* M
husk

cartolina [KAR•to•LEE•na] *n* F
card (postal)

cartolina postale
[KAR•to•LEE•na pos•TAH•le]
n F post card

cartone [kar•TOH•ne] *n* M
cardboard

cartone animáto [kar•TOH•ne
•ani•MAH•to] *n* M cartoon

casa [KAH•za] *n* F home; house

casalinga [KA•za•LEEN•ga] *n*
F housewife

casamento [KA•za•MEHN•to]
n M tenement

cascata [kas•KAH•ta] *n* F
waterfall

caserma [ka•SEHR•ma] *n* F
barracks

caserma dei pompieri
[ka•ZEHR•ma deh•i
pom•PYEH•ri] *n* F fire station

caserma di polizia
[ka•ZEHR•ma dee
PO•lit•SEE•a] *n* F police
station

caso [KAH•zo] *n* M case (in ~
of); chance; event; instance; **a
caso** *adj* MF random

cassa 1 [KAHS•sa] *n* F cash
register; till

cassa 2 [KAHS•sa] *n* F crate

cassetta [kas•SEHT•ta] *n* F
cassette

cassettiera [KAS•set•TIEH•ra]
n F chest of drawers; bureau
(dresser)

cassetto [kas•SEHT•to] *n* M
drawer

cast [kahst] *n* M cast (film)

castagna [kas•TAH•nya] *n* F
chestnut

castello [kas•TEHL•lo] *n* M
castle

castigare [KAS•ti•GAH•re] *vt*
chastise

castitá [kas•ti•TA'] *n* F chastity

casto; casta [KAHS•to]; [KAHS•ta] *adj* MF chaste

castoro [kas•TOH•ro] *n* M beaver

casuale [ka•SUAH•le] *adj* casual; haphazard

catacumeno [KA•ta•kuh•ME•no] *n* M convert

catalogare [KA•ta•lo•GAH•re] *vt* catalogue

catalogo [KA•tah•LO•go] *n* M catalogue

catapulta [KA•ta•PUHL•ta] *n* F catapult

catapultare [KA•ta•pul•TAH•re] *vt* catapult

catastrofe [KA•tas•TROH•fe] *n* F catastrophe

categoria [KA•te•go•REE•ah] *n* F category

categorico; catgorica [KA•te•goh•RI•ko]; [KA•te•goh•RI•ka] *adj* categorical

catena [ka•TEH•na] *n* F chain

cateratta [KA•ter•AHT•ta] *n* F cataract

catterale [KAT•te•DRAH•le] *n* F cathedral

cattiva condotta [kat•TEE•va kon•DOHT•ta] *n* F misconduct

cattivo; cattiva [kat•TEE•vo]; [kat•TEE•va] *adj* MF bad; evil

cattivo uso [kat•TEE•vo UH•zo] *n* M misuse

cattolico; cattolica [kat•TOH•li•ko]; [kat•TOH•li•ka] *adj n* MF Catholic

cattura [kat•TUH•ra] *n* F capture

catturare [KAT•tu•RAH•re] *vt* nab; capture

causa [KAUH•za] *n* F cause; lawsuit; litigation; a causa di\ *prep* because of

causare [kau•ZAH•re] *vt* cause

caustico; caustica [KAH•u•STI•ko];[kah•u•sti•ka] *adj* caustic

cautela [kau•TEH•la] *n* F caution

cauto; cauta [KAH•uto]; [KAH•uta] *adj* cautious; wary; deliberate

cauzione [kau•TSIOH•ne] *n* F bail

cava [KAH•va] *n* F quarry (stone)

cavalcare [KA•val•KAH•re] *vt* ride (horseback)

cavalcatura [KA•val•ka•TUH•ra] *n* F mount

cavaliere [KA•va•LYEH•re] *n* M knight

cavalla [ka•VAHL•la] *n* F mare

cavalleria [KA•val•le•REE•ah] *n* F cavalry; chivalry

cavallerizzo; cavallerizza [KA•val•le•REE•tso]; [KA•val•le•REE•tsa] *n* MF rider

cavalletta [KA•val•LEHT•ta] *n* F locust

cavalletto [KA•val•LEHT•to] *n* M trestle

cavallo [ka•VAHL•lo] *n* M
horse; a cavallo *adj adv* (on)
horseback

cavatappi [KAH•va•TAHP•pi]
n M corkscrew

caverna [ka•VEHR•na] *n* F
cave

cavezza [ka•VEH•tsa] *n* F
halter

cavia [KAH•vya] *n* F guinea pig

cavillare [KA•vil•LAH•re] *vi*
haggle; quibble

cavitá [kah•vi•TA'] *n* F cavity;
sinus

cavo [KAH•vo] *n* M cable;
hollow

cavolfiore [KA•vol•FYOH•re] *n*
M cauliflower

cavolo [kah•VO•lo] *n* M
cabbage

cazzuola [ka•TSUOH•la] *n* F
trowel

ceco; ceca [TSHEH•ko];
[TSHEH•ka] *adj* MF Czech

Cecoslovacchia
[TSHE•ko•slo•VAH•kya] *n* F
Czechoslovakia

cedere [tsheh•DE•re] *vt vi* cede

cedilla [tshe•DEEL•la] *n* F
cedilla

cedro [TSHEH•dro] *n* M cedar

celare [tshe•LAH•re] *vt* conceal

celebrare [TSHE•le•BRAH•re]
vt celebrate

celebrazione
[TSHE•le•bra•TSIOH•ne] *n* F
celebration

celebritá [TSHE•lebri•TA'] *n* F
celebrity

celestiale [TSHE•les•TYAH•le]
adj heavenly

celibe [tsheh•LI•be] *adj* M
celibate

cella [TSHEHL•la] *n* F cell;
dungeon

celtico; celtica [TSHEL•TI•ko];
[TSHEL•TI•ka] *adj* Celtic

cemento [tshe•MEHN•to] *n* M
cement; concrete

cenere [tsheh•ne•re] *n* F ash;
cinder

Cenerentola
[TSHE•ne•REHN•to•la] *n* F
Cinderella

cenno del capo [TSHEHN•no
dehl KAH•po] *n* M nod

censimento
[TSHEN•si•MEHN•to] *n* M
census

censore [tshen•SOH•re] *n* M
censor

censura [tschen•SUH•ra] *n* F
censorship

centenario
[TSHEN•te•NAH•rio] *n* M
centennial

centesimo 1
[TSHEN•teh•ZI•mo] *n* M
penny

centesimo 2; centesima
[tshen•TEH•zimo];
[tshen•TEH•zi•ma] *adj*
hundredth

centigrado
[TSHEN•tee•GRA•do] *n* M
centigrade

centimetro
[TSHEN•tee•ME•tro] *n* M
centimeter

cento [TSHEHN•to] *num*
hundred

•

centrale [tshen•TRAH•le] *adj*
central

centralinista
[TSHEN•tra•li•NEES•ta] *n*
MF operator (telephone)

centralino
[TSHEN•tra•LEE•no] *n* M
switchboard

centro [TSHEN•tro] *n* M
center; hub; pivot

ceppo [TSHEHP•po] *n* M log

cera [TSHEH•ra] *n* F wax

ceramica [TSHE•rah•MI•ka] *n*
F ceramic; pottery

cerbiatto [tsher•BYAHT•to] *n*
M fawn

cercare [tsher•KAH•re] *vi*
search; *vt* seek

cerchio [TSHEHR•kyo] *n* M
circle; hoop

cereale [tshe•REH•ale] *n* M
cereal

cerimonia [TSHE•ri•MOH•nia]
n F ceremony

cerniera [tsher•NYEH•ra] *n* F
zipper

certamente
[TSHER•ta•MEHN•te] *adv*
certainly

certezza [tsher•TEH•tsa] *n* F
certainty

certificare
[TSHER•ti•fi•KAH•re] *vt*
certify

certificato
[TSHER•ti•fi•KAH•to] *n* M
certificate

certo; certa
[TSHEHR•to];[TSHEHR•ta]
adj MF certain

cervello [tsher•VEHL•lo] *n* M
brain

cervo [TSHEHR•vo] *n* M stag

cesellare [TSHE•sel•LAH•re] *vt*
chisel

cespuglio [tshes•PUH•lyo] *n* M
bush; shrub

cessare [tshes•SAH•re] *v* cease

cessare il fuoco [tshes•SAH•re
il FUOH•ko] *n* M cease-fire

cestino [tshes•TEE•no] *n* M
waste-paper basket

ceto medio
[TSHEH•to•MEH•dyo] *n* M
middle class

cetra [TSHEH•tra] *n* F zither

cetriolo [TSHE•tri•OH•lo] *n* M
cucumber

champagne [sham•PAH•n] *n*
M champagne

charter [TSHAHR•ter] *n* M
charter (flight)

che [keh] *pron* which

che cosa [keh KOH•za] *pron*
what; al che; *adv* thereon;
thereupon

che esercita la professione
[keh ezehr•TSHI•ta la
PRO•fes•SYOH•ne] *adj*
practicing

che fa colpo [keh fah
KOHL•po] *adj* striking

che fa soffrire [keh fah
sof•FREE•re] *adj* hurtful

che ha successo [keh ah
su•TSHESH•so] *adj* successful

che lavora [keh la•VOH•ra] *adj*
working

che non fa distinzioni [keh
nohn fah DIS•tin•TSYOH•ni]
adj undiscriminating

che pesa troppo [keh PEH•za TROHP•po] *adj* overweight

chela [KEH•la] *n* F claw (lobster)

cherosene [KE•ro•SEH•ne] *n* M kerosene

chi [kee] *pron* who; whom; **di chi** *pron* whose

chi rinunzia facilmente [kee ri•NUHN•tsya FA•tshil•MEHN•te] *n* M quitter

chiaccherare [KYAK•ke•RAH•re] *vi* chat

chiaccherone; chiaccherona [KYAK•ke•ROH•ne]; [KYIAK•ke•ROH•na] *n* MF chatterbox; talker; tattle-tale

chiamare [kya•MAH•re] *vt* call

chiamata [kya•MAH•ta] *n* F call

chiaramente [KEE•ar•ah•MEN•te] *adv* clearly; plainly

chiarezza [kya•REH•tsa] *n* F clarity

chiarificare [KYA•ri•fi•KAH•re] *vt* clarify

chiarire [kya•REE•re] *vt* clear

chiaro; chiara [KYAH•ro]; [KYAH•ra] *adj* MF clear; manifest; patent

chiaro di luna [KYA•ro•di•LUH•na] *n* M moonlight

chiave [KYAH•ve] *n* F key

chiave di violino [KYAH•ve dee vyo•LEE•no] *n* F treble clef

chiave inglese [KYAH•ve in GLEH•ze] *n* F wrench

chiazza [KYAH•tsa] *n* F fleck

chicco [KEEK•ko] *n* M kernel

chicco d'uva [KEE•ko DUH•va] *n* M grape

chicco di grandine [KEEK•ko di GRAHN•di•ne] *n* M hailstone

chiea [KIEH•za] *n* F church

chilogrammo [KI•lo•GRAHM•mo] *n* M kilogram

chilometro [ki•LOH•metro] *n* M kilometer

chilowatt [kee•LO•vat] *n* M kilowatt

chimica [ki•MEE•ka] *n* F chemistry

chimico; chimica [ki•MEE•ko]; [ki•MEE•ka] *n* MF *adj* chemical

chinino [ki•NEE•no] *n* M quinine

chiocciare [kyo•TSHAH•re] *vi* cluck

chiodo [KYOH•do] *n* M nail

chiodo di garofano [KYOH•do di ga•ROH•fa•no] *n* M clove

chiosco [KYOHS•ko] *n* M stall

chiostro [KYOH•stro] *n* M cloister

chitarra [ki•TAHR•ra] *n* F guitar

chiudere [kyuh•DE•re] *vt* shut; *vt* close

chiunque [ki•UHN•qwe] *pron* M anyone (anybody); whomever

chiuso; chiusa [KYUH•zo]; [KYUH•za] *adj* MF

close; near; inner; withdrawn;
al chiuso\ indoor

cialda [TSHAHL•da] *n* F waffle

ciambella [TSHI•am•BEHL•la]
n F bun

cianfrusaglie
[TSHAN•fru•ZAH•lye] *n* F
junk

ciao [TSHAH•o] *excl* hello

ciarlatano; ciarlatana
[THSAR•la•TAH•no];
[TSHAR•la•TAH•na] *n* MF
quack

cibo [TSHEE•bo] *n* M food

cicatrice [TSHI•ka•TREE•tshe]
n F scar

ciclo [TSHEE•klo] *n* M cycle

ciclomotore
[TSHEE•klo•mo•TOH•re] *n* M
motorcycle

ciclone [tshi•KLOH•ne] *n* M
cyclone

cicogna [tshi•KOH•nya] *n* F
stork

cieco; cieca
[TSHEH•ko];[TSHEH•ka] *adj*
MF blind

cielo [TSHEH•lo] *n* M heaven;
sky

cifra [TSHEE•fra] *n* F figure
(number); digit

ciglia [TSHI•lya] *n* F eyelash

cigno [TSHEE•nyo] *n* M swan

cigolare [TSHI•go•LAH•re] *vi*
creak; squeak

Cile [TSHEE•le] *n* M Chile

ciliegia [tshi•LYEH•dja] *n* F
cherry

cilindro [tshi•LEEN•dro] *n* M
cylinder

cimelio di casa [tshi•MEH•lyo
di KAH•za] *n* M heirloom

cimitero [TSHI•mi•TEH•ro] *n*
M cemetery

Cina [TSHEE•na] *n* F China

cinema [tshee•NE•ma] *n* M
cinema

cinese [tshi•NEH•se] *adj*
Chinese

cinghia [TSHEEN•gya] *n* F
webbing

cinghiale [tshin•GYAH•le] *n* M
boar; wild boar

cinguettare
[TSHIN•guet•TAH•re] *vi*
chirp (bird)

cinguettio
[TSHIN•guet•TEE•o] *n* M
twitter

cinico; cinica [tshee•NI•ko];
[tshee•NI•ka] *n* MF cynic; *adj*
cynical

cinquanta [tshin•KWAHN•ta]
num fifty

**cinquantesimo;
cinquantesima**
[TSHIN•kwan•teh•ZI•mo];
[TSHIN•kwan•teh•ZI•ma] *adj*
fiftieth

cinque [TSHIN•kwe] *num* five

cintura [tshin•TUH•ra] *n* F belt

cintura di salvataggio
[tshin•TUH•ra di
SAL•va•TAH•djo] *n* F life
jacket

ciò [tscho] this; that; con ciò\
therefore; di ció\ *adv* thereof;
in ció\ *adv* therein

ciocca [TSHOHK•ka] *n* F tress

cioccolata [TSHOK•ko•LAH•ta]
n F chocolate; fudge

ciondolare [TSHON•do•LAH•re] *vt*
dangle

cipiglio [tshi•PEE•lyo] *n* M
frown; scowl

cipolla [tshi•POHL•la] *n* F
onion

cipresso [tshi•PREHS•so] *n* M
cypress

circa [TSHEER•ka] *adv* about;
prep concerning

**circdato da mura; circondata
da mura**
[TSHIR•kon•DAH•to dah
MUH•ra];
[TSHIR•kon•DAH•ta dah
MUH•ra] *adj* MF walled

circo [TSHEER•ko] *n* M circus

circolare [TSHIR•ko•LAH•re]
adj circular; *vi* circulate

circolazione
[TSHIR•ko•la•TSIOH•ne] *n* F
circulation

circoncisione
[TSHIR•kon•tshi•ZIOH•ne] *n*
F circumcision

circondare
[TSHIR•kon•DAH•re] *vt*
enclose

circonferenza
[TSHIR•kon•fe•REHN•tsa] *n*
F girth; circumference

circonflesso; circonflessa
[TSHIR•kon•FLEHS•sso];
[TSHIR•kon•FLEHS•sa] *adj*
MF circular

circostanza
[TSHIR•kos•TAHN•tsa] *n* F
circumstance

circuito [TSHIR•kuh•I•to] *n* M
circuit

ciste [TSHEE•ste] *n* F cyst

citare [tshi•TAH•re] *vt* cite;
quote

citazione [TSHI•ta•TSYOH•ne]
n F quotation

citofono [TSHI•toh•fo•no] *n* M
intercom

cittá [tshit•TA'] *n* F city; town

cittadino; cittadina
[TSHIT•ta•DEE•no];
[TSHIT•ta•DEE•na] *n* MF
citizen

ciuffo [TSHUHF•fo] *n* M tuft

ciurma [TSHUHR•ma] *n* F crew

civetta [tshi•VEHT•ta] *n* F flirt

civico; civica
[tshee•VI•KO];[tshee•VI•KA]
adj civic

civile [tshi•VEE•le] *adj* civil

civilizzare [TSHI•vil•it•SAH•re]
vt civilize

civiltá [tshi•vil•TA'] *n* F
civilization

clamore [kla•MOH•re] *n* M
clamor

clan [klahn] *n* M clan

clandestino; clandestina
[KLAN•de•STEE•no];
[KLAN•de•STEE• na] *adj* MF
clandestine; underhanded

clarinetto [KLA•ri•NEHT•to] *n*
M clarinet

classe [KLAHS•se] *n* F class

classe turistica
[KLAHS•se•tu•rees•ti•ka] *n* F
coach (class)

classico; classica
[KLAHS•si•ko];
[KLAHS•si•ka] *adj n* MF
classic; classical

classificare
[KLAS•si•fi•KAH•re] *vt*
classify; sort; class

classificato; classificata
[KLAS•si•fi•KAH•to];
[KLAS•si•fi•KAH•ta] *adj*
classified

clausola [klou•SO•lah] *n* F
clause

clausola condizionale
[klou•SO•lah
KON•di•tsyo•NAH•le] *n* M
proviso

clavicembalo
[KLA•vi•TSHEHM•ba•lo] *n*
M harpsichord

clericale [KLE•ri•KAH•le] *adj*
clerical

clero [KLEH•ro] *n* M clergy

clessidra [kles•SEE•dra] *n* F
hourglass

cliente [kli•EHN•te] *n* MF
client; customer; patron

clientela [KLI•ent•EH•la] *n*
clientele

clima [KLEE•ma] *n* M climate

clinica [kli•NEE•ka] *n* F clinic

clinico; clinica
[KLI•NEE•ko];[KLI•NEE•ka]
adj clinical

clorofilla [KLO•ro•FEEL•la] *n*
F chlorophyll

clown [KLAH•un] *n* clown

club [kluhb] *n* M club (social)

cocaina [KO•ka•EE•na] *n* F
cocaine

coccodrillo
[KOK•ko•DREEL•lo] *n* M
crocodile

coccolare [KOK•ko•LAH•re] *vt*
pamper

cocktail [kok•TEH•il] *n* cocktail

cocnetto [kon•TSHEHT•to] *n*
M concept

cocorita [KO•ko•REE•ta] *n* F
parakeet

coda [KOH•da] *n* F tail

coda di cavallo [KOH•da dee
ka•VAHL•lo] *n* F ponytail

codardia [KO•dar•DEE•a] *n* F
cowardice

codice [ko•DEE•tshe] *n* M code

codificare [KO•di•fi•KAH•re] *vt*
code

coercitivo; coercitiva
[KOER•tshi•TEE•vo];
[KOER•tshi•TEE•va] *adj* MF
compulsive

coerente [KO•e•REHN•te] *adj*
coherent

coferenza [KON•fe•REHN•tsa]
n F conference

cognata [ko•NYAH•ta] *n* F
sister-in-law

cognato [ko•NYAH•to] *n* M
brother-in-law

cognome [ko•NYOH•me] *n* M
last name

cognome da nubile
[ko•NYOH•me dah
•NUH•bi•le] *n* M maiden
name

coincidenza
[KO•in•tshi•DEHN•tsa] *n* F
coincidence

coincidere [KO•in•tshee•DE•re]
vi coincide

coinvolgere
[KO•in•VOHL•dje•re] *vt*
involve

colare [ko•LAH•re] *vi* seep

colare lentamente [ko•LAH•re LEN•ta•MEHN•te] *vi* ooze

colazione [KO•lat•SIOH•ne] *n* F breakfast; lunch

colera [ko•LEH•ra] *n* M cholera

colibrí [ko•LI•bree] *n* M humming-bird

colino [ko•LEE•no] *n* strainer

colla [KOHL•la] *n* F glue

collaborare [KOL•la•bo•RAH•re] *vi* collaborate

collant [KOL•lahnt] *n* M pantyhose

collasso [kol•LAHS•soh] *n* M breakdown

collaterale [KOL•la•te•RAH•le] *n* collateral

collega [kol•EH•ga] *n* MF colleague

collegamento [KOL•le•gam•EHN•to] *n* M liaison

collegio [kol•LEH•djo] *n* M boarding school

collera [kohl•LE•ra] *n* F anger

colletto [kol•LEHT•to] *n* M collar

collezionare [KOL•let•syo•NAH•re] *n* collect

collina [kol•LEE•na] *n* F hill

collinoso; collinosa [KOL•li•NOH•zo]; [KOL•li•NOH•za] *adj* hilly

collisione [KOL•li•SYOH•ne] *n* F shock

collo [KOHL•lo] *n* M neck

collottola [KOL•loht•TO•la] *n* F scruff of neck

collusione [KOL•lu•ZYOH•ne] *n* F graft (financial)

colluttorio [KOL•lut•TOH•ryo] *n* M mouthwash

colomba [ko•LOHM•ba] *n* F dove

colon [KOH•lon] *n* M colon

colonia [ko•LOH•nya] *n* F colony

colonia [ko•LOH•nya] *n* F toilet water

colonna [ko•LOHN•na] *n* F column

colonna vertebrale [ko•LOHN•na VER•te•BRAH•le] *n* F spinal column

color ruggine [KO•lor ruh•DJI•ne] *adj* russet

colorare [KO•lo•RAH•re] *vt* color

colore [ko•LOH•re] *n* M color; paint

colorire [KO•lo•RAH•re] *vt* tint

colossale [KO•los•SAH•le] *adj* colossal

colpa [KOHL•pa] *n* F fault; guilt

colpevole [KOL•peh•VO•le] *n* MF culprit; *adj* guilty

colpo [KOHL•po] *n* M coup; hit; stroke

colpo apoplettico [KOHL•po APO•pleht•TI•ko] *n* M stroke (medical)

colpo fortunato [KOHL•po FOR•tu•NAH•to] *n* M fluke

coltello [kol•TEHL•lo] *n* M knife

coltivare [KOL•ti•VAH•re] *vt* cultivate; grow; raise

coltivatore diretto
[KOL•ti•VATOH•re di REHT•to] *n* M yeoman

coma [KOH•ma] *n* coma

comandante
[KO•mahn•DAHN•te] *n* M commander

comando [ko•MAHN•do] *n* M command; leadership; lead

combattere [kom•BAHT•te•re] *vi* combat; spar; fight

combattimento
[KOM•bat•ti•MEHN•to] *n* M combat

combinare [KOM•bi•NAH•re] *vt* combine

combinazione
[KOM•bi•nat•SYOH•ne] *n* F combination

combriccola
[KOM•breek•KO•la] *n* F gang

combustibile
[KOM•bus•TEE•bi•le] *adj* flammable

come [KOH•me] *conj* as; *adv* how

come sopra [KOH•me SOH•pra] *prep* ditto

cometa [ko•MEH•ta] *n* F comet

comico [koh•MI•ko] *n* M comedian; comic actor

comico; comica [koh•MI•ko]; [koh•MI•ka] *adj* humorous

cominciare
[KO•min•TSHYAH•re] *vt* begin; start

comitato [KO•mi•TAH•to] *n* M committee

commedia [kom•MEH•dya] *n* F comedy

commemorativo; commemorativa
[KOM•me•mora•TEE•vo]; [KOM•me•mora•TEE•va] *adj* MF memorial

commendare
[KOM•men•DAH•re] *vt* commend

commensale
[KOM•men•SAH•le] *n* MF diner

commentare
[KOM•men•TAH•re] *vi* comment

commento [kom•MEHN•to] *n* M comment

commerciale
[KOM•mer•TSHAH•le] *adj* trading

commerciante
[KOM•mer•TSHAHN•te] *n* MF dealer; merchant; trader

commercio [KOM•MEHR•tsho] *n* M commerce; dealings; trade

commesso [kom•MEHS•so] *n* M clerk

commesso di banca; commessa di banca
[kom•MEHS•so dee BAHN•ka]; [kom•MEHS•sa dee BAHN•ka] *n* MF teller

commestibile
[KOM•me•STEE•bi•le] *adj* edible

commestibili
[KOM•me•STEE•bi•li] *npl* M groceries

commettere
[KOM•met•TEH•re] *vt* commit (a crime)

commissione
[KOM•mis•SYOH•ne] *n* F
commission; errand

commovente
[KOM•mo•VEHN•te] *adj*
moving; stirring; touching

commutare
[KOM•mu•TAH•re] *vt*
commute (a sentence)

comó [KO•moh] *n* M dresser

comodo; comod [koh•MO•do];
[koh•MO•da] *adj* comfortable

compact disc [KOHM•pakt
deesk] *n* compact disc

compagnia [KOM•pa•NEE•ah]
n F company; outfit

compagno; compagna
[kom•PAH•nyo];
[kom•PAH•nya] *n* MF
companion; comrade; mate

compagno di camera;
compagna di camera
[kom•PAH•nyo dee
KAH•ME•ra]; [kom•PAH•nyo
dee KAH•ME•ra] *n* MF
roommate

compassione
[KOM•pas•SYOH•ne] *n* F
compassion

compassionevole
[KOM•pas•syo•neh•VO•le]
adj compassionate

compasso [kom•PAHS•so] *n* M
compass

compatibile
[KOM•pa•tee•bi•le] *adj*
compatible

compatto; compatta
[kom•PAHT•to];
[kom•PAHT•ta] *adj* MF
compact; firm

compendio [kom•PEHN•dyo] *n*
M epitome

compensare
[KOM•pen•SAH•re] *vt*
compensate

compenso [kom•PEHN•so] *n*
M compensation

comperè [KOHM•pe•re] *n* F
shopping

competente
[KOM•pe•TEHN•t]e *adj*
competent

competenza
[KOM•pe•TEHN•tsa] *n* F
competence

competere [KOM•peh•TE•re]
vi compete

competizione
[KOM•pe•tit•SYOH•ne] *n* F
competition

compiacente
[KOM•pya•TSHEN•te] *adj*
obliging

compiaciuto; compiaciuta
[KOM•pyah•TSHU•to];
[KOM•pyah•TSHU•ta] *adj*
MF complacent; pleased

compiti di casa [kohm•PI•ti di
KAH•za] *npl* M homework

compito [kohm•PI•to] *n* M task

compito; compita
[kom•PEE•to]; [kom•PEE•ta]
adj prim

compiuto; compiuta
[kom•PYUH•to];
[kom•PYUH•ta] *adj* MF
thorough

compleanno
[KOM•ple•AHN•no] *n* M
birthday

complessivamente
[KOM•ples•si•va•MEHN•te]
adv overall

complesso; complessa
[kom•PLEHS•so];
[kom•PLEHS•sa] *adj* MF
complex

completamente 1
[KOM•plet•a•MEHN•te] *adv*
altogether; thoroughly; wholly

completamente 2
[KOM•ple•ta•MEHN•te] *adv*
stark

completare 1
[KOM•ple•TAH•re] *vt*
complement

completare 2
[KOM•ple•TAH•re] *vt*
complete

completo; completa
[kom•PLEH•to];
[kom•PLEH•ta] *adj* MF
complete

complicare [KOM•pli•KAH•re]
vt complicate

complicato; complicata
[KOM•pli•KAH•to];
[KOM•pli•KAH•ta] *adj* MF
complicated; tricky

complice [kohm•PLIT•she] *n*
MF accomplice

complimentare
[KOM•pli•men•TAH•re] *vt*
compliment

complimento
[KOM•pli•MEHN•to] *n* M
compliment

complotto [kom•PLOHT•to] *n*
M conspiracy

componente
[KOM•po•NEHN•te] *n* M
component

comporre [kom•pohr•re] *vt*
compose

comportamento
[kom•por•ta•MEHN•to] *n* M
behavior; demeanor

comportare
[KOM•por•TAH•re] *vt* entail

comportarsi
[KOM•por•TAHR•si] *vi*
behave

comportarsi male
[KOM•por•TAHR•si MAH•le]
vi misbehave

compositore
[KOM•po•si•TOH•re] *n* M
composer

composizione
[KOM•po•si•TSYOH•ne] *n* F
composition

composto; composta
[kom•POHS•to];
[kom•POHS•ta] *adj* compound

comprare [kom•PRAH•re] *vt*
buy

compratore
[KOM•pra•TOH•re] *n* M
buyer; shopper

comprendere
[kom•PREHN•de•re] *vt*
comprehend; encompass

comprensibile
[KOM•pren•SEE•bi•le] *adj*
understandable

comprensione
[KOM•pren•TSYOH•ne] *n* F
comprehension; sympathy;
understanding

comprensivo; comprensiva
[KOM•pren•SEE•vo];
[KOM•pren•SEE•va] *adj*
comprehensive; sympathetic

compreso; compresa
[kom•PREH•zo];

[kom•PREH•za] *adj* MF
including

comprimere
[kom•PREE•me•re] *vt*
compress

compromesso
[KOM•pro•MEHS•so] *n* M
compromise

compromettere
[KOM•pro•meht•TE•re] *vt*
compromise

computer [kom•PUH•ter] *n* M
computer

computerizzare
[KOM•pu•te•ri•TSAH•re] *vt*
computerize

comune 1 [ko•MUH•ne] *n* M
borough; township

comune 2 [ko•muh•ne] *adj*
common

comunemente
[KO•mu•ne•MEHN•te] *adv*
commonly

comunicare
[KO•mu•ni•KAH•re] *vt*
communicate

comunicato commerciale
[KO•muni•KAH•to
KOM•mer•TSHAH•le] *n* M
commercial

comunione
[KO•mu•NYOH•ne] *n* F
communion

comunismo
[KO•mu•NEEZ•mo] *n* M
communism

comunista [KO•mu•NEES•ta] *n*
adj communist

comunitá [KO•mu•ni•TA'] *n* F
community; town

Comunitá Europea
[KO•muni•TAH euro•PEH•a]
n F European Community

comunque [ko•MUHN•keh]
adv anyway; *conj* however

con [kohn] *conj* with

con aria condizionata [kohn
AH•ria KON•dit•sion•ah•ta]
adj M air-conditioned

con gratitudine [kohn
GRA•ti•TUH•di•ne] *adv*
thankfully

con precauzione [kohn
PRE•kau•TSYOH•ne] *adv*
gingerly

con questo mezzo [kon
•KWEH•sto MEH•tso] *conj*
hereby

con riluttanza [kohn
RI•lut•TANH•tsa] *adv*
reluctantly

concedere [KON•tsheh•DE•re]
vt allow; bestow

concedersi
[KON•tsheh•DER•si] *vi* indulge

concentrare
[KON•tshen•TRAH•re] *vt*
concentrate (reduce)

concentrarsi
[KON•tshen•TRAHR•si] *vi*
concentrate

concepire [KON•tshe•PEE•re]
vt conceive

conceria [KON•tshe•REE•a] *n* F
tannery

concerto [kon•TSHEHR•to] *n*
M concert

concessione
[KON•tshes•SYOH•ne] *n* F
concession; grant

concetto errato
[kon•TSHEHT•to er•RAH•to]
n M misconception

concilio [kon•TSHEE•lyo] *n* M
council

conciso; concisa
[kon•TSHEE•so];
[kon•TSHEE•sa] *adj* MF
concise

concludere [kon•KLUH•de•re]
vt conclude

conclusivo; conclusiva
[KON•klu•SEE•vo];
[kon•klu•see•va] *adj* MF
eventual

concorrenziale
[KON•kor•ren•TSYAH•le] *adj*
competitive

concreto; concreta
[kon•KREH•to];
[kon•KREH•ta] *adj* concrete

condannare
[KON•dan•NAH•re] *vt*
condemn

condannato; condannata
[KON•dan•NAH•to];
[KON•dan•NAH•ta] *adj* MF
doomed

condensare [KON•den•SAH•re]
vt condense

condimento
[KON•di•MEHN•to] *n* M
seasoning

condiscendente
[KON•dit•shen•DEHN•te] *adj*
condescending; patronizing

condizione
[KON•dit•SHYOH•ne] *n* F
condition; plight

condizioni metereologiche
[KON•di•TSYOH•ni
ME•te•reo•LOH•ji•ke] *n* F
weather conditions

condoglianze
[KON•do•LYANH•tse] *npl* F
condolences

condonare [KON•do•NAH•re]
vt condone

condotta [kon•DOHT•ta] *n* F
conduct

conduttura [KON•dut•TUH•ra]
n F duct

confederazione
[KON•fede•rat•SYOH•ne] *n* F
confederation

conferenza
[KON•fe•REHN•za] *n* F
lecture

conferire [KON•fe•REE•re]
vt/vi confer

conferma [kon•FEHR•ma] *n* F
confirmation

confermare [KON•fer•ma•re] *vt*
confirm

confessare [KON•fes•SAH•re]
vt confess

confessione
[KON•fes•SYOH•ne] *n* F
confession

confidare [KON•fi•DAH•re] *vt*
confide

confidente [KON•fi•DEHN•te]
n MF confidant

confidenza
[KON•fi•DEHN•tsa] *n* F
confidence

confidenziale
[KON•fi•den•TSHYAH•le] *adj*
confidential

confisca [kon•FEES•ka] *n* F
sequestration

confiscare [KON•fis•KAH•re] *vt* confiscate

conflitto [kon•FLEET•to] *n* M conflict; strife

confondere [KON•fohn•DE•re] *vt* confuse; dumbfound; conform

conformista [KON•for•MEES•ta] *adj n* MF conformist

confortante [KON•for•TAHN•te] *adj* heartwarming

confortare [KON•for•TAH•re] *vt* comfort

conforto [ko•FOHR•to] *n* M comfort

confraternita [KON•fra•TEHR•nita] *n* F fraternity

confrontare [KON•fron•TAH•re] *vt* confront

confusione [KON•fu•TSYOH•ne] *n* F commotion

confusione [KON•fu•ZYOH•ne] *n* F confusion; muddle

confutare [KON•fu•TAH•re] *vt* M disprove

congedare [KON•dje•DAH•re] *vt* dismiss

congedo [kon•DJEH•do] *n* M dismissal

congegno [kon•DJEH•nyo] *n* M gadget

congelamento [KON•dje•LAMHN•to] *n* M frostbite

congelare [KON•dje•LAH•re] *vt* freeze

congelatore [KON•dje•la•TOH•re] *n* M freezer

congestione [KON•djes•TYOH•ne] *n* F congestion

congettura [KON•djet•TUH•ra] *n* F guess

congintivo [KON•djun•TEE•vo] *n* M subjunctive

congiungere [KON•djuhn•DJE•re] *vt* splice

congiunzione [KON•djun•TSYOH•ne] *n* F conjunction; junction

congratulare [KON•gra•tu•LAH•re] *vt* congratulate

congregarsi [KON•gre•GAHR•si] *vi* congregate

congregazione [KON•gre•gat•SYOH•ne] *n* F congregation

conigliera [KO•ni•LYEH•ra] *n* F hutch

coniglio [ko•NEE•lyo] *n* M rabbit

coniugazione [KON•yu•gat•SYOH•ne] *n* F conjugation

coniuge [ko•NYU•dje] *n* MF spouse

connazionale [KON•nat•syo•NAH•le] *n* MF countryman

connettere [KON•neht•TE•re] *vt* connect

cono [KOH•no] *n* M cone

conoscenza
[KO•no•SHEHN•dsa] *n* F
acquaintance

conquista [kon•KWIS•ta] *n* F
conquest

conquistare
[KON•kwis•TAH•re] *vt*
conquer

conquistatore
[KON•kwis•ta•TOH•re] *n* M
conqueror

consacrare [KO•sa•KRAH•re]
vt consecrate

consacrato; consacrata
[KON•sa•KRAH•to];
[KON•sa•KRAH•ta] *adj* MF
hallowed

consapevolezza
[KON•sa•pe•VOLEH•tsa] *n* F
knowledge

conscio; concia
[KOHN•tshyo];[KOHN•tshya]
adj aware; conscious

consecuivo; consecutiva
[KON•se•ku•TEE•vo];
[KON•se•ku•TEE•va] *adj*
consecutive

consegna [kon•SEH•nya] *n* F
delivery

consegnare
[KON•se•NYAH•re] *vt* deliver

conseguenza
[KON•se•GUEHN•tsa] *n* F
consequence

consenso [kon•SEHN•so] *n* M
consent

consentire [KON•sen•TEE•re]
vt acquiesce

consenziente
[KON•sen•TSIEHN•te] *adj*
agreeable

conservare [KON•ser•VAH•re]
vt preserve

conservativo; conservativa
[KON•ser•va•TEE•vo];
[KON•ser•va•TEE•va] *n adj*
MF conservative

conservazione
[KON•ser•vat•SYOH•ne] *n* F
conservation

considerando
[KON•si•de•RAHN•do] *prèp*
given

considerare
[KON•si•de•RAH•re] *vt*
consider

considerazione
[KON•si•de•ra•TSYOH•ne] *n*
F regard

considerevole
[KON•si•de•REH•VO•le] *adj*
considerable

consigliare [KON•sil•YAH•re]
vt advise

consigliere [KON•sil•YEH•re]
n M counselor; advisor

consiglio [kon•SEEL•yo] *n* M
advice; counsel

consistente
[KON•sis•TEHN•te] *adj*
consistent

consistenza
[KON•sis•TEHN•tsa] *n* F
consistency

consistere [KON•sees•TE•re] *vi* .
consist

consolare [KON•so•LAH•re] *vt*
console

consolato [KON•so•LAH•to] *n*
M consulate

consolazione
[KON•so•la•TSYOH•ne] *n* F
consolation

consolidare
[KON•so•li•DAH•re] *vt*
consolidate

consonante [KON•so•NAN•te]
n F consonant

consuetudine
[KON•sue•tuh•DI•ne] *n* F
custom

consultare [KON•sul•TAH•re]
vt consult

consultazione segreta
[KQN•sul•tah•TSYOH•ne
se•GREH•ta] *n* F huddle

consumare [KON•su•MAH•re]
vt consume; consummate

consumatore
[KON•su•ma•TOH•re] *n* M
consumer

consumo [kon•SUH•mo] *n* M
consumption

consunto; consunta
[kon•SUHN•to];
[kon•SUHN•ta] *adj* MF
threadbare

contabile [KON•tah•BI•le] *n*
MF bookkeeper

contabilitá [KON•tabi•li•TA'] *n*
F bookkeeping

contadino; contadina
[KON•ta•DEE•no];
[KON•ta•DEE•na] *n* MF
peasant

contagioso; contagiosa
[KON•ta•DJYOH•so];
[KON•ta•DJYOH•sa] *adj* MF
contagious

contaminare
[KON•ta•mi•NAH•re] *vt*
contaminate; taint

contanti [kon•TAHN•ti] *npl* M
cash

contare [kon•TAH•re] *vt* count

contatto [kon•TAHT•to] *n* M
contact

contea [kon•TEH•a] *n* F county

contemplare
[KON•tem•PLAH•re] *vt*
contemplate

contemporaneo;
contemporanea
[KON•tem•po•RAH•ne•o];
[KON•tem•po•RAH•ne•a] *adj*
n MF contemporary

contendere [KON•tehn•DE•re]
vi contend

contenere [KON•te•NEH•re] *vt*
contain

contenitore
[KON•te•ni•TOH•re] *n* M
container; holder

contentissimo; contentssima
[KON•tehn•tis•SI•mo];
[KON•tehn•tis•SI•ma] *adj* MF
delighted

contento; contenta
[kon•TEHN•to];[kon•TEHN•ta]
adj content; glad

contenuto [KON•te•NUH•to] *n*
M contents

contessa [kon•TEHS•sa] *n* F
countess

contestare [KON•tes•TAH•re]
vt contest

contesto [kon•TEHS•to] *n* M
context

continente [KON•ti•NEHN•te]
n M continent; mainland

contingenza
[KON•tin•DJEHN•tsa] *n* F
contingency; eventuality

continuamente
[KON•ti•nua•MEHN•te] *adv*
continually

continuare [KON•ti•nu•AH•re]
vt continue

continuazione
[KON•ti•nua•TSYOH•ne] *n* F
continuation

continuo; continua
[kon•TEE•nuo];
[kon•TEE•nua] *adj* nonstop;
continual

conto [KOHN•to] *n* M account;
bill; check (bill)

conto di partecipazione
[KOHN•to di
PAR•te•tshi•pa•TSYOH•ne] *n*
M joint account

contorcersi
[KON•tohr•TSHER•si] *vi*
writhe

contorno [kon•TOHR•no] *n* M
outline

contraddire
[KON•trad•DEE•re] *vt*
contradict

contraddizione
[KON•trad•dit•SYOH•ne] *n* F
discrepancy; contradiction

contrapporsi
[KON•trap•POHR•si] *vi*
counteract

contrario; contraria
[kon•TRAH•ryo];
[kon•TRAH•rya] adj; *n* MF
contrary

contrarre [kon•TRAHR•re] *vt*
contract; twitch

contrastare
[KON•tra•STAH•re] *vi vt*
contrast

contrasto [kon•TRAH•sto] *n* M
contrast

contratto [kon•TRAHT•to] *n* M
contract

contratto d'affitt
[kon•TRAHT•to daf•FEET•to]
n M lease

contrazione
[KON•trat•SYOH•ne] *n* F
contraction

contribuente
[KON•tri•BUEHN•te] *n* MF
taxpayer

contribuire [KON•tri•bu•EE•re]
vt contribute

contribuzione
[KON•tri•but•SYOH•ne] *n* F
contribution

contrito; contrita
[kon•TREE•to];
[kon•TREE•ta] *adj* MF rueful

contro [KOHN•tro] *prep* against

controllare [kon•trol•LAH•re]
vt check; rein; control

controllo [kon•TROHL•lo] *n* M
control

controllo delle nascite
[kon•TROHL•lo DEL•le
nah•SHI•te] *n* M birth control

controllore [KON•trol•LOH•re]
n M conductor

controversia
[KON•tro•VEHR•sya] *n* F
controversy

convalescente
[KON•va•le•SHEHN•te] *adj/n*
convalescent

convalescenza
[KON•va•le•SHEHN•tsa] *n* F
convalescence

conveniente
[KON•ve•NYEHN•te] *adj*
convenient

convenienza
[KON•ve•NYEHN•tsa] *n* F
convenience

convento [kon•VEHN•to] *n* M
convent

convergere [KON•vehr•DJE•re]
vi converge

conversare [KON•ver•SAH•re]
vi converse

conversazione
[KON•ver•sat•SYOH•ne] *n* F
conversation

conversione
[KON•ver•SYOH•ne] *n* F
conversion

converso; conversa
[kon•VEHR•so];
[kon•VEHR•sa] *n* MF
converse

convertire [KON•ver•TEE•re]
vt convert

convesso; convessa
[kon•VEHS•so];
[kon•VEHS•sa] *adj* convex

convincente
[KON•vin•TSHEHN•te] *adj*
convincing

convincere
[KON•veen•TSHE•re] *vt*
convince

convocare [KON•vo•KAH•re]
vt convene

convoglio [kon•VOH•lyo] *n* M
convoy

cooperare [KO•op•ERAH•re] *vi*
cooperate

cooperazione
[KO•op•erah•TSYOH•ne] *n* F
cooperation

coordinare [KO•ordi•NAH•re]
vt coordinate

coordinazione
[KO•or•di•na•TSYOH•ne] *n* F
coordination

coperchio [ko•PEHR•kyo] *n* F
lid; *n* M top

coperta [ko•PEHR•ta] *n* F
blanket

copertina [KO•per•TEE•na] *n* F
wrapper

coperto; coperta (di nubi)
[ko•PEHR•to]; [ko•PEHR•ta]
adj overcast

**coperto d'erbacce; coperta
d'erbacce** [ko•PEHR•to der
BAH•tshe]; [ko•PEHR•ta
der•BAH•tshe] *adj* weedy

copertura [KO•per•TUH•ra] *n*
F covering

copertura di paglia
[KO•per•TUH•ra dee
PAH•lya] *n* F thatch

copia [KOH•pya] *n* F copy;
facsimilie

copioso; copiosa
[ko•PYOH•so];[ko•PYOH•sa]
adj MF copious

coppia [KOHP•pya] *n* F couple

coprifuoco
[KOH•pri•FUOH•ko] *n* M
curfew

coprire [ko•PREE•re] *vt* cover

coraggio [ko•RAH•djyo] *n* M
bravery; courage

coraggioso; coraggiosa
[kora•DJYOH•so];
[kora•DJYOH•sa] *adj* MF
brave; courageous

corallo [ko•RAHL•lo] *n* M coral

corda [KOHR•da] *n* F cord; rope

cordiale [kor•DYAH•le] *adj*
hearty

cordicella
[KOR•di•TSHEHL•la] *n* F
twine

Corea [ko•REH•a] *n* F Korea

coridoio [KOR•ri•DOH•yo] *n*
M corridor

cornamusa
[KOR•nah•MUH•sa] *n* F
bagpipes

cornice [kor•NEE•tshe] *n* F
frame

cornicione
[KOR•nit•SHYOH•ne] *n* M
cornice

corno [kohr•nò] *n* M horn

coro [KOH•ro] *n* M choir;
chorus

corona [ko•ROH•na] *n* F crown

coroner [koh•RO•ner] *n* M
coroner

corpo [KOHR•po] *n* M body

corpo legislativo [KOHR•po
LE•djis•la•TEE•vo] *n* M
legislature

corporazione
[KOR•po•rat•SYOH•ne] *n* F
guild

corpulento; corpulenta
[KOR•pu•LEHN•to];
[KOR•pu•LEHN•ta] *adj* portly

corredo [kor•REH•do] *n* M
trousseau

correggia [kor•REH•dja] *n* F
thong

corrente 1 [kor•REHN•te] *adj*
current; *adj* running; working;
al corrente\ *adj* up-to-date

corrente 2 [kor•REHN•te] *n* F
draft

corrente 3 [kor•REHN•te] *n* F
stream; current

correre [kohr•RE•re] *vi* run;
race; zip

correttamnte
[KOR•ret•ta•MEHN•te] *adv*
correctly

corretto; corretta
[kor•REHT•to];[kor•REHT•ta]
adj MF correct

correzione
[KOR•ret•SYOH•ne] *n* F
correction

corridoio [kor•RI•DOH•yo] *n*
M aisle

corridore [kor•RI•DOH•re] *n* M
racer; runner; courier

corrispondente 1
[KOR•ris•pon•DEHN•te] *adj*
corresponding

corrispondente 2
[KOR•ris•pon•DEHN•te] *n*
MF correspondent

corrispondenza
[KOR•ris•pon•DEHN•tsa] *n* F
correspondence

corrispondere
[KOR•ris•pohn•DE•re] *vi*
correspond

corrodere [KOR•roh•DE•re] *vt*
corrode

corrompere [KOR•rohm•PE•re]
vt bribe

corrosione [KOR•roz•YOH•ne]
n F corrosion

corrotto; corrotta
[kor•ROHT•to];[kor•ROHT•ta]
adj MF corrupt

corrugare [KOR•ru•GAH•re] *vt*
pucker

corruzione
[KOR•rut•SYOH•ne] *n* F
corruption

Corsica [kohr•SI•ka] *n* F
Corsica

corsivo [kor•SEE•vo] *n* M
script; *adj* italic

corso [KOHR•so] *n* M course

corte [KOHR•te] *n* F court

corteccia [kor•TEH•tshya] *n* F
bark

corteggiare [KOR•te•DJAH•re]
vt woo; court

corteggiatore
[KOR•te•dja•TOH•re] *n* M
swain; lover; young man

cortese [kor•TEH•ze] *adj*
courteous; gracious

cortesia [KOR•te•SEE•a] *n* F
courtesy

cortile [kor•TEE•le] *n* M
backyard; courtyard; yard

corto; corta [KOHR•to];
[kohr•ta] *adj* MF short

corvo [KOHR•vo] *n* M crow;
raven

cosa [KOH•za] *n* F thing

coscia [KOH•sha] *n* F thigh

coscienza [ko•TSHEHN•tsa] *n*
F conscience

coscienzioso; coscienziosa
[KO•tshen•TSYOH•so];
[KO•tshen•TSYOH•sa] *adj*
conscientious

così [KO•see] *adv* so; thus

cosmetico [KOZ•meh•TI•ko] *n*
M cosmetic

cosmetico per ciglia
[KOZ•meh•TI•ko pehr
TSHEE•lya] *n* M mascara

cosmopolita
[KOS•mo•poh•LI•ta] *adj n*
MF cosmopolitan

cospicuo; cospicua
[kos•PEE•kuo];[kos•PEE•kua]
adj MF conspicuous

costa [KOHS•ta] *n* F coast

costante [kos•TAHN•te] *adj*
contant; undeviating

costellazione
[KOS•tel•lat•TSYOH•ne] *n* F
constellation

costernazione
[KOS•ter•na•TSYOH•ne] *n* F
dismay; consternation

costituzione
[KOS•ti•tu•TSYOH•ne] *n* MF
constitution

costo [KOHS•to] *n* M cost; price

costola [kohs•TO•la] *n* F rib

costoso; costosa
[kos•TOH•zo];[kos•TOH•za]
adj costly; expensive

costrizione
[KOS•trit•SYOH•ne] *n* F
constraint

costruire [KO•stru•EE•re] *vt*
build; construct; erect

costruttore [KOS•trut•TOH•re]
n M builder

costume [kos•TUH•me] *n* M
costume

costume da bagno
[kos•TUH•me dah BAH•nyo]
n M bathing suit; swimsuit

cotogna [ko•TOH•nya] *n* F
quince

cotoletta [KO•to•LEHT•ta] *n* F
cutlet

cotone [ko•TOH•ne] *n* M cotton

cotta [KOHT•ta] *n* F crush
(romantic)

covare [ko•VAH•re] *vt* hatch

covone [ko•VOH•ne] *n* M
haystack

cowboy [KAH•u•BOH•i] *n* M
cowboy

cracker [krehk] *n* M cracker

crampo [KRAHM•po] *n* M
cramp

cratere [kra•TEH•re] *n* M crater

cravatta [kra•VAHT•ta] *n* F tie
cravatta a farfalla
[kra•VAHT•ta ah
far•FAHL•la] *n* F bow tie
creare [kre•AH•re] *vt* create
creativo; creativa
[KRE•ah•TEE•vo];
[KRE•ah•TEE•va] *adj* MF
creative
creatore [KRE•at•OH•re] *n* M
creator
creatura [KRE•at•UH•ra] *n* F
creature
creazione [KRE•at•SYOH•ne] *n*
F creation
credenza 1 [kre•DEHN•tsa] *n* F
belief
credenza 2 [kreh•DEN•tsa] *n* F
cupboard; sideboard
credere [KREH•dere] *vi* believe
credibile [kre•DEE•BI•le] *adj*
credible
credito [kreh•DITO] *n* M credit
credo [KREH•do] *n* M créed;
belief
credulone; credulona
[KRE•du•LOH•ne];
[KRE•du•LOH•na] *adj* MF
gullible
crema [KREH•ma] *n* F custard;
cream
cremoso; cremosa
[kre•MOH•zo];[kre•MOH•za]
adj MF creamy
crepuscolo [KRE•puhs•KO•lo]
n dusk; nightfall; twilight
crescere [kreh•SHE•re] *v* grow
crescita [kreh•SHI•ta] *n* F
growth
cresciuto troppo
[kre•SHOO•to TROH•poh]
adj overgrown

cresima [kreh•SI•ma] *n* F
confirmation (religious)
crespo da lutto [KREHS•po
dah LUHT•to] *n* M crape
cresta [KREH•sta] *n* F crest
creta [KREH•ta] *n* F clay
cretino [kre•TEE•no] *n* M jerk;
cretin; idiot
cricco [KREEK•ko] *n* M jack
criminale [KRI•mi•NAH•le] *adj*
n MF criminal; felon
crimine [krih•MI•ne] *n* M
crime; felony
criniera [kri•NYEH•ra] *n* F
mane
crisantemo [KRI•san•TEH•mo]
n M chrysanthemum
crisi [KREE•si] *n* F crisis
cristallo [kris•TAHL•lo] *n* M
crystal
cristiano; cristiana
[kris•TYAH•no];
[kris•TYAH•na] *adj n* MF
Christian
cristinitá [KRIS•tya•NI•ta] *n* F
Christianity
Cristo [KREE•sto] *n* M Christ
criterio [kri•TEH•ryo] *n* M
criterion
critica [kree•TI•ka] *n* F criticism
criticare [KRI•ti•KAH•re] *vt*
criticize
critico [kree•TI•ko] *n* M critic
crivello [kri•VEHL•lo] *n* M jig
(tool)
croccante [kro•KAH•te] *adj*
crisp
croce [KROH•tshe] *n* F cross
crociata [kro•TSHYAH•ta] *n* F
crusade
crociera [kro•TSHEH•ra] *n* F
cruise

crocifisso [KRO•tshi•FEES•so] *n* M crucifix

crollare [krol•LAH•re] *vi* collapse; fall down

crollo [KROHL•lo] *n* M collapse

cromo [KROH•mo] *n* M chrome

cronaca [kroh•NA•ka] *n* F chronicle

cronico; cronica [kroh•NI•ko]; [kroh•NI•ka] *adj* MF chronic

cronologico; cronologica [KRO•no•loh•DJI•ko]; [KRO•no•loh•DJI•ka] *adj* MF chronological

cronometrista [KRO•no•me•TREES•ta] *n* MF timekeeper

cronometro [KRO•noh•ME•tro] *n* M stopwatch; timer

crosta [KROH•sta] *n* F crust

crostata [kros•TAH•ta] *n* F tart

crucciarsi [kru•TSHAHR•si] *vi* fret

cruciale [kru•TSHYAH•le] *adj* crucial

cruciverba [KRU•tshi•VEHR•ba] *n* M crossword (puzzle)

crudele [kru•DEH•le] *adj* cruel

crudo; cruda [KRUH•do]; [KRUH•da] *adj* MF raw; crude

cruento; cruenta [kru•EHN•to]; [kru•EHN•ta] *adj* MF gory; bloody

crusca [KRUH•ska] *n* F bran

cruscotto [krus•KOHT•to] *n* M dashboard

Cuba [KUH•ba] *n* F Cuba

cubano; cubana [ku•BAH•no]; [ku•BAH•na] *adj* MF Cuban

cubetto di ghiaccio [ku•BEHT•to di GYAH•tsho] *n* M ice cube

cubico; cubica [kuh•BI•ko]; [kuh•BI•ka] *adj* MF cubic

cubo [KUH•bo] *n* M cube

cucchiaiata [KUK•kya•YAH•ta] *n* F spoonful

cucchiaino [KUK•kya•EE•no] *n* M teaspoon

cucchiaio [kuk•KYAH•yo] *n* M spoon

cucciolo [kuh•TSHO•lo] *n* M pup

cucina [ku•TSHEE•na] *n* F cooking; kitchen

cucinare ai ferri [KU•tshi•NAH•re ahi FEHR•ri] *vt* broil

cucire [ku•TSHEE•re] *vt* sew

cucire con graffette [ku•TSHEE•re kon graf•FEHT•te] *vt* staple

cucito [ku•TSHEE•to] *n* M sewing

cucito; cucita [ku•TSHEE•to]; [ku•TSHEE•ta] *p. part* MF sewn

cucitura [KU•tshi•TUH•ra] *n* F seam

cuffia 1 [KUHF•fya] *n* F bonnet; hat

cuffia 2 [KUHF•fya] *n* F headphones

cugino; cugina [ku•DJEE•no];[ku•DJEE•na] *n* MF cousin

culla [KUHL•la] *n* F cradle

culminare [KUL•mi•NAH•re] *vi* culminate

culmine [kuhl•MI•ne] *n* M climax; highlight

culto [KUHL•to] *n* M cult

cultura [kul•TUH•ra] *n* F
culture; education; learning

culturale [KUL•tu•RAH•le] *adj*
cultural

cumulativo; cumulativa
[KU•mu•la•TEE•vo];
[KU•mu•la•TEE•va] *adj* MF
cumulative

cumulo di neve [KUH•mulo
dee NEH•ve] *n* M snowdrift

cuneo [KUH•neo] *n* M wedge

cuocere in acqua
[kwoh•TSHE•re in AH•kwa]
vt poach

cuocere nel forno
[ku•OH•tshere nel FOHR•no]
vt bake

cuoco; cuoca [KUOH•ko];
[KUOH•ka] *n* MF cook

cuoio [KWOH•yo] *n* M leather

cuore [KWOH•re] *n* M heart

cupola [kuh•PO•la] *n* F dome

cura [KUH•ra] *n* F care; cure

curare [ku•RAH•re] *vt* look
after; edit

curato [ku•RAH•to] *n* M curate

curcolionide
[KUR•ko•lyoh•NI•de] *n* M
weevil

curiosità [KUR•io•zi•TAH] *n* F
curiosity

curioso; curiosa
[ku•RYOH•zo];
[ku•RYOH•za] *adj* MF
curious; inquisitive; nosy

curry [KUHR•ri] *n* M curry

curva [KUHR•va] *n* F bend;
curve

curvare [kur•VAH•re] *vt* bow;
bend

curvo; curva [KUHR•vo];
[KUHR•va] *adj* hunched

cuscino [ku•SHEE•no] *n* M
cushion; pillow

custode [kus•TOH•de] *n* MF
custodian

custodia [kus•TOH•dya] *n* F
custody

D

da [dah] *prep* from; at; to; as;
like; since; by; from

dabasso [da•BAHS•so] *adv*
downstairs

dado [DAH•do] *n* M dice

dai [dy] *prep art* da i

daina [DAH•ina] *n* F doe

daino [DAH•ino] *n* M deer

dal dall dal' [dahl] *prep art*
da la

del dell del' [dehl] *prep art*
de la

dollo [DOH•lo] *prep art* da lo

daltonica; daltonica
[DAL•toh•NI•ko];
[DAL•toh•NI•ka] *adj*
color-blind

damigella d'onore
[DAH•mi•DJEHL•la
do•NOH•re] *n* F bridesmaid

Danimarca [DA•ni•MAHR•ka]
n F Denmark

danno [DAHN•no] *n* M damage

dannoso; dannosa
[dan•NOH•zo]; [dan•NOH•za]
adj MF harmful; detrimental

danza [DAHN•tsa] *n* F dance

dappertutto
[DAH•per•TUHT•to] *adv*
everywhere

dardo [DAHR•do] *n* M dart

dare 1 [DAH•re] *n* M debit

dare 2 [DAH•re] *vt* give

dare un pugno [DAH•re uhn
PUH•nyo] *vi* punch

dare una stoccata [DAH•re
uhna stok•KAH•ta] *vi* lunge

data [DAH•ta] *n* F date

dati [DAH•ti] *npl* M data

datore di lavoro [da•TOH•re
di la•VOH•ro] *n* M employer

dattilografo; dattilografa
[DAT•ti•loh•GRA•fo];
[DAT•ti•loh•GRA•fa] *n* MF
typist

davanzale [DA•van•TSAH•le]
n M sill; windowsill

dea [DEH•a] *n* F goddess

debito [deh•BI•to] *n* M debt

debitore [DE•bi•TOH•re] *n* M
debtor

debole [DEH•bole] *adj* faint;
feeble; weak

debolmente
[DE•bol•MEHN•te] *adv*
weakly

debutto [de•BUHT•to] *n* M
debut

decadente [DE•ka•DEHN•te]
adj decadent

decadenza [DE•ka•DEHN•tsa]
n F decadence

decano [de•KAH•no] *n* M dean

decapitare [DE•ka•pi•TAH•re]
vt behead

deceduto; deceduta
[DE•tshe•DUH•to];
[DE•tshe•DUH•ta] *adj* MF
deceased

decennio [de•TSHEHN•nyo] *n*
M decade

decente [de•TSHEHN•te] *adj*
decent

decenza [de•TSHEHN•tsa] *n* F
decency

decidere [DE•tshee•DE•re] *vt*
decide; resolve

decifrare [DE•tshi•FRAH•re] *vt*
decipher; decode

decima [deh•TSHI•ma] *n* F tithe

decimale [DEH•tshi•MAH•le] *n*
M decimal

decimare [DEH•tshi•MAH•re]
vt decimate

decimo; decima
[deh•TSHI•mo];
[deh•TSHI•ma] *adj* tenth

decisamente
[DE•tshi•sa•MEHN•te] *adv*
definitely

decisione [DE•tshi•ZIOH•ne] *n*
F decision

decisivo; decisiva
[DE•tshi•SEE•vo];
[DE•tshi•SEE•va] *adj* MF
decisive; fateful

declino [de•KLEE•no] *n* M
decline

decolleté [de•KOL•te'] *n* M
cleavage

decomporsi
[DE•kom•PORH•si] *vi*
decompose

decorare [DE•ko•RAH•re] *vt*
decorate

decorazione
[DE•ko•ra•TSYOH•ne] *n* F
decoration

decoro [de•KOH•ro] *n* M
decorum

decoroso; decorosa
[DE•ko•ROH•zo];
[DE•ko•ROH•za] *adj* MF
proper

decrepito; decrepita
[de•KREH•PI•to];
[de•KREH•PI•ta] *adj* MF
decrepit

decrescere [de•KREH•SHE•re]
vi subside

decreto [de•KREH•to] *n* M
decree

dedica [deh•DI•ka] *n* F
dedication; devotion

dedicare [de•DI•KAH•re] *vt*
dedicate; devote

dedurre [de•DUHR•re] *vt* infer

deficiente [de•FIT•SHEHN•te]
adj deficient

deficienza [de•FIT•SHEHN•tsa]
n F deficiency; shortage

deficit [de•FIT•shit] *n* M deficit

definire [DE•fi•NEE•re] *vt*
define

definito; definita
[DE•fi•NEE•to];
[DE•fi•NEE•ta] *adj* MF
definite; in definitiva
[IN•de•fi•NI•TEE•va] *adv*
after all; ultimately

definizione
[DE•fi•ni•TSYOH•ne] *n* F
definition

deflettere [de•FLEHT•tere] *vt*
deflect; turn away

deformare [DE•for•MAH•re] *vt*
warp

deformato; deformata
[DE•for•MAH•to];
[DE•for•MAH•ta] *adj* warped

deforme [de•FOHR•me] *adj*
deformed

defraudare [DE•frau•DAH•re]
vt defraud

degenerare
[DE•dje•ne•RAH•re] *vi*
degenerate

degenerato; degenerata
[DE•dje•ne•RAH•to];
[DE•dje•ne•RAH•ta] *adj*
degenerate

degno; degna [DEH•nyo];
[deh•nya] *adj* worthy

degradante [DE•gra•DAHN•te]
adj degrading

degradare [DE•gra•DAH•re] *vt*
abase; degrade

delegato; delegata
[DE•le•GAH•to];
[DE•le•GAH•ta] *n* MF
delegate; representative

delegazione
[DE•le•gat•SYOH•ne] *n* F
delegation

delfino [del•FEE•no] *n* M
dolphin

deliberare [DE•li•be•RAH•re]
vi deliberate; discuss

delicato; delicata
[DE•li•KAH•to];

[DE•li•KAH•ta] *adj* MF
delicate

delinquente [de•lin•kwehn•te]
n MF delinquent

delirante [DE•li•RAHN•te] *adj*
delirious

delirare [DE•li•RAH•re] *vi* rave

delizia [de•LEE•tsya] *n* F
delight

delizioso; deliziosa
[DE•lit•SYOH•zo];
[DE•lit•SYOH•za] *adj* MF
darling; delicious

deludente [DE•lu•DEHN•te]
adj disappointing

deludere [DE•luh•DE•re] *vt*
disappoint

delusione [DE•lu•ZYOH•ne] *n*
F delusion; disappointment

demagogo [DE•ma•GOH•go] *n*
M demagogue

demente [de•MEHN•te] *adj*
demented

demerito [DE•meh•RI•to] *n* M
demerit

democratico; democratica
[DE•mo•krah•TI•ko];
[DE•mo•krah• TI•ka] *n* MF
democrat; *adj* democratic

democrazia
[DE•mo•krat•SEE•a] *n* F
democracy

demolire [DE•mo•LEE•re] *vt*
demolish

demonietto
[DE•mo•NYEHT•to] *n* M
goblin

demonio [de•MOH•nio] *n* M
fiend

demoralizzare
[DE•mo•ra•li•TSAH•re] *vt*
demoralize

denaro [de•NAH•ro] *n* M
money

densitá [den•SI•tah] *n* M
density

denso; densa [DEHN•so];
[DEHN•sa] *adj* MF dense

dentale [den•TAH•le] *adj*
dental

dente [DEHN•te] *n* M tooth

dentifricio [DEN•ti•FREE•tsho]
n M toothpaste

dentista [den•TEE•sta] *n* MF
dentist

dentro [DEHN•tro] *prep* into

denunciare
[DE•nun•TSHYAH•re] *vt*
denounce

dépliant [de•pli•ahnt] *n* M
brochure

deplorare [DE•plo•RAH•re] *vt*
deplore

deplorevole
[DE•plo•REH•vole] *adj*
deplorable

deporre [de•POHR•re] *vt*
depose

deportare [DE•por•TAH•re] *vt*
deport

deposito [DE•poh•SI•to] *n* M
deposit; down payment

depressione
[DE•pres•SYOH•ne] *n* F
depression

depresso; depressa
[de•PREHS•so];[de•PREHS•sa]
adj MF depressed

deprezzare [DE•prets•AH•re]
vi cheapen; depress

deprimente [DE•pri•MEHN•te]
adj depressing

deprimere [DE•pree•ME•re] *vt*
depress

deragliare [DE•ra•LYAH•re] *vt*
derail

deridere [de•REE•dere] *vt*
deride; mock; scoff

derivare [DE•ri•VAH•re] *vt*
derive

derivazione
[DE•ri•vat•SYOH•ne] *n* F
derivation; source; shunt

derrate [der•RAH•te] *npl* F
commodity

derubare [DE•ru•BAH•re] *vt*
rob

descrivere [DES•kree•VE•re] *vt*
describe

descrizione
[DES•krit•SYOH•ne] *n* F
description; portrayal

deserto [de•ZEHR•to] *n* M
desert

desiderabile
[DE•zi•de•RAH•bi•le] *adj*
desirable

desiderare [DE•zi•de•RAH•re]
vt covet

desiderare [DE•side•RAH•re]
vt crave; wish; yearn

desiderio [DE•zi•deh•RI•o] *n*
M desire; wish; yearning

designare [DE•zi•NYHA•re] *vt*
designate

designer [de•ZAY•ner] *n* M
designer

desistere [DE•zee•STE•re] *vi*
desist

desolato; desolata
[DE•zo•LAH•to];
[DE•zo•LAH•ta] *adj* MF
desolate; heartbroken

despota [dehs•PO•ta] *n* despot

destinatario; desinataria
[DES•ti•na•TAH•ryo];
[DES•ti•na•TAH•rya] *n* MF
receiver; recipient

destinato; destinata
[DES•ti•NAH•to];
[DES•ti•NAH•ta] *adj* MF
bound

destinazione
[DES•ti•nat•SYOH•ne] *n* F
destination

destino [des•TEE•no] *n* M
destiny; doom

destituto; destituta
[DES•ti•TUH•to];
[DES•ti•TUH•ta] *adj* destitute

destrezza [des•TREH•tsa] *n* F
sleight

destriero [des•TRYEH•ro] *n* M
steed

destro; destra [DEHS•tro];
[DEHS•tra] *adj* deft

detenzione
[DE•ten•TSYOH•ne] *n* F
detention

deteriorare
[DE•te•ryò•RAH•re] *vi*
deteriorate

determinare
[DE•ter•mi•NAH•re] *vt*
determine

detersivo [DE•ter•SEE•vo] *n* M
detergent; cleaner (product)

detestare [DE•tes•TAH•re] *vt*
detest; loathe

detonare [DE•to•NAH•re] *vt*
detonate

detrarre [de•TRAHR•re] *vt*
deduct; detract

dettagliante
[DET•ta•LYAHN•te] *n* MF
retailer

dettaglio [det•TAH •yo] *n* M
detail; retail

dettare [det•TAH•re] *vt* dictate

dettato [det•TAH•to] *n* M
dictation

devastante [DE•vas•TAHN•te]
adj devastating

devastare [DE•va•STAH•re] *vt*
devastate; ravage

deviare [de•VYAH•re] *vi*
deviate; divert; avert one's
eyes; swerve

deviazione
[DE•vya•TSYOH•ne] *n* F
detour

devoto; devota [de•VOH•to];
[de•VOH•ta] *adj* MF devout;
devoted

devozione [DE•vo•TSYOH•ne]
n devotion

di [dee] *prep* of; *conj* than

diabete [dya•BEH•te] *n* M
diabetes

diabetico; diabetica
[DYA•beh•TI•ko];
[DYA•beh•TI•ka] adj; *n* MF
diabetic

diabolico; dibolica
[DYA•boh•LI•ko];
[DYA•boh•LI•ka] *adj* fiendish

diagnosi [DY•ah•NYO•zi] *n* F
diagnosis

diagnosticare
[DYA•nyo•sti•KAH•re] *vt*
diagnose

diagonale [DYA•go•NAH•le]
adj diagonal

diagramma
[DYA•GRAHM•ma] *n* M
diagram

dialetto [dya•LEHT•to] *n* M
dialect

dialogo [dyah•LO•go] *n* M
dialog

diametro [dyah•ME•tro] *n* M
diameter

diario [DI•ah•RYO] *n* M diary;
journal

diatriba [DIA•TREE•ba] *n* F
tirade

diavoletto [DYA•vo•LEHT•to]
n M imp

diavolo [DY•ah•VO•lo] *n* M
devil

dibattito [DI•baht•TI•to] *n* M
debate

dicembre [di•TSHEHM•bre] *n*
M December

dichiarare [DI•kya•rah•re] *vt*
declare

diciannove [DI•tshan•NOH•ve]
num nineteen

diciassette [DI•tshas•SEHT•te]
num seventeen

**diciassettesimo;
diciassettesima**
[DI•tshas•SET•teh•ZI•mo];
[DI•tshas•SET•teh•ZI•ma] *adj*
MF seventeenth

diciottesimo; diciottesima
[DI•TSHY•ot•teh•SIM•o];
[DI•TSHY•ot•teh•SIM•a] *adj*
eighteenth

diciotto [di•TSHYOHT•to] *num*
eighteen

didascalia [DI•das•ka•LEE•ah]
n F caption

didietro [di•DIEH•tro] *n* M
behind

dieci [DYEH•tshi] *num* ten

dieta [di•EH•ta] *n* F diet

dietro [DIEH•tro] *prep* behind

difendere [DI•fehn•DE•re] *vt* defend

difensivo; difensiva [DI•fen•SEE•vo]; [DI•fen•SEE•va] *adj* MF defensive

difesa [di•FEH•za] *n* F defense

difetto [di•FEHT•to] *n* M defect; flaw; shortcoming

difettoso; difettosa [DI•fet•TOH•zo]; [DI•fet•TOH•za] *adj* MF faulty

diffamare [DIF•fa•MAH•re] *vt* defame

diffamazione [DIF•fama•TSYOH•ne] *n* F defamation; libel

differente [DIF•fe•REHN•te] *adj* different

differenza [DIF•fe•REHN•tsa] *n* F difference

differenziare [DIF•fe•ren•TSYAH•re] *vi* differentiate; diversify

differire [DIF•fe•REE•re] *vt* defer; differ; delay

difficile [DIF•fee•TSHI•le] *adj* difficult

difficoltá [DIF•fee•KOL•tah] *n* M difficulty

diffidente [DIF•fi•DEHN•te] *adj* distrustful

diffidenza [DIF•fi•DEHN•tsa] *n* F distrust; mistrust

diffondere [DIF•fohn•DE•re] *vt* diffuse

diffondersi [DIF•fohn•DER•si] *vi* waft

dificile [DIF•fee•TSHI•le] *adj* trying

diga [DEE•ga] *n* F dam

digerire [DI•dje•REE•re] *vt* digest

digestione [DI•dje•STYOH•ne] *n* F digestion

dignitá [di•ni•TAH] *n* F dignity

dignitoso; dignitosa [DI•ni•TOH•zo]; [DI•ni•TOH•za] *adj* MF dignified

digrignare [DI•gri•NJAH•re] *vt* gnash

dilatare [DI•la•TAH•re] *vt* dilate; expand

dilazione [DI•lat•SYOH•ne] *n* F respite

dilemma [di•LEHM•ma] *n* M dilemma

dilettante [DI•let•TAHN•te] *adj n* MF amateur

diligente [DI•li•DJEHN•te] *adj* diligent

diligenza [DI•li•DJEHN•tsa] *n* F diligence

diluire [di•LUEE•re] *vt* dilute

diluvio [di•LUH•vyo] *n* M deluge

dimenare [DI•me•NAH•re] *vt* wag

dimenarsi [DI•me•NAHR•si] *vi* squirm

dimensione [DI•men•SYOH•ne] *n* F dimension

dimenticare [DI•men•ti•KAH•re] *vt* forget

dimentico; dimentica [di•MEHN•ti•ko]; [di•MEHN•ti•ka] *adj* MF oblivious

dimettersi [DI•met•TEHR•si] *vi* resign

diminuire [DI•mi•NUEE•re] *vt*
diminish; lessen; *vi* dwindle

diminuzione
[DI•mi•nu•TSYOH•ne] *n* F
decrease

dimora [di•MOH•ra] *n* F abode

dimorare [DI•mo•RAH•re] *vi*
dwell

dimostrare [DI•mo•STRAH•re]
vt demonstrate

dimostrazione
[DI•mo•stra•TSYOH•ne] *n* F
demonstration

dinamica [DI•nah•MI•ka] *n adj*
-o -a\ dynamic

dinamite [DI•na•MEE•te] *n* F
dynamite

dinastia [DI•nas•TEE•a] *n* F
dynasty

dinghy [DIN•gi] *n* M dinghy

diniego [di•NYE•go] *n* M
denial

dinosauro [DI•no•SAH•uro] *n*
M dinosaur

Dio [DEE•o] *n* M God

diocesi [DIOH•TSHE•zi] *n* F
diocese

dipendenza
[DI•pen•DEHN•tza] *n* F
addiction

dipendere [DI•pehn•DE•re] *vi*
depend

dipingere [DI•peen•GE•re] *vt*
portray

dipinto [di•PEEN•to] *n* M
painting

diploma [di•PLOH•ma] *n* M
degree (academic); diploma;
bachelor (degree)

diplomarsi [DI•plo•MAHR•si]
vi graduate

diplomatico; diplomatica
[DI•plo•MAH•ti•ko];
[DI•plo•MAH•ti•ka] *adj* MF
diplomatic; *n* MF diplomat

diplomazia
[DI•plo•ma•TSEE•a] *n* F
diplomacy

dire [DEE•re] *vt* tell

direttamente
[DI•ret•ta•MEHN•te] *adv*
firsthand

diretto; diretta [di•REHT•to];
[di•REHT•ta] *adj* direct;
outright

direttore [DI•ret•TOH•re] *n* M
director; manager

direzione [DI•ret•SYOH•ne] *n*
F direction; management

dirigere [DI•ree•DJE•re] *vt*
manage; conduct

diritti umani [di•REET•ti
u•MAH•ni] *n* M human rights

diritto [di•REET•toh] *n* M
claim; right

diritto d'autore
[di•REET•todau•TOH•re] *n*
copyright

disaccordo [DIZ•ak•KOHR•do]
n M disagreement

disagio [diz•AHD•jyo] *n* M
discomfort; a disagio\ *adj* ill at
ease; uneasy

disapprovare
[DIZ•ap•pro•VAH•re] *vt*
disapprove

disapprovazione
[DIZ•ap•PRO•va•TSYOH•ne]
n F disapproval

disarmare [DIZ•ar•MAH•re] *vt*
disarm

disastro [di•ZAHS•tro] *n* M
disaster; *adj* disastrous

discendere [di•SHEHN•DE•re] *vt* descend

discepolo [di•SHEH•PO•lo] *n* M disciple

discernere [di•SHEHR•NE•re] *vt* discern

discesa [di•SHEH•sa] *n* F descent

disciplina [DI•shi•PLEE•na] *n* F discipline

disciplinato; disciplinata [DI•shi•pli•NAH•to]; [DI•shi•pli•NAH•ta] *adj* MF orderly

disco [DEES•ko] *n* M disk

disco volante [DEES•ko vo•LAHN•te] *n* M flying saucer

discordi [dis•KOHR•dee] *n* F discord

discorso [dis•KOHR•so] *n* M discourse; patter; speech

discorso inintelligibile [dis•KOHR•zo in•INTEL•li•DJEE•bile] *n* M gibberish

discredito [dis•KREH•DI•to] *n* M discredit

discrezione [di•KRE•TSYOH•ne] *n* F discretion

discriminare [dis•KRI•mi•NAH•re] *vi* discriminate

discussione [dis•KUS•SIOHN•e] *n* M argument; *n* F discussion

discutere [dis•KUHT•ere] *vt* argue; *vt* discuss

discutibile [dis•KU•TEE•bi•le] *adj* questionable

disdicevole [DIZ•di•TSHEH•vo•le] *adj* unbecoming

disegno [di•ZEH•nyo] *n* M design; drawing

disertare [di•ZER•TAH•re] *vt* desert

disertore [di•ZER•TOH•re] *n* M deserter; runaway

disfare [dis•FAH•re] *vt* undo

disfarsi (di) [dis•FAHR•si] *vi* dispose (of something)

disgelare [DIZ•dje•LAH•re] *vt* defrost

disgraziato; disgraziata [DIZ•gra•TSYAH•to]; [DIZ•gra•TSYAH•ta] *adj* MF wretched; disgraced; embarassed

disgusto [diz•GUHS•to] *n* M disgust

disgustoso; disgustosa [DIZ•gus•TOH•zo]; [DIZ•gus•TOH•za] *adj* MF disgusting

disidratare [DI•zi•dra•TAH•re] *vt* dehydrate

disimpegnare [DIS•im•pen•YAH•re] *vt* disengage

disinfettante [DIZ•in•fet•TAHN•te] *n* M disinfectant

disinfettare [DIZ•in•fet•TAH•re] *vt* disinfect

disingannare [DIZ•in•gan•NAH•re] *vt* undeceive

disinganno [DIZ•in•GAHN•no] *n* M disillusion

disintegrare
[DIZ•in•te•GRAH•re] *vi*
disintegrate

disinteressato; disinteressata
[DIZ•in•ter•ES•SAH•to];
[DIZ•inter•ES•SAH•ta] *adj*
MF disinterested

disinvolto; disinvolta
[DIZ•in•VOHL•to];
[DĬZ•in•VOHL•ta] *adj* MF
offhand; casual

dislocare [DIZ•lo•KAH•re] *vt*
dislocate

disobbediente
[DIZ•ob•be•DYEHN•te] *adj*
disobedient

disobbedire
[DIZ•ob•be•DEE•re] *vi*
disobey

disoccupato; disoccupata
[DIZ•ok•ku•PAH•to];
[DIZ•ok•ku•PAH•ta] *adj n*
MF unemployed

disoccupazione
[DIZ•ok•ku•pa•TSYOH•ne] *n*
F unemployment

disonesto; disonesta
[DIZ•on•EHS•to];
[DIZ•on•EHS•ta] *adj*
dishonest

disonore [DIZ•on•OH•re] *n* M
dishonor

disordinato; disordinata
[DI•zor•di•NAH•to];
[DI•zor•di•NAH•ta] *adj* MF
messy

disordine [DIZ•ohr•DI•ne] *n* M
clutter; disarray; disorder;
untidiness

**disorganizzato;
disorganizzata**
[DIZ•orga•nit•SAH•to];
[DIZ•orga•nit•SAH•ta] *adj*
MF disorganized

disorientato; disorientata
[DIZ•or•i•en•TAH•to];
[DIZ•or•i•en•TAH•ta] *adj* MF
disoriented

dispensa [dis•PEHN•za] *n* F
pantry

dispensare [DIS•pen•SAH•re]
vt dispense

disperato; disperata
[DIS•pe•RAH•to];
[DIS•pe•RAH•ta] *adj* MF
desperate

disperazione
[DIS•pe•rat•SYOH•ne] *n* F
despair; desperation

disperdere [DIS•pehr•DE•re] *vt*
disperse

dispetto [dis•PEHT•to] *n* M
spite

dispiacere
[DIS•pya•TSHEH•re] *vt*
displease

dispiaciuto; dispiaciuta
[DIS•pya•TSHUH•to];
[DIS•pya•TSHUH•ta] *adj* MF
displeased

disponibile [DIS•po•NEE•bile]
adj available

disporre [dis•POHR•re] *vt*
dispose

disporre in tabella
[dis•POHR•re in ta•BEHL•la]
vt tabulate

dispositivo [DIS•po•zi•TEE•vo]
n M device (mechanical)

disposizione
[DIS•pozi•TSYOH•ne] *n* F
disposal; disposition

disposto; disposta
[dis•POHS•to]; [dis•POHS•ta]
adj MF disposed

dispotico; dispotica
[DIS•poh•TI•ko];
[DIS•poh•TI•ka] *adj* MF
domineering

disprezzare [DIS•prets•AH•re]
vt despise; scorn; contempt;
disdain

disputa [DEES•put•a] *n* F
dispute

disreto; discreta
[dis•KREH•to]; [dis•KREH•ta]
adj MF discreet

disseminare
[DIS•se•mi•NAH•re] *vt*
disseminate

dissenso [dis•SEHN•so] *n* M
dissent

dissezionare
[DIS•se•tsyo•NAH•re] *vt*
dissect

dissimulare
[DIS•si•mu•LAH•re] *vt*
dissimulate

dissipare [DIS•si•PAH•re] *vt*
dispel; dissipate

dissociare [DIS•so•TSHAH•re]
vt dissociate

dissolutezza
[DIS•sol•ut•EH•tsa] *n* F
debauchery

dissoluto; dissoluta
[DIS•so•LUH•to];
[DIS•so•LUH•ta] *adj* MF
dissolute

dissolvere [DIS•sohl•VE•re] *vt*
dissolve

dissuadere [DIS•suah•DE•re] *vt*
deter; hold off; keep off;
dissuade

distante [dis•TAHN•te] *adj*
distant

distanza [dis•TAHN•tsa] *n* F
distance

distillare [DIS•til•LAH•re] *vt*
distill

distilleria [DIS•til•le•REE•a] *n*
F distillery

distinguere [DIS•teen•GUE•re]
vt distinguish

distinto; distinta
[dis•TEEN•to]; [dis•TEEN•ta]
MF *adj* distinct

distorcere [DIS•tohr•TSHE•re]
vt distort

distrarre [dis•TRAHR•re] *vt*
distract; sidetrack

distratto; distratta
[dis•TRAHT•to] *adj* MF
absent-minded; distracted

distretto [dis•TREHT•to] *n* M
district

distribuire [DIS•tri•bu•EE•re]
vt distribute

distributore
[DIS•tri•bu•TOH•re] *n* M
dispenser

distribuzione
[DIS•tri•bu•TSYOH•ne] *n* F
distribution

distruggere [DIS•tru•DJEH•re]
vt destroy

distruttivo; distruttiva
[DIS•trut•TEE•vo];
[DIS•trut•TEE•va] *adj* MF
destructive

distruzione
[DIS•tru•TSYOH•ne] *n* F
destruction

disturbare [DIS•tur•BAH•re] *vt*
disturb; disrupt

disuguale [DI•zu•GUAH•le] *adj* unequal

ditale [di•TAH•le] *n* M thimble

dito [DEE•to] *n* M finger

dito del piede [DEE•to deh PYEH•de] *n* M toe

ditta [DEET•ta] *n* F company

dittatore [DIT•ta•TOH•re] *n* M dictator

dittatura [DIT•ta•TUH•ra] *n* F dictatorship

diventare [DI•ven•TAH•re] *vt* become

divergere [DI•vehr•DJE•re] *vi* diverge

diversitá [DI•ver•si•TAH] *n* F diversity

divertente [DI•ver•TEHN•te] *adj* entertaining

divertimento [DI•ver•ti•MEHN•to] *n* M entertainment; fun

divertire [DI•ver•TEE•re] *vt* amuse

dividere [DI•vee•DE•re] *vt* divide; split

divieto [di•VIEH•to] *n* M ban

divinitá [DI•vi•ni•TAH] *n* F deity; divinity

divino; divina [di•VEE•no]; [di•VEE•na] *adj* MF divine

divisione [DI•vi•SYOH•ne] *n* F division; partition

divorare [DI•vo•RAH•re] *vt* devour

divorzio [di•vohr•tsyo] *n* M divorce

divulgare 1 [DI•vul•GAH•re] *vt* divulge

divulgare 2 [DI•vul•GAH•re] *vt* popularize

dizionario [DI•tsyo•NAH•ri•o] *n* M dictionary (foreign language)

doccia [DOH•tsha] *n* F shower

doccione [dotsh•YOH•ne] *n* M gargoyle

docile [doh•TSHI•le] *adj* docile; yielding

documento [DO•ku•MEHN•to] *n* M document; record

dodicesimo; dodicesima [DO•di•tsheh•ZI•mo]; [DO•di•tsheh•ZI•ma] *adj* twelfth

dodici [doh•DIT•shi] *num* twelve

dogana [do•GAH•na] *n* F custom (border)

dogma [DOHG•ma] *n* M dogma

dogmatico; dogmatica [dog•MAH•TI•ko]; [dog•MAH•TI•ka] *adj* opinionated

dolce [DOHL•tshe] *n* M dessert; *adj* sweet

dolcezza [dol•TSHEH•tsa] *n* F sweetness

dollaro [dohl•LA•ro] *n* M dollar

dolore [do•LOH•re] *n* M ache; pain; grief; sorrow; woe

doloroso; dolorosa [DO•lo•ROH•zo]; [DO•lo•ROH•za] *adj* grievous; painful

domanda [do•MAHN•da] *n* F application; query; question

domandare [DO•man•DAH•re] *vt* ask

domani [do•MAH•ni] *n* M tomorrow

Domenica delle palme
[do•MEH•ni•KA dehl•le
•PAHL•me] *n* F Palm Sunday

domestico; domestica
[do•MEHS•ti•ko];
[do•MEHS•ti•ka] *adj*
domestic; *n* MF housekeeper

dominante [DO•mi•NAHN•te]
adj dominant

dominare [DO•mi•NAH•re] *vt*
dominate

dominio [do•MEE•nyo] *n* M
domain

donare [do•NAH•re] *vt* donate

donatore [DO•na•TOH•re] *n* M
donor

donazione [DO•nat•SYOH•ne]
n F donation

**donchisciottesco;
donchisciottesca**
[DON•ki•TSHOT•TEHS•ko];
[DON•ki•TSHOT•TEHS•ka]
adj MF quixotic

dondolare [DON•do•LAH•re]
vt swing

donna [DOHN•na] *n* F woman

donna delle pulizie
[DOHN•na DEHL•le
PU•li•TSEE•eh] *n* F cleaning
lady

donna di servizio [DOHN•na
di ser•VEE•tsyo] *n* F maid

donnola [doh•NO•la] *n* F
weasel

dono dal cielo [DOH•no dahl
TSHEH•lo] *n* M godsend

dopo [DOH•po] *adv* after

doppiamente
[DOP•pya•MEHN•te] *adv*
doubly

doppiato; doppiata
[dop•PYAH•to];
[dop•PYAH•ta] *adj* MF
dubbed

doppio; doppia [DOHP•pyo];
[DOHP•pya] *adj* dual; double;
a doppio petto *adj*
double-breasted

dorato; dorata [do•RAH•to];
[do•RAH•ta] *adj* MF gilded;
golden

dormicchiare
[DOR•mik•KYAH•re] *vi* doze;
nap

dormiente [dor•MYEHN•te]
adj sleeping

dormire [dor•MEE•re] *vi* sleep

dormitorio [DOR•mi•TOH•ryo]
n M dormitory

dose [DOH•se] *n* F dose

dotato; dotata [do•TAH•to];
[do•TAH•ta] *adj* MF gifted

dote [DOH•te] *n* F dowry

dotto; dotta [doht•to];
[DOHT•ta] *adj* scholarly

dottore [dot•TOH•re] *n* M
doctor

dottrina [dot•TREE•na] *n* F
doctrine

dove [DOH•ve] *adv* where

dovere 1 [do•VEH•re] *n* M
duty

dovere 2 [do•VEH•re] *vi* must;
ought; owe

dovunque [do•VUHN•kwe]
adv wherever

dozzina [do•TSEE•na] *n* F
dozen

drago [DRAH•go] *n* M dragon

dramma [DRAHM•ma] *n* M
drama

drammatico; drammatica
[DRAM•mah•TI•ko];
[DRAM•mah•TI•ka] *adj*
dramatic

drammatizzare
[DRAM•ma•ti•TSAH•re] *vt*
dramatize

drammaturgo
[DRAM•ma•TUHR•go] *n* M
dramatist; playwright

drappeggiare
[DRAP•ped•JAH•re] *vt* drape

drastico; drastica
[DRAH•sti•ko];
[DRAH•sti•ka] *adj* MF drastic

drettamente
[DI•ret•ta•MEHN•te] *adv*
directly

dritto; dritta [DREET•to];
[DREET•ta] *adj* straight

drizzare [dri•TSAH•re] *vt*
straighten

droga [DROH•ga] *n* F drug

dubbio [DUHB•byo] *n* M doubt

dubbio; dubbia [DUHB•byo];
[DUHB•bya] *adj* MF dubious;
doubtful

Dublino [du•BLEE•no] *n* F
Dublin

duc [DUH•ka] *n* M duke

duchessa [du•KEHS•sa] *n* F
duchess

due [duhe] *num* two

due settimane
[DUHE•set•TIMAH•ne] *npl* F
fortnight

due volte [duhe•VOHL•te] *adv*
twice

duello [du•EHL•lo] *n* M duel;
fight

duetto [du•EHT•to] *n* M duet

duna [DUH•na] *n* F dune

duplicitá [DU•pli•TSHI•tah] *n*
F duplicity

durata [du•RAH•ta] *n* F
duration; lifespan

durevole [DU•reh•VO•le] *adj*
durable; lasting

durezza [du•REH•tsa] *n* F
toughness

duro; dura [DUH•ro];
[DUH•ra] *adj* MF hard; tough

duty-free [du•TEE•free] *adj*
duty-free

E

e; ed (in front of vowel)
[eh];[ed] *conj* and

ebano [eh•BA•no] *adj* M ebony

ebollizione
[EH•bol•lit•SIOH•ne] *n* F
boiling point

ebreo; ebrea [e•BREH•o];
[e•BREH•a] *n* MF Jew

ebreo; ebrea [e•BREH•o];
[e•BREH•a] *adj* MF Jewish

eccedente [E•tshe•DEHN•te]
adj excess

eccedere [E•tshe•DE•re] *vt*
exceed

eccellente [E•tshel•lehn•te] *adj*
excellent

eccellenza [E•tshel•LEHN•tsa] *n* F excellence

eccellere [E•tshehl•LE•re] *vi* excel

eccentrico; eccentrica [e•TSHEN•triko]; [e•TSHEN•trika] *adj n* MF eccentric

eccessivo; eccessiva [ET•shes•SEE•vo]; [ET•shes•SEE•va] *adj* MF outrageous

eccetto [e•TSHEHT•to] *prep* except

eccezionale [E•tshe•tSYO•NAH•le] *adj* exceptional

eccezione [E•tshe•TSYOH•ne] *n* F exception

eccitamento [ET•shi•ta•MEHN•to] *n* M stimulation

eccitante [E•tshi•TAHN•te] *adj* stimulant

eccitare [E•tshi•TAH•re] *vt* excite

eccitarsi [e•tshi•TAHR•si] *vi* flutter

eccitato; eccitata [E•tshi•TAH•to]; [E•tshi•TAH•ta] *adj* MF excited

ecclesistico; ecclesiastica [EK•kle•SYAHS•tiko]; [EK•kle•SYAHS•tika] *adj* MF ecclesiastic

eclisse [ek•LEES•se] *n* F eclipse

eco [EH•ko] *n* M echo

ecologia [EKO•lo•DJEE•a] *n* F ecology

economia [EKO•no•MEE•a] *n* F economics; economy

economico; economica [EKO•noh•MI•ko]; [EKO•noh•MI•ka] *adj* MF cheap; economic; economical

edera [eh•DE•ra] *n* F ivy

editore [edi•TOH•re] *n* M publisher

editoriale [EDI•to•RYAH•le] *n* M editorial

edizione [E•dit•SYOH•ne] *n* F edition

edizione economica [E•di•TSYOH•ne E•ko•NOH•mi•ka] *n* F paperback

educare [E•du•KAH•re] *vt* educate

educativo; educativa [E•du•ka•TEE•vo]; [E•du•ka•TEE•va] *adj* MF educational

effervescenza [EF•fer•ve•SHEN•tsa] *n* F fizz

effettivamente [EF•fet•ti•va•MEHN•te] *adv* actually

effettivo; effettiva [EF•fet•TEE•vo]; [EF•fet•TEE•va] *adj* MF effective

effetto [ef•FEHT•to] *n* M effect

efficente [EF•fi•TSHEN•te] *adj* efficient

efficenza [EF•fi•TSHEHN•tsa] *n* F efficiency

Egitto [e•DJEET•to] *n* M Egypt

egiziano; egiziana [E•dji•TSYAH•no]; [E•dji•TSYAH•no] *adj* MF Egyptian

egoismo [E•go•EEZ•mo] *n* M selfishness

egoista [EGO•EES•ta] *adj*
self-centered; selfish

egotista [EGO•TEES•ta] *n* MF
egotist

eguaglianza
[E•gua•LYAHN•tsa] *n* F
equality

egualmente [E•gual•MEHN•te]
adv equally

ehi [EH•i] *excl* hey

elaborare [E•la•bo•RAH•re] *vt*
elaborate; expand upon

elaborato; elaborata
[E•la•bo•RAH•to];
[ela•bo•rah•ta] *adj* MF fancy;
elaborate

elastico [E•LAHS•ti•ko] *n* M
elastic; *adj* elastic

elefante [E•le•FAHN•te] *n* M
elephant

elegante [E•le•GAHN•te] *adj*
elegant; stylish

eleganza [E•le•GAHN•tsa] *n* F
elegance

eleggere [E•leh•DJE•re] *vt* elect

elementare [E•le•men•TAH•re]
adj elementary

elemento [E•le•MEHN•to] *n* M
element

elencare [e•len•kah•re] *vt*
itemize

elenco [e•LEHN•ko] *n* M
directory

elettore [E•let•TOH•re] *n* M
constituent

elettricitá [E•let•tri•TSHI•TAH]
n F electricity

elettrico; elettrica
[E•leht•TRI•ko];
[E•leht•TRI•ka] *adj* MF
electric

elettronico; elettronica
[E•let•TROH•ni•ko];
[E•let•TROH•ni•ka] *adj* MF
electronic

elevare [E•le•VAH•re] *vt*
elevate

elezione [E•le•TSYOH•ne] *n* F
election

elica [eh•LI•ka] *n* F propeller

elicottero [ELI•koht•tE•RO] *n*
M helicopter

eliminare [ELI•mi•NAH•re] *vt*
eliminate

elitista [eli•TEES•ta] *adj n* MF
elitist; snob

elmo [EHL•mo] *n* M helmet

elogio [e•LOH•djo] *n* M praise

eloquente [elo•KWEHN•te] *adj*
eloquent

eloquenza [elo•KWEHN•tsa] *n*
F eloquence; oratory; speech

elsa [EHL•sa] *n* F hilt

eludere [E•luh•DE•re] *vt* elude

emaciato; emaciata
[ema•TSHAH•to];
[ema•TSHAH•ta] *adj* MF
emaciated; shrunken; gaunt

emanare 1 [ema•NAH•re] *vt*
emanate

emanare 2 [ema•NAH•re] *vt*
enact

emancipazione
[e•man•tshi•pa•TSYOH•ne] *n*
F emancipation

emblema [em•BLEH•ma] *n* M
emblem; badge

embrione [em•BRYOH•ne] *n*
M embryo

emendare [EH•men•DAH•re]
vt amend (law); amendment
M

emergenza [E•mer•DJEHN•tsa] *n* F emergency

emergere [E•mehr•DJE•re] *vi* emerge

emettere [em•EHT•te•re] *vt* emit; utter

emicrania [emi•KRAH•nya] *n* F migraine

emigrante [E•mi•GRAHN•te] *n* MF emigrant

emigrare [E•mi•GRAH•re] *vi* emigrate; migrate

eminente [E•mi•NEHN•te] *adj* eminent

eminenza [E•mi•NEHN•tsa] *n* F eminence

emisfero [E•mi•SFEH•ro] *n* M hemisphere

emissario; emissaria [E•mis•SAH•ryo]; [E•mis•SAH•rya] *n* MF emissary

emissione [E•mis•SYOH•ne] *n* F emission

emoraggia [E•mo•ra•DJEE•a] *n* F hemorrhage

emorroidi [E•mor•ROHY•di] *n* F hemorrhoids

emozionante [EMO•tsyo•NAHN•te] *adj* exciting

emulare [emu•LAH•re] *vt* emulate

enciclopedia [EN•tshi•klo•pe•DEE•a] *n* F encyclopedia

energia [EN•er•DJEE•a] *n* F energy

energico; energica [EN•ehr•DJI•ko]; [EN•ehr•DJI•ka] *adj* MF energetic; forceful

energumeno; energumena [EN•er•guh•ME•no]; [EN•er•guh•ME•na] *n* MF thug; ruffian

enfasi [ehn•FA•si] *n* F emphasis

enfatizzare [EN•fa•ti•TSAH•re] *vt* emphasize

enigma [e•NEEG•ma] *n* M enigma

enorme [en•OHR•me] *adj* enormous; huge

entitá [en•TI•tah] *n* F entity

entrambi; entrambe [en•TRAHM•bi]; [en•TRAHM•be] *adj* MF both

entrare [en•TRAH•re] *vi* enter

entrata 1 [en•TRAH•ta] *n* F entrance

entrata [en•TRAH•ta] *n* F income; revenue

entrata di servizio [en•TRAH•ta dee ser•VEE•tsyo] *n* F stage door

entro [EHN•tro] *prep* within

entusiasmo [EN•tu•ZYAH•zmo] *n* M MF enthusiasm

entusiastico; entusiastica [EN•tu•ZYAH•stiko]; [EN•tu•ZYAH•stika] *adj* MF enthusiastic

enumerare [ENU•me•RAH•re] *vt* enumerate

epico; epica [EH•pi•ko]; [EH•pi•ka] *adj* MF epic

epidemia [EPI•de•MEE•a] *n* F epidemic

episodio [epi•ZOH•dyo] *n* M episode

epistola [EP•ee•STO•la] *n* F
epistle

epitaffio [epi•TAHF•fyo] *n* M
epitaph

epoca [eh•POK•a] *n* F epoch

equatore [E•kwa•TOH•re] *n* M
equator

equazione [E•kwa•TZYOH•ne]
n F equation

equilibrio [E•kwi•lee•BREE•oh]
n M balance; poise

equipaggiamento
[E•kwi•pa•dja•MEHN•to] *n* M
kit; equipment; baggage

equipaggiare
[E•kwipa•DJAH•re] *vt* equip;
outfit

equivalente
[E•kwi•va•LEHN•te] *adj n*
MF equivalent

era [EH•ra] *n* F era

erba [EHR•ba] *n* F grass; herb

erba cipollina [EHR•ba
TSHI•pol•LEE•na] *n* F chive

erbaccia [er•BAH•tsha] *n* F
weed

erboso; erbosa [er•BOH•zo];
[er•BOH•za] *adj* grassy

erede [er•EH•de] *n* MF heir

ereditá [er•e•DI•TAH] *n* F
inheritance

ereditare [ER•e•di•TAH•re] *vt*
inherit

ereditarietá
[ER•e•di•ta•RYE•tah] *n* F
heredity

ereditario; ereditaria
[E•re•di•TAH•ryo];
[E•re•di•TAH•rya] *adj* MF
hereditary

erediteira [E•re•dit•IEH•ra] *n*
heiress

eremita [E•re•MEE•ta] *n* M
hermit

eresia [E•re•SEE•a] *n* F heresy

eretto; eretta [er•EHT•to];
[er•EHT•ta] *adj* MF erect

erezione [E•re•TSYOH•ne] *n* F
erection

ergastolo [ER•gas•TOH•lo] *n*
M life sentence

erica [EH•rika] *n* F heather;
hernia

erodere [er•oh•DE•re] *vt* erode

eroe [e•rohe] *n* M hero

eroico; eroica [ER•oh•I•ko];
[ER•oh•I•ka] *adj* MF heroic

eroina 1 [E•ro•EE•na] *n* F
heroine

eroina 2 [E•ro•EE•na] *n* F
heroin

eroismo [ero•EEZ•mo] *n* M
heroism

erosione [ero•ZYOH•ne] *n* F
erosion

errare 1 [er•RAH•re] *vi* err;
blunder; error; *n* M mistake;
lapse; in errore *adj* \ mistaken

erudito; erudita [eru•DEE•to];
[eru•DEE•ta] *adj* erudite;
educated; intellectual

eruttare [erut•TAH•re] *vi* erupt

eruzione 1 [e•ru•TSYOH•ne] *n*
F eruption; outburst

eruzione 2 [e•ru•TSYOH•ne] *n*
F rash (med)

esagerare [E•za•ge•RAH•re] *vi*
exaggerate

esagerazione
[E•za•dje•ra•TSYOH•ne] *n* F
exaggeration

esagono [E•zah•GO•NO] *n* M
hexagon

esalare [E•za•LAH•re] *vt* exhale

esalazione [E•za•lat•SYOH•ne]
n F fumes

esaltare [E•zal•TAH•re] *vt* exalt

esame [e•ZAH•me] *n* M exam;
test

esame del sangue [e•ZAH•me
dehl SAHN•gue] *n* test
(blood)

esaminare [E•za•mi•NAH•re]
vt examine

esasperare [E•zas•pe•RAH•re]
vt exasperate

esatto; esatta [e•ZAHT•to];
[e•ZAHT•ta] *adj* exact

esaurimento
[E•za•uri•MEHN•to] *n* M
exhaustion

esaurire [E•zau•REE•re] *vt*
deplete; exhaust

esaurito; esaurita
[E•za•u•REE•to];
[E•za•u•REE•ta] *adj* used up

esausto; esausta
[E•zah•US•to]; [E•zah•UST•a]
adj MF exhausted

esca 1 [ES•skah] *n* F bait;
decoy; lure

esca 2 [ES•ka] *n* F tinder

esclamare [ES•kla•MAH•re] *vi*
exclaim

escludere [ES•kluh•DE•re] *vt*
exclude

escogitare [ES•ko•dji•TAH•re]
vt devise

escremento [ES•kre•MEHN•to]
n M excrement

escursione [ES•kur•SYOH•ne]
n F excursion

esecutivo; esecutiva
[E•ze•ku•TEE•vo];
[E•ze•ku•TEE•va] *adj* MF
executive

esecuzione
[E•ze•kut•SYOH•ne] *n* F
execution

eseguire [E•ze•GUEE•re] *vt*
perform

esempio [e•ZEHM•pyo] *n* M
example

esemplare 1 [E•zem•PLAH•re]
adj exemplary

esemplare 2 [E•zem•PLAH•re]
n M example; specimen

esemplificare
[E•zem•pli•fi•KAH•re] *vt*
exemplify

esente [e•ZEHN•te] *adj* exempt

esercitare [E•zer•tshi•TAH•re]
vt exert

esercito [E•zehr•TSHI•to] *n* M
army

esercizio [E•zer•tshee•tsyo] *n* M
exercise

esigente [E•zi•DJEHN•te] *adj*
demanding

esilarante [E•zi•la•RAHN•te]
adj exhilarating

esile [EH•zile] *adj* slight

esiliare [EH•sil•YAH•re] *vt*
banish

esilio [e•ZEE•lyo] *n* M exile

esistenza [E•zis•TEHN•tsa] *n* F
existence

esistere [e•ZEES•ste•re] *vi* exist

esitante [e•zi•TAHN•te] *adj*
hesitant

esitare [e•zi•TAH•re] *vi* hesitate

esitazione
[E•zi•tah•TSYOH•ne] *n* F
hesitation

esito [EH•zit•o] *n* M upshot

esodo [eh•zo•do] *n* M exodus

esonerare [e•ZO•ne•rah•re] *vt* exonerate

esotico; esotica [E•zoh•TI•KO]; [E•hzo•TI•KA] *adj* MF exotic

espandere [es•PAHN•dere] *vt* expand

espansione [es•PAHN•ZYOH•ne] *n* F expansion

espansivo; espansiva [ES•pan•SEE•vo]; [ES•pan•SEE•va] *adj* MF outgoing

espellere [es•PEHL•lere] *vt* eject; expel; oust

esperienza [ES•per•YEHN•tsa] *n* F experience

esperimento [ES•pe•ri•MEHN•to] *n* M experiment

esperto; esperta [es•PEHR•to]; [es•PEHR•ta] *adj* experienced; expert; skilled

esplodere [es•PLOH•dere] *vi* explode

esplorare [ES•plo•RAH•re] *vt* explore; scout

esploratore [ES•plo•ra•TOH•re] *n* M explorer

esplorazione [ES•plo•ra•TSYOH•ne] *n* F exploration; export

esposizione [ES•po•zi•TSYOH•ne] *n* F exposure

espressione [ES•pres•SYOH•ne] *n* F expression; utterance

espressivo; espressiva [ES•pres•SEE•vo]; [ES•pres•SEE•va] *adj* MF expressive; telling

espresso [es•PREHS•so] *n* M espresso; *adv* express

essenza [es•SEHN•tsa] *n* F essence

essenziale [ES•sen•TSYAH•l] *adj* essential

essenzialmente [ES•sen•tsyal•MEHN•te] *adv* essentially

essere 1 [ehs•SE•re] *v* be

essere 2 [ehs•SE•re] *n* M being

essere in conflitto [ehs•SE•re in kon•FLEET•to] *vi* conflict

essere in disaccordo [ehs•SE•re in DIZ•ak•KOHR•do] *vi* disagree

essere umano [ehs•SE•re u•MAH•no] *n* M human being

essi; esse [EHS•si]; [EHS•se] *per pron* MF they

esso; essa [EHS•soo]; [EHS•sa] *pron* MF it

est [ehst] *n* M east

estasi [ehs•TA•zi] *n* F ecstasy; rapture

estatico; estatica [ES•tah•TI•ko]; [ES•tah•TI•ka] *adj* MF ecstatic; rapt

estendere [es•TEHN•dere] *vt* extend

estendersi [es•TEHN•dersi] *vi* sprawl

estensione [ES•ten•SYOH•ne] *n* F extension

estensivo; estensiva [ES•ten•SEE•vo]; [ES•ten•SEE•va] *adj* MF extensive

estenuante [ES•te•NUAHN•te] *adj* grueling

esteriore [ES•ter•RYOH•re] *adj* outward

esternamente [ES•ter•na•MEHN•te] *adv* outwardly

esterno; esterna *adj* [es•TEHR•no]; [es•TEHR•na] outside; exterior; external; *n* MF exterior

esteso; estesa [es•TEH•zo]; [es•TEH•za] *adj* widespread

estinguese [ES•teen•GUE•re] *vt* extinguish

estinto; estinta [es•TEEN•to]; [es•TEEN•ta] *adj* MF extinct

estirpare [ES•tir•PAH•re] *vt* eradicate

estorcere [ES•tohr•TSHE•re] *vt* extort

estradare [ES•tra•DAH•re] *vt* extradite

estraneo; estranea [ES•trah•NE•o]; [ES•trah•NE•a] *n* MF outsider

estrarre [es•TRAHR•re] *vt* extract

estratto [es•TRAHT•to] *n* M extract

estremista [ES•tre•MEES•ta] *adj n* MF extremist

estremo; estrema [es•TREH•mo]; [es•TREH•ma] *adj n* MF extreme; terminal; ultimate; utmost

estro [EHS•tro] *n* M flair

estroverso; estroversa [ES•tro•VEHR•so]; [ES•tro•VEHR•sa] *adj n* MF extrovert

esuberante [EZU•be•RAHN•te] *adj* exuberant

esultante [ezul•TAHN•te] *adj* elated

esultanza [ezul•TAHN•tsa] *n* F rejoicing

esultare [ezul•TAH•re] *vi* exult

esultare silenziosamente [e•zul•TAH•re si•LEN•tsyo•za•MEHN•te] *vi* gloat

etá [etah] *n* F age

eternitá [e•TER•ni•TAH] *n* F eternity

eterno; eterna [e•TEHR•no]; [e•TEHR•na] *adj* MF eternal

eterosessuale [EH•te•ro•ses•SUAH•le] adj; *n* MF heterosexual

etica [eh•tika] *n* F ethic

etichetta 1 [eti•KEHT•ta] *n* F etiquette

etichetta 2 [eti•KEHT•ta] *n* F label

etico; etica [EH•tiko]; [EH•tika] *adj* MF ethical

Etiopia [ETYOH•pya] *n* F Ethiopia

etnico; etnica [EHT•ni•ko]; [eht•nika] *adj* MF ethnic

eufemismo [EU•fe•MEEZ•mo] *n* M euphemism

eulogia [EU•lo•DJEE•a] *n* F eulogy

Europa [eu•ROH•pa] *n* F Europe

europeo; europea [EU•ro•PEH•o]; [EU•ro•PEH•a] *adj* MF European

eutanasia [EU•ta•NAH•zya] *n* F euthanasia

evacuare [eva•KWAH•re] *vt* evacuate

evadere [EVAH•de•re] *vt* evade

evaporare [E•va•po•RAH•re] *vi* evaporate

evasivo; evasiva [eva•ZEE•vo]; [eva•ZEE•va] *adj* MF evasive

evidente [evi•DEHN•te] *adj* evident

evidenza [evi•DEHN•tsa] *n* F evidence

evitare [EH•vi•TAH•re] *vt* avoid; dodge

evocare [evo•KAH•re] *vt* evoke

evoluzione [E•vo•lut•SYOH•ne] *n* F evolution

evolvere [E•vohl•VE•re] *vi* evolve

extra [EHX•tra] *adj* extra

F

fa [fah] *adv* ago

fabbrica [FAHB•brika] *n* F factory; mill

fabbricante [FAB•bri•KAHN•te] *n* M manufacturer

fabbricare [FAB•bri•KAH•re] *vt* fabricate

fabbro [FAHB•bro] *n* M blacksmith

faccenda [fa•TSHEHN•da] *n* F affair; matter

faccetta [fa•TSHEHT•ta] *n* F facet

faccia [FAH•tshya] *n* F face

facciata [fa•TSHYAH•ta] *n* F facade

faceto; faceta [fa•TSHEH•to]; [fa•TSHEH•ta] *adj* MF facetious

facile [fah•TSHI•le] *adj* easy

facilmente [FA•tshil•MEHN•te] *adv* easily

facoltá [fa•KOL•tah] *n* F faculty

facoltá di giurisprudenza [fa•KOL•tah di DJU•ris•pru•DEHN•tsa] *n* F law school

facoltativo; facoltativa [FA•kol•ta•TEE•vo]; [FA•kol•ta•TEE•va] *adj* optional

faggio [FAH•djo] *n* M beech

fagiolo [fad•JOH•lo] *n* M bean; sophomore

fagotto [fa•GOHT•to] *n* M bassoon; bundle

falce [FAHL•tshe] *n* F scythe; sickle

falciare [fal•TSHAH•re] *vt* mow

falcone [fal•KOH•ne] *n* M falcon

falda [FAHL•da] *n* F flap

falegname [FAL•e•NYAH•me] *n* M carpenter; woodworker

falena [fa•LEH•na] *n* F moth

fallimento [FAL•li•mehn•to] *n* M bankruptcy; failure

fallire [fal•LEE•re] *vt* fail

fallito; fallita 1 [fal•LEE•to];[fal•LEE•ta] *adj* bankrupt

fallito; fallita 2 [fal•LEE•to]; [fal•LEE•ta] *adj* unsuccessful; failed

faló [fa•LO'] *n* M bonfire

falsificare [fal•si•fi•kah•re] *vt* falsify

falso; falsa [FAHL•so]; [fahl•sa] *adj* MF phony; untrue; counterfeit; false

fama [FAH•ma] *n* F fame

fame [FAH•me] *n* F hunger

famelico; famelica [fa•MEH•liko]; [fa•MEH•lika] *adj* famished; ravenous

famigerato; famigerta [FA•mi•djer•AH•to]; [FA•mi•djer•AH•ta] *adj* notorious

famiglia [fa•MI•lya] *n* F family

familiare [FA•mil•YAH•re] *adj* colloquial; familiar

familiarizzarsi [fa•mi•lya•riz•ZAR•si] *vt* familiarize

famoso; famosa [fa•MOH•zo]; [fa•MOH•za] *adj* famous

fanatico; fanatica [FA•nah•TI•ko]; [FA•nah•TI•ka] *n* MF zealot

fanghiglia [fan•GY•lya] *n* F slime

fango [FAHN•go] *n* M mud

fangoso; fangosa [fan•GOH•zo]; [fan•GOH•za] *adj* MF muddy

fannullone; fannullona [FAN•nul•LOH•ne]; [FAN•nul•LOH•na] *n* MF slacker

fantasia [FAN•ta•SEE•a] *n* F fantasy

fantasioso; fantasiosa [FAN•ta•ZYOH•zo]; [FAN•ta•ZYOH•za] *adj* MF imaginative

fantasma [fan•TAHZ•ma] *n* M ghost; phantom

fantastico; fantastica [fan•TAHS•tiko]; [fan•TAHS•tika] *adj* MF fantastic

fanteria [FAN•te•REE•a] *n* F infantry

fantino [fan•TEE•no] *n* M jockey

far cenno [fahr•tshehn•no] *vi* beckon

far disperare [FAHR•dis•pe•RAH•re] *vt* madden

far fronte [fahr•FROHN•te] *vi* cope

far girare [fahr dji•RAH•re] *vt* twirl

far pagare in piú [fahr pa•GAH•re een pyuh] *vt* overcharge

far piacere [fahr pya•TSHEH•re] *vi* please

farabutto [FA•ra•BUHT•to] *n* M scoundrel

fardello [far•DEHL•lo] *n* M burden

fare [FAH•re] *vt* do; make

fare a pezzi [FAH•re ah PEH•tsi] *vt* hack

fare acquisti [FAH•re a•KWEES•ti] *vi* shopping (to go)

fare amicizia [FAH•re am•i•TSHEE•tsya] *vi* befriend

fare causa [FAH•re KAU•za] *vt* sue

fare cilecca [FAH•re tshi•LEH•ka] *vi* misfire

fare da intermediario [FAH•re dah IN•ter•me•DYAH•ryo] *vi* mediate

fare domanda [fah•re do•MAHN•da] *vt* apply

fare giochi di destrezza [FAH•re DJOH•ki di des•TREH•tsa] *vi* juggle

fare il broncio [FAH•re il BROHN•tsho] *vi* pout

fare il burro [FAH•re il BUHR•ro] *vi* churn (butter)

fare il footing [FAH•re il FUH•ting] *vi* jog

fare il pendolare [FAH•re il PEN•do•LAH•re] *vi* commute

fare l'autostop [FAH•re lahu•to•STOHP] *vi* hitchhike

fare la pubblicità [FAH•re lah •PUB•bli•TSHI•tah] *vi* publicize

fare le fusa [FAH•re leh FUH•za] *vi* purr

fare male [FAH•re MAH•le] *vt* hurt

fare rappresaglie [FAH•re RAP•pre•ZAH•lye] *vi* retaliate

fare risatine [FAH•re RI•za•TEE•ne] *vi* giggle

fare scavi [FAH•re SKAH•vi] *vi* excavate

fare un favore [FAH•re uhn•fa•VOH•re] *vi* oblige

fare un infuso [FAH•re un•in•FUH•zo] *vi* brew

fare un'escursione [FAH•re unes•kur•ZYOH•ne] *vi* hike

fare una campagna [FAH•re uh•na•kam•PAH•nya] *v* campaign

fare una digressione [FAH•re uh•na•DI•gres•SYOH•ne] *vi* digress

farfalla [far•FAHL•la] *n* F butterfly

farina [fa•REE•na] *n* F flour

farinaceo; farinacea [FA•ri•nah•TSHE•o]; [FA•ri•nah•TSHE•a] *adj* MF starchy

farmacia [FAR•ma•TSHEE•a] *n* F pharmacy

farmacista [FAR•mat•SHEE•sta] *n* MF druggist; pharmacist

faro 1 [FAH•ro] *n* M headlight

faro 2 [FAH•ro] *n* M lighthouse

farsa [FAHR•sa] *n* F farce

farsi piccolo [FAHR•si PEEK•KO•lo] *vi* cringe

fasciare [fa•SHAH•re] *vt* swathe

fasciatura [FAH•shia•TUH•ra] *n* F bandage

fascino [fah•SHI•no] *n* M charm; fascination

fascismo [fa•SHEE•zmo] *n* M fascism

fase [FAH•ze] *n* F phase

fastidioso; fastidiosa [FAS•tee•di•OH•so]; [FAS•tee•di•OH•sa] *adj* MF annoying

fata [FAH•ta] *n* F fairy

fatale [fa•TAH•le] *adj* fatal

fatica [fa•TEE•ka] *n* F labor; toil

faticoso; faticosa [FA•ti•KOH•zo]; [FA•ti•KOH•za] *adj* MF wearisome

fato [FAH•to] *n* M fate

fatti [FAHT•ti] *n* M doings

fattibile [fat•TEE•bile] *adj* feasible

fatto [FAHT•to] *n* M fact

fatto a mano; fatta a mano [FAHT•to•ah•MAHNO]; [FAHT•ta•ah•MAHNO] *adj* MF handmade

fatto in casa [FAHT•to•in•KAH•za] *adj* homemade

fattore [fat•TOH•re] *n* M factor

fattoria [FAT•to•REE•a] *n* F farm

fattura [fat•TUH•ra] *n* F invoice

fatuo; fatua [FAH•tuo]; [FAH•tua] *adj* MF fatuous

fauna [FAH•una] *n* F fauna

favoloso; favolosa [FA•vo•LOH•zo]; [fa•vo•loh•zà] *adj* MF fabulous

favore [fa•VOH•re] *n* M favor

favoreggiare [FA•vo•re•DJAH•re] *vt* abet

favorevole [FA•vo•REH•vole] *adj* favorable

favorito; favorita [FA•vo•REE•o]; [FA•vo•REE•ta] *n* MF favorite

fazzoletto [FAT•so•LEHT•to] *n* M handkerchief

febbraio [feb•RAH•yo] *n* February

febbre [FEHB•bre] *n* F fever

febbricitante [FEB•bri•TSHI•TAHN•te] *adj* feverish

febbrile [feb•BREE•le] *adj* hectic

feccia [feh•TSHA] *n* F scum

fede [FEH•de] *n* F faith

fedele [FE•DEH•le] *adj* faithful; staunch; worshipper

fedeltá [FE•DEL•tah] *n* F fidelity

federa [feh•DERA] *n* F pillowcase

federale [FE•de•RAH•le] *adj* federal

fegato [feh•GATO] *n* M liver

felce [fehl•TSHE] *n* F fern

felice [fe•LEE•tshe] *adj* happy

felicissimo; felicissima [FE•li•TSHEES•simo]; [FE•li•TSHEES•sima] *adj* MF overjoyed

felicitá [FE•li•TSHI•tah] *n* F happiness

feltro [FEHL•tro] *n* M felt

femmina [fehm•MI•na] *adj* F female

femminile [FEM•mi•NEE•le] *adj* feminine; womanly

femminilitá [FEM•mi•NI•LI•tah] *n* F womanhood

fendere [FEHN•dere] *vt* slit; slice

fenicottero [FENI•koht•TERO] *n* M flamingo

fenomeno [FE•noh•ME•no] *n*
M phenomenon

feretro [fe•REH•tro] *n* M
coffin; casket (funeral)

ferire [fe•REE•re] *vt* injure

ferita [fe•REE•ta] *n* F injury;
hurt; wound

fermaglio [FER•MAH•lyo] *n* M
clasp

fermare [FER•MAH•re] *vt* stop;
halt

fermentare [FER•MEN•tah•re]
vi ferment

fermento [fer•MEHN•to] *n* M
ferment

fermezza [fer•MEH•tsa] *n* F
steadiness; firmness

fermo [FEHR•mo] *n* M
embargo; forbid; close off

fermo; ferma [FEHR•mo];
[FEHR•ma] *adj* MF set; firm

feroce [fe•ROH•tshe] *adj*
ferocious; fierce

ferramenta [FER•ra•MEHN•ta]
n F hardware

ferro [FEHR•ro] *n* M iron

ferro battuto
[FEHR•ro•bat•TUH•to] *n* M
wrought iron

ferro di cavallo
[FEHR•ro•di•ka•VAHL•lo] *n*
M horseshoe

ferrovia [FER•ro•VEE•a] *n* F
railroad; railway

ferroviere [FER•ro•VYEH•re] *n*
M trainman

fertile [fehr•TILE] *adj* fertile

fertilitá [fer•TI•li•TAH] *n* F
fertility

fertilizzante
[FER•ti•li•TSAHN•te] *n* M
fertilizer

fertilizzare
[FER•ti•li•TSAH•re] *vt*
fertilize

fervido; fervida [fehr•VIDO];
[fehr•VIDA] *adj* MF fervent

fessura [fes•SUH•ra] *n* F crack;
crevice; fissure

festa [FEH•sta] *n* F holiday;
party

feste [FEHS•te] *npl* F Yuletide

festival [FEHS•tival] *n* festival

festoso; festosa [fes•TOH•zo];
[fes•TOH•za] *adj* MF festive

feto [FEH•to] *n* M fetus

fetta [FEHT•ta] *n* F slice

feud [FEH•udo] *n* M feud

feudale [feu•DAH•le] *adj*
feudal

fiaba [FYAH•ba] *n* F fable;
fairy tale

fiala [FYAH•la] *n* F vial

fiamma [FIA•hm•ma] *n* F
blaze; flame

fiammeggiante
[FYAM•me•DJAHN•te] *adj*
fiery; blazing

fiammifero [FYAM•MEE•fero]
n M match

fianco 1 [FYAHN•ko] *n* M
flank

fianco 2 [FYAHN•ko] *n* M hip

fiaschetta [fyaz•KEHT•ta] *n* F
flask

fibbia [FEEB•bya] *n* F buckle

fibra [FEE•bra] *n* F fiber

fico [FEE•ko] *n* M fig

fidanzamento
[FI•dan•TSA•MEHN•to] *n* M
engagement

fidanzata [FI•dan•TSAH•ta] *n*
F fiancée; *adj* engaged

fidanzato [FI•dan•TSAH•to] *n*
M fiancé; *adj* engaged

fidarsi [fi•DAHR•si] *vi* rely;
trust

fidato; fidata [fi•DAH•to];
[fi•dah•ta] *adj* MF trusty;
trustworthy

fiducia [fi•DUH•tsha] *n* F
reliance

fiduciario [FI•duh•TSHAH•ryo]
n M trustee

fiducioso; fiduciosa
[FI•dut•SHOH•so];
[FI•dut•SHOH•sa] *adj* MF
confident; hopeful

fieno [FYEH•no] *n* M hay

figlia [FEE•lya] *n* F daughter

figliastra [fi•LYAHS•tra] *n* F
stepdaughter

figliastro [fi•LYAHS•tro] *n* M
stepson

figliastro; figliastra
[FI•LYAHS•tro];
[FI•LYAHS•tra] *n* MF
stepchild

figlio [FEE•lyo] *n* M son

figlioccia [fi•LYOH•tsha] *n* F
goddaughter

figura [fi•GUH•ra] *n* F figure

figurativo; figurativa
[FI•gura•TEE•vo];
[FI•gura•TEE•va] *adj* MF
figurative

fil di ferro
[FEEL•dee•FEHR•ro] *n* M
wire

fila [FEE•la] *n* F rank; row

filastrocca [FI•la•STROHK•ka]
n F nursery rhyme

filatoio [FI•la•TOH•yo] *n* M
spinning-wheel

filatrice [FI•la•TREE•tshe] *n* F
spinner

filetto 1 [FI•LEHT•to] *n* M
fillet

filetto 2 [FI•LEHT•to] *n* M
sirloin; tenderloin

film [feelm] *n* M movie

filo 1 [FEE•lo] *n* M floss;
strand; thread

filo 2 [FEE•lo] *n* M tread

filo spinale
[FEE•lo•spi•NAH•le] *n* M
spinal cord

filosofia [FILO•zo•FEE•a] *n* F
philosophy

filosofico; filosofica
[FILO•zoh•FI•ko];
[FILO•zoh•FI•ka] *adj* MF
philosophical

filosofo [FI•loh•SO•fo] *n* M
philosopher

filtro [FEEL•tro] *n* M filter

finale [FI•NAH•le] *adj* final

finalmente [FI•nal•MEHN•te]
adv eventually; finally

finanza [FI•NAHN•tsa] *n* F
finance

finanziario; finanziaria
[FI•nan•TSYAH•rio];
[FI•nan•TSYAH•ria] *adj* MF
financial

finché [FIN•keh] *adv* until

fine [FEE•ne] *n* F end; ending

finestra [FI•NEHS•tra] *n* F
window

fingere [FEEN•dje•re] *vt* feign;
pretend

finimenti [FINI•MEHN•ti] *npl*
M harness

finitura [fi•NITUH•ra] *n* F
finish

finlandese [FIN•lan•DEH•ze] *n* Finn; *adj* Finnish

Finlandia [FIN•lahn•DYA] *n* F Finland

finora [fin•OH•ra] *adv* hitherto; thus far

finto; finta [FEEN•to]; [FEEN•ta] *adj* fake

fiocchi d'avena [FYOH•ki•da•VEH•na] *n* M oatmeal

fiocco [FYOH•ko] *n* M flake; tassel

fiocco [FIO•hk•ko] *n* M bow (knot)

fiocco di neve [FYOHK•ko dee NEH•ve] *n* M snowflake

fiore [FIOH•re] *n* M blossom; flower; il fior fiore *n* M elite

fiorire [fio•REE•re] *vi* bloom; flower

fiorista [fyo•REES•ta] *n* M florist

firma [FEER•ma] *n* F signature

firmare [fir•MAH•re] *vt* execute (document); sign

fiscale [fis•KAH•le] *adj* fiscal

fischi [FEES•ki] *n* M boos

fischiare [FIS•ki•AH•re] *vt* boo; whistle

fisica [FEE•ZI•ka] *n* F physics

fisico [FEE•ZI•ko] *n* M physique

fisico; fisica1 [FEE•ZI•ko]; [FEE•ZI•ka] *adj* MF physical

fisico; fisica 2 [FEE•ZI•ko]; [FEE•ZI•ka] *n* MF physicist

fissare [fis•SAH•re] *vt* implant

fissazione [FIS•sa•TSYOH•ne] *n* F fixation

fissione [fis•SYOH•ne] *n* F fission

fisso; fissa [FEES•so]; [FEES•sa] *adj* MF fixed

fitta [FEET•ta] *n* F pang; twinge

fiume [FYUH•me] *n* M river

fiutare [fyu•TAH•re] *vt* snort

flagellazione [FLA•djel•la•TSYOH•ne] *n* F flogging; whipping

flagello 1 [fla•DJEHL•lo] *n* M pest

flagello 2 [fla•DJEHL•lo] *n* M scourge

flagrante [fla•GRAHN•te] *adj* flagrant

flanella [fla•NEHL•la] *n* F flannel

flauto [FLAH•uto] *n* M flute

flemmatico; flemmatica [flem•MAH•ti•ko]; [flem•MAH•ti•ka] *adj* MF stolid

flessibile [fles•SEE•bile] *adj* flexible; pliable

flettere [FLEHT•tere] *vt* flex

flora [FLOH•ra] *n* F flora; plant life

flotta [FLOHT•ta] *n* F fleet

fluido [FLUH•ido] *n* M fluid; -o -a\ *adj* fluid

fluorescente [FLUO•re•SHEHN•te] *adj* fluorescent

fluoro [FLUOH•ro] *n* M fluoride

flusso [FLUHS•so] *n* M flow

fluttuare [flut•TUAH•re] *vi* fluctuate

foca [FOH•ka] *n* F seal

focaccia [fo•KAH•tsha] *n* F
scone

focale [fo•KAH•le] *adj* focal

focena [fo•TSHEH•na] *n* F
porpoise

focolare [fo•KOLAH•re] *n* M
hearth

fodera [foh•DE•ra] *n* F lining

foglia [FOH•lya] *n* F leaf

fogliame [fo•LYAH•me] *n* M
foliage

fogna [FOH•nya] *n* F sewer

folla [FOHL•la] *n* F crowd;
mob; throng

follia [fol•LEE•a] *n* F folly; alla
follia *adv* madly

fomentare [FO•men•TAH•re]
vt foment

fomentatore
[FO•men•TA•TOH•re] *n* M
trouble maker

fondamenta
[FON•da•MEHN•ta] *npl* F
foundation (building)

fondamentale
[FON•da•MEN•TAH•le] *adj*
fundamental

fondatore [fon•DATOH•re] *n*
M founder

fondazione
[FON•da•TSYOH•ne] *n* F
foundation; basis

fondina [fon•DEE•na] *n* F
holster

fondo 1 [FOHN•do] *n* M
bottom; di fondo; *adj*
cross-country

fondo 2 [FOHN•do] *n* M fund

fonetica [FO•neh•TI•ka] *n* F
phonetics

fontana [fon•TAH•na] *n* F
fountain

fonte [FOHN•te] *n* F source

footing [FUH•ting] *n* M
jogging

foraggio [fo•RAH•djyo] *n* M
fodder; forage

forbici [fohr•BI•tshi] *npl* F
scissors

forca 1 [FOHR•ka] *n* F gallows

forca 2 [FOHR•ka] *n* F prong

forchetta [for•KEHT•ta] *n* F
fork

forcina [for•TSHEE•na] *n* F
hairpin

forcipe [fohr•TSHI•pe] *n* M
forceps

forcone [for•KOH•ne] *n* M
pitchfork

foresta [fo•REHS•ta] *n* F forest

forfora [fohr•FO•ra] *n* F
dandruff

forma [FOHR•ma] *n* F form; in
forma *adj* fit

formaggio [for•MAH•djo] *n* M
cheese

formale [for•MAH•le] *adj*
formal

formalitá [for•MALI•tah] *n* F
formality

formica [for•MEE•ka] *n* F ant

formicolare
[for•MIKO•LAH•re] *vi* teem

formidabile [for•MIDAH•bile]
adj formidable

formula [FOHR•mula] *n* F
formula

fornace [for•NAH•tshe] *n* F
furnace; kiln

fornello [for•NEHL•lo] *n* M
hot-plate

fornitore [FOR•ni•TOH•re] *n*
M provider

forno [FOHR•no] *n* M oven;
bakery; forse [fohr•se] *conj*
perhaps

forte 1 [FOHR•te] *n* M fort

forte 2 [FOHR•te] *adj* strong;
stout

forte e magro; forte e magra
[FOHR•te•eh•MAH•gro];
[FOHR•te•eh•MAH•gra] *adj*
MF wiry

fortemente [FOR•te•MEHN•te]
adv strongly

fortezza [for•TEH•tsa] *n* F
fortress

fortificare [FOR•ti•FIKAH•re]
vt fortify

fortificazione
[FOR•ti•FIKAT•SYOH•ne] *n*
F fortification

fortuito; fortuita
[for•TUH•ito]; [for•TUH•ita]
adj MF fortuitous; incidental;
lucky

fortuna [for•TUH•na] *n* F luck;
fortune

fortuna inaspettata
[FOR•tuh•na
INAS•pet•TAH•ta] *n* F
windfall

fortunatamente
[FOR•tu•NA•ta•MEHN•te]
adv fortunately; happily;
luckily

fortunato; fortunata
[for•tu•nah•to];
[FOR•tu•NAH•ta] *adj* MF
fortunate; lucky

foruncolo [fo•RUHN•kolo] *n* M
pimple

forza [FOHR•tsa] *n* F force;
might; strength

forza d'animo
[FOHR•tsa•DAH•nimo] *n* F
fortitude

forzare [for•TSAH•re] *vt*
coerce; force; impel

forzato [for•TSAH•to] *n* M
convict

foschia [fos•KEE•a] *n* F haze

fosco; fosca [FOHS•ko];
[FOHS•ka] *adj* MF somber;
dark; gloomy

fossato [fos•SAH•to] *n* M moat

fossetta [fos•SEHT•ta] *n* F
dimple

fossile [FOHS•sile] *n* M fossil

fosso [FOHS•so] *n* M ditch

foto [FOH•to] *n* F photo

fotografia [FOTO•gra•FEE•a] *n*
F photograph; photography

fotografo; fotografa
[fotoh•GRA•fo];
[fotoh•GRA•fa] *n* MF
photographer

fra [frah] *prep* among

fra poco [frah•POH•ko] *adv*
shortly

frac [frahk] *n* M tuxedo

fraganza [fra•GAHN•sah] *n* F
toilet

fragile [FRAH•djile] *adj* fragile

fragola [frah•GO•la] *n* F
strawberry

fragoroso; fragorosa
[fra•GO•ROH•zo];
[fra•GO•ROH•za] *adj* MF
loud; thunderous

fragrante [fra•GRAHN•te] *adj*
fragrant

fragranza [fra•GRAHN•tsa] *n* F fragrance

frammento [fram•MEHN•to] *n* M fragment

frana [FRAH•na] *n* F landslide

francese [fran•TSHEH•ze] *adj* French

franchigia [fran•KEE•dja] *n* F franchise

Francia [FRAHN•tshya] *n* F France

franco 1 [FRAHN•ko] *n* M franc

franco; franca 2 [FRAHN•ko]; [FRAHN•ka] *adj* MF frank; outspoken

frangia [FRAHN•dja] *n* F fringe

frase [FRAH•ze] *n* F phrase; sentence

frastagliato; frastagliata [FRAS•ta•LYAH•to]; [FRAS•ta•LYAH•ta] *adj* MF jagged

frate [FRAH•te] *n* M friar

fratello [fra•TEHL•lo] *n* M brother

fraterno; fraterna [fra•TEHR•no]; [fra•TEHR•na] *adj* MF fraternal

frattura [frat•TUH•ra] *n* F fracture; break

fraudolento; fraudolenta [FRAU•do•LEHN•to]; [FRAU•do•LEHN•ta] *adj* fraudulent

frazione [fra•TSYOH•ne] *n* F fraction

freccia 1 [FREE•tsha] *n* F arrow

freccia 2 [FREH•tshya] *n* F blinker (car)

freddo [FREHD•do] *n* M chill; -o -a\ *adj* chilly; cold

fregagione [FRE•ga•DJOH•ne] *n* F rub-down; massage

fremere [FREH•ME•re] *vi* thrill

frenare [FRE•NAH•re] *vt* restrain; brake

frenesia [FRE•NEZEE•a] *n* F frenzy

frenetico; frenetica [fre•NEH•tiko]; [fre•NEH•tika] *adj* frantic

freno [FREH•no] *n* M brake

frequentare [FRE•kwen•TAH•re] *vt* attend (school, etc); frequent; haunt

frequente [fre•KWEH•te] *adj* frequent

frequenza [fre•KWEHN•tsa] *n* F frequency

freschezza [fres•KEH•tsa] *n* F freshness

fresco; fresca [FREHS•ko];[FREHS•ka] *adj* MF cool; fresh; di fresco\ *adv* newly

frescura [fres•KUH•ra] *n* F coolness

fretta [FREHT•ta] *n* F hurry; hustle; haste; rush; in fretta\ *adv* hastily

frettolosamente [FRET•to•lo•za•MEHN•te] *adv* hurriedly

friggere [FREE•djere] *vt* fry

frigido; frigida [FREE•DJI•do]; [FREE•DJI•da] *adj* MF frigid

fringuello [frin•GUEHL•lo] *n* M finch

frittata [frit•TAH•ta] *n* F omelet

frittella [frit•TEHL•la] *n* F
pancake

frivolo; frivola [FREE•volo];
[FREE•vola] *adj* MF
frivolous; silly

frizione 1 [fri•TSYOH•ne] *n* F
clutch (auto)

frizione 2 [fri•TSYOH•ne] *n* F
friction

frizzo [FREE•tso] *n* M quip;
witticism

frode [FROH•de] *n* F fraud

fronte [FROHN•te] *n* F
forehead; di fronte\ *prep*
facing; *adj* front; *adj* opposite

frontiera [fron•TYEH•ra] *n* F
frontier

frottole; assurdita'
[FRO•to•lai];
[AH•soor•DEE•tah] *n* F
nonsense

frugale [fru•GAH•le] *adj* frugal;
economic

frugare [fru•GAH•re] *vi*
ransack; sack

frullino [frul•LEE•no] *n* M
whisk

frusta [FRUH•sta] *n* F whip

frustrare [frus•TRAH•re] *vt*
frustrate

frustrazione
[FRUS•tra•TSYOH•ne] *n* F
frustration

fruttare [frut•TAH•re] *vt* yield

frutteto [frut•TEH•to] *n* M
orchard

frutto [FRUHT•to] *n* M fruit

fucile [fu•TSHEE•le] *n* M gun;
rifle; shotgun

fucina [fu•TSHEE•na] *n* F forge

fuga [FUH•ga] *n* F escape

fuggi fuggi [FUH•dji FUH•dji]
n M stampede

fuggiasco; fuggiasca
[fu•DJAHS•ko]; [fu•DJAS•ka]
n adj MF runaway

fuggire [FUDJEE•re] *vi* escape;
elope; flee

fuggitivo; fuggitiva
[FUDJI•tee•vo];
[FUDJI•tee•va] *adj* fugitive

fuliggine [fu•LEE•DJI•ne] *n* F
soot

fulligginoso; fulliggiosa
[FU•li•DJINOH•zo];
[FU•li•DJINOH•za] *adj* MF
sooty

fulminare [ful•MINAH•re] *vt*
electrocute

fulmine [fuhl•MI•ne] *n* M
thunderbolt

fumetti [fu•MEHT•ti] *npl* M
comics (comic strip)

fumigare [FU•mi•GAH•re] *vt*
fumigate

funerale [fu•NERAH•le] *n* M
funeral

fungo [FUHN•go] *n* M fungus;
mushroom

funzione [FUN•TSYOH•ne] *n*
F function

fuochi artificiali
[FUOH•ki•ar•TIFI•tshah•li]
npl M fireworks

fuoco 1 [FUOH•ko] *n* M fire

fuoco 2 [FUOH•ko] *n* M focus

fuoco incrociato
[FUOH•ko•in•KRO•TSHAH
•to] *n* M crossfire

fuori [FUOH•ri] *adv* out; *adv*
prep outside

fuori bordo
[FUOH•ri•BOHR•do] *adv*
overboard

fuori dal comune
[FUOH•ri•DAHL•ko•MUH•ne]
adj uncommon

fuori legge [FUOH•ri•LEH•dje]
n MF outlaw

fuori moda
[FUOH•ri•MOH•da] *adj*
outmoded; outdated;
old-fashioned

furbo; furba [FUHR•bo];
[FUHR•ba] *adj* MF clever

furetto [fu•REHT•to] *n* M
ferret

furfante [fur•FAHN•te] *n* MF
villain

furia [FUH•rya] *n* F fury

furioso; furiosa [fu•RYOH•zo];
[fu•RYOH•za] *adj* MF furious

furtivo; furtiva [fur•TEE•vo];
[fur•TEE•va] *adj* MF furtive

furto [FUHR•to] *n* M larceny;
robbery; theft

fusibile [fu•ZEE•bile] *n* M fuse

fusione [fu•ZYOH•ne] *n* F
fusion

fustigare [fus•TIGAH•re] *vt*
flog

futile [FUH•tile] *adj* futile;
useless

futuro; futura [fu•TUH•ra] *adj*
MF future

G

gabbia [GAHB•ya] *n* F bird
cage

gabbia [GAHB•bya] *n* F cage

gabinetto 1 [ga•BIN•EHT•toh]
n M cabinet

gabinetto 2 [ga•BI•NEHT•to] *n*
M lavatory

gaelico; gaelica [ga•EH•liko];
[ga•EH•lika] *adj n* MF Gaelic

gagliardetto
[ga•LYAR•DEHT•to] *n* M
pennant

gaio; gaia [GAH•yo]; [GA•ya]
adj MF gay; merry;
homosexual (coll)

galleggiare [GAL•le•DJAH•re]
vi float

galleria [gal•LEREE•a] *n* F
gallery

gallina [gal•LEE•na] *n* F hen

gallo [GAHL•lo] *n* M cock

gallone [gal•LOH•ne] *n* M
gallon

galoppo [ga•LOHP•po] *n* M
gallop

gamba [GAHM•ba] *n* F leg

gambero [GAHM•BE•ro] *n* M
shrimp

gambero di fiume
[GAHM•BE•ro•di•FYUH•me]
n M crayfish

gambo [GAHM•bo] *n* M stalk
(plant)

gangster [GAHNG•ster] *n* M
gangster; racketeer

gara [GAH•ra] *n* F contest

garage [ga•RAH•dje] *n* M
garage

garante [ga•RAHN•te] *n* MF
sponsor

garanzia [GA•ran•TSEE•a] *n* F
guarantee

gareggiare [GA•re•DJAH•re] *vi*
vie

gargarizzare
[GAR•ga•ri•TSAH•re] *vi*
gargle

garofano [GA•roh•FA•no] *n* M
carnation

garza [GAHR•tsa] *n* F gauze

gas [GAH•s] *n* M gas

gasoso; gasosa [gas•OH•zo];
[gas•OH•za] *adj* gaseous

gattino; gattina [gat•TEE•no];
[gat•TEE•na] *n* MF kitten

gatto [GAHT•to] *n* M tomcat

gatto; gatta [GAHT•to];
[GAHT•ta] *n* MF cat

gazzetta [ga•TSEHT•ta] *n* F
gazette

gelatina [DJE•la•TEE•na] *n* F
gelatin; jelly

gelato [dje•LAH•to] *n* M
ice-cream

gelo [DJEH•lo] *n* M frost

gelosia [DJE•lo•ZEE•a] *n* F
jealousy

geloso; gelosa [dje•LOH•zo];
[dje•LOH•za] *adj* MF jealous

gemello; gemella
[dje•MEHL•lo];
[dje•MEHL•la] *n adj* MF twin

gemere [djeh•ME•re] *vt*
whimper

gemito [djeh•MI•to] *n* M cry;
groan; moan; wail

gemma [DJEHM•ma] *n* F gem

gene [DJEH•ne] *n* M gene

generale [DJEN•er•AH•le] *adj*
n MF general; master

generalizzare
[DJEN•er•al•I•TSAH•re] *vt*
generalize

generalizzazione
[DJE•nera•LITSA•TSYOH•ne]
n F generalization

generalmente
[DJE•ne•ral•MEHN•te] *adv*
generally

generare [DJE•ne•RAH•re] *vt*
generate; sire; spawn

generatore
[DJE•ne•ra•TOH•re] *n* M
generator

generazione
[DJE•ne•ra•TSYOH•ne] *n* F
generation

genere [dje•NEH•re] *n* M
gender

genero [djeh•NERO] *n* M
son-in-law

generositá [dje•ne•ro•zi•tah] *n*
F generosity

generoso; generosa
[DJE•ne•ROH•zo];
[DJE•ne•ROH•za] *adj* MF
generous

genetico; genetica
[dje•NEH•tiko];
[dje•NEH•tika] *adj* genetic

genio [DJEH•nyo] *n* M genius

genitale [DJE•ni•TAH•le] *adj*
npl MF genitals

genitore [DJE•ni•TOH•re] *n* M
parent

gennaio [djen•NAH•yo] *n* M
January

gente [DJEHN•te] *n* F people

gentile [djen•TEE•le] *adj* kind;
nice; gentle

gentilezza [DJEN•ti•LEH•tsa]
n F kindness; gentleness

gentilmente
[DJEN•til•MEHN•te] *adv*
gently; kindly

gentiluomo
[DJEN•ti•LUOH•mo] *n* M
gentleman

genuino; genuina
[dje•NUEE•no];
[dje•NUEE•na] *adj* genuine;
real; veritable

geografia [DJEO•gra•FEE•a] *n*
F geography

geologia [DJE•olo•DJEE•a] *n* F
geology

geometria [DJEO•me•TREE•a]
n F geometry

geometrico; geometrica
[djeo•MEH•triko];
[djeo•meh•trika] *adj* MF
geometric

gerarchia [DJE•rar•KEE•a] *n* F
hierarchy

gergo [DJEHR•go] *n* M jargon;
lingo; slang

Germania [djer•MAH•nya] *n* F
Germany

germe [DJEHR•me] *n* M germ

germinare [DJER•mi•NAH•re]
vi germinate

germogliare
[DJER•mo•LYAH•re] *vi*
sprout; germinate; bud

gesso [DJEHS•so] *n* M chalk

gesso [DJEHS•so] *n* M plaster

gesticolare [DJE•ti•ko•LAH•re]
vi gesticulate

gesto [DJEHS•to] *n* M gesture

gettare [djet•TAH•re] *vt* fling;
chuck; toss

gettare via
[DJET•tah•re•VEE•a] *vt* throw
out

getto 1 [DJEHT•to] *n* M gush;
fountain

getto 2 [DJEHT•to] *n* M jet

gettone [djet•TOH•ne] *n* M
token

ghepardo [ge•PAHR•do] *n* M
cheetah

gherone [ge•ROH•ne] *n* M
gusset

ghiacciaio [GYA•TSHA•yo] *n*
M glacier

ghiacciato; ghiacciata
[gya•TSHAH•to];
[gya•TSHAH•ta] *adj* MF icy

ghiaccio [GYAH•tsho] *n* M ice

ghiaia [GYAH•ya] *n* F gravel

ghiandola [giahn•DO•la] *n* F
gland

ghigliottina [GI•lyot•TEE•na]
n F guillotine

ghiotto; ghiotta [GYOHT•to];
[GYOHT•ta] *adj* MF
gluttonous

ghiottone; ghiottona
[gyot•TOH•ne]; [gyot•toh•na]
n MF glutton

ghiottoneria
[GYOT•to•NE•ree•] *n* F
delicacy; gluttony

ghirlanda [gir•LAHN•da] *n* F
garland; wreath

giá [JIA'] *adv* already

giacca [DJAH•ka] *n* F jacket

giacere [dja•TSHE•re] *vi* recline

giacinto [dja•TSHEEN•to] *n* M
hyacinth

giallo; gialla [DJAHL•lo];
[djahl•la] *adj* MF yellow

Giappone [djap•POH•ne] *n* M
Japan

giapponese [djap•PONEH•ze]
adj Japanese

giardino [djahr•DI•no] *n* M
garden

giarrettiera
[DJAR•ret•TYEH•ra] *n* F
garter

giavellotto [DJA•vel•LOHT•to]
n M javelin

giga [DJEE•ga] *n* F jig

gigante [dji•GAHN•te] *n* M
giant

gigantesco; gigantesca
[DJI•gan•TEHS•ko];
[DJI•gan•TEHS•ka] *adj* MF
gigantic

gilé [DJI•leh'] *n* M vest

gingillo [djin•DJEEL•lo] *n* M
trinket

ginnasta [djin•NAHS•ta] *n* MF
gymnast

ginnastica [djin•NAHS•tika] *n*
F gymnastics

ginocchio [dji•NOHK•kyo] *n* M
knee

giocatore [djo•KATOH•re] *n* M
player; competitor

giocattolo [DJO•kaht•TO•lo] *n*
M plaything

giocattolo [DJO•kaht•TO•lo] *n*
M toy

gioco [DJYOH•ko] *n* M game;
play

gioco di parole [DJOH•ko
DEE PA•ROH•le] *n* M pun

gioco di pazienza [DJOH•ko
DI PA•TSYEHN•tsa] *n* M
jigsaw (puzzle); puzzle

giocoliere [DJO•ko•LYEH•re] *n*
M juggler

giocoso; giocosa
[DJO•KOH•zo];
[DJO•KOH•za] *adj* MF
playful

giogo [DJOH•go] *n* M yoke

gioia [DJOH•ya] *n* F joy

gioielli [djo•YEHL•li] *n* M
jewelry

gioielliere [DJO•yel•LYEH•re]
n M jeweler

gioiello [djo•YEL•lo] *n* M jewel

gioioso; gioiosa
[DJO•YOH•zo];
[DJO•YOH•za] *adj* MF joyful

giornale [djohr•NAH•le] *n* M
newspaper

giornalismo
[DJOR•na•LEEZ•mo] *n* M
journalism

giornalista [DJOR•na•LEES•ta]
n MF journalist; reporter

giorno [DJOHR•no] *n* M day; a
mezza giornata\ *adj adv* MF
part-time

giorno feriale [DJOHR•no
fe•RYAH•le] *n* M weekday

giorno lavorativo [DJOHR•no
LA•vo•ra•TEE•vo] *n* M
workday

giostra [DJOH•stra] *n* F
merry-go-round

giovane [djoh•VA•ne] *adj*
young

giovanile [djo•VA•NEE•le] *adj*
youthful

giovedí [djo•VE•dee] *n* M
Thursday

gioviale [djo•VYAH•le] *adj*
genial; jovial

giovincello; giovincella
[DJO•vin•TSHEHL•lo];
[DJO•vin•TSHEHL•la] *n* MF
youth; youngster

giovinezza [DJO•vi•NEH•tsa] *n*
F youth

giradischi [DJI•ra•DEES•ki] *n*
M turntable

giraffa [dji•RAHF•fa] *n* F
giraffe

girare 1 [dji•RAH•re] *vt* endorse
(a check)

girare 2 [dji•RAH•re] *vt* flip

girare vorticosamente
[DJI•rah•re•VOR•ti•ko•sa
•MEHN•te] *vi* reel; swirl

girino [dji•REE•no] *n* M tadpole

giro [DJEE•ro] *n* M ride; tour

giro in macchina
[DJEE•ro•in•MAHK•ki•na] *n*
M drive (car)

gironzolare
[DJI•ron•tso•LAH•re] *vi*
ramble

gita [DJEE•ta] *n* F outing

giú [djuh] *adv* down; in giú\
prep downward

giubilante [DJU•bi•LAHN•te]
adj jubilant

giudicare male
[DJU•di•KAH•re•MAH•le] *vt*
misjudge

giudice [djuh•DIT•she] *n* M
judge

giudiziale [DJU•di•TSYAH•le]
adj judicial

Giudizio Universale
[dju•DEE•tsyo
UNI•ver•SAH•le] *n* M
doomsday

giudizioso; giudiziosa
[DJU•di•TSYOH•zo];
[DJU•di•TSYOH•za] *adj* MF
judicious

giugno [DJUH•nyo] *n* M June

giungere a un compromesso
[DJUHN•djere ah uhn
KOM•pro•MEHS•so] *vi*
compromise (on an issue)

giungla [DJUHN•gla] *n* F
jungle

giuramento
[DJU•ra•MEHN•to] *n* M oath

giurare [dju•RAH•re] *vi* swear;
curse

giurato; giurata [dju•RAH•to];
[dju•RAH•ta] *n* MF juror

giuria [dju•REE•a] *n* F jury

giurisdizione
[DJU•ris•DITSYOH•ne] *n* F
jurisdiction

giustapporre
[DJUS•tap•POHR•re] *vt*
juxtapose

giustificare
[DJUS•ti•FIKAH•re] *vt* justify

giustizia [djus•TEE•tsya] *n* F
justice

giustiziare
[DJU•sti•TSYAH•re] *vt*
execute (a prisoner)

giusto; giusta [DJUH•sto];
[DJUH•sta] *n* MF fair; just;
right

glassa [GLAHS•sa] *n* F icing

globale [glo•BAH•le] *adj*
global; overall; comprehensive

globo [GLOH•bo] *n* M globe

gloria [GLOH•rya] *n* F glory

glorificare [GLO•ri•fi•KAH•re]
vt glorify

glossario [glos•SAH•ryo] *n* M
glossary

glucosio [glu•KOH•syo] *n* M
glucose

gobba [GOHB•ba] *n* F hump

gobbo; gobba [GOHB•bo];
[GOHB•ba] *n* MF hunchback

goccia [GOH•tshya] *n* F drop

goccia di pioggia
[GOH•tsha•dee•PYOH•ja] *n* F
raindrop

gocciolio [GO•tsho•LEE•o] *n*
trickle

goffo; goffa
[GOHF•fo];[GOHF•fa] *adj*
awkward

gola [GOH•la] *n* F gorge;
gullet; gully; throat

goletta [go•LEHT•ta] *n* F
schooner

golf 1 [gohlf] *n* M cardigan

golf 2 [gohlf] *n* M golf

golfo [GOHL•fo] *n* M gulf

Golfo Persico
[GOHL•fo•PEHR•si•ko] *n* M
Persian Gulf

gomitata [GO•mi•TAH•ta] *n* F
nudge

gomito [goh•MITO] *n* M elbow

gomma [GOHM•ma] *n* F gum;
eraser; rubber

gomma a terra
[GOHM•ma•ah•TEHR•ra] *n* F
tire (flat)

gonfiare [gon•FYAH•re] *vt*
inflate

gonfiarsi [gon•FYAHR•si] *vi*
swell; expand; blow up; bloat

gonfio; gonfia
[gohn•FYO];[gøhn•FYA] *adj*
MF bloated; swollen

gonfiore [gon•FYOH•re] *n* M
bulge; swelling

gong [gohng] *n* M gong

gonna [GOHN•na] *n* F skirt

gorgheggiare
[GOR•ge•DJAH•re] *vi* warble

gorgogliare
[GOR•go•LYAH•ree] *vi*
gurgle

gorilla [go•REEL•la] *n* M
gorilla

gotico; gotica [goh•TIKO];
[goh•TIKA] *adj* MF gothic

gotta [GOHT•ta] *n* F gout

governante
[GO•ver•NAHN•te] *n* F
governess

governare [GO•ver•NAH•re] *vt*
govern; rule

governatore
[GO•ver•NATOH•re] *n* M
governor

governo [go•VEHR•no] *n* M
government

gracchiare [GRAK•KYAH•re]
vi cackle

gracidare [GRA•tshi•DAH•re]
vi croak

gradevole [GRA•deh•VOLE]
adj enjoyable; pleasing;
agreeable; comfortable

grado [K•do] *n* M grade; degree

graduale [gra•DUAH•le] *adj*
gradual

graffetta [graf•FEHT•ta] *n* F
clip

graffiare [graf•FYAH•re] *vt*
claw (at); scratch

grafico [GRAH•fiko] *n* M
graph; -o -a\ *adj* graphic

grammatica
[GRAM•mah•TIKA] *n* F
grammar

grammaticale
[GRAM•mah•TIKA•le] *adj*
grammatical

grammo [GRAHM•mo] *n* M
gram

Gran Bretagna
[GRAHN•bre•TAH•nya] *n* F
Great Britain

grana [GRAH•na] *n* F texture

granaio [GRA•nah•YO] *n* M
barn; granary

granata [gra•NAH•ta] *n* F
grenade

granchio [GRAHN•kyo] *n* M
crab

grande [GRAHN•de] *adj* big;
large; great

grande magazzino
[GRAHN•de
MA•ga•TSEE•no] *n* M
department store

grandezza [GRAHN•detsa] *n* F
greatness

grandine [GRAHN•dine] *n* F
hail

grandioso; grandiosa
[GRAN•DYOH•zo];
[GRAN•DYOH•za] *adj* MF
grandiose

granello [GRA•NEHL•lo] *n* M
granule

graniglia [GRA•NEE•lya] *n* F
grit

granito [gra•NEE•to] *n* M
granite

grano [GRAH•no] *n* M grain;
wheat

granoturco
[GRAH•no•TUHR•ko] *n* M
corn

grappolo [GRAHP•po•lo] *n* M
cluster

grasso [GRAHS•so] *n* M
shortening

grasso di bue
[GRAHS•so•dee•BU•he] *n* M
suet

grasso; grassa [GRAHS•so];
[GRAHS•sa] *adj* MF fat

grassottello; grassottella
[GRAS•sot•TEHL•lo];
[GRAS•sot•TEHL•la] *adj*
plump; pudgy

graticcio [gra•TEE•tsho] *n* M
trellis

gratifica [GRAH•ti•FEE•ka] *n*
F bonus; extra; gratification

gratitudine
[GRA•ti•TUH•dine] *n* F
gratitude

grato; grata
[GRAH•to];[GRAH•ta] *adj*
MF grateful; thankful

grattacielo
[GRAT•ta•TSHEH•lo] *n* M
skyscraper

grattugia [grat•TUH•dja] *n* F
grater

grave [GRAH•ve] *adj* grave;
serious

gravidanza
[GRA•vi•DAHN•tsa] *n* F
pregnancy

gravitá [gra•VITAH] *n* F
gravity

grazia [GRAH•tsya] *n* F grace

grazioso; graziosa
[gra•TSYOH•zo];
[gra•TSYOH•za] *adj* MF
lovely

Grecia [GREH•tsha] *n* F Greece

greco; greca [GREH•ko];
[GREH•ka] *adj* MF Greek

gregge [GREH•dje] *n* M drove;
flock

grembo [GREHM•bo] *n* M lap

gridare [gri•DAH•re] *vi* bawl;
yell; shout; outcry

grido rauco
[GREE•do•RAH•u•ko] *n* M
squawk

grigio [GREE•djo] *n* M gray; -o
-a\ *adj* gray

griglia [GREE•lya] *n* F grid;
grill

grilletto [gril•LEHT•to] *n* M
trigger

grillo [GREEL•lo] *n* M cricket;
grasshopper

Groenlandia
[GRO•en•LAHN•dia] *n* F
Greenland

grondaia [GRON•DAH•ya] *n* F
gutter

groppa [GROHP•pa] *n* F rump

grossa [GROHS•sa] *n* F gross

grossolano; grossolana
[GROS•so•LAH•no];
[GROS•so•LAN•na] *adj* MF
coarse; crude; rough

grottesco; grottesca
[grot•TEHS•ko];
[grot•TEHS•ka] *adj* MF
grotesque

groviglio [gro•VEE•lyo] *n* M
tangle

gru [gruh] *n* F crane

gruccia [GRUH•tsha] *n* F perch

grugnito [gru•NEE•to] *n* M
grunt

grugno [GRUH•nyo] *n* M snout

gruppo [GRUHP•po] *n* M
group; clump

gruppo di cinque gemelli
[GRUHP•po•dee•TSHEEN
•kwe•dje•MEHL•li] *n* M
quintuplet

guadagnare
[GUA•da•NYAH•re] *vt* earn;
gain

guadagno [gua•DAH•nyo] *n* M
gain

guadare [GUA•dah•re] *vt* wade

guado [GUAH•do] *n* M ford (a
stream)

guaio [GUAH•yo] *n* M trouble

guancia [gu•AHN•tsha] *n* F
cheek

guanto [GUAHN•to] *n* M
glove; gauntlet

guardare [GUAR•DAH•re] *vt*
look at; view

guardare a bocca aperta
[GUAR•DAH•re ah BOHK•ka
APEHR•ta] *vi* gape

guardare furtivamente
[GUAR•dah•RE
fur•ti•VA•MENH•te] *vt* peep

guardaroba
[GUAR•da•ROH•ba] *n* M
wardrobe

guardarsi [guar•DAHR•si] *vi*
beware (of)

guardia [GUAHR•dya] *n* F
guard; warden

guardia del corpo
[GUAHR•dya del KOHR•po]
n F bodyguard

guardiano [guar•DYAH•no] *n*
M watchman; guardian;
keeper

guarigione [GUA•ri•DJOH•ne]
n F recovery

guarire [gua•REE•re] *vt* heal

guarnire [guar•NEE•re] *vt*
garnish

guarnizione
[GUAR•ni•TSYOH•ne] *n* F
gasket; washer

guastare [gua•STAH•re] *vt*
mar; hurt

guerra [GUEHR•ra] *n* F war

guerriero [guer•RYEH•ro] *n* M
warrior; -o -a\ *adj* warlike

guerrilla [guer•RIL•la] *n* M
guerrilla

gufo [GUH•fo] *n* M owl

guglia [GUH•lya] *n* F spire

guida [GUEE•da] *n* F guidance

guidare [gui•DAH•re] *vt* guide

guinzaglio [guyn•TSAH•lyo] *n*
F lash

guinzaglio [guin•TSAH•lyo] *n*
M leash

guizzare [gui•TSAH•re] *vi*
flicker

gustare [gus•TAH•re] *vt* relish;
enjoy

gusto [GUHS•to] *n* M zest

gustoso; gustosa
[gus•TOH•zo]; [gus•TOH•za]
adj MF delicious; tasty;
palatable

H

Haiti [ha•EE•ti] *n* M Haiti

hamburger [ham•BUHR•ger] *n*
M hamburger

handicap [hahn•DI•kap] *n* M
handicap

hangar [AHN•gar] *n* M hangar

hobby [OHB•bi] *n* M hobby

hockey [OH•key] *n* M hockey

hostess [OHS•tes] *n* F
stewardess

I

i su; la sua [il•SUH•o];
[lah•suh•a] *poss pron* its

iarda [YAHR•da] *n* F yard

ibrido; ibrida [ib•REE•do];
[ib•REE•da] *adj n* MF
hybrid

iceberg [AHYS•berg] *n* iceberg

idea [id•EH•a] *n* F idea

ideale [id•EAH•le] *adj n* MF
ideal

idealismo [id•EA•LEEZ•mo] *n*
M idealism

idealistico; idealistica
[ID•ea•LIS•TIKO];
[ID•ea•LIS•TIKA] *adj* MF
idealistic

identico; identica
[id•EHN•tiko]; [id•EHN•tika]
adj MF identical

identificare
[ID•en•ti•fi•KAH•re] *vt*
identify

identitá [ID•en•TI•tah] *n* F
identity

ideologia [ID•eo•lo•DJEE•a] *n*
F ideology

idiota [id•YOH•ta] *n* MF idiot;
moron; *adj* idiotic

idolatrare [IDO•la•TRAH•re] *vt*
idolize

idolo [EE•DO•lo] *n* M idol

idoneo; idonea [IDOH•neo];
[IDOH•nea] *adj* MF eligible

idrante [id•RAHN•te] *n* M
hydrant

idraulico 1 [EE•drou•LEE•ko] *n*
M plumber

idraulico; idraulica 2
[ID•rah•ULIKO];
[ID•rah•ULIKO] *adj* hydraulic

idrogeno [ID•roh•DJE•no] *n* M
hydrogen

iena [YEH•na] *n* F hyena

ieri [YEH•ri] *n* M yesterday

igiene [i•GEH•ne] *n* F hygiene

ignaro; ignara [INYAH•ro];
[INYAH•ra] *adj* MF unaware

ignorante [INYO•RAHN•te]
adj ignorant; uniformed;
unaware

ignoranza [INYO•RAHN•tsa] *n*
F ignorance

ignorare [INYO•RAH•re] *vt*
ignore

il; la; lo [eel]; [lah]; [loh] *art* the

illecito; illecta
[IL•leh•TSHI•to];
[IL•leh•TSHI•ta] *adj* MF
illicit

illegale [il•LEGAH•le] *adj*
illegal

illegittimo; illegittima
[IL•le•DJEET•timo];
[IL•le•DJEET•tima] *adj* MF
illegitimate

illividire [IL•li•vi•DEE•re] *vt*
bruise

illogico; illogica
[il•LOH•DJI•ko];
[il•LOH•DJI•ka] *adj* MF
illogical

illuminare [IL•lu•MINAH•re] *vt*
enlighten; illuminate

illuminazione
[IL•lu•MINA•TSYOH•ne] *n* F
lighting

Illuminismo
[IL•lumi•NEEZ•mo] *n* M
Enlightenment

illusione [IL•lu•ZYOH•ne] *n* F
illusion

illustrare [IL•lus•TRAH•re] *vt*
illustrate; draw; picture

illustrazione
[il•lus•tra•TSYOH•ne] *n* F
illustration

illustre [il•LUHS•tre] *adj*
illustrious; notable

imballaggio [IM•bal•LAH•djo]
n M packing

imbarazzante
[IM•ba•RAT•SAHN•te] *adj*
embarrassing

imbarazzare
[IM•ba•RAT•SAH•re] *vt*
embarrass

imbarazzato; imbarazzata
[IM•ba•RAT•SAH•to];
[IM•ba•RAT•SAH•ta] *adj* MF
embarrassed

imbarazzo [IM•ba•RAHT•so] *n*
M embarrassment

imbastire [IM•ba•STEE•re] *vt*
baste

imbecille [IM•be•TSHEEL•le] *n*
MF imbecile

imbestialire
[IM•bes•TYA•LEE•re] *vt*
enrage

imbiancare [IM•byan•KAH•re]
vt whitewash

imboscarsi [IM•bos•KAHR•si]
vi skulk

imbottire [IM•bot•TEE•re] *vt*
stuff; cram

imbottitura [IM•bot•ti•TUH•ra]
n F padding; upholstery

imbracatura
[IM•bra•ka•TUH•ra] *n* F sling

imbrogliare [IM•brol•YAH•re]
vt cheat; hoodwink

imbroglione; imbrogliona
[IM•bro•LYOH•ne];
[IM•bro•LYOH•na] *n* MF
cheater

imburrare [IM•bur•RAH•re] *vt*
butter

imbuto [im•BUH•to] *n* M
funnel

imitare [imi•TAH•re] *vt* imitate

imitazione [IMI•ta•TSYOH•ne]
n F imitation

immacolato; immacolata
[IM•ma•KO•LAH•to];
[IM•ma•KO•LAH•ta] *adj* MF
immaculate; pure

immagazinamento
[IM•ma•GA•tsina•MEHN•to]
n M storage

immaginare
[IM•ma•DJI•NAH•re] *vt*
imagine

immaginario; immaginaria
[IM•ma•DJI•NAH•ryo];
[IM•ma•DJI•NAH•rya] *adj* MF
imaginary

immaginazione
[IM•ma•DJINA•TSYOH•ne] *n*
imagination

immagine [IM•mah•DJINE] *n*
F image

immagini [IM•mah•DJI•ni] *npl*
F imagery

immateriale
[IM•ma•TERYAH•le] *adj*
immaterial

immatricolazione
[IM•ma•tri•KOLA•TSYOH•ne]
n F matriculation

immaturo; immatura
[IM•ma•TUH•ro];
[IM•ma•TUH•ra] *adj* MF
immature

immediatamente
[IM•me•DYATA•MEHN•te]
adv immediately; right away

immediato; immediata
[IM•me•DYAH•to];
[IM•me•DYAH•ta] *adj* MF
immediate

immemor [IM•meh•MORE] *adj*
forgetful

immenso; immensa
[im•MEHN•so];
[im•MEHN•sa] *adj* MF
immense; huge

immergere [im•MEHR•djere]
vt immerse

immeritato; immeritata
[IM•me•ri•TAH•to];
[IM•me•ri•TAH•ta] *adj*
unearned

immeritevole
[IM•me•ri•TEH•vole] *adj*
worthless

immigrante
[IM•mi•GRAHN•te] *n* MF
immigrant

immigrazione
[IM•mi•GRA•TSYOH•ne] *n* F
immigration

imminente [IM•mi•NEHN•te]
adj imminent

immobile [IM•moh•BI•le] *adj*
immobile; still

immobilizzare
[IM•mo•bil•ITSAH•re] *vt*
immobilize

immorale [IM•mo•RAH•le] *adj*
immoral

immoralità [IM•mo•ra•LI•tah]
n F immorality

immortale [IM•mor•TAH•le]
adj immortal

immortalità [IM•mora•LI•tah]
n MF immortality

immune [im•MUH•ne] *adj*
immune

immunità [IM•mu•NI•tah] *n* F
immunity

immunizzare
[IM•mu•ni•TSAH•re] *vt*
immunize

immutabile
[IM•mu•TAH•BI•le] *adj*
unchangeable; immutable

immutato; immutata
[IM•mu•TAH•to];
[IM•mu•TAH•ta] *adj*
unchanged

impacciato; impacciata
[IM•pat•SHAH•to];
[IM•pat•SHAH•ta] *adj* MF
self-conscious

impaccio [im•PAH•tsho] *n* M
hindrance

impadronirsi
[IM•pa•dro•NEER•si] *vi* seize

imparare [IM•pa•RAH•re] *vt*
learn

imparare a memoria
[IM•pa•RAH•re ah
ME•moh•RYA] *vt* memorize

imparentato; imparentata
[IM•pa•ren•TAH•to];
[IM•pa•ren•TAH•ta] *adj* MF
related

impartire [IM•par•TEE•re] *vt*
impart

imparziale [IM•par•TSYAH•le]
adj impartial; unbiased

impastare [IM•pas•TAHRE] *vt*
knead

impastoiare
[IM•pas•to•YAH•re] *vt* hobble

impatto [im•PAHT•to] *n* M
impact

impavido; impavida
[IM•pah•VIDO];
[IM•pah•VIDA] *adj* MF
fearless

impaziente
[IM•pa•TSYEHN•te] *adj*
impatient

impazienza
[IM•pa•TSYEHN•tsa] *n* F
impatience

impedimento
[IM•pe•di•MEHN•to] *n* M
impediment

impedire [IM•pe•DEE•re] *vt*
impede; hinder

impegnare [IM•pe•NYAH•re]
vt engage

impegno [im•PEH•nyo] *n* M
commitment

impemeabile
[IM•per•MEAH•BI•le] *n* M
slicker

impennarsi [IM•pen•NAHR•si]
vi buck; prance

impensabile
[IM•pen•SAH•BI•le] *adj*
unthinkable

imperativo; imperativa
[IM•pe•ra•TEE•vo];
[IM•pe•ra•TEE•va] *adj*
imperative

imperatore [IM•pera•TOH•re]
n M emperor

imperatrice
[IM•pera•TREE•tshe] *n* F
empress

imperfetto; imperfetta
[IM•per•FEHT•to];
[IM•per•FEHT•ta] *adj* MF
imperfect

imperiale [IM•per•YAH•le] *adj*
imperial

imperioso; imperiosa
[IM•per•YOH•zo];
[IM•per•YOH•za] *adj* MF
imperious

imperituro; imperitura
[IM•pe•ri•TUH•ro];
[IM•pe•ri•TUH•ra] *adj* MF
undying

impermeabile
[IM•per•MEAH•BI•le] *adj*
waterproof

impero [im•PEH•ro] *n* M
empire

impersonale
[IM•per•so•NAH•le] *adj*
impersonal

impersonare
[IM•per•so•NAH•re] *vt*
impersonate

impertinente
[IM•per•ti•NEHN•te] *adj*
impertinent; naughty

impervio; impervia
[im•PEHR•vyo];
[im•PEHR•vya] *adj* MF
impervious

impeto [EEM•pe•to] *n* M
impetus

impetuoso; impetuosa
[IM•pe•TUOH•zo];
[IM•pe•TUOH•za] *adj*
hot-tempered

impetuoso; impetuosa
[IM•pet•UOH•zo];
[IM•pet•UOH•za] *adj* MF
impetuous

impiallacciatura
[IM•pyal•LAT•sha•TUH•ra] *n*
F veneer

impianti [im•PYAHN•ti] *n* M
facilities

impianto idraulico
[IM•pyahn•to
IDRAU•ul•I•KO] *n* M
plumbing

impiccione; impicciona
[IM•pit•SHYOH•ne];
[IM•pit•SHYOH•na] *n* MF
busybody

impiegare [IM•pye•GAH•re] *vt*
employ; expend

impiegato; impiegata
[IM•pye•GAH•to];
[IM•pye•GAH•ta] *n* MF
employee

impiegato statale
[IM•pye•GAH•to•STA•TAH•le]
n M servant (civil)

impiego [im•PYEH•go] *n* M
employment

implicar [IM•pli•KAH•re] *vt*
purport

implicare [IM•pli•KAH•re] *vt*
implicate

implicito; implicita
[IM•plee•TSHI•to];
[IM•plee•TSHI•ta] *adj* MF
implicit

implorare [IM•plo•RAH•re] *vt*
implore

imponente [IM•po•NEHN•te]
adj impressive

imporre [im•POHR•re] *vt*
enforce; impose

imporsi [im•POHR•si] *vi*
intrude

importante [IM•por•TAHN•te]
adj important; *n* MF
momentous

importanza
[IM•por•TAHN•tsa] *n* F
importance; magnitude

importare [IM•por•TAH•re] *vt*
import; (a qualcuno) *vi* care
(about)

importunare
[IM•por•tu•NAH•re] *vt* pester

importuno; importuna
[IM•por•TUH•no];
[IM•por•TUH•na] *adj* MF
troublesome

imposizione
[IM•po•ZITSYOH•ne] *n* F
imposition

impossibile [IM•pos•SEE•bile]
adj impossible

imposta 1 [im•POHS•ta] *n* F
levy

imposta 2 [in•POHS•ta] *n* F
shutter

imposta su redditi
[IM•poh•STA su REHD•DI•ti]
n F tax (income)

imposta su stato tax (state
tax)

imposta sui redditi
[IM•POHS•ta•suhi•REHD
•DITI] *n* F income tax

impostore [im•POS•TOH•re] *n*
M impostor

impotente [im•PO•TEHN•te]
adj impotent; powerless

**imprenditore di pompe
funebri**
[IM•pren•di•TOH•re•dee
•POHM•pe•FUH•NEB RI] *n*
M undertaker

impresa [im•PREH•za] *n* F
enterprise; exploit; feat;
undertaking

impressione
[IM•pres•SYOH•ne] *n* F
impression; hunch

imprigionare
[IM•pri•DJO•NAH•re] *vt*
imprison

imprimere [im•PREE•mere] *vt*
impress

improbabile
[im•PRO•bah•BILE] *adj*
improbable

impronta [im•PROHN•ta] *n* F
imprint

impronta digitale
[IM•PROHN•ta•DI•GITAH•le]
n F fingerprint

improprio; impropria
[IM•PROH•pryo];
[IM•PROH•prya] *adj* MF
inappropriate

improvvisamente
[IM•prov•vi•ZA•MEHN•te]
adv suddenly

improvvisare
[IM•prov•VIZAH•re] *vt*
improvise

improvviso; improvvisa
[IM•prov•VEE•zo];
[IM•prov•VEE•za] *adj* sudden

imprudente [IM•pru•DEHN•te]
adj imprudent; unwise

impudente [IM•pu•DEHN•te]
adj impudent

impulsivo; impulsiva
[IM•pul•SEE•vo];
[IM•pul•SEE•va] *adj* MF
impulsive

impulso [im•PUHL•so] *n* M
urge

impunitá [IM•pu•NITAH] *n* F
impunity

impuntarsi [IM•pun•TAHR•si]
vi balk

impuritá [IM•pu•RITAH] *n* F
impurity

impuro; impura [im•PUH•ro];
[im•PUH•ra] *adj* MF impure

imputato; imputata
[IM•pu•TAH•to];
[IM•pu•TAH•ta] *n* MF
defendant

in [een] *prep* in

inabilitá [INA•bi•LI•tah] *n* F
inability

inaccessbile
[IN•atshes•SEE•BI•le] *adj*
unapproachable

inaccurato; inaccurata
[INAK•ku•RAH•to];
[INAK•ku•RAH•ta] *adj* MF
inaccurate

inadatto; inadatta
[ina•DAHT•to];
[ina•DAHT•ta] *adj* MF
unsuitable

inadeguato; indeguata
[IN•ade•GUAH•to];
[IN•ade•GUAH•ta] *adj*
inadequate

inalare [ina•LAH•re] *vt* inhale

inane [INAH•ne] *adj* inane

inanimato; inanimata
[INA•ni•MAH•to];
[INA•ni•MAH•ta] *adj*
inanimate; senseless; lifeless

inaridito; inaridita
[INA•ri•DEE•to];
[INA•ri•DEE•ta] *adj* parched

inaspettatamente
[IN•as•PET•tah•ta•mehn•te]
adv unawares

inattaccabile
[IN•at•tak•KAH•bile] *adj*
unassailable

inattivo; inattiva
[inat•TEE•vo]; [inat•tee•va]
adj MF inactive

inaugurazione
[IN•ugu•RAT•SYOH•ne] *n* F
inauguration

incanalare [IN•kana•LAH•re] *vt*
channel (water)

incantare [IN•kan•TAH•re] *vt*
enchant; charm; entrance

incantato; incantata
[IN•kan•TAH•to];
[IN•kan•TAH•ta] *adj*
spellbound

incantesimo
[IN•kan•TEH•ZI•mo] *n* M
spell

incantevole
[IN•kan•TEH•VO•le] *adj*
delightful; enchanting

incapace [IN•ka•PAH•tshe] *adj*
incapable; unable

incatenare [IN•ka•TENAH•re]
vt shackle

incauto; incauta [in•KAH•uto];
[in•KAH•uta] *adj* unwary

incenso [in•TSHEHN•so] *n* M
incense

incentivo [IN•tshen•TEE•vo] *n*
M incentive

incerto; incerta
[IN•TSHEHR•to];
[in•tshehr•ta] *adj* MF
uncertain

incessante [IN•tshes•SAHN•te]
adj incessant; unceasing

inchiesta [n•KYEHS•ta] *n* F
poll

inchinarsi [IN•ki•NAHR•si] *vi*
bow

inchiostro [IN•KYOHS•tro] *n*
M ink

inciamparsi
[IN•tsham•PAHR•si] *vi*
stumble

incidente [IN•tshi•DEHN•te] *n*
M incident; accident

incidere [IN•tshee•DERE] *vt* M
engrave

incinta [in•TSHEEN•ta] *adj* F
pregnant

incisione [IN•tshi•ZYOH•ne] *n*
F engraving

incitare [IN•tshi•TAH•re] *vt*
impel; incite

incivile [IN•tshi•VEE•le] *adj*
uncivil

inclinare [IN•kly•NAH•re] *vt*
tilt

inclinazione
[IN•kli•nat•SYOH•ne] *n* F
penchant; slant

includere [in•KLUH•dere] *vt*
comprise; include

incollerirsi [in•KOL•ler•EER•si]
vi bristle

incolto; incolta [in•KOHL•to];
[in•KOHL•to] *adj* MF
uncultured

incomodo; incomoda
[in•KOH•MO•do];
[in•KOH•MO•da] *adj* MF
inconvenient

incomparabile
[in•KOM•pa•RAH•bile] *adj*
incomparable

incompatibile
[in•KOM•pa•TEE•bile] *adj*
incompatible

incompetente
[in•KOM•pe•TEHN•te] *adj*
incompetent

incompleto; incompleta
[in•KOM•PLEH•to];
[in•KOM•PLEH•ta] *adj* MF
incomplete

incondizionato;
incondizionata
[in•KON•di•TSYO•NAH•to];
[in•KON•di•TSYO•NAH•ta]
adj unconditional

inconscio; inconscia
[in•KOHN•sho];
[in•KÓHN•sha] *adj* MF
unconscious

inconsistente
[IN•kon•sis•TEHN•te] *adj*
inconsistent

incontrare [in•KON•TRAH•re]
vt meet

incontro [in•KON•tro] *n* M
encounter; meeting

incontrollabile
[in•KON•trol•LAH•BI•le] *adj*
uncontrollable

incoraggiamento
[in•KO•ra•dja•MEHN•to] *n* M
encouragement

incoraggiare
[IN•ko•RADJAH•re] *vt*
encourage

incoronazione
[IN•koro•na•TSYOH•ne] *n* F
coronation

incorporamento
[IN•KOR•po•ra•MEHN•to] *n*
M merger

incorporare
[IN•KOR•po•RAH•re] *vt*
incorporate

incorrere [IN•kor•REH•re] *vt*
incur

incoscienza
[IN•ko•SHEHN•tsa] *n* F
unconsciousness

incostante [IN•kos•TAHN•te]
adj fickle

incredibile [IN•kre•DEE•BI•le]
adj incredible; unbelievable

incredulo; incredula
[in•KREH•DU•lo];
[in•KREH•DU•la] *adj* MF
incredulous; unbelieving

increspatura
[in•KRES•pa•TUH•ra] *n* F
ripple

incriminare
[in•KRI•mi•NAH•re] *vt*
incriminate

incrocio [in•KROH•tsho] *n* M
intersection

incrollabile
[in•KROL•lah•BI•le] *adj*
steadfast

incubo [een•KU•bo] *n* M
nightmare

incurabile [in•KU•rah•BI•le]
adj incurable

incursione [in•KUR•SYOH•ne]
n incursion

incurvarsi [in•KUR•VAHR•si]
vi stoop

indaco [EEN•dako] *adj n* MF
indigo

indagare [IN•da•GAH•re] *vi*
inquire

indagine [IN•dah•DJINE] *n* F
inquiry

indebitato; indebitata
[IN•de•bi•TAH•to];
[IN•de•bi•TAH•ta] *adj* MF
indebted

indebolire [IN•de•bo•LEE•re]
vt weaken

indecente [IN•de•TSHEHN•te]
adj indecent; lewd

indeciso; indecisa
[IN•de•TSHEE•zo];
[IN•de•TSHEE•za] *adj* MF
undecided

indefinito; indefinita
[IN•de•fi•NEE•to];
[IN•de•fi•NEE•ta] *adj* MF
indefinite

indegno; indegna
[IN•DEH•nyo]; [IN•DEH•nya]
adj MF unworthy

indennitá [IN•den•NI•tah] *n* F
indemnity

India [EEN•dya] *n* F India

indiano; indiana
[in•DYAH•no]; [in•DYAH•na]
adj MF Indian

indicare [IN•di•KAH•re] *vt*
indicate

indicatore [IN•di•KA•TOH•re]
n M indicator

indice [EEN•DI•tshe] *n* M
index; index finger; pointer

indietreggiare 1
[IN•dyetre•DJAH•re] *vi* flinch;
recoil

indietreggiare 2
[IN•die•tre•JYAH•re] *vi* F
back

indietro [in•DIEH•tro] *adv*
back; backward; behind

indifeso; indifesa
[IN•di•FEH•zo]; [in•di•feh•za]
adj MF helpless

indifferente
[IN•dif•fer•EHN•te] *adj*
indifferent

indigeno; indigena
[in•DEE•DJE•no];
[in•DEE•DJE•na] *adj*
indigenous; *n* MF native

indigestione
[IN•di•djes•TYOH•ne] *n* F
indigestion

indignato; indignata
[IN•di•NYAH•to];
[IN•di•NYAH•ta] *adj* MF
indignant

indipendente
[IN•di•PEN•DEHN•te] *adj*
independent

indipendenza
[IN•di•PEN•DEHN•tsa] *n* F
independence

indiposto; indisposta
[IN•dis•POHS•to];
[IN•dis•POHS•ta] *adj* MF
indisposed

indirizzare [IN•di•RIT•SAH•re]
vt address

indirizzo [IN•di•REE•tso] *n* M
address

indirizzo del mittente
[IN•di•REE•tso dehl
MIT•TEHN•te] *n* M return
address

indirtto; indiretta
[in•DI•REHT•to];
[in•di•reht•ta] *adj* MF indirect

indiscreto; indiscreta
[in•DIS•KREH•to];
[in•DIS•KREH•ta] *adj* MF
indiscreet

indispensabile
[in•DIS•pen•SAH•bile] *adj*
indispensable

indistinto; indistinta
[IN•dis•TEEN•to];
[IN•dis•TEEN•ta] *adj* MF
indistinct

indistruttibile
[IN•dis•TRUT•TEE•bile] *adj*
indestructible

indisturbato; indisturbata
[IN•dis•TUR•BAH•to];
[IN•dis•TUR•BAH•ta] *adj* MF
undisturbed

individuale
[IN•di•VI•DUAH•le] *adj*
individual

individuare
[IN•di•VI•DUAH•re] *vt* locate

indizio [in•DEE•tsyo] *n* M clue

indolenzito; indolenzita
[IN•do•LEN•TSEE•to];
[in•do•len•tsee•ta] *adj* MF
sore

indolore [IN•do•LOH•re] *adj*
painless

Indonesia [IN•do•NEH•zia] *n* F
Indonesia

indossare [IN•dos•SAH•re] *vt*
wear

indovenoso; indovenosa
[IN•do•VEN•oh•ZO];
[IN•do•VEN•oh•ZA] *adj* MF
intravenous

indovinello
[IN•do•VIN•EHL•lo] *n* M
riddle

indovino; indovina
[IN•do•VEE•no];
[IN•do•VEE•na] *n* MF
soothsayer

indú [induh] *n* MF Hindu

indugiare [IN•du•DJAH•re] *vi*
lag; linger; tarry

indumento [IN•du•MEHN•to]
n M garment

indurire [IN•du•REE•re] *vt*
harden; toughen

indurre [in•DUHR•re] *vt* induce

industria [in•DUHS•trya] *n* F
industry

industriale [IN•dus•TRYAH•le]
adj industrial

industrioso; industriosa
[IN•dus•TRYOH•zo];
[IN•dus•TRYOH•za] *adj* MF
industrious

inebriato; inebriata
[ine•BRYAH•to];
[ine•BRYAH•ta] *adj* MF
inebriated; intoxicated

inedia [i•NEH•dya] *n* F
starvation

inefficace [INEF•fi•KAH•tshe]
adj ineffective

ineguaglianza
[INE•gua•LYAHN•tsa] *n* F
inequality

inerente [IN•er•EHN•te] *adj*
inherent

inerme [INEHR•me] *adj*
unarmed

inesperto; inesperta
[INES•PEHR•to];
[INES•PEHR•ta] *adj* MF
inexperienced; untrained

inesplorato; inesplorata
[IN•es•plo•RAH•to];
[IN•es•plo•RAH•ta] *adj* MF
uncharted

inestimabile
[IN•es•ti•MAH•bi•le] *adj*
invaluable; priceless

inevitabile [INE•VITAH•bile]
adj inevitable; unavoidable

infallibile [IN•fal•LEE•bile] *adj*
infallible

infantile [IN•fan•TEE•le] *adj*
childish

infanzia [IN•fahn•TSYA] *n* F
childhood; infancy

infastidire [IN•fah•STIDEE•re]
vt annoy; bother

infatti [in•FAHT•ti] *adv* indeed

infedeltà [IN•fe•DEL•tah] *n* F
infidelity

infelice [IN•fe•LEE•tshe] *adj*
sorrowful; wretched

inferiore [IN•fe•RYOH•re] *adj*
n MF inferior

infermiera [IN•fer•MYEH•ra] *n*
F nurse

infernale [IN•fer•NAH•le] *adj*
hellish

inferno [in•FEHR•no] *n* M hell

inferriata [infer•RYAH•ta] *n* F
grate

infestato; infestata
[IN•fes•TAH•to];
[IN•fes•TAH•ta] *adj* MF
overrun

infettare [IN•fet•TAH•re] *vt*
infect

infettivo; infettiva
[IN•fet•TEE•vo];
[IN•fet•TEE•va] *adj* MF
infectious

infezione [IN•fe•TSYOH•ne] *n*
F infection

infiammare
[in•FYAM•MAH•re] *vt*
inflame

infinitá [in•FI•NI•tah] *n* MF
infinity

infinito; infinita
[in•FI•NEE•to];
[in•FI•NEE•ta] *adj* endless;
infinite; unending; *adj n* MF
infinitive

inflessibile [IN•fles•SEE•BI•le]
adj relentless; unbending;
unyielding

inflessione [IN•fles•SYOH•ne]
n F inflection

infliggere [IN•flee•DJE•re] *vt*
inflict

influenza [IN•flu•EHN•tsa] *n* F
influence; flu; influenza

influsso [IN•FLUHS•so] *n* M
influx

infondato; infondata
[IN•fon•DAH•to];
[IN•fon•DAH•ta] *adj*
groundless

informare [IN•for•MAH•re] *vt*
inform

informare male
[IN•for•MAH•re•MAH•le] *vt*
misinform

informatore; informatrice
[IN•for•MA•TOH•re];
[IN•for•MA•TREE•tshe] *n* MF
stool pigeon

informazione
[IN•for•MAT•SYOH•ne] *n* F
information

infortunio [IN•for•TUH•nyo] *n*
M mishap

infrangibile
[IN•fran•DJEE•BI•le] *adj*
unbreakable

infruttuoso; infruttuosa
[IN•frut•TUOH•zo];
[IN•frut•TUOH•za] *adj* MF
fruitless

infuriare [IN•fu•RYAH•re] *vt*
infuriate

ingaggiare [IN•ga•DJAH•re] *vt*
hire; engage

ingannare [IN•gan•NAH•re] *vt*
deceive; trick

ingannevole
[IN•gan•NEH•vole] *adj*
deceitful; tricky; misleading

inganno [in•GAHN•no] *n* M
deceit; deception; trickery

ingegnere [IN•dje•NYEH•re] *n*
M engineer

ingegneria [IN•dje•NYE•ree•a]
n F engineering

ingegnoso; ingegnosa
[IN•dje•NYOH•zo];
[IN•dje•NYOH•za] *adj* MF
ingenious

ingenuo; ingenua
[IN•DJEH•nuo];
[IN•DJEH•nua] *adj* MF naive

ingessatura
[IN•djes•SA•TUH•ra] *n* F cast

Inghilterra [IN•gil•TEHR•ra] *n*
F England

inginocchiarsi
[IN•dji•NOK•KYAHR•si] *vi*
kneel

ingiuriare [IN•dju•RYAH•re] *vt*
revile

ingiustificato; ingiustificata
[IN•djus•TI•FI•KAH•to];
[IN•djus•TI•FI•KAH•ta] *adj*
MF unwarranted; unjust

ingiustiziia [IN•djus•TEE•tsya]
n F injustice

inglese [in•GLEH•se] *adj*
British; English

ingoiare [IN•go•YAH•re] *vt*
swallow

ingombrare
[IN•gom•BRAH•re] *vt* clutter

ingrandire [IN•gran•DEE•re] *vt*
enlarge; magnify

ingrassare [IN•gra•SAH•re] *vt*
fatten

ingratitudine
[IN•gra•TI•tuh•DI•ne] *n* F
ingratitude; thanklessness;
ingratitude

ingrato; ingrata [in•GRAH•to];
[in•GRAH•ta] *adj* MF
thankless; ungrateful

ingrediente
[IN•gre•DYEHN•te] *n* M
ingredient

ingresso [in•GREHS•so] *n* M
entry

ingrosso [in•GROHS•so] *adj*
wholesale

inguine [een•GUI•ne] *n* M
groin

inibire [ini•BEE•re] *vt* inhibit

iniettare [INI•et•TAH•re] *vt*
inject

iniziale [ini•TSYAH•le] *adj. n*
MF initial; *adj* opening;
beginning

iniziare [I•ni•TSYAH•re] *vi*
commence; *vt* initiate

innamorato; innamorata
[IN•na•mo•RAH•to];
[IN•na•mo•RAH•ta] *adj* MF
enamored; in love (with)

innato; innata [in•NAH•to];
[in•NAH•ta] *adj* MF innate;
native

innegabile [IN•ne•GAH•bi•le]
adj undeniable

innesto [in•NEHS•to] *n* M graft

inno [EEN•no] *n* M hymn

innocente [in•NO•TSHEN•te]
adj innocent

innocenza
[IN•no•TSHEHN•tsa] *n* F
innocence

innocuo; innocua
[IN•noh•KWUO];
[IN•noh•KWUA] *adj* MF
harmless

innovazione
[IN•no•VATSYOH•ne] *n* F
innovation

innumerevole
[IN•nu•ME•REH•vole] *adj*
countless; untold (number)

inoculare [IN•o•KULAH•re] *vt*
inoculate

inoltre [in•OHL•tre] *prep adv*
besides; *adv* furthermore

inondare [IN•on•DAH•re] *vt*
inundate; overflow

inondazione
[IN•on•da•TSYOH•ne] *n* F
flood

inorganico; inorganica
[IN•or•GAH•niko];
[IN•or•GAH•nika] *adj* MF
inorganic

inossidabile
[IN•os•si•DAH•BI•le] *adj*
stainless

inquietante
[IN•kwye•TAHN•te] *adj*
disturbing

inquieto; inquieta
[IN•KWYEH•to];
[IN•KWYEH•ta] *adj* MF
restless

inquietudine
[IN•kwye•TUH•DI•ne] *n* F
restlessness

inquilino; inquilina
[IN•kwi•LEE•no];
[IN•kwi•LEE•na] *n* MF
lodger; tenant

inquinamento
[IN•kwi•NAMEHN•to] *n* M
pollution

inquinare [IN•KWINAH•re] *vt*
pollute

inquisizione
[IN•kwi•ZI•TSYOH•ne] *n* F
inquisition

insalata [IN•sa•LAH•ta] *n* F
salad

insalata di cavolo
[IN•sa•LAH•ta dee
KAH•volo] *n* F slaw

insanguinato
[IN•sahn•GUIN•AH•to] *adj*
bloody

insaziabile [IN•sa•TSYAH•bile]
adj insatiable

insegnamento
[IN•se•NYA•MEHN•to] *n* M
teaching .

insegnante [IN•se•NYAHN•te]
n MF teacher

insegnare [IN•se•NYAH•re] *vt*
teach

insegne regali
[IN•seh•NYE•re•GAH•li] *npl*
F regalia

inseguimento
[IN•se•GUI•MEHN•to] *n* M
pursuit

inseguire [IN•se•GUEE•re] *vt*
pursue

inseguire furtivamente
[IN•se•GUEE•re
FUR•ti•VAMEHN•te] *vt* stalk

insenatura [IN•se•NA•TUH•ra]
n F cove

insensibile [IN•sen•SEE•bile]
adj insensitive; numb

inseparabile
[IN•se•PARAH•bile] *adj*
inseparable

inserire [IN•se•REE•re] *vt* insert

inserviente [IN•ser•VIEHN•te]
n M porter

inserzione [IN•ser•TSIOH•ne]
n F advertisement; classified
ad; insertion

insetticida
[IN•set•ti•TSHEE•da] *n* M
insecticide

insetto [in•SEHT•to] *n* M bug;
insect

insieme [in•SYEH•me] *adv*
together

insieme di fatti e tradizione
[in•SYEH•me di FAHT•ti e
TRA•di•TSYOH•ne] *n* M lore

insignificante
[IN•si•nyfi•KAHN•te] *adj*
inconspicuous

insignificante
[IN•si•nyfi•KAHN•te] *adj*
insignificant; petty

insinuare [IN•si•NUAH•re] *vt*
imply

insinuazione
[IN•si•nua•TSYOH•ne] *n* F
innuendo; hint; indication

insipido; insipida
[in•SEE•PI•do];
[in•SEE•PI•da] *adj* MF
insipid; tasteless

insistente [IN•sis•TEHN•te] *adj*
insistent

insistere [IN•sis•TEH•re] *vi*
insist

insolente [IN•so•LEHN•te] *adj*
brash; insolent

insonne [in•SOHN•ne] *adj*
sleepless

insonnia [in•SOHN•nya] *n* F
insomnia

insopportabile
[in•SOP•por•TAH•BI•le] *adj*
unbearable

insospettato; insospettata
[IN•sos•PET•TAH•to];
[IN•sos•PET•TAH•ta] *adj* MF
unsuspected

insostituibile
[IN•sos•TI•tuee•BI•le] *adj*
irreplaceable

insozzare [IN•sot•SAH•re] *vt*
defile

installare [IN•stal•LAH•re] *vt*
install

installazione
[IN•stal•LAT•SYOH•ne] *n* F
installation

instancabile
[IN•stan•KAH•BI•le] *adj*
tireless; untiring

instillare [IN•stil•LAH•re] *vt*
instill

instupidire [IN•stu•PI•DEE•re]
vt stupefy; astound

insufficiente
[IN•suf•FIT•SHEHN•te] *adj*
insufficient

insulso; insulsa
[IN•SUHL•so];[IN•SUHL•sa]
adj vapid

insulto [in•SUHL•to] *n* M insult

intanto [in•TAHN•to] *adv*
meanwhile

intatto; intatta [in•TAHT•to];
[in•TAHT•ta] *adj* MF intact;
unbroken; untouched

integrale [IN•te•GRAH•le] *adj*
integral

integrazione
[IN•te•GRA•TSYOH•ne] *n* F
integration

integritá [IN•te•GRI•tah] *n* F
integrity

intellettuale
[IN•tel•LET•TUAH•le] *adj n*
MF intellectual

intelligente
[IN•tel•LI•DJEHN•te] *adj*
intelligent

intelligenza
[IN•tel•LI•DJEHN•tsa] *n* F
intelligence

intendente [IN•ten•DEHN•te]
n M steward

intenerirsi [IN•te•ne•REER•si]
vi relent

intensificare
[IN•tn•sifi•KAH•re] *vt*
enhance; intensify

intensitá [IN•ten•SI•tah] *n* F
intensity

intensivo; intensiva
[IN•ten•SEE•vo];
[IN•ten•SEE•va] *adj* MF
intensive

intenso; intensa [in•TEH•so];
[in•TEHN•sa] *adj* intense

intentare [in•TEN•TAH•re] *vt*
prosecute

intentato; intentata
[in•TEN•TAH•to];
[in•TEN•TAH•ta] *adj* MF
untried

intento; intenta [in•TEHN•to];
[in•tehn•ta] *adj* MF intent

intenzione
[in•TEN•TSYOH•ne] *n* F
intention

interamente
[in•TE•RAMEHN•te] *adv*
entirely

intercettare
[in•TER•tshet•TAH•re] *vt*
intercept

interessante
[in•TE•res•SAHN•te] *adj*
interesting

interesse [in•TE•REHS•se] *n* M
concern; interest

interferenza
[IN•ter•fer•EHN•tsa] *n* F
interference

interferire [IN•ter•FEREE•re]
vi interfere

interiore [IN•ter•YOH•re] *adj*
inner; interior

intermediario
[IN•ter•ME•DYAH•ryo] *n* M
mediator

intermedio; intermedia
[IN•ter•MEH•dyo];
[in•ter•meh•dya] *adj*
intermediate

interminabile
[IN•ter•MI•NAH•bi•le] aj
interminable

internazionale
[IN•ter•NA•TSYO•nah•le] *adj*
international

interno [in•TEHR•no] *n* M
intern; interior

interno; interna [in•TEHR•no];
[in•TEHR•na] *adj* MF inside;
interior; internal; inward

intero; intera [in•TEH•ro];
[in•TEH•ra] *adj* MF entire;
whole

interpretare
[in•TER•pre•TAH•re] *vt*
construe; interpret

interpretare male
[in•TER•pre•TAHRE•MAH•le]
vt misconstrue

interpretazione
[IN•ter•PRE•tat•SYOH•ne] *n*
F interpretation

interprete [IN•tehr•PRE•te] *n*
MF interpreter

interrogare [IN•ter•ro•GAH•re]
vt interrogate

interrogazione
[INTER•ro•gat•SYOH•ne] *n* F
interrogation

interrompere
[IN•ter•ROHM•pere] *vt*
interrupt

interrompere con critiche
[IN•ter•ROHM•pe•re KON
KREE•tike] *vt* heckle

interruttore
[IN•ter•rut•TOH•re] *n* M
switch

interruzione
[IN•ter•RUT•SYOH•ne] *n* F
interruption

intersecare [IN•ter•se•KAH•re]
vt intersect

intervallo [IN•ter•VAHL•lo] *n*
M intermission; interval; recess

intervenire [IN•ter•ve•NEE•re]
vt intervene

intervento [IN•ter•VEHN•to] *n*
M intervention

intervista [IN•ter•VEE•sta] *n* F
interview

intestazione
[IN•tes•tat•SYOH•ne] *n* F
heading

intestino [IN•tes•TEE•no] *n* M
intestine

intimi [een•TI•mi] *npl* M
lingerie

intimidire [IN•ti•mi•DEE•re] *vt*
daunt

intimitá [IN•ti•MI•tah] *n* F
intimacy; privacy

intimo; intima [een•TI•mo];
[een•TI•ma] *adj* MF cozy;
inmost; intimate

intollerabile
[IN•tol•ler•AH•bile] *adj*
intolerable

intollerante
[IN•tol•ler•AHN•te] *adj*
intolerant

intolleranza
[IN•tol•ler•AHN•tsa] *n* F
intolerance

intonaco [IN•toh•NA•ko] *n* M
stucco

intorno [IN•TOHR•no] *adv*
around

intorpidito; intorpidita
[IN•tor•pi•DEE•to];
[IN•tor•pi•DEE•ta] *adj* MF
torpid

intransigente
[IN•tran•zi•DJEHN•te] *adj*
uncompromising

intraprendente
[IN•tra•PREN•dehn•te] *adj*
enterprising

intraprendere
[IN•tra•PREHN•dere] *vt*
undertake

intrattenere
[IN•trat•TENEH•re *vt*
entertain

intrecciare
[IN•tre•TSHYAH•re] *vt* braid

intrecciarsi
[IN•tre•TSHAHR•si] *vi*
interlock; intertwine

intricato; intricata
[IN•tri•KAH•to];
[IN•tri•KAH•ta] *adj* MF
intricate

intrigo [in•TREE•go] *n* M
intrigue

introdurre [IN•troo•DUHR•re]
vt introduce

introduzione
[IN•tro•DUTSYOH•ne] *n* F
introduction

intromettersi
[IN•tro•MEHT•tersi] *vi*
meddle

introverso; introversa
[IN•tro•VEHR•so];
[IN•tro•VEHR•sa] *n* MF
introvert; *adj* introverted

intrusione [IN•tru•ZYOH•ne] *n*
F intrusion

intruso; intrusa [in•TRUH•zo];
[in•TRUH•za] *n* MF intruder

intuito [in•TUH•i•to] *n* M
insight; intuition

inumano; inumana
[inu•MAH•no]; [inu•MAH•na]
adj inhuman

inumidire [IN•u•MI•DEE•re] *vt*
dampen; moisten

inutile [IN•uh•TI•le] *adj*
needless; useless; pointless

inutilitá [I•nu•ti•LI•TAH] *n* F
uselessness

invadere [in•VAH•dere] *vt*
encroach; invade

invalido; invalida
[IN•vah•LI•do];
[IN•vah•LI•da] *adj* disabled;
adj n MF invalid

invariabilmente
[IN•va•RYA•bil•MEHN•te]
adv invariably

invasione [IN•vaz•YOH•ne] *n*
F invasion

invece [in•VEH•tshe] *adv*
instead

inventare [IN•ven•TAH•re] *vt*
contrive; invent

inventario [IN•ven•TAH•ryo] *n*
M inventory

inventivo; inventiva
[IN•ven•TEE•vo];
[IN•ven•TEE•va] *adj* MF
inventive

inventore [IN•ven•TOH•re] *n*
M inventor

invenzione
[IN•ven•TSYOH•ne] *n* F
invention

invernale [IN•ver•NAH•le] *adj*
wintry

inverno [IN•VEHR•no] *n* M
winter

investigare [IN•ves•ti•GAH•re]
vt investigate

investigatore
[IN•ves•ti•GA•TOH•re] *n* M
sleuth

investigazione
[IN•ves•ti•GA•TSYOH•ne] *n*
F investigation

investimento
[IN•ves•TI•MEHN•to] *n* M
investment; venture (business)

investire 1 [IN•ves•TEE•re] *vt*
induct

investire 2 [IN•ves•TEE•re] *vt*
invest

investitore [IN•ves•TI•TOH•re]
n M investor

inviato; inviata [in•VIAH•to];
[in•VIAH•ta] *n* MF envoy

invidia [in•VEE•dya] *n* F envy

invidioso; invidiosa
[IN•vi•DYOH•so];
[IN•vi•DYOH•sa] *adj* MF
envious

invincibile
[IN•vin•TSHEE•bi•le] *adj*
invincible

invisibile [IN•vi•ZEE•bile] *adj*
invisible

invitare [IN•vi•TAH•re] *vt*
invite

invito [in•VEE•to] *n* M
invitation

invitto; invitta [in•VEET•to];
[in•veet•ta] *adj* MF
unconquered

invocare [IN•vo•KAH•re] *vt*
invoke

involontario; involontaria
[IN•vo•lon•TAH•ryo];
[IN•vo•lon•TAH•rya] *adj* MF
inadvertent; involuntary

inzuppare [IN•tsup•PAH•re] *vt*
drench; sop

io 1 [EE•o] *n* M ego; self

io 2 [EE•o] *pers pron* I

io stesso; io stessa
[EE•o•STEHS•so];
[EE•o•STEHS•sa] *pron* MF
myself

iperattivo; iperattiva
[I•per•at•TEE•vo];
[I•per•at•TEE•va] *adj* MF
hyperactive

ipnosi [ip•NOH•zi] *n* F
hypnosis

ipnotico; ipnotica
[ip•NOH•tiko]; [ip•NOH•tika]
adj MF hypnotic

ipnotizzare [IP•noti•TSAH•re]
vt hypnotize; mesmerize

ipocrisia [I•po•kri•ZEE•a] *n* F
hypocrisy

ipocrita [I•poh•KRI•ta] *n* MF
hypocrite; *adj* hypocritical

ipoteca [IPO•TEH•ka] *n* F
mortgage

ipotesi [I•poh•TESI] *n* F
hypothesis

ipotetico; ipotetica
[I•po•TEH•tiko];
[I•po•TEH•tika] *adj* MF
hypothetical

ippopotamo [IP•po•POH•tamo]
n M hippopotamus

ira [EE•ra] *n* F wrath

iracheno; irachena
[IRA•keh•no]; [IRA•keh•na]
adj MF Iraqi

Irak [irahk] *n* M Iraq

Iran [[EE•ran] *n* M Iran

iraniano; iraniana
[IRA•NYAH•no];
[IRA•NYAH•na] *adj* MF
Iranian

irato; irata [ir•AH•to];
[ir•AH•ta] *adj* MF angry

ireos [ee•RE•os] *n* M iris

Irlanda [ir•LAHN•da] *n* F
Ireland

Irlanda del Nord
[ir•LAHN•da•dehl•NOHRD] *n*
F Northern Ireland

irlandese [ir•LAN•DEH•ze] *adj*
Irish

ironia [iro•NEE•a] *n* F irony

ironico; ironica [iroh•NI•ko];
[iroh•NI•ka] *adj* MF ironic

irrazionale
[IR•ra•TSYO•NAH•le] *adj*
irrational

irregolare [IR•re•GOLAH•re]
adj irregular

irregolaritá
[IR•re•GOLA•ri•TAH] *n* F
irregularity

irreparabile
[IR•re•par•AH•BI•le] *adj*
irreparable

irresistibile
[IR•rezi•STEE•BI•le] *adj*
compelling; irresistible

irresponsabile
[IR•res•pon•SAH•BI•le] *adj*
irresponsible; unaccountable

irrgidire [IR•ri•dji•DEE•re] *vt*
stiffen

irrigare [IR•ri•GAH•re] *vt*
irrigate

irrigazione
[IR•ri•ga•TSYOH•ne] *n* F
irrigation

irrilevante [IR•ri•lev•AHN•te]
adj irrelevant

irrisorio; irrisoria
[IR•ri•ZOH•ryo];
[IR•ri•ZOH•rya] *adj* MF
paltry

irritabile [IR•ri•TAH•bile] *adj*
irritable

irritante [IR•ri•TAHN•te] *adj*
irritating

irritare [IR•ri•TAH•re] *vt* irritate

irriverenza
[IR•ri•VEREHN•tsa] *n* F
disrespect

irruvidire [IR•ru•vi•DEE•re] *vt*
roughen

iscrivere [IS•KREE•vere] *vt*
enroll; register

iscrizione [IS•KRI•tsyoh•ne] *n*
F inscription; registration

Islamismo [IZ•la•MEEZ•mo] *n*
M Islam

Islanda [iz•LAHN•da] *n* F
Iceland

isola [ee•ZO•la] *n* F island

isolamento [IZO•la•MEHN•to]
n M isolation; insulation

isolare [I•so•LAH•re] *vt*
insulate; isolate; sequester

isolato 1 [IS•o•LAH•to] *n* M
block (street)

isolato; isolata 2
[I•zo•LAH•to]; [I•zo•LAH•ta]
adj MF lonely

isolato acusticamente;
isolataacusticamente
[IZO•LAH•to
akus•TI•kmehn•te];
[IZO•LAH•ta
akus•TI•kmehn•te] *adj*
soundproof

ispanico; ispanica
[is•PAH•niko]; [is•PAH•nika]
adj MF Hispanic

ispessire [IS•pes•SEE•re] *vt*
thicken

ispettore [IS•pet•TOH•re] *n* M
inspector

ispezionare
[IS•pe•TSYO•NAH•re] *vt*
inspect

ispezione [IS•PETSYOH•ne] *n*
F inspection

ispirare [IS•pi•RAH•re] *vt*
inspire

ispirazione
[IS•pi•rat•SYOH•ne] *n* F
inspiration

istantaneo; istantanea
[IS•tan•TAH•neo];
[IS•tan•TAH•nea] *adj* MF
instant

isterico; isterica [is•TEH•riko];
[is•TEH•rika] *adj* MF
hysterical

istigare [IS•ti•GAH•re] *vt*
instigate

istinto [is•TEEN•to] *n* M
instinct

istituto [IS•ti•TUH•to] *n* M
institute

istruire [IS•tru•EERE] *vt*
instruct

istruttore [IS•trut•TOH•re] *n* M
instructor

istruzione [IS•tru•TSYOH•ne]
n F instruction

italiano; italiana
[ITA•LYAH•no]; [ita•lyah•na]
adj MF Italian

itinerario [ITI•NERAH•ryo] *n*
M itinerary

itterizia [IT•te•REE•tsya] *n* F
jaundice

J

jazz [DJEH•ts] *n* M jazz

jeans [DJEE•ntz] *npl* M jeans

jukebox [DJUHK•boks] *n* M
jukebox

K

Kenya [KEH•nya] *n* M Kenya
kilt [keelt] *n* M kilt

Kuwait [ku•UEH•it] *n* M
Kuwait

L

l'uno e l'altro; l'una e l'altra
[LUH•no•eh•LAHL•tro];
[LUH•na•eh•LAHL•tra] *adj*
MF either
lá [lah] *adv* there
labbro [LAHB•bro] *n* M lip
labirinto [LA•bi•REEN•to] *n* M
maze
laboratorio
[LA•bo•RATOH•ryo] *n* M
lab; laboratory
lacca 1 [LAHK•ka] *n* F
hairspray
lacca 2 [LAHK•ka] *n* F lacquer
lacrima [lah•KRI•ma] *n* F tear
ladro; ladra [LAH•dro];
[LAH•dra] *n* MF thief;
burglar; robber
lagnanza [la•NYAHN•tsa] *n* F
complaint; grievance
lagnarsi [la•NYAHR•si] *vi*
complain
lago [LAH•go] *n* M lake
laguna [la•GUH•na] *n* F lagoon
lama [LAH•ma] *n* F blade
lamentare [LÁ•men•TAH•re] *vt*
lament
lamentela [LA•men•TEH•la] *n*
F gripe
laminare [LA•mi•NAH•re] *vt*
laminate

lampada [lahm•PADA] *n* F
lamp
lampo [LAHM•po] *n* M
lightning
lampone [lam•POH•ne] *n* M
raspberry
lana [LAH•na] *n* F wool; di
lana\ *adj* woolen
lancia [LAHN•tsha] *n* F lance;
spear
lanciare [lan•TSHAH•re] *vt*
hurl; throw; launch; toss
languido; languida
[lahn•GUYDO];
[lahn•GUYDA] *adj* MF
dreamy; languid
lanoso; lanosa [la•NOH•zo];
[la•NOH•za] *adj* MF woolly
lanterna [lan•TEHR•na] *n* F
lantern
lanugine [LA•nuh•DJENE] *n* F
fluff
lanuginoso; lanuginosa
[LA•nudji•NOH•zo];
[LA•nudji•NOH•za] *adj* MF
fuzzy
lapide [lah•PI•de] *n* F marker;
tombstone
largamente
[LAR•ga•MEHN•te] *adv*
widely

larghezza [lar•GEH•tsa] *n* F
breadth; width

largo; larga
[LAHR•go];[LAHR•ga] *adj*
MF broad; wide

larva [LAHR•va] *n* F grub

lasciapassare
[LAH•sha•PAS•SAH•re] *n* M
pass

lasciare [la•SHAH•re] *vt* let

lasciare (per testamento)
[la•SHIAH•re] *vt* bequeath

lasciato; lasciata
[la•SHAH•to]; [la•SHAH•ta]
pp MF left

lascivo; lasciva [la•SHEE•vo];
[la•SHEE•va] *adj* MF
lecherous

lassativo [LAS•sa•TEE•vo] *n* M
laxative

lastra [LAHS•tra] *n* F slab

lastricare [LAS•tri•KAH•re] *v*
pave

lastrico [lahs•TRI•ko] *n* M
pavement

latente 1 [la•TEHN•te] *adj*
latent

latente 2 [la•TEHN•te] *adj*
potential

laterale [la•TERAH•le] *adj*
sideways

latino; latina [la•TEE•no];
[la•TEE•na] *adj n* MF Latin

latitudine [LA•ti•TUH•dine] *n*
F latitude

lato superiore
[LAH•to•SU•pe•RYOH•re] *n*
M upside; a lato di *prep*
beside

latrina [la•TREE•na] *n* F
outhouse

latta [LAHT•ta] *n* F tin

latte [LAHT•te] *n* M milk

latteria [LAT•te•REE•a] *n* F
dairy

latticino [LAT•ti•TSCHEE•no]
n M dairy (product)

lattina [lat•TEE•na] *n* F tin can

lattuga [lat•TUH•ga] *n* F
lettuce

Latvia [LAHT•vya] *n* F Latvia

laurea [LAH•ur•E•a] *n* F
doctorate

lava [LAH•va] *n* F lava

lavaggio [la•VAH•djo] *n* M
washing

lavagna [la•VAH•nya] *n* F
blackboard

lavandino [LA•van•DEE•no] *n*
M sink

lavandino di cucina
[LA•van•DEE•no•di•KU•TSCHI
•na] *n* M kitchen sink

lavare [la•VAH•re] *vt* wash;
launder

lavastoviglie
[LAH•va•STO•VEE•lye] *n* F
dishwasher

lavatrice [LA•va•TREE•tshe] *n*
F washing-machine

lavorare a maglia
[LA•vo•RAH•re•ah•MAH•lya]
vi knit

lavorare eccessivamente
[LA•vo•RAH•re
et•SHES•si•va•MEHN•te] *vi*
overwork

lavoratore [LA•vo•RATOH•re]
n M worker; -tore -trice\ *adj*
hardworking

lavorazione
[LA•vo•ra•TSYOH•ne] *n* F
workmanship

lavori di casa
[LA•voh•RI•di•KAH•za] *npl*
M housework

lavoro [la•VOH•ro] *n* M chores;
job; work

lavoro a maglia
[la•VOH•ro•ah•MAH•lya] *n*
M knitting

lavoro di gruppo
[la•VOH•ro•dee•GRUHP•po]
n M teamwork

leale [LEAH•le] *adj* loyal

lealtá [le•AHL•tah] *n* F loyalty

lebbra [LEHB•bra] *n* F leprosy

lebbroo; lebbrosa
[leb•BROOH•zo];
[leb•BROH•za] *n* MF leper

lecca lecca [LEHK•ka•LEH•ka]
n F lollipop

leccare [lek•KAH•re] *vt* lick

lecita; lecita [leh•TSHI•to] *adj*
MF kosher

lega [LEH•ga] *n* F league; di
buona lega *adj* sterling

legale [le•GAH•le] *adj* legal

legalizzare [LE•ga•LITSAH•re]
vt legalize

legame [le•GAH•me] *n* M bond

legamento [LE•ga•MEHN•to]
n M ligament

legare [le•GAH•re] *vt* hitch

legare come un salame
[le•GAH•re KOH•me uhn
sa•LAH•me] *vt* truss

legge [LEH•dje] *n* F law

leggenda [le•DJEHN•da] *n* F
legend

leggendario; leggendaria
[le•DJEN•DAH•ryo];
[le•DJEN•DAH•rya] *adj* MF
legendary

leggere [LEH•djere] *vt* read

leggere le labbra
[LEH•djere•le•LAHB•bra] *vi*
lip-read

leggerezza [LEDJE•reh•tsa] *n*
F lightness

leggermente
[ledj•ERMEHN•te] *adv*
lightly; slightly

leggero; leggera
[ledj•EHRO]; [ledj•EHRA]
adj light; flimsy; flippant

leggiadro; leggiadra
[ledj•AH•dro]; [ledj•AD•dra]
adj MF graceful

leggibile [LEDJ•ee•BILE] *adj*
legible

legislazione
[LE•djiz•lat•SYOH•ne] *n* F
legislation

legittima difesa
[LE•djeet•TI•ma•di•FEH•za] *n*
F self-defense

legittimo; legittima
[LE•djeet•TI•mo];
[LE•djeet•TI•ma] *adj* MF
lawful; legitimate

legna da ardere
[LEH•nya•da•AHR•dere] *n* F
firewood

legname [le•NYAH•me] *n* M
lumber; timber

legno [LEH•nyo] *n* M wood

legno compensato
[LEH•nyo•kom•PEN•SAH•to]
n M plywood

lei [LEH•i], *per pron* F her

lei stessa [LEH•i STEHS•sa]
pron F herself

lente [LEHN•te] *n* F lens

lente d'ingrandimento [LEHN•te din•GRAN•di•MEHN•to] *n* F magnifying glass

lento; lenta [LEHN•to]; [LEHN•ta] *adj* MF slack

leone [LEOH•ne] *n* M lion

leonessa [le•ONEHS•sa] *n* F lioness

leopardo [leo•PAHR•do] *n* M leopard

lepre [LEH•pre] *n* F hare

lesbica [lehz•BI•ka] *n* F lesbian

letale [le•TAH•le] *adj* lethal

letame [le•TAH•me] *n* M manure

letargo [le•TAHR•go] *n* M lethargy; hibernation

lettera [let•TEH•ra] *n* F letter

letterale [let•TE•rah•le] *adj* literal

letterario; letteraria [LET•te•RAH•ryo]; [let•te•rah•rya] *adj* MF literary

letteratura [LET•te•RATUH•ra] *n* F literature

letteratura d'immaginazione [LET•te•ra•TUH•ra DIM•ma•DJINA•TSYOH•ne] *n* F fiction

letti a castello [LEHT•ti a KA•STEHL•lo] *npl* M bunk beds

lettino [let•TEE•no] *n* M crib

letto [LEHT•to] *n* M bed

lettore; lettrice [let•TOH•re]; [let•TREE•tshe] *n* MF reader

lettura [let•TUH•ra] *n* F reading

leva 1 [LEH•va] *n* F lever

leva 2 [LEH•va] *n* F draft (military)

levatrice [LE•va•TREE•tshe] *n* F midwife

lezione [le•TSYOH•ne] *n* F lesson

Libano [LEE•bano] *n* M Lebanon

libbra [LEEB•bra] *n* F pound

libellula [li•BEHL•LU•la] *n* M dragonfly

libera scelta [LEE•be•ra•SHEL•ta] *n* F free will

liberale [LI•be•RAH•le] *adj n* MF liberal

liberare [LI•be•RAH•re] *vt* liberate

liberazione [li•be•RAT•SYOH•ne] *n* F liberation; release

libero; libera [LEE•bero]; [LEE•bera] *adj* MF free

libero scambio [LEE•be•ro•SKAHM•byo] *n* M free trade

libertá [li•BER•tah] *n* F freedom; liberty

libertá di parola [LI•ber•TAH di pa•ROH•la] *n* F free speech

Libia [LEE•bya] *n* F Libya

librarsi in volo [li•BRAHR•si een VOH•lo] *vi* soar

libreria [LI•bre•REE•ah] *n* F bookstore

libretto d'assegni [LI•BREHT•to•das•SEH•ni] *n* M checkbook

libro [LEE•bro] *n* M book

libro di testo [LEE•bro•dee•TEHS•to] *n* M textbook

libro mastro
[LEE•bro•MAHS•tro] *n* M
ledger

libro paga [LEE•bro•PAH•ga]
n M payroll

licenza [li•TSHEHN•tsa] *n* F
licence

licenziare [LI•shen•TSYAH•re]
vt terminate

licenzioso; licenziosa
[LI•tshen•TSYOH•zo];
[LI•tshen•TSYOH•za] *adj* MF
wanton

liceo [li•TSHEH•o] *n* M high
school

lievito di birra [LYEH•vito dee
BEER•ra] *n* M yeast

liguetta [lin•GUEHT•ta] *n* F
tab

limitare [LI•mi•TAH•re] *vt*
restrict; stint

limite [lee•MI•teh] *n* M
boundary; limit; extent

limite di velocitá [lee•MI•te
dee VE•lo•TSHI•TAH] *n* M
speed limit

limonata [LI•mo•NAH•ta] *n* F
lemonade

limone [li•MOH•ne] *n* M lemon

limone verde [li•MOH•ne
VEHR•de] *n* M lime

limousine [li•MU•zeen] *n* F
limousine

linciare [lyn•TSHAH•re] *vt*
lynch

linea [lee•NE•a] *n* F line

linea di condotta [lee•NEA
dee KON•DOHT•ta] *n* F
policy

lineetta [li•NE•EHT•ta] *n* F
hyphen

lingua [LEEN•gua] *n* F
language; tongue

linguaggio [lin•GUAH•djo] *n*
M parlance

linguistica [lin•GUEES•TI•ka]
n F linguistics

lino [LEE•no] *n* M flax; linen

liquefatto; liquefatta
[LI•kwe•FAHT•to];
[LI•kwe•FAHT•ta] *adj* MF
molten

liquidare 1 [LI•kwi•DAH•re] *vt*
liquidate

liquidare 2 [LI•kwi•DAH•re] *vt*
pay off; dismiss

liquido [lee•KWI•do] *n* M
liquid; -o -a; *adj* liquid

lirico; lirica [LEE•riko];
[LEE•rika] *adj* MF lyric;
lyrical

liscio; liscia [li•SCI•o];
[li•SCI•o] *adj* slick

lista [LEE•sta] *n* F list

litigare [LI•ti•GAH•re] *vi*
bicker; quarrel; litigate

livello [li•VEHL•lo] *n* M
standard

livido 1 [lee•VI•do] *n* M bruise

livido; livida 2 [lee•VI•do];
[lee•VI•da] *adj* MF livid

lobo [LOH•bo] *n* M lobe

locale [loh•KA•le] *adj* local

localitá [LO•ka•LI•tah] *n* F
locality

localizzatore di guasti
[LO•ka•LIT•sa•TOH•re dee
GUAH•sti] *n* M trouble
shooter

locanda [lo•KAHN•da] *n* F inn

locomotiva
[LO•ko•MOTEE•va] *n* F
locomotive

loggia [LOH•dja] *n* F lodge

logica [loh•DJI•ka] *n* F logic

logico; logica [loh•DJI•ko];
[loh•DJI•ka] *adj* MF logical

logoro; logora [loh•GO•ro];
[loh•GO•ra] *adj* MF frayed

logotipo [LO•go•TEE•po] *n* M
logo

Londra [LOHN•dra] *n* F
London

longitudine
[LON•dji•TUH•di•ne] *n* F
longitude

lontano; lontana
[lon•TAH•no]; [lon•TAH•na]
adj MF far; il piú lontano\ *adj*
adv furthest; -o -a\ *adj*
farthest

lontra [LOHN•tra] *n* F otter

lonza [LOHN•tsa] *n* F loin

loquace [lo•KWAH•tshe] *adj*
talkative; loquacious; glib

loro [LOH•ro] *adj pos* their;
pron pos theirs; *per pron*
them

loro stessi; loro stesse
[LOH•ro•STEHS•si]; [LOH•ro
STEHS•se] *per pron* MF
themselves

lotta [LOHT•ta] *n* F fight;
struggle

lottare [lot•TAH•re] *vi* grapple;
wrestle

lotteria [LOT•te•REE•a] *n* F
raffle; lottery

lozione [lo•TSYOH•ne] *n* F
lotion

lubrificante
[LU•bri•fi•KAHN•te] *n*
lubricant

lubrificare [LU•bri•FIKAH•re]
vt lubricate

lucchetto [luk•KEHT•to] *n* M
padlock

luce della ribalta
[LUH•tshe•DEHL•la•ri•BAHL
•ta] *n* F limelight

lucentezza
[LU•tshen•TEHT•sa] *n* F
brilliance; gloss; luster

lucernario [LU•tsher•NAH•ryo]
n M skylight

lucertola [LU•tsher•TOH•la] *n*
F lizard

lucido 1 [LUH•TSHI•do] *n* M
polish; -o -a\ *adj* glossy

lucido; lucida 2
[LUH•TSHI•do];
[LUH•TSHI•da] *adj* MF lucid

luglio [LUH•lyo] *n* M July

lui [luhi] *pers pron* M he; him

lui stesso [LUH•i•STEHS•so]
pers pron M himself

luminoso; luminosa
[LU•mi•NOH•zo];[LU•min
•OH•za] *adj* MF bright;
luminous

luna [LUH•na] *n* F moon

luna di miele
[LUH•na•di•MYEH•le] *n* F
honeymoon

luna piena [LUH•na•PYEH•na]
n F full moon

lunare [lu•NAH•re] *adj* lunar

lunatico; lunatica
[lu•NAH•ti•ko];
[lu•NAH•ti•ka] *adj* MF
lunatic; moody

lunedì [LU•ne•DEE] *n* M
Monday

lunghezza [lun•GEH•tsa] *n* F
length

lunghezza d'onda
[lun•GEH•tsa•DOHN•da] *n* F
wavelength

lungo [LUN•go] *prep* along; -o
-a\ *adj* long

luogo [lu•WOH•goh] *n* place; in
nessun luogo\ *adv* nowhere; in
primo luogo\ *adv* primarily; in
qualche luogo\ *adv*
somewhere; in qualunque
luogo\ *adv* anywhere

lupo [LUH•po] *n* M wolf

lupo manarro
[LUH•po•ma•NAHR•ro] *n*
M werewolf

lusingare [LU•zin•GAH•re] *vt*
flatter

lusinghiero; lusinghiera
[LU•zin•GIEH•ro];
[LU•zin•GIEH•ra] *adj* MF
flattering

lusso [LUHS•so] *n* M luxury

lussuoso; lussuosa
[lus•SUOH•zo]; [lus•suoh•za]
adj MF luxurious

lussuria [lus•SUH•rya] *n* F lust

lustrino [lus•TREE•no] *n* M
spangle

lustro; lustra [LUHS•tro];
[LUHS•tra] *adj* MF sleek

lutto [LUHT•to] *n* M mourning

M

ma [mah] *conj* but

macchia 1 [MAH•kia] *n* F
blemish; spot

macchia 2 [MAHK•kya] *n* F
shrubbery

macchia [MAHK•kya] *n* F spot

macchiato; macchiata
[mak•KYAH•to];
[mak•KYAH•ta] *adj* MF
spotted

macchiettare
[MAK•kyet•TAH•re] *vt*
speckle

macchina [MAH•ki•na] *n* F
machine; automobile; car

macchina da cucire
[MAHK•kina DAH
ku•TSHEE•re] *n* F sewing
machine

macchina da scrivere
[MAHK•ki•na DAH
SKREE•vere] *n* F typewriter

macchina fotografica
[MAHK•ki•na
FOTO•grah•FI•ca] *n* F camera

macchinario
[MAK•ki•nah•RYO] *n* M
machinery

macellaio [ma•TSHEL•lahyo] *n*
M butcher

macellare [ma•TSHEL•LAH•re]
vt slaughter

macelleria
[MAT•shel•le•REE•ah] *n* F
butcher (shop)

macerare [ma•TSHE•RAH•re]
vt steep

machinetta per tosare
[MAK•ki•NEHT•ta•PEHR•to
•ZAH•re] *n* F clippers

macinare [MA•tshi•NAH•re] *vt*
grind

macinino [MA•TSHIEE•no] *n*
M grinder (coffee~)

madre [MAH•dre] *n* F mother

madrina [ma•DREE•na] *n* F godmother

maestá [me•ESTAH] *n* F majesty

maestoso; maestosa [maes•TOH•zo]; [maes•TOH•za] *adj* MF majestic; stately

maestro di scuola [ma•EHSTRO•dee•SKUOH•la] *n* M schoolteacher

magazzino 1 [MA•gats•EE•no] *n* M depot

magazzino 2 [MA•ga•TSEE•no] *n* M stockroom; warehouse

maggio [MAH•djo] *n* M May

maggioranza [MADJ•or•AHN•tsa] *n* F majority

maggiordomo [MA•djor•DOH•mo] *n* M butler

maggiore [ma•DJOH•re] *adj* major; elder

magico; magica [mah•DJI•ko]; [mah•dji•ka] *adj* MF magic; magical

magistrato [ma•DJIS•TRAH•to] *n* M magistrate

maglietta [ma•LYEHT•ta] *n* F jersey; undershirt

maglione [ma•LYOH•ne] *n* M sweater

magnetico; magnetica [ma•NYEH•TI•ko]; [ma•NYEH•TI•ka] *adj* MF magnetic

magnificenza [ma•NIFI•TSHEHN•tsa] *n* F grandeur; magnificence

magnifico; magnifica [ma•NEE•FIKO]; [ma•NEE•FIKA] *adj* MF gorgeous; magnificent

mago [MAH•go] *n* M magician; sorcerer; wizard

magrezza [ma•GREH•tsa] *n* F thinness

magro; magra [MAH•gro]; [mah•gra] *adj* lean; skinny; meagre

mai [mahi] *adv* ever; never

maiale [ma•YAH•le] *n* M hog; pig; pork

maionese [mayo•NEH•ze] *n* F ~mayonnaise

mal di denti [MAHL dee DEHN•ti] *n* M toothache

mal di stomaco [MAHL dee STOH•ma•ko] *n* M stomachache

mal di testa [MAHL di TEHS•ta] *n* M headache

malamente [MA•la•MEHN•te] *adv* badly

malanimo [MAL•ah•NI•mo] *n* M grudge; ill will

malaticcio; malaticcia [MA•latee•TSHO]; [MA•latee•TSHO] *adj* sickly

malato; malata [ma•LAH•tp]; [ma•LAH•ta] *adj* MF ill; sick

malattia [MA•lat•TEE•a] *n* F disease; illness; sickness

malcontento; malcontenta [MAL•kon•TEHN•to]; [MAL•kon•TEHN•ta] MF *adj* disgruntled

maldestro; maldestra
[mal•DEH•stro];
[mal•DEH•stra] *adj MF*
clumsy

male in arnese [MAH•le een
ar•NEH•ze] *adj* shabby

maledizione
[MAHLE•dit•SYOH•ne] *n F*
curse

maleducato; maleducata
[MAL•ed•UKAH•to];
[MAL•ed•UKAH•ta] *adj MF*
rude; crass

malfamato; malfamata
[MAL•fa•MAH•to];
[MAL•fa•MAH•ta] *adj MF*
infamous

malgrado [mal•GRAH•do] *prep*
despite

malignare [MA•li•NYAH•re] *vt*
malign

maligno; maligna
[ma•LEE•nyo]; [ma•LEE•nya]
adj MF malicious; malignant

malincuore
[MAL•in•KWOH•re] a
malincuore\ *adv* reluctant;
half-hearted

malinteso [MA•lin•TEH•zo] *n*
M misunderstanding

malizia [ma•LEE•tsya] *n F*
malice

malizioso; maliziosa
[MA•li•TSYOH•zo];
[MA•li•TSYOH•za] *adj MF*
mischievous; wicked

malpena [MA•la•PEH•na] *adv*
hardly

malsano; malsana
[MAL•SAH•no];
[MAL•SAH•na] *adj MF*
unwholesome

malsicuro; malsicura
[MAL•si•KUH•ro];
[MAL•si•KUH•ra] *adj MF*
insecure

maltrattare [MAL•trat•TAH•re]
vt mistreat

malvagitá [MAL•va•DJI•tah] *n*
F wickedness

mammella [mam•MEHL•la] *n*
F udder

mammifero; mammifera
[mam•MEE•FE•ro];
[mam•MEE•FE•ra] *n MF*
mammal

mancante [man•KAHN•te] *adj*
missing

mancanza [man•KAHN•tsa] *n*
F default; lack

mancare [man•KAH•re] *vt* miss

mancia [MAHN•tsha] *n F*
gratuity; tip

manciata [man•TSHAH•ta] *n F*
handful

mancino; mancina
[man•TSHEE•no];
[man•TSHEE•na] *adj MF*
left-handed

mandare [man•DAH•re] *vt* send

mandare un cablogramma
[man•DAH•re•un•KAH•blo
•GRAHM•ma] *vi* cable

mandarino [MAN•da•REE•no]
n M tangerine

mandato [man•DAH•to] *n M*
mandate; writ

mandato di comparizione
[man•DAH•to dee
KOM•pa•RITSYOH•ne] *n M*
subpoena

mandato di perquisizione
[man•DAH•to dee

PER•kwi•ZITSYOH•ne] *n* M
search warrant

mandria [MAHN•drya] *n* F
herd

manette [ma•NEHT•te] *npl* F
handcuff

mangiare [man•DJAH•re] *vt* eat

mangime [man•DJEE•me] *n* M
feed

mania [ma•NEE•a] *n* F craze;
fad; mania

manica [mah•NI•ka] *n* F sleeve

manichetta [MA•ni•KEHT•ta]
n F hose

manichino [MA•ni•KEE•no] *n*
M dummy

manico [MAH•niko] *n* M
handle

manicure [ma•NI•kuhr] *n* M
manicure

maniera [ma•NYEH•ra] *n* F
manner

manifattura
[MANI•fat•TUH•ra] *n* F
manufacture

manifesto [MA•ni•FEHS•to] *n*
M poster

manipolare
[MA•ni•po•LAH•re] *vt*
manipulate

mannaia [MAN•nah•YA] *n* F
cleaver

mano [MAH•no] *n* F hand; di
seconda mano\ *adj*
second-hand; used

manodopera
[MAH•no•DOH•pera] *n* F
manpower

manomettere
[MA•no•MEHT•te•re] *vt*
tamper

manopola [ma•NOH•POLA] *n*
F mitten

manoscritto
[ma•NO•SKREET•to] *n* M
manuscript

manovale [MA•no•VAH•le] *n*
M laborer

manovella [MAH•no•VEHL•la]
n F crank

manovra [ma•NOH•vra] *n* F
maneuver

mansueto; mansueta
[man•SUEH•to];
[man•SUEH•ta] *adj* MF meek

mantella [man•TEHL•la] *n* F
cape (clothing)

mantello [man•TEL•lo] *n* M
cloak

mantenere [MAN•te•NEH•re]
vt keep; maintain

mantenuta [MAN•te•NUH•ta]
n F mistress

manuale [ma•NUAH•le] *adj n*
MF manual

manutenzione
[MA•nu•ten•TSYOH•ne] *n* F
maintenance; upkeep

manzo [MAH•tso] *n* M beef

Mar dei Caraibi [MAHR deh•i
ka•RAH•ibi] *n* M Caribbean
(Sea)

mara [MAHR•ka] *n* F brand;
trademark

maratona [MA•ra•TOH•na] *n* F
marathon

marchiare [mar•KYA•re] *vt*
brand

marchio [MAHR•kyo] *n* M
badge

marchio di fabbrica
[MAHR•kyo•dee•FAHB•ri•ka]
n M trademark

marcia [MAHR•tsha] *n* F march

marciapiede
[MAR•tsha•PYEH•de] *n* M
sidewalk

marciare [MAR•TSHAH•re] *vi*
march

marcio; marcia [MAHR•tsho];
[MAHR•tsha] *adj* rotten

marcire [mar•TSHEE•re] *vi* rot

mare [MAH•re] *n* M sea

marea [MA•REH•a] *n* F tide;
della marea\ *adj* tidal

maresciallo [MA•re•SHAL•lo]
n M marshal

margarina [MAR•ga•REE•na]
n F margarine

margherita [MAR•ge•REE•ta]
n F daisy

marginale [MAR•dji•NAH•le]
adj marginal

margine [mahr•DJI•ne] *n* M
margin; verge; edge

marijuana [MA•riu•AH•na] *n* F
marijuana

marina [ma•REE•na] *adj* F
navy

marinaio [MA•ri•NAH•yo] *n* M
sailor

marinare [MA•ri•NAH•re] *vt*
marinate

marinare (la scuola)
[ma•rinah•re (la•SKWOH•la)]
vt hooky (to play)

marine [ma•REEN] *n* M marine

marino; marina [ma•REE•no];
[ma•ree•na] *adj* MF marine

marito [ma•REE•to] *n* M
husband

marmellata
[MAR•mel•LAH•ta] *n* F jam;
marmalade

marmellata d'arance
[MAR•mel•LAH•ta
da•RAHN•tshe] *n* F orange
marmalade

marmitta [mar•MEET•ta] *n* F
kettle

marmo [MAHR•mo] *n* M
marble

Marocco [ma•ROHK•ko] *n* M
Morocco

marrone [mar•ROH•ne] *adj*
brown

marrone rossastro
[mar•ROH•ne•ros•SAHS•tro]
adj maroon

Marte [MAHR•te] *n* M Mars

martedí [mar•TE•dee] *n* M
Tuesday

martedí grasso
[mar•TE•dee•GRAHS•so] *n* M
Shrove Tuesday

martello [mar•TEHL•lo] *n* M
hammer

martire [mahr•TI•re] *n* MF
martyr

marziale [mar•TSYAH•le] *adj*
martial

marzo [MAHR•tso] *n* M march

mascella [ma•SHEHL•la] *n* F
jaw

maschera [MAHS•kera] *n* F
mask

mascherata [MAS•ke•RAH•ta]
n F masquerade

maschio [MAHS•kyo] *adj n* M
male; *adj* masculine

massa [MAHS•sa] *n* F lump;
mass

massacro [mas•SAH•kro] *n* M
massacre

massaggio [mas•SAH•djo] *n* M
massage

massiccio; massiccia
[mas•SEE•tsho];
[mas•SEE•tsha] *adj* massive

massimo [MAHS•simo] *n* M
maximum; -o -a\ *adj*
maximum; il massimo\ *adj*
most

masso [MAHS•so] *n* M boulder

masticare [MAS•ti•KAH•re] *vt*
chew

mastodontico; mastodontica
[MAS•to•DOHN•ti•ko];
[MAS•to•DOHN•ti•ka] *adj*
MF mammoth

matassa [ma•TAHS•sa] *n* F
skein

matematica [MA•te•MAH•tika]
n F mathematics

materasso [MA•te•RAHS•so] *n*
M mattress

materia [ma•TEH•rya] *n* F
matter

materia prima [MA•teh•RYA
PREE•ma] *n* F raw material

materiale [MA•te•RYAH•le]
adj material

materialista
[MA•te•RYA•LEES•ta] *n* MF
materialist

materialistico; materialistica
[MA•te•RYA•LEES•tiko];
[MA•te•RYA•LEES•tika] *adj*
MF materialistic

maternitá [MA•ter•NI•tah] *n* F
motherhood

materno; materna
[ma•TEHR•no];
[ma•TEHR•na] *adj* MF
maternal; motherly

matita [ma•TEE•ta] *n* F pencil

matrice [ma•TREE•tshe] *n* F
matrix

matricola [ma•TREE•kola] *n* F
freshman

matrigna [ma•TREE•nya] *n* F
stepmother

matrimonio
[MA•tri•MOH•nyo] *n* M
marriage; matrimony; wedding

mattiniero; mttiniera
[MAT•ti•NYEH•ro];
[MAT•ti•NYEH•ra] *adj* MF
early

mattino [mat•TEE•no] *n* M
morning

matto; matta [MAHT•to];
[MAHT•ta] *adj* MF crazy;
mad

mattone [mat•TOH•ne] *n* M
brick

maturitá [MA•tu•RITAH] *n* F
maturity

maturo; matura [ma•TUH•ro];
[ma•tuh•ra] *adj* MF mature;
ripe

mazza [MAH•tsa] *n* F bat

mazzo [MAH•tso] *n* M bunch

mazzuolo [ma•TSUOH•lo] *n* M
mallet

me [meh] *pers pron* me

meccanico [mek•KAH•niko] *n*
M mechanic

meccanico; meccanica
[mek•KAH•niko];
[mek•KAH•nika] *adj* MF
mechanical

meccanismo
[MEK•ka•NEEZ•mo] *n* M
gear; mechanism

medaglia [me•DAH•lya] *n* F
medal

medaglione [ME•da•LYOH•ne]
n M medallion

media [MEH•dya] *n* F average

medicare [me•DIKAH•re] *vt*
medicate

medicina [ME•di•TSHEE•na] *n*
F medicine

medico [meh•DI•ko] *n* M
physician; -o -a\ *adj* medical

medievale [ME•dye•VAH•le]
adj medieval

medio; media
[MEH•dyo];[MEH•dya] *adj*
average; medium

Medio Oriente
[MEH•dyo•or•YEHN•te] *n* M
Middle East

mediocre [me•DYOH•kre] *adj*
mediocre; undistinguished

Medioevo [MEH•dyo•EH•vo] *n*
M Middle Ages

meditare [ME•di•TAH•re] *vt*
meditate

medusa [me•DUH•za] *n* F
jellyfish

megafono [ME•gah•FONO] *n*
M megaphone

meglio [MEH•lyo] *adv* best

mela [MEH•lah] *n* F apple

melanconico; melanconica
[ME•ln•KOH•niko];
[ME•lan•KOH•nika] *adj* MF
melancholy

melanzana [ME•lan•TSAH•na]
n F eggplant

melassa [me•LAHS•sa] *n* F
molasses

melma [MEHL•ma] *n* F silt

melodia [ME•lo•DEE•a] *n* F
melody

melone [me•LOH•ne] *n* M
melon

**membro della sinistra;
membra della sinistra**
[MEHM•bro
DEHL•la•si•NEES•tra];
[MEHM•bra
DEHL•la•si•NEES•tra] *adj*
MF leftist

membro; membra
[MEHM•bro]; [MEHM•bra] *n*
MF member

memore [MEH•more] *adj*
mindful

memoria [ME•MOH•rya] *n* F
memory

memoria [me•MOH•rya] *n* F
recollection; rote

mendicante
[MEN•di•KAHN•te] *n* MF
beggar

meno [MEH•no] *adv* less; *prep*
minus

menomare [ME•no•MAH•re] *vt*
impair

menopausa [ME•no•PAH•usa]
n F menopause

mensile [men•SEE•le] *adj n* MF
monthly

menta [MEHN•ta] *n* F mint

menta peperita [MEHN•ta
PE•pe•REE•ta] *n* F
peppermint

mentale [men•TAH•le] *adj*
mental

mentalitá [MEN•ta•LITAH] *n*
F mentality

mente [MEHN•te] *n* F mind

mento [MEHN•to] *n* M chin

mentre [MEHN•tre] *conj* while

menú [MEN•uh] *n* M menu

menzionare
[MEN•tsyo•NAH•re] *vt*
mention

meraviglia [ME•ra•VEE•lya] *n*
F marvel; wonder

meravigliato; meravigliata
[ME•ra•VILYAH•to];
[ME•ra•VILYAH•ta] *adj MF*
gaping

meraviglioso; meravigliosa
[ME•ra•VIL•yoh•zo];
[ME•ra•VIL•yoh•za] *adj MF*
marvelous; wonderful

mercanteggiare
[MER•KAN•te•JAH•re] *vi*
bargain

mercato [mer•KAH•to] *n* M
market

mercato nero
[mer•KAH•to•NEH•ro] *n* M
black market

merce [MEHR•tshe] *n* F
merchandise; ware

mercenario; mercenaria
[MER•tshe•NAH•ryo];
[MER•tshe•NAH•rya] *adj n*
MF mercenary

mercoledí [MER•ko•LE•dee] *n*
M Wednesday

mercurio [mer•KU•ryo] *n* M
mercury; quicksilver

meridionale
[ME•ri•DYO•NAH•le] *adj*
southerner

meritare [ME•ri•TAH•re] *vt*
deserve

meritevole [ME•ri•TEH•vo•le]
adj deserving

merito [meh•RI•to] *n* M merit

merlo [MEHR•lo] *n* M
blackbird

merluzzo [mer•LUH•tso] *n* M
cod

mero; mera [MEH•ro];
[MEH•ra] *adj* MF mere

mescolare [MES•ko•LAHRE]
vt mingle; mix; stir

mese [MEH•ze] *n* M month

messa [MEHS•sa] *n* F mass
(church)

messa in moto
[MEHS•sa•in•MOH•to] *n* F
ignition

messaggero
[MES•sa•DJEH•ro] *n* M
messenger

messaggio [MES•SAH•djo] *n*
M message

messicano; messicana
[MES•si•KAH•no];
[MES•si•KAH•na] *adj MF*
Mexican

Messico [mes•SEE•ko] *n* M
Mexico

mestiere [mes•TIEH•re] *n* M
craft

mestolata [MES•to•LAH•ta] *n*
F scoop

mestolo [MEHS•tolo] *n* M
ladle

mestruazioni
[MES•trua•TSYOH•ni] *n* F
menstruation

metá [me•Tá] *adj* mid

metafora [me•TAH•fo•RA] *n* F
metaphor

metallico; metallica
[me•TAHL•LI•ko];
[me•TAHL•LI•ka] *adj MF*
metallic

metallo [me•TAHL•lo] *n* M
metal

metallo grezzo
[me•TAHL•lo•GREH•tso] *n*
M ore

meteora [ME•teh•OR•a] *n* F
meteor

meteorologia
[me•TEO•rolo•GEE•a] *n* F
meteorology

meticoloso; meticolosa
[ME•ti•ko•LOH•zo];
[ME•ti•ko•LOH•za] *adj* MF
meticulous; painstaking

metodo [MEH•to•do] *n* M
method

metrico; metrica
[meh•TRI•ko]; [meh•TRI•ka]
adj MF metric

metro [MEH•tro] *n* M meter;
yardstick

**metropolitano;
metropolitana**
[ME•tro•PO•li•TAH•no];
[ME•tro•PO•li•TAH•na] *adj*
MF metropolitan

mettere [meht•TEH•re] *vt* put

mettere a repentaglio
[met•TEH•re•ah•RE•pen•
TAH•lyo] *vt* jeopardize

mettere i denti [MET•teh•re ee
DEHN•ti] *vi* teethe

mettere in gioco [MET•teh•re
in DJOH•ko] *vt* stake

mettere in grado di
[MEHT•te•re in
GRAH•DO•di] *vi* enable

mettere in guardia
[MEHT•te•re in GUAHR•dya]
vt caution

mettere in pericolo
[MEHT•tere in
pe•REE•KO•lo] *vt* endanger

mettersi in contatto
[MET•tehr•SI in
kon•TAHT•to] *vi* contact

mezz'ora [met•ZOH•ra] *n* F
half-hour

mezza cartuccia [MEH•tsa
KAR•tuh•TSHA] *n* MF runt

mezzaluna [meh•TSA•LUH•na]
n F crescent

mezzano [me•TSAH•no] *n* M
pimp

mezzano; mezzana
[me•TSAH•no];
[me•TSAH•na] *n* MF
go-between

mezzanotte
[MEH•tsa•NOHT•te] *n* F
midnight

mezzi [MEH•tsi] *n* M means;
npl M wherewithal

mezzi di comunicazione
[MEH•tsi di
KO•mu•NIKA•TSYOH•ne] *n*
M media

mezzo [MEH•tso] *n* M middle;
midst

mezzo; mezza [MEH•tso];
[meh•tsa] *adj* MF half

mezzogiorno
[MET•so•DJOHR•no] *n* M
noon

micro onde
[MEE•kro•OHN•de] *n* M
microwave

microchip *n* F microchip

microfono [mi•KROH•fono] *n*
M microphone

microscopico; microscopica
[MI•kros•KOH•piko];
[MI•kros•KOH•pika] *adj* MF
microscopic

microscopio
[MI•kro•SKOH•pyo] *n* M
microscope

miele [MYEH•le] *n* M honey

miglio [MEE•lyo] *n* M mile

miglioramento
[MI•lyo•ra•MEHN•to] *n* M
improvement

migliorare [MI•lyo•RAH•re] *vt*
improve; upgrade

migliore [MIL•YOH•re] *adj*
best

migratore [MI•gra•TOH•re] *n*
M migrant

miliardo [mil•YAHR•do] *num*
M billion

milionario; milionaria
[MI•lyo•NAH•ryo];
[MI•lyo•NAH•rya] *n adj* MF
millionaire

milione [mi•LYOH•ne] *n* M
million

militante [MI•li•TAHN•te] *adj*
n MF militant

militare [MI•li•TAH•re] *adj*
military

milizia [mi•LEE•tsya] *n* F
militia

mille [MEEL•le] *num* thousand

millennio [mil•LEHN•nyo] *n* M
millenium

millepiedi [MEEL•le•PIEH•di]
n M centipede

millesimo; millesima
[MIL•leh•ZI•mo];
[MIL•leh•ZI•ma] *adj* MF
thousandth

milza [MEEL•tsa] *n* F spleen

mimo; mima [MEE•mo];
[MEE•ma] *n* MF mimic

minaccia [mi•NAH•tsha] *n* F
menace; threat

minacciare [mi•NA•TSHAH•re]
vt threaten; meance

minaccioso; minacciosa
[mi•NAH•TSHO•zo];
[mi•NAH•TSHO•za] *adj* MF
menacing; threatening

minare [mi•NAH•re] *vt*
undermine

minerale [MI•ne•RAH•le] *adj*.
n MF mineral

minestra [MI•NEHS•tra] *n* F
soup

miniatura [ME•nya•TUH•ra] *n*
F·miniature; in miniatura; *adj*
miniature

miniera [mi•NYEH•ra] *n* F
mine

minimo; minima [mee•NI•mo];
[mee•NI•ma] *adj* least;
minimum; *n* MF minimum

ministero [mi•NI•STEH•ro] *n*
M ministry

ministro [mi•NEE•stro] *n* M
minister

minoranza [MI•no•RAHN•tsa]
n F minority

minore [mi•NOH•re] *adj* junior;
lesser; *adj n* MF minor

minuto; minuta [mi•NUH•to];
[mi•NUH•ta] *adj n* MF minute

mio; mia [MEE•ō]; [MEE•a]
poss adj my

miope [MEE•ope] *adj*
near-sighted

mira [MEE•ra] *n* F aim

miracolo [mi•RAH•KO•lo] *n* M
miracle

miracoloso; miracolosa
[mi•RA•KO•LOH•zo];

[mi•RA•KO•LOH•za] *adj* MF
miraculous

miraggio [mi•RAH•djo] *n* M
mirage

mirtillo [mir•TEEL•loh] *n* M
blueberry

mirtillo rosso
[mir•TEEL•lo•ROHS•so] *n* M
cranberry

misantropo
[mi•ZAHN•TRO•po] *n* M
misanthropist

miscelare [MI•she•LAH•re] *vt*
blend

miscellaneo; miscellanea
[mi•SHEL•lah•NEO];
]mi•SHEL•lah•NEA] *adj* MF
miscellaneous

mischiare (le carte)
[mis•KYAH•re leh KAHR•te]
vt shuffle (cards)

miscredente
[MIS•kre•DEHN•te] *n* MF
unbeliever

miscuglio [mis•KUH•lyo] *n* M
mixture

misericordia
[MI•se•ri•KOHR•dya] *n* F
mercy

**misericordioso;
misericordiosa**
[MI•zeri•kor•DYOH•zo];
[MI•zeri•kor•DYOH•za] *adj*
MF merciful

misfatto [mis•FAHT•to] *n* M
misdeed

missile [MEES•sile] *n* M
missile

missionario; missionaria
[MIS•syo•NAH•rio];

[MIS•syo•NAH•rya] *n* MF
missionary

missione [mis•SYOH•ne] *n* F
mission

misterioso; misteriosa
[MIS•ter•YOH•z];
[MIS•ter•YOH•za] *adj*
mysterious; uncanny

mistero [mis•TEH•ro] *n* M
mystery

mistico; mistica [mees•TI•ko];
[mees•TI•ka] *n* MF mystic;
adj mystical

misura [mi•SUH•ra] *n* F gauge;
measure; measurement; in
gran misura *adv* largely

mite [MEE•te] *adj* gentle; mild

mitico; mitica [mee•TI•ko];
[mee•ti•ka] *adj* mythical

mitigante [MI•ti•GAHN•te] *adj*
mitigating

mito [MEE•to] *n* M myth

mitologia [MI•to•lo•DJEE•a] *n*
F mythology

mitragliatrice
[MI•tra•lya•TREE•tshe] *n* F
machine gun

mittente [mit•TEHN•te] *n* MF
sender

mobile [moh•BI•le] *adj* mobile;
movable

mobili [moh•BILI] *n* M
furniture

mobilizzare
[MO•bi•LIT•SAH•re] *vt*
mobilize

moccio per pavimenti
[MOH•tsho PEH
PA•vi•MEHN•ti] *n* M mop

moda [MOH•da] *n* F fashion

modello [mo•DEHL•lo] *n* MF
model; *n* M pattern

moderare [MO•de•RAH•re] *vt*
moderate

moderato; moderata
[MO•de•RAH•to];
[MO•de•RAH•ta] *adj n* MF
moderate

moderazione
[MO•de•rat•SYOH•ne] *n* F
moderation

modernizzare
[MO•der•nit•SAH•re] *vt*
modernize

moderno; moderna
[mo•DEHR•no];
[mo•DEHR•na] *adj* MF
modern

modestia [mo•DEHS•tya] *n* F
modesty

modesto; modesta
[mo•DEHS•to]; [mo•DEHS•ta]
adj MF demure; modest;
unassuming

modificare [MO•di•fi•KAH•re]
vt modify

modo [MOH•do] *n* M mode;
fashion; style; way; alla moda\
adv fashionable; in modo stu-
pendo\ *adv* wonderfully; in
qualche modo\ *adv* somehow

modo di vivere
[MOH•do•di•VEE•vere] *n* M
lifestyle

modulo per rintracciare
[MOH•dulo PEHR
rin•TRA•TSHAH•re] *n* tracer

mogano [mo•GAH•no] *n* M
mahogany

moglie [MOH•lye] *n* F wife

molare [mo•LAH•re] *n* M
molar

molestare [MO•les•TAH•re] *vt*
molest

molla [MOHL•la] *n* F spring

molle [MOHL•le] *adj* limp

mollusco [mol•LUH•sko] *n* M
mollusk

molo [MOH•lo] *n* M jetty

molti; molte [MOHL•ti];
[MOHL•te] *adj* MF many

moltiplicare
[MOL•ti•pli•KAH•re] *vt*
multiply

moltiplicazione
[MOL•ti•pli•KA•TSYOH•ne]
n F multiplication

moltitudine
[MOL•ti•TUH•di•ne] *n* F
multitude

molto [MOHL•to] *adv* very; -o
-a\ *adj* much; a lot; lots of

momento [mo•MEHN•to] *n* M
moment

monaco [MOH•nako] *n* M
monk

monarca [mo•NAHR•ka] *n* M
monarch

monarchia [mo•NAR•KEEA] *n*
F monarchy

monastero [MO•nas•TEH•ro] *n*
M monastery

moncherino
[MON•ke•REE•no] *n* M
stump

mondano; mondana
[MON•DAH•no];
[MON•DAH•na] *adj* MF
mundane; worldly

mondo [MOHN•do] *n* M world

monello [mo•NEHL•lo] *n* M
brat

monello; monella
[mo•NEHL•lo];
[mo•NEHL•la] *n* MF urchin

moneta [mo•NEH•ta] *n* F coin

monetario; monetaria
[MO•ne•TAH•ryo];
[MO•ne•TAH•rya] *adj* MF
monetary

monologo [MO•no•LOH•go] *n*
M monologue

monopolio [MO•no•to•NEE•a]
n M monopoly

monopolizzare
[MONO•po•lit•SAH•re] *vt*
monopolize

monotonia [MO•no•TONEE•a]
n F monotony; F monotone

monotono; monotona
[mo•NOH•TO•no];
[mo•NOH•TO•na] *adj* MF
dull; monotonous; boring

monsone [mon•SOH•ne] *n* M
monsoon

montaggio [mon•TAH•jo] *n* M
assembly (mech)

montanaro; montanara
[MON•ta•NAH•ro];
[MON•ta•NAH•ra] *n* MF
mountaineer

monte dei pegni
[MOHN•te•dei•PEH•ni] *n* M
pawnshop

montone [mon•TOH•ne] *n* M
mutton

montuoso; montuosa
[mon•TUOH•zo];
[mon•TUOH•za] *adj* MF
mountainous

monumentale
[MO•nu•MEN•TAH•le] *adj*
monumental

monumento
[MO•nu•MEHN•to] *n* M
monument

mora [MOH•ra] *n* F blackberry

morale [mo•RAH•le] *n* MF
moral; *n* M morale

moralitá [MO•ra•li•TAH] *n* F
morality

morbidezza [MO•bi•DEH•tsa]
n F softness

morbido; morbida
[mohr•BI•do]; [mohr•BI•da]
adj MF soft

morbillo [mor•BEEL•lo] *n* M
measles

morboso; morbosa
[mor•BOH•zo]; [mor•BOH•za]
adj MF morbid

mordere [mohr•DE•re] *vt* bite

mordicchiare
[MOR•dik•KYAH•re] *vt*
nibble

morente [mo•REHN•te] *adj*
dying

morire [mo•REE•re] *vi* die

mormorare [MOR•mo•RAH•re]
vt whisper

mormorio [MOR•mor•EE•o] *n*
M murmur

Moro [MOH•ro] *n* M Moor

morsa [MOHR•sa] *n* F clamp;
vice (tool)

morso [MOHR•zo] *n* M bite
(insect, snake)

mortaio [mor•TAH•yo] *n* M
mortar

mortale [mor•TAH•le] *adj*
deadly; *adj n* MF mortal

mortalitá [MOT•ta•LITAH] *n* F
mortality

morte [MOHR•te] *n* F death

mortificare
[MOR•ti•fi•KAH•re] *vt*
mortify

morto; morta [MOHR•to];
[mohr•ta] *adj* MF dead

mosaico [mo•ZAH•yko] *n* M
mosaic

mosca [MOHS•ka] *n* F fly

Mosca [MOHZ•ka] *n* F Moscow

moscerino [MO•she•REE•no] *n*
M gnat

moschea [mos•KEH•a] F
mosque

mossa [MOHS•sa] *n* F move

mostra [MOH•stra] *n* F display;
exhibit

mostrare [mos•TRAH•re] *vt*
show

mostro [MOHS•tro] *n* M
monster

mostruositá
[mos•TRUOU•sitah] *n* MF
monstrosity

mostruoso; mostruosa
[mo•STRUOH•zo];
[mos•TRUOH•za] *adj* MF
monstrous

motivare [MO•ti•VAH•re] *vt*
motivate

motivo 1 [mo•TEE•vo] *n* M
motif

motivo 2 [mo•TEE•vo] *n* M
motive

moto [MOH•to] *n* M motion

motore [MO•TOH•re] *n* M
engine; motor

motoscafo [MO•to•SKAH•fo] *n*
M motorboat

motto [MOHT•to] *n* M motto

movimento [MO•vi•MEHN•to]
n M movement

mozione [mo•TZYOH•ne] *n* F
motion (legal)

mozzicone [MO•tsi•KOH•ne] *n*
M butt (of cigarette); stub

mucchio [MUH•kyo] *n* M heap;
pile

mucosa [mu•KOH•za] *n* F
mucous (membrane)

muffa [MUHF•fa] *n* F mildew;
mold

muffin [MUHF•fin] *n* M muffin

muggire [muh•DJEE•re] *vi*
bellow

muggito [muh•DJEE•to] *n* M
moo.

mulino a vento
[mu•LEE•no•ah•VEHN•to] *n*
M windmill

mulo [MUH•le] *n* M mule

multiplo [muhl•TI•plo] *n* M
multiple; -o -a\ *adj* multiple

mummia [MUHM•mya] *n* F
mummy

municipale
[MU•ni•tshi•PAHLE] *adj*
municipal

municipalitá
[MU•ni•tshi•PALI•TAH] *n* F
municipality

municipio [MU•ni•TSHEE•pyo]
n M city hall

muratore [MU•ra•TOH•re] *n* M
mason

muratura [MU•ra•TUH•ra] *n* F
stonework

muro [MUH•ro] *n* M wall

musa [MUH•za] *n* F muse

muscio [MUHS•kyo] *n* M moss

muscolo 1 [muhs•KO•lo] *n* M
brawn; muscle

muscolo 2 [muhs•KOLO] *n* M
mussel

muscoloso; muscolosa
[MUS•ko•LOH•zo] *adj* MF
muscular

museo [mu•ZEH•o] *n* M
museum

museruola [MU•ze•RUOH•la]
n F muzzle

musica [MUH•zika] *n* F music

musicale [MU•zi•KAH•le] *adj*
musical

musicista [MU•zi•TSHEES•ta]
n MF musician

mussulmano; mussulmana
[MUS•sul•MAH•no];
[MUS•sul•MAH•na] *adj* MF
Muslim

mutandine [MU•tan•DEE•ne] *n*
F panties

mutilare [MU•ti•LAH•re] *vt*
maim; mutilate

muto; muta [MUH•to];
[MUH•ta] *adj n* MF mute

N

nano; nana [NAH•no];
[NAH•na] *n* MF dwarf

narciso [nahr•TSHEE•zo] *n* M
daffodil

narcotico [nar•KOH•TI•ko] *n*
M dope; narcotic; -o -a\ *adj*
narcotic

narice [na•REE•tshe] *n* F nostril

narrare [nar•RAH•re] *vt* narrate

narrativo; narrativa
[NAR•ra•TEE•vo];
[NAR•ra•TEE•va] *adj* MF
narrative

narratore [NAR•ra•TOH•re] *n*
M narrator

narrazione
[NAR•ra•TSYOH•nw] *n* F
narration

nasale [na•ZAH•le] *adj* nasal

nascita [nah•SHI•ta] *n* F birth

nascondere [NAS•kohn•DERE]
vt hide; secrete; shroud

nascondersi
[NAS•kon•DEHR•si] *vi* lurk

nascondiglio
[NAS•kon•DEE•lyo] *n* M
hiding place

nascosto; nascosta
[nas•KOHS•to];
[nas•KOHS•ta] *adj* MF hidden

naso [NAH•zo] *n* M nose

nastro [NAHS•tro] *n* M ribbon;
tape

nasturzio [nas•TUHR•tsyo] *n*
M nasturtium

Natale [na•TAH•le] *n* M
Christmas

natica [nah•TI•ka] *n* F buttock

Natività [NA•ti•VIT•ah] *n* F
Nativity

nato; nata [NAH•to]; [NAH•ta]
adj MF born (to be)

natura [na•TUH•ra] *n* F nature

naturale [NA•tu•RAH•le] *adj*
natural

naturalizzare
[NA•tura•LIT•SAH•re] *vt*
naturalize

naturalmente
[NA•tu•RAL•MEHN•te] *adv*
naturally

nausea [nah•U•ZEA] *n* F
nausea

nauseabondo; nauseabonda
[NA•uz•ea•BOHN•do];
[NA•uz•ea•BOHN•da] *adj* MF
nauseous

nauseare [nau•ZEAH•re] *vt*
nauseate

nauseato; nauseata
[nau•ZEAH•to];
[nau•ZEAH•ta] *adj* MF
seasick

nausebondo; nauseabonda
[NAU•zea•BOHN•do];
[NAU•zea•BOHN•da] *adj* MF
sickening

navale [na•VAH•le] *adj* naval

nave da guerra
[NAH•ve•DAH•GUEH•ra] *n* F
battleship

navigare [NA•vi•GAH•re] *vt*
navigate

navigatore [NA•vi•ga•TOH•re]
n M navigator

navigazione
[NA•vi•ga•TSYOH•ne] *n* F
navigation; sailing

nazionale [NA•tsyo•NAH•le]
adj national

nazionalitá
[NA•tsyo•NA•li•TAH] *n* F
nationality

nazionalizzare
[NA•tsyo•NA•lit•SAH•re] *vt*
nationalize

nazione [na•TSYOH•ne] *n* F
nation

né [neh] *conj* nor

nebbia [NEHB•bya] *n* F fog;
mist

nebbioso; nebbiosa
[neb•BYOH•zo];
[neb•BYOH•za] *adj* hazy;
misty

necessario; necessaria
[NE•tshes•SAH•ryo];
[NE•tshes•SAH•ryo] *adj* MF
necessary

necessitá [NE•tshes•SI•tah] *n* F
necessity; requirement

necrologia [NE•kro•lo•DJEE•a]
n F obituary

negare [ne•GAH•re] *vt* deny

negativo; negativa
[NE•ga•TEE•vo];
[NE•ga•TEE•va] *adj* MF
negative

negligente [NE•gli•DJEHN•te]
adj lax; negligent; remiss

negligenza
[NE•gli•DJEHN•tsa] *n*
negligence

negoziante
[NE•go•TSYAHN•te] *n* M
shopkeeper; tradesman

negoziare [NE•go•TSYAH•re]
vt transact; negotiate

negozio [ne•GOH•tsyo] *n* M
shop

negozio d'alimentari
[ne•GOH•tsyo
DALI•men•TAH•ri] *n* M
grocery (store)

negro; negra [NEH•gro];
[NEH•gra] *adj n* MF Negro

nei dintorni
[NAI•din•TOHR•ni] *adv*
thereabouts

nel frattempo
[NEHL•frat•TEHM•po] *adv*
meantime

nella presente
[NEHL•la•PRE•ZEHN•te] *adv*
herein

nemico; nemica [ne•MEE•ko];
[ne•MEE•ka] *n MF* enemy;
nemesis; foe

neonato; neonata
[NE•ho•NAH•to];
[NE•ho•NAH•to] *n MF* baby;
infant

nero; nera [NEH•ro]; [NEH•ra]
adj n MF black

nervo [NEHR•vo] *n M* nerve

nervoso; nervosa
[ner•VOH•zo]; [ner•VOH•za]
adj MF nervous

nessuno [nes•SUH•no] *pron*
nobody

**nessuno dei due; nessuna
delle due**
[nes•SUH•no•DEHI•DUHE];
[nes•SUH•na•DEHL•le•DUHE]
adj MF neither

nessuno; nessuna
[nes•SUH•no]; [nes•SUH•na]
pron adj none

Nettuno [net•TUH•no] *n M*
Neptune

neutrale [NE•ut•RAH•le] *adj*
neutral

neutralitá [NE•utra•ti•TAH] *n
F* neutrality

neutralizzare
[NE•utra•lit•SAH•re] *vt*
neutralize

neutro; neutra [neh•UT•ro];
[neh•UT•ra] *adj MF* neuter

neve [NEH•ve] *n F* snow

nevicata [NE•vi•KAH•ta] *n F*
snowfall

nevischio [ne•VEES•kyo] *n M*
sleet

nevrosi [ne•VROH•zi] *n F*
neurosis

nevrotico; nevrotica
[ne•VROH•TI•ko];
[ne•VROH•TI•ka] *adj n MF*
neurotic

nicchia [NEEK•kya] *n F* niche

nicotina [NI•ko•TEE•na] *n F*
nicotine

nido [NEE•do] *n M* nest

nightclub [NAH•IT•kluhb] *n M*
nightclub

ninfa [NEEN•fa] *n F* nymph

ninna; nanna
[NEEN•na•NAHN•na] *n F*
lullaby

nipote [ni•POH•te] *n F*
granddaughter

nipote [ni•POH•te] *n MF*
grandson; nephew; niece

nitrire [ni•TREE•re] *vi* neigh

no [noh] *conj* no

nobile [noh•BILE] *adj* noble

nobilitare [NO•bi•li•TAH•re] *vt*
dignify

nobiltá [NO•bil•TAH] *n F*
gentry; nobility

nocca [NOHK•ka] *n F* knuckle

nocciola [no•TSHOH•la] *n F*
hazelnut

nocciolo [noh•TSHO•lo] *n M*
gist

noce [NOH•tshe] *n F* nut;
walnut

noce di cocco
[NOH•tshe•di•KOH•ko] *n F*
coconut

nocivo; nociva
[no•TSHEE•vo];
[no•TSHEE•va] *adj* MF
noxious

nodo [NOH•do] *n* M knot

nodoso; nodosa [no•DOH•zo];
[no•DOH•za] *adj* MF gnarled

noi [NOH•i] *pers pron* us; we

noi stessi; noi stesse
[NOHI•STEHS•si];
[NOHI•STEHS•se] *pron pl*
ourselves

noia [NOH•ya] *n* F boredom

noioso; noiosa [noy•OH•zo];
[noy•OH•za] *adj* MF boring;
cranky; stuffy; tiresome

nolo [NOH•lo] *n* M freight

nome 1 [NOH•me] *n* M first
name; name

nome 2 [NOH•me] *n* M noun

nomignolo [no•MEE•NYO•lo]
n M nickname

nomina [NOH•mi•na] *n* F
nomination

nominale [NO•mi•NAH•le] *adj*
nominal

nominare [NO•mi•NAH•re] *vt*
appoint; nominate

non [nohn] *adv* not

non- [nohn] *pref* un-

non avvezzo; non avvezza
[NOHN•av•VEH•tso];
[NOHN•av•VEH•tsa] *adj* MF
unaccustomed

non disponbile [NOHN
DIS•po•NEE•bi•le] *adj*
unavailable

non fumatore [NON
fu•MA•TOH•re] *n* M
nonsmoker

non lavato; non lavata
[NOHN la•VAH•to];
[NOHN•la•VAH•ta] *adj* MF
unwashed

non pagato; non pagata
[NOHN pa•GAH•to];
[NOHN•pa•GAH•ta] *adj* MF
delinquent

**non reclamato; non
reclamata** [NOHN
re•KLA•MAH•to];
[NOHN•re•KLA•MAH•ta] *adj*
MF unclaimed

**non riconosciuto; non
riconosciuta** [NOHN
ri•KO•no•SHUH•to; [NOHN
ri•KO•no•SHUH•ta] *adj*
unacknowledged

**non sospettoso; non
sospettosa**
[nohn•sos•pet•toh•zo];
[nohn•sos•pet•toh•za] *adj* MF
unsuspecting

non ufficiale [NOHN
UF•fi•TSHAH•le] *adj*
informal

non usato; no usata [NOHN
u•ZAH•to]; [NOHN
u•ZAH•ta] *adj* MF unused

nonconformista
[NON•kon•for•MEES•ta] *adj*
nonconformist

noncurante
[NON•ku•RAHN•te] *adj*
nonchalant; unconcerned

noncuranza
[NON•ku•RAHN•tsa] *n* F
disregard

nondimeno [NON•di•MEH•no]
adv nonetheless

nonna [NOHN•na] *n* F
grandmother; grandmanonni

[NOH•ni] *npl* M grandparents

nonno [NOHN•no] *n* M
grandfather

nonno [NOHN•no] *n* M
grandpa

nono; nona [NOH•no];
[NOH•na] *num* ninth

nonostante
[NON•os•TAHN•te] *adv*
notwithstanding

nord [nohrd] *n* M north; a nord
adj north

nord america
[NOHRD•ameh•RIKA] *n* M
North America

norma [NOHR•ma] *n* F norm

normale [nor•MAH•le] *adj*
normal

normalmente
[nor•MAL•MEHN•te] *adv*
ordinarily; normally; usually

norvegese [NOR•ve•DJEH•ze]
adj Norwegian

Norvegia [nor•VEH•dja] *n* F
Norway

nostalgia [NOS•tal•DJEE•a] *n*
F nostalgia

nostalgico; nostalgica
[NOS•tahl•DJI•ko];
[NOS•tahl•DJI•ka] *n* MF
homesick

nostro; nostra [NOHS•tro];
[NOH•stra] *poss adj* our;
ours

nota [NOH•ta] *n* F note

nota a pié pagina
[NOH•ta•ah•PIEH•pah•DJI•na]
n F footnote

notabile [no•TAH•bile] *adj*
notable

notaio [no•TAH•yo] *n* M notary

notevole [no•TEH•vole] *adj*
noteworthy; remarkable;
substantial

notevolmente
[NO•te•VOL•MEHN•te] *adv*
notably

notificare [NO•ti•FI•KAH•re]
vt notify

notizia [no•TEE•tsya] *n* F news

notiziario [NO•ti•TSYAH•ryo]
n M newscast

notizie [NO•TEE•tsye] *n* F
tidings

notorietá [NO•to•RYE•tah] *n* F
notoriety

notte [NOHT•te] *n* F night

notturno; notturna
[not•TUHR•no];
[not•TUHR•na] *adj* MF
nightly; nocturnal

novanta [no•VAHN•ta] *num*
ninety

nove [NOH•ve] *num* nine

novella [no•VEHL•la] *n* F short
story

novembre [no•VEHM•bre] *n* M
November

novitá [no•VI•tah] *n* F novelty

novizio; novizia
[no•VEE•TSYO];
[no•VEE•TSYA] *n* MF novice

nozione [no•TSYOH•ne] *n* F
notion

nucleare [nu•KLE•AH•re] *adj*
nuclear

nucleo [nuh•KLEO] *n* M
nucleus

nudista [nu•DEES•ta] *n* MF
nudist

nuditá [NU•dit•AH] *n* F
nakedness; nudity

nudo; nuda
[NUH•do];[NUH•da] *adj* bare;
naked; adj; *n* MF nude

nulla [NUHL•la] *n* F nothing

nullo; nulla [NUHL•lo];
[nuhl•la] *adj* MF null; nothing

numerale [NU•me•RAH•le] *n*
MF numeral

numero 1 [NUH•mero] *n* M
number

numero 2 [NUH•me•ro] *n* M
issue (magazine)

numero di telefono
[NUH•mero DEE
te•LEH•fo•no] *n* M telephone
number

numeroso; numerosa
[NU•me•ROH•zo];
[NU•me•ROH•za] *adj* MF
numerous

nuora [NUOH•ra] *n* F
daughter-in-law

nuotare [nuo•TAH•re] *vi*
swim

nuotatore; nuotatrice
[NUO•ta•TOH•re];

[NUO•ta•TREE•tshe] *n* MF
swimmer

nuoto [NUOH•to] *n* M
swimming

**nuovo di zecca; nuova di
zecca** [NU•ohvo di ZEH•ka];
[NU•ohva] *adj* MF brand-new

nuovo; nuova [NUOH•vo];
[NUOH•va] *adj* MF new; di
nuovo\ *adv* again

nuovo ricco; nuova ricca
[NUOH•vo•REEK•ko];
[NUOH•va•REEK•ka] *n* MF
upstart

nutriente [nu•TRYEHN•te] *adj*
nourishing; nutritious

nutrimento [NU•tri•MEHN•to]
n M nourishment

nutrire [nu•TREE•re] *vt*
nourish

nutrizione [NU•tri•TSYOH•ne]
n F nutrition

nuvola [NUH•vola] *n* F cloud

nuvoloso; nuvolosa
[NU•vo•LOH•zo];
[NU•vo•LOH•za] *adj* MF
cloudy

nuziale [nut•see•ah•le] *adj*
bridal; nuptial

nylon [NAHI•lon] *n* M nylon

O

o [oh] *conj* or

oasi [OHA•zi] *n* F oasis

obbediente
[OB•be•DYEHN•te] *adj*
obedient

obbedienza
[OB•be•DYEHN•tsa] *n* F
obedience

obbedir [OB•be•DEE•re] *vi*
obey

obbiettivo [ob•BYET•TEE•vo]
n M objective

obbligare [OB•bli•GAH•re] *vt*
compel

obbligatorio; obbligatoria
[OB•bli•ga•TOH•ryo];
[OB•bli•ga•TOH•rya] *adj* MF
obligatory; obliged; mandatory

obbligo [ohb•BLI•go] *n* M
obligation

obeso; obesa [OBEH•zo];
[OBEH•za] *adj* MF obese; fat

obiezione [OB•ye•TSYOH•ne]
n F objection

obitorio [OBI•TOH•ryo] *n* M
morgue

oblio [OBLEE•o] *n* M oblivion

obliquo; obliqua 1
[ob•LEE•kwo]; [ob•LEE•kwa]
adj MF oblique

obliquo; obliqua 2
[o•BLEE•kwo];
[o•BLEE•kwa] *adj* MF wry

obló [OB•loh] *n* M porthole

oca [OH•ka] *n* F goose

occasionale
[OK•ka•SYONAH•le] *adj*
occasional

occasionalmente
[OK•ka•SI•o•NAL•MEHN•te]
adv occasionally

occasione 1 [OK•ka•SIOH•ne]
n F bargain

occasione 2 [OK•ka•SYOH•ne]
n F occasion

occhiali [ok•KYAH•li] *npl* M
glasses

occhiali di protezione
[ok•KYAH•li di
PRO•te•TSYOH•ne] *npl* M
goggles

occhiata maliziosa
[ok•KYAH•ta
MA•lit•SYOH•za] *n* F leer

occhio [OHK•kyo] *n* M eye

occidentale
[OTSHI•den•TAH•le] *adj*
western; *n* MF westerner

occulto; occulta
[ok•KUHL•to]; [ok•kuhl•ta]
adj MF occult

occupante [OK•ku•PAHN•te] *n*
MF occupant

occupare [OK•ku•PAH•re] *vt*
occupy

occuparsi (di)
[OK•ku•PAHR•si] *vt/vi* attend

occupato; occupata
[OK•ku•PAH•to];
[OK•ku•PAH•ta] *adj* MF busy

occupazione
[OK•ku•PAT•SYOH•ne] *n* F
occupation

oceano [o•TSHEH•ano] *n* M
ocean

odine [ohr•DI•ne] *n* M order

odio [OH•dyo] *n* M hate; hatred

odioso; odiosa [ODYOH•zo];
[ODYOH•za] *adj* MF hateful;
loathsome; odious

odore [o•DOH•re] *n* M odor

offendere [OF•fehn•DE•re] *vt*
offend

offensivo; offensiva
[OF•fen•SEE•vo];
[of•fen•see•va] *adj* MF
offensive

offerta [of•FEHR•ta] *n* F bid;
offering; tender

offesa [of•FEH•za] *n* F offense;
umbrage

officina [OF•fi•TSHEE•na] *n* F
workshop

offrire [of•FREE•re] *vt* offer; bid

offuscato; offuscata [OF•fus•KAH•to]; [OF•fus•KAH•ta] *adj MF* blurry

oggettivo; oggettiva [OD•jet•TEE•vo]; [OD•jet•TEE•va] *adj MF* objective

oggetto [ODJEHT•to] *n M* object

oggetto ricordo [ODJ•eht•TO•ri•KOHR•do] *n M* keepsake

oggi [OH•dji] *n M* today; dall'oggi al domani\ *adj* overnight

ogni [OH•ni] *adj* every

ogniqualvolta [OHNY•kwah•VOHL•ta] *adv* whenever

ognuno [ONY•uhno] *pron M* everybody

ognuno; ognuna [on•YUH•no]; [on•YUH•na] *adj MF* each

oioso; odiosa [od•YOH•zo]; [od•YOH•za] *adj MF* obnoxious

Olanda [ol•AHN•da] *n F* Holland

olandese [olan•DEH•se] *adj* Dutch

oleoso; oleosa [ole•OHZO]; [ole•OHZA] *adj MF* oily

olio [OH•lyo] *n M* oil

oliva [oh•LEE•va] *n F* olive

olivastro; olivastra [O•li•VAHS•tro]; [O•li•VAHS•tra] *adj MF* swarthy; olive-colored

olmo [OHL•mo] *n M* elm

olocausto [olo•KAH•usto] *n M* holocaust

oltraggio [ol•TRAH•djo] *n M* outrage

oltre [OHL•tre] *prep* beyond

oltremare [OHL•tre•MAH•re] *adv* overseas

oltrepassare [OL•tre•pas•SAH•re] *vt* overstep

oltrepassare i confini [OL•tre•PAS•SAH•re ee kon•FEE•ni] *vi* trespass

oltremare [OL•tre•MAH•re] *adj* overseas

oltretomba [OL•tre•TOHM•ba] *n M* underworld

ombelico [OM•be•LEE•ko] *n M* navel; umbilicus

ombra [OHM•bra] *n F* shade

ombrello [om•BREHL•lo] *n M* umbrella

ombroso; ombrosa [om•BROH•zo]; [om•BROH•za] *adj MF* skittish

omettere [o•MEHT•tere] *vt* omit

omicida [omi•TSHEE•da] *adj* murderous

omicidio [o•mi•TSHEE•dyo] *n M* homicide; murder

omicidio colposo [O•mi•TSHEE•dyo kol•POH•zo] *n M* manslaughter

omissione [O•mis•SYOH•ne] *n F* omission

omosessuale [O•mo•SES•SUAH•le] *adj n MF* homosexual

oncia [OHN•tsha] *n F* ounce

onda [OHN•da] *n* F wave

ondata di caldo [ON•DAH•ta di KAHL•do] *n* F heatwave

ondulare [ON•du•LAH•re] *vi* sway; wave; *vt* undulate

ondulato; ondulata [ON•du•LAH•to]; [ON•du•LAH•ta] *adj* MF wavy

onestá [on•ESTAH] *n* F honesty

onesto; onesta [o•NEH•sto]; [o•NEH•sta] *adj* MF honest

onfine [on•fee•ne] *n* M border

onnipotente [ON•ni•po•TEHN•te] *adj* omnipotent

onnisciente [ON•ni•SHEHN•te] *adj* omniscience

onorario [ono•RAH•ryo] *n* M fee

onore [ONOH•re] *n* M honor

onorevole [O•no•REH•vole] *adj* honorable

opaco; opaca [o•PAH•ko]; [o•pah•ka] *adj* MF opaque

opale [OPAH•le] *n* M opal

opera [OH•pera] *n* F opera

operaio [OPE•RAH•yo] *n* M workman

operare [OPE•RAH•re] *vt* operate

operatore [OPE•ra•TOH•re] *n* M operator (machine)

operazione [OPE•ra•TSYOH•ne] *n* F operation

opinone [OPI•NYOH•ne] *n* F opinion

opporre [op•POHR•re] *vt* oppose

opportunista [OP•por•tu•NEES•ta] *n* MF opportunist

opportunitá [OP•por•tu•NI•tah] *n* F opportunity

opportuno; opportuna [OP•por•TUH•no]; [OP•por•TUH•na] *adj* MF opportune

opposizione [OP•po•zit•SYOH•ne] *n* F opposition

opposto; opposta [op•POHS•to]; [op•POHS•ta] *adj* MF opposing; opposed

oppressione [OP•pres•SYOH•ne] *n* F oppression

oppressivo; oppressiva [op•PRES•SEE•vo]; [op•PRES•SEE•va] *adj* MF oppressive

opprimere [OP•pree•ME•re] *vt* oppress

optare [op•TAH•re] *vi* opt

opulento; opulenta [opu•LEHN•o]; [opu•LEHN•ta] *adj* MF opulent

opulenza [opu•LEH•tsa] *n* F opulence

opuscolo [o•PUHS•KOLO] *n* M pamphlet

opzione [op•TSYOH•ne] *n* F option

ora 1 [OH•ra] *n* F hour; o'clock

ora 2 [OH•ra] *adv* now; d'ora in avanti *adv* henceforth

ora di pranzo [OHRA•di•PRAHN•tso] *n* F lunch hour

ora di punta
[OHRA•dee•PUHN•ta] *n* F
rush-hour

oracolo [OR•ah•KO•lo] *n* M
oracle

orario [ORAH•ryo] *n* M
schedule; timetable

orario; oraria [o•RAH•ryo];
[o•RAH•rya] *adj* MF hourly

oratore [ora•TOH•re] *n* M
orator

orbita [OHR•BI•ta] *n* F orbit

orchestra [or•KEHS•tra] *n* F
orchestra

orchestrale [OR•kes•TRAH•le]
adj orchestral

orchidea [OR•ki•DEH•a] *n* F
orchid

ordinario; ordinaria
[OR•di•NAH•ryo];
[OR•di•NAH•rya] *adj*
commonplace; ordinary

ordinato; ordinata
[ORDI•NAH•to];
[OR•DINAH•ta] *adj* MF neat;
tidy; ordered

ordine 1 [ohr•DI•ne] *n* M
tidiness; order

ordine 2 [ohr•DI•ne] *n* M tier

ordine del giorno [ohr•DINE
dehl DJOHR•no] *n* M agenda

orecchioni [OREK•KYOH•ni]
npl M mumps

orecchino [OREK•KEE•no] *n*
M earring

orecchio [o•REK•KYO] *n* M
ear

orfano; orfana [ohr•FA•no];
[ohr•fa•na] *n* MF orphan

orfanotrofio
[or•FA•not•ROH•fyo] *n* M
orphanage

organico; organica
[OR•gah•NI•ko];
[OR•gah•NI•ka] *adj* MF
organic

organismo [OR•ga•NEEZ•mo]
n M organism

organizzare
[OR•ga•nit•SAH•re] *vt*
organize

organizzazione
[OR•ga•nit•SA•TSYOH•ne] *n*
F organization

organo [ohr•GA•no] *n* M organ

orgasmo [or•GAHZ•mo] *n* M
orgasm

orgia [OHR•dja] *n* F orgy

orgoglio [or•GOH•lyo] *n* M
pride

orgoglioso; orgogliosa
[OR•go•LYOH•zo];
[OR•go•LYOH•za] *adj* MF
proud

orientale [OR•yen•TAH•le] *adj*
n MF oriental; east; eastern

orientamento
[OR•yen•ta•MEHN•to] *n* M
orientation

orientare [OR•yen•TAH•re] *vt*
orientate

orificio [O•ri•FEE•tsho] *n* M
orifice

origano [oree•GA•no] *n* M
oregano

originale [ORI•gi•NAH•le] *adj*
n MF original

originalitá [ORI•gi•NA•LIT•ah]
n F originality

originare [ORI•dji•NAH•re] *vt*
originate

originariamente
[ORI•dji•NAR•ya•MEHN•te]
adv originally

origine [O•ree•DJI•ne] *n* F
origin

orina [o•REE•na] *n* F urine

orinare [ori•NAH•re] *vi* urinate

orizzontale [ORI•tson•TAH•le]
adj horizontal

orizzonte [ORI•TSOHN•te] *n*
M horizon

orlo [OHR•lo] *n* M edge; hem;
rim

orlo del marciapiede
[OHR•lo•dehl•MAHR•tsha
•PIEH•de] *n* M curb

orma [OHR•ma] *n* F footprint

ormone [or•MOH•ne] *n* M
hormone

ornamentale
[OR•na•MEN•TAH•le] *adj*
ornamental; decorative

ornamento [OR•na•MEHN•to]
n M ornament; decoration

ornato; ornata [or•NAH•to];
[or•NAH•ta] *adj* MF ornate

oro [OH•ro] *n* M gold

orologio [O•ro•LOH•djo] *n* M
clock

orologio [O•ro•LOH•djo] *n* M
timepiece; watch

oroscopo [O•roh•SKO•po] *n* M
horoscope

orrendo; orrenda
[OR•REHN•do];
[OR•REHN•da] *adj* MF
ghastly; hideous; horrendous

orribile [or•REE•bile] *n* MF
grisly; *adj* horrible

orrido; orrida [ohr•RIDO];
[ohr•RIDA] *adj* MF horrid

orrore [or•ROH•re] *n* M horror

orso [OHR•so] *n* M bear

ortica [or•TEE•ka] *n* F nettle

ortodosso; ortodossa
[OR•to•DOHS•so];
[OR•to•DOHS•sa] *adj* MF
orthodox

ortografia [OR•to•gra•FEE•a] *n*
F spelling

orzaiolo [OR•tsa•YOH•lo] *n* F
sty (eye)

orzo [OHR•tso] *n* M barley

osare [o•ZAH•re] *vi* dare

oscenitá [O•she•NI•tah] *n* F
obscenity

osceno; oscena [o•SHEH•no];
[o•SHEH•na] *adj* bawdy;
obscene

oscillare [OS•hil•LAH•re] *vi*
oscillate; swing; wave

oscillazione
[OSHIL•la•TSYOH•ne] *n* F
swing

oscurare [OSKU•RAH•re] *vt*
darken

oscuritá [OS•ku•RI•tah] *n* F
darkness; gloom; obscurity

oscuro; oscura [os•KUH•ro];
[os•KUH•ra] *adj* obscure

ospedale [OS•pe•DAH•le] *n* M
hospital

ospitale [OS•pi•TAH•le] *adj*
hospitable

ospitalitá [OS•pi•TA•LI•tah] *n*
F hospitality

ospitare [OS•pi•TAH•re] *vt*
accommodate

ospite 1 [ohs•PITE] *n* MF guest

ospite 2 [ohs•PI•TE] *n* MF
host; hostess

ossequente
[OS•se•KWEHN•te] *adj*
subservient

osservante [OS•ser•VAHN•te]
adj observant

osservanza [OS•ser•VAHN•tsa]
n F observance

osservare [OS•ser•VAH•re] *vt*
observe

osservatore
[OS•ser•VATOH•re] *n* M
observer

osservatorio
[OS•ser•va•TOH•ryo] *n* M
observatory

osservazione
[OS•ser•va•TSYOH•ne] *n* F
observation; remark

ossessionare
[OS•ses•SYONAH•re] *vt*
obsess

ossessione [OS•ses•SYOH•ne]
n F obsession

ossessivo; ossessiva
[OS•ses•SEE•vo];
[OS•ses•SEE•va] *adj* MF
obsessive

ossigeno [OS•see•DJE•no] *n* M
oxygen

osso [OHS•so] *n* M bone

ostacolare [O•sta•ko•LAH•re]
vt thwart

ostacolo [os•TAH•kolo] *n* M
hurdle; obstacle

ostaggio [os•TAH•djo] *n* M
hostage

oste [OHS•te] *n* M innkeeper

ostentare [OS•ten•TAH•re] *vt*
flaunt

ostentato; ostentata
[OS•ten•TAH•to];
[OS•ten•TAH•ta] *adj* MF
ostentatious

ostia [OHS•tya] *n* F wafer

ostile [os•TEE•le] *adj* hostile

ostilitá [OS•ti•LI•tah] *n* F
hostility

ostinatezza
[OS•ti•na•TEHT•sa] *n* F
obstinacy

ostinato; ostinata
[OS•ti•NAH•to];
[OS•ti•NAH•ta] *adj*
headstrong; obstinate;
pig-headed

ostrica [ohs•TRI•ka] *n* F oyster

ostruire [OS•tru•EERE] *vt*
obstruct

ostruzione [OS•tru•TSYOH•ne]
n F obstruction; stoppage;
blockage

ottagono [ot•tah•go•no] *n* m
octagon

ottanta [ot•TAHN•ta] *num*
eighty

ottavo; ottava [ot•TAH•vo];
[ot•TAH•va] *adj* eighth

ottenere [OH•ten•AIR•eh] *vt*
get; to obtain

ottica [OHT•ti•ka] *n* F point of
view

ottico [OHT•ti•ko] *n* M
optician; -o -a\ *adj* optical

ottimismo [OT•ti•MEEZ•mo] *n*
M optimism

ottimista [OT•ti•MEES•ta] *n*
MF optimist

ottimistico; ottimistica
[OT•ti•MEES•TI•ko];
[OT•ti•MEES•TI•ka] *adj* MF
optimistic

otto [OHT•to] *num* eight

ottobre [ot•TOH•bre] *n* M
October

ottone [ot•TOH•ne] *n* M brass

otturare [OT•tu•RAH•re] *vt*
clog

ottuso; ottusa [ot•TUH•zo];
[ot•TUH•za] *adj* MF obtuse

ovaia [OVAH•ya] *n* F ovary

ovale [VAH•le] *adj n* MF oval

ovazione [o•VAH•TSYOH•ne]
n F ovation

ovest [oh•VEST] *n* M west

ovviamente
[ov•VYA•MEHN•te] *adv*
obviously

ovvio; ovvia [OHV•vyo];
[OHV•vya] *adj* MF obvious

ozioso; oziosa [ot•SYOH•zo];
[ot•SYOH•za] *adj* MF idle

P

pacchetto [PAK•KEHT•to] *n*
M pack; parcel; packet

pacco [PAHK•ko] *n* M package

pace [PAH•tshe] *n* F peace

Pacifico [pa•TSHEE•FI•ko] *adj*
Pacific

pacifico; pacifica
[pa•TSHEE•FI•ko];
[pa•TSHEE•FI•ka] *adj* MF
peaceful

padella [pa•DEHL•la] *n* F
skillet

padiglione [PA•di•LYOH•ne] *n*
M pavilion

padre [PAH•dre] *n* M father

padrigno [pa•DREE•nyo] *n* M
stepfather

padrino [pa•DREE•no] *n* M
godfather

padrona [pa•DROH•na] *n* MF
mistress (owner)

padrona di casa
[pa•DROH•na•di•KAH•za] *n*
F landlady

padrone [pa•DROH•ne] *n* M
master

padrone di casa
[pa•DROH•ne•di•KAH•za] *n*
M landlord

paese [pa•EH•ze] *n* M country
(nation)

Paesi Bassi [pa•EH•zi•BAHS•si]
n M Netherlands

paesinò [pae•ZEE•no] *n* M
hamlet

paffuto; paffuta
[paf•FUH•to];[paf•FUH•ta]
adj MF chubby

paga [PAH•ga] *n* F pay; wages

pagabile [pa•GAH•BILE] *adj*
payable

pagaia [pa•GAH•ya] *n* F paddle

pagamento [PA•ga•MEHN•to]
n M payment

pagano; pagana [pa•GAH•no];
[pa•GAH•na] *adj n* MF pagan

pagare inadeguatamete
[pa•GAH•re
INA•de•GUA•ta•MEHN•te] *vt*
underpay; da pagarsi
[DH•pa•GAHR•si] *adj* due

pagina [pah•DJI•na] *n* F page

pagnotta [pa•NYOHT•ta] *n* F
loaf

paio [PAH•yo] *n* M pair; brace

Pakistan [pa•KIS•tahn] *n* M
Pakistan

palanchino [PA•lan•KEE•no] *n*
M crowbar

palato [pa•LAH•to] *n* M palate

palazzo [pa•LAHT•so] *n* M
building; mansion; palace

palcoscenico
[PAL•ko•SHEH•NI•ko] *n* M
stage

Palestina [PA•les•TEE•na] *n* F
Palestine

palestra [pa•LEHS•tra] *n* F
gymnasium; gym

paletta [pa•LEHT•ta] *n* F
dustpan

palla [PAHL•la] *n* F ball

palla di neve [PAHL•la dee
NEH•ve] *n* F snow ball

pallacanestro
[PAHL•la•KAN•EH•stro] *n* F
basketball

pallido; pallida [PAHL•li•do];
[PAHL•li•da] *adj* MF dim;
pale; wan; pallid

pallone 1 [pal•LOH•ne] *n* M
balloon

pallone 2 [pal•LOH•ne] *n* M
football

pallottolina
[PAL•LOT•to•LEE•na] *n* F
pellet

palmo [PAHL•mo] *n* M palm

palo [PAH•lo] *n* M post

palo del lampione
[PAH•lo•del•LAM•PYOH•ne]
n M lamp-post

palpabile [pal•PAH•bile] *adj*
palpable

palpebra [pahl•PE•bra] *n* F
eyelid

palude [pa•LUH•de] *n* F bog;
marsh; swamp

paludoso; paludosa
[pa•LU•DOOH•zo];
[pa•LU•DOH•za] *adj* marshy

pan di Spagna
[PAHN•di•SPAH•nya] *n* M
sponge cake

pan di zenzero
[PAHN•di•TSEHN•TSE•ro] *n*
M gingerbread

pan tostato
[PAHN•tos•TAH•to] *n* M
toast (bread)

panacea [PA•na•TSHEH•a] *n* F
panacea

Panama [pa•NAH•ma] *n* F
Panama

panca [PAHN•ka] *n* F bench

pancetta affumicata
[PAN•tsheht•TA
af•FUMIKAH•ta] *n* F bacon

pancia [PAHN•tshya] *n* F belly

panda [PAHN•da] *n* M panda

pane [PAH•ne] *n* M bread

panettiere [PAH•net•TIEH•re]
n M baker

panico [pah•NI•ko] *n* M panic;
stage fright

panna [PAHN•na] *n* F cream
(dairy)

panne [PAH•ne] *n* M
breakdown (machine)

pannello [pan•NEHL•lo] *n* M
panel

pannier [PAN•nie'] *n* M bustle
(fashion)

pantaloni [PAN•ta•LOH•ni] *npl* M pants

pantano [pan•TAH•no] *n* M quagmire

pantera [pan•TEH•ra] *n* F panther

pantofola [PAN•toh•FO•la] *n* F slipper

papá [PA•pah] *n* M dad; papa

papa [PAH•pa] *n* M pope

papale [pa•PAH•le] *adj* papal

papavero [PA•pah•VE•ro] *n* M poppy

pappa d'avena [PAHP•pa•DA•VEH•na] *n* F porridge

pappagallo [PAP•pa•GAHL•lo] *n* M parrot

parabola [pa•RAH•BOLA] *n* F parable

parabrezza [PA•ra•BREH•tsa] *n* M windshield

paracadute [PA•ra•ka•DUH•te] *n* M parachute

paradiso [PA•ra•DEE•zo] *n* M paradise

paradosso [PA•ra•DOHS•so] *n* M paradox

paragonare [PA•ra•go•NAH•re] *vt* compare

paragone [PA•ra•GOH•ne] *n* M comparison

paragrafo [PA•rah•GRA•fo] *n* M paragraph; break; pause

Paraguay [PA•ra•GUAH•i] *n* M Paraguay

paralisi [PA•rah•LI•zi] *n* F paralysis

paralizzare [PA•ra•lit•SAH•re] *vt* paralyze

parallelo; parallela [PA•ral•LEH•lo]; [PA•ral•LEH•la] *adj* MF parallel

paranco [pa•RAHN•ko] *n* M tackle

paranoico; paranoica [PA•ra•NOH•yko]; [PA•ra•NOH•yka] *adj* MF paranoid

parare [pa•RAH•re] *vt* fend; ward (off)

parasole [PA•ra•SOH•le] *n* M parasol

parassita [PA•ras•SEE•ta] *n* M parasite

parata [pa•RAH•ta] *n* F parade

paraurti [PA•ra•UHR•ti] *n* M bumper (of car); fender

parcheggio [par•KEH•djo] *n* M parking; parking lot

parco [PAHR•ko] *n* M park

parecchi; parecchie [pa•REH•ki];[pa•REH•kye] *adj pl* MF several

pareggio [pa•REH•djo] *n* M balance

parente [pa•REHN•te] *n* MF relative

parentel [pa•REHN•te] *n* MF kin

parentesi [PA•rehn•TE•si] *n* F parenthesis

parentesi quadra [PA•reh•NTE•si KWAH•dra] *n* F bracket (in writing)

pari [PAH•ri] *n* F par; *n* M peer

parlamentare [PAR•la•men•TAH•re] *adj* parliamentary

parlamento [PAR•la•MEHN•to] *n* M parliament

parlante [par•LAHN•te] *adj*
talking

parlare [par•LAH•RE] *vi* speak;
vi talk

parodia [PA•ro•DEE•a] *n* F
parody; travesty

parola [pa•ROH•la] *n* F word

parola d'onore [pa•OH•la
do•NOH•re] *n* F parole

parola d'ordine [pa•ROH•la
DOHR•DI•ne] *n* F password

parole di canzone [pa•ROH•le
di kan•TSOH•ne] *n* F lyrics

parrocchia [par•ROHK•kya] *n*
F parish

parrocchiale
[PAR•rok•KYAH•le] *adj*
parochial

parrucca [par•RUH•ka] *n* F wig

parrucchiere
[PAR•ruk•KYEH•re] *n* M
hairdresser

parte [PAHR•te] *n* F part; side;
a parte; *adv* aside; in parte
adv partly

partecipante
[PA•te•tshi•PAHN•te] *n* MF
participant

partecipare
[PAR•te•tshi•PAH•re] *vi*
participate

partecipazione
[PAR•te•tshi•PAT•SYOH•ne]
n F participation

partenza [pahr•TEHN•tsa] *n* F
departure; di partenza *adj*
starting (from)

partgiano; partigiana
[PAR•ti•DJAH•no];
[PAR•t•DJAH•na] *adj n* MF
partisan

particella [PAR•ti•TSHEHL•la]
n F particle; whit

particolare
[PAR•ti•ko•LAH•re] *adj*
particular; peculiar

particolarmente
[PAR•ti•ko•LAR•MEHN•te]
adv particularly

partire [par•TEE•re] *vi* depart
leave; set out

partito laburista [par•TEE•to
la•BUREE•sta] *n* M Labor
Party

parto [PAHR•to] *n* M
childbirth; delivery (of a
baby)

parziale [par•TSYAH•le] *adj*
partial

parzialitá [PAR•tsya•LI•tah] *n*
F partiality

parzialmente
[PAR•tsyal•MEHN•te] *adv*
partially

pascolare [pas•KOLAH•re] *vi*
graze (sheep)

pascolo [pahs•KO•lo] *n* M
pasture

Pasqua [PAHS•kwa] *n* F Easter

passaggio [pas•SAH•djyo] *n* M
gangway; lift; passage

passante [pas•SAHN•te] *n* MF
passerby

passaporto [PAS•sa•POHR•to]
n M passport

passare l'aspirapolvere
[PAS•SAAH•re
las•PEE•ra•POHL•vere] *vi*
vacuum

passare rasente [PAS•sah•RE
ra•ZEHN•te] *vi* graze

passato; passata
[pas•SAH•to]; [pas•SAH•ta]
adj MF past

passeggero; passeggera
[pas•SEDJEH•ro];
[pas•SEDJEH•ra] *n* MF
passenger

passeggiata [pas•SEDJ•ahta] *n*
F promenade; stroll

passero [PAHS•sero] *n* M
sparrow

passero di mare
[PAHS•sero•di•MAH•re] *n* M
halibut

passione [pas•SYOH•ne] *n* F
passion

passivo; passiva [pas•SEE•vo];
[pas•SEE•va] *adj* MF passive

passo [PAHS•so] *n* M footstep;
gait; pace; step

pasta [PAH•sta] *n* F pasta;
macaroni; dough; paste

pasta da spalmare [PAHS•ta•
dah•SPAL•MAH•re] *n* F
spread

pastella [pas•TEHL•la] *n* F
batter

pastello [pas•TEHL•lo] *n* M
pastel

pastello a olio [pas•TEHL•lo
ah OH•lyo] *n* M crayon

pasticceria
[PAS•tit•she•REE•ah] *n* F
confectionery; pastry; pastry
shop

pasticcio [pas•TEE•tsho] *n* M
mess

pastinaca [PAS•ti•NAH•ka] *n* F
parsnip

pasto [PAHS•to] *n* M meal

pastoia [pas•TOH•ya] *n* F
tether

pastore [pas•TOH•re] *n* M
parson; pastor; elder

pastorizzare
[PAS•to•rit•SAH•re] *vt*
pasteurize

patata [pa•TAH•ta] *n* F potato

patata dolce
[pah•TAH•ta•DOHL•tshe] *n* F
sweet potato

patatine fritte
[pa•TA•TEE•ne•FREET•te] *n*
F french fries

pâté [PA•teh] *n* M pâté

paternità [pa•TER•ntah] *n* F
paternity

paterno; paterna
[pa•TEHR•no]; [pa•TEHR•na]
adj MF fatherly; paternal

patetico; patetica
[PA•teh•TI•ko];
[PA•teh•TI•ka] *adj* MF
pathetic

patologia [PA•to•lo•DJEE•a] *n*
F pathology

patria [PAH•tria] *n* F
fatherland; homeland

patrimonio [PA•tri•MOH•nyo]
n M holding

patriota [PA•try•OH•ta] *n* MF
patriot

patriottico; patriottica
[PA•try•OHT•ti•ko];
[PA•try•OHT•ti•ka] *adj* MF
patriotic

patriottismo
[PA•try•ot•TEEZ•mo] *n* M
patriotism

patrocinare
[PA•tro•tshi•NAH•re] *vt*
patronize

pattinaggio sul ghiaccio
[PAT•ti•NAH•djo suhl
GYAH•tsho] *n* M ice skating

pattinare [PAT•ti•NAH•re] *vi*
skate

pattinare sul ghiaccio
[PAT•ti•NAH•re suhl
GYAH•tsho] *vi* ice-skate

pattino [paht•TI•no] *n* M skate
(ice)

pattino a rotelle [paht•TI•no
ah RO•TEHL•le] *n* M skate
(roller)

patto [PAHT•to] *n* M pact

pattuglia [pat•TUH•lya] *n* F
patrol

pattuire [pat•TUEE•re] *vt*
condition

paura [pa•UH•ra] *n* F fear

pauroso; paurosa
[pau•ROH•zo]; [pau•ROH•za]
adj MF fearful

pausa [PAH•u•za] *n* F pause;
coffee break

pavimento [PA•vi•MEHN•to] *n*
M floor

pavone [pa•VOH•ne] *n* M
peacock

paziente [pa•TSYEHN•te] *adj*
n MF patient

pazienza [pa•TSYEHN•tsa] *n* F
patience

pazzia [pa•TSEE•a] *n* F
insanity; madness

pazzo; pazza
[PAH•tso]; [PAH•tsa] *adj* MF
deranged; insane; crazy;
loony; MF lunatic; madman

peccatare [PEK•kah•TAH•re] *vt*
sin

peccato [pek•KAH•to] *n* M sin

peccatore; peccatrice
[PEK•ka•TOH•re];
[PEK•ka•TREE•tshe] *n* MF
sinner

pece [PEH•tshe] *n* F tar

pecora [pe•KOH•ra] *n* F ewe

pedaggio [pe•DAH•djo] *n* M
toll

pedale [pe•DAH•le] *n* M pedal

pedante [pe•DAHN•te] *n* MF
pedant

pedantesco; pedantesca
[PE•dan•TEHS•ko];
[PE•dan•TEHS•ko] *adj* MF
pedantic

pedestallo [PE•des•TAHL•lo] *n*
M pedestal

pedina [pe•DEE•na] *n* F pawn

pedone [pe•DOH•ne] *n* M
pedestrian

peggiore [pe•DJOH•re] *adj*
worse; worst

pegno [PEH•nyo] *n* M pledge

pelame [pe•LAH•me] *n* M coat
(of an animal)

pelle [PEL•le] *n* F skin; pelt

pellegrinaggio
[PEL•le•GREE•nah•DJO] *n* M
pilgrimage

pellegrino; pellegrina
[PEL•le•GREE•no];
[PEL•le•GREE•na] *n* MF
pilgrim

pelliccia [pel•LEE•tsha] *n* F fur

pellicola [pel•LEE•kola] *n* F
film

pellucida [PEL•luh•TSHI•da] *n*
F patent leather

peloso; pelosa [pe•LOH•zo];
[pe•LOH•za] *adj* MF hairy;
furry

pelucco [pe•LUHK•ko] *n* M lint

peluche [pe•LUH•sh] *n* M
plush

penale [pe•NAH•le] *adj* penal

penalitá [PE•na•LI•tah] *n* F
penalty

pendente [pen•DEHN•te] *n* M
hanging

pendenza [pen•DEHN•tsa] *n* F
slope

pendere [PEEHN•dere] *vi*
hang; slope; incline; sag

pendio [pen•DEE•O] *n* M
hillside; incline

pendolo [pehn•DOLO] *n* M
pendulum

pene [PEH•ne] *n* M penis

penetrare [PE•ne•TRAH•re] *vt*
penetrate

penicillina
[PE•nit•SHIL•LE•na] *n* F
penicillin

penisola [PE•nee•ZO•la] *n* F
peninsula

penitenza [pe•NITEHN•tsa] *n*
F penance

penna [PEHN•na] *n* F pen;
quill

pennello [pen•NEHL•lo] *n* M
paintbrush

pensare [pen•SAH•re] *vi*
think

pensatore [PEN•sa•TOH•re] *n*
M thinker

pensier [pen•SYEH•ro] *n* M
thought

pensione [pen•SYOH•ne] *n* F
pension; retirement

pensoso; pensosa
[pen•SOH•zo]; [pen•SOH•za]
adj MF pensive; thoughtful;
wistful

pentirsi [pen•TEER•si] *vi* repent

pentola [PEHN•tola] *n* F pot

pepe [PEH•pe] *n* M pepper
adv mostly

per cento [pehr TSHEHN•to]
adv percent

per conto di [PER KOHN•to
DI] *prep* behalf

per lo piú [PEHR loh PIUH]
adv mostly

per mezzo [PEHR MEH•tso]
adv thereby

per sempre [PEHR SEHM•pre]
adv forever

pera [PEH•ra] *n* F pear

percentuale
[PER•tshen•TUAH•le] *n* F
percentage

percepire [PER•tshe•PEE•re] *vt*
detect; perceive

percezione
[PER•tshe•TZYOH•ne] *n* F
perception; realization

perché [PER•ke'] *conj* because;
why

perció [PEHR•tshoh] *adv* hence:
conj wherefore

percuotere [per•KWUOH•tre]
vt wallop

perdere [PEHR•dere] *vt* forfeit;
lose

perdita [pehr•DITA] *n* F
discharge; leak; loss

perdonare [per•DONAH•re] *vt*
forgive

perdono [per•DOH•no] *n* M
pardon ·

perduto; perduta
[per•DUH•to];[per•DUH•ta]
adj MF lost

perenne [pe•REHN•ne] *adj*
perennial

perfettamente
[PER•fet•TA•MEHN•te] *adv*
perfectly

perfetto; perfetta
[per•FEHT•to]; [per•FEHT•ta]
adj MF perfect

perfezione
[PER•fe•TSYOH•ne] *n* F
perfection

perfezionista
[PER•fet•syo•NEES•ta] *n* MF
perfectionist

perforare [PER•fo•RAH•re] *vt*
perforate

pergamena [PER•ga•MEH•na]
n F parchment

pericolo [PE•ree•KO•lo] *n* M
danger; hazard; peril

pericoloso; pericolosa
[PE•ri•KO•LOH•zo];
[PE•ri•KO•LOH•za] *adj* MF
dangerous

pericosa; pericolosa
[PERI•ko•LOH•zo];
[PERI•ko•LOH•za] *adj* MF
hazardous

periferia [PE•ri•fe•REE•a] *n* F
outskirts

perimetro [PE•ree•ME•tro] *n* M
perimeter

periodico [PER•yoh•DI•ko] *n*
M periodical; -o -a\ *adj*
periodic

periodo [pe•REE•odo] *n* M
period

perire [pe•REE•re] *vi* perish

perla [PEHR•la] *n* F bead; pearl

permaloso; permalosa
[PER•ma•LOH•zo];
[PER•ma•LOH•za] *adj* MF
resentful

permanente
[PER•ma•NEHN•te] *n* F
perm; *adj* permanent

permeare [PER•me•AH•re] *vt*
permeate

permess [PER•MEHS•so] *n* M
permission

permesso [PER•MEHS•so] *n* M
leave; permit

permettere [PER•MEHT•tere]
vt afford; permit

pernice [PER•NEE•tshe] *n* F
partridge

perno [PEHR•no] *n* M pivot

perpendicolare [PER•pen
DI•ko•LAH•re] *adj n* MF
perpendicular

perpetrare [PER•pe•TRAH•re]
vt perpetrate

perpetuo; perpetua
[per•PEH•tuo]; [per•PEH•tua]
adj perpetual

perplesso; perplessa
[per•PLEHS•so];
[per•PLEHS•sa] *adj* MF
perplexed

perquisire [PER•kwi•SEE•re] *vt*
frisk (search)

perseguitare
[PER•se•GUY•TAH•re] *vt*
persecute

perseveranza
[PER•se•VER•AHN•tsa] *n* F
perseverance

perseverare
[PER•se•VE•RAH•re] *vi*
persevere

persiana per•SYAH•na *n* F
window shade

persistente [PER•sis•TEHN•te] *adj* persistent

persistenza [PER•sis•TEHN•tsa] *n* F persistence

persistere [per•SEES•TE•re] *vi* persist

persona [per•SOH•na] *n* F person; fellow

persona insignificante [per•SOH•na in•SI•ni•FI•KAHN•te] *n* F nonentity

personale 1 [per•SONAH•le] *adj* personal

personale 2 [PER•so•NAH•LE] *n* M personnel; staff

personalitá [PER•so•NA•li•TAH] *n* F personality

persuadere [PER•suah•DE•re] *vt* coax; persuade

persuasione [PER•sua•ZYOH•ne] *n* F persuasion

persuasivo; persuasiva [PER•sua•ZEE•vo]; [PER•sua•ZEE•va] *adj* MF persuasive

pertinente [PER•ti•NEHN•te] *adj* pertinent

perverso; perversa [per•VEHR•so]; [per•VEHR•sa] *adj* MF perverse

pervertire [PER•ver•TEE•re] *vt* pervert

pervertito; pervertita [PER•ver•TEE•to]; [PER•ver•TEE•ta] *adj* MF kinky; perverted; *n* MF pervert

pesante [pe•ZAHN•te] *adj* heavy; unwieldy; weighty

pesantemente [pe•ZAN•te•MEHN•te] *adv* heavily

pesare [pe•ZAH•re] *vt* weigh

pesca [PEHS•ka] *n* F peach

pescare [pes•KAH•re] *vt* fishing

pescatore [PES•ka•TOH•re] *n* M fisherman

pesce [PEH•she] *n* M fish

pesce rosso [PEH•tshe ROHS•so] *n* M goldfish

peso [PEH•zo] *n* M weight

pessimismo [PES•si•MEEZ•mo] *n* M pessimism

pessimista [PES•si•MEES•ta] *n* MF pessimist

pessimistico; pessimistica [PES•si•MEES•tiko]; [PES•si•MEES•tika] *adj* MF pessimistic

peste [PEHS•te] *n* F plague

petalo [pe•TAH•lo] *n* M petal

petizione [PE•ti•TSYOH•ne] *n* F petition

petrificato; petrificata [PE•tri•fi•KAH•to]; [PE•tri•fi•KAH•ta] *adj* MF petrified

petroliera [PE•tro•LYEH•ra] *n* F tanker

petrolio [pe•TROH•lyo] *n* M petroleum

pettegolezzo [PET•te•go•LEHT•so] *n* M gossip; rumor

pettinare [PET•ti•NAH•re] *vt* comb

pettinatura
[PET•ti•na•TUH•ra] *n* F
hairstyle
pettine [peht•TI•ne] *n* M comb
pettirosso [PET•ti•ROHS•so] *n*
M robin
petto [PEHT•to] *n* M bosom;
breast
petulante [PE•tu•LAHN•te] *adj*
shrewish
pezza [PEH•tsa] *n* F patch
pezzetto [pet•SEHT•to] *n* M bit
pezzo [PEH•tso] *n* M piece
piacere [pya•TSHEH•re] *n* M
pleasure
piacevole [PYA•TSHEH•vole]
adj pleasant
pianerottolo
[PYA•ne•ROHT•tolo] *n* M
landing
pianeta 1 [pya•NEH•ta] *n* M
planet
pianeta 2 [pya•NEH•ta] *n* F
vestment; official attire
piangente [PYAN•DJEHN•te]
adj weeping
piangere [PYAHN•djere] *vt*
mourn; *vi* weep
pianista [pya•NEES•ta] *n* MF
pianist
piano 1 [PYAH•no] *n* M piano;
adj -o -a\ soft
piano 2 [PYAH•no] *n* M plane;
floor
piano 3 [PYAH•no] *n* M story
(of house); al piano superiore
adv upstairs; -o -a *adj* level;
adj tabular
piano terra
[PYAH•no•TEHR•ra] *n* M
ground floor

pianta [PYAHN•ta] *n* F plant
piantare in asso
[PYAN•tah•RE in AHS•so] *vt*
jilt
pianuzza [pia•NUH•tsa] *n* F
flounder
piastrellare
[PYAS•trel•LAH•re] *vt* tile
piattaforma
[PYAT•ta•FOHR•ma] *n* F
platform
piatto 1 [PYAHT•to] *n* M dish;
plate; -o -a\ flat
piatto 2 [PYAHT•to] *n* M
jackpot
piatto forte
[PYAHT•to•FOHR•te] *n* M
main course
piatto grande
[PYAHT•to•GRAHN•de] *n* M
platter
piazza [PYAH•tsa] *n* F square
picchetto [pik•KEHT•to] *n* M
picket
picchio [PEEK•kyo] *n* M
woodpecker
piccione [pi•TSHOH•ne] *n* M
pigeon
picco [PEEK•ko] *n* M peak
piccolo; piccola [PEEK•kolo];
[PEEK•kola] *adj* little; tiny
pidocchio [pi•DOH•kyo] *n* M
louse
piede [PYEH•de] *n* M foot; a
piedi nudi\ *adv* barefoot
piega [PYEH•ga] *n* F fold; pleat
piegare [PI•e•GAH•re] *vt* bend;
fold
pieno; piena [PYEH•no];
[pyeh•na] *adj* MF full
pietá [PYE•tah] *n* F pity

pietoso; pietosa [pie•TOH•zo]; [pie•TOH•za] *adj* MF piteous; pitiful

pietra [PYEH•tra] *n* F stone; di pietra\ *adj* stony

pietra focaia [PYEH•tra FO•KAH•ya] *n* F flint

pietrisco [pye•TREES•ko] *n* M rubble

pigiama [pi•DJAH•ma] *n* M pajamas

pigmento [pig•MEHN•to] *n* M pigment

pigro; pigra [PEE•gro]; [pee•gra] *adj* MF lazy

pila [PEE•la] *n* F flashlight

pilastro [pi•LAHS•tro] *n* M pillar

pillola [PEEL•lola] *n* F pill

pilone [pi•LOH•ne] *n* M pylon

pilota [pi•LOH•ta] *n* MF pilot

pinguino [pin•GUEE•no] *n* M penguin

pinna [PEEN•na] *n* F fin

pinnacolo [pin•NAH•KO•lo] *n* M pinnacle

pino [PEE•no] *n* M pine

pinta [PEEN•ta] *n* F pint

pintagione [PYAN•ta•DJOH•ne] *n* F plantation

pinza [PEEN•tsa] *n* F pliers; tongs

pinzetta [pin•TSEHT•ta] *n* F tweezers

pio; pia [PEE•o]; [PEE•a] *adj* MF pious

pioggerella [PYO•dje•REHL•la] *n* F drizzle

pioggia [PYOH•dja] *n* F rain

piombino [pyom•BEE•no] *n* M plummet; fall

piombo [PYOHM•bo] *n* M lead

pioniere; pioniera [pyo•NYEH•re]; [pyo•NYEH•ra] *n* MF pioneer

pioppo [PYOHP•po] *n* M poplar

piovoso; piovosa [pyo•VOH•zo]; [pyo•VOH•za] *adj* MF rainy

pipistrello [PI•pi•STREHL•lo] *n* M bat

piramide [PI•rah•MI•de] *n* F pyramid

pirata [pi•RAH•ta] *adj* pirate

piroscafo [PI•rohs•KA•fo] *n* M steamer; steamship

piscina [pi•SHEE•na] *n* F pool; swimming pool

pisello [pi•ZEHL•lo] *n* M pea

pista [PEES•ta] *n* F track; trail

pista da corsa [PEES•ta dah KOHR•sa] *n* F speedway

pista per pattinaggio [PEES•ta PEHR PAT•ti•NAH•djo] *n* F rink

pistola [pis•TOH•la] *n* F pistol

pistone [pis•TOH•ne] *n* M piston

pittore [pit•TOH•re] *n* M painter

pittoresco; pittoresca [PIT•to•REHS•ko]; [PIT•to•REHS•ka] *adj* MF colorful; picturesque

piú [piuh] *adj* more; in piú\ *adv* moreover

piú avanti [PIUH a•VAHN•ti] *adv* ahead (of)

piú basso; piú bassa [PIUH BAHS•so]; [piuh•bahs•sa] *adj* MF lower

piú buono; piú buona [PIU' BU•oh•no];[piu'•bu•oh•na] *adj* MF better

piú lontano; piú lontana [PIUH lon•TAH•no]; [piuh•lon•tah•na] *adj* farther

piú vecchio; piú vecchia [PIUH VEHK•kyo]; [piuh•vehk•kya] *adj* MF senior

piuma [PIUH•ma] *n* F feather; plume

piuolo [pyu•OH•lo] *n* M peg

piuttosto [piut•TOHS•to] *adv* rather; *pron* somewhat

pizzico [pee•TSI•ko] *n* M pinch

pizzo [PEE•tso] *n* M lace

placare [pla•KAH•re] *vt* pacify; placate

placca [PLAHK•ka] *n* F plaque

placcato; placcata [plak•KAH•to]; [plak•KAH•ta] *adj* MF plated

placcato ; placcata d'oro [plak•KAH•to]; [plak•KAH•ta (DOH•ro)] *adj* gold-plated

placido; placida [plah•TSHI•do]; [plah•TSHI•da] *adj* MF placid; peaceful

plastica [plahs•TI•ka] *n* F plastic; di plastica\ *adj* plastic

platano [PLAH•tano] *n* M sycamore

platino [plah•TI•no] *n* M platinum

playboy [PLEHY•boi] *n* M playboy

plebaglia [ple•BAH•lya] *n* F populace; rabble

plurale [plu•RAH•le] *adj n* M plural

pochi; poche [POH•ki]; [POH•ke] *adj pl* MF few

poco attraente [POH•ko at•TRA•EHN•te] *adj* unattractive

poco costoso; poco costosa [POH•ko•KOS•TOH•zo]; [POH•ko•KOS•TOH•za] *adj* MF inexpensive

poesia [poe•SEE•a] *n* F poem; poetry

poeta [POEH•ta] *n* M poet

poetico; poetica [POEH•ti•ko]; [POEH•ti•ka] *adj* MF poetic

poggiatesta [POH•dja•TEHS•ta] *n* M headrest

poiché [POY•keh] *conj* whereas

poker [POH•ker] *n* M poker (game)

polacco; polacca [po•LAHK•ko]; [po•LAHK•ka] *adj* Polish; *n* MF Pole

polare [po•LAH•re] *adj* polar

Polinesia [PO•li•NEH•zia] *n* F Polynesia

polipo [poh•LIPO] *n* M octopus

politica [PO•lee•TIKA] *n* F politics

politico; politica [PO•lee•TIKO]; [PO•lee•TIKA] *adj* MF political

polizia [PO•li•TSEE•a] *n* F police

poliziotta [PO•li•TSYOHT•ta] *n* F policewoman

poliziotto [PO•lit•SYOHT•to] *n* M cop; policeman; police officer

pollaio [pol•LAH•yo] *n* M coop; hen-house

pollame [pol•LAH•me] *n* M poultry

pollice 1 [pohl•LIT•she] *n* M inch

pollice 2 [pohl•LIT•she] *n* M thumb

polline [pohl•LINE] *n* M pollen

pollo [POHL•lo] *n* M chicken; fowl

polmone [pol•MOH•ne] *n* M lung

polmonite [POL•mo•NEE•te] *n* F pneumonia

polo1 [POH•lo] *n* M pole

polo 2 [POH•lo] *n* M polo

polo nord [POH•lo•NOHRD] *n* M North Pole

Polonia [PO•loh•NYA] *n* F Poland

polpa [POHL•pa] *n* F pulp

polpaccio [pol•PAHTSH•yo] *n* M calf (anat)

polpetta [pol•PEHT•ta] *n* F meatball

polsino [pol•SEE•no] *n* M cuff

polso 1 [POHL•so] *n* M pulse

polso 2 [POHL•so] *n* M wrist

poltrona [pohl•TROH•nah] *n* F armchair

poltrone; poltrona [pol•TROH•ne]; [pol•TROH•na] *n* MF loafer; slacker; truant

polvere [pohl•VE•re] *n* F dust; powder; **in polvere** *adj* powdered

polvere da sparo [pohl•VERE dah SPAH•ro] *n* F gunpowder

polverizzare [POL•ve•rit•SAH•re] *vt* pulverize

pomeriggio [PO•me•REE•djo] *n* M afternoon

pomice [poh•MI•tshe] *n* F pumice

pomodoro [PO•mo•DOH•ro] *n* M tomato

pomolo [poh•MO•lo] *n* M knob

pompa 1 [POHM•pa] *n* F pomp

pompa 2 [POHM•pa] *n* F pump

pompelmo [pom•PEHL•mo] *n* M grapefruit

pompiere [pom•PYEH•re] *n* M fireman

pomposo; pomposa [pom•POH•zo]; [pom•POH•za] *adj* MF pompous

ponte [POHN•te] *n* M bridge

ponte a pedaggio [POHN•te ah PE•DAH•djo] *n* M toll-bridge

pontile [pon•TEE•le] *n* M wharf

pony [POH•ni] *n* M pony

popolare [PO•po•LAH•re] *adj* folk; popular; *vt* populate

popolaritá [PO•po•la•RI•tah] *n* F popularity

popolazione [PO•po•lat•SYOH•ne] *n* F population

porcellana [POR•tscel•LAH•na] *n* F china; porcelain

porcle [por•TSHEE•le] *n* M pigsty

porcospino [POR•ko•SPEE•no] *n* M porcupine

pornografia
[POR•no•gra•FEE•a] *n*
pornography

poro [POH•ro] *n* M pore

poroso; porosa [po•ROH•zo];
[po•ROH•za] *adj* porous

porro [POHR•ro] *n* M leek;
wart

porta [POHR•ta] *n* F door; a
porta accanto\ *adj* next-door

porta d'ingresso
[POHR•ta•din•GREHS•so] *n* F
front door

portacenere
[POHR•ta•TSHEH•ne•re] *n* M
ashtray

portachiavi
[POHR•ta•KYAH•vi] *n* M key
ring

portafoglio [POR•ta•FOH•lyo]
n M wallet

portare [por•TAH•re] *vt* bring;
carry

portata [por•TAH•ta] *n* F
reach; scope

portatile [POR•tah•TI•le] *adj*
portable

portavoce [POR•ta•voh•TSHE]
n MF spokesperson

portinaio [POR•ti•NAH•yo] *n*
M janitor

porto [POHR•to] *n* M harbor

porto [POHR•to] *n* M port

Portogallo [POR•to•GAHL•lo]
n M Portugal

portoghese [POR•to•GEH•ze]
adj Portuguese

porzione [por•TSYOH•ne] *n* F
helping

porzione [por•TSYOH•ne] *n* F
portion

posa [POH•za] *n* F sitting

posare [po•ZAH•re] *vi* pose; *vt*
posture

posate [po•ZAH•te] *npl* F
cutlery

posato; posata [po•ZAH•to];
[po•ZAH•ta] *adj* MF sedate

poscia [PAH•sha] *adv* thereafter

posdatare [poz•DATAH•re] *vt*
postdate

positivo; positiva
[PO•zi•TEE•vo];
[PO•zi•TEE•va] *adj* positive

posizione [PO•zi•TSYOH•ne] *n*
F location; position; standing

posporre [pos•POHR•re] *vt*
postpone

possedere [POS•se•DEH•re] *vt*
possess

possesso [pos•SEHS•so] *n* M
ownership; possession

possibile [pos•SEE•BI•le] *adj*
possible

possibilità [POS•si•BI•LI•tah] *n*
F possibility

possibilmente
[POS•si•BIL•MEHN•te] *adv*
possibly

posta [POH•sta] *n* F mail

posta aerea [POH•stah
ah•EREH•ah] *n* F airmail

postale [pos•TAH•le] *adj* postal

posteriore [POS•ter•YOH•re]
adj; rear; back; *adj n* MF
posterior

postino [pos•TEE•no] *n* M
mailman; postman

posto [POHS•to] *n* M place;
seat

posto vacante
[POH•sto•va•KAHN•te] *n* M
vacancy

postribolo [pos•TREE•bolo] *n*
M brothel

postumo; postuma
[pohs•TU•mo]; [pohs•TU•ma]
adj MF posthumous

potassio [po•TAHS•syo] *n* M
potassium

potent [po•TEHN•te] *adj*
potent; mighty; powerful

potenza cavalli [po•TEHN•tsa
ka•VAHL•li] *n* F horsepower

potenziale [PO•ten•TSYAH•le]
n M potential

potenzialmente
[PO•ten•TSYAL•MEHN•te]
adv potentially

potere [po•TEH•re] *vi* can;
may; power

povero; povera [poh•VE•ro];
[poh•VE•ra] *adj* MF poor

povertá [po•VER•tah] *n* F
poverty

pozione [po•TSYOH•ne] *n* F
potion

pozzanghera [pots•AHN•gera]
n F puddle

pozzo [POH•tso] *n* M well

pozzo di petrolio [POH•tso
DEE pe•TROH•lyo] *n* M well
(oil)

pranzare [pran•ZAH•re] *vi* dine

pranzo [PRAHN•tso] *n* M
dinner

prateria [PRA•te•REE•a] *n* F
prairie

pratica [prah•TI•ka] *n* F
practice

pratico; pratica [prah•TI•ko];
[prah•TI•ka] *adj* MF practical;
serviceable

prato [PRAH•to] *n* M lawn;
meadow

precario; precaria
[pre•KAH•ryo];
[pre•KAH•rya] *adj* MF
precarious

precauzione
[PRE•kau•TSYOH•ne] *n* F
precaution

precedente
[PRE•tshe•DEHN•te] *adj*
former; previous; prior *n* M
precedent; *n* F precedence

precedere [pre•TSHE•dere] *vt*
precede

precipitare
[PRE•tshi•PI•TAH•re] *vi*
precipitate

precipitazione
[PRE•tshi•PI•tat•SYOH•ne] *n*
F precipitation; rainfall

precisamente
[PRE•tshi•za•MEHN•te] *adv*
precisely

precisione
[PRE•tshi•ZYOH•ne] *n* F
precision

preciso; precisa
[pre•TSHEE•zo];
[pre•TSHEE•za] *adj* MF
precise

precludere [pre•KLUH•dere] *vt*
preclude

precoce [pre•KOH•tshe] *adj*
precocious

precursore [PRE•kur•SOH•re]
n MF forerunner

preda [PREH•da] *n* F prey;
quarry

predatore [PRE•da•TOH•re] *n*
M predator

predecessore
[PRE•de•TSHES•soh•re] *n* M
predecessor

predestinato; predestinata
[pre•DES•ti•NAH•to];
[PRE•des•TINAH•ta] *adj* MF
predestined

predicare [PRE•di•KAH•re] *vi*
preach

predicato [PRE•di•KAH•to] *n*
M predicate

predicatore
[PRE•di•KA•TOH•re] *n* M
preacher

predire [pre•DEE•re] *vt* foretell

predisposto; predisposta
[PRE•dis•POHS•to];
[PRE•dis•POHS•ta] *adj* MF
predisposed

predizione [PRE•dit•SYOH•ne]
n F prediction

predominante
[PRE•do•mi•NAHN•te] *adj*
predominant

prefazione [PRE•fat•SYOH•ne]
n F foreword; preface

preferenza [PRE•fe•REHN•tsa]
n F preference

preferenziale
[PRE•fe•ren•TSYAH•le] *adj*
preferential

preferibile [PRE•fe•REE•BI•le]
adj preferable

preferibilmente
[PRE•fe•RIB•il•MEHN•te]
adv preferably

preferire [PRE•fe•REE•re] *vt*
prefer

preferito; preferita
[PRE•fe•REE•to];
[PRE•fe•REE•ta] *adj* MF
favorite

prefisso [pre•FEES•so] *n* M
prefix

pregare [pre•GAH•re] *vt* beg; *vi*
pray

preghiera [pre•GYEH•ra] *n* F
prayer

pregiudizio
[PRE•dju•DEE•tsyo] *n* M
prejudice; bias

prelievo [pre•LYEH•vo] *n* M
withdrawal

preliminare
[PRE•li•mi•NAH•re] *adj*
preliminary

preludio [pre•LUD•dyo] *n* M
prelude

prematrimoniale
[PRE•ma•TRI•MONYAH•le]
adj premarital

prematuro; prematura
[PRE•ma•TUH•ro];
[PRE•ma•TUH•ra] *adj*
premature; untimely

premeditato; premeditata
[PRE•me•di•TAH•to];
[PRE•me•di•TAH•ta] *adj* MF
intentional

premessa [pre•MEHS•sa] *n* F
premise

premio [PREH•myo] *n* M prize

premonizione
[PRE•mo•NITSYOH•ne] *n* F
premonition

premura [pre•MUH•ra] *n* F
thoughtfulness

prendere [PREHN•dere] *vt* take

prendere a prestito
[PREHN•dere ah
PREH•STI•to] *vt* borrow

prendere a randellate
[PREHN•de•re ah
RAN•DEL•lah•te] *vt* bludgeon

prendere nota [PREHN•de•re NOH•ta] *vi* jot

prenotazione [PRE•no•tat•SYOH•ne] *n* F reservation

preoccuparsi [PRE•ok•ku•PAHR•si] *vi* worry; bother

preoccupato; preoccupata [PREOK•ku•PAH•to]; [PREOK•ku•PAH•ta] *adj* MF preoccupied

preoccupazione [PRE•ok•ku•PAT•SYOH•ne] *n* F worry

prepagato; prepagata [PRE•pa•GAH•to]; [PRE•pa•GAH•ta] *adj* MF prepaid

preparare [PRE•pa•RAH•re] *vt* prepare

preparare cibi da asporto [PRE•pa•RAH•re TSHEE•bi dah as•POHR•to] *vi* cater (banquet, etc)

preparazione [PRE•pa•rat•SYOH•ne] *n* F preparation

preposizione [PRE•po•zi•TSYOH•ne] *n* F preposition

prepotente [PRE•po•TEHN•te] *n adj* bully

prerogativa [PRE•ro•ga•TEE•va] *n* F prerogative

presa 1 [PREH•za] *n* F grasp; grip; hold

presa 2 [PREH•za] *n* F socket

presavare [PREH•seh•VAHR•ai] preserve; keep; maintain

prescrivere [PRES•kree•VE•re] *vt* prescribe

presentabile [PRE•sen•TAH•bi•le] *adj* presentable

presentare [PRE•zen•TAH•re] *vt* tender; present

presentazione [PRE•zen•tat•SYOH•ne] *n* F presentation

presente [pre•SEHN•te] *adj* present

presenza [pre•ZEHN•tsa] *n* F presence

preside [preh•SI•de] *n* M schoolmaster

presidente [PRE•si•DEHN•te] *n* M chairman; MF president

presidio [pre•SEE•dyo] *n* M garrison

pressione [pres•SYOH•ne] *n* F pressure

prestare [pres•TAH•re] *vt* lend

prestigio [pres•TEE•djo] *n* M prestige

prestito [prehs•TI•to] *n* M loan

presto [PREHS•to] *adv* soon

presumabilmente [PRE•zu•ma•BIL•MEHN•te] *adv* presumably

presumere [pre•ZUH•ME•re] *vt* presume

presuntuoso; presuntuosa [PRE•zun•TUOH•zo]; [PRE•zun•TUOH•za] *adj* MF stuck-up

presunzione [PRE•zun•TSYOH•ne] *n* F presumption; pretension

prete [PREH•te] *n* M priest

pretendere [PRE•ten•DEH•re]
  vt claim

pretenzioso; pretenziosa
  [PRE•ten•TSYOH•zo];
  [PRE•ten•TSYOH•za] *adj* MF
  pretentious

pretesa [pre•TEH•sa] *n* F
  demand

pretesto [pre•TEHS•to] *n* M
  pretext

prevalente [PRE•va•LEHN•te]
  adj prevailing; prevalent

prevalere [PRE•v•LEH•re] *vi*
  prevail

prevaricazione
  [PRE•va•ri•KATSYOH•ne] *n*
  F malpractice

prevedere [PRE•ve•DEH•re] *vt*
  foresee

prevedibile
  [PRE•ve•DEE•bi•le] *adj*
  predictable

preveggenza
  [PRE•ve•DJEHN•tsa] *n* F
  foresight

prevenire [PRE•ve•NEE•re] *vt*
  prevent

preventivo; preventiva
  [PRE•ven•TEE•vo];
  [PRE•ven•TEE•va] *adj* MF
  preventive

prevenuto; prevenuta
  [PRE•ve•NUH•to];
  [PRE•ve•NUH•ta] *adj* MF
  biased; narrow-minded;
  prejudiced

previsione [pre•VIZYOH•ne] *n*
  F forecast

prevosto [pre•VOHS•to] *n* M
  provost

prezioso; preziosa
  [pre•TSYOH•zo];
  [pre•TSYOH•za] *adj* MF
  precious

prezzemolo [pretseh•MO•lo] *n*
  M parsley

prezzo [PREH•tso] *n* M charge;
  price; a metá prezzo *adj* MF
  half-price

prigione [pri•DJOH•ne] *n* F
  prison

prigioniero; prigioniera
  [PRI•djo•NIEH•ro];
  [PRI•djo•NIEH•ra] *n* MF
  captive; prisoner

prima [PREE•ma] *adj adv*
  before; first; prime; di prima
  classe\ *adj* first-class; di prima
  qualitá\ *adj* prime

primario; primaria
  [pri•MAH•ryo];[pri•mah•rya]
  adj MF primary

primate [pri•MAH•te] *n* M
  primate

primitivo; primitiva
  [PRI•mi•TEE•vo];
  [PRI•mi•TEE•va] *adj* MF
  primitive

primo [PREE•mo] *n* M
  premiere; -o -a *adj* first;
  premier

primo piano [PREE•mo
  PYAH•no] *n* M foreground

primula [pree•MU•la] *n* F
  primrose

principale 1
  [PRIN•tshi•PAH•le] *n* M boss;
  principal

principale 2
  [PRIN•tshi•PAH•le] *adj*
  foremost; leading; main

principe [preen•TSHI•pe] *n* M
prince

principessa
[PRIN•tshi•PEHS•sa] *n* F
princess

principiante
[PRIN•tshi•PYAHN•te] *n* MF
beginner

principio 1 [prin•TSHEEP•yo] *n*
M beginning; outset

principio 2 [prin•TSHEE•pyo] *n*
M principle

prioritá [PRI•o•RI•tah] *n* F
priority

prisma [PREEZ•ma] *n* M prism

privare [pri•VAH•re] *vt* deprive

privato; privata [pri•VAH•to];
[pri•VAH•ta] *adj* MF private

privazione [PRI•vat•SYOH•ne]
n F privation

privilegio [PRI•vi•LEH•djo] *n*
M privilege

privo; priva [PREE•vo];
[PREE•va] *adj* MF devoid

probabile [PRO•bah•BILE] *adj*
likely; probable

probabilitá [PRO•ba•BI•LI•tah]
n F probability

probabilmente
[PRO•ba•bil•MEHN•te] *adv*
probably

probazione
[PRO•bat•SYOH•ne] *n* F
probation

problema [pro•BLEH•ma] *n* M
problem

probo; proba [PROH•bo];
[PROH•ba] *adj* MF
law-abiding

proboscide [PRO•boh•SHI•de]
n F trunk

procedere [pro•TSHEH•dere] *vi*
proceed

procedimento furtivo
[pro•TSHE•di•MEHN•to
fur•TEE•vo] *n* M stealth

procedura [PRO•tshe•DUH•ra]
n F procedure

processione
[PRO•tshes•SYOH•ne] *n* F
procession

processo [pro•TSHEHS•so] *n*
M process; trial

procione [pro•TSHYOH•ne] *n*
M raccoon

proclamare [PRO•kla•MAH•re]
vt proclaim

procrastinare
[PRO•kras•ti•NAH•re] *vi*
procrastinate

procura [pro•KUH•ra] *n* F
proxy

procurare [PRO•ku•RAH•re] *vt*
procure

prodezza [PRO•DEH•tsa] *n* F
prowess

prodigio [pro•DEE•djo] *n* M
prodigy; genius

prodigo; prodiga
[proh•DIGO]; [proh•DIGA]
adj MF prodigal

prodotto [pro•DOHT•to] *n* M
product

prodotto principale
[pro•DOHT•to
PRIN•tshi•PAH•le] *n* M staple

produrre [pro•DUHR•re] *vt*
produce

produttivo; produttiva
[PRO•dut•TEE•vo];
[PRO•dut•TEE•va] *adj* MF
productive

produttore [PRO•dut•TOH•re]
n M producer

produzione
[PRO•du•TSYOH•ne] *n* F
production; output

profano; profana
[pro•FAH•no]; [pro•FAH•na]
adj MF profane

professionale
[PRO•fes•SYONAH•le] *n* MF
professional

professione
[PRO•fes•SYOH•ne] *n* F
profession

professionista
[PRO•fes•syo•NEES•ta] *n* MF
pro; professional

professore; professoressa
[PRO•fes•SOH•re];
[PRO•fes•SOREHS•sa] *n* MF
professor

profeta [pro•FEH•ta] *n* M
prophet

profetizzare
[PRO•fe•tit•SHA•re] *vt*
predict; prophesy

profezia [PRO•fe•TSEE•a] *n* F
prophecy

profilo [pro•FEE•lo] *n* M profile

profitto [pro•FEET•to] *n* M
proceeds; profit

profonditá [PRO•fon•DI•tah] *n*
F depth

profondo; profonda
[PRO•FOHN•do];
[PRO•FOHN•da] *adj* MF
deep; profound

profumo [pro•FUH•mo] *n* M
perfume

progettazione
[PRO•djet•ta•TSYOH•ne] *n* F
planning

progetto [pro•DJEHT•to] *n* M
blueprint; plan; project

programma [pro•GRAHM•ma]
n M program

progredire [PRO•gre•DEE•re]
vi progress

progressivo; progressiva
[PRO•gres•SEE•vo];
[PRO•gres•SEE•va] *adj* MF
progressive

progresso [pro•GREHS•so] *n*
M headway; progress; stride

proibire [proy•BEE•re] *vt*
forbid; prohibit

proibizione
[PROY•bi•TSYOH•ne] *n* MF
prohibition

proiettare [PRO•yet•TAH•re]
vt project

proiettile [PRO•yeht•TI•le] *n*
M bullet

proiezione
[PRO•yet•SYOH•ne] *n* F
projection

prole [PROH•le] *n* F offspring

proletariato
[PRO•le•tar•YAH•to] *n* M
proletariat

prolungare [PRO•lun•GAH•re]
vt prolong

promemoria
[PRO•me•MOH•rya] *n* M
reminder

promessa [pro•MEHS•sa] *n* F
promise

promettente
[PRO•met•TEHN•te] *adj*
promising

prominente
[PRO•mi•NEHN•te] *adj*
prominent

promiscuo; promiscua
[pro•MEES•kwo];
[pro•MEES•kwa] *adj* MF
promiscuous

promotore [PRO•mo•TOH•re]
n M promoter

promozione
[PRO•mo•TSYOH•ne] *n* F
promotion

promuovere [pro•MUOH•vere]
vt promote

pronipote [PRO•ni•POH•te] *n*
F great-granddaughter; *n* M
great-grandson

prono; prona [PROH•no];
[proh•na] *adj* MF prone

pronome [pro•NOH•me] *n* M
pronoun

pronosticare
[PRO•nos•TIKAH•re] *vt*
forecast

prontamente
[PRON•ta•MEH•te] *adv*
promptly; readily

prontezza [pron•TEH•tsa] *n* F
readiness

pronto; pronta [PROHN•to];
[PROHN•ta] *adj* MF ready;
excl (answering telephone)
hello!.

pronto soccorso
[PROHN•to•sok•KOHR•so] *n*
M first aid

pronuncia [pro•NUHN•tsha] *n*
F pronunciation

pronunciare
[PRO•nun•TSHAH•re] *vt*
pronounce

pronunciato; pronunciata
[PRO•nun•TSHAH•to];

[PRO•nun•TSHA•ta] *adj* MF
pronounced

propaganda
[PRO•pa•GAHN•da] *n* F
propaganda

proporre [pro•POHR•re] *vt*
propose

proposito [PRO•poh•SEE•toh]
n regard; di proposito\ *adv*
regarding

proporzione
[PRO•por•TSYOH•ne] *n* F
proportion

proposta [pro•POHS•ta] *n* F
proposal; proposition

proprietá [pro•PRIE•tah] *n* F
estate; property

proprietá terriera [PRO•prye
TAH•ter•YEH•ra] *n* F manor

proprietario
[PRO•prie•TAH•ryo] *n* M
proprietor; -o -a\ *n* MF owner

proprietario terriero
[PRO•prietah•RYO
ter•RTEH•ro] *n* M landowner

proprio; propria [PROH•pryo];
[PROH•prya] *adj* own; *adv*
quite

prosa [PROH•za] *n* F prose

prosciutto [pro•SHUHT•to] *n*
M ham

prosperare [PROS•pe•RAH•re]
vi flourish; *vt* prosper

prosperare [PROS•per•AH•re]
vi thrive

prosperitá [PROS•pe•RI•tah] *n*
F prosperity

prosperoso; prosperosa
[PROS•pe•ROH•zo];
[PROS•pe•ROH•za] *adj* MF
prosperous

prospettiva
[PROS•pet•TEE•va] *n* F
outlook; perspective; prospect;
vista

prospettivo; prospettiva
[PROS•pet•TEE•vo];
[PROS•pet•TEE•va] *adj* MF
prospective

prossimitá [PROS•i•MI•tah] *n*
F proximity

prossimo; prossima
[PROHS•SI•mo];
[PROHS•SI•ma] *adj* MF
coming; forthcoming; next

prostituta [PROS•ti•TUH•ta] *n*
F prostitute; whore

prostrato; prostrata
[pros•TRAH•to];
[pros•TRAH•ta] *adj* MF
prostrate

proteggere [PRO•teh•DJE•re]
vt protect

proteina [PRO•te•EE•na] *n* F
protein

protesta [pro•TEHS•ta] *n* F
protest

protestante
[PRO•tes•TAHN•te] *adj*
Protestant

protettivo; protettiva
[PRO•tet•TEE•vo];
[PRO•tet•TEE•va] *adj* MF
protective

protettore [PRO•tet•TOH•re] *n*
M protector

protezione
[PRO•te•TSYOH•ne] *n* F
protection

protoplasma
[PRO•to•PLAHZ•ma] *n* M
protoplasm

protrarre [pro•TRAHR•re] *vt*
protract

protrudere [pro•TRUH•DE•re]
vi protrude

protuberanza
[pro•TU•ber•AHN•tsa] *n* F
protuberance; F bump

prova 1 [PROH•va] *n* F proof

prova 2 [PROH•va] *n* F
rehearsal

provare 1 [pro•VAH•re] *vt*
prove

provare 2 [pro•VAH•re] *vt*
rehearse; try

provare gusto a
[pro•VAH•re•GUH•sto•ah] *vt*
enjoy

proverbio [pro•VEHR•byo] *n*
M proverb

provetta [pro•VEHT•ta] *n* F
test tube

provincia [pro•VEEN•tsha] *n* F
province

provincial
[PRO•vin•TSHAH•le] *adj*
provincial

provino [pro•VEE•no] *n* M
audition (film)

provocare [PRO•vo•KAH•re] *vt*
provoke

provvedere
[PROV•ve•DEH•re] *vt* provide

provvedimento
[PROV•ve•di•MEHN•to] *n* M
provision

provvidenza
[PROV•vi•DEHN•tsa] *n* F
providence

provvisorio; provvisoria
[PROV•vi•ZOH•ryo];
[PROV•vi•ZOH•rya] *adj* MF
interim; tentative

prua [PRUH•a] *n* F prow

prudente [pru•DEHN•te] *adj* prudent

prudenza [pru•DEHN•tsa] *n* F prudence

prugna [PRUH•nya] *n* F plum

prugna secca [PRUH•nya•SEHK•ka] *n* F prune

pruriginoso; pruriginosa [PRU•ri•dji•NOH•zo]; [PRU•ri•dji•NOH•za] *adj* MF itchy

prurito [pru•REE•to] *n* M itch

pseudonimo [pse•UDOH•NI•mo] *n* M pseudonym

psichiatra [PSI•kyah•TRA] *n* MF psychiatrist

psichiatria [PSI•kya•TREE•a] *n* F psychiatry

psicologia [PSI•ko•la•DJEE•a] *n* F psychology

psicologico; psicologica [PSI•ko•loh•DJI•ko]; [PSI•ko•LOH•DJI•ka] *n* MF psychological

psicologo; psicologa [PSI•koh•LO•go]; [PSI•koh•LO•ga] *n* MF psychologist

pubblicare su diversi giornali [PUB•bli•KAH•re suh di•VEHR•si DJOR•nah•li] *vt* syndicate

pubblicazione [PUB•bli•kat•SYOH•ne] *n* F publication

pubblico [puhb•BLI•ko] *n* M audience

pubblico ministero [PUHB•bli•KO•MI•nis•TEH•ro] *n* M prosecutor

pubblico; pubblica [PUHB•bli•KO]; [PUHB•bli•KA] *adj* MF public

pudibondo; pudibonda [PU•di•BOHN•do]; [PU•di•BOHN•da] *n* MF prude

pugilato [PU•dji•LAH•to] *n* M boxing

pugilatore [PU•dji•la•TOH•re] *n* M boxer

pugnalare [PU•nya•LAH•re] *vt* stab

pugno [PUH•nyo] *n* M fist

pulce [PUHL•tshe] *n* F flea

pulcino [pul•TSHEE•no] *n* M chick

puledro [pu•LEH•dro] *n* M colt

pulire [pu•LEE•re] *vt* clean; scrub

pulito; pulita [PU•LEE•to]; [PU•LEE•ta] *adj* MF clean

pulitore [PU•li•TOH•re] *n* M cleaner

pulizia [PU•li•TSEE•ah] *n* F cleanliness

pulmino [pul•MEE•no] *n* M van

pulpito [puhl•PI•to] *n* M pulpit

pulsare [pul•SAH•re] *vi* pulsate; throb

pulsazione [PUL•sa•TSYOH•ne] *n* F heartbeat; pulsation

pungente [pun•DJEHN•te] *adj* barbed

pungere [puhn•DJE•re] *vt*
prick; sting

pungitopo
[PUHN•dji•TOH•po] *n* M
holly

pungolare [PUN•go•LAH•re] *vt*
prod

punire [pu•NEE•re] *vt* punish

punizione [PU•nit•SYOH•ne] *n*
F punishment

punta del dito [PUHN•ta del
DEE•to] *n* F fingertip

a puntate [AH•pun•TAH•te]
adj MF serial

puntare a [PUN•tah•RE•ah] *n*
M aim

punteggiatura
[PUN•tedja•TUH•ra] *n* F
punctuation

punteggio [pun•TEH•djo] *n* M
score

puntello [pun•TEHL•lo] *n* M
prop

puntina [pun•TEE•na] *n* F tack

puntino [pun•TEE•no] *n* dot

punto [PUHN•to] *n* M point;
period (grammar); stitch

punto di domanda [PUHN•to
dee do•MAHN•da] *n* M
question mark

punto di partenza [PUHN•to
dee par•TEHN•tsa] *n* M
starting point

punto di riferimento
[PUHN•to di
ri•fe•RIMEHN•to] *n* M
landmark

punto e virgola [PUHN•to eh
VEER•go•la] *n* M semicolon

punto esclamativo [PUHN•to
es•KLA•MATEE•vo] *n* M
exclamation point

punto in discussione
[PUHN•to in
DIS•kus•SYOH•ne] *n* M issue

puntone [pun•TOH•ne] *n* M
strut

puntuale [pun•TUAH•le] *adj*
punctual

puntura [pun•TUH•ra] *n* F
puncture

pupilla [pu•PEEL•la] *n* F pupil

puramente [PU•ra•MEHN•te]
adv merely

purezza [pu•REH•tsa] *n* F
purity

purgare [pur•GAH•re] *vt* purge

purgatorio [PUR•ga•TOH•ryo]
n M purgatory

purificare [PU•ri•fi•KAH•re] *vt*
purify

puro; pura [PU•ro]; [PU•ra] *adj*
MF pure

purosangue
[PUH•ro•SAHN•gue] *n adj*
thoroughbred

putrefare [PU•tre•FAH•re] *vi*
putrefy

putrefazione
[PUTRE•fat•SYOH•ne] *n* F
decay

putrido; putrida [puh•TRI•do];
[puh•TRI•da] *adj* MF putrid

puzzare [put•SAH•re] *vi* reek;
stink

puzzo [PUH•tso] *n* M stench

puzzola [puh•TSOLA] *n* F
skunk

Q

quaderno [kwa•DEHR•no] *n* M
notebook

quadrante 1 [kwa•DRAHN•te]
n M dial

quadrante 2 [kwa•DRAHN•te]
n M quadrant

quadrilatero; qudrilatera
[KWA•dri•LAH•tero];
[KWA•dri•LAH• tera] *adj* MF
quadrilateral

quadro [KWAH•dro] *n* M
picture

quaglia [KWAH•lya] *n* F quail

qualche [KWAHL•ke] *adj* some

qualche volta
[KWAHL•ke•VOHL•ta] *adv*
sometimes

qualcosa [kwal•KOH•za] *pron*
F something

qualcuno [kwal•KUH•no] *pron*
M somebody; someone

qualificare
[KWA•li•fi•KAH•re] *vt*
qualify

qualificazione
[KWA•li•fi•ka•TSYOH•ne] *n*
F qualification

qualitá [kwa•LI•tah] *n* F
quality; di qualitá inferiore\
adj second-rate

qualitativo; qualitativa
[KWA•li•ta•TEE•vo];
[KWA•li•ta•TEE•va] *adj* MF
qualitative

qualsiasi [kwahl•SEE•asi] *adj*
any; whatever

qualsiasi cosa [KWAL•see•ASI
KO•sah] *pron* F anything

qualunque [kwa•LUHN•kwe]
adj whichever

quando [KWAHN•do] *adv*
when

quantitá [kwan•TI•TAH] *n* F
quantity

quantotativo; quantitativa
[KWAN•ti•ta•TEE•vo];
[KWAN•ti•ta•TEE•va] *adj* MF
quantitative

quaranta [kwa•RAHN•ta] *num*
forty

quarantina [KWA•ran•TEE•na]
n F quarantine

Quaresima [KWA•reh•ZI•ma] *n*
F Lent

quartetto [kwar•TEHT•to] *n* M
quartet

quartier generale
[KWAR•tyehr
DJE•ne•RAH•le] *n* M
headquarters

quarto [KWAHR•to] *n* M
quarter

quarto di gallone [KWAHR•to
dee GAL•LOH•ne] *n* M quart

quarto; quarta [KWAHR•to];
[KWAHR•ta] *num* MF fourth

quarzo [KWAHR•tso] *n* M
quartz

quasi [KWAH•si] *adv* almost;
nearly

quattordici [kwat•TOHR•ditshi]
num fourteen

quattro [KWAHT•tro] *num*
four
quelli; quelle [KWEHL•li];
[KWEHL•le] *adj pl MF* those
quello lá; quella lá
[KWEHL•lo•lah];
[KWEHL•la•lah] *adj MF* that
(one); those; yonder
quello; quella [KWEHL•lo];
[KWEHL•la] *adj MF* that
(one)
quercia [KWEHR•tsha] *n F* oak
querelante [KWE•re•LAHN•te]
n MF plaintiff
questi; queste [KWEHS•ti];
[KWEHS•te] *adj pl MF* these
questionario
[KWES•tyo•NAH•ryo] *n M*
questionnaire
questo; questa [KWEHS•to];
[KWEHS•ta] *adj* this
questore [kwes•TOH•re] *n M*
commissioner (police)
qui [kwee] *adv* here
qui accluso; qui acclusa
[KWEE•ak•KLUH•zo];
[KWEE•ak•KLUH•za] *adv*
MF *phr* herewith

quiescenza [KWYE•shehn•tsa]
n F quiescence
quiete [KWYEH•te] *n F*
quietness; stillness
quindi [KWEEN•di] *adv*
therefore
quindicesimo; quindicesima
[KWIN•di•TSHEH•ZI•mo];
[KWIN•di•TSHEH•ZI•ma] *adj*
MF fifteenth
quindici [kween•DIT•shi] *num*
fifteen
quintetto [kwin•TEHT•to] *n M*
quintet
quinto; quinta [KWEEN•to];
[KWEEN•ta] *adj MF* fifth
quiz [kweets] *n M* quiz
quorum [KWOH•rum] *n M*
quorum
quota [KWOH•ta] *n F* quota;
part; portion
quotidiano; quotidiana
[KWO•tid•YAH•no];
[KWO•tid•YAH•na] *adj MF*
daily; everyday
quoziente [kwo•TSYEHN•te] *n*
M quotient

R

rabarbaro [RA•bahr•BA•ro] *n*
M rhubarb
rabbia [RAHB•bya] *n F* rage
rabbino [rab•BEE•no] *n M*
rabbi
rabbioso; rabbiosa
[RAB•BYOH•zo];

[RAB•BYOH•za] *adj MF*
rabid; vicious
rabbrividire
[RAB•bri•vi•DEE•re] *vi*
shiver
rabbuffare [RAB•buf•FAH•re]
vt snub

racchetta [rak•KEHT•ta] *n* F
racket

raccogliere [rak•KOH•lyere] *vt*
gather; reap

raccolto [rak•KOHL•to] *n* M
crop; harvest

raccomandare
[RAK•ko•MAHN•DA•re] *vt*
recommend

raccomandazione
[RAK•ko•MAN•DAH•re] *n* F
recommendation

racconto [rak•KOHN•to] *n* M
recital

radere al suolo [RAH•de•RE
ahl SUOH•lo] *vt* raze

radiatore [RA•dia•TOH•re] *n*
M radiator

radiazione
[RA•dya•TSYOH•ne] *n* F
radiation

radicale [RA•di•KAH•le] *adj*
radical

radice [ra•DEE•tshe] *n* F root

radio [RAH•dyo] *n* F radio

radiositá [RA•dio•ZI•tah] *n* F
radiance

rado; rada [RAH•do];
[RAH•da] *adj* MF sparse

radunare [RA•du•NAH•re] *vt*
muster

raduno [ra•DUH•no] *n* M
convention

radura [ra•DUH•ra] *n* F
clearing

rafano [RAH•fano] *n* M
horseradish

raffica [RAHF•fika] *n* F gust
(of wind)

raffiguraree
[RAF•fi•gu•RAH•re] *vt*
visualize

raffinare [RAF•fi•NAH•re] *vt*
refine

raffinatezza
[RAF•fi•na•TEH•tsa] *n* F
refinement

raffinato; raffinata
[RAF•f•NAH•to];
[raf•fi•nah•ta] *adj* MF refined

raffineria [RAF•fi•ne•REE•a] *n*
F refinery

raffreddare
[RAF•fred•DAH•re] *vt* chill

raffreddore
[RAF•fred•DOH•re] *n* M cold

ragazza [ra•GAH•tsa] *n* F girl;
girlfriend; da ragazza\ *adj*
juvenile; girlish

ragazza che fa tappezzeria
[ra•GAH•tsa keh FAH
TAP•pe•TSE•REE•a] *n* F
wallflower

ragazzino; ragazzina
[RA•GATS•ee•no];
[RA•GATS•ee•na] *n* MF kid

ragazzo [ra•GAHT•so] *n* M
boy; da ragazzo\ *adj* juvenile;
boyish

raggi x [rah•DJI•eeks] *n* M
X-ray

raggiante [radj•AHN•te] *adj*
radiant

raggio [RAH•djo] *n* M radius;
ray; spoke

raggrinzito; raggrinzita
[rag•GRIN•TSEE•to];
[rag•GRIN•TSEE•ta] *adj* MF
shrunk

ragionamento
[RA•djo•na•MEHN•to] *n* M
reasoning

ragione [ra•DJOH•ne] *n* F
reason

ragionevole
[RA•djo•NEH•vole] *adj*
reasonable; rationale; thinking

ragionevolmente
[RA•djo•ne•vol•MEHN•te]
adv reasonably

ragliare [ra•LYAH•re] *vi* bray

ragnatela [RA•nya•TEH•la] *n*
F cobweb; web

ragno [RAHN•yo] *n* M spider

raion [RAH•yon] *n* M rayon

rallegrare [RAL•le•GRAH•re]
vt cheer; cheer up

rallegrarsi [RAL•le•GRAHR•si]
vi rejoice

ramanzina [RA•man•TSEE•na]
n F scolding

rame [RAH•me] *n* M copper

rammendare
[RAM•men•DAH•re] *vt* darn

ramo [RAH•mo] *n* M branch;
limb

rampicante
[RAM•pi•KAHN•te] *n* M vine

rancido; rancida
[RAHN•TSHI•do];
[RAHN•TSHI•da] *adj* MF
rancid

rancore [ran•KOH•re] *n* M
rancor

ranocchio [ra•NOHK•kyo] *n* M
frog

rapa [RAH•pa] *n* F turnip

rapidamente
[RA•pi•da•MEHN•te] *adv*
quickly; speedily

rapiditá [RA•pi•DI•tah] *n* F
quickness; swiftness

rapido; rapida [rah•PI•do];
[rah•PI•da] *adj* MF rapid;
speedy; swift

rapimento [RA•pi•MEHN•to] *n*
M kidnaping

rapina a mano armata
[RA•pee•NA ah MAH•no
ar•MAH•ta] *n* F holdup

rapire [ra•PEE•re] *vt* abduct;
kidnap; ravish

rapitore [RA•pi•TOH•re] *n* M
kidnapper

rapporto [rap•POHR•to] *n* M
intercourse; ratio; relationship;
statement

rapprendere
[RAP•prehn•de•re] *vt* curdle

rappresaglia [RAP•pre•ZA•lya]
n F retaliation

rappresentare
[RAP•pre•SEN•TAH•re] *vt*
depict; embody; represent

rappresentazione
[RAP•pre•ZEN•tat•SYOH•ne]
n F performance; representation

raramente [RA•ra•MEHN•te]
adv seldom

raritá [ra•RITAH] *n* F rarity

raro [RAH•ro]; [RAH•ra] *adj*
MF rare

raschiare [RAS•KYAH•re] *vt*
scrape

raschietto [ras•KYEHT•to] *n* M
scraper

rasoio [ra•ZOH•yo] *n* M razor

raspa [RAHS•pa] *n* F rasp

rassegnazione
[RAS•se•nya•TSYOH•ne] *n* F
resignation

rastrelliera [RAS•trl•LYEH•ra]
n F rack

ratto [RAHT•to] *n* M rat

rattristare [RAT•tris•TAH•re]
vt sadden

rauco; rauca [RAH•uko];
[RAH•uka] *adj* MF hoarse

ravanello [RA•va•NEHL•lo] *n*
M radish

ravvivare [RAV•vi•VAH•re] *vt*
liven

razionale [RA•tsyo•NAH•le]
adj rational

razza [RAH•tsa] *n* F race;
breed; pedigree; *adj* de razza\
pedigreed

razzo [RAH•tso] *n* M flare;
rocket

re [reh] *n* M king

reagire [RE•ad•JEE•re] *vi* react

realismo [RE•al•EEZ•mo] *n* M
realism

realista [RE•alees•TA] *n* MF
realist

realistico; realistica
[re•ALEES•ti•ko];
[re•ALEES•ti•ka] *adj* MF
realistic; lifelike

realizzare [RE•ali•DSAH•re] *vt*
accomplish

realtá [re•ALTAH] *n* F reality

reame [re•AH•me] *n* M
kingdom

reazionario; reazionaria
[RE•at•syo•NAH•ryo];
[RE•at•syo•NAH•rya] *adj n*
MF reactionary

reazione [RE•at•SYOH•ne] *n* F
reaction

reazione sfavorevole
[RE•atsyoh•NE
SFAVO•reh•VO•le] *n* F
backlash

recedere [re•TSEH•dere] *vi*
recede

recensione
[re•TSHEN•TSYOH•ne] *n* F
review

recente [re•TSHEHN•te] *adj*
recent

recidere [re•TSHEE•de•re] *vt*
sever

**recinto per animali da
macello** [re•TSHEEN•to
PEHR AN•i•MAH•li DAH
MA•TSHEHL•lo] *n* M
stockyards

reciprocare
[RE•tshi•pro•KAH•re] *vt*
reciprocate

reciproco; reciproca
[RE•tshi•PRO•ko];
[RE•tshi•PRO•ka] *adj* MF
reciprocal; mutual

recitare [RE•tshi•TAH•re] *vt*
recite

recluso; reclusa [re•KLUH•zo];
[re•KLUH•za] *adj* MF recluse

reclutare [RE•klu•TAH•re] *vt*
recruit

recuperare [RE•ku•pe•RAH•re]
vt regain

redattore [RE•dat•TOH•re] *n*
M editor

redazione (di)
[DI•re•DAH•TSYOH•ne] *adj*
editorial

redentore [RE•den•TOH•re] *n*
M redeemer

redenzione
[re•DEN•TSYOH•ne] *n* F
redemption

redimere [re•DEE•ME•re] *vt*
reclaim; redeem

referenza [RE•fe•REHN•tsa] *n*
F reference

refrigeramento
[RE•fri•DJE•ra•MEHN•to] *n*
M refrigeration

refutare [RE•fu•TAH•re] *vt*
refute

regale [re•GAH•le] *adj* regal

regalo [re•GAH•lo] *n* M gift;
present

reggimento [redji•MEHN•to] *n*
M regiment

reggiseno [REH•dji•SEH•no] *n*
M bra

regime [re•DJEE•me] *n* M
regime

regina [re•DJEE•na] *n* F queen

regione [re•DJOH•ne] *n* F
region

registro [re•DJIS•tro] *n* M
register

regno [REH•nyo] *n* M realm;
reign

regola [REH•gola] *n* F canon

regolamento
[RE•go•la•MEHN•to] *n* M
regulation

regolare [RE•go•LAH•re] *adj*
regular; regulate

regolarmente
[RE•go•lar•MEHN•te] *adv*
regularly

reietto; reietta [re•YEHT•to];
[re•yeht•ta] *n* MF outcast

reiterare [RE•it•er•AH•re] *vt*
reiterate

relazione [RE•lat•SYOH•ne] *n*
F relation

relazione amorosa
[RE•la•TSYOH•ne
amo•ROH•za] *n* F love affair

relegare [re•LEGAH•re] *vt*
confine

religione [RE•li•DJOH•ne] *n* F
religion

religioso; religiosa
[RE•li•DJOH•zo];
[RE•li•DJOH•za] *adj* MF
religious

reliquiario
[RE•li•KWYAH•ryo] *n* M
shrine; reliquary

relitto [re•LEET•to] *n* M wreck

reminiscenza
[RE•mi•ni•SHEHN•tsa] *n* F
reminiscence

remisssione
[RE•mis•SYOH•ne] *n* F
remission

remo [REH•mo] *n* M oar

remoto; remota [re•MOH•to];
[re•MOH•ta] *adj* MF remote

rendere [REHN•dere] *vt* render

rendere perplesso
[REHN•dere per•PLEHS•so]
vt perplex

rene [REH•ne] *n* M kidney

renna [REHN•na] *n* F reindeer

reparto [re•PAHR•to] *n* M
department

replica [reh•PLI•ka] *n* F replica

reprimere [RE•pree•ME•re] *vt*
quell; repress; subdue

repubblica [RE•pub•BLI•ka] *n*
F republic

repubblicano; repubblicana
[RE•pub•bli•KAH•no];
[RE•pub•bli•KAH•na] *adj* MF
republican

reputazione
[RE•pu•tat•SYOH•ne] *n* F
reputation; repute

requisito primo
[RE•kwi•SEE•to PREE•mo] *n*
M prerequisite

residenza [RE•zi•DEHN•tsa] *n*
F residence

residuo [re•ZEE•duo] *n* M
residue

resistenza [RE•zi•STEHN•tsa]
n F endurance

resistenza [RE•zis•TEHN•tsa] *n*
F resistance

resistere [RE•sis•TE•re] *vi*
resist; *vt* withstand

respingere [RES•peen•DJE•re]
vt repel; refuse; turn down;
spurn

respirare [RES•pi•RAH•re] *vt*
breathe

respiro [res•PEE•roh] *n* M
breath

responsabile
[RES•pon•SAH•BI•le] *adj*
liable; responsible

responsabilitá
[RES•pon•SA•BEE•li•TAY] *n*
F liability; responsibility

restaurare [RES•tau•RAH•re]
vt restore

restauro [RES•TOU•ro] *n* M
restoration

resti [REHS•ti] *npl* M remains

restituzione
~[RES•ti•tut•SYOH•ne] *n* F
restitution

resto [REHS•to] *n* M remainder

restringere
[res•TREEN•DJE•re] *vt* shrink

restringimento
[RES•trin•dji•MEHN•to] *n* M
shrinkage

restrizione
[RES•tri•TSYOH•ne] *n* F
limitation; restriction

retaggio [re•TAH•djo] *n* M
heritage; legacy

rete [REH•te] *n* F net; network;
mesh

reticente [RE•ti•TSHEHN•te]
adj secretive

retorica [RE•toh•RI•ka] *n* F
rhetoric

retro [REH•tro] *n* M back

retroattivo; retroattiva
[RE•troat•TEE•vo];
[RE•troat•TEE•va] *adj* MF
retroactive

retrospettiva
[REH•tro•SPET•tee•va] *n* F
flashback

retta [REHT•ta] *n* F tuition

rettangolo [RET•tahn•GO•lo] *n*
M rectangle

rettificare [RET•ti•fi•KAH•re]
vt rectify

rettile [REHT•tile] *n adj* reptile

rettitudine [RET•ti•TUH•di•ne]
n F righteousness

retto; retta [REHT•to];
[REHT•ta] *adj* MF righteous

rettore [ret•TOH•re] *n* M rector

reumatismo
[REU•mat•EEZ•mo] *n* M
rheumatism

reverendo; reverenda
[RE•ve•REHN•do];
[RE•ve•REHN•da] *adj* MF
reverend

revisionare
[RE•vi•SYO•NAH•re] *vt*
overhaul

revisione [RE•vi•SYONE] *n* F
revision

revocare [RE•vo•KAH•re] *vt*
revoke

riacaduta [RI•ka•DUH•ta] *n* F
relapse

riapparire [RI•ap•pa•REE•re] *vi*
reappear

riaprire [ri•APREE•re] *vt*
reopen

riassestare [RI•as•ses•TAH•re]
vt readjust

riassicurare
[RI•as•si•KU•RAH•re] *vt*
reassure

ribelle [ri•BEHL•le] *n adj* rebel;
adj rebellious; wayward

ribellione [ri•BEL•LYOH•ne] *n*
F rebellion

ribes [REE•bes] *n* M currant

ribollire [RI•bol•LEE•re] *vi*
seethe; bubble

ricambio 1 [ri•KAHM•byo] *n*
M refill

ricambio 2 [ri•KAHM•byo] *adj*
duplicate

ricamo [ri•KAH•mo] *n* M
embroidery

ricattare [ri•KAT•TAH•re] *vt*
blackmail

ricchezza [rik•KEH•tsa] *n* F
wealth

riccio [ree•TSHO] *n* M
hedgehog

ricciolo [ree•TSHO•lo] *n* M curl

ricciuto; ricciuta [rit•SHUH•to];
[rit•SHUH•ta] *adj* curly

ricco; ricca [REEK•ko];
[REEK•ka] *adj* rich; wealthy

ricerca [ri•TSHEHR•ka] *n* F
quest; research

ricetta [ri•TSHET•ta] *n* F
prescription; recipe

ricettacolo [ri•TSHET•tah•kolo]
n M receptacle

ricevere [ri•TSHEH•VE•re] *vt*
receive

ricevimento
[RI•tshe•vi•MEHN•to] *n* M
reception

ricevimento da the
[RI•tshe•vi•MEHN•to DAH
teh] *n* M tea party

ricevitore [RI•tshe•VI•TOH•re]
n M receiver (telephone)

ricevuta [RI•tshe•VUH•ta] *n* F
receipt

richiamare [RI•kya•MAH•re] *vt*
recall

richiedere [RI•kyeh•DE•re] *vt*
require

richiesta [ri•KYEHS•ta] *n* F
request

ricognizione
[RI•ko•nit•SYOH•ne] *n* F
reconnaissance

ricompensa [RI•kom•PEHN•sa]
n F award; premium;
recompense; reward;
gratification

riconciiare [RI•kon•TSHI•lyare]
vt reconcile

riconciliazione
[RI•kon•TSHI•lya•TSYOH•ne]
n F reconciliation

ricongiungere
[RI•kon•DJUHN•DJE•re] *vt*
rejoin

riconoscere
[RI•ko•noh•SHE•re] *vt*
recognize

riconoscimento
[RI•ko•no•SHI•MEHN•to] *n*
M identification; recognition

riconsiderare
[RI•kon•SUDE•RAH•re] *vt*
reconsider

ricontare [RI•kon•TAH•re] *vt*
recount

ricoprire [RI•ko•PREE•re] *vt*
coat

ricordare [RI•kor•DAH•re] *vt*
recollect; remember; *vi* remind

ricordo [RI•KOR•do] *n* M
souvenir

ricorrere [RI•kohr•RE•re] *vi*
recur; resort

ricorso [ri•KOHR•so] *n* M
recourse

ricostruire [ri•KOS•tru•EE•re]
vt rebuild; reconstruct

ricoverato; ricoverata
[RI•ko•ve•RAH•to];
[RI•ko•ve•RAH•ta] *n* MF
inmate

ridacchiare [RI•dak•KYAH•re]
vi chuckle

ridere [REE•dere] *vi* laugh

ridicolo [RI•dee•KO•lo] *n* M
ridicule

ridicolo; ridicola
[RI•dee•KO•lo];
[RI•dee•KO•la] *adj* MF
ludicrous; ridiculous

ridurre [ri•DUHR•re] *vt* curtail;
reduce

ridurre ai minimi termini
[RI•duhr•RE ahi MEE•ni•MI
tehr•MI•ni] *vt* minimize

riempire [RI•em•PEE•re] *vt* fill

rientrare [RI•en•TRAH•re] *vi*
re-enter

riesaminare
[RI•eza•MI•NAH•re] *vt* revise

riferire [RI•fe•REE•re] *vt* relate

rifiutare [RI•fyu•TAH•re] *vt*
refuse; decline; reject

rifiuti [RIFIU•ti] *n* F garbage;
npl M litter; rubbish; M trash;
waste

rifiuto [ri•FYUH•to] *n* M
refusal

riflessione [RI•fles•SYOH•ne] *n*
F reflection

riflessivo; riflessiva
[RI•fles•SEE•vo];
[RI•fles•SEE•va] *adj* MF
reflexive

riflettere [RI•fleht•TERE] *vi*
ponder; reflect

riflettore [RI•flet•TOH•re] *n* M
floodlight

riflusso [RI•fluhs•SO] *n* M ebb

riforma [ri•FOHR•ma] *n* F
reform

rifornire [RI•for•NEE•re] *vt*
replenish

rifrazione [RI•fra•TSYOH•ne]
n F refraction

rifugio [ri•FUH•djo] *n* M
haven; refuge

rigidezza [RI•dji•DEH•tsa] *n* F
stiffness

rigiditá [RI•dji•DIT•ah] *n* F
rigidity

rigido; rigida [ree•DJI•do];
[ree•DJI•da] *adj* MF rigid;
stiff

rigore [ri•GOH•re] *n* M rigor

riguardoso; riguardosa
[ri•GUAR•doh•SO];
[ri•GUAR•doh•SA] *adj*
considerate

rilasciare [RI•la•SHAH•re] *vt*
release

rilassamento
[RI•las•sa•MEHN•to] *n* M
relaxation

rilassare [RI•las•SAH•re] *vt*
relax

rilevante [RI•le•VAHN•te] *adj*
noticeable; outstanding;
relevant

rilucere [RI•luh•TSHERE] *vi*
glitter

riluttante [RI•lut•TAHN•te] *adj*
reluctant; unwilling

riluttanza [RI•lut•TAHN•tsa] *n*
F unwillingness

rima [REE•ma] *n* F rhyme

rimanere [RI•ma•NEH•re] *vi*
remain; stay

rimbalzare [RIM•bal•TSAH•re]
vi vt bounce

rimbalzo [RIM•BAHL•tso] *n* M
bounce

rimborsare [RIM•bor•SAH•re]
vt reimburse; refund

rimborso [rim•BOHR•so] *n* M
refund

rimedio [ri•MEH•dyo] *n* M
remedy

rimettere [ri•MEHT•TE•re] *vt*
remit

rimorchio [ri•MOHR•kyo] *n* M
towing; trailer

rimorso [ri•MOHR•so] *n* M
qualm; remorse

rimosso; rimossa
[ri•MOHS•so]; [ri•MOHS•sa]
adj MF removed

rimozione [RI•mo•TSYOH•ne]
n F removal

rimpiangere
[RIM•pyahn•DJE•re] *vt* regret

rimpianto [rim•PYAHN•to] *n*
M regret

rimpinzarsi
[RIM•pin•ZAHR•si] *vi* guzzle

rimproverare
[RIM•pro•VE•RAH•re] *vt*
rebuke; reprimand; scold;
upbraid

rimprovero [RIM•proh•VERO]
n M reproof

rimuovere [ri•MUOH•VERE]
vt displace; remove

rinascimento
[RI•na•tshi•MEHN•to] *n* M
renaissance

rinascita [RI•nah•SHI•ta] *n* F
rebirth

rinforzare [RIN•for•TSAH•re]
vt reinforce; strengthen

rinfrescante
[RIN•fres•KAHN•te] *adj*
refreshing

rinfrescare [RIN•fres•KAH•re]
vt freshen; refresh

rinfresco [RIN•FREHS•ko] *n* M
refreshment

ringhiare [rin•GYAH•re] *vi*
growl

ringhiera [rin•GYEH•ra] *n* F
rail

ringiovanire
[RIN•djo•VA•NEE•re] *vt*
rejuvenate

ringraziamento
[RIN•gra•TSYA•MEHN•to] *n*
M thanksgiving

ringraziare
[RIN•gra•TSYAH•re] *vt* thank

rinnegare [RIN•ne•GAH•re] *vt*
disavow; disown

rinnovamento
[RIN•no•va•MEHN•to] *n* M
renewal

rinnovare [RIN•no•VAH•re] *vt*
renew; renovate

rinoceronte
[RI•no•TSHE•ROHN•te] *n* M
rhinoceros

rinomanza [RI•no•MAHN•tsa]
n F renown

rinomato; rinomata
[RI•no•MAH•to];
[RI•no•MAH•ta] *adj* MF
famed

rintanarsi [RIN•ta•NAHR•si] *vi*
burrow

rintoccare [RIN•tok•KAH•re] *vi*
toll

rintracciare
[RIN•trat•SHAH•re] *vt*
retrieve

rinunciare: rinunziare
[RI•nun•TSHAH•re (ah)] *vi*
waive

rinvigorente
[RIN•vi•GOR•EHN•te] *adj*
invigorating

riordinamento
[RI•or•DI•na•MEHN•to] *n* M
turnover

ripagare [RI•pa•GAH•re] *vt*
repay; redress; repair

riparazione
[RI•pa•RAT•SYOH•ne] *n* F
reparation

ripercussione
[RI•per•KUS•SYOH•ne] *n* F
rebound

ripetere [ri•PEH•tere] *vt* repeat

ripetizione
[RI•pe•tit•SYOH•ne] *n* F
repetition

ripicco [ri•PEEK•ko] *n* M pique

ripido; ripida [REE•PI•do];
[REE•PI•da] *adj* steep

ripiegare [RI•pye•GAH•re] *vt*
tuck

ripieno [ri•PYEH•no] *n* M
filling; stuffing

riporre [ri•POHR•re] *vt* store

riporre male [RI•pohr•RE
MAH•le] *vt* misplace

riposante [RI•po•ZAHN•te] *adj*
restful

riposarsi [RI•po•ZAHR•si] *vi*
rest

riposo [ri•POH•zo] *n* M repose

riprendere [RI•prehn•DERE] *vt*
recover; resume

riprendersi [RI•prehn•DER•si]
vi rally

ripristinare [RI•pris•ti•NAH•re]
vt remodel

ripristino [ri•PREES•TI•no] *n*
M revival

riprodurre [ri•PRO•DUHR•re]
vt reproduce

riproduzione
[ri•PRO•dut•SYOH•ne] *n* F
reproduction

ripudiare [ri•PU•DYAH•re] *vt*
repudiate

ripugnante [ri•PU•NYAH•te]
adj repugnant

ripugnanza
[ri•PU•NYAH•tsa] *n* F
distaste

ripulsa [ri•PUHL•sa] *n* F
repulse

ripulsivo; ripulsiva
[RI•pul•SEE•vo];
[RI•pul•SEE•va] *adj* MF
repulsive

risarcire [RI•zahr•TSHI•re] *vt*
recoup

risata [ri•ZAH•ta] *n* F guffaw;
laughter; laugh

riscaldamento
[ris•KAL•da•MEHN•to] *n* M
heating

riscatto [ri•KAHT•to] *n* F
ransom

rischio [REES•kyo] *n* M risk

riscontrare [RIS•kon•TRAH•re]
vt tally

riscrivere [RIS•kree•VERE] *vt*
rewrite

risentirsi [RI•sen•TEER•si] *vi*
resent

riserva [ri•SEHR•va] *n* F
reserve

risiedere [RI•syeh•DE•re] *vi*
reside

riso [REE•zo] *n* M rice

risolutezza [RI•so•lu•TEH•tsa]
n F determination

risoluto; risoluta
[RI•so•LUH•to];
[RI•so•LUH•ta] *adj* MF
resolute

risoluzione
[RI•solu•TSYOH•ne] *n* F
resolution; settlement

risolvere [RI•sohl•VERE] *vt*
solve

risonante [RI•so•NAHN•te] *adj*
resonant

risonanza [RI•so•NAHN•tsa] *n*
F resonance

risorsa [ri•SOHR•sa] *n* F
resource

risparmiare
[ris•PAR•MYAH•re] *vt* spare

risparmio [RIS•pahr•MYO] *n*
M thrift

rispettabile
[RIS•pet•TAH•BI•le] *adj*
reputable; respectable

rispettivo; rispettiva
[RIS•pet•TEE•vo];
[RIS•pet•TEE•va] *adj* MF
respective

rispetto [ris•PEHT•to] *n* M
respect; reverence

rispettoso; rispettosa
[RIS•pet•TOH•zo];
[RIS•pet•TOOH•za] *adj* MF
respectful; reverent

rispondere [ris•POHN•dere] *vi*
answer; respond; reply

risposta [ris•POHS•ta] *n* F
reply; response; retort

rissa [REES•sah] *n* F brawl

ristabilire [RIS•ta•BI•LEE•re]
vt re-establish

ristabilirsi [RIS•ta•BI•LEER•si]
vi recuperate

ristorante [RIS•to•RAHN•te] *n*
M restaurant; diner

risucchio 1 [ri•SUHK•kyo] *n* M
suction

risucchio 2 [ri•SUH•kyo] *n* M
undertow

risultante [RI•zul•TAHN•te]
adj ensuing

risultati (elettorali)
[RI•zul•TAH•ti
(ELT•to•RAH•li)] *n* M returns
(election)

risultato [RI•zul•TAH•to] *n* M
outcome; result

risuscitare [RI•su•SHI•TAH•re]
vt resuscitate

ritardardato; ritardata
[ri•TAHR•DATO];
[ri•TAHR•DATA] *adj* MF
backward

ritardare [RI•tar•DAH•re] *vt*
retard

ritardo [RI•TAHR•do] *n* M
delay

ritirare [RI•ti•RAH•re] *vt* retire;
withdraw

ritirarsi [RI•ti•RAHR•si] *vi*
cower; retreat; duck; *n* F
retreat

ritirata [RI•ti•RAH•ta] *n* F
withdrawal; retreat

ritmo [REET•mo] *n* M rhythm

rito [REE•to] *n* M rite

ritorcere [RI•tohr•TSHE•re] *vt*
twist

ritornare [RI•tor•NAH•re] *vi*
revert

ritornello [RI•tor•NEHL•lo] *n*
M refrain

ritorno [RI•TOHR•no] *n* M
comeback; return

ritrarre [ri•TRAHR•re] *vt* retract

ritratto [ri•TRAHT•to] *n* M
portrait

ritroso; ritrosa [ri•TROH•zo];
[ri•TROH•za] *adj* MF coy

ritto; ritta [REET•to];
[REET•ta] *adj* upright

rituale [ri•TUAH•le] *adj* ritual

riunione [RIU•NYOH•ne] *n* F
gathering; assembly; reunion

riunire [RI•un•EE•re] *vt*
assemble; reunite

riuscire [ryu•SHEE•ree] *vi*
succeed

rivale [ri•VAH•le] *n* MF rival

rivalitá [RI•va•LIT•ah] *n* F
rivalry

rivelare [RI•ve•LAH•re] *vt*
reveal

rivelatore; rivelatrice
[RI•ve•la•TOH•re];
[RI•ve•la•TREE•tshe] *adj* MF
telltale

rivelazione
[RI•ve•lat•ZYOH•ne] *n* F
disclosure; revelation

rivendicare
[RI•ven•DI•KAH•re] *vt*
vindicate

riverbero [RI•vehr•BERO] *n* M
glare

riverire [RI•ve•REE•re] *vt*
revere

rivestitura [RI•ves•TI•TUH•ra]
n F siding

rivista [ri•VEE•sta] *n* F
magazine

rivista scandalistica
[RI•VEES•ta
SKAN•da•LEES•ti•ka] *n* F
tabloid

rivolta [ri•VOHL•ta] *n* F
uprising

rivoltare [RI•vol•TAH•re] *vt*
revolt

rivoluzionario; rivoluzionaria
[RI•vo•lut•SYO•NAH•ryo];
[RI•vo•LUTSYO•NAH•rya]
adj MF revolutionary

rivoluzione
[RI•vo•LUT•SYOH•ne] *n* F
revolution

robusto; robusta
[ro•BUHS•to]; [ro•BUHS•ta]
adj MF hardy; husky; robust;
stalwart; sturdy

roccaforte [ROK•ka•FOHR•te]
n F stronghold

roccia [ROH•tsha] *n* F rock

roccioso; rocciosa
[ro•TSHOH•zo];
[ro•TSHO•za] *adj* rocky

rodere [ROH•dere] *vt* gnaw

romano; romana
[ro•MAH•no]; [ro•MAH•na]
adj MF Roman

romanticismo
[RO•man•ti•TSHEEZ•mo] *n*
M romanticism

romantico; romantica
[ro•MAHN•ti•ko];
[ro•MAHN•ti•ka] *adj* MF
romantic; *n* MF romanticist

romanziere
[ro•MAHN•TSYEH•re] *n* M
novelist

romanzo [ro•MAHN•tso] *n* M
novel

rombare [rom•BAH•re] *vi*
boom; whir

rombo [ROHM•bo] *n* M
rumble; boom

romboidale
[ROM•boi•DAH•le] *adj*
diamond-shaped

rompere [rohm•PE•re] *vt* break;
rupture

rondine [rohn•DI•ne] *n* F
swallow

ronzare intorno
[RON•tsah•RE•in•TOHR•no]
vi hover

ronzio [rohn•TSEE•oh] *n* M
buzz (of insect); *n* M whiz

rosa [ROH•za] *adj n* MF pink;
n F rose

rosario [ro•ZAH•ryo] *n* M
rosary

roseo; rosea [ROH•zeo];
[ROH•zea] *adj* MF rosy

rospo [ROHS•po] *n* M toad

rossetto [ros•SEHT•to] *n* M
lipstick

rosso d'uovo
[ROHS•so•DUOH•vo] *n* M
yolk

rosso; rossa [ROHS•so];
[ROHS•sa] *adj* MF red

rotante [ROTAHN•te] *adj*
rotary

rotare [ro•TAH•re] *vi* revolve

rotazione [ro•TAT•SYOH•ne]
n F rotation

roteare [ro•TEAH•re] *vt* spin

rotolarsi [RO•to•LAHR•si] *vi*
wallow

rotolo [ROH•tolo] *n* M roll

rotolo di pergamena
[ROH•to•lo dee
PER•ga•MEH•na] *n* M scroll

rotondo; rotonda
[ro•TOHN•do]; [ro•TOHN•da]
adj MF round

rottura [rot•TUH•ra] *n* F break

rotula [roh•TULA] *n* F kneecap

rovesciare [RO•ve•SHAH•re] *vt*
overthrow; reverse; *vt* tip

rovina [ro•VEE•na] *n* F havoc

rovinare [RO•vi•NAH•re] *vt*
ruin; spoil

rovinoso; rovinosa
[RO•vi•NOH•zo];
[RO•vi•NOH•za] *adj* MF
wasteful

rozzo; rozza [ROH•tso];
[ROH•tsa] *adj* MF crude;
uncouth; uneducated

rubacchiare
[RU•bak•KYAH•re] *vt* swipe
rubare [ru•BAH•re] *vt* steal
rubinetto [RU•bi•NEHT•to] *n*
M faucet; spigot; tap
rubino [ru•BEE•no] *n* M ruby
ruga [RUH•ga] *n* F wrinkle
ruggine [RUH•djne] *n* F rust
rugginoso; rugginosa
[RU•dji•NOH•zo];
[RU•dji•NOH•za] *adj* MF rusty
ruggire [ru•DJEE•re] *vi* roar
rugiada [ru•DJAH•da] *n* F dew
rum [RUH•m] *n* M rum
ruminare [RU•mi•NAH•re] *vi*
ruminate
rumore [ru•MOH•re] *n* M din;
noise
rumoroso; rumorosa
[RU•mo•ROH•zo];

[RU•mo•ROH•za] *adj* MF
boisterous; noisy
ruolo [RUOH•lo] *n* M role
ruota [RUOH•ta] *n* F wheel
ruota di scorta
[RUOH•ta•dee•SKOHR•ta] *n*
F tire (spare)
ruotare [ruo•TAH•re] *vi* gyrate;
swivel
rurale [ru•RAH•le] *adj* rural
ruscello [ru•SHEHL•lo] *n* M
brook; creek
Russia [RUHS•sya] *n* F Russia
russo; russa [RUHS•so];
[RUHS•sa] *adj* Russian
rustico; rustica [RUHS•ti•ko];
[RUHS•ti•ka] *adj* MF rustic
ruvido; ruvida [ruh•VI•do];
[ruh•VI•da] *adj* MF harsh;
rough; rugged

S

sabato [SAH•BA•to] *n* M
Sabbath
sabbie mobili
[SAHB•bye•MOH•bi•li] *npl* F
quicksand
sabotaggio [SA•bo•TAH•djo]
n M sabotage
saccentone; saccentona
[SATSHEN•toh•ne];
[SATSHEN•toh•na] *n* MF
know-it-all
saccentone; saccentona
[sa•TSHEN•TOH•ne];
[sa•TSHEN•TOH•na] *n* MF
wiseacre

saccheggiare
[SAK•ke•DJAH•re] *vt*
plunder
sacco [SAHK•ko] *n* M sack
sacerdozio
[SA•tsher•DOH•tsyo] *n* M
priesthood
sacramento [SA•kra•MEHN•to]
n M sacrament
sacrestano [SA•kres•TAH•no]
n M sexton
sacrificio [SA•kri•FEE•tsho] *n*
M sacrifice
sacro; sacra [SAH•kro];
[SAH•kra] *adj* MF sacred

sadico; sadica [SAH•DI•ko]; [SAH•DI•ka] *adj* MF sadistic

sagace [SA•gah•TSHE] *adj* sagacious; shrewd

sagacia [SA•gah•TSHA] *n* F sagacity

saggezza [sa•DJEH•tsa] *n* F wisdom

saggio [SAH•djo] *n* M essay; -o -a\ *adj* wise; sage

saggistica [SADJEE•STI•ka] *n* F nonfiction

sagrestia [sa•GRES•TEE•a] *n* F vestry

sala [SAH•la] *n* F hall

sala d'aspetto [SAH•la•DAS•PEHT•to] *n* F lounge

sala d'attesa [SAH•la•DAT•TEH•za] *n* F waiting-room

sala da pranzo [SAH•la•DAH•PRAHN•tso] *n* F dining room

salassare [SA•las•SAH•re] *vt* bleed

saldamente [SAL•da•MEHN•te] *adv* steadily

saldare [sal•DAH•re] *vt* solder; weld

saldo; salda [SAHL•do]; [SAHL•da] *adj* MF steady

salice [sah•LIT•she] *n* M willow

saliscendi [SAH•li•SHEHN•di] *n* M latch

salita [sa•LEE•ta] *n* F upgrade

salmo [SAHL•mo] *n* M psalm

salmodiare [SAL•mo•DIAH•re] *vi* chant

salotto [sa•LOHT•to] *n* M parlor; sitting-room

salsa [SAHL•sa] *n* F dressing; gravy

salsa Rubra [SAHL•sa•RUH•bra] *n* F ketchup

salsiccia [sal•SEE•tsha] *n* F hot dog

saltare [sal•TAH•re] *vt* skip

saltellare [SAL•tel•LAH•re] *vi* frisk; *vt* hop

saltimbanco [SAL•tim•BAHN•ko] *n* M tumbler

salto [SAHL•to] *n* M jump

salumeria [SA•lu•ME•REE•a] *n* F delicatessen

salutare1 [SA•lu•TAH•re] *vt* greet

salutare 2 [SA•lu•TAH•re] *adj* wholesome

salute [sa•LUH•te] *n* F cheers; health

saluto [sa•LUH•to] *n* M greeting

salvataggio [SAL•va•TAH•djo] *n* M rescue

salvia [SAHL•vya] *n* F sage (bot.)

sangue [SAHN•gueh] *n* M blood; gore; a sangue freddo\ *adv* cold-blooded

sanguinare [SAN•gui•NAH•re] *vi* bleed

sanguisuga [SAN•gui•SUH•ga] *n* F leech

sano; sana [SAH•no]; [SAH•na] *adj* MF healthy

santitá [SAN•ti•TAH] *n* F holiness

santo; santa [SAHN•to]; [SAHN•ta] *adj* holy; saintly; *n* MF saint

sanzionare [SAN•tsyo•NAH•re] *vt* ratify

sapere [sa•PEH•re] *vt* know

sapone [sa•POH•ne] *n* M soap

sapore [sa•POH•re] *n* M flavor; taste

saprofago; saprofaga [SA•proh•FA•go]; [SA•proh•FA•ga] *n* MF scavenger

sarta [SAHR•ta] *n* F seamstress

sarto [SAHR•to] *n* M tailor

sassolino [SAS•so•LEE•no] *n* M pebble

satira [SA•tira] *n* F lampoon

saturazione [SA•tu•ra•TSYOH•ne] *n* F glut

sbadato; sbadato [ZBA•DAH•to]; [ZBA•DAH•ta] *adj* MF careless

sbadiglio [zba•DEE•lyo] *n* M yawn

sbagliare l'ortografia [zba•LYAH•re LOR•to•gra•FEE•a] *vi* misspell; *vt* miscount

sbagliato; sbagliata [zba•LYAH•to]; [zba•LYAH•ta] *adj* MF wrong

sbaglio di stampa [sbah•LYO di STAHM•pa] *n* M misprint

sbalordire [ZBA•lor•DEE•re] *vt* dazzle

sbarazzare [ZBA•rat•SAH•re] *vt* rid

sbattere [ZBAHT•tere] *vt* slam

sbavare [sba•VAH•re] *vi* slobber

sbiadire [zbya•DEE•re] *vt* fade

sbiancare [ZBYAN•KAH•re] *vt* whiten

sbieco [SBIEH•ko] *n* M bias

sbilanciato; sbilanciata [ZBI•lan•TSHAH•to]; [ZBI•lan•TSHAH•ta] *adj* unbalanced

sbirciare [sbir•TSHAH•re] *vt* peek

sbocco [ZBOHK•ko] *n* M outlet

sbottonare [ZBOT•to•NAH•re] *vt* unbutton

sbraitare [SBRA•it•AH•re] *vi* rant

sbriciolare [SBRI•tsho•LAH•re] *vt* crumble

sbrindellato; sbrindellata [SBRIN•del•LAH•to]; [SBRIN•del•LAH•ta] *adj* MF tattered

sbuffare [zbuf•FAH•re] *v* puff

scacchi [SKAH•ki] *npl* M chess

scadente [ska•DEHN•te] *adj* shoddy

scadenza [ska•DEHN•tsa] *n* F deadline

scadere [ska•DEH•re] *vi* expire

scafo [SKAH•fo] *n* M hull (of a ship)

scala [SKAH•la] *n* F stair

scala a pioli [SKAH•la•ah•PYOH•li] *n* F ladder; stepladder

scala mobile [SKAH•la•MOH•bile] *n* F escalator

scalare [ska•LAH•re] *vt* escalate

scalpello [skal•PEHL•lo] *n* M
chisel

scaltrezza [skal•TREH•tsa] *n* F
guile

scaltro; scaltra [SKAHL•tro];
[SKAHL•tra] *adj* wily

scalzo; scalza
[SKAHL•tso];[SKAHL•tsa]
adj MF barefoot

scambiare [skam•BYAH•re] *vt*
swap

scambiare [skam•BYAH•re] *vt*
switch; interchange

scambio [SKAHM•byo] *n* M
exchange; interchange

scampagnata
[SKAM•pan•YAH•ta] *n* F
picnic

scampanare
[SKAM•pa•NAH•re] *vt* peal;
vi chime

scampanio
[SKAM•pa•NEE•oh] *n* M
chime

scampolo [SKAHM•po•lo] *n* M
remnant

scapolo [SKAH•po•lo] *n* M
bachelor

scappamente
[SKAP•pa•MEHN•to] *n* M
exhaust

scappare [skap•PAH•re] *vi* get
away

scappatella
[SKAP•pa•TEHL•la] *n* F
caper

scappatoia [SKAP•pa•TOH•ya]
n F loophole

scarabeo [SKA•ra•BEH•oh] *n*
M beetle; scarab

scarabocchiare
[SKA•ra•bok•KYAH•re] *vt*
doodle; scrawl

scarafaggio
[SKA•ra•FAH•djyo] *n* M
cockroach

scarica [skah•RI•ka] *n* F volley

scaricare [SKA•ri•KAH•re] *vt*
dump; unload; discharge;
unburden; unwind

scaricarsi [SKA•ri•KAHR•si] *vi*
run-down

scarico [skah•RI•ko] *n* M drain;
overflow

scarlatto; scarlatta
[skar•LAHT•to];
[skar•LAHT•ta] *adj* MF
scarlet

scarpa [SKAHR•pa] *n* F shoe

scarsamente
[SKAR•sa•MEHN•te] *adv*
thinly

scarso; scarsa [SKAHR•so];
[SKAHR•sa] *adj* MF meager;
scarce

scartare [skar•TAH•re] *vt*
discard

scatola [skah•TO•la] *n* F box;
in scatola\ *adj* tinned

scatolone [SKA•to•LOH•ne] *n*
M carton

scatto finale
[SKAHT•to•FINAH•le] *n* M
sprint

scaturire [SKA•tu•REE•re] *vt*
spew

scavare [ska•VAH•re] *vt* dig

scavezzacollo
[SKA•veh•tsa•KOHL•lo] *n*
MF daredevil

scavo [SKAH•vo] *n* M mining

scegliere [SHEH•lye•re] *vt*
choose; select

scelleratezza
[SHEL•le•ra•TEH•tsa] *n* F
villainy

scellerato; scellerata
[SHEL•le•RAH•to];
[SHEL•le•RAH•ta] *n* MF
ruffian; *adj* villainous

scelta [SHEHL•ta] *n* F choice

scena [SHEH•na] *n* F scene

scenario [she•NAH•ryo] *n* M
scenery

sceneggiatura
[SHE•ne•DJA•tuh•ra] *n* F
scenario

scettico; scettica
[SHEHT•ti•ko];
[SHEHT•ti•ka] *adj n* MF
skeptic

scettro [SHEHT•tro] *n* M
scepter

schedario [ske•DAH•ryo] *n* M
file

scheggia [SKEH•djah] *n* F
chip; sliver; splinter

scheggiare [ske•DJAH•re] *vt*
chip

scheletro [skeh•LET•ro] *n* M
skeleton

schema [SKEH•ma] *n* M
scheme

scherma [SKEHR•ma] *n* F
fencing

schermo [SKEHR•mo] *n* M
screen (movies)

schernire [sker•NEE•re] *vt* jeer;
taunt

scherzo [SKEHR•tso] *n* M
banter; jest; joke; practical
joke

schiaccianoci
[SKYAH•sha•NOH•tshi] *n* M
nutcracker

schiacciare [SKYA•TSHAH•re]
vt mash; squash; swat

schiaffeggiare
[SKYAF•fe•DJAH•re] *vt* slap

schiavitú [SKYA•vitu'] *n* F
bondage

schiavo; schiava [SKYAH•vo];
[skyah•va] *n* MF slave

schiena [SKIEH•na] *n* F back
(anat.)

schietto; schietta
[SKYEHT•to]; [skyeht•ta] *adj*
straightforward

schisto [SKEES•to] *n* M schist

schiuma [SKYUH•ma] *n* F
foam; froth; lather; suds

schiumare [skyu•MAH•re] *vt*
skim

schizzare [ski•TSAH•re] *vt*
spatter; splash; squirt

schizzinoso; schizzinosa
[SKI•tsi•NOH•zo];
[SKI•tsi•NOH•za] *adj* MF
fastidious; squeamish

schizzo [SKEE•tso] *n* M sketch

sciabola [shah•BO•la] *n* F saber

sciacallo [sha•KAHL•lo] *n* M
jackal

sciacquare [sha•KWAH•re] *vt*
flush; rinse

scialacquare
[SHA•la•KWAH•re] *vt*
squander; waste

scialbo; scialba [SHAHL•bo];
[SHAHL•ba] *adj* MF homely

scialuppa di salvataggio
[SHA•LUHP•pa di

SAL•va•TAH•djo] *n* F
lifeboat

sciamare [sha•MAH•re] *vi*
swarm

sciare [shi•AH•re] *vi* ski

sciarpa [SHAHR•pa] *n* F scarf

sciattona [shat•TOH•na] *n* F
slattern

scientifico; scientifica
[shen•TEE•FI•ko];
[shen•TEE•FI•ka] *adj* MF
scientific

scienza [SHYEHN•tsa] *n* F
science

scienziato [shen•TSYAH•to] *n*
M scientist

scimmi [SHEEM•ya] *n* F
monkey

scimmione
[SHEEM•mee•OH•nai] *n* M
ape

scimpanzé [shim•PAN•tse'] *n*
M chimpanzee

scintilla [shin•TEEL•la] *n* F
spark

scintillante
[SHIN•til•LAHN•te] *adj*
sparkling

scintillare [SHIN•til•LAH•re] *vi*
glisten; sparkle; twinkle

sciocchezza [shok•KEH•tsa] *n*
F trifle

sciocco; sciocca
[SHYOHK•ko];
[SHYOHK•ka] *n* MF fool *adj*
foolish; silly; absurd

sciogliere [shoh•LYE•re] *vt*
melt; loosen

scioltamente
[SHOL•ta•MEHN•te] *adv*
loosely

scioltezza [shyol•TEH•tsa] *n* F
fluency

sciolto; sciolta [SHOHL•to];
[shohl•ta] *adj* MF loose

scioperante [SHO•per•AHN•te]
n MF striker

sciopero [SHOH•pero] *n* M
strike

sciroppo [shi•ROHP•po] *n* M
syrup

scisma [SHEE•zma] *n* M schism

sciupato; sciupata
[shyu•PAH•to]; [shyu•PAH•ta]
adj disreputable

scivolare [shi•VOLAH•re] *vi*
glide

scivolare [SHI•vo•LAH•re] *vi*
skid; slip

scivolata [SHI•vo•LAH•ta] *n* F
slide

scivolo [shee•VO•lo] *n* M chute

scivoloso; scivolosa
[SHI•vo•LOH•zo];
[SHI•vo•LOH•za] *adj* MF
slippery

scodella [sko•DEHL•la] *n* F
bowl

scogliera [sko•LYEH•ra] *n* F
cliff; reef

scoiattolo [SKO•yaht•TOLO] *n*
M squirrel

scolaro [sko•LAH•ro] *n* M
schoolboy

scolastico; scolastica
[SKO•lahs•TI•ko];
[SKO•lahs•TI•ka] *adj*
scholastic

scolpire [skol•PEE•re] *vt* carve

scolpire nel legno
[skol•PEE•re•NEHL•LEH•nyo]
vt whittle

scommessa [skom•MEHS•sa] *n*
F bet; wager

scommettere
[SKOM•meht•TE•re] *vt* bet

scomodo; scomoda
[SKOH•MO•do];
[SKOH•MO•da] *adj* MF
uncomfortable

scompartimento
[SKOM•par•ti•MEHN•to] *n* M
compartment; division

sconcertante
[SKON•tsher•TAHN•te] *adj*
confusing

sconfinato; sconfinata
[SKON•fi•NAH•to];
[SKON•fi•NAH•ta] *adj*
unbounded

sconfitta [skon•FEET•ta] *n* F
defeat

scontentare
[SKON•ten•TAH•re] *vt*
dissatisfy

sconto [SKOHN•to] *n* M
discount; rebate

scontrare [skon•TRAH•re] *vt*
clash

scontrarsi [skon•TRAHR•si] *vi*
collide (with)

scontro [SKOHN•tro] *n* M
clash

sconvolgere
[SKON•vohl•DJE•re] *vt*
confound; perturb

sconvolgimento
[SKON•vol•dji•MEHN•to] *n*
M upheaval

sconvolto; sconvolta
[SKON•VOHL•to];
[SKON•VOHL•ta] *adj* MF
upset

scopa [SKOH•pa] N F broom

scopare [sko•PAH•re] *vt*
sweep

scoperta [sko•PEHR•ta] *n* F
detection; discovery; find

scoperto; scoperta
[sko•PEHR•to];
[sko•PEHR•ta] *adj* overdrawn

scopo [SKOH•po] *n* M aim;
goal; purpose

scoppiare [skop•PYAH•re] *vt*
burst

scoppio [SKOP•pi•o] *n* M blast;
crash; outbreak

scoppio di tuono [SKOHP•pyo
dee TUOH•no] *n* M
thunderclap

scoprire 1 [sko•PREE•re] *v*
discover; uncover; unearth

scoprire 2 [sko•PREE•re] *vt*
overdraw (an account)

scoprite [sko•PREE•re] *vt*
unveil

scoraggiare [SKO•rad•JAH•re]
vt discourage; dishearten

scorciatoia
[SKOR•tsha•TOHYA] *n* F
shortcut

scoria [SKOH•rya] *n* F slag

scorpione [skor•PYOH•ne] *n* M
scorpion

scorreria [SKOR•re•REE•a] *n* F
raid

scorretto; scorretta
[skor•REHT•to];
[skor•REHT•ta] *adj* MF
improper; incorrect

scorta [SKOHR•ta] *n* F escort

scortese [skor•TEH•ze] *adj*
impolite

scosceso; scoscesa
[sko•SHEH•zo];
[sko•SHEH•za] *adj MF*
uphill

scosiderato; sconsiderata
[skon•SIDE•RAH•to];
[skon•SIDE•RAH•ta] *adj MF*
inconsiderate

scossa [SKOHS•sa] *n F* jolt

scoutismo [SKO•u•TEEZ•mo]
n M scouting

Scozia [SKOH•tsya] *n F*
Scotland

scozzese [SKOTSEH•ze] *n MF*
Scot

scribacchiare
[SKRI•bak•KYAH•re] *vt*
scribble

scrigno [SKREE•nyo] *n M*
casket

scritto [SKREET•to] *n M*
writing

scrittore; scrittrice
[skrit•TOH•re];
[skrit•TREE•tshe] *n MF*
writer

scrittura [skrit•TUH•ra] *n F*
handwriting

Scrittura [skrit•TUH•ra] *n F*
scripture (Biblical)

scrivania [SKRI•va•NEE•a] *n F*
desk

scrivano [skri•VAH•no] *n M*
scribe

scrivere [skree•VE•re] *vt* write

scroccone; scroccona
[skrok•KOH•ne];
[skrok•KOH•na] *n MF*
sponger

scrofa [SKROH•fa] *n F* sow

scrupolo [SKRUH•po•lo] *n M*
scruple

scrupoloso; scrupolosa
[SKRU•po•LOH•zo];
[SKRU•po•LOH•za] *adj MF*
scrupulous

scrutare [skru•TAH•re] *vi* pry;
vt scrutinize

scrutinio [skru•TEE•nyo] *n M*
scrutiny

scudiero [sku•DYEH•ro] *n M*
squire

sculacciare [SKU•lat•SHAH•re]
vt spank

sculacciata [SKU•lat•SHAH•ta]
n F spanking

scultore [skul•TOH•re] *n M*
sculptor

scultura [skul•TUH•ra] *n F*
sculpture

scuola [SKUOH•la] *n F* school

scuola elmentare
[SKWOH•la•ele•MEN•TAH
•re] *n F* grade school

scuola industriale
[SKWOH•la•in•DUS•TRYAH
•le] *n F* trade school

scuotere [SKUOH•te•re] *vt*
rattle

scuro; scura [SKUH•ro];
[skuh•ra] *adj MF* dark;
obscure; gloomy

scurrile [skur•REE•le] *adj*
scurrilous

scusa [SKUH•za] *n F* excuse;
plea

scusarsi [sku•ZAHR•si] *vt*
apologize

scuse (pl) [SKUH•ze] *n F*
apology

scutinio [skru•TEEN•yo] *n M*
ballot

se [seh] *conj* if; whether

sé stesso; sé stessa
[seh•STEHS•so];
[seh•STEHS•sa] *pron* itself;
oneself

seccatura [SEK•ka•TUH•ra] *n*
F nuisance; bother

secchio [SEH•kyo] *n* M bucket;
pail

secchio dei rifiuti
[SEHK•kio•DEHI•ri•FYUH•ti]
n M garbage can

secco; secca [SEHK•ko];
[SEHK•ka] *adj* MF dried

secedere [se•TSHEH•dere] *vi*
secede

secernere [SE•tshehr•NERE] *vt*
secrete

secessione
[SE•tshes•SYOH•ne] *n* F
secession

secludere [se•KLUH•dere] *vi*
seclude

seclusione [se•KLU•ZYOH•ne]
n F seclusion

secolare [SE•ko•LAH•re] *adj*
secular

secolarizzare
[SE•ko•la•RIT•SAH•re] *vt*
secularize

secolo [seh•KO•lo] *n* M century

seconda colazione
[se•KOHN•da
KO•la•TSYOH•ne] *n* F lunch

secondariamente
[SE•kon•DA•rya•MEHN•te]
adv secondly

secondario; secondaria
[SE•ko] *adj* MF secondary

secondo [se•KOHN•do] *prep*
according; -o -a\ *adj* second;

il secondo; la seconda\ *adj*
latter

secrezione [SE•kre•TSYOH•ne]
n F secretion

sedativo [SE•da•TEE•vo] *n* M
sedative

sede [SEH•de] *n* F seat; venue;
office; residence

sedentario; sedentaria
[SE•den•TAH•ryo];
[SE•den•TAH•rya] *adj* MF
sedentary

sedere [se•DEH•re] *vi* sit

sedia [SEH•dya] *n* F chair

sedia a dondolo [SEH•dya ah
DOHN•do•lo] *n* F rocking
chair

sedia a rotelle [SEH•dya ah
RO•TEHL•le] *n* F wheelchair

sedia girevole [SEH•dya
dji•REH•vole] *n* F swivel
chair

sedicente [SE•di•TSHEHN•te]
adj would-be; so-called

sedicesimo; sedicesima
[SE•di•TSHEH•ZI•mo];
[SE•di•TSHEH•ZI•ma] *adj*
MF sixteenth

sedici [seh•DIT•shi] *num* sixteen

sedimento [SE•di•MEHN•to] *n*
M sediment

sedizione [SE•di•TSYOH•ne] *n*
F sedition

sedizioso; sediziosa
[SE•dit•SYOH•zo];
[SE•dit•SYOH•za] *adj* MF
seditious

seducente [SE•du•TSHEHN•te]
adj enticing; seductive

sedurre [se•DUHR•re] *vt*
seduce

seduttore [SE•dut•TOH•re] *n*
M seducer

seduzione [SE•du•TSYOH•ne]
n F seduction

sega a catena
[SEH•ga•ah•KA•TEH•na] *n* F
chain saw

segala [SEH•gala] *n* F rye

seghetta [se•GEHT•ta] *n* F
hacksaw

segmento [seg•MEHN•to] *n* M
segment

segnalare [SE•nya•LAH•re] *vi*
mean; mark; signalize

segnale [se•NYAH•le] *n* M
signal

segno [SEH•nyo] *n* M mark;
sign

sego [SEH•go] *n* M tallow

segregare [SE•gre•GAH•re] *vt*
segregate

segretario segretaria
[SE•gre•TAH•ryo];
[SE•gre•TAH•rya] *n* MF
secretary

segretezza [SE•gre•TEH•tsa] *n*
F secrecy

segreto [se•GREH•to] *n* M
secret

seguace [se•GUAH•tsh] *n* MF
follower

seguire [se•GUEE•re] *vt* follow;
heed; tag along

seguito [se•GUEE•to] *n* M
following; retinue

sei [SEH•i] *num* six

selettivo; selettiva
[SE•let•TEE•vo];
[SE•let•TEE•va] *adj* MF
selective

selezionare
[SE•letsyo•NAH•re] *vt* screen

selezione [SE•let•SYOH•ne] *n*
F selection

self-service [self-SEHR•vis] *n*
M cafeteria

sella [SEHL•la] *n* F saddle

selvaggio; selvaggia
[SEL•VAH•djo];
[SEL•VAH•dja] *adj* MF wild

sembianza [sem•BYAHN•tsa]
n F semblance

sembrare [sem•BRAH•re] *vi*
seem

seme [SEH•me] *n* M seed

semestrale [SE•mes•TRAH•le]
adj semiannual

seminario [SE•mi•NAH•ryo] *n*
M seminary

seminterrato
[SE•mi•nter•RAH•to] *n* M
basement

semplice [sehm•PLI•tshe] *adj*
plain; simple; unaffected

sempliciotto; sempliciotta
[SEM•pli•TSHOHT•to];
[SEM•pli•TSHOHT•ta] *n* MF
simpleton

semplicitá [SEM•pli•TSHI•tah]
n F simplicity

semplificare
[SEM•pli•fi•KAH•re] *vt*
simplify

semplificazione
[SEM•pli•fi•kah•TSYOH•ne] *n*
F simplification

sempre [SEHM•pre] *adv*
always; da sempre\ *adv*
lifelong

sempre piú [SEHM•pre•PIUH]
adv increasingly

sempreverde
[SEHM•pre•VEHR•de] *n adj*
evergreen

senape [seh•NAPE] *n* F
mustard

senato [se•NAH•to] *n* M senate

senatore [SE•na•TOH•re] *n* M
senator

senile [se•NEE•le] *adj* senile

senilità [SE•nee•LI•TAH] *n* F
senility

sensato; sensata
[sen•SAH•to]; [sen•SAH•ta]
adj MF sensible

sensazionale
[SEN•sa•TSYO•NAH•le] *adj*
lurid

sensazione
[SEN•sa•TSYOH•ne] *n* F
sensation

sensibile [sen•SEE•BI•le] *adj*
sensitive

sensibilità [sen•SI•bi•LI•TAH]
n F sensibility; sensitivity

senso [SEHN•so] *n* M sense; a
senso unico\ *adj* one-way; in
senso orario\ *adv* clockwise

sensuale [sen•SUAH•le] *n* MF
sensual

sentenza [sen•TEHN•tsa] *n* F
sentence (death)

sentiero [sen•TYEH•ro] *n* M
footpath

sentiero [sen•TYEH•ro] *n* M
lane; path; pathway

sentimentalismo
[SEN•ti•MEN•ta•LEEZ•mo] *n*
M sentimentality

sentimento [SEN•ti•MEHN•to]
n M feeling; sentiment

sentinella [SEN•ti•NEHL•la] *n*
F sentinel

sentire [sen•TEE•re] *vt* feel

sentito dire [SEN•tee•to
DEE•re] *n* M hearsay

senza [SEHN•tsa] *prep* without

senza cuore [SEHN•tsa
KWUOH•re] *adj* heartless

senza Dio [SEHN•tsa DEE•o]
adj godless

senza fiato [SEHN•tsa
FEE•AH•to] *adv* breathless

senza fili [SEHN•tsa FEE•li]
adj wireless

senza peccato [SEHN•tsa
pek•KAH•to] *adj* sinless

senza pericolo [SEHN•tsa
PE•ree•KO•lo] *adv* safely

senza preconcetti [SEHN•tsa
PRE•kon•TSHEHT•ti] *adj*
open-minded

senza scrupoli [SEHN•tsa
SKRUH•poli] *adj* mean

senza tetto [SEHN•tsa
TEHT•to] *adj n* MF homeless

senza un soldo [SEHN•tsa
UHN•SOHL•do] *adj* penniless

separabile [SE•pa•rah•BI•le] *n*
MF separable

separare [SE•pa•RAH•re] *vt*
separate

separatamente
[SE•pa•rata•MEHN•te] *adv*
separately

separatismo
[SE•para•TEEZ•mo] *n* M
separatism

separazione
[SE•pa•rat•SYOH•ne] *n* F
parting; separation

sepolcro [se•POHL•kro] *n* M
sepulcher

sepoltura [SE•pol•TUH•ra] *n* F
burial

seppellire [SEP•pel•LEE•re] *vt*
bury

sequela [se•KWEH•la] *n* F
sequel

sequenza [se•KWEHN•tsa] *n* F
sequence

sequestro [se•KWEHS•tro] *n*
M seizure

sera [SEH•ra] *n* F evening

serbatoio [SER•ba•TOH•yo] *n*
M tank (gasoline)

serenata [se•RENAH•ta] *n* F
serenade

serenitá [SE•re•NI•tah] *n* F
serenity

sereno; serena [se•REH•no];
[se•reh•na] *adj* MF serene

sergente [ser•DJEHN•te] *n* M
sergeant

seriamente [SE•rya•MEHN•te]
adv seriously

serie [SEH•rye] *n* F series;
range

serie completa
[SEH•rye•kom•PLEH•ta] *n* F
set

serietá [se•RYE•tah] *n* F
seriousness

serio; seria [SEH•ryo];
[seh•rya] *adj* MF earnest;
serious

sermone [ser•MOH•ne] *n* M
sermon

serpente [ser•PEHN•te] *n* M
serpent

serpente a sonagli
[SER•PEHN•te ah
so•NAH•ly] *n* M rattlesnake

serra [SEHR•ra] *n* F greenhouse

serratura [SER•ra•TUH•ra] *n* F
lock

servile [ser•VEE•le] *adj* menial

servile [ser•VEE•le];
[ser•vee•le] *adj* servile; slavish

servire [ser•VEE•re] *vt* serve

servitú [ser•VI•tuh] *n* F
servitude; service

servizio [ser•VEE•tsyo] *n* M
coverage

servizio pubblico
[ser•VEE•tsyo•PUHB•BLI•ko]
n M utility

servo; serva [SEHR•vo];
[sehr•va] *n* MF servant

sessanta [ses•SAHN•ta] *num*
sixty

sessantesimo; sessantesima
[ses•SAN•teh•ZI•mo];
[ses•SAN•teh•ZI•ma] *adj*
sixtieth

sessione [ses•SYOH•ne] *n* F
session

sesso [SEHS•so] *n* M sex

sessuale [ses•SUAH•le] *adj*
sexual

sesto; sesta [SEHS•to];
[sehs•ta] *adj* MF sixth

seta [SEH•ta] *n* F silk; di seta
adj silken

setacciare [se•TATSHAH•re] *vt*
sift

setaccio [se•TAH•tsho] *n* M
sieve

sete [SEH•te] *n* F thirst

setta [SEHT•ta] *n* F sect

settanta [set•TAHN•ta] *num*
seventy

settario; settaria
[set•TAH•ryo]; [set•TAH•rya]
adj MF sectarian

sette [SEHT•te] *num* seven

settembre [set•TEHM•bre] *n* M
September

settentesimo; settantesima
[set•TAN•teh•ZI•mo];
[set•TAN•teh•ZI•ma] *adj* MF
seventieth

settentrionale
[SET•ten•TRYO•NAH•le] *adj*
northern

settico; settica [seht•TI•ko];
[seht•TI•ka] *adj* MF septic

settimana [SET•ti•MAH•na] *n*
F week

settimana di Pentecoste
[SET•ti•MAH•na dee
PEN•te•KOHS•te] *n* F
Whitsuntide

settimanale
[SET•ti•ma•NAH•le] *adj*
weekly

settimo; settima
[SEHT•TI•mo]; [seht•ti•ma]
adj MF seventh

settore [SET•TOH•re] *n* M
sector

severo; severa [se•VEH•ro];
[se•VEH•ra] *adj* MF severe;
stern; strict

sezione [SETSYOH•ne] *n* F
section

sfaccendare
[sfa•TSHEN•DAH•re] *vi*
putter

sfacchinare [SFAK•ki•NAH•re]
vi plod

sfacelo [sfa•TSHEH•lo] *n* M
debacle

sfera [SFEH•ra] *n* F sphere

sferico; sferica [SFEH•ri•ko];
[SFEH•ri•ka] *adj* MF
spherical

sfida [SFEE•da] *n* F dare;
challenge; defiance

sfidare [sfi•DAH•re] *vt* defy;
brave; challenge

sfiduciato; sfiduciata
[SFI•du•TSHAH•to];
[SFI•du•TSHAH•ta] *adj* MF
hopeless

sfogo [SFOH•go] *n* M vent

sfondo [SFOHN•do] *n* M
background (in the)

sfortuna [sfor•TUH•na] *n* F
misfortune

sfortunato; sfortunata
[SFOR•tu•NAH•to];
[SFOR•tu•NAH•ta] *adj* MF
hapless

sforzarsi [sfor•TSAHR•si] *vi*
strive

sforzo [SFOHR•tso] *n* M effort;
endeavor; strain; stress; force

sfrattare [sfrat•TAH•re] *vt* evict

sfrecciare [sfre•TSHAH•re] *vi*
zoom

sfregiare [sfre•DJAH•re] *vt*
deface; disfigure

sfrenato; sfrenata
[sfre•NAH•to]; [sfre•NAH•ta]
adj MF overwhelming;
uncontrolled

sfrigolare [SFRI•go•LAH•re] *vi*
sizzle

sfrontato; sfrontata
[sfron•TAH•to];
[sfron•TAH•ta] *adj* MF
forward

sfruttare [sfrut•TAH•re] *vt*
exploit

sfuggire [sfu•DJEE•re] *vt* shun

sfumatura [SFU•ma•TUH•ra] *n*
F nuance; sense; tinge

sgabello [sga•BEHL•lo] *n* M
stool

sgattaiolare
[SGAT•ta•yo•LAH•re] *vi* slink

sgelare [zdje•LAH•re] *vt* thaw

sgocciolio [SGO•tshyo•LEE•o]
n M drip

sgomberare
[ZGOM•be•RAH•re] *vt* vacate

sgombro [ZGOHM•bro] *n* M
mackerel

sgonfiare [zgon•FYAH•re] *vt*
deflate

sgradevole [SGRA•deh•VOLE]
adj nasty; mean

sgradito; sgradita
[sgrah•DEE•to];
[sgrah•DEE•to] *adj* MF
unwelcome

sgranocchiare
[SGRA•nok•KYH•re] *vt*
crunch; munch

sguaiato; sguaiata
[sgua•YAH•to];
[sgua•YAH•ta] *adj* MF
raucous

sguardo [ZGUAHR•do] *n* M
glance; look

sguardo fisso
[SGUAHR•do•FEES•so] *n* M
gaze

si [see] *n* M yes; yeah

sibilare [SI•bi•LAH•re] *vi* hiss

sibilla [si•BEEL•la] *n* F sibyl

siccità [sit•SHI•tah] *n* F drought

sicurezza [SI•ku•REHT•sa] *n* F
safety; security; confidence
(self~)

sicuro di sé; sicura di sé
[SI•kuh•ro•DEE•seh];
[SI•kuh•ra•DEE•seh] *adj* MF
self-confident

sicuro; sicura [si•KUH•ro];
[si•KUH•ra] *adj* MF safe;
secure

SIDA [SEE•da] *n* F AIDS

sidro [SEE•dro] *n* M cider

siepe [SYEH•pe] *n* F hedge

siero [SYEH•ro] *n* M serum

sifone [si•FOH•ne] *n* M siphon

sigarett [SI•ga•REHT•ta] *n* F
cigarette

sigaro [see•GA•ro] *n* M cigar

sigillo [si•DJEEL•lo] *n* M signet

significare [SI•ny•fi•KAH•re] *vi*
signify

significativo; significativa
[SI•ny•fi•ka•TEE•vo];
[SI•ny•fi•ka•TEE•va] *adj* MF
significant

significato [SI•ni•fi•KAH•to] *n*
M meaning; significance; drift

signora [si•NYOH•ra] *n* F lady;
madam

signore [si•NYOH•re] *n* M
mister; sir; lord

signorina [SI•nyo•REE•na] *n* F
Miss

silenziatore
[SI•len•TSYA•TOH•re] *n* M
silencer

silenzio [SI•lehn•TSYO] *n* M
hush; silence

silenziosamente
[SI•len•TSYO•za•MEHN•te]
adv silently

silenzioso; silenziosa
[SI•len•TSYOH•zo];
[SI•len•TSYOH•za] *adj* MF
soundless

sillaba [SEEL•la•ba] *n* F
syllable

sillabario [SIL•la•BAH•ryo] *n*
M primer

sillogismo [SIL•lo•DJEEZ•mo] *n* M syllogism

siluetta [si•LUEHT•ta] *n* F silhouette

simbolico; simbolica [sim•BOH•LI•ko]; [sim•BOH•LI•ka] *adj* MF symbolic

simbolo [SEEM•bo•lo] *n* M symbol

simile [SEE•mi•le] *adj* alike; like; similar

similmente [SI•mil•MEHN•te] *adv* similarly

simmetrico; simmetrica [SIM•meh•TRI•ko]; [SIM•meh•TRI•ka] *adj* MF symmetrical.

simpatia [SIM•pa•TEE•a] *n* F liking

simpatico; simpatica [sim•PAH•tiko]; [sim•PAH•tika] *adj* MF nice; sympathetic; friendly; likeable

simulare [si•MULAH•re] *vt* dissemble; simulate

simultaneo; simultanea [SI•mul•TAH•neo]; [SI•mul•TAH•nea] *adj* MF simultaneous

sinagoga [SI•na•GOH•ga] *n* F synagogue

sincerità [SIN•tshe•RI•tah] *n* F sincerity; truthfulness

sincero; sincera [sin•TSHEH•ro]; [sin•TSHEH•ra] *adj* MF sincere

sincronizzare [SIN•kro•ni•TSAH•re] *vt* synchronize

sindacato [SIN•da•KAH•to] *n* M labor union; syndicate; trade-union

sindaco [SEEN•dako] *n* M mayor

sinfonia [SIN•fo•NEE•a] *n* F symphony

singhiozzare [SIN•gyo•TSAH•re] *vi* sob

singhiozzo [sin•GYOH•tso] *n* M hiccup

singolare [SIN•go•LAH•re] *adj* singular

singolarità [SIN•go•LAH•RI•tah] *n* F strangeness

singolo; singola [SEEN•go•lo]; [SEEN•go•la] *adj* MF single; sole

sinistro; sinistra [si•NEES•tro]; [si•NEES•tra] *adj* MF ominous; sinister; di sinistra\ left-wing

sinonimo; sinonima [SI•noh•NI•mo]; [SI•noh•NI•ma] *adj* MF synonymous

sintassi [sin•THS•si] *n* F syntax

sintesi [seen•TE•zi] *n* F synthesis

sintomatico; sintomatica [SIN•to•MAH•ti•ko]; [SIN•to•MAH•ti•ka] *adj* MF symptomatic

sintomo [seen•TO•mo] *n* M symptom

sinusite [SI•nu•ZEE•te] *n* F sinusitis

sipario [si•PAH•ryo] *n* M curtain (theater)

sirena [si•REH•na] *n* F mermaid; siren

Siria [SEE•rya] *n* F Syria

siriano; siriana [si•RYAH•no];
[si•RYAH•na] *adj* Syrian

siringa [si•REEN•ga] *n* F
syringe

sistema [sis•TEH•ma] *n* M
system

sistemare [SIS•te•MAH•re] *vt*
arrange; settle

sistematico; sistematica
[SIS•te•MAH•ti•ko];
[sis•te•mah•ti•ka] *adj* MF
systematic

situare [si•TUAH•re] *vt* situate

situazione [SI•tua•TSYOH•ne]
n F situation

situazione difficile
[SI•tua•TSYOH•ne
dif•FEE•TSHI•le] *n* F
predicament

sketch [SKEH•tsh] *n* M skit

slancio [ZLAHN•tsho] *n* M
dash

slattare [zlat•TAH•re] *vt* wean

sleale [zle•AHLE] *adj* disloyal

slegare [zle•GAH•re] *vt* untie

slitta [SLEET•ta] *n* F sledge;
sleigh

slogan [SLOH•gan] *n* M slogan

slogatura [SLO•ga•TUH•ra] *n*
F sprain

sloop [sluhp] *n* M sloop

smalto [ZMAHL•to] *n* M
enamel

smeraldo [zme•RAHL•do] *n* M
emerald

smilzo; smilza [SMEEL•tso];
[smeel•tsa] *adj* MF slim

smobilitare
[ZMO•bi•li•TAH•re] *vt*
demobilize

smontare [zmon•TAH•re] *vi*
dismount

smorfia [SMOHR•fya] *n* F
grimace

smorzare [zmor•TSAH•re] *vt*
muffle

smuovere [ZMUOH•vere] *vi vt*
budge

snonimo [SI•noh•NI•mo] *n* M
synonym

sobbollire [SOB•bol•LEE•re] *vt*
simmer

sobriamente
[SO•brya•MEHN•te] *adv*
soberly

sobrietá [so•BRYE•tah] *n* F
sobriety

sobrio; sobria [SOH•bryo];
[SOH•brya] *adj* MF sober;
staid

socchiudere gli occhi
[SOK•kyuh•DERE•lee•OHK
•ki] *vi* squint

socchiuso; socchiusa
[sot•SHYU•so•sot•SHYU•sa]
adj MF ajar

soccombere
[sok•KOHM•BE•re] *vi*
succumb

soccorso [sok•KOHR•so] *n* M
succor

sociale [so•TSHAH•le] *adj*
social

socialismo [SO•tsha•LEEZ•mo]
n M socialism

socialista [SO•tsha•LEES•ta] *n*
adv socialist

societá [so•TSHE•tah] *n* F
society; company; partnership

**societá a responsabilitá
limitata** [so•TSHET•ah ah
RES•pon•SABILI•tah
li•MITAH•ta] *n* F corporation

socievole [so•TSHYEH•vole]
adj sociable

socio; socia [SOH•tsho];
[SOH•tsha] *n* MF partner

sociologia
[so•TSHO•lo•DJEE•a] *n* F
sociology

soddisfare [SOD•dis•FAH•re]
vt fulfill

soddisfazione
[SOD•dis•FATSYOH•ne] *n* F
fulfillment

sodio [SOH•dyo] *n* M sodium

sofá [SO•fah] *n* F couch; sofa

sofferenza [SOF•fe•REHN•tsa]
n F misery; suffering

soffiare [sof•FIAH•re] *vt* blow

soffione [sof•FYOH•ne] *n* M
dandelion

soffitta [sohf•FIT•tah] *n* F attic

soffocamento
[SOF•fo•ka•MEHN•to] *n* M
suffocation

soffocare [SOF•fo•KAH•re] *vt*
squelch; stifle; suffocate

soffocare per il caldo
[SOF•fo•KAH•re PEHR eel
KAHL•do] *vi* swelter

soffondere [sof•FOHN•DE•re]
vt suffuse

soffrire [sof•FREE•re] *vi* suffer

sofisticato; sofisticata
[SO•fis•ti•KAH•to];
[SO•fis•ti•KAH•ta] *adj* MF
sophisticated

sofisticazione
[SO•fis•ti•KA•TSYOH•ne] *n*
sophistication

soggettivo; soggettiva
[SO•djet•TEE•vo];

[SO•djet•TEE•va] *adj* MF
subjective

soggetto [SODJ•eht•to] *n* M
subject

sogghigno [sog•GIN•yo] *n* M
grin

soggiogare [SO•djo•GAH•re]
vt subjugate

soggiorno [so•DJOHR•no] *n* M
sojourn

soglia [SOH•lya] *n* F doorstep;
threshold

sognare ad occhi aperti
[so•NYAH•re ahd OHK•ki
APEHR•ti] *vi* daydream

sogno [SO•nyo] *n* M dream

solamente [SO•la•MEHN•te]
adv alone

solare [so•LAH•re] *adj* solar

solco [SOHL•ko] *n* M groove

soldato [sol•DAH•to] *n* M
soldier

soldato [sol•DAH•to] *n* M
trooper

solecismo [SO•le•TSHEEZ•mo]
n M solecism

solenne [so•LEHN•ne] *adj*
solemn

solennitá [SO•len•NI•tah] *n* F
solemnity

solennizzare
[SO•len•nit•SAH•re] *vt*
solemnize

solidarietá [SO•li•DARYE•tah]
n F solidarity

solidificare
[SO•li•di•fi•KAH•re] *vt*
solidify

soliditá [SO•li•DI•tah] *n* F
solidity

solido; solida [soh•LI•do];
[soh•LI•da] *adj* MF solid
soliloquio [SOLI•loh•KWYO] *n*
M soliloquy
solitario; solitaria
[SO•li•TAH•ryo];
[SO•li•TAH•rya] *adj* MF lone;
single; solitary
solito; solita [SOH•LI•to];
[SOH•LI•ta] *adj* MF habitual;
usual; ordinary; di solito\ *adv*
ordinarily
solitudine [SO•li•TUH•dine] *n*
F loneliness; solitude
sollecitare [SOL•letshi•TAH•re]
vt elicit; solicit
sollecitazione
[SOL•le•TSHI•tat•SYOH•ne]
n F solicitation
sollecito; sollecita
[SOL•leh•TSHI•to];
[SOL•leh•TSHI•to] *adj* MF
prompt; solicitous
solleticare [SOL•le•ti•KAH•re]
vt tickle
solletico [SOL•leh•TI•ko] *n* M
tickle
sollevare [SOL•le•VAH•re] *vt*
hoist; heave; uplift
sollievo [sol•LYEH•vo] *n* M
relief; solace
solo; sola [SOH•lo];[SOH•la]
adj MF alone; a solo\ solo; da
sola\ single-handed
solstizio [sol•STEE•tsyo] *n* M
solstice
soluzione [SO•lu•TSYOH•ne] *n*
F solution
solvente [sol•VEHN•te] *adj*
solvent

somiglianza
[SO•mi•LYAHN•tsa] *n* F
resemblance; likeness;
similitude
somma [SOM•mah] *n* F amount
sommario [som•MAH•ryo] *n* M
summary
sommergere
[SOM•mehr•DJERE] *vt*
engulf; submerge
somministrare
[SOM•mi•ni•STRAH•re] *vt*
administer
sommitá [som•MI•tah] *n* F
hilltop
sonata [so•NAH•ta] *n* F sonata
sonda [SOHN•da] *n* F probe
sonetto [so•NEHT•to] *n* M
sonnet
sonnellino [SON•nel•LEE•no]
n M nap
sonnolento; sonnolenta
[SON•no•LEHN•to];
[SON•no•LEHN•ta] *adj* MF
drowsy; sleepy; somnolent
sono (essere) [SOH•no] *v* am
(be)
sonoro; sonora [so•NOH•ro];
[so•NOH•ra] *adj* sonorous
sopore [so•POH•re] *n* M
sleepiness
soporifico; soporifica
[SO•po•REE•fiko];
[SO•po•REE•fika] *adj* MF
soporific
soppalco [sop•PAHL•ko] *n* M
loft
sopportabile
[SOP•por•TAH•BI•le] *adj*
tolerable

sopportare [SOP•por•TAH•re] *vt* abide (by)

sopra [SOH•pra] *prep* above

sopra [SOH•pra] *prep* unto; upon; di sopra\ *adj* over

soprabito [SO•prah•BI•to] *n* M topcoat

sopracciglio [SOH•pra•TSHEE•lyo] *n* M eyebrow

sopraffare [SO•praf•FAH•re] *vt* overcome; overpower; overwhelm

soprano [so•PRAH•no] *n* M soprano; treble voice

sopravvivenza [SO•prav•vi•VEHN•tsa] *n* F survival

sopravvivere [SO•prav•VEE•vere] *vt* outlive; survive

soprintendente [SO•prin•TEN•DEHN•te] *n* MF overseer

soprintendere [SO•prin•TEHN•dere] *vt* oversee

sordido; sordida [SOHR•DI•do]; [SOHR•DI•da] *adj* MF sordid

sordo; sorda [SOHR•do]; [SOHR•da] *adj* deaf

sorella [so•REHL•la] *n* F sister

sorgere [sohr•DJE•re] *vi* rise

sorpassare [SOR•pas•SAH•re] *vt* overtake

sorprendente [SOR•pren•DEHN•te] *adj* amazing

sorprendere [SOR•PREHN•dere] *vt* startle

sorso [SOHR•so] *n* M sip

sorveglianza [SOR•ve•LYAHN•tsa] *n* F keeping

sospendere [SOS•pehn•DE•re] *vt* suspend; in sospeso\ *adj* pending

sospettare [SOS•pet•TAH•re] *vt* suspect

sospetto [sos•PEHT•to] *n* M suspicion

sospiro [sos•PEE•ro] *n* M sigh

sosta [SOHS•ta] *n* F halt

sostantivo [SOS•tan•TEE•vo] *n* M substantive

sostanza [sos•TAHN•tsa] *n* F substance

sostanza chimica [SOS•tahn•TSA ki•MEE•ka] *n* F chemical

sostenere [SOS•te•NEH•re] *vt* sustain; uphold

sostenibile [SOS•te•NEE•BI•le] *adj* tenable

sostentamento [SOS•ten•ta•MEHN•to] *n* M sustenance

sostituire [SOS•ti•TU•eere] *vt* replace

sostituto; sostituta [SOS•ti•TUH•to]; [SOS•TITUH•ta] *n* MF counterpart; substitute; deputy; understudy

sottaceto [SOT•tat•SHEH•to] *n* M pickle

sotterranea [SOT•ter•RAH•nea] *n* F subway

sotterraneo; sotterranea [SOT•ter•RAH•neo];

[SOT•ter•RAH•nea] *adj* MF
subterranean

sotterraneo; sotterranea
[SOT•ter•RAH•neo];
[SOT•ter•RAH•nea] *adj* MF
underground

sottile [sot•TEE•le] *adj* subtle;
thin

sotto [SOHT•to] *adv* beneath;
prep under; di sotto *adv*
below; underneath

sotto la media
[SOHT•to•lah•MEH•dya] *adj*
undersized

sottobosco [SOT•to•BOHS•ko]
n M underbrush

sottocomitato
[SOT•to•ko•mi•TAH•to] *n* M
subcommittee

sottolineare
[SOT•to•lin•EAH•re] *vt*
underline; stress

sottomano
[SOHT•to•MAH•no] *adv*
handy (near); nearby

sottomarino
[SOT•to•ma•REE•no] *n* M
submarine

sottomettere
[SOT•to•MEHT•te•re] *vt*
submit

sottomissione
[SOT•to•MIS•SYOH•ne] *n* F
submission

sottoscritto; sottoscritta
[SOT•to•SKREET•to] *adj* MF
undersigned

sottoscrivere
[SOT•to•SKREE•ve•re] *vt*
underwrite

sottosopra [SOT•to•SOH•pra]
adj topsy-turvy

sottostante
[SOT•to•STAHN•te] *adj*
underlying

sottovalutare
[SOT•to•va•LU•TAH•re] *vt*
underestimate

sottrarre [sot•TRAHR•re] *vt*
subtract; deduct

sottrazione
[SOT•tra•TSYOH•ne] *n* F
subtraction

Soviet [SOH•vyet] *n* M Soviet

sovrano; sovrana
[so•VRAH•no];
[so•VRAH•na] *adj* MF
sovereign

sovrapporre
[SO•vrap•POHR•re] *vt* overlap

sovrintendente
[SOH•vrin•TEN•DEHN•te] *n*
M controller

sovvenzionare
[SOV•ven•TSYO•NAH•re] *vt*
subsidize

sovversivo; sovversiva
[SOV•ver•SEE•vo];
[SOV•ver•see•va] *adj*
subversive

spada [SPAH•da] *n* F sword

spagnolo; spagnola
[spa•NYOH•lo];
[spa•NYOH•la] *n* MF
Spaniard; *adj* Spanish

spago [SPAH•go] *n* M string

spalla [SPAHL•la] *n* F shoulder

spaniel [SPAH•nyel] *n* M
spaniel

sparare [spa•RAH•re] *vi* shoot;
vt discharge; shoot off

sparatoria [SPA•ra•TOH•rya] *n* F gunfire

spargere [spahr•DJE•re] *vt* scatter; sprinkle

sparire [spa•REE•re] *vi* disappear

sparo [SPAH•ro] *n* M gunshot; shot

sparpagliare [SPAR•pa•LYAH•re] *vt* strew

sparpagliarsi [SPAR•pa•LYAHR•si] *vi* straggle

sparuto; sparuta [spa•RUH•to]; [spa•RUH•ta] *adj* MF haggard

sparviero [spar•VYEH•ro] *n* M hawk

spasimo [spah•ZI•mo] *n* M spasm

spassionato; spassionata [spa•SYONAH•to]; [spas•SYONAH•ta] *adj* MF dispassionate; uninterested

spaventare [SPA•ven•TAH•re] *vt* frighten; scare

spaventato; spaventata [SPAH•ven•TAH•to]; [SPAH•ven•TAH•ta] *adj* MF afraid (to be)

spavento [spa•VEHN•to] *n* M fright

spaventoso; spaventosa [SPA•ven•TOH•so]; [SPA•ven•TOH•sa] *adj* MF dreadful; frightening

spazio [SPAH•tsyo] *n* M space

spazio a capoverso [SPAH•tsyo ah KAPO•VEHR•so] *n* M indent

spazioso; spaziosa [spa•TSYOH•zo]; [spa•TSYOH•za] *adj* MF roomy; spacious

spazzaneve [SPAH•tsa•NEH•ve] *n* M snowplow

spazzino [spa•TSEE•no] *n* M sweeper

spazzola [spah•TSO•la] *n* F brush; hairbrush

spazzolare [spa•TSOLAH•re] *vt* brush

specchio [SPEH•kyo] *n* M mirror

speciale [spe•TSHAH•le] *adj* special

specialista [SPE•tsha•LEES•ta] *n* MF specialist

specializzarsi [SPE•tsha•li•TSAHR•si] *vi* specialize

specialmente [SPE•tshal•MEHN•te] *adv* especially

specie [SPEH•tshe] *n* F species

specificare [SPE•tshi•fi•KAH•re] *vi* specify

specifico; specifica [SPE•TSHEE•fi•ko]; [SPE•TSHEE•fi•ka] *adj* MF specific

specioso; speciosa [spe•TSHOH•zo]; [spe•TSHOH•za] *adj* MF specious

speculare [SPE•ku•LAH•re] *vi* speculate

speculativo; speculativa [SPE•ku•LA•TEE•vo];

[SPE•ku•LA•TEE•va] *adj* MF
speculative

speculatore; speculatrice
[SPE•ku•LA•TOH•re];
[SPE•ku•LA•TREE•tshe] *n*
MF speculator

speculazione
[SPE•ku•lat•SYOH•ne] *n* F
speculation

spedito; spedita [spe•DEE•to];
[spe•DEE•ta] *adj* MF fluent

spedizione
[SPE•DITSYOH•ne] *n* F
expedition

spegnere [speh•NYE•re] *vt*
quench

spegnere [speh•NYERE] *vt*
turn off

spendaccione; spendacciona
[SPEN•da•TSHOH•ne];
[SPEN•da•TSHOH•na] *n* MF
spendthrift

spendere [SPEHN•dere] *vt*
spend

spensierato; spensierata
[SPEN•sye•RAH•to];
[SPEN•sye•RAH•ta] *adj* MF
carefree

speranza [spe•RAHN•tsa] *n* F
hope

spergiuro [sper•DJUH•ro] *n* M
perjury

spericolato; spericolata
[SPE•rik•o•LAH•to];
[SPE•rik•o•LAH•ta] *adj* MF
daring

sperone [spe•ROH•ne] *n* M
spur

spesa [SPEH•za] *n* F
expenditure; expense

spesso [SPEHS•so] *adv* often;
-o -a\ *adj* MF thick

spessore [spes•SOH•re] *n* M
thickness

spettacolare
[SPET•ta•ko•LAH•re] *adj* F
spectacular

spettacolo [SPET•tah•KO•lo] *n*
M show; spectacle

spettatore; spettatrice
[SPET•ta•TOH•re];
[SPET•ta•TREE•tshe] *n* MF
spectator; audience (pl)

spettegolare
[SPET•te•go•AH•re] *vi* tattle

spettro 1 [SPEHT•tro] *n* M
specter; spook; ghost

spettro 2 [SPEHT•tro] *n* M
spectrum

spezeia [SPEH•tsya] *n* F spice⁻

spia [SPEE•a] *n* F spy

spiacente [SPYA•TSHEHN•te]
adj sorry

spiaggia [SPIAH•jdja] *n* F
beach; shore

spiare [spi•AH•re] *vi* spy

spiattellare
[SPI•aht•tel•LAH•re] *vt* blab

spiedo [SPYEH•do] *n* M
skewer

spiegare [spye•GAH•re] *vt*
explain

spiegazione
[SPYE•ga•TSYOH•ne] *n* F
explanation

spiegazzare
[SPYE•gat•ZAH•re] *vt* rumple

spietato; spietata
[spye•TAH•to]; [spye•TAH•ta]
adj MF merciless; pitiless;
ruthless

spigolare [spi•GOLAH•re] *vt* glean

spigolo [SPEE•golo] *n* M ridge

spilla [SPEEL•la] *n* F brooch

spillare [spil•LAH•re] *vt* tap

spillo [SPEEL•lo] *n* M pin

spilorcio; spilorcia [spi•LOHR•tsho] *n* MF tightwad

spina [SPEE•na] *n* F thorn

spinaci [spi•NAH•tshi] *npl* M spinach

spinale [spi•NAH•le] *adj* spinal

spingere [SPEEN•dje•re] *vt* boost; poke; push; shove

spingere avanti [SPIN•DJEH•re av•AHN•ti] *vt* propel

spinta [SPEEN•ta] *n* F thrust

spionaggio [spyo•NAH•djo] *n* M espionage

spioncino [spyon•TSHEE•no] *n* M peephole

spirale [SPI•RAH•le] *adj n* F spiral

spirito [spee•RI•to] *n* M spirit

spiritosaggine [SPI•ri•to•ZAH•DJI•ne] *n* F wisecrack

spirituale [SPI•ri•TUAH•le] *adj* spiritual

spiritualismo [SPI•ri•TUA•LEEZ•mo] *n* M spiritualism

spiritualitá [SPI•ri•tu•AL•I•tah] *n* F spirituality

splendente [splen•DEHN•te] *adj* glowing

splendido; splendida [splehn•DI•do]; [splehn•DI•da] *n* MF glorious; *adj* grand; splendid

splendore [splen•DOH•re] *n* M glow; splendor

spogliare [spo•LYAH•re] *vt* strip (clothes)

spola 1 [SPOH•la] *n* F shuttle

spola 2 [SPOH•la] *n* F spool

spontaneitá [SPON•ta•NEY•tah] *n* F spontaneity

spontaneo; spontanea [spon•TAH•neo]; [spon•TAH•nea] *adj* MF spontaneous

sporco [SPOHR•ko] *n* M dirt

sporco; sporca [SPOHR•ko]; [SPOHR•ka] *adj* MF dingy; dirty; foul; grubby; unclean

sporgenza [spor•DJEHN•tsa] *n* F ledge

sport [spohrt] *n* M sport

sport acquatici [SPOH•rt•AKWAH•TIT•shi] *n* M water sports

sportivo; sportiva [spor•TEE•vo]; [spor•TEE•va] *n* MF sportsman

sposa [SPOH•za] *n* F bride

sposare [spo•ZAH•re] *vt* marry; wed

sposato; sposata [spo•ZAH•to]; [spo•ZAH•ta] *adj* MF married; wedded

sposo [SPOH•zo] *n* M bridegroom; groom

spostato; spostata [spos•TAH•to]; [spos•tah•ta] *n* MF misfit

sprazzo [SPRAH•tso] *n* M gleam; shine; sparkle

sprecare [spre•KAH•re] *vt*
waste

spregevole [spre•DJEH•VO•le]
adj contemptible; despicable;
vile

sprezzante [spre•TSAHN•te]
adj disparaging

sprofondare
[SPRO•fon•DAH•re] *vi* sink

sproporzionato;
sproporzionata
[SPRO•por•TSYO•NAH•to];
[SPRO•por•TSYO•NAH•ta]
adj MF undue; undeserved;
disproportionate

spruzzare [spru•TSAH•re] *vt*
spray

spruzzata [spru•TSAH•ta] *n* F
dash (quantity)

spruzzatore
[spru•TSA•TOH•re] *n* M
sprayer

spugna [SPUH•nya] *n* F sponge

spuntare [spun•TAH•re] *vt* trim

spuntato; spuntata
[SPUN•TAH•to];
[SPUN•TAH•ta] *adj* MF blunt

sputare [spu•TAH•re] *vt* spit

squadra [SKWAH•dra] *n* F
team

squadriglia [skwa•DREE•lya] *n*
F squadron

squalificare
[SKWA•li•fi•KAH•re] *vt*
disqualify

squallido; squallida
[skwahl•LI•do];
[skwahl•LI•da] *adj* MF
squalid

squilibrio [skwi•LEE•bryo] *n* M
imbalance

squisito; squisita
[skwi•SEE•to]; [skwi•SEE•ta]
adj MF exquisite

stabile [stah•BI•le] *adj* stable

stabilire [sta•BILEE•re] *vt*
establish

stabilitá [sta•BI•LI•tah'] *n* F
stability

stabilizzare
[STA•bi•li•TSAH•re] *vt*
stabilize

staccare [stak•KAH•re] *vt*
detach; disconnect; take off

stadio [STAH•dyo] *n* M
stadium

staffa [STAHF•fa] *n* F stirrup

staffetta [staf•FEHT•ta] *n* F
relay

stagione [sta•DJOH•ne] *n* F
season; di stagione\ *adj*
seasonable

stagnante [sta•NYAHN•te] *adj*
stagnant

stagno [STAH•nyo] *n* M pond;
-o -a\ *adj* MF watertight

stagnola [STA•nyoh•LA] *n* F
foil; tin foil

staio [STAH•yo] *n* M bushel

stalla [STAHL•la] *n* F stable

stallare [stal•LAH•re] *vt* stall

stallone 1 [stal•LOH•ne] *n*
stallion; horse (male)

stallone 2 [stal•LOH•ne] *n* M
stud (animal)

stampa [STAHM•pa] *n* F press

stampa [STAHM•pa] *n* F print

stampella [stam•PEHL•la] *n* F
crutch

stampino [stam•PEE•no] *n* M
stencil

stampo [STAHM•po] *n* M
mold (shape)

stancaresi [stan•KAHR•si] *vi*
tire

stanchezza [stan•KEH•tsa] *n* F
fatigue; tiredness; weariness

stanco; stanca [STAHN•ko];
[STAHN•ko] *adj* MF jaded;
tired; weary

stand [stend] *n* M booth; stand

standardizzare
[STAN•dar•DITSAH•re] *vt*
standardize

standardizzazione
[STAN•dar•DITSA•TSYOH•ne]
n F standardization

stanotte [sta•NOHT•te] *n* F
tonight

stantio; stantia [stan•TEE•o];
[stan•TEE•a] *adj* MF stale

stantuffo [stan•TUHF•fo] *n* M
plunger

stanza 1 [STAHN•tsa] *n* F
room

stanza 2 [STAHN•tsa] *n* F
stanza; verse

stanza degli ospiti
[STAHN•tsa deh•ly OHS•piti]
n F guestroom

stappare [stap•PAH•re] *vt*
uncork

stare [STAH•re] *vi* stay; remain;
live; be

stare a cavalcioni [STAH•re ah
KA•val•TSHOH•ni] *vi*
straddle

stare in piedi [STAH•re in
PYEH•di] *vi* stand

statico; statica [stah•TI•ko];
[stah•TI•ka] *adj* MF static

statista [sta•TEES•ta] *n* M
statesman

statistica [sta•TEES•TI•ka] *n* F
statistics

stato 1 [STAH•to] *n* M state;
status

stato; stata 2
[STAH•to];[stah•ta] *v pp* stare;
been

statua [STAH•tua] *n* F statue

statuto [sta•TUH•to] *n* M
statute

stazionario; stazionaria
[STA•tsyo•NAH•ryo];
[STA•tsyo•NAH•rya] *adj* MF
stationary

stazione [sta•TSYOH•ne] *n* F
railroad station; station;
terminal

stecca 1 [STEHK•ka] *n* F splint

stecca 2 [STEHK•kah] *n* F
carton (cigarette)

steccato [stek•KAH•to] *n* M
fence

stecchino [stek•KEE•no] *n* M
toothpick

stecco [STEHK•ko] *n* M twig

stecconata [STEK•ko•NAH•ta]
n F stockade

stella [STEHL•la] *n* F star

stella filante
[STEHL•la•fi•LAN•te] *n* F
streamer

stelo [STEH•lo] *n* M stem

stendere [sten•DEH•re] *vt* lay

stendere [stehn•DERE] *vt*
spread

stenografia
[STE•no•gra•FEE•a] *n* F
shorthand

stenografo; stenografa
[STE•noh•GRA•fo];
[STE•noh•GRA•fa] *n* MF
stenographer

stentare la crescita
[STEN•TAH•re lah
KREH•SHI•ta] *vi* stunt

sterco [STEHR•ko] *n* M dung

stereo [STEH•reo] *n* M stereo

stereotipo [STE•reoh•TY•po] *n*
M stereotype

sterile [STEHR•I•le] *adj* barren;
sterile

sterilitá [STE•ri•LI•tah] *n* F
sterility

sterilizzare
[STE•ri•li•TSAH•re] *vt*
sterilize

sterlina [ster•LEE•na] *n* F quid

sterminare [STER•mi•NAH•re]
vt exterminate

sterzare [ster•TSAH•re] *vt* steer

stetoscopio
[STE•to•SKOH•pyo] *n* M
stethoscope

stia [STEE•a] *n* F sty

stigma [STEEG•ma] *n* M
stigma

stile [STEE•le] *n* M style

stima [STEE•ma] *n* F esteem;
estimate

stimare [sti•MAH•re] *vt* deem

stimolare [sti•MO•LAH•re] *vt*
stimulate

stimolo [stee•MO•lo] *n* M
motivation; stimulus

stipare [sti•PAH•re] *vt* cram;
stow

stipendio [sti•PEHN•dyo] *n* M
stipend

stipolare [STI•po•LAH•re] *vt*
stipulate

stiratura [STI•rat•UH•ra] *n* F
ironing

stivale [stiv•AH•le] *n* M boot

stivatore [STI•va•TOH•re] *n* M
stevedore

stizza [STEE•tsa] *n* F huff

stoccata [stok•KAH•ta] *n* F jab

stoffa [STOHF•fa] *n* F cloth;
fabric

stoffa scozzese [STOHF•fa
SKOT•SEH•ze] *n* F plaid

stoicismo [sto•YTSHEEZ•mo]
n M stoicism

stoico; stoica [STOH•yko];
[STOH•yka] *n adj* MF stoic

stoino [sto•EE•no] *n* M mat

stola [STOH•la] *n* F stole

stomaco [stoh•MA•ko] *n* M
stomach

stoppia [STOHP•pya] *n* F
stubble

stoppino [stop•PEE•no] *n* M
wick

stordire [stor•DEE•re] *vt* fluster;
stun; stupefy

stordito; stordita
[stor•DEE•to]; [stor•DEE•ta]
adj MF dizzy

storia [STOH•rya] *n* F history;
story; tale

storico [stoh•RI•ko] *n* M
historian

storico; storica [stoh•RI•ko];
[stoh•RI•ka] *adj* MF historic

storione [sto•RYOH•ne] *n* M
sturgeon

storpio; storpia [STOHR•pyo];
[STOHR•pya] *n* MF cripple

storto; storta
[STOHR•to];[stohr•ta] *adj* MF
bent; crooked

stoviglie [sto•VEE•lye] *n* F
tableware

stracciato; stracciata
[stra•TSHAH•to];
[stra•TSHAH•ta] *adj* MF
ragged

straccio [STRAH•tsho] *n* M rag

strada [STRAH•da] *n* F road;
route; street; a metá strada
adv halfway

strafare [stra•FAH•re] *vt* overdo

stranezza [stra•NEH•tsa] *n* F
oddity

strangolamento
[STRAN•go•la•MEHN•to] *n*
M strangulation

strangolare
[STRAN•go•LAH•re] *vt*
strangle

straniero; straniera
[STRA•NYEH•ro];
[STRA•NYEH•ra] *adj* foreign;
alien; *n* MF foreigner;
stranger

strano; strana [STRAH•no];
[STRAH•na] *adj* MF odd;
queer; strange

straordinario
[STRA•or•di•NAH•ryo] *n* M
overtime; -o -a\ *adj*
extraordinary; terrific

strappare [strap•PAH•re] *vt*
pluck; tear; wrest

strappo [STRAHP•po] *n* M tear

strategia [STRA•te•DJEE•a] *n*
F strategy

strategico; strategica
[STRA•teh•DJI•ko];

[STRA•teh•DJI•ka] *adj* MF
strategic

strato [STRAH•to] *n* M layer

stratosfera [STRA•tos•FEH•ra]
n F stratosphere

strattagemma
[STAT•ta•DJEHM•ma] *n* M
device

strattone [strat•TOH•ne] *n* M
yank

stravagante
[STRA•va•GAHN•te] *adj*
extravagant

stravaganza
[STRA•va•GAHN•tsa] *n* F
extravagance

strega [STREH•ga] *n* F witch

strenuo; strenua
[STREH•nuo]; [STREH•nua]
adj MF strenuous

stretta di mano [STREHT•ta
di MAH•no] *n* F handshake

stretto [STREHT•to] *n* M strait;
tight spot; -o -a\ *adj* narrow;
snug; tight

stria [STREE•a] *n* F streak

striare [stri•AH•re] *vt* stripe

stridente [stri•DEHN•te] *adj*
grating; shrill; strident

strillare [stril•LAH•re] *vi*
squeal; *vi* screech

strillo [STREEL•lo] *n* M
screech; shriek

stringa [STREEN•ga] *n* F
shoelace

stringere [strin•DJEH•re] *vt*
clench; clamp

stringersi [strin•DJEHR•si] *vi*
cling

striscia [STREE•sha] *n* F strip

striscia [STREE•shya] *n* F stripe

strisciare [stri•SHAH•re] *vi*
crawl; creep; grovel; slither

strizzare [stri•TSAH•re] *vt*
squeeze; wring

strofinaccio
[STRO•fi•nah•TSHO] *n* M
wiper

strofinare [STRO•fi•NAH•re] *vt*
scour

stroncare [stron•KAH•re] *vt*
scathe

strozzare [stro•TSAH•re] *vt*
choke; strangle; throttle

strumento [stru•MEHN•to] *n*
M instrument

strumento appuntito
[stru•MEHN•to
ap•PUN•TEE•to] *n* M pick

strutto [STRUHT•to] *n* M lard

struttura [strut•TUH•ra] *n* F
structure

strutturale
[STRUT•tu•RAH•le] *adj*
structural

struzzo [STRUH•tso] *n* M
ostrich

stucco [STUHK•ko] *n* M putty

studente [stu•DEHN•te] *n* MF
student

studente d'universitá
[stu•DEHN•te
du•NI•ver•SI•tah] *n* MF
undergraduate

studio [STUH•dyo] *n* M studio;
study; den

studioso; studiosa
[stu•DYOH•zo];
[stu•DYOH•za] *n* MF scholar

stufa [STUH•fa] *n* F heater;
stove

stufato [stu•FAH•to] *n* M stew

stuoino [STU•o•EE•no] *n* M
doormat

stupendo; stupenda
[stu•PEHN•do]; [stu•pehn•da]
adj MF stupendous

stupidaggine
[stu•PIDAH•DJI•ne] *n* F
drivel

stupiditá [STU•pi•DI•tah] *n* F
stupidity

stupido; stupida [stuh•PI•do];
[stuh•PI•da] *adj* dumb; stupid
adj n MF idiot; fool

stupire [stu•PEE•re] *vt* amaze;
astonish

stupore [stu•POH•re] *n* M daze;
stupor

stuzzicare [stutsi•KAH•re] *vt*
tease

su [ssuh] *prep* on; up; in su\ *adv*
upward

subaffittare
[SUB•af•FI•TAH•re] *vt* sublet

subcosciente
[SUB•ko•SHEHN•te] *adj n*
MF subconscious

subire [su•BEE•re] *vt* undergo

subitaneitá [SU•bi•ta•NEI•tah]
n F suddenness

sublime [su•BLEE•me] *adj*
sublime

subordinato; subodinata
[SU•bor•di•NAH•to];
[SU•bor•di•NAH•ta] *n adj* MF
subordinate

suburbano; suburbana
[SU•bur•BAH•no];
[SU•bur•BAH•na] *adj* MF
suburban

suburbo [su•BUHR•bo] *n* M
suburb

successione
[SU•tshes•SYOH•ne] *n* F
succession

successo [su•TSHEHS•so] *n* M
success

succhiare [suk•KYAH•re] *vt*
suck

succo [SUHK•ko] *n* M juice

succolento; succolenta
[SUK•ko•LEHN•to];
[SUK•ko•LEHN•ta] *adj* MF
succulent; luscious

sud [suhd] *n* M south

Sud America
[SUHD•a•MEH•rika] *n* M
South America

sud est [SUHD•ehst] *n* M
southeast

sud ovest [SUHD•oh•VEST] *n*
M southwest

sudare [su•DAH•re] *vi* perspire

sudario [su•DAH•ryo] *n* M
shroud

suddivisione
[SUD•di•VIZYOH•ne] *n* F
subdivision

sudicio; sudicia [suh•DIT•sho];
[suh•dit•sha] *adj* MF filthy;
grimy

sudiciume [SU•di•TSHUH•me]
n M filth; grime

sudore [su•DOH•re] *n* M sweat

sufficiente
[SUF•fi•TSHEHN•te] *adj*
sufficient

sufficienza
[SUF•fi•TSHEHN•tsa] *n* F
sufficiency

suffragio [suf•FRAH•djo] *n* M
suffrage

suggerimento
[su•DJE•ri•MEHN•to] *n* M
cue; hint; suggestion

suggerire [SUDJE•REE•re] *vt*
suggest; hint (at)

suggestivo; suggestiva
[SU•djes•TEE•vo];
[SU•djes•TEE•va] *adj* MF
suggestive

sugoso; sugosa [su•GOH•zo];
[su•GOH•za] *adj* MF juicy

suicidio [sui•TSHEE•dyo] *n* M
suicide

suo; sua [SUH•o]; [SUH•a] *pos*
adj his; hers

il suo; la sua [il•SUH•o];
[lah•SUH•a] *poss pron* hers

suocera [SUOH•tshe•ra] *n* F
mother-in-law

suoceri [SUOH•tshe•ri] *n* M
in-laws

suocero [SUOH•tshe•o] *n* M
father-in-law

suola [SUOH•la] *n* F sole

suolo [SUOH•lo] *n* M soil

suono [SUOH•no] *n* M sound;
suono del clakson *n* M\ horn
(auto); honk

superare [su•PERAH•re] *vi*
exceed; go beyond; surpass; *vt*
pass; overtake

superare in importanza
[su•PERAH•re in
IM•por•TAHN•tsa] *vt*
outweigh

superare in numero
[SU•pe•RAH•re in
NUH•mero] *vt* outnumber

superbia [su•PEHR•bya] *n* F
conceit

superbo; superba
[su•PEHR•bo];
[su•PEHER•ba] *adj* MF
conceited

superficiale
[SU•per•fit•SHA•le] *adj*
skin-deep

superiore [SU•pe•RYOH•re]
adj upper

superstite [SU•pehr•STI•te] *n*
MF survivor

supplementare
[SUP•ple•men•TAH•re] *adj*
additional

supplicare [SUP•pli•KAH•re] *vt*
plead

suscettibile
[SU•tshet•TEE•BI•le] *adj*
susceptible; touchy

suscettibilitá
[SU•shet•TI•BI•li•tah] *n* F
susceptibility

suspense [sus•PAHNS] *n* M
suspense

susseguente
[SUS•se•GUEHN•te] *adj*
subsequent

sussistere [SUS•sees•TE•re] *vi*
subsist

sutura [su•TUH•ra] *n* F suture

svago [ZVAH•go] *n* M
recreation

svalutare [ZVA•lu•TAH•re] *vt*
depreciate

svalutazione
[ZVA•lu•TATSYOH•ne] *n* F
inflation

svanire [zva•NEE•re] *vt* vanish

svantaggio [zvan•TAH•djyo] *n*
M disadvantage

svedese [zve•DEH•ze] *n* MF
Swede; *adj* Swedish

sveglia [SVE•lia] *n* F alarm
clock

svegliare [zve•LYAH•re] *vt*
rouse; waken

svegliarsi [zve•LYAHR•si] *vi*
wake

sveglio; sveglia
[ZVEH•lio];[ZVEH•lia] *adj*
MF awake; wide awake

svelare [zve•LAH•re] *vt*
disclose; expose

svelto; svelta
[ZVEHL•to];[ZVEHL•ta] *adj*
MF brisk; quick

svendere [svehn•DE•re] *vt*
undersell

svendita [ZVEHN•dita] *n* F
clearance

svenire [sve•NEE•re] *vi*
swoon

sventatezza
[ZVEN•ta•TEH•sa] *n* F
thoughtlessness

sventato; sventata
[ZVEN•TAH•to];
[ZVEN•TAH•ta] *adj* MF
thoughtless; unthinking

svernare [zver•NAH•re] *vi*
hibernate

svestire [zves•TEE•re] *vt*
undress

Svezia [ZVEH•tsya] *n* F
Sweden

svilire [zvi•LEE•re] *vt* debase

sviluppare [ZVI•lup•PAH•re] *vt*
develop

sviluppo [ZVI•luhp•PO] *n* M
development

Svizzera [svi•TSEH•ra] *n* F
Switzerland

svizzero; svizzera
[svi•TSEH•ro]; [svi•TSEH•ra]
n adj MF Swiss

svolgere [ZVOHL•dje•re] *vt*
unwrap

T

tabaccaio; tabaccaia
[ta•BAK•KAH•yo];
[ta•BAK•KAH•ya] *n* MF
tobacconist

tabacco [ta•BAHK•ko] *n* M
tobacco

tabacco da fiuto
[ta•BAHK•ko•dah•FYUH•to]
n snuff

tabella [ta•BEHL•la] *n* F table

tacca [TAHK•ka] *n* F nick;
notch

taccagno; taccagna
[tak•KAH•nyo];
[tak•KAH•nya] *n* MF skinflint

tacchino [tak•KEE•no] *n* M
turkey

tacitare [TA•tshi•TA•re] *vt*
cover-up (scandal, etc)

tacito; tacita [tah•TSHI•to];
[ta•TSHI•ta] *adj* MF tacit

taciturno; taciturna
[TA•tshi•TUHR•no];
[TA•tshi•TUHR•na] *adj* MF
taciturn

tacometro [TA•koh•ME•tro] *n*
M tachometer

taffetá [taf•FE•tah] *n* M taffeta

taglia [TAH•lya] *n* F size

taglia erba [TAH•lya•EHR•ba]
n M lawn mower

tagliare [ta•LYAH•re] *vt* cut;
chop; slash; clip

tagliare a metá [TA•lyah•re ah
ME•tah] *vt* halve

tagliatelle [TA•lya•TEHL•le]
npl F noodles

taglio [TAH•lyo] *n* M cut

taglio dei capelli
[TAH•lyo•dehi•KA•PEHL•li]
n M haircut

talco [TAHL•ko] *n* M talcum

tale [TAH•le] *adj* such

talento [ta•LEHN•to] *n* M
talent

talpa [TAHL•pa] *n* F mole

tamburino [TAM•bu•REE•no]
n M drummer

tamburo [tam•BUH•ro] *n* M
drum

tampone [tam•POH•ne] *n* M
swab; wad

tana [TAH•na] *n* F burrow; den
(of an animal); lair

tandem [tahn•dem] *n* M tandem

tangente [TAN•DJEHN•te] *n* F
tangent

Tangeri [tan•DJEH•ri] *n* F
Tangiers

tangibile [tan•DJEE•bi•le] *adj*
tangible

tantalizzare
[TAN•ta•li•TSAH•re] *vt*
tantalize

tappeto [tap•PEH•to] *n* M
carpet; rug; tapestry

tappezzare [TAP•pe•TSAH•re]
vt upholster

tappo [TAHP•po] *n* M cork;
plug; stopper

tara [TAH•ra] *n* F tare

tarchiato; tarchiata
[tar•KYAH•to];
[tar•KYAH•ta] *adj* MF stocky

tardivo; tardiva [tar•DEE•vo];
[tar•DEE•va] *adj* tardy

tardo; tarda
[TAH•rdo];[TAH•rda] *adj* MF
belated; late

targa [TAHR•ga] *n* F placard

tariffa [ta•REEF•ta] *n* F fare;
tariff

tartaro [TAHR•taro] *n* M tartar

tartaruga [TAR•ta•RUH•ga] *n*
M tortoise; turtle

tasca [TAHS•ka] *n* F pocket

tassare [tas•SAH•re] *vt* tax

tassí [TAS•see] *n* M taxi

tasso [TAHS•so] *n* M rate

tasso di nascite [TAHS•so di
NAH•SHI•te] *n* M birthrate

tastiera [tas•TYEH•ra] *n* F
keyboard

tattica [taht•TI•ka] *n* F tactics

tattico; tattica [taht•TI•ko];
[taht•TI•ka] *adv* MF tactical

tattile [taht•TI•le] *adj* tactile

tatto [TAHT•to] *n* M tact

tatuaggio [ta•TUAH•djo] *n* M
tattoo

tatuare [ta•TUAH•re] *vt* tattoo

taverna [ta•VEHR•na] *n* F
tavern

tavoletta [TA•vo•LEHT•ta] *n* F
tablet

tavolo [tah•VO•lo] *n* M table
(card)

tavolozza [TA•vo•LOH•tsa] *n*
F palette

taxi [TA•xi] *n* M cab

tazza [TAH•tsa] *n* F cup

tazza da the
[TAH•tsa•DAH•teh] *n* F
teacup

tazzina da caffé
[TA•tsee•na•da•KAF•feh] *n* F
coffee cup

teatrale [TE•a•TRAH•le] *adj*
theatrical

teatro [TEAH•tro] *n* M theater

tecnico; tecnica [tehk•NI•ko];
[tehk•NI•ka] *adj* technical; *n*
MF technician

tedesco; tedesca
[te•DEHS•ko]; [te•DEHS•ka]
adj n MF German

tedioso; tediosa
[te•DYOH•zo]; [te•DYOH•za]
adj MF tedious

tegame [te•GAH•me] *n* M pan

teiera [te•YEH•ra] *n* F teapot

tela [TEH•la] *n* F canvas

telaio [te•LAH•yo] *n* M loom;
undercarriage

telefonata [TELE•fo•NAH•ta]
n F phone call

telefono [te•LEH•fono] *n* M
phone; telephone

telefono pubblico
[TE•leh•FONO PUHB•bli•ko]
n M pay phone

telegrafo [TE•leh•GRA•fo] *n*
M telegraph

telegramma
[TE•le•GRAHM•ma] *n* M
telegram

telescopio [TE•les•KOH•pyo] *n*
M telescope

teletrasmettere
[TE•le•traz•MEHT•te•re] *vt*
televise

televisione
[TE•le•VIS•YOH•ne] *n* F
television

televisione a colori
[TE•le•VIZ•YOH•ne ah
KO•LOH•ri] *n* F color
television

televisore [TE•le•VI•ZOH•re] *n*
M television set

telfonare [TE•le•fo•NAH•re] *vi*
call (by phone)

telone [te•LOH•ne] *n* M
tarpaulin

tema [TEH•ma] n] M theme

temerarietá
[te•ME•ra•RYE•tah] *n* F
temerity

temperamatite
[TEHM•pe•ra•MA•TEE•te] *n*
M pencil sharpener

temperamento
[TEM•pe•ra•MEHN•to] *n* M
temperament

temperanza
[TEM•pe•RAHN•tsa] *n* F
temperance

temperato; temperata
[TEM•pe•RAH•to];
[TEM•pe•RAH•ta] *adj* MF
temperate

temperatura
[TEM•pe•ra•TUH•ra] *n* F
temperature

temperino [TEM•pe•REE•no] *n*
M pocketknife

tempesta [tem•PEHS•ta] *n* F
storm; tempest

tempestivo; tempestiva
[TEM•pes•TEE•vo];
[TEM•pes•TEE•va] *adj* MF
timely

tempestoso; tempestosa
[TEM•pes•TOH•zo];
[TEM•pes•TOH•za] *adj* MF
stormy; tempestuous

tempia [TEHM•pya] *n* F
temple

tempio [TEHM•pyo] *n* M
temple

tempo [TEHM•po] *n* M tense;
time; weather

tempo antico
[TEHM•po•an•TEE•ko] *n* M
yore

tempo pieno (a)
[TEHM•po•PYEH•no] *adj adv*
MF full-time

temporale [TEM•po•RAH•le] *n*
M temporal; thunderstorm

temporaneo; temporanea
[TEM•po•RAH•neo];
[TEM•po•RAH•nea] *adj* MF
temporary

temporeggiare
[TEM•po•re•DJAH•re] *vi*
temporize

tenace [te•NAH•tshe] *adj*
tenacious

tenacia [te•NAH•tsha] *n* F
tenacity

tenda [TEHN•da] *n* F curtain;
tent; drapes

tendenza [ten•DEHN•tsa] *n* F
tendency; trend

tendere [tehn•DE•re] *vi* tend

tendine [tehn•DI•ne] *n* M
sinew; tendontenendo in conto
[te•NEHN•do•in•KOHN•to]
prep considering

tenente [te•NEHN•te] *n* M
lieutenant

tenerezza [TE•ne•REH•tsa] *n* F
tenderness

tenero; tenera [teh•NE•ro];
[teh•ne•ra] *adj* MF tender

tennis [TEHN•nis] *n* M tennis

tenore [te•NOH•re] *n* M tenor

tensile [tehn•SI•le] *adj* tensile

tensione [ten•SYOH•ne] *n* F
tension

tentare [ten•TAH•re] *vt* attempt
(to); tempt

tentazione
[TEN•ta•TSYOH•ne] *n* F
temptation

tenue [TEH•nue] *adj* tenuous

tenuta [te•NUH•ta] *n* F
tightness

teologia [TEO•lo•DJEE•a] *n* F
theology

teorema [TEO•REH•ma] *n* M
theorem

teoretico; teoretica
[TEO•reh•TI•ko];
[TEO•reh•TI•ka] *adj* MF
theoretical

teoria [teo•REE•a] *n* F theory

teppista [tep•PEE•sta] *n* MF
hoodlum

terapeutico; terapeutica
[TE•ra•POI•tiko];
[TE•ra•POI•tika] *adj* MF
therapeutic

termico; termica [tehr•MI•ko];
[tehr•MI•ka] *adj* MF thermal

termine [TEHR•mine] *n* M
term

termometro
[TER•moh•ME•tro] *n* M
thermometer

termostato [TER•moh•STA•to]
n M thermostat

terra [TEHR•ra] *n* F dirt
(earth); earth; ground; land

terrazzo [ter•RAH•tso] *n* M
terrace

terremoto [ter•REMOH•to] *n*
M earthquake

terreno [ter•REH•no] *n* M site;
terrain

terreno boscoso [ter•REH•no
BOS•KOOH•zo] *n* M
woodland

terrestre [ter•REHS•tre] *adj*
terrestrial

terribile [ter•REE•BI•le] *adj*
awful; dire; terrible

territorio [TER•ri•TOH•ryo] *n*
M territory

terrore [ter•ROH•re] *n* M terror

terrorizzare
[TER•ro•rit•SAH•re] *vt*
terrorize

terso; tersa [TEHR•o];
[TEHR•sa] *adj* MF terse

terzo; terza [TEHR•tso];
[THER•tsa] *adj* MF third; in
terzo luogo\ *adv* thirdly

teschio [TEHS•kyo] *n* M skull

tesi [TEH•zi] *n* F thesis

teso; tesa [TEH•zo]; [TEH•za]
adj MF tense

tesoreria [TE•zo•re•REE•a] *n* F
treasury

tesoriere; tesoriera
[TE•zo•RYEH•re];

[TE•zo•RYEH•ra] *adj* MF
treasurer

tesoro 1 [te•ZOH•ro] *n* M
hoard; treasure

tesoro 2 [te•ZOH•ro] *n* M
darling

tessile [tehs•SI•le] *adj* textile

tessuto [tes•SUH•to] *n* M tissue

testamento [TES•ta•MEHN•to]
n M testament

testardaggine
[TES•tar•dah•DJI•ne] *n* F
stubbornness

testardo; testarda
[TES•TAHR•do];
[TES•TAHR•da] *adj* MF
stubborn

testimone [TES•ti•MOH•ne] *n*
MF witness

testimone oculare
[TES•ti•MOH•ne
oku•LAH•re] *n* MF eye
witness

testimonianza
[TES•ti•MO•NYAHN•tsa] *n* F
testimony

testo [TEHS•to] *n* M text

tetano [teh•TA•no] *n* M tetanus

tetro; tetra [TEH•tro];
[TEH•tra] *adj* MF dismal;
dreary; glum

the [teh] *n* M tea

tiara [TYAH•ra] *n* tiara

tibia [TEE•bya] *n* F tibia

ticchettare [TIK•ket•TAH•re]
vi tick

tiepido; tiepida [tyeh•PI•do];
[tyeh•PI•da] *adj* MF
lukewarm; tepid

tifo [TEE•fo] *n* M typhus

tifoideo; tifoidea
[TI•fo•YDEH•o];
[TI•fo•YDEH•a] *adj* typhoid

tifone [ti•FOH•ne] *n* M typhoon

tigre [TEE•gre] *n* MF tiger;
tigress

timidezza [TI•mi•DEHT•sa] *n*
F shyness

timido; timida [TEEM•I•do];
[TEEM•I•da] *adj* MF bashful;
shy; timid

timo [TEE•mo] *n* M thyme

timone [ti•MOH•ne] *n* M helm;
rudder

timore [ti•MOH•re] *n* M dread

timpani [teem•PA•ni] *n* M
tympani

timpano [teem•PANO] *n* M
gable

tino [TEE•no] *n* M vat

tinta [TEEN•ta] *n* F dye; hue

tintinnare [TIN•tin•NAH•re] *vi*
tinkle

tintura [tin•TUH•ra] *n* F
tincture

tintura d'iodio
[TIN•tuh•ra•DYOH•dyo] *n* F
iodine

tipico; tipica [TEE•pi•ko];
[tee•pi•ka] *adj* MF typical

tipo 1 [TEE•po] *n* M guy

tipo 2 [TEE•po] *n* M type

tipografia [TI•po•grah•FEE•a]
n F typography

tipografo [TI•poh•GRA•fo] *n*
M printer

tirannia [TI•ran•NEE•a] *n* F
tyranny

tirannico; tirannica
[TI•rahn•NI•ko];
[TI•rahn•NI•ka] *adj* MF
tyrannical

tiranno; tiranna [ti•RAHN•no];
[ti•RAHN•na] *n* MF tyrant

tirare [ti•RAH•re] *vt* pull;
stretch; tighten; tug

tiratore [TI•ra•TOH•re] *n* M
shooter

tiratura [TI•ra•TUH•ra] *n* F
printing

tiro [TEE•ro] *n* M prank

titolare [TI•to•LAH•re] *adj*
titular

titolo [TEE•tolo] *n* M headline;
title

toboga [to•BOH•ga] *n* M
toboggan

tocco [TOHK•ko] *n* M touch

tolda [TOHL•da] *n* F deck

tollerante [TOL•le•RAHN•te]
adj tolerant

tolleranza [TOL•le•RAHN•tsa]
n F tolerance

tollerare [TOL•le•RAH•re] *vt*
tolerate

tomba [TOHM•ba] *n* F tomb

tonante [to•NAHN•te] *adj*
thundering

tonico [toh•NI•ko] *n* M tonic

tonnellaggio
[TON•nel•LAH•djo] *n* M
tonnage

tonnellata [TON•nel•LAH•ta] *n*
F ton

tonno [TOHN•no] *n* M tuna

tono [TOH•no] *n* M tone

tonsilla [ton•SEE•la] *n* F tonsil

tonsillite [TON•sil•LEE•te] *n* F
tonsillitis

tonsura [TON•SUH•re] *n* F
tonsure

topazio [to•PAH•tsyo] *n* M
topaz

topi [TOH•pi] *n* M mice

topo [TOH•po] *n* M mouse

topografia [TO•po•gra•FEE•a]
n F topography

torace [to•RAH•tshe] *n* M chest

torba [TOHR•ba] *n* F peat

torbido; torbida [TOHR•bido];
[TOHR•bida] *adj* murky;
turbid

torcia [TOHR•tsha] *n* F torch

tordo [TOHR•do] *n* M thrush

tormenta [tohr•MEHN•ta] *n* F
blizzard

tormentare [tor•MEN•TAH•re]
vt harass

tormentatore; tormentatrice
[tor•men•ta•toh•re];
[TOR•men•TA•TREE•tshe] *n*
MF tormentor

tormento [tor•MEHN•to] *n* M
torment

tornado [tor•NAH•do] *n* M
tornado

torneo [tor•NE•ho] *n* M
tournament

toro [TOH•ro] *n* M bull

torpedine [TOR•peh•DI•ne] *n*
F torpedo

torre [TOHR•re] *n* F tower

torreggiare [TOR•redj•AH•re]
vi tower

torrente [tor•REHN•te] *n* M
torrent

torretta [tor•REH•ta] *n* F turret

torrido; torrida [tor•REE•do];
[tor•REE•da] *adj* MF torrid

torta [TOHR•tah] *n* F cake; pie

torto [TOHR•to] *n* M harm

tortuoso; tortuosa
[tor•TUOH•zo];
[tor•TUOH•za] *adj* MF
devious; tortuous; winding

tortura [tor•TUH•ra] *n* F torture

torvo; torva [TOHR•vo];
[TOHR•va] *adj MF* grim

tosse [TOHS•se] *n F* cough

tossico; tossica [tohs•SI•ko];
[tohs•SI•ka] *adj MF* toxic

tossicodipendente
[TOHS•si•ko•di•PEN•DEHN•te]
n MF addict; drug addict

tossina [tos•SEE•na] *n F* toxin

totale [to•TAH•le] *n M* total

totalitá [TO•ta•LITAH] *n F*
entirety; totality

totalitario totalitaria
[TO•ta•li•TAH•ryo];
[TO•ta•li•TAH•rya] *adj*
totalitarian

totalmente [TO•tal•MEHN•te]
adv totally

tovagliolo [TO•va•LYOH•lo] *n*
M napkin

tozzo; tozza [TOH•tso];
[TOH•tsa] *adj MF* squat

tra [trah] *prep* between

tra le quinte
[TRAH•le•KWEEN•te] *adj*
adv offstage

tra poco [trah•POH•ko] *adv*
presently

traballare [TRA•bal•LAH•re] *vi*
topple

traccia [TRAH•tsha] *n F* trace

tracciato [tra•TSHAH•to] *n M*
layout

trachea [tra•KEH•a] *n F* trachea

tradimento
[TRA•di•MEHN•to] *n M*
betrayal; treachery; treason

tradire [tra•DEE•re] *vt* betray

traditore [TRA•di•TOH•re] *n*
M betrayer; traitor

traditore; traditrice
[TRA•di•TOH•re];
[TRA•di•TREE•tshe] *adj MF*
treacherous

tradizione
[TRA•di•TSYOH•ne] *n F*
tradition

tradurre [tra•DUHR•re] *vt*
translate

traduttore; traduttrice
[TRA•dut•TOH•re];
[TRA•dut•TREE•tshe] *n MF*
translator

traduzione
[TRA•du•TSYOH•ne] *n F*
translation

traffico [trahf•FI•ko] *n M* traffic

tragedia [tra•DJEH•dya] *n F*
tragedy

traghetto [tra•GEHT•to] *n M*
ferry

tragico; tragica [trah•DJI•ko];
[trah•DJI•ka] *adj MF* tragic

traguardo [tra•GUAHR•do] *n*
M finish (~line)

traiettoria [TRA•yet•TOH•rya]
n F trajectory

trainare [tra•YNAH•re] *vt* tow

traliccio [tra•LEE•tsho] *n M*
lattice

tram [trahm] *n M* streetcar;
tram; trolley

trama 1 [TRAH•ma] *n F* plot

trama 2 [TRAH•ma] *n F*
weave; woof (fabric)

tramare [trah•MA•re] *vt* plot;
plan

trambusto [TRAM•BUH•sto] *n*
M bustle; fuss

tramite cui
[TRAH•mi•te•KUH•i] *pron*
whereby

trampolo [TRAHM•po•lo] *n* M
stilt

trance [TRAHN•s] *n* F trance

trangugiare
[TRAN•gu•DJAH•re] *vt*
gobble; gulp

tranquillamente
[tran•KWIL•la•MEHN•te] *adv*
quietly

tranquillitá [tran•KWIL•li•tah]
n F tranquillity

tranquillo; tranquilla
[tran•KWEEL•lo];
[tran•KWEEL•la] *adj* MF
quiet; tranquil

transazione
[tran•ZA•TSYOH•ne] *adj* F
transaction

transetto [tran•ZEHT•to] *n* M
transept

transitivo; transitiva
[tran•ZI•TEE•vo];
[tran•ZI•TEE•va] *adj* MF
transitive

transito [TRAHN•zi•to] *n* M
transit

transitorio; transitoria
[TRAN•zi•TOH•ryo];
[TRAN•zi•TOH•rya] *adj* MF
momentary; transient;
transitory

transizione
[TRAN•zi•TSYOH•ne] *n* F
transition

trapano [trah•PAN•o] *n* M drill

trapezio [tra•PEH•tsyo] *n* M
trapeze

trapiantare
[TRA•pyan•TAH•re] *vt*
transplant

trappola [trap•POH•la] *n* F trap

trapunta [tra•PUHN•ta] *n* F
quilt

trasalire [TRA•sa•LEE•re] *vi*
wince

trascendere
[TRA•shehn•DE•re] *vt*
transcend

trascinare [TRA•shi•NAH•re]
vt drag; lug

trascinare i piedi
[TRA•shi•NAH•re EE
PYEH•di] *vt* shuffle

trascrivere [TRAS•kree•VE•re]
vt transcribe

trascurare [TRAS•KURAH•re]
vt overlook

trascuratezza
[TRAS•ku•ra•TEH•tsa] *n* F
neglect

trascurato; trascurata
[tras•KURAH•to];
[tras•KURAH•ta] *adj* MF
forlorn

trasferire [TRAS•fe•REE•re] *vt*
transfer

trasformare
[TRAS•for•MAH•re] *vt*
transform

trasformatore
[TRAS•for•MATOH•re] *n* M
transformer

trasformazione
[TRAS•for•MA•TSYOH•ne] *n*
F transformation

trasfusione
[TRAS•fu•SYOH•ne] *n* F
transfusion

trasgredire [TRAS•gre•DEE•re]
vi transgress

trasgressione
[TRAS•gres•SYOH•ne] *n* F
transgression

trasgressore
[TRAZ•gres•SOH•re] *n* M
trespasser

traslucido; traslucida
[TRAZ•luh•TSHI•do] *adj* MF
translucent

trasmettere
[TRAZ•meht•TE•re] *vt*
broadcast; transmit

trasmettitore
[TRAZ•met•ti•TOH•re] *n* M
transmitter

trasmissione
[TRAZ•mis•YOH•ne] *n* F
broadcast; transmission

trasparente
[TRAS•pa•REHN•te] *adj*
transparent

traspirazione
[TRAS•pi•rat•syoh•ne] *n* F
perspiration

traspirazione
[TRAS•pi•rah•TSYOH•ne] *n*
F transpiration

trasporre [tras•POHR•re] *vt*
transpose

trasportare
[TRAS•por•TAH•re] *vt* carry;
transport; cart; convey; haul

trasportatore a cinghia
[TRAS•por•TATOH•re ah
TSHEEN•gya] *n* M conveyer
belt

trasporto [tras•POHR•to] *n* M
transport

trastullarsi
[TRAS•tul•LAHR•si] *vi* frolic

trasversale [TRAZ•ver•SAH•le]
adj transverse; traverse

traversarse
[TRAZ•ver•SAR•se] *vt* cross;
traverse; go through

trattabile [trat•TAH•BI•le] *adj*
tractable

trattamento
[TRAT•ta•MEHN•to] *n* M
treatment

trattare [trat•TAH•re] *vt*
negotiate; treat; deal with

trattativa [TRAT•ta•TEE•va] *n*
F negotiation

trattato [trat•TAH•to] *n* M tract

trattato [trat•TAH•to] *n* M
treatise; treaty; dissertation;
essay

trattenere [TRAT•te•NEH•re]
vt detain; withhold

trattenersi [TRAT•te•NEHR•si]
vi refrain; hold back (from)

trattenuta [TRAT•te•NUH•ta]
n F deduction

tratto [TRAHT•to] *n* M trait

trattore [trat•TOH•re] *n* M
tractor

trave [TRAH•ve] *n* F beam;
rafter

trave maestra
[TRAH•ve•ma•EHS•tra] *n* F
girder

traversa [tra•VEHR•sa] *n* F
transom

travestimento
[TRA•ves•TIMEHN•to] *n* M
disguise

trazione [tra•TSYOH•ne] *n* F
traction

tre [treh] *num* three

tre volte [treh•VOHL•te] *adv*
thrice

trebbiare [treb•BYAH•re] *vt*
thresh

trebbiatura
[TREB•bya•TUH•ra] *n* F
threshing

treccia [TREH•shya] *n* F braid

tredicesimo; tredicesima
[TRE•di•TSHEH•ZI•mo];
[RE•di•tSHEH•ZI•ma] *adj* MF
thirteenth

tredici [treh•DIT•shi] *num*
thirteen

tregua [TREH•gua] *n* F truce;
peace

tremare [tre•MAH•re] *vi* falter;
quake; quaver; tremble

tremendo [tre•MEN•do]
tremendous

trementina [TRE•men•TEE•na]
n F turpentine

tremito [treh•MI•to] *n* M
tremor

tremulo; tremula
[treh•MU•lo]; [treh•MU•la]
adj MF tremulous

trench coat [trehn•TSH•kot] *n*
M trench coat

treno espresso
[TREH•no•es•PREHS•so] *n* M
train (express)

trenta [TREHN•ta] *num* thirty

trentesimo; trentesima
[TREN•teh•ZI•mo];
[TREN•teh•ZI•ma] *adj*
thirtieth

trentunesimo; trentunesima
[TREN•tu•NEH•ZI•mo];
[TREN•tuneh•ZI•ma] *adj* MF
thirty-first

treppiedi [trep•PYEH•di] *n* M
tripod

triangolo [TRI•AHN•GO•lo] *n*
M triangle

tribolazione
[TRI•bo•lah•TSYOH•ne] *n* F
tribulation

tribordo [tri•BOHR•do] *n* M
starboard

tribú [TRI•buh] *n* F tribe

tribuna [tri•BUH•na] *n* F
tribune

tribunale [TRI•bu•NAH•le] *n*
M tribunal

tributario; tributaria
[TRI•bu•TAH•ryo];
[TRI•bu•TAH•rya] *adj* MF
tributary

trifoglio 1 [tri•FOH•lyo] *n* M
clover

trifoglio 2 [tri•FOH•lyo] *n* M
trefoil

trillo [TREEL•lo] *n* M trill

trimestrale
[TRI•mes•TRAH•le] *adj*
quarterly (by trimester)

trincarino [TRIN•ka•REE•no] *n*
M waterway

trincea [tryn•TSHEH•a] *n* F
trench

trio [TREE•o] *n* M trio

trionfalmente
[TRION•fal•MEHN•te] *adv*
triumphantly

trionfante [TRI•on•FAHN•te] *n*
MF triumphant

trionfo [TRIOHN•fo] *n* M
triumph

triplicare [TRI•pli•KAH•re] *vt*
treble

triplo; tripla [TREE•plo];
[TREE•pla] *adj* MF triple

triste [TREE•ste] *adj* miserable;
sad; despondent

tristezza [tris•TEH•tsa] *n* F
sadness; misery; gloom

tritare [tri•TAH•re] *vt* mince

trito; trita [TREE•to]; [TREE•ta] *adj* MF trite; overworn; hackneyed

trofeo [tro•FEH•o] *n* M trophy

troglodita [TRO•glo•DEE•tah] *n* MF caveman

tromba [TROHM•ba] *n* F trumpet; bugle

trombone [trom•BOH•ne] *n* M trombone

tronco [TROHN•ko] *n* M trunk; stump (tree); -o -a\ *adj* cut off; truncated

trono [TROH•no] *n* M throne

tropicale [TRO•pi•KAH•le] *adj* tropical

tropico [TROH•pi•ko] *n* M tropic

troppo [TROH•poh] *adj* too; too-much; too many

trottare [trot•TAH•re] *vi* trot

trotto [TROHT•to] *n* M trot

trovare [tro•VAH•re] *vt* find

trovatello; trovatella [TRO•va•TEHL•lo]; [TRO•va•TEHL•la] *n* MF waif

trovato; trovata [tro•VAH•to]; [tro•VAH•ta] *pp* found

trucco1 [TRUHK•ko] *n* M make-up

trucco 2 [TRUHK•ko] *n* M ruse; trick

truffa [TRUHF•fa] *n* F swindle; hocus-pocus

truffare [truf•FAH•re] *vt* swindle

truffatore [TRUT•FATOH•re] *n* M crook

truogolo [TRUOH•golo] *n* M trough

truppa [TRUHP•pa] *n* F troop

tu [tuh] *per pron* you; thou

tu stesso; tu stessa [tuh•STEHS•so]; [tuh•STEHS•sa] *per pron* yourself

tubare [tu•BAH•re] *vi* coo

tubatura [TU•ba•TUH•ra] *n* F pipe

tubazione [TU•ba•TSYOH•ne] *n* F tubing

tubercolare [TU•ber•KOLAH•re] *adj* tubercular

tubercolosi [TU•ber•ko•LOH•zi] *n* F tuberculosis

tubetto [tu•BEHT•to] *n* M tube

tuffo [TUHF•fo] *n* M dip; dive; plunge

tugurio [TU•GUH•ryo] *n* M hovel

tulipano [TU•li•PAH•no] *n* M tulip

tulle [TUHL•le] *n* M tulle

tumore [tu•MOH•re] *n* M tumor

tumulo [tuh•MU•lo] *n* M mound

tumulto [tu•MUHL•to] *n* M riot; tumult; uproar

tumultuoso; tumultuosa [TU•mul•TUOH•zo]; [TU•mul•TUOH•za] *adj* MF tumultuous

tunica [tuh•NI•ka] *n* F robe; tunic

tunnel [TUHN•nel] *n* M tunnel

tuo; tua [TUH•o]; [tuh•a] *adj* MF your; yours

tuono [TUOH•no] *n* M thunder

turbato; turbata [tur•BAH•to];
[tur•BAH•ta] *adj* MF
distraught

turbina [tur•BEE•na] *n* F
turbine

turbinare [TUR•bi•NAH•re] *vi*
whirl

turbine [tuhr•BINE] *n* M flurry;
whirlwind

turbolento; turbolenta
[TUR•bo•LEHN•to];
[TUR•bo•LEHN•ta] *adj* MF
turbulent

turchese [tur•KEH•ze] *adj*
turquoise

Turchia [tur•KEE•a] *n* F
Turkey

turco; turca [TUHR•ko];
[TUHR•ka] *n* MF Turk; *adj*
Turkish

turgido; turgida
[TUHR•DJI•do];
[TUHR•DJI•da] *adj* MF turgid

turista [tu•REES•ta] *n* MF
tourist

turno [TUHR•no] *n* M turn

turpitudine
[TUR•pi•TUH•DI•ne] *n* F
turpitude

tuta [TUH•ta] *n* F overalls

tutore [tu•TOH•re] *n* M tutor

tuttavia [TUT•ta•VEE•a] *adv*
nevertheless; *conj* yet

tutto [TUHT•to] *pron* M
everything; -o -a\ *adj* all

tuttora [TUT•TOH•ra] *adv* still

tweed [tueed] *n* M tweed

U

ubicazione
[UBI•ka•TSYOH•ne] *n* F
whereabouts

ubriachezza [U•bri•AK•EH•tsa]
n F drunkenness

ubriaco; ubriaca
[ub•RIAH•ko]; [ub•riah•ka]
adj MF drunk

uccello [UTSH•el•loh] *n* M bird

uccello canterino
[u•TSHEHL•lo
KAN•te•REE•no] *n* M
song-bird

uccidere [ut•SHEE•dere] *vt* kill

udienza [OO•dee•EN•sah] *n* F
audience

udire [UDEE•re] *vt* hear

udire per caso
[UDEE•re•pehr•KAH•zo] *vt*
overhear

udito [UDEE•to] *n* M hearing

ufficiale [uf•fi•TSHAH•le] *n* M
officer; *adj* official

ufficio [UF•fee•TSHYO] *n* M
bureau; office

ufficio postale [uf•FEE•tsho
POS•TAH•le] *n* M post office

uggiolio [udjo•LEE•o] *n* M
whine

ugola [uh•GO•la] *n* F uvula

uguale [u•GUAH•le] *adj* equal

ulcera [uhl•TSHERA] *n* F ulcer

ulcerazione
[ul•TSHE•rah•TSYOH•ne] *n* F
ulceration

ulteriore [ul•TERYOH•re] *adj*
further; ulterior

ultimo; ultima [uhl•TI•mo];
[uhl•TI•ma] *adj* MF last

ululo [uh•LULO] *n* M howl

umanitá [U•ma•NI•TAH] *n* F
humanity; mankind

umanitario; umanitaria
[u•MA•ni•TAH•ryo];
[u•MA•ni•TAH•rya] *adj* MF
humanitarian

umano; umana [u•MAH•no];
[u•MAH•na] *adj* MF human;
humane

umiditá [U•mi•DI•tah] *n* F
humidity; moisture

umido; umida [uh•MI•do];
[uh•MI•da] *adj* MF damp;
humid; moist

umile [uh•MI•le] *adj* humble;
lowly

umiliare [U•mi•LYAH•re] *vt*
humiliate

umiliazione
[u•MI•lya•TSYOH•ne] *n* F
humiliation

umiltá [u•MIL•tah] *n* F humility

umore [uh•MOH•re] *n* M mood

umorismo [U•mo•REEZ•mo] *n*
M humor

un altro; un'altra
[un•AHL•tro]; [un•AHLTRA]
adj another

un; una [uhn]; [uhna] *art* MF a;
one

una volta [UH•na•VOHL•ta]
adv once

unanime [U•nah•NIME] *adj*
unanimous

unanimitá [UNA•ni•MI•tah']* n*
F unanimity

uncinetto [UN•tshi•NEHT•to] *n*
M crochet

uncino [un•TSHEE•no] *n* M
hook

undicesimo; undicesima
[UN•di•TSHEH•SI•mo];
[UN•di•TSHEH•SI•ma] *adj*
MF eleventh

undici [UHN•ditshi] *num* eleven

ungherese [un•GE•REH•ze]
adj Hungarian

Ungheria [UN•ge•REE•a] *n* F
Hungary

unghia [UHN•gya] *n* F nail
(finger)

unghia del piede [UHN•gya
DEHL PYEH•de] *n* F toenail

unguento [un•GUEHN•to] *n* M
ointment

unico; unica [UHN•i•ko];
[UHN•i•ka] *adj* MF only

unilaterale
[U•ni•la•TER•AH•le] *adj*
one-sided

unire [un•EE•re] *vt* join

unito; unita [un•EE•to];
[un•EE•ta] *adj* MF joint

universitá [UNI•ver•SI•tah] *n* F
college

uno; una [UH•no]; [UH•na]
num one

unto [UHN•to] *n* M grease

untuoso; untuosa
[un•TUOH•zo];
[un•TUOH•zo] *adj* MF
unctuous

unzione [un•TSYOH•ne] *n* F
unction

uomo [UOH•mo] *n* M man

uomo (donna) d'affari
[UOH•mo (DOHN•na)
daf•FAH•ri] *n* MF
businessman; ~woman

uomo politico [UOH•mo
po•LEE•tiko] *n* M politician

uovo [UOH•vo] *n* M egg

uovo sodo [U•OH•vo•SOH•do]
n M boiled egg

uragano [ura•GAH•no] *n* M
hurricane

uranio [URAH•nyo] *n* M
uranium

urbano; urbana [ur•BAH•no];
[ur•BAH•na] *adj* MF urban

urgente [uhr•DJEHN•te] *adj*
pressing; urgent

urgentemente
[ur•DJEN•te•MEHN•te] *adv*
urgently

urgenza [uhr•DJEHN•tsa] *n* F
urgency

urlare [URLAH•re] *vi* scream;
whoop

urlo [UHR•lo] *n* M hoot

urna [UHR•na] *n* F urn

urtare [ur•TAH•re] *vt* bump;
use

usciere [u•SHEH•re] *n* M usher

uscire [u•SHEE•re] *vi* exit

uscita [u•SHEE•ta] *n* F exit

uscita d'emergenza
[USH•ee•TA
demer•DJEHN•tsa] *n* F
emergency exit

usgnolo [uzi•NYOH•lo] *n* M
nightingale

uso [UH•zo] *n* M usage; di uso
semplicissimo\ *adj* foolproof

usura [u•ZUH•ra] *n* F usury

usuraio; usuraia
[U•zu•RAH•yo];
[U•zu•RAH•ya] *n* MF usurer

usurpare [U•zur•PAH•re] *vt*
usurp

utensile [U•tehn•SI•le] *n* M
utensil

utero [uh•TE•ro] *n* M womb

utile [uh•TILE] *adj* useful

utilizzare [U•ti•LI•TSAH•re] *vt*
utilize

uvetta [UVEHT•ta] *n* F raisin

V

vacante [VA•KAHN•te] *adj*
vacant

vacanza [va•KAHN•tsa] *n* F
vacation

vacca [VAHK•ka] *n* F cow

vaccinare [VA•tshi•NAH•re] *vt*
vaccinate

vaccino [va•TSHEE•no] *n* M
vaccine

vacillare [VA•tshil•LAH•re] *vt*
vacillate

vagabondare
[VA•ga•BON•DAH•re] *vi*
roam; wander

vagabondo; vagabonda
[VA•ga•BOHN•do];
[VA•ga•BOHN•da] *n* MF

hobo; tramp; wanderer; *adj* vagabond

vagare [va•GAH•re] *vi* stray

vagare in cerca di bottino [VA•GAH•re een TSHEHR•ka dee BOT•TEE•no] *vi* prowl

vago; vaga [VAH•go]; [vah•ga] *adj* MF vague

vagone [va•GOH•ne] *n* M wagon

vagone letto [va•GOH•ne LEHT•to] *n* M sleeper

vale a dire [VAH•le ah DEE•re] *adv* namely

validitá [VA•li•DI•TAH] *n* F validity

valido; valida [VAH•li•do]; [vah•li•da] *adj* MF valid

valigetta [VA•li•DJEHT•ta] *n* F briefcase

valigia [va•LEE•dja] *n* F valise

vallata [val•LAH•ta] *n* F valley

valletto [val•LEHT•to] *n* M valet

valore [va•LOH•re] *n* M valor; value; worth; di gran valore\ *adj* valuable

valore commerciale [VA•loh•re KOM•mer•TSHAH•le] *n* M value (market)

valore corrente [VA•loh•re KOR•REHN•te] *n* M market value

valoroso; valorosa [va•LOROH•zo]; [va•LOROH•za] *adj* MF gallant; valiant; valorous

valuta [va•LUH•ta] *n* F currency

valutare [va•LUTAH•re] *vt* evaluate; appraise

valutazione [VA•luh•TAT•SIOH•ne] *n* F appraisal; rating

valutazione approssimativa [VA•lu•TAT•SYOH•ne ap•PROS•SI•ma•TEE•va] *n* F rough estimate

valvola [VAHL•vola] *n* F valve

valvola dell'aria [VAHL•vo•la del•LAH•rya] *n* F choke (of car)

valzer [VAHL•tser] *n* M waltz

vanga [VAHN•ga] *n* F shovel; spade

vangelo [van•DJEH•lo] *n* M gospel

vaniglia [va•NEE•lya] *n* F vanilla

vanitá [va•NI•tah] *n* F vanity

vanitoso; vanitosa [va•NI•TOH•zo]; [va•NI•TOH•za] *adj* MF vain

vantaggio [van•TAH•djo] *n* M advantage; benefit; usefulness; vantage

vantaggioso; vantaggiosa [VAN•ta•DJOH•so]; [VAN•ta•DJOH•sa] *adj* MF advantageous

vantaggioso; vantaggiosa [VAN•tad•JOH•so]; [VAN•tad•JOH•sa] *adj* MF beneficial; profitable

vantare [van•TAH•re] *vt* vaunt

vantarsi [van•TAHR•si] *vi* boast; brag; swagger

vapore 1 [va•POH•re] *n* M
steam; vapor

vapore 2 [va•POH•re] *n* M
steamboat

vaporiera [VA•po•RYEH•ra] *n*
F steam engine

vaporizzare
[VA•po•RIT•SAH•re] *vt*
vaporize

variabile [VA•rya•BI•le] *adj*
variable

variare [va•RYAH•re] *vi* vary

variato; variato [va•RYAH•to];
[va•RYAH•to] *adj* MF varied

variazione
[VA•rya•TSYOH•ne] *n* F
variance; variation

varicella [va•ri•TSHEHL•la] *n*
F chicken pox

variegato; variegata
[VA•rye•GAH•to];
[VA•rye•GAH•ta] *adj* MF
variegated

varietá 1 [va•RYE•tah] *n* F
variety

varietá 2 [va•RYE•tah] *n* M
vaudeville

vario; varia [VAH•ryo];
[VAH•rya] *adj* MF various;
diverse

vasc da bagno
[VAHS•ka•dah•BAH•nyo] *n* F
bathtub

vasca [VAHS•ka] *n* F tank; tub

vascello [va•SHEHL•lo] *n* M
vessel

vasetto di vetro [va•ZEHT•to
di VEH•tro] *n* M jar

vaso [VAH•zo] *n* M vase

vassoio [vas•SOH•yo] *n* M tray

vastitá [vas•TI•tah] *n* F vastness

vasto; vasta [VAHS•to];
[VAHS•ta] *adj* MF vast;
sweeping

vecchiaia [vek•KYAH•ya] *n* F
old age

vecchio; vecchia [VEH•kyo];
[VEH•kya] *adj* MF old; aged

vece [VEH•tshe] *n* F place;
stead

vedere [ve•DEH•re] *vt* see

vedere doppio [ve•DEH•re
DOHP•pyo] *vt* double vision

vedova [VEH•dova] *n* F
widow

vedovo [veh•DO•vo] *n* M
widower

veemente [ve•e•MEHN•te] *adj*
impassioned; vehement

veemenza [ve•e•MEHN•tsa] *n*
F vehemence; passion

vegetare [VE•dje•TAH•re] *vi*
vegetate

vegetariano; vegetariana
[VE•dje•ta•RYAH•no];
[VE•dje•ta•RYAH•na] *n adj*
MF vegetarian

vegetazione
[VE•dje•TAT•SYOH•ne] *n* F
vegetation

veggente [ve•DJEHN•te] *n* MF
seer

veglia [VEH•lya] *n* F vigil

veglia funebre [VEH•lya
FUH•NE•bre] *n* F wake

veicolo [VE•ee•KO•lo] *n* M
vehicle

veicolo pubblico [VE•eeko•lo
PUHB•BLI•ko] *n* M livery

velato; velata [ve•LAH•to];
[ve•LAH•ta] *adj* MF covert

veleggiare [VE•le•DJAH•re] *vi*
sail

veleno [VELEH•no] *n* M
poison; venom

velenoso; velenosa
[VE•le•NOH•zo];
[VE•le•NOH•za] *adj* MF
poisonous; venomous

velina [ve•LEE•na] *n* F
tissue-paper

vello [VEHL•lo] *n* M fleece

velluto [vel•LUH•to] *n* M
velvet

velluto a coste [VEL•luh•to ah
KOHS•te] *n* M corduroy

velo [VEH•lo] *n* M veil

veloce [ve•LOH•tshe] *adj* fast

velocitá [VE•lo•TSH•itah] *n* F
speed; velocity

vena [VEH•na] *n* F vein

vendemmia
[VEN•DEHM•mya] *n* F
vintage

vendere [vehn•DERE] *vt* sell

vendere al minuto
[VEHN•dere ahl MI•NUH•to]
vt peddle

vendetta [ven•DEHT•ta] *n* F
revenge; vengeance

vendicare [VEN•di•KAH•re] *vt*
avenge

vendicativo; vendicativa
[VEN•di•ka•TEE•vo];
[VEN•di•ka•TEE•va] *adj* MF
vindictive

venditore; venditrice
[VEN•di•TOH•re];
[VEN•di•TREE•tshe] *n* M
vendor

venerabile [VE•ne•RAH•BI•le]
adj venerable

venerare [VE•ne•RAH•re] *vt*
venerate; worship

venerazione
[VE•ne•RAH•TSYOH•ne] *n* F
veneration; worship

venerdí [ve•NEHR•dee] *n* M
Friday

venire [ve•NEE•re] *vi* come

venire via [ve•NEE•re•VEE•ah]
vi come away

ventesimo; ventesima
[VEN•teh•ZI•mo];
[VEN•teh•ZI•ma] *adj*
twentieth

venti [VEHN•ti] *num* twenty

venti alisei [VEHN•ti
ALI•ZE•hi] *n* M tradewind

ventilare [VEN•ti•LAH•re] *vt*
ventilate

ventilatore [VEN•ti•la•TOH•re]
n M ventilator

ventilazione
[VEN•ti•lat•SYOH•ne] *n* F
ventilation

vento [VEHN•to] *n* M wind

ventola [VEHN•tola] *n* F fan

ventoso; ventosa
[VEN•TOH•zo];
[VEN•TOH•za] *adj* MF windy

ventriera [ven•TRIEH•ra] *n* F
girdle

veramente [VE•ra•MEHN•te]
adv really; truly

veranda [ve•RAHN•da] *n* F
porch; verandah

verbale [ver•BAH•le] *n* M
report; *adj* verbal

verbo [VEHR•bo] *n* M verb

verboso; verbosa
[ver•BOH•zo]; [ver•BOH•za]
adj MF verbose; long-winded

verde [VEHR•de] *adj n* MF
green

verde blu [VEHR•de•BLUH]
adj teal

verdetto [ver•DEHT•to] *n* M
verdict

verdura [ver•DUH•ra] *n* F
vegetable

verdure [ver•DUH•re] *n* F
produce

vergine [vehr•DJI•ne] *adj n* MF
virgin

verginitá [VER•dji•NI•tah] *n* F
virginity

vergogna [ver•GOH•nya] *n* F
disgrace; -o -a\ *adj* disgraced
ashamed (to be)

vergognoso; vergognosa
[VER•go•NYOH•zo];
[VER•go•NYOH•za] *adj* MF
disgraceful; shameful

verifica [ve•REE•FI•ka] *n* F
verification

verificare [ve•RI•FIKAH•re] *vt*
verify

veritá [ve•RITAH] *n* F truth

veritiero; veritiera
[VE•ri•TYEH•ro];
[VE•ri•TYEH•ra] *adj* MF
truthful

verme [VEHR•me] *n* M worm

vermiglio; vermiglia
[ver•MEE•lyo]; [ver•MEE•lya]
adj MF crimson

vernacolo [VER•nah•KOLO] *n*
M vernacular

vernice [VER•NEE•tshe] *n* F
glaze; varnish; shellac

verniciare [VER•ni•TSHAH•re]
vt varnish; glaze

vero; vera [VEH•ro]; [VEH•ra]
n MF truth; reality; *adj* true;
real

versare [ver•SAH•re] *vt* pour;
spill

versato; versata
[ver•SAH•to];[ver•SAH•ta]
adj MF conversant; versed;
knowledgeable

versione [ver•SYOH•ne] *n* F
version

verso 1 [VEHR•so] *prep*
towards

verso 2 [VEHR•so] *n* M verse

verso casa [VEHR•so•KAH•za]
adv homeward

verso l'interno [VEHR•zo
lin•TEHR•no] *adv* inward

verso ovest [VEHR•so
oh•VEST] *adv* westward

verso sud [VEHR•so SUHD]
adv southward

versonord [VEHR•so NOHRD]
adv northward(s)

vertebra [VEHR•tebra] *n* F
vertebra

verticale [VER•ti•KAH•le] *adj*
vertical; upright

vertigine [VER•tee•DJI•ne] *n* F
vertigo

vertiginoso; vertiginosa
[VER•ti•dji•NOH•zo];
[VER•ti•dji•NOH•za] *adj*
giddy

vescica 1 [ve•SHEE•ka] *n* F
bladder

vescica 2 [ve•SHEE•ka] *n* F
blister

vescovo [vehs•KO•vo] *n* M
bishop

vespa 1 [VEHS•pa] *n* F hornet;
wasp

vespa 2 [VEHS•pa] *n* F motor
scooter (coll)

vespro [VEHS•pro] *n* M
vespers

vessare [ves•SAH•re] *vt* vex;
irritate

vessazione
[VES•sa•TSYOH•ne] *n* F
harassment

vestiario [ves•TYAH•RI•o] *n* M
clothing

vestibolo [ves•TEE•bolo] *n* M
hallway; vestibule

vestigiale [ves•TEE•DJAH•le]
adj vestigial

vestigio [ves•TEE•djo] *n* M
vestige

vestire [ves•TEE•re] *vt* clothe;
dress; get dressed

veterano; veterana
[VE•te•RAH•no] *adj n* MF
veteran

veterinario [VE•te•ri•NAH•ryo]
n M veterinarian; -o -a\ *adj*
veterinary

veto [VEH•to] *n* M veto

vetriolo [VE•tri•OH•lo] *n* M
vitriol

vetro [VEH•tro] *n* M glass;
drinking glass; pane (of glass)

vettovaglie [VET•to•VAH•lye]
n F victuals

vezzeggiare
[VETS•EDJAH•re] *vt* fondle

via [VEE•ah] *adv* away; by; via

viadotto [vya•DOHT•to] *n* M
viaduct

viaggiatore; vaggiatrice
[VYA•dja•TOH•re];
[VYA•dja•TREE•tshe] *n* MF
traveler

viaggio [VIAH•djo] *n* M
journey; trip; voyage; da
viaggio\ *adj* traveling

viale [vi•AH•le] *n* M avenue

viatico [VYAH•TI•ko] *n* M
viaticum

vibrare [vi•BRAH•re] *n* tingle;
vibration; *vi* twang; vibrate

vibrazione
[vi•BRAH•TSYOH•ne] *n* F
vibration

vicinanza [VI•tshi•NAHN•tsa] *n*
F vicinity

vicinato [vi•TSHEE•NAH•to] *n*
M neighborhood •

vicino [vit•SHEE•no] *prep* by
(near to); close

vicino; vicina [vi•TSHEE•no];
[vi•TSHEE•na] *adj* close;
near; nearby; MF neighbor

viggiare [via•DJAH•re] *vi* travel

vigilante [vij•il•AHN•te] *adj*
alert

vigile [vee•DJI•le] *adj* vigilant

vigilia [vi•DJEE•lya] *n* F eve

vigilia di Ognissanti
[VI•DJEE•lya di
ONY•SAHN•ti] *n* F
Halloween

vigliacco; vigliacca
[vi•LYAHK•ko];
[vi•LYAK•ka] *n* MF coward;
adj cowardly

vigneto [vi•NYEH•to] *n* M
vineyard

vigore [vi•GOH•re] *n* M vigor;
stamina

vigoroso; vigorosa
[VI•go•ROH•zo];
[VI•go•ROH•za] *adj* MF
vigorous

villa [VEEL•la] *n* F villa

villaggio [vil•LAH•djo] *n* M
village

villino [vil•LEE•no] *n* M cottage

vimine [vee•MI•ne] *n* M wicker

vincente [VIN•TSHEHN•te] *adj*
winning

vincere [veen•TSHE•re] *vt*
vanquish; win

vincitore [VIN•tshi•TOH•re] *n*
M victor; -o -a; MF winner

vino [VEE•no] *n* M wine

viola [VIOH•la] *n adj* purple

viola del pensiero [VYOH•la
dehl PEN•SYEH•ro] *n* F
pansy

violare [vyo•LAH•re] *vt*
infringe; violate

violazione
[V•i•o•la•TSI•OH•ne] *n* F
breach (of contract); violation

violentare [VYO•len•TAH•re]
vt rape

violento; violenta
[vyo•LEHN•to];
[vyo•LEHN•ta] *adj* MF
violent

violenza [vyo•LEHN•tsa] *n* F
violence

violenza sessuale
[vyo•LEHN•tsa
SES•SUAH•le] *n* F rape

violetta [vyo•LEHT•ta] *n* M
violet

violinista [VYO•lin•EES•ta] *n*
MF violinist

violino [vyo•LEE•no] *n* M
fiddle; violin

violoncello
[VIO•lont•SHEHL•lo] *n* M
cello

vipera [VEE•pera] *n* F viper

vireo; vitrea [vee•TREO];
[vee•trea] *adj* MF vitreous

virgola [veer•GO•la] *n* F
comma

virile [vi•REE•le] *adj* virile

virilitá [VI•ri•LI•tah] *n* F
manhood; virility

virtuale [vir•TUAH•le] *adj*
virtual

virtualmente
[vr•TUAL•MEHN•te] *adv*
virtually

virulenza [VI•ru•LEHN•tsa] *n* F
virulence

virus [VEE•rus] *n* M virus

viscere [VEE•shere] *n* F viscera

viscositah [VIS•ko•ZI•tah] *n* F
viscosity

visibile [vi•ZEE•BI•le] *adj*
visible

visibiltá [vi•ZI•bi•LI•tah] *n* MF
visibility

visiera [vi•ZYEH•ra] *n* F visor

visionario; visionaria
[vi•ZYO•NAH•ryo];
[vi•ZYO•NAH•rya] *adj n* MF
visionary

visione [vi•ZYOH•ne] *n* F
glimpse; vision

visita [VEE•zita] *n* F visit

visita turistica [VEE•zi•ta
tu•REES•TI•ka] *n* F
sightseeing

visita ufficiale [VEE•zita
uf•FIT•SHAH•le] *n* F
visitation

visitatore; visitatrice
[VI•zi•TA•TOH•re];
[VI•zi•TA•TREE•tshe] *n* MF
visitor

visivo; visiva [vi•ZEE•vo];
[vi•ZEE•va] *adj* visual

viso [VEE•zo] *n* M visage

visone [vi•ZOH•ne] *n* M mink

vista [VEE•sta] *n* F sight; view;
eyesight

vista aerea [VEES•ta AEH•rea] *n* F view (bird's eye)

visto [VEES•to] *n* M visa

vistoso; vistosa [vis•TOH•zo]; [vis•TOH•za] *adj* MF flashy; gaudy; showy

vita 1 [VEE•ta] *n* F life

vita 2 [VEE•ta] *n* F waist

vita presunta [VEE•ta pre•SUHN•ta] *n* F life expectancy

vitale [vi•TAH•le] *adj* vital

vitalitá [VI•ta•LI•tah] *n* F vitality

vitamina [VI•ta•MEE•na] *n* F vitamin

vite [VEE•te] *n* F screw

vitello [vit•EHL•lo] *n* M calf; veal

viticcio [vi•TEE•tsho] *n* M tendril

vitreo; vitrea [VEE•treo]; [VEE•trea] *adj* glassy

vittima [vit•TEE•ma] *n* M victim

vittoria [vit•TOH•rya] *n* F victory

vittorioso; vittoriosa [VIT•to•RYOH•zo]; [VIT•to•RYOH•za] *adj* MF victorious

vivace [vi•VAH•tshe] *adj* frisky; spirited; vivacious; lively

vivacitá [VI•va•TSHI•tah] *n* F vivacity

vivanda [vi•VAHN•da] *n* F viands

vivente [vi•VEHN•te] *adj* living

vivido; vivida [vee•VI•do]; [vee•VI•da] *adj* MF vivid

vivo; viva [VEE•vo]; [VEE•va] *adj* MF alive; live

viziare [vi•TSYAH•re] *vt* spoil (a child)

vizio [VEE•tsyo] *n* M vice

vocabolario [VO•ka•bo•LAH•ryo] *n* M vocabulary; dictionary

vocale1 [vo•KAH•le] *adj* vocal

vocale 2 [vo•KAH•le] *n* F vowel

vocazione [VO•ka•TSIOH•ne] *n* F calling; vocation

voce [VOH•tshe] *n* F voice; a voce alta\ *adv* aloud

voga [VOH•ga] *n* F vogue; style

voglia [VOH•lya] *n* F birthmark

volatile [VO•lah•TEE•le] *adj* volatile

volato [VOLAH•to] flown

volentieri [VO•len•TIEH•ri] *adv* gladly; willingly

volere [vo•LEH•re] *vt* want

volgare [vol•GAH•re] *adj* vulgar; gross

volgaritá [VOL•ga•RI•tah] *n* F vulgarity

volo [VOH•lo] *n* M flight

volontá [vo•LON•tah] *n* F will

volontario; volontaria [VO•lon•TAH•ryo]; [VO•lon•TAH•rya] *adj* voluntary; willing; *n* MF volunteer

volpe [VOHL•pe] *n* F fox

volt [vohlt] *n* M volt

volta [VOHL•ta] *n* F vault

voltaggio [vol•TAH•djo] *n* M voltage

volte; a volte [ah•VOHL•te]
adv sometime

volume [vo•LUH•me] *n* M
volume

voluttuoso; voluttuosa
[VO•lut•TUOH•zo];
[VO•lut•TUOH•za] *adj* MF
voluptuous

vomitare [VO•mi•TAH•re] *vt*
throw up; vomit

vongola [VOHN•GO•la] *n* F
clam

vorace [VO•rah•TSHE] *adj*
voracious

vortice [VOHR•TI•tshe] *n* M
whirlpool

votante [vo•TAHN•te] *n* MF
voter; *adj* voting

votare [vo•TAH•re] *vi* vote

voto [VOH•to] *n* M vow

vulcanico; vulcanica
[VUL•kah•NI•ko];
[VUL•kah•NI•ka] *adj* MF
volcanic

vulcano [vul•KAH•no] *n* M
volcano

vulnerabile
[VUL•ne•RAH•BI•le] *adj*
vulnerable

vuoto [VUOH•to] *n* M void; -o
-a\ *adj* MF empty; void;
devoid; hollow

whiskey [UYS•kee] *n* M
whiskey

xenofobo; xenofoba
[XE•noh•FO•bo];
[XE•noh•FO•ba] *n* MF
xenophobe

xilofono [XI•loh•FO•no] *n* M
xylophone

xilografia [XI•lo•GRA•FE•a] *n*
F xylography

yacht [YAH•kt] *n* M yacht

yog [YOH•ga] *n* M yoga

Z

zafferano [TSAF•fe•RAH•no] *n*
M saffron

zaino [TSAH•IN•oh] *n* M
backpack; knapsack

Zaire [TSA•eer] *n* M Zaire

zampa [ZAHM•pa] *n* F paw

zampillaare
[TSAM•pil•LAH•re] *vt* spurt

zangola [TSAHN•GO•la] *n* F
churn (butter)

zanna [TSAHN•na] *n* F fang;
tusk

zanzara [tsan•TSAH•ra] *n* F
mosquito

zar [tsahr] *n* M czar

zattera [TSAHT•tera] *n* F raft

zebra [TSEH•bra] *n* F zebra

zecca [TSEH•ka] *n* F tick
(insect)

zefiro [tseh•FI•ro] *n* M zephyr

zelante [tse•LAHN•te] *adj*
zealous

zelo [TSEH•lo] *n* M zeal

zenith [TSEH•nit] *n* zenith

zenzero [TSEH•TSE•ro] *n* M
ginger

zeppelin [TSEHP•PE•lin] *n*
zeppelin

zero [TSEH•ro] *n* M zero

zia [TSEE•ah] *n* F aunt

zinco [TSEEN•ko] *n* M zinc

zingaro; zingara
[TSEEN•GA•ro];

[TSEEN•GA•ra] *n* MF *adj*
gypsy

zio [TSEE•o] *n* M uncle

zoccolo [TSOHK•kolo] *n* M
hoof

zodiacale [TSO•dya•KAH•le]
adj zodiacal

zodiaco [TSO•DEE•ako] *n* M
zodiac

zolla [TSOHL•la] *n* F sod

zolla erbosa
[TSOHL•la•EHR•BOH•za] *n*
F turf

zona [ZOH•na] *n* F area; zone

zoo [TZOH•o] *n* M zoo

zoologia [TSO•olo•DJEE•a] *n*
F zoology

zoologico; zoologica
[TSO•oloh•DJI•ko];
[TSO•oloh•DJI•ka] *adj* MF
zoological

zoppo; zoppa [TSOHP•po];
[TSOHP•pa] *adj* MF lame

zoticone [tso•TIKOH•ne] *n* M
lout

zucca [TSUH•ka] *n* F gourd;
pumpkin

zuccheriera
[TZUK•ke•RYEH•ra] *n* F
sugar bowl

zucchero [TSUHK•KE•ro] *n* M
sugar

A

a [u or ai] (before vowel or silent 'h') *indef article* an [en] *art* un; una; number one; ratio per \$5 ~ week\ \$5 alla settimana

A.M. antimeridiano; antimeridiana

abandon [u•BAN•dun] *vt* abbandonare

abase [u•BAIS] *vt* abbassare; degradare

abbey [a•BEE] *n* abbazia; badia F

abbreviate [u•BREE•vee•AIT] *vt* abbreviare

abbreviation [u•BREE•vee•AI•shn] *n* abbreviazione F

abdomen [AB•du•men] *n* addome M

abduct [ub•DUHKT] *vt* rapire

abet [u•BET] *vt* favoreggiare; aiutare

abhor [ub•HAUR] *vt* abborrire

abide (by) [u•BUYD] *vi* sopportare

ability [u•BI•li•tee] *n* abilitá F

able [AI•bl] *adj* capace ; be ~\ essere capace di fare

abnormal [ab•NAUR•ml] *adj* anormale

abode [u•BOD] *n* dimora F

abolish [u•BAH•lish] *vt* abolire

abominable [u•BAH•mi•nu•bl] *adj* abominevole

abortion [u•BAUR•shn] *n* aborto M

about [u•BOUT] *adv* circa; quasi; (place) qua; *prep* su; di; (place) per

above [u•BUHV] *prep* sopra

abrupt [u•BRUHPT] *adj* brusco; brusca

absent [AB•sunt] *adj* assente

absent-minded [~MUYN•did] *adj* distratto; distratta

absolute [AB•su•LOOT] *adj* assoluto; assoluta

absolutely [AB•su•LOOT•lee] *adv* assolutamente

absorb [ub•ZAURB] *vt* assorbire; be ~ed by\ immerso

abstain [ab•STAIN] *vi* astenersi

absurd [ub•SURD] *adj* assurdo; assurda

abundant [u•BUHN•dunt] *adj* abbondante

abuse [u•BYOOS] *n* abuso M; *vt* abusare

abyss [u•BIS] *n* abisso M

academy [u•KA•du•mee] *n* accademia F

accent [AK•sent] *n* accento M

accept [ak•SEPT] *vt* accettare

access [AK•ses] *n* accesso M

accident 1 [AK•si•dunt] *n*
accidente M

accident 2 [AK•si•dunt] *n*
incidente M

accidental [AK•si•DEN•tl] *adj*
accidentale

accommodate
[uh•KAH•mu•DAIT] *vt*
adattare; ospitare

accompany [u•CUHM•pu•nee]
vt accompagnare

accomplice [u•KAHM•plis] *n*
complice

accomplish [u•KAHM•plish] *vt*
realizzare

accord [u•KAURD] *n*
accordo M

according [u•KAUR•ding] *prep*
secondo

accost [u•KAUST] *vt* abbordare

account [u•KOUNT] *n* conto
M; *n* descrizione F; *npl* conti

accumulate
[u•KYOO•myu•LAIT] *vt*
accumulare

accurate [A•kyu•ret] *adj*
accurato; accurata

accuse [u•KYOOZ] *vt* accusare

accustom [u•KUH•stum] *vt*
abituare

ache [aik] *n* dolore M

acid 1 [A•sid] *n* acido M

acid 2 [A•sid] *adj* acido; acida

acknowledge [ek•NAH•lij] *vt*
ammettere

acquaintance [u•KWAIN•tuns]
n conoscenza F

acquiesce 1 [a•kwee•YES] *vi*
aderire

acquiesce 2 [a•kwee•YES] *vi*
consentire

acquire [u•KWUYUR] *vt*
acquisire

acquit [u•KWIT] *vt* assolvere

acre [AI•kur] *n* acro M

acrid [A•krid] *adj* acre

across [u•KRAUS] *adv*
attraverso; dall'altra parte di

act [akt] *n* atto M; (law)
numero; *vi* agire; fingere

action [AK•shn] *n* azione F

active [AK•tiv] *adj* attivo; attiva

actor [AK•tur] *n* attore M

actress [AK•tris] *n* attrice F

actually [AK•chu•lee] *adv*
effettivamente

acute [u•KYOOT] *adj* acuto;
acuta

adapt [u•DAPT] *vt* adattare

add [ad] *vt* aggiungere

addict [A•dikt] *n*
tossicodipendente

addiction [u•DIK•shn] *n*
dipendenza F

addition [u•DI•shn] *n*
addizione F

additional [u•DI•shun•ul] *adj*
supplementare

address [n. A•dres v. u•DRES]
n indirizzo M; *vt* indirizzare

adequate [A•de•kwet] *adj*
adeguato; adeguata

adjective [A•jik•tiv] *n*
aggettivo M

adjourn [u•JURN] *vt vi*
aggiornare

adjust [u•JUHST] *vt* adattare

administer [ud•MI•ni•stur] *vt*
somministrare

admire [ud•MUYR] *vt*
ammirare

admission [ud•MI•shun] *n*
ammissione; ingresso F

admit [ud•MIT] *vt* ammettere

admonish [ud•MAH•nish] *vt*
ammonire

adolescence [A•du•LE•suns] *n*
adolescenza F

adopt [u•DAHPT] *vt* adottare

adoption [u•DAHP•shun] *n*
adozione F

adore [u•DAUR] *vt* adorare

adult [u•DUHLT] *n* adulto;
adulta; *adj* adulto; adulta

adultery [u•DUHL•tu•ree] *n*
adulterio M

advance [ed•VANS] *vt/vi*
avanzare; *vt* anticipare; *n*
avanzamento

advantage [ed•VAN•tej] *n*
vantaggio M

advantageous
[AD•VUN•TAI•jus] *adj*
vantaggioso; vantaggiosa

Advent [AD•vent] *n*
Avvento M

adventure [ed•VEN•chur] *n*
avventura F

adventurous [ed•VEN•chu•rus]
adj avventuroso; avventurosa

adverb [AD•vurb] *n*
avverbio M

adversity [ad•VUR•si•tee] *n*
avversitá F

advertise [AD•vur•TUYZ] *vt*
annunziare

advertisement
[AD•vur•TUYZ•munt] *n*
inserzione F

advice [ad•VUYS] *n*
consiglio M

advise [ad•VUYZ] *vt*
consigliare

affair [u•FAIR] *n* faccenda F;
affare M; relazione F amorosa

affect [u•FEKT] *vt* affettare

affection [u•FEK•shn] *n*
affezione F

afford [uh•FAWRD] *vt*
permettere

Afghanistan [af•GA•ni•STAN]
n Afganistan M

afraid (to be) [u•FRAID] *adj*
spaventato; spaventata

Africa [A•fri•ku] *n* Africa F

after [AF•tur] *adv* dopo

afternoon [AF•tur•NOON] *n*
pomeriggio M

again [uh•GEN] *adv* di nuovo

against [uh•GENST] *prep*
contro

age [aij] *n* etá F; *vt vi*
invecchiare

aged [AI•jud / aij'd] *adj*
vecchio; vecchia

agency [AI•jun•cee] *n*
agenzia F

agenda [uh•JEN•duh] *n* ordine
del giorno M

agent [AI•junt] *n* agente

aggravate [A•gru•VAIT] *vt*
aggravare

aggressive [u•GRE•siv] *adj*
aggressivo; aggressiva

ago [uh•GO] *adv* fa

agree [uh•GREE] *vi* accordarsi

agreeable [u•GREE•u•bl] *adj*
consenziente; gradevole

agreement [u•GREE•munt] *n*
accordo M

agriculture [A•gri•CUL•chur] *n*
agricoltura F

ahead (of) [uh•HED] *adv* piú
avanti

aid [aid] *n* aiuto M; *vt* aiutare

AIDS [aids] *n* SIDA F

aim [aim] *n* scopo M; mira F;
vt puntare a

air [air] *n* aria F; *vt* aerare; on
the ~\ in onda

air conditioning
[~ kuhn•DI•shuh•ning] *n* aria
condizionata F

air-conditioned
[~ kuhn•DI•shuhnd] *adj* con
aria condizionata M

airmail [AIR•mail] *n* posta
aerea F

airplane [AIR•plain] *n*
aeroplano M

airport [AIR•paurt] *n*
aeroporto M

airtight [AIR•tuyt] *adj* a tenuta
d'aria

aisle [uyl] *n* corridoio M

ajar [uh•JAHR] *adj* socchiuso;
socchiusa

alarm [u•LAHRM] (vt: alarmer)
n allarme M; *vt* allarmare

alarm clock [u•LAHRM clahk]
n sveglia F

alas [uh•LAS] *excl* ahimé

Albania [al•BAI•nee•yuh] *n*
Albania F

album [AL•bum] *n* album M

alcohol [AL•ku•HAL] *n* alcool

alcoholic [AL•ku•HAU•lik] *adj*
alcolico; alcolica; *n* alcolista

alert [uh•LUHRT] *adj* vigilante;
vt avvertire

algebra [AL•je•bru] *n* algebra F

Algeria [AL•jee•ree•yu] *n*
Algeria F

alibi [A•li•BUY] *n* alibi M

alike [uh•LUYK] *adj* simile

alive [uh•LUYV] *adj* vivo; viva

all [awl] *adj* tutto; tutta

allegation [A•lu•GAI•shun] *n*
asserzione F

allergic ¡u•LUR•jik] *adj*
allergico; allergica

allergy [A•luhr•jee] *n* allergia F

alliance [u•LUY•yuns] *n*
alleanza F

allow [uh•LOW] *vt* concedere

allusion [u•LOO•zhuhn] *n*
allusione F

almost [AWL•most] *adv* quasi

alone [uh•LON] *adj* solo; sola;
adv solamente; leave ~\
lasciare

along [uh•LAWNG] *prep* lungo

aloud [uh•LOWD] *adv* a voce
alta

alphabet [AL•fu•BET] *n*
alfabeto M

already [awl•RE•dee] *adv* giá

also [AWL•so] *adv* anche

alternate (with)
[AUL•tur•NAIT] *vi* alternare

although [awl•THO] *conj*
benché

altogether
[AWL•too•GE•thuhr] *adv*
completamente

always [AWL•waiz] *adv*
sempre

am (be) [am] *v* sono (essere)

amateur [A•mu•CHUR] *adj n*
dilettante ·

amaze [u•MAIZ] *vt* stupire

amazing [u•MAI•zing] *adj*
sorprendente

ambassador [am•BA•su•dur] *n*
ambasciatore M

ambiguous [am•BI•gyoo•wus]
adj ambiguo; ambigua

ambitious [am•BI•shus] *adj*
ambizioso; ambiziosa

amend (law) [u•MEND]
amendment: amendment m *vt*
emendare

America [u•ME•ri•ku] *n*
America F

amnesty [AM•ni•stee] *n*
amnistia F

among [u•MUHNG] *prep* fra;
tra; in mezzo a

amount [u•MOWNT] *n* somma;
ammontare M

amuse [u•MYOOZ] *vt* divertire;
dilettare

analogy [u•NA•lu•jee] *n*
analogia F

analysis [u•NA•lu•sis] *n*
analisi F

analyze [A•nu•LUYZ] *vt*
analizzare

anarchy [A•nahr•kee] *n*
anarchia F

ancestor [AN•SE•stur] *n*
antenato M

anchor [AN•kur] *n* ancora F

ancient [AIN•shunt] *adj* antico;
antica

and [and] or [end] *conj* e; ed (in
front of vowel)

angel [AIN•jul] *n* angelo M

anger [ANG•gur] *n* collera F

angle [ANG•gl] *n* angolo M

angry [ANG•gree] *adj* irato;
irata; essere in collera con; *vi*
arrabbiarsi

anguish [AN•gwish] *n*
angoscia F

animal [A•ni•ml] *n* animale M

animate [A•ni•mut] *adj*
animato; animata

anniversary [A•ni•VUR•su•ree]
n anniversario M

announce [u•NOUNS] *vt*
annunziaren; annuncio M

annoy [u•NOI] *vt* infastidire

annoying [u•NOI•ying] *adj*
fastidioso; fastidiosa

annual [A•nyoo•ul] *adj* annuale

another [u•NUH•thur] *adj* un
altro; un'altra; *pron* un altro;
un'altra; ancora

answer [AN•sur] *vt* rispondere;
n riposta; soluzzione F

ant [ant] *n* formica F

anthology [an•THAH•lu•jee] *n*
antologia F

antique [an•TEEK] *adj* antico;
antica

antisocial [AN•ti•SO•shul] *adj*
antisociale

anxiety [ang•ZUY•yu•tee] *n*
ansietá F

anxious [ANK•shus] *adj*
ansioso; ansiosa

any [E•nee] *adj* qualsiasi; del
de; (phrases) ogn; un

anyone (anybody)
[E•nee•WUHN] *pron*
chiunque M

anything [E•nee•THING] *pron*
qualsiasi cosa F

anyway [E•nee•WAI] *adv*
comunque

anywhere [E•nee•WAIR] *adv*
in qualunque luogo

apartment [u•PAHRT•munt] *n*
appartamento M

ape [aip] *n* scimmione M

apologize [u•PAH•lu•JUYZ] *vi*
scusarsi

apology [u•PAH•lu•jee] *n pl*
scuse F

apology *n* apologia F

apparently [u•PA•runt•lee] *adv*
apparentemente

appear [u•PEER] *vi* apparire

appearance [u•PEER•uns] *n*
apparenza F

appetite [A•pu•TUYT] *n*
appetito M

appetizer [A•pu•TUY•zur] *n*
antipasto M

applaud [u•PLAUD] *vt*
applaudire

apple [A•pl] *n* mela F

application [A•pli•KAI•shn] *n*
domanda F; applicazione F

apply [uh•PLUY] *vt* applicare;
fare domanda

appoint [u•POINT] *vt* nominare

appointment [u•POINT•ment]
n appuntamento M

appraisal [u•PRAI•zl] *n*
valutazione F

appraise [u•PRAIZ] *vt* valutare

appreciate [u•PREE•shee•AIT]
vt apprezzare

approach [u•PROCH] *vt*
avvicinare

appropriate [u•PRO•pree•IT]
adj appropriato; appropriata

approval [u•PROO•vl] *n*
approvazione F

approve [uh•PROOV] *vt*
approvare

approximately
[u•PRAHK•su•mit•lee] *adv*
approssimativamente

apricot [A•pri•KAHT] *n*
albicocca F

April [AI•pril] *n* Aprile M

arbitrary [AHR•bi•TRE•ree]
adj arbitrario; arbitraria

arch [ahrch] *n* arco M

archaeology
[AHR•kee•AH•lu•jee] *n*
archeologia F

archaic [ahr•KAI•ik] *adj*
arcaico; arcaica

architect [AHR•ki•TEKT] *n*
architetto M

architecture
[AHR•ki•TEK•chur] *n*
architettura F

area [A•ree•u] *n* zona F

argue [AHR•gyoo] *vt* discutere

argument [AHR•gyu•mint] *n*
discussione M

arid [A•rid] *adj* arido; arida

arm [ahrm] *n* braccio M; *n* arma
F; *vt* armmere

armchair [AHRM•chair] *n*
poltrona F

armor [AHR•mur] *n* armatura F

army [AHR•mee] *n* esercito M

aroma [u•RO•mu] *n* aroma M

around [u•ROWND] *adv*
intorno; attorno; *prep* inorno a

arrange [u•RAINJ] *vt* sistemare

arrest [u•REST] *vt* arrestare

arrival [u•RUY•vl] *n* arrivo M;
(person) arrivato

arrive [u•RUYV] *vi* arrivare

arrogant [A•ru•gent] *adj*
arrogante

arrow [A•ro] *n* freccia F

art [ahrt] *n* arte F

artery [AHR•tuh•ree] *n* arteria F

article [AHR•ti•kl] *n* articolo M

articulate [ahr•TI•cyu•LAIT] *vt vi* articolare

artificial [AHR•ti•FI•shl] *adj* artificiale

artist [AHR•tist] *n* artista

as [az] *conj* come; mentre; (since) dal; (concerning) quanto per quanto; ~ if \como se

ash [ash] *n* cenere F

ashamed (to be) [u•SHAIMD] *adj* vergognoso; vergognosa

ashtray [ASH•trai] *n* portacenere M

aside [u•SUYD] *adv* a parte

ask [ask] *vt* domandare

asleep [u•SLEEP] *adj* addormentato; addormentata

asparagus [u•SPA•ru•gus] *n* asparago M

aspect [A•spekt] *n* aspetto M

aspirin [A•sprin] *n* aspirina F

assassinate [u•SA•si•NAIT] *vt* assassinare

assassination [u•SA•si•NAI•shun] *n* assassinio M

assemble [u•SEM•bl] *vt* riunire

assembly 1 [u•SEM•blee] *n* riunione F

assembly 2 (mech) [u•SEM•blee] *n* montaggio M

assign [u•SUYN] *vt* assegnare

associate [u•SO•shee•AIT] *vt* associare

association [u•SO•see•AI•shn] *n* associazione F

assume [u•SOOM] *vt* assumere

astonish [u•STAH•nish] *vt* stupire

astrology [u•STRAH•lu•jee] *n* astrologia F

astronaut [A•stru•NAHT] *n* astronauta

astronomy [a•STRAH•nu•mee] *n* astronomia F

at [at] *prep* a; (activity) al (cause) da; per

attach [u•TACH] *vt* attaccare; *vt* allegare

attack [u•TAK] *vt* attaccare

attempt (to) [u•TEMPT] *vt* tentare

attend 1 [u•TEND] *vt* occuparsi (di)

attend 2 (place) [u•TEND] *vt* frequentare

attention [u•TEN•shn] *n* attenzione F

attentive [u•TEN•tiv] *adj* attento; attenta

attic [A•tik] *n* soffitta F

attitude [A•ti•TOOD] *n* attitudine F

attract [u•TRAKT] *vt* attrarre

attraction [u•TRAK•shn] *n* attrazione F

attractive [u•TRAK•tiv] *adj* attraente

audience [AU•dee•uns] *n* pubblico M; udienza F

audition 1 [au•DI•shun] *n* audizione F

audition 2 (film) *n* provino M

August [AU•gust] *n* Agosto M

aunt [ant or ahnt] *n* zia F

Australia [au•STRAIL•yu] *n* Australia F

Austria [AU•stree•u] *n*
Austria F

authentic [au•THEN•tik] *adj*
autentico; autentica

author [AU•thur] *n* autore;
autrice

authority [u•THAU•ri•tee] *n*
autoritá F

autobiography
[AU•to•buy•AH•gru•fee] *n*
autobiografia F

autograph [AU•tu•GRAF] *n*
autografo M

automatic [AU•to•MA•tik] *adj*
automatico; automatica

autumn [AU•tum] *n* autunno M

auxiliary [awg•ZIL•yu•ree] *adj*
n ausiliario; ausiliaria

available [u•VAI•lu•bl] *adj*
disponibile

avenge [u•VENJ] *vt* vendicare

avenue [A•vu•NYOO] *n*
viale M

average [A•vur•ij] *n* media F;
adj medio; media; *vt* fare
de/in media

avoid [u•VOID] *vt* evitare

awake [u•WAIK] *adj* sveglio;
sveglia

award [u•WAURD] *n* ricompensa F; *vt* aggiudicare M

aware [u•WAIR] *adj* conscio;
concia

away [u•WAI] *adv* via

awful [AU•ful] *adj* terribile

awkward [AU•kwurd] *adj*
goffo; goffa

axe [ax] *n* ascia F; *vt* abolire;
(jobs) sopprimere

axis [AK•sis] *n* asse F

axle [AK•sl] *n* asse F

B

babble [BA•bl] *vi* balbettare

baby [BAI•bee] *n* neonato;
neonata

bachelor 1 [BA•chu•lur] *n*
scapolo M

bachelor 2 (degree)
[BA•chu•lur] *n* diploma M

back [bak] *adv* indietro; *adj*
posteriore; *n* retro M; *vi*
indietreggiare F; (anat.) *n*
schiena F

background (in the)
[BAK•grownd] *n* sfondo M

backlash [BAK•lash] *n* n F

backpack [BAK•pak] *n*
zaino M

backward 1 [BAK•wurd] *adv*
adj indietro

backward 2 [BAK•wurd] *adj*
ritardardato; ritardata

backyard [bak•YAHRD] *n*
cortile M

bacon [BAI•kun] *n* pancetta
affumicata F

bad [bad] *adj* cattivo; cattiva

badge [baj] *n* marchio M;
(official) insegno M

badly [BAD•lee] *adv* malamente

bag [bag] *n* borsa F

baggage [BA•gij] *n* bagaglio M

bagpipes [BAG•puyps] *npl*
cornamusa F

bail [bail] *n* cauzione F; *vt*
concedere la libertà

bait [bait] *n* esca F

bake [baik] *vt* cuocere nel forno

baker [BAI•kur] *n* panettiere M

bakery [BAI•ker•ee] *n* forno M;
panetteria

balance [BA•luns] *n*
equilibrio M

balance sheet [BA•lens sheet]
n bilancio M

balcony [BAL•ku•nee] *n*
balcone M

bald [bauld] *adj* calvo; calva

bale [baiul] *n* balla F

balk [bauk] *vi* impuntarsi

ball [bawl] *n* palla F

ballad [BA•lud] *n* ballata F

ballerina [BA•lu•REE•nu] *n*
ballerina F

ballet [BA•lai] *n* balletto M

balloon [bu•LOON] *n*
pallone M

ballot [BA•lut] *n* scutinio M;

bamboo [bam•BOO] *n*
bambu' M

ban [ban] *n* divieto M;
interdizione F; *vt* interdire

banal [bu•NAL] *adj* banal

banana [bu•NA•nu] *n* banana F

band [band] *n* banda F; *vi* ~
together\ collegarsi

bandage [BAN•dij] *n*
fasciatura F

banish [BA•nish] *vt* esiliare

bank [bank] *n* banca F; (river)
sponda F (earth) banco (aviat)
vi inclinarsi in virata

banknote [BANK•not] *n*
banconota F

banker [BANG•kur] *n*
bancario M

bankrupt [BANK•ruhpt] *adj*
fallito; fallita

bankruptcy
[BANK•RUHPT•see] *n*
fallimento M

banner [BA•nur] *n* bandiera F

banquet [BANG•kwet] *n*
banchetto M

banter [BAN•tur] *n* scherzo M

baptism [BAP•tizm] *n*
battesimo M

baptize [bap•TUYZ] *vt*
battezzare

bar [bahr] barra; sbarra F;
restrizione F; (pub) *n* bar M;
vt sbarre

barbarian [bahr•BE•ree•un] *adj*
n barbaro; barbara

barbed [bahrbd] *adj* pungente

barber [BAHR•bur] *n*
barbiere M

bare [bair] *adj* nudo; nuda

barefoot 1 [BAIUR•fut] *adj*
scalzo; scalza

barefoot 2 [BAIUR•fut] *adj* a
piedi nudi

barely [BAIR•lee] *adv* appena

bargain [BAHR•gin] *n*
occasione F; *vi*
mercanteggiare

barge [bahrj] *n* battello M

bark [bahrk] *n* corteccia F; (at)
vi abbaiare

barley [BAHR•lee] *n* orzo M

barn [bahrn] *n* granaio M

barometer [bu•RAH•mi•tur] *n*
barometro M

baroque 1 [bu•ROK] *adj*
barocco; barocca

Baroque 2 [bu•ROK] *n*
Barocco M

barracks [BA•ruks] *npl*
caserma F

barrel [BA•rul] *n* botte F

barren [BA•run] *adj* sterile

barricade [BA•ri•KAID] *n*
barricata F

barrier [BA•ree•ur] *n* barriera F

bartender [BAHR•TEN•dur] *n*
barista M

base [bais] *n* base F; *vt* basare

baseball [BAIS•bawl] *n*
baseball M

basement [BAIS•munt] *n*
seminterrato M

bashful [BASH•ful] *adj* timido;
timida

basic [BAI•sik] *adj* basilare

basil [baizl] *n* basilico M

basis [BAI•sis] *n* base F

basket [BA•skit] *n* canestro M

basketball [BA•skit•BAWL] *n*
pallacanestro F

bass (mus) [bais] *n* basso M

bassoon [bu•SOON] *n*
fagotto M

bastard 1 [BA•sturd] *n*
bastardo M

bastard 2 [BA•sturd] *adj*
bastardo; bastarda

baste [baist] *vt* imbastire

bat 1 [bat] *n* pipistrello M

bat 2 [bat] *n* mazza F

bath [bath] *n* bagno M

bather [BAI•thur] *n* bagnante

bathing suit [BAI•thing ~] *n*
costume da bagno M

bathrobe [BATH•rob] *n*
accappatoio M

bathroom [BATH•room] *n*
bagno M

bathtub [BATH•tuhb] *n* vasca
da bagno F

baton [bu•TAHN] *n* bacchetta F

battalion [bu•TA•lyun] *n*
battaglione M

batter [BA•tur] *n* pastella F

battery [BA•tu•ree] *n* batteria F

battle [batl] *n* battaglia F

battleship [BA•tl•SHIP] *n* nave
da guerra F

bawdy [BAU•dee] *adj* osceno;
oscena

bawl [baul] *vt vi* gridare

bay [bai] *n* baia F

bayonet [BAI•u•net] *n*
baionetta F

bazaar [bu•ZAHR] *n* bazar M

BC (before Christ) AC

be [bee] *aux v* essere; estere
(weather) fare

beach [beech] *n* spiaggia F

bead [beed] *n* perla F

beagle [BEE•gl] *n* beagle M

beak [beek] *n* becco M

beam [beem] *n* trave F

bean [been] *n* fagiolo M

bear [bair] *n* orso M

beard [beerd] *n* barba F

beast [beest] *n* bestia F;
animale M

beastly [BEE•stlee] *adj* bestiale

beat [beet] *vt* battere

beating [BEE•ting] *n* battuta F

beautiful [BYOO•ti•ful] *adj*
bello; bella

beauty [BYOO•tee] *n*
bellezza F

beaver [BEE•vur] *n* castoro M

because 1 [bi•CAWZ] *conj* perché

because 2 (of) [bi•CAWZ] *prep* a causa di

beckon [BE•kun] *vt* far cenno

become [bi•CUHM] *vi* diventare

becoming [bi•CUH•ming] *adj* appropriato; appropriata

bed [bed] *n* letto M

bedroom [BED•room] *n* camera da letto F

bee [bee] *n* ape F

beech [beech] *n* faggio M

beef [beef] *n* manzo M

beehive [BEE•huyv] *n* alveare M

been [bin] *v* stato; stata

beer [bee'ur] *n* birra F

beet [beet] *n* bietola F

beetle [beetl] *n* scarabeo M

before [bi•FAWR] *adv* prima

befriend [bu•FREND] *vt* fare amicizia

beg [beg] *vt* pregare

beggar [BE•gur] *n* mendicante

begin [bi•GIN] *vt vi* cominciare; iniziare

beginner [bu•GI•nur] *n* principiante

beginning [bi•GI•ning] *n* principio M

behalf [bi•HAF] *n* per conto di

behave [bi•HAIV] *vi* comportarsi

behavior [bi•HAI•vyur] *n* comportamento M

behead [bi•HED] *vt* decapitare

behind [bi•HUYND] *prep* dietro; *adv* indietro; *n* didietro M

beige [baizh] *adj* beige; *n* beige M

being [BEE•ing] *n* essere M

belated [bi•LAI•tid] *adj* tardo; tarda

belfry [BEL•free] *n* campanile M

Belgian [BEL•jun] *adj* belga

Belgium [BEL•jum] *n* Belgio M

belief [bi•LEEF] *n* credenza F

believe [bi•LEEV] *vt vi* credere

bell [bel] *n* campana F

bellow [BE•lo] *vi* muggire

belly [BE•lee] *n* pancia F; venture M

belong [bi•LAUNG] *vi* appartenere

beloved [bi•LUVHVD] *adj* beneamato; beneamata

below [bi•LO] *adv prep* sotto; di sotto; giù

belt [belt] *n* cintura F

bench [bench] *n* panca F

bend [bend] *vt* piegare; *n* curva F

beneath [bi•NEETH] *adv* sotto; di sotto; giù

benediction [BE•ni•DIK•shun] *n* benedizione F

benefactor [BE•ni•FAK•tur] *n* benefattore M

beneficial [BE•nu•FI•shl] *adj* vantaggioso; vantaggiosa

benefit [BE•ni•FIT] *n* vantaggio M; *vt* avvantaggiare

benign [bi•NUYN] *adj* benigno; benigna

bent [bent] *adj* storto; storta

bequeath [bi•KWEETH] *vt* lasciare (per testamento)

beret [bu•RAI] *n* basco M

berry [BE•ree] *n* bacca F

beside [bi•SUYD] *prep* a lato di

besides [bi•SUYDS] *prep adv* inoltre

besiege [bi•SEEJ] *vt* assediare

best [best] *adj* migliore; *adv* meglio

bestow [bi•STO] *vt* concedere

bet [bet] *n* scommessa F; *vt* scommettere

betray [bi•TRAI] *vt* tradire

betrayal [bi•TRAI•ul] *n* tradimento M

betrayer [bi•TRAI•ur] *n* traditore M

better [BE•tur] *adj* piú buono; piú buona

between [bi•TWEEN] *prep* tra; in mezzo a

beverage [BE•vu•rij] *n* bevanda F

beware (of) [bi•WAIR] *vi* guardarsi

bewitching [bi•WI•ching] *adj* ammaliante

beyond [bi•YAHND] *prep* oltre

bias [BUY•us] *n* sbieco M; pregiudizio M

biased [BUY•ust] *adj* prevenuto; prevenuta

bib [bib] *n* bavaglino M

Bible [BUY•bl] *n* Bibbia F

bicker [BI•kur] *vi* litigare

bicycle [BUY•si•kul] *n* bicicletta F

bid [bid] *n* offerta F; *vi* offrire

big [big] *adj* grande; grosso; importante

bigamy [BI•gu•mee] *n* bigamia F

bigot [BI•gut] *n* bigotto; bigotta

bike [buyk] *n* bici F

bikini [bi•KEE•nee] *n* bikini M

bile [buyl] *n* bile F

bilingual [BUY•LING•gwul] *adj* bilingue

bill [bil] *n* conto M

billiards [BIL•yurdz] *n* bigliardo M

billion [BIL•yun] *num* miliardo M

bin (for garbage) [bin] *n* bidone M

binoculars [bi•NAH•kyu•lurz] *npl* binocolo M

biography [buy•AH•gru•fee] *n* biografia F

biology [buy•AH•lu•jee] *n* biologia F

birch [burch] *n* betulla F

bird [burd] *n* uccello M

birdcage [BURD•kaij] *n* gabbia F

birth [burth] *n* nascita F

birth control [~ kon•TROL] *n* controllo delle nascite M

birthday [BURTH•dai] *n* compleanno M

birthmark [BURTH•mahrk] *n* voglia F

birthrate [BURTH•rait] *n* tasso di nascite M

bishop [BI•shup] *n* vescovo M

bit [bit] *n* pezzetto M

bitch [bich] *n* cagna F

bite [buyt] *vt* mordere

bite (insect; snake) [buyt] *vt* morso M

bitter [BI•tur] *adj* amaro; amara

bitterness [BI•tur•NIS] *n* amarezza F

blab [blab] *vi vt* spiattellare

black [blak] *adj n* nero; nera

black market [~ MAHR•kit] *n* mercato nero M

blackberry [BLAK•BU•ree] *n* mora F

blackbird [BLAJ•burd] *n* merlo M

blackboard [BLAK•baurd] *n* lavagna F

blacken [BLA•kun] *vt* annerire

blackmail [BLAK•mail] *n* ricattare

blacksmith [BLAK•smith] *n* fabbro M

bladder [BLA•dur] *n* vescica F

blade [blaid] *n* lama F; ~ of grass\ filo d'erba

blame [blaim] *vt* biasimare

bland [bland] *adj* blando; blanda

blank [blank] *n* in bianco

blanket [BLANG•kit] *n* coperta F

blaspheme [blas•FEEM] *vt vi* bestemmiare

blast [blast] *n* scoppio M

blatant [BLAI•tunt] *adj* appariscente

blaze [blaiz] *n* fiamma F; *vt* ardere; divampare

bleach [bleech] *n* candeggina F

bleed [bleed] *vi* sanguinare; *vt* salassare

blemish [BLE•mish] *n* macchia F

blend [blend] *vt* miscelare

bless [bles] *vt* benedire

blessing [BLE•sing] *n* benedizione F

blind [bluynd] *adj* cieco; cieca

blindfold [BLUYND•fold] *n* benda F

blink [blink] *vt* ammiccare

blinker (car) [bling•kur] *n* freccia F

bliss [blis] *n* beatitudine F

blister [BLI•stur] *n* vescica F

blizzard [BLI•zurd] *n* tormenta F

bloated [BLO•tid] *adj* gonfio; gonfia

block [blahk] *n* blocco M; *vt* bloccare; (street) *n* isolato M

blockade [blah•KAID] *n* blocco M

blockage [BLAH•kij] *n* blocco M

blonde [blahnd] *adj* biondo; bionda

blood [bluhd] *n* sangue M

bloody [BLUH•dee] *adj* insanguinato

bloom [bloom] *vi* fiorire

blossom [BLAH•sum] *n* fiore M

blouse [blous] *n* camicetta F

blow [blo] *vt* soffiare

bludgeon [BLUH•jn] *vt* prendere a randellate

blue [bloo] *adj n* blú; azzurro

blueberry [BLOO•BE•ree] *n* mirtillo M

blueprint [BLOO•print] *n* progetto M

bluff [bluhf] *n* bluff M; *vt* ingannare

blunder [BLUHN•dur] *n* errore M

blunt [bluhnt] *adj* spuntato; spuntata

blurry [BLU•ree] *adj* offuscato; offuscata

blush [bluhsh] *vi* arrossire; *n* rossore M

boar [baur] *n* cinghiale M

board [baurd] (lumber) *n* asse F; (on board) *vt* abbordare

boarding school [BAUR•ding ~] *n* collegio M

boast [bost] *vi* vantarsi

boat [bot] *n* barca F; batello M

boating [BO•ting] *n* canottaggio M

body [BAH•dee] *n* corpo M

bodyguard [BAH•dee•GAHRD] *n* guardia del corpo F

bog [bahg] *n* palude F

boil [boil] *vt* bollire

boiled egg [boild ~] *n* uovo sodo M

boiling point [BOI•ling ~] *n* ebollizione F

boisterous [BOI•stu•rus] *adj* rumoroso; rumorosa

bold [bold] *adj* audace

boldness [BOLD•nes] *n* audacia F

bolt [bolt] *n* bullone M

bomb [bahm] *n* bomba F

bombard [BAHM•bahrd] *vt* bombardare

bomber [BAH•mur] *n* bombardiere M

bombing [BAH•ming] *n* bombardamento M

bond [bahnd] *n* legame M; vincolo M

bondage [BAHN•dij] *n* schiavitú F

bone [bon] *n* osso M

bonfire [BAHN•fuyur] *n* faló M

bonnet [BAH•nit] *n* cuffia F

bonus [BO•nus] *n* gratifica F

boo [boo] *vt vi* fischiare

book [bük] *n* libro M

bookkeeper [BÜK•KEE•pur] *n* contabile

bookkeeping [BÜK•KEE•ping] *n* contabilitá F

bookstore [BÜK•staur] *n* libreria F

boom [boom] *vi n* rombare; *n* rombo M

boomerang [BOO•mu•RANG] *n* boomerang M

boos [booz] *npl* fischi M

boost [boost] *vt* spingere

boot [boot] *n* stivale M

booth [booth] *n* stand M

booty [BOO•tee] *n* bottino M

border [BAUR•dur] *n* onfine M

bore [baur] *vt* annoiare

boredom [BAUR•dum] *n* noia F

boring [BAU•ring] *adj* noioso; noiosa

born (to be) [baurn] *adj* nato; nata

borough [BUH•ro] *n* comune M

borrow [BAH•ro] *vt* prendere a prestito

Bosnia [BAHZ•nee•u] *n* Bosnia F

Bosnian [BAHZ•nee•un] *adj n* bosniaco; bosniaca

bosom [BU•zum] *n* petto M

boss [baus] *n* principale M

botany [BAH•tu•nee] *n* botanica F

both [both] *adj* entrambi; entrambe

bother [BAH•thur] *vt* infastidire

bottle [BAH•tl] *n* bottiglia F

bottom [BAH•tum] *n* fondo M

boulder [BOL•dur] *n* masso M

bounce [bouns] *vi vt* rimbalzare; *n* rimbalzo M

bouncer [BOUN•sur] *n* buttafuori M

bound [bound] *adj* (to be ~ for) destinato; destinata

boundary [BOUN•du•ree] *n* limite M

bout [bout] *n* attacco M

bovine [BO•vuyn] *adj* bovino; bovina

bow 1 [bou] *vi* inchinarsi; *vt* curvare

bow 2 (archery) [bou] *n* arco M

bow 3 (knot) [bou] *n* fiocco M

bow tie [BOW ty] *n* cravatta a farfalla F

bowels [boulz] *npl* budella F

bowl [bol] *n* scodella F

bowling [BO•ling]] *n* bowling M

box [bahks] *n* scatola F

box office [bahx AW•fis] *n* botteghino M

boxer [BAH•ksur] *n* pugilatore M

boxing [BAH•ksing] *n* pugilato M

boy [boi] *n* ragazzo M

boycott 1 [BOI•kaht] *vt* boicottare

boycott 2 [BOI•kaht] *n* boicotto M

bra [brah] *n* reggiseno M

brace [brais] *n* paio M

bracelet [BRAI•slit] *n* braccialetto M

bracket (in writing) [BRA•kit] *n* parentesi quadra F

brag [brag] *vi* vantarsi

braid 1 [braid] *n* treccia F

braid 2 [braid] *vt* intrecciare

braille [brail] *n* braille M

brain [brain] *n* cervello M

brake [braik] *n vi* freno M; *vi* frenare

bran [bran] *n* crusca F

branch [branch] *n* ramo M

brand [brand] *n* mara F; *vt* (cattle, etc) marchiare

brand-new [brand•NOO] *adj* nuovo di zecca; nuova di zecca

brandy [BRAN•dee] *n* brandy M

brash [brash] *adj* insolente

brass [bras] *n* ottone M

brat [brat] *n* monello M

brave [braiv] *adj* coraggioso; coraggiosa; *vt* sfidare

bravery [BRAI•vu•ree] *n* coraggio M

brawl [braul] *n* rissa F

brawn [braun] *n* muscolo M

bray [brai] *vi* ragliare

breach (in wall) [breech] *n vt* breccia F; (of contract) *n* violazione F

bread [bred] *n* pane M

breadth [bredth] *n* larghezza F

break [braik] *vt vi* rompere; *n* rottura F

breakdown 1 [BRAIK•doun] *n* collasso M

breakdown 2 (machine) [BRAIK•doun] *n* in panne

breakfast [BREK•fust] *n* (prima) colazione F

breast [brest] *n* petto M

breath [breth] *n* respiro M

breathe [breeth] *vi* respirare

breathless [BRETH•lis] *adj* senza fiato

breed 1 (animals) [breed] *vt* allevare

breed 2 (race) [breed] *n* razza F

breeze [breez] *n* brezza F

brevity [BRE•vi•tee] *n* brevitá F

brew [broo] *vt* fare un infuso

brewer [BROO•ur] *n* birraio M

brewery [BROO•u•ree] *n* birreria F

bribe [bruyb] *n* bustarella F; *vt* corrompere

brick [brik] *n* mattone M

bridal [BRUY•dl] *adj* nuziale

bride [bruyd] *n* sposa F

bridegroom [BRUYD•groom] *n* sposo M

bridesmaid [BRUYDZ•maid] *n* damigella d'onore F

bridge [brij] *n* ponte M; *vt* congiungere

brief [breef] *adj* breve

briefcase [BREEF•kais] *n* valigetta F

briefly [BREE•flee] *adv* brevemente

bright [bruyt] *adj* luminoso; luminosa

brilliance [BRIL•lyuns] *n* lucentezza F

brilliant [BRIL•lyunt] *adj* brillante

bring [bring] *vt* portare

brisk [brisk] *adj* svelto; svelta

bristle [BRI•sl] *vi* incollerirsi

British [BRI•tish] *adj* inglese

broad [braud] *adj* largo; larga

broadcast [BRAUD•kast] *vt* trasmettere; *n* trasmissione F

brocade [bro•KAID] *n* broccato M

broccoli [BRAH•klee] *n* broccoli M

brochure [bro•SHUR] *n* dépliant M

broil [broil] *vt* cucinare ai ferri

broker [BRO•kur] *n* agente

bronze [brahnz] *n adj* bronzo

brooch [broch] *n* spilla F

brook [brük] *n* ruscello M

broom [broom] *n* scopa F

broth [brauth] *n* brodo M

brothel [BRAH•thl] *n* postribolo M

brother [BRUH•thur] *n* fratello M

brother-in-law [BRUH•thur•in•LAU] *n* cognato M

brown [braun] *adj n* marrone

bruise [brooz] *n* livido M; *vt* illividire

brunette [BROO•net] *n* brunetta F

brush [bruhsh] *n* spazzola F; *vt* spazzolare

Brussels [BRUH•slz] *n* Bruxelles M

brutal [BROO•tl] *adj* brutale

brute [broot] *n* bruto M

bubble [BUH•bl] *n* bolla F; *vi* ribollire

buck [buhk] *vi* impennarsi

bucket [BUH•kit] *n* secchio M

buckle [BUH•kl] *n* fibbia F; *vt*
allacciare con una fibbia

bud [buhd] *n* bocciolo M; *vi*
germogliare

Buddhism [BOO•DI•zm] *n*
Buddismo M

budge [buhj] *vi vt* smuovere

budget [BUH•jit] *n* bilancio M

buffalo [BUH•fu•LO] *n* bufalo;
bufala

buffet [buh•FAI] *n* buffet M

bug [buhg] *n* insetto M

bugle [BYOO•gl] *n* tromba F

build [bild] *vt* costruire

builder [BIL•dur] *n* costruttore
M; palazzo M

bulb [buhlb] *n* bulbo M

Bulgaria [BUHL•GAI•ree•u] *n*
Bulgheria F

bulge [buhlj] *n* gonfiore M

bull [bül] *n* toro M

bulldozer [BÜL•do•zur] *n*
bulldozer M

bullet [BÜ•lit] *n* proiettile M

bulletin [BÜ•lu•tin] *n*
bollettino M

bully [BÜ•lee] *n* prepotente

bumblebee [BUHM•bl•BEE] *n*
calabrone M

bump [buhmp] *vt* urtare; *n*
protuberanza F

bumper (of car) [BUHM•pur] *n*
paraurti M

bun [buhn] *n* ciambella F

bunch [buhnch] *n* mazzo M

bundle [BUHN•dl] *n* fagotto M

bunk beds [buhnk ~] *npl* letti a
castello M

buoy [BOO•ee] *n* boa F

burden [BUR•dn] *n* fardello M;
vt caricare

bureau [BYÜ•ro] *n* ufficio M;
(dresser) cassettiera F

bureaucracy
[byü•RAH•kru•see] *n*
burocrazia F

burglar [BUR•glur] *n* ladro;
ladra

burial [BU•ree•ul] *n* sepoltura F

Burma [BUR•mu] *n* Burma F

Burmese [bur•MEEZ] *adj*
burmese

burn [burn] *vi vt* bruciare

burner [BUR•nur] *s*
bruciatore M

burrow [BUH•ro] *n* tana F; *vt*
rintanarsi

burst [burst] *vt* scoppiare

bury [BU•ree] *vt* seppellire

bus [buhs] *n* autobus M

bush [büsh] *n* cespuglio M

bushel [BÜ•shul] *n* staiò M

business [BIZ•nis] *n* affari M;
adj d'affari

businessman ~woman
[BIZ•nis•MAN] *n* uomo
(donna) d'affari

bust (of statue) [buhst] *n* busto
M

bustle [BUH•sl] *n* trambusto M;
vi affacendarsi; (fashion) *n*
pannier M

busy [BI•zee] *adj* occupato;
occupata

busybody [BIZ•ee•BAH•dee] *n*
impiccione; impicciona

but [buht] *conj* ma

butcher 1 [BU•chur] *n*
macellaio M

butcher 2 (shop) [BU•chur] *n*
macelleria F

butler [BUHT•lur] *n*
maggiordomo M

butt (of cigarette) [buht] *n*
mozzicone M

butter [BUH•tur] *n vt* burro M;
vt imburrare

butterfly [BUH•tur•FLUÝ] *n*
farfalla F

buttock [BUH•tuk] *n* natica F

button [BUH•tn] *n* bottone M

buy [buy] *vt* comprare

buyer [BUY•ur] *n*
compratore M

buzz (of insect) [buhz] *n*
ronzio M

by [buy] *prep* da; con; a; di;
per; entro; near to\ *prep*
vicino

C

cab [kab] *n* taxi M

cabbage [CA•bij] *n* cavolo M

cabin [CA•bin] *n* cabina F

cabinet [KA•bi•nit] *n*
gabinetto M

cable [KAI•bl] *vi/vt* mandare un
cablogramma; *n* cavo M

cackle [KA•kl] *vi* gracchiare

cactus [KAK•tes] *n* cacto M

cadaver [ku•DA•vur] *n*
cadavere M

cadet [ku•DET] *n* cadetto M

cafeteria [KA•fi•TEE•ree•u] *n*
self-service M

cage [kaij] *n* gabbia F

cake [kaik] *n* torta F

calcium [KAL•see•um] *n*
calcio M

calculate [KAL•kyoo•LAIT] *vt*
calcolare

calculator [KAL•kyoo•LAI•tur]
n calcolatore M

calendar [KA•lin•dur] *n*
calendario M

calf [kaf] *n* vitello M; (anat) *n*
polpaccio M

call [caul] *n* chiamata F; *vt*
chiamare; (by phone) *vt*
telfonare

calling [KAU•ling] *n*
vocazione F

calm [kahm] *adj* calmo; calma

calm down [kalm down] *vt*
calmare

Cambodia [kam•BO•dyu] *n*
Cambogia F

camel [KA•mul] *n* cammello M

cameo [KA•mee•O] *n*
cammeo M

camera [KA•mu•ru] *n* macchina
fotografica F

cameraman [KA•mu•ru•MAN]
n cameraman M

camp [kamp] *n* campo M; *vi*
campeggiare

campaign [kam•PAIN] *n*
campagna F; *vi* fare una
campagna

campground [KAMP•ground]
n campeggio M

can [kan] *n* barattolo M; *vi-aux*
potere

Canada [KA•nu•du] *n*
Canadá M

canal [ku•NAL] *n* canale M

canary [ku•NA•ree] *n*
canarino M

cancel (call off) [KAN•suhl] *vt*
cancellare

cancer [KAN•sur] *n* cancro M

candid [KAN•did] *adj* candido;
candida

candidate [KAN•di•DUT] *n*
candidato; candidata

candle [KAN•dl] *n* candela F

candor [KAN•dur] *n* candore M

candy [KAN•dee] *n* caramella F

cane [kain] *n* canna F; (walking
stick) *n* bastone M

canine [KAI•nuyn] *adj* canino;
canina

cannibal [KA•ni•bl] *n* cannibale

cannon [KA•nun] *n* cannone M

canoe [ku•NOO] *n* canoa F

canon [KA•nun] *n* regola F

canopy [KA•nu•pee] *n*
baldacchino M

canvas [KAN•vus] *n* tela F

canyon [KA•nyun] *n* canyon M

cap [kap] *n* berretto M

capacity [ku•PA•ci•tee] *n*
capacitá F

cape (clothing) [kaip] *n*
mantella F; (geog) *n* capo M

caper [KAI•pur] *n* scappatella
F; (food) *n* cappero M

capital [KA•pi•tl] *n* capitale M

capitalism [KA•pi•tu•LI•zm] *n*
capitalismo M

capsule [KAP•sul] *n* capsula F

captain [KAP•tin] *n* capitano
M; *n* didascalia F

captive [KAP•tiv] *n* prigioniero;
prigioniera

capture [KAP•chur] *vt n* cattura
F; *vt* catturare

car [kahr] *n* automobile F;
machina F

carbon [KAHR•bun] *n*
carbone M

carcass [KAHR•kus] *n*
carcassa F

card [kahrd] *n* carta F; (postal)
n cartolina F

cardboard [KAHRD•baurd] *n*
cartone M

cardiac [KAHR•dee•AK] *adj*
cardiaco; cardiaca

cardigan [KAHR•di•gun] *n*
golf M

cardinal [KAHR•di•nl] *n*
cardinale M

care [kair] *n* cura F; premura F;
(about) *vi* curare; importare (a
qualcuno)

career [ku•REER] *n* carriera F

carefree [KAIR•free] *adj*
spensierato; spensierata

careful [KAIR•ful] *adj* attento;
attenta

careless [KAIR•lis] *adj* sbadato;
sbadato

caress [ku•RES] *n* carezza F; *vt*
accarezzare

cargo [KAHR•go] *n* carico M

Caribbean (Sea)
[KU•ri•BEE•un] *n* Mar dei
Caraibi M

carnal [KAHR•nul] *adj* carnale

carnation [kahr•NAI•shun] *n*
garofano M

carnival [KAHR•nu•vl] *n*
carnevale M

carnivorous [kahr•NI•vu•rus] *adj* carnivoro; carnivora

carp [kahrp] *n* carpa F

carpenter [KAHR•pun•tur] *n* falegname M

carpet [KAHR•put] *n* tappeto M

carriage [KA•rij] *n* carrozza F; portamento M

carrot [KA•rut] *n* carota F

carry [KA•ree] *vt* portare; transportare

cart [kahrt] *n* carro M; *vt* trasportare

carton 1 [KAHR•tn] *n* scatolone M

carton 2 (cigarette) [KAHR•tn] *n* stecca F

cartoon [kahr•TOON] *n* cartone animato M

carve [kahrv] *vt vi* scolpire

case [kais] *n* astuccio M; (in ~ of) *n* caso M

cash [kash] *n* contanti M

cash register [KASH RE•jis•tur] *n* cassa F

cask [kask] *n* barile M

casket [KA•skit] *n* scrigno M; (funeral) *n* feretro M

cassette [ku•SET] *n* cassetta F

cast [kast] *n* ingessatura F; *vt* assegnare una parte; (film) *n* cast M

castle [KA•sl] *n* castello M

casual [KA•zhoo•ul] *adj* casuale

cat [kat] *n* gatto; gatta

catalogue [KA•tu•LAHG] *n vt* catalogo M; *vt* catalogare

catapult [KA•tu•PUHLT] *n* catapulta F; *vt* catapultare

cataract [KA•tu•RAKT] *n* cateratta F

catastrophe [ku•TA•stru•fee] *n* catastrofe F

catch [kach] *vt* acchiappare; *n* preda F; cattura; retata

categorical [KA•tu•GAU•ri•kl] *adj* categorico; catgorica

category [KA•tu•GAU•ree] *n* categoria F

cater (banquet, etc) [KAI•tr] *vt* preparare cibi da asporto

caterpillar [KA•tur•PI•lur] *n* bruco M

cathedral [ku•THEE•drul] *n* catterale F

Catholic [KATH•lik] *adj n* cattolico; cattolica

cattle [KA•tl] *npl* bestiame M

cauliflower [KAH•lee•FLOU•ur] *n* cavolfiore M

cause [kauz] *n* causa F; *vt* causare

caustic [KAU•stik] *adj* caustico; caustica

caution [KAU•shun] *n* cautela F; *vt* mettere in guardia

cautious [KAU•shus] *adj* cauto; cauta

cavalry [KA•vl•ree] *n* cavalleria F

cave [kaiv] *n* caverna F

caveman [KAIV•man] *n* troglodita

cavity [KA•vi•tee] *n* cavitá F; (dental) *n* carie F

cease [sees] *vt vi* cessare

cease-fire [CEES•FUYUR] *n* cessare il fuoco M

cedar [SEE•dur] *n* cedro M

cede [seed] *vt vi* cedere

cedilla [si•DI•lu] *n* cedilla F

celebrate [SE•li•BRAIT] *vt vi*
celebrare

celebration [SE•li•BRAI•shun]
n celebrazione F

celebrity [si•LE•bri•tee] *n*
celebritá F

celibate [CE•li•but] *adj*
celibe M

cell [sel] *n* cella F

cellar [SE•lur] *n* cantina F

cello [CHE•lo] *n* violoncello M

Celtic [KEL•tik] *adj* celtico;
celtica

cement [si•MENT] *vt n*
cemento M

cemetery [SE•mi•TE•ree] *n*
cimitero M

censor [SEN•sur] *n vt*
censore M

censorship [SEN•sur•SHIP] *n*
censura F

census [SEN•sus] *n*
censimento M

centennial [sen•TEN•ee•ul] *n*
centenario M

center [SEN•tur] *n* centro M; *vt*
centrare; accentrare

centigrade [SEN•ti•GRAID]
adj centigrado M

centimeter [SEN•ti•MEE•tur] *n*
centimetro M

centipede [SEN•ti•PEED] *n*
millepiedi M

central [SEN•trul] *adj* centrale

century [SEN•chu•ree] *n*
secolo M

ceramic [si•RA•mik] *adj*
ceramica F

cereal [SI•ree•ul] *n* cereale M

ceremony [SE•ri•MO•nee] *n*
cerimonia F

certain [SUR•tn] *adj* certo; certa

certainly [SUR•tn•lee] *adv*
certamente

certainty [SUR•tn•tee] *n*
certezza F

certificate [sur•TI•fi•kut] *n*
certificato M

certify [SUR•tu•FUY] *vt*
certificare

chain [chain] *n* catena F

chain saw [CHAIN sau] *n* sega
a catena F

chair [chai'ur] *n* sedia F; seggio
M; *vt* presiedere

chairman [CHAI'UR•mun] *n*
presidente M

chalk [chauk] *n* gesso M

challenge [CHA•linj] *n* sfida F;
vt sfidare

chamber [CHAIM•bur] *n*
camera F

chameleon [ku•MEEL•yun] *n*
camaleonte M

champagne [sham•PAIN] *n*
champagne M

champion [CHAM•pyun] *n*
campione M; *vi* difendere;
sostenere

chance [chans] *n* caso M

chancellor [CHAN•su•lur] *n*
cancelliere M

change [chainj] *n* cambio M; *vt
vi* cambiare

channel (TV, radio) [CHA•nul]
n canale M; (water) *vt*
íncanalare

chant (rel) [chant] *vt vi*
salmodiare; *n* canto M

chaos [KAI•ahs] *n* caos M

chapel [CHA•pl] *n* cappella M

chaplain [CHA•plen] *n*
cappellano M

chapter [CHAP•tur] *n*
capitolo M

character [KA•ruk•tur] *n*
carattere M

characteristic
[KA•ruk•tu•RI•stik] *n*
caratteristica F; *adj*
caratteristico; caratteristica

charcoal [CHAHR•col] *n*
carbone M

charge [charj] *n* prezzo M; *vi vt*
addebitare; *vi* accusare

charity [CHA•ru•tee] *n* caritá F

charm [chahrm] *n* fascino M; *vt*
incantare

charming [CHAHR•ming] *adj*
affascinante

chart [chahrt] *n* carta F

charter (flight) [CHAHR•tur] *n*
charter M

chase [chais] *n* caccia F; *vt*
cacciare

chasm [KA•zm] *n* baratro M

chaste [chaist] *adj* casto; casta

chastise [cha•STUYZ] *vt*
castigare

chastity [CHA•sti•tee] *n*
castitá F

chat [chat] *vi* chiaccherare

chatterbox [CHA•tur•BAHKS]
n chiaccherone; chiaccherona

chauffeur [SHO•fur] *n*
autista M

cheap [cheep] *adj* economico;
economica

cheapen [CHEE•pn] *vt*
deprezzare

cheat [cheet] *vt vi* imbrogliare

cheater [CHEE•tr] *n*
imbroglione; imbrogliona MF

check [chek] *vt* controllare; bill\
n conto M; currency\ *n*
assegno M

checkbook [CHEK•buk] *n*
libretto d'assegni M

cheek [cheek] *n* guancia F

cheer [cheer] *n* applauso M *vt*
rallegrare; applaudire; ~ up *vi*
rallegrare

cheerful [CHEER•ful] *adj*
allegro; allegra

cheers (drinking toast)
[cheerz] *excl* salute F

cheese [cheez] *n* formaggio M

cheetah [CHEE•tu] *n*
ghepardo M

chef [shef] *n* capo; cuoco M

chemical 1 [KE•mi•kul] *n*
sostanza chimica F

chemical 2 [KE•mi•kul] *adj*
chimico; chimica

chemist [KE•mist] *n* chimico;
chimica

chemistry [KE•mi•stree] *n*
chimica F

cherish [CHE•rish] *vt* amare;
nutrire

cherry [CHE•ree] *n* ciliegia F

chess [ches] *n* scacchi M

chest [chest] *n* torace M

chest of drawers
[~ DRAW•urz] *n* cassettiera F

chestnut [CHEST•nuht] *n*
castagna F

chew [choo] *vt* masticare

chick [chik] *n* pulcino M

chicken [CHI•kin] *n* pollo M

chicken pox [~ pahks] *n*
varicella F

chief [cheef] *n* capo M; *adj* capo; principale

child [chuyld] *n* bambino; bambina

childbirth [CHUYLD•burth] *n* parto M

childhood [CHUYLD•hud] *n* infanzia F

childish [CHUYL•dish] *adj* infantile

Chile [CHI•lee] *n* Cile M

chill [chil] *n* freddo M; *vi vt* raffreddare

chilly [CHI•lee] *adj* freddo; fredda

chime [chuym] *n* scampanio M; *vi* scampanare

chimney [CHIM•nee] *n* camino M

chimpanzee [chim•PAN•ZEE] *n* scimpanzé M

chin [chin] *n* mento M

China 1 [CHUY•nu] *n* Cina F

china 2 [chuy•nu] *n* porcellana F

Chinese [chuy•NEEZ] *adj* cinese

chip [chip] *n* scheggia F; *vt* scheggiare

chirp [churp] *vi* cinguettare

chisel [CHI•zl] *n* scalpello M; *vt* cesellare

chivalry [SHI•vl•ree] *n* cavalleria F

chive [chuyv] *n* erba cipollina F

chlorophyll [KLAU•ru•FIL] *n* clorofilla F

chocolate [CHAU•ku•lut] *n* cioccolata F

choice [chois] *n* scelta F

choir [kwuyr] *n* coro M

choke [chok] *vt vi* strozzare; ~of car\ *n* valvola dell'aria F

cholera [KAH•lu•ru] *n* colera M

choose [chooz] *vi vt* scegliere

chop [chahp] *vt* tagliare; (of meat) *n* braciola F

chord [kaurd] *n* accordo M

chores [chaurz] *npl* lavoro M

chorus [KAU•rus] *n* coro M

Christ [kruyst] *n* Cristo M

christen [KRI•sn] *vt* battezzare

Christian [KRI•schun] *adj n* cristiano; cristiana

Christianity [KRI•schee•A•nu•tee] *n* cristinitá F

Christmas [KRIS•mus] *n* Natale M

chrome [krom] *n* cromo M

chronic [KRAH•nik] *adj* cronico; cronica

chronicle [KRAH•ni•kl] *n* cronaca F

chronological [KRAH•nu•LAH•ji•kl] *adj* cronologico; cronologica

chrysanthemum [kri•SAN•thi•mum] *n* crisantemo M

chubby [CHUH•bee] *adj* paffuto; paffuta

chuck [chuhk] *vt* gettare

chuckle [CHUH•kl] *vi* ridacchiare

chunk [chuhnk] *n* bel pezzo M

church [church] *n* chiea F

churn (butter) [churn] *n* zangola F; *vt* fare il burro

chute [shoot] *n* scivolo M

cider [SUY•dur] *n* sidro M

cigar [si•GAHR] *n* sigaro M

cigarette [SI•gu•RET] *n*
sigarett F

cinder [SIN•dur] *n* cenere F

Cinderella [SIN•du•RE•lu] *n*
Cenerentola F

cinema [SI•nu•mu] *n* cinema M

cinnamon [SI•nu•mun] *n*
cannella F

circle [SUR•kl] *n* cerchio M;
circolo M; *vt* girarre attorno

circuit [SUR•kit] *n* circuito M

circular [SUR•cyu•lur] *adj*
circolare

circulate [SUR•kyu•LAIT] *vi vt*
circolare

circulation
[SUR•kyu•LAI•shun] *n*
circolazione F

circumcision
[SUR•cuhm•SI•zhun] *n*
circoncisione F

circumference
[sur•CUHM•fu•runs] *n*
circonferenza F

circumflex [SUR•cuhm•FLEKS]
adj circonflesso; circonflessa

circumstance
[SUR•cum•STANS] *n*
circostanza F

circus [SUR•kus] *n* circo M

cite [suyt] *vt* citare

citizen [SI•ti•zn] *n* cittadino;
cittadina

city [SI•tee] *n* città F

city hall [SIT•tee HALL] *n*
municipio M

civic [SI•vik] *adj* civico; civica

civil [CI•vl] *adj* civile

civilization [SI•vi•li•ZAI•shun]
n civiltà F

civilize [SI•vi•LUYZ] *vt*
civilizzare

claim [klaim] *n* diritto M; *vt*
pretendere

clam [klam] *n* vongola F

clamor [CLA•mur] *n* clamore M

clamp [klamp] *n* morsa F; *vt*
stringere

clan [klan] *n* clan M

clandestine [klan•DE•stin] *adj*
clandestino; clandestina

clap [klap] *vi* battere le mani;
applaudire

clarify [KLA•ri•FUY] *vt*
chiarificare

clarinet [KLA•ri•NET] *n*
clarinetto M

clarity [CLA•ri•tee] *n*
chiarezza F

clash [klash] *n* scontro M; *vt*
scontrare

clasp [klasp] *n* fermaglio M; *vt*
afferrare

class [klass] *n* classe F; *vt*
classificare

classic [KLA•sik] *adj n* classico;
classica

classical [KLA•si•kl] *adj*
classico; classica

classified [KLA•si•FUYD] *adj*
classificato; classificata

classified ad [KLA•si•FUYD
AD] *n* inserzione F

classify [KLA•si•FUY] *vt*
classificare

classroom [KLAS•rum] *n*
aula F

clause [klauz] *n* clausola F;
articulo M

claw [clau] *n* artiglio M; ~ *at vi*
graffiare; (lobster, etc.) *n*
chela F

clay [klay] *n* creta F

clean [kleen] *adj* pulito; pulita; *vt* pulire

cleaner [KLEE•nur] *n* pulitore M; (product) *n* detersivo M

cleaning lady [KLEE•ning LAI•dee] *n* donna delle pulizie F

cleanliness [KLEN•lee•nis] *n* pulizia F

clear [kleer] *adj* chiaro; chiara; *vt* chiarire

clearance [CLEE•runs] *n* svendita F

clearing [KLEE•ring] *n* radura F

clearly [KLEER•lee] *adv* chiaramente

cleavage [KLEE•vij] *n* decolleté M

cleaver [KLEE•vur] *n* mannaia F

clench [klench] *vt* stringere

clergy [KLUR•jee] *n* clero M

clerical [KLE•ri•kl] *adj* clericale

clerk [clurk] *n* commesso M

clever [KLE•vur] *adj* furbo; furba

client [KLUY•unt] *n* cliente

clientele [KLUY•un•TEL] *n* clientela

cliff [klif] *n* scogliera F

climate [KLUY•mit] *n* clima M

climax [KLUY•maks] *n* culmine M

climb [cluym] *n* ascesa F; *vt/vi* arrampicarsi

cling [kling] *vi* stringersi

clinic [KLI•nik] *n* clinica F

clinical [KLI•ni•kl] *adj* clinico; clinica

clip [klip] *n* graffetta F; *vt* tagliare

clippers [KLI•purz] *npl* machinetta per tosare F

cloak [klok] *n* mantello M

clock [klahk] *n* orologio M

clockwise [KLAHK•wuyz] *adj adv* in senso orario

clog [klahg] *vt/vi* otturare

cloister [KLOI•stur] *n* chiostro M; *vt* rinchiudere in convento

close 1 [klos] *adj* vicino; vicina; *n* recinto M

close 2 [kloz] *vt/vi* chiudere concludere

closet [KLAH•zit] *n* armadio a muro M

cloth [klauth] *n* stoffa F

clothe [kloth] *vt* vestire

clothes [klothz] *npl* abiti M

clothing [KLO•thing] *n* vestiario M

cloud [kloud] *n* nuvola F

cloudy [KLOU•dee] *adj* nuvoloso; nuvolosa

clove [klov] *n* chiodo di garofano M

clover [KLO•vur] *n* trifoglio M

clown [kloun] *n* clown

club [kluhb] *n* bastone M; *vt* bastonare; (social) *n* club M

cluck [cluhk] *vi* chiocciare

clue [kloo] *n* indizio M

clump [kluhmp] *n* gruppo M

clumsy [KLUHM•zee] *adj* maldestro; maldestra

cluster [KLUH•stur] *n* grappolo M; (auto) *n* frizione F

clutter [KLUH•tur] *n* disordine M; *vt* ingombrare

coach [koch] *n* carrozza F
   (class) *n* classe turistica F;
   (sports) *n* allenatore M; *vt*
   allenare

coal [kol] *n* carbone M

coarse [caurs] *adj* grossolano;
   grossolana

coast [kost] *n* costa F; *vi* andare
   a ruota libera

coat [kot] *n* cappotto M;
   soprabito M; *vt* ricoprire; (of
   an animal) *n* pelame M

coax [koks] *vt* persuadere

cobblestones
   [KAH•bl•STONZ] *npl*
   acciottolato M

cobweb [KAHB•web] *n*
   ragnatela F

cocaine [ko•KAIN] *n* cocaina F

cock [kahk] *n* gallo M; (a gun)
   vt alzare il cane

cockroach [KAHK•roch] *n*
   scarafaggio M

cocktail [KAHK•tail] *n* cocktail

cocoa [KO•ko] *n* cacao M

coconut [KO•ku•nuht] *n* noce
   di cocco F

cocoon [ku•KOON] *n*
   bozzolo M

cod [kahd] *n* merluzzo M

code [kod] *n* codice M; *vt*
   codificare

coerce [ko•URS] *vt* forzare

coffee [KAU•fee] *n* caffé M

coffee break [KAW•fee
   BRAIK] *n* pausa F

coffee cup [KAW•fee KUP] *n*
   tazzina da caffé F

coffee pot [KAW•fee POT] *n*
   caffettiera F

coffee shop [KAW•fee SHOP]
   n bar M

coffin [KAU•fin] *n* feretro M

coherent [ko•HEE•runt] *adj*
   coerente

coil [koil] *vt/vi* avvolgere;
   (electrical) *n* bobina F

coin [koin] *n* moneta F

coincide [KO•in•SUYD] *vi*
   coincidere

coincidence [ko•IN•si•duns] *n*
   coincidenza F

cold [kold] *n* raffreddore M; dj
   freddo; fredda; be ~\ aver
   freddo; (weather) far freddo;
   have a ~\ essere raffreddato

cold-blooded [~ BLU•did] *adj*
   a sangue freddo

collaborate [ku•LA•bu•RAIT]
   vi collaborare

collapse [ku•LAPS] *n* crollo M;
   vi crollare

collar [KAH•lur] *n* colletto M

collateral [ku•LA•tu•rul] *n*
   collaterale

colleague [KAH•leeg] *n* collega

collect [KU•lekt] *vt/vi*
   collezionare

college [KAH•lij] *n* universitá F

collide (with) [ku•LUYD] *vi*
   scontrarsi

colloquial [ku•LO•kwee•ul] *adj*
   familiare

colon [KO•lun] *n* colon M

colony [KAH•lu•nee] *n*
   colonia F

color [KUH•lur] *n* colore M; *vt*
   colorare

color television
   [~ TEL•i•VI•shn] *n*
   televisione a colori F

color-blind [KUH•lor•blynd]
adj daltonica; daltonica

colorful [KUH•lur•ful] *adj*
pittoresco; pittoresca

colossal [ku•LAH•sul] *adj*
colossale

colt [kolt] *n* puledro M

column [KAH•luhm] *n* colonna
F; (newspaper) rubrica F

coma [KO•mu] *n* coma

comb [kom] *n* pettine M; *vt*
pettinare

combat [KAHM•bat] *n*
combattimento M; *vt/vi*
combattere

combination
[KAHM•bi•NAI•shn] *n*
combinazione F

combine [kum•BUYN] *vt*
combinare

come 1 [kuhm] *vi* venire

come 2 (away) [kuhm] venire
via

comeback [KUHM•bak] *vi*
ritorno M

comedian [ku•MEE•dee•un] *n*
comico M

comedy [KAH•mi•dee] *n*
commedia F

comet [KAH•mit] *n* cometa F

comfort [KUHM•furt] *n*
conforto M; *vt* confortare

comfortable [KUHMF•tur•bl]
adj comodo; comod

comics (comic strip)
[KAH•miks] *npl* fumetti M

coming [KUH•ming] *adj*
prossimo; prossima

comma [KAH•mu] *n* virgola F

command [ku•MAND] *n*
comando M; *vt* commandare

commander [ku•MAN•dur] *n*
comandante M

commence [ku•MENS] *vt/vi*
iniziare

commend [ku•MEND] *vt*
commendare

comment [KAH•ment] *n*
commento M; *vi* commentare

commerce [KAH•murs] *n*
commercio M

commercial [ku•MUR•shl] *n*
comunicato commerciale M

commission [ku•MI•shn] *n*
commissione F

commissioner (police)
[ku•MI•shu•nur] *n* questore M

commit [ku•MIT] *vt* affidare; (a
crime) *vt* commettere

committee [ku•MI•tee] *n*
comitato M

committment [ku•MIT•munt] *n*
impegno M

commodity [ku•MAH•di•tee] *n*
derrate F

common [KAH•mun] *adj*
comune ; ~ sense\ *n* buon
senso M

commonly [KAH•mun•lee] *adv*
comunemente

commonplace
[KAH•mun•PLAIS] *adj*
ordinario; ordinaria

commotion [ku•MO•shn] *n*
confusione F

communicate
[ku•MYOO•ni•KAIT] *vt/vi*
comunicare

communion [ku•MYOO•nyun]
n comunione F

communism
[KAH•myu•NI•zm] *n*
comunismo M

communist [KAH•myu•nist]
adj n comunista

community [ku•MYOO•nu•tee]
n comunitá F

commute 1 [ku•MYOOT] *vi*
fare il pendolare

commute 2 (a sentence)
[ku•MYOOT] *vt* commutare

compact 1 [kahm•PAKT] *adj*
compatto; compatta

compact 2 [KAHM•pakt] *n*
accordo M; patto M

compact disc [KAM•pakt
DISK] *n* compact disc

companion [kum•PA•nyun] *n*
compagno; compagna

company [KUHM•pu•nee] *n*
compagnia F; *n* ditta F

compare [kum•PAIR] *vt*
paragonare

comparison [kum•PA•ri•sn] *n*
paragone M

compartment (division)
[kum•PAHRT•munt] *n*
scompartimento M

compass [KAHM•pus] *n*
compasso M; (nav) *n*
bussola F

compassion [kum•PA•shn] *n*
compassione F

compassionate
[kum•PA•shu•nit] *adj*
compassionevole

compatible [kum•PA•ti•bl] *adj*
compatibile

compel [kum•PEL] *vt* obbligare

compelling [kum•PE•ling] *adj*
irresistibile

compensate
[KAHM•pun•SAIT] *vt*
compensare

compensation
[KAHM•pun•SAI•shn] *n*
compenso M

compete [kum•PEET] *vi*
competere

competence [KAHM•pi•tuns] *n*
competenza F

competent [KAHM•pi•tunt] *adj*
competente

competition
[KAHM•pu•TI•shn] *n*
competizione F

competitive [kum•PE•tu•tiv]
adj concorrenziale

complacent [kum•PLAI•sunt]
adj compiaciuto; compiaciuta

complain [kum•PLAIN] *vi*
lagnarsi

complaint [kuhm•PLAINT] *n*
lagnanza F

complement [KAHM•pli•munt]
vt completare

complete [kum•PLEET] *adj*
completo; completa; *vt*
completare

complex [kahm•PLEKS] *adj*
complesso; complessa

complexion [kum•PLEK•shn] *n*
carnagione F

complicate [KAHM•pli•KAIT]
vt complicare; *adj* complicato;
complicata

compliment [KAHM•pli•ment]
n complimento M; *vt*
complimentare

comply [kum•PLUY] *vi* aderire

component [kum•PO•nunt] *n*
componente M

compose [kum•POZ] *vt*
comporre

composer [kum•PO•zur] *n*
compositore M

composition
[KAHM•pu•ZI•shn] *n*
composizione F

composure [kum•PO•zhur] *n*
calma F

compound [KAHM•pound] *adj*
composto; composta

comprehend
[KAHM•pree•HEND] *vt*
comprendere

comprehension
[KAHM•pree•HEN•shn] *n*
comprensione F

comprehensive
[KAHM•pree•HEN•siv] *adj*
comprensivo; comprensiva

compress [kum•PRES] *vt*
comprimere

comprise [kum•PRUYZ] *vt*
includere

compromise 1
[KAHM•pru•MUYZ] *n*
compromesso M

compromise 2
[KAHM•pru•MUYZ] *vt/vi*
compromettere; (on an issue)
vt/vi giungere a un
compromesso

compulsive [kum•PUHL•siv]
adj coercitivo; coercitiva

computer [kum•PYOO•tur] *n*
computer M

computerize
[kum•PYOO•tu•RUYZ] *vt*
computerizzare

comrade [KAHM•rad] *n*
compagno; compagna

conceal [kun•SEEL] *vt* celare

concede [kun•SEED] *vt/vi*
ammettere

conceit [kun•SEET] *n*
superbia F

conceited [kun•SEE•tid] *adj*
superbo; superba

conceive [kun•SEEV] *vt/vi*
concepire

concentrate
[KAHN•sun•TRAIT] *vi*
concentrarsi; (reduce) *vt*
concentrare

concept [KAHN•sept] *n*
cocnetto M

concern [kun•SURN] *n*
interesse M

concerning [kun•SUR•ning]
prep circa

concert [KAHN•surt] *n*
concerto M

concession [kun•SE•shn] *n*
concessione F; (commercial)
n appalto M

concise [kun•SUYS] *adj*
conciso; concisa

conclude [kun•KLOOD] *vt/vi*
concludere

concrete [kahn•KREET] *n*
cemento M; *adj* concreto;
concreta

condemn [kun•DEM] *vt*
condannare

condense [kun•DENS] *vt/vi*
condensare

condescending
[KAHN•di•SEN•ding] *adj*
condiscendente

condition [kun•DI•shn] *n*
condizione F; *vt* pattuire; *n*
condizione F

condolences [kun•DO•lun•ciz] *npl* condoglianze F

condone [kun•DON] *vt* condonare

conduct [n. KAHN•duhkt v. kun•DUHKT] *n* condotta F; *vt* dirigere

conductor [kun•DUHK•tur] *n* controllore M

cone [kon] *n* cono M

confectionery [kun•FEK•shu•NE•ree] *n* pasticceria F

confederation [kun•FE•du•RAI•shn] *n* confederazione F

confer [kun•FUR] *vt/vi* conferire

conference [KAHN•fu•runs] *n* coferenza F

confess [kun•FES] *vt/vi* confessare

confession [kun•FE•shn] *n* confessione F

confidant [KAHN•fi•DAHNT] *n* confidente

confide [kun•FUYD] *vt/vi* confidare

confidence [KAHN•fi•duns] *n* confidenza F; *n* sicurezza F

confident [KAHN•fi•dunt] *adj* fiducioso; fiduciosa

confidential [KAHN•fi•DEN•shl] *adj* confidenziale

confine [kun•FUYN] *vt* relegare

confirm [kun•FURM] *vt* confermare

confirmation [KAHN•fur•MAI•shn] *n* conferma F; (religious) *n* cresima F

confiscate [KAHN•fi•SKAIT] *vt* confiscare

conflict [n. KAHN•flikt v. kun•FLIKT] *n* conflitto M; *vi* essere in conflitto

conform [kun•FAURM] *vt/vi* conformare

conformist [kun•FAUR•mist] *adj n* conformista

confound [kun•FOUND] *vt* sconvolgere

confront [kun•FRUHNT] *vt* confrontare

confuse [kun•FYOOZ] *vt* confondere

confusing [kun•FYOO•zing] *adj* sconcertante

confusion [kun•FYOO•zhn] *n* confusione F

congestion [kun•JES•chn] *n* congestione F

congratulate [kung•GRA•chu•LAIT] *vt* congratulare

congregate [KAHNG•gri•GAIT] *vi* congregarsi

congregation [KAHNG•gri•GAI•shn] *n* congregazione F

conjugation [KAHN•joo•GAI•shn] *n* coniugazione F

conjunction [kun•JUHNK•shn] *n* congiunzione F

connect [ku•NEKT] *vt* connettere

conquer [KAHGN•kur] *vt* conquistare

conqueror [KAHNG•ku•rur] *n*
conquistatore M

conquest [KAHNG•kwest] *n*
conquista F

conscience [KAHN•shuns] *n*
coscienza F

conscientious
[KAHN•shee•EN•shus] *adj*
coscienzioso; coscienziosa

conscious [KAHN•shus] *adj*
conscio; conscia

consecrate [KAHN•se•KRAIT]
vt consacrare

consecutive [kun•SE•cyu•tiv]
adj consecutivo; consecutiva

consent [kun•SENT] *n*
consenso M; *vi* acconsentire

consequence
[KAHN•si•KWENS] *n*
conseguenza F

conservation
[KAHN•sur•VAI•shn] *n*
conservazione F

conservative [kun•SUR•vu•tiv]
n/adj conservativo;
conservativa

consider [kun•SI•dr] *vt*
considerare

considerable [kun•SI•du•ru•bl]
adj considerevole

considerate [kun•SI•du•rit] *adj*
riguardoso; riguardosa

considering [kun•SI•du•ring]
prep tenendo in conto

consist [kun•SIST] *vi* consistere

consistency [kun•SI•stun•see] *n*
consistenza F

consistent [kun•SIS•tunt] *adj*
consistente

consolation
[KAHN•su•LAI•shn] *n*
consolazione F

console [kun•SOL] *vt/n*
consolare

consolidate
[kun•SAH•lu•DAIT] *vt*
consolidare

consonant [KAHN•su•nunt] *n*
consonante F

conspicuous [kun•SPI•kyoo•us]
adj cospicuo; cospicua

conspiracy [kun•SPI•ru•see] *n*
complotto M

constant [KAHN•stunt] *n adj*
costante

constellation
[KAHN•stu•LAI•shn] *n*
costellazione F

constituent [kun•STI•choo•int]
n elettore M

constitution
[KAHN•sti•TOO•shn] *n*
costituzione F

constraint [kun•STRAINT] *n*
costrizione F

construct [kun•STRUHKT] *vt*
costruire

construe [kun•STROO] *vt*
interpretare

consulate [KAHN•su•lit] *n*
consolato M

consult [kun•SUHLT] *vt/vi*
consultare

consume [kun•SOOM] *vt*
consumare

consumer [kun•SOOM•ur] *n*
consumatore M

consummate
[KAHN•su•MAIT] *vt*
consumare

consumption
[kun•SUHMP•shn] *n*
consumo M

contact [KAHN•takt] *n* contatto
M; *vt* mettersi in contatto;
contattare

contagious [kun•TAI•jus] *adj*
contagioso; contagiosa

contain [kun•TAIN] *vt*
contenere

container [kun•TAI•nur] *n*
contenitore M

contaminate
[kun•TA•mi•NAIT] *vt*
contaminare

contemplate
[KAHN•tum•PLAIT] *vt/vi*
contemplare

contemporary
[kun•TEM•pu•RE•ree] *adj n*
contemporaneo;
contemporanea

contempt [kun•TEMPT] *n*
disprezzo M

contemptible
[kun•TEMP•tu•bl] *adj*
spregevole

contend [kun•TEND] *vi*
contendere

content [kun•TENT] *adj*
contento; contenta

contents [KAHN•tents] *npl*
contenuto M

contest [n. KAHN•test v.
kun•TEST] *n* gara F; *vt*
contestare

context [KAHN•tekst] *n*
contesto M

continent [KAHN•ti•nunt] *n*
continente M

contingency [kun•TIN•jun•see]
n contingenza F

continual [kun•TI•nyoo•ul] *adj*
continuo; continua

continually [kun•TI•nyoo•u•lee]
adv continuamente

continuation
[kun•TI•nyoo•AI•shn] *n*
continuazione F

continue [kun•TI•nyoo] *vt*
continuare

contract [n. KAHN•trakt v.
kun•TRAKT] *n* contrato M;
accordo M; *vt* contrarre

contraction [kun•TRAK•shn] *n*
contrazione F

contradict [KAHN•tru•DIKT]
vt contraddire

contradiction
[KAHN•tru•DIK•shn] *n*
contraddizione F

contrary [KAHN•TRE•ree] *adj;
n* contrario; contraria

contrast [n. KAHN•trast v.
kun•TRAST] *n* contrasto M;
vt contrastare

contribute [kun•TRI•byoot]
vt vi contribuire

contribution
[KAHN•tri•BYOO•shn] *n*
contribuzione F

contrive [kun•TRUYV] *vt*
inventare

control [kun•TROL] *n* controllo
M; *vt* controllare

controller [kun•TRO•lur] *n*
sovrintendente M

controversy
[KAHN•tru•VUR•see] *n*
controversia F

convalescence
[KAHN•vu•LE•suns] *n*
convalescenza F

convalescent
[KAHN•vu•LE•sunt] *adj/n*
convalescente

convene [kun•VEEN] *vi*
convocare

convenience [kun•VEE•nyuns]
n convenienza F

convenient [kun•VEE•nyunt]
adj conveniente

convent [KAHN•vent] *n*
convento M

convention [kun•VEN•shn] *n*
raduno M

converge [kun•VURJ] *vi*
convergere

conversant [kun•VUR•sunt] *adj*
versato; versata

conversation
[KAHN•vur•SAI•shn] *n*
conversazione F

converse 1 [kun•VURS] *vi*
conversare

converse 2 [KAHN•vurs] *n*
converso; conversa

conversion [kun•VUR•zhn] *n*
conversione F

convert 1 [KAHN•vurt] *n*
catacumeno M

convert 2 [kun•VURT] *vt*
convertire

convex [kahn•VEKS] *adj*
convesso; covessa

convey [kun•VAI] *vt* trasportare

conveyer belt [kun•VAI•ur ~]
n trasportatore a cinghia M

convict [n. KAHN•vikt v.
kun•VIKT] *n* forzato M

convince [kun•VINS] *vt*
convincere

convincing [kun•VIN•sing] *adj*
convincente

convoy [KAHN•voi] *n*
convoglio M

coo [koo] *vi* tubare

cook [kuk] *n* cuoco; cuoca; *vt*
cuocere; cucinare; far la
cucina

cookie [KU•kee] *n* biscottino M

cooking [KU•king] *n* cucina F

cool [kool] *adj* fresco; fresca

coolness [KOOL•nis] *n*
frescura F

coop [koop] *n* pollaio M

cooperate [ko•AH•pu•RAIT] *vi*
cooperare

cooperation
[ko•AH•pu•RAI•shn] *n*
cooperazione F

coordinate [n. ko•AUR•di•nit
v. ko•AUR•di•NAIT] *vt*
coordinare

coordination
[ko•AUR•di•NAI•shn] *n*
coordinazione F

cop [kahp] *n* poliziotto M (coll)

cope [kop] *vi* far fronte

copious [KO•pee•us] *adj*
copioso; copiosa

copper [KAH•pur] *n* rame M

copy [KAH•pee] *n* copia F; *vt*
copiare; riprodurre; imitare

copyright [KAH•pee•RUYT] *n*
diritto d'autore

coral [KAU•rul] *n* corallo M

cord [kaurd] *n* corda F

corduroy [KAUR•du•ROI] *s*
velluto a coste M

cork [kaurk] *n* tappo M

corksrew [KAURK•skroo] *n*
cavatappi M

corn [kaurn] *n* granoturco M

corner [KAUR•nur] *n* angolo M

cornice [KAUR•nis] *n*
cornicione M

coronation [KAU•ru•NAI•shn]
n incoronazione F
coroner [KAU•ru•NUR] *n*
coroner M
corporal [KAUR•pu•rul] *adj n*
caporale M
corporation
[KAUR•pu•RAI•shn] *n* societá
a responsabilitá limitata F;
coproarzione F; ente M
corpse [kaurps] *n* cadavere M
correct [ku•REKT] *adj* corretto;
corretta; guisto; guista; *vt*
correggere
correction [ku•REK•shn] *n*
correzione F
correctly [ku•REKT•lee] *adv*
correttamnte
correspond [KAU•ri•SPAHND]
vi corrispondere
correspondence
[KAU•ri•SPAHN•duns] *n*
corrispondenza F
correspondent
[KAU•ri•SPAHN•dunt] *n*
corrispondente
corresponding
[KAU•ri•SPAHN•dunt] *adj*
corrispondente
corridor [KAU•ri•daur] *n*
coridoio M
corrode [ku•ROD] *vt* corrodere
corrosion [ku•RO•zhn] *n*
corrosione F
corrupt [ku•RUHPT] *adj*
corrotto; corròtta; *vt*
corrompere
corruption [ku•RUHP•shn] *n*
corruzione F
Corsica [KAUR•si•ku] *n*
Corsica F

cosmetic [kahz•ME•tik] *n*
cosmetico M
cosmopolitan
[KAHZ•mu•PAH•li•tn] *adj*
cosmopolita
cost [kaust] *n* costo M
costly [KAUST•lee] *adj*
costoso; costosa
costume [KAH•styoom] *n*
costume M
cot [kaht] *n* branda F
cottage [KAH•tij] *n* villino M
cotton [KAH•tn] *n* cotone M
couch [kouch] *n* sofá F;
divano M
cough [kauf] *n* tosse F
council [KOUN•sl] *n* concilio M
counsel [KOUN•sl] *n*
consiglio M
counselor [KOUN•su•lur] *n*
consigliere M
count [koun•sl] *vt vi* contare
counter [KOUN•tur] *n* banco M
counteract [KOUN•tur•AKT]
vt contrapporsi
counterfeit [KOUN•tur•FIT]
adj falo; falsa
counterpart
[KOUN•tur•PAHRT] *n*
sostituto; sostituta
countess [KOUN•tis] *n*
contessa F
countless [KOUNT•lis] *adj*
innumerevole
country [KUHN•tree] *n*
campagna M; (nation) *n*
paese M
countryman [KUHN•tree•mun]
n connazionale; paesano M
county [KOUN•tee] *n* contea F
coup [koo] *n* colpo M

couple [KUH•pl] *n* coppia F

coupon [KOO•pahn] *n* buono sconto M

courage [KU•rij] *n* coraggio M

courageous [ku•RAI•jus] *adj* coraggioso; coraggiosa

courier [KU•ree•ur] *n* corriere M

course [kaurs] *n* corso M; (food) piatto M

court [kaurt] *n* corte F; *vt* corteggiare; far la corte a

courteous [KUR•tee•us] *adj* cortese

courtesy [KUR•ti•see] *n* cortesia F

courtyard [KAURT•yahrd] *n* cortile M

cousin [KUH•zin] *n* cugino; cugina

cove [kov] *n* insenatura F

covenant [KUH•vu•nunt] *n* accordo M

cover [KUH•vur] *vt* coprire

cover-up (scandal, etc) *vt* tacitare

coverage [KUH•vu•rij] *n* servizio M

covering [KUH•vu•ring] *n* copertura F

covert [KO•vurt] *adj* velato; velata

covet [KUH•vit] *vt* desiderare

cow [kou] *n* vacca F

coward [KOU•urd] *n* vigliacco; vigliacca

cowardice [KOU•ur•dis] *n* codardia F

cowardly [KOU•urd•lee] *adj* vigliacco; vigliacca

cowboy [KOU•boi] *n* cowboy M

cower [KOU•ur] *vi* ritirarsi

coy [koi] *adj* ritroso; ritrosa

cozy [KO•zee] *adj* intimo; intima

crab [krab] *n* granchio M

crack [krak] *n* fessura F

cracker [KRA•kur] *n* cracker M

cradle [KRAI•dl] *n* culla F

craft [kraft] *n* mestiere M

crafty [KRAF•tee] *adj* astuto; astuta

cram [kram] *vt* stipare

cramp [kramp] *n* crampo M

cranberry [KRAN•BE•ree] *n* mirtillo rosso M

crane [krain] *n* gru F

crank [krank] *n* manovella F

cranky [KRANG•kee] *adj* noioso; noiosa

crape [kraip] *n* crespo da lutto M

crash [krash] *n* scoppio M

crate [krait] *n* cassa F

crater [KRAI•tur] *n* cratere M

crave [kraiv] *vt* desiderare

crawl [kraul] *vi* strisciare; *n* craw (swim)

crayfish [KRAI•fish] *n* gambero di fiume M

crayon [KRAI•un] *n* pastello a olio M

craze [kraiz] *n* mania F

crazy [KRAI•zee] *adj* matto; matta

creak [kreek] *vi* cigolare

cream [kreem] *n* crema F; (dairy) *n* panna F

creamy [KREE•mee] *adj* cremoso; cremosa

create [kree•AIT] *vt* creare

creation [kree•AI•shn] *n*
creazione F

creative [kree•AI•tiv] *adj*
creativo; creativa

creator [kree•AI•tur] *n*
creatore M

creature [KREE•chur] *n*
creatura F

credible [KRE•di•bl] *adj*
credibile

credit [KRE•dit] *n* credito M

credit card [KRE•dit KARD] *n*
carta di credito F

creed [kreed] *n* credo M

creek [kreek] *n* ruscello M

creep [kreep] *vi* strisciare

crescent [KRE•snt] *n*
mezzaluna F

crest [krest] *n* cresta F

crevice [KRE•vis] *n* fessura F

crew [kroo] *n* ciurma F

crib [krib] *n* lettino M

cricket [KRI•kit] *n* grillo M

crime [kruym] *n* crimine M

criminal [KRI•me•nl] *adj n*
criminale

crimson [KRIM•sun] *adj*
vermiglio; vermiglia

cringe [krinj] *vi* farsi piccolo

cripple [KRI•pl] *n* storpio;
storpia

crisis [KRUY•sis] *n* crisi F

crisp [krisp] *adj* croccante

criterion [kruy•TEER•ree•un] *n*
criterio M

critic [KRI•tik] *n* critico M

criticism [KRI•ti•SI•zm] *n*
critica F

criticize [KRI•ti•SUYZ] *vt vi*
criticare

croak [krok] *vi* gracidare

crochet [kro•SHAI] *n*
uncinetto M

crocodile [KRAH•ku•DUYL] *n*
coccodrillo M

crook [kruk] *n* truffatore M

crooked [KRU•kid] *adj* storto;
storta

crop [krahp] *n* raccolto M

cross [kraus] *n* croce F

cross-country
[KROS•KUN•tree] *adj* di
fondo

crossfire [KRAUS•fuyr] *n*
fuoco incrociato M

crossroads [KRAUS•rodz] *n*
bivio M

crossword (puzzle)
[KRAUS•wurd] *n*
cruciverba M

crow [kro] *n* corvo M

crowbar [KRO•bahr] *n*
palanchino M

crowd [kroud] *n* folla F

crown [kroun] *n* corona F

crucial [KROO•shl] *adj* cruciale

crucifix [KROO•si•FIKS] *n*
crocifisso M

crude [krood] *adj* rozzo; rozza

cruel [krooul] *adj* crudele

cruise [krooz] *n* crociera F

crumb [kruhm] *n* briciola F

crumble [KRUHM•bl] *vt*
sbriciolare

crunch [kruhnch] *vt*
sgranocchiare

crusade [kroo•SAID] *n*
crociata F

crush (romantic) [kruhsh] *n*
cotta F

crust [kruhst] *n* crosta F

crutch [kruhch] *n* stampella F

cry [kruy] *n* gemito M

crystal [KRI•stl] *n* cristallo M

Cuba [KYOO•bu] *n* Cuba F

Cuban [KYOO•bun] *adj n*
cubano; cubana

cube [kyoob] *n* cubo M

cubic [KYOO•bik] *adj* cubico;
cubica

cucumber [KYOO•kuhm•bur] *n*
cetriolo M

cuddle [KUH•dl] *vt* abbracciare

cue [kyoo] *n* suggerimento M

cuff [kuhf] *n* polsino M

culminate [KUHL•mi•NAIT] *vi*
culminare

culprit [KUHL•prit] *n* colpevole

cult [kuhlt] *n* culto M

cultivate [KUHL•ti•VAIT] *vt*
coltivare

cultural [KUHL•chu•rul] *adj*
culturale

culture [KUHL•chur] *n*
cultura F

cumulative [KYOO•myu•lu•tiv]
adj cumulativo; cumulativa

cunning [KUH•ning] *adj* astuto;
astuta

cup [kuhp] *n* tazza F

cupboard [KUH•burd] *n*
credenza F

curate [KYOO•rit] *n* curato M

curb [kurb] *n* orlo del
marciapiede M

curdle [KUR•dl] *vt* rapprendere

cure [kyoour] *n* cura F

curfew [KUR•fyoo] *n*
coprifuoco M

curiosity
[KYOOUR•ree•AH•si•tee] *n*
curiositá F

curious [KYOOUR•ree•us] *adj*
curioso; curiosa

curl [kurl] *n* ricciolo M

curly [KUR•lee] *adj* ricciuto;
ricciuta

currant [KUH•runt] *n* ribes M

currency [KU•run•see] *n*
valuta F

current [KU•runt] *adj* corrente

curry [KU•ree] *n* curry M

curse [kurs] *n* maledizione F

curtail [kur•TAIL] *vt* ridurre

curtain [KUR•tn] *n* tenda F;
(theater) *n* sipario M

curve [kurv] *n* curva F

cushion [KU•shn] *n* cuscino M

custard [KUH•sturd] *n* crema F

custodian 1 [KUH•STO•dyun]
n custode

custodian 2 (school)
[KUH•STO•dyun] *n* bidello;
bidella

custody [KUH•stu•dee] *n*
custodia F

custom [KUH•stum] *n*
consuetudine F; (border) *n*
dogana F

customer [KUH•stu•mur] *n*
cliente

cut [kuht] *n* taglio M; *vt* tagliare

cute [kyoot] *adj* carino; carina

cutlery [KUHT•lu•ree] *n*
posate F

cutlet [KUHT•lit] *n* cotoletta F

cycle [SUY•kl] *n* ciclo M

cyclone [SUY•klon] *n*
ciclone M

cylinder [SI•lin•dur] *n*
cilindro M

cynic [SI•nik] *n* cinico; cinica

cynical [SI•ni•kl] *adj* cinico;
cinica
cypress [SUY•pris] *n*
cipresso M
cyst [sist] *n* ciste F

czar [zahr] *n* zar M
Czech [chek] *adj* ceco; ceca
Czechoslovakia
[che•KO•slo•vah•KEE•uh] *n*
Cecoslovacchia F

D

dachsund [DAHK•sund] *n*
bassotto M
dad [dad] *n* papá M
daffodil [DA•fu•DIL] *n*
narciso M
daily [DAI•lee] *adj* quotidiano;
quotidiana
dairy 1 [DAI•ree] *n* latteria F
dairy 2 (product) [DAI•ree]
adj latticino M
daisy [DAI•zee] *n* margherita F
dam [dam] *n* diga F
damage [DA•mij] *n* danno M
damp [damp] *adj* umido; umida
dampen [DAM•pun] *vt*
inumidire
dance [dans] *n* danza F
dancer [DAN•sur] *n* ballerino;
ballerina
dandelion [DAN•di•LUY•un] *n*
soffione M
dandruff [DAN•druhf] *n*
forfora F
danger [DAIN•jur] *n*
pericolo M
dangerous [DAIN•ju•rus] *adj*
pericoloso; pericolosa
dangle [DANG•gl] *vt*
ciondolare
dare [dair] *n* sfida F; *vi* osare

daredevil [DAIR•DE•vl] *n*
scavezzacollo
daring [DAI•ring] *adj*
spericolato; spericolata
dark [dahrk] *adj* scuro; scura
darken [DAHR•kn] *vt* oscurare
darkness [DAHRK•nis] *n*
oscuritá F
darling [DAHR•ling] *adj*
delizioso; deliziosa; *n*
tesoro M
darn [dahrn] *vt* rammendare
dart [dahrt] *n* dardo M; *v*
balzare
dash [dash] *n* slancio M;
(quantity) *n* spruzzata F;
vuttare; urtare
dashboard [DASH•baurd] *n*
cruscotto M
data [DAI•tu] *n* dati M
date [dait] *n* data F;
(appointment) *n*
appuntamento M
daughter [DAU•tur] *n* figlia F
daughter-in-law
[DAU•tur•in•LAU] *n* nuora F
daunt [daunt] *vt* intimidire
dawdle [DAU•dl] *vi*
bighellonare
dawn [daun] *n* alba F

day [dai] *n* giorno M; good ~\
buon giorno

daybreak [DAI•braik] *n* alba F

daydream [DAI•dreem] *vi*
sognare ad occhi aperti

daze [daiz] *n* stupore M; *vi*
sblaordire; stordire

dazzle [DA•zl] *vt* sbalordire

dead [ded] *adj* morto; morta;
defunto; defunta

deadline [DED•luyn] *n*
scadenza F

deadly [DED•lee] *adj* mortale

deaf [def] *adj* sordo; sorda

deafen [DE•fn] *vt* assordare

deafening [DE•fu•ning] *adj*
assodante

deal [deel] *n* affare M; (cards)
dare le carte; ~ with\ occupare

dealer [DEE•lur] *n*
commerciante

dealings [DEE•lingz] *npl*
commercio M

dean [deen] *n* decano M

dear [deer] *adj* caro; cara

death [deth] *n* morte F

debacle [du•BAH•kl] *n*
sfacelo M

debase [di•BAIS] *vt* svilire

debate [di•BAIT] *n* dibattito M;
vt dibattere

debauchery [di•BAU•chu•ree]
n dissolutezza F

debit [DE•bit] *n* dare M; *vt*
addebitare

debt [det] *n* debito M

debtor [DE•tur] *n* debitore M

debut [DAI•byoo] *n* debutto M;
debuttare

decade [DE•kaid] *n* decennio M

decadence [DE•ku•duns] *n*
decadenza F

decadent [DE•ku•dunt] *adj*
decadente

decanter [di•KAN•tur] *n*
caraffa F

decay [di•KAY] *n* putrefazione
F; *vi* deperirie; putrefare

deceased [di•SEEST] *adj*
deceduto; deceduta

deceit [di•SEET] *n* inganno M

deceitful [di•SEET•ful] *adj*
ingannevole

deceive [di•SEEV] *vt vi*
ingannare

December [di•SEM•bur] *n*
dicembre M

decency [DEE•sn•see] *n*
decenza F

decent [DEE•sunt] *adj* decente

deception [di•SEP•shn] *n*
inganno F

decide [di•SUYD] *vt* decidere

decimal [DE•si•ml] *n*
decimale M

decimate [DE•si•MAIT] *vt*
decimare

decipher [di•SUY•fur] *vt*
decifrare

decision [di•SI•zhn] *n*
decisione F

decisive [di•SUY•siv] *adj*
decisivo; decisiva

deck [dek] *n* tolda F; *v* ornare

declare [di•KLAIR] *vt*
dichiarare

decline [di•KLUYN] *n* declino
M; (refuse) rifutare

decode [dee•KOD] *vt* decifrare

decompose [DEE•kum•POZ] *vi*
decomporsi

decorate [DE•ku•RAIT] *vt*
decorare

decoration [DE•ku•RAI•shn] *n*
decorazione F

decorum [di•KAU•rum] *n*
decoro M

decoy [DEE•coi] *n* esca F

decrease [dee•CREES] *n*
diminuzione F

decree [di•KREE] *n* decreto M;
v decretare

decrepit [di•KRE•pit] *adj*
decrepito; decrepita

dedicate [de•di•KAIT] *vt*
dedicare

dedication [DE•di•KAI•shn] *n*
dedica F

deduct [di•DUHKT] *vt* detrarre

deduction [di•DUHK•shn] *n*
trattenuta F

deed [deed] *n* atto M

deem [deem] *vt* stimare

deep [deep] *adj* profondo;
profonda

deepen [DEEP•n] *vt*
approfondire

deer [deer] *n* daino M

deface [di•FAIS] *vt* sfregiare

defamation [DE•fu•MAI•shn]
n diffamazione F

defame [di•FAIM] *vt* diffamare

default [di•FAULT] *n*
mancanza F

defeat [di•FEET] *n* sconfitta F

defect [n. DEE•fekt v.
di•FEKT] *n* difetto M; *vt*
disertare

defend [di•FEND] *vt* difendere

defendant [di•FEN•dunt] *n*
imputato; imputata

defense [di•FENS] *n* difesa F

defensive [di•FEN•siv] *adj*
difensivo; difensiva

defer [di•FUR] *vt* differire

defiance [di•FUY•uns] *n*
sfida F

deficiency [di•FI•shun•see] *n*
deficienza F

deficient [di•FI•shunt] *adj*
deficiente

deficit [DE•fi•sit] *n* deficit M

defile [di•FUYL] *vt* insozzare

define [di•FUYN] *vt* definire

definite [DE•fi•nit] *adj* definito;
definita

definitely [DE•fi•nit•lee] *adv*
decisamente

definition [DE•fi•NI•shn] *n*
definizione F

deflate [di•FLAIT] *vt* sgonfiare;
deflettere

deformed [di•FAURMD] *adj*
deforme

defraud [di•FRAUD] *vt*
defraudare

defrost [di•FRAUST] *vt*
disgelare

deft [deft] *adj* destro; destra

defy [di•FUY] *vt* sfidare

degenerate [adj. di•JE•nu•rit v.
di•JE•nu•RAIT] *adj*
degenerato; degenerata; *vi*
degenerare

degrading [di•GRAI•ding] *adj*
degradante

degree 1 [di•GREE] *n* grado M

degree 2 (academic)
[di•GREE] *n* diploma M

dehydrate [di•HUY•drait] *vt*
disidratare

deity [DAI•i•tee] *n* divinitá F

dejected [di•JEK•tid] *adj*
abbattuto; abbattuta

delay [di•LAI] *n* ritardo M; *vt*
differire

delegate [n. DE•li•gut v.
DE•li•GAIT] *n* delegato;
delegata

delegation [DE•li•GAI•shn] *n*
delegazione F

delete [di•LEET] *vt* cancellare

deliberate 1 [di•LI•brut] *adj*
cauta

deliberate 2 [du•LI•bu•RAIT]
vi deliberare

delicacy [DE•li•ku•see] *n*
ghiottoneria F

delicate [DE•li•kut] *adj*
delicato; delicata

delicatessen [DE•li•ku•TE•sun]
n salumeria F

delicious [di•LI•shus] *adj*
delizioso; deliziosa

delight [di•LUYT] *n* delizia F

delighted [di•LUY•tid] *adj*
contentissimo; contentissima

delightful [di•LUYT•ful] *adj*
incantevole

delinquent [di•LING•kwunt]
adj non pagato; non pagata; *n*
delinquente

delirious [di•LI•ree•us] *adj*
delirante

deliver [di•LI•vur] *vt*
consegnare

delivery [di•LI•vu•ree] *n*
consegna F; (of a baby) *n*
parto M

deluge [DE•lyooj] *n* diluvio M

delusion [di•LOO•zhn] *n*
delusione F

demagogue [DE•mu•GAHG] *n*
demagogo M

demand [di•MAND] *n* pretesa
F; *vt* esigere; pretendere

demanding [di•MAN•ding] *adj*
esigente

demeanor [di•MEE•nur] *n*
comportamento M

demented [di•MEN•tid] *adj*
demente

demerit [di•ME•rit] *n*
demerito M

demobilize [di•MO•bi•LUYZ]
vt smobilitare

democracy [di•MAH•kru•see] *n*
democrazia F

democrat [DE•mu•KRAT] *n*
democratico; democratica

democratic [DE•mu•KRA•tik]
adj democratico; democratica

demolish [di•MAH•lish] *vt*
demolire

demonstrate
[DE•mun•STRAIT] *vt*
dimostrare

demonstration
[DE•mun•STRAI•shn] *n*
dimostrazione F

demonstrative
[di•MAHN•stru•tiv] *adj*
affettuoso; affettuosa

demoralize
[di•MAU•ru•LUYZ] *vt*
demoralizzare

demure [di•MYOOR] *adj*
modesto; modesta

den [den] *n* studio M; (of an
animal) *n* tana F

denial [di•NUYL] *n* diniego M

Denmark [DEN•mahrk] *n*
Danimarca F

denounce [di•NOUNS] vt
denunciare

dense [dens] adj denso; densa

density [DEN•si•tee] n
densitá M

dent [dent] n ammaccatura F; vt
intaccare; ammaccare

dental [DEN•tl] adj dentale

dentist [DEN•tist] n dentista

deny [di•NUY] vt negare

depart [di•PAHRT] vi partire

department [di•PAHRT•munt]
n reparto M

department store
[dee•PART•mint STOR] n
grande magazzino M

departure [di•PAHR•chur] n
partenza F

depend [di•PEND] vi dipendere

dependable [di•PEND•u•bl]
adj affidabile

depict [di•PIKT] vt
rappresentare

deplete [di•PLEET] vt esaurire

deplorable [di•PLAU•ru•bl] adj
deplorevole

deplore [di•PLAUR] vt
deplorare

deport [di•PAURT] vt deportare

depose [di•POZ] vt deporre

deposit [di•PAH•zit] n
deposito M

depot [DEE•po] n
magazzino M

depreciate [di•PREE•shee•AIT]
vi vt svalutare

depress [di•PRES] vt deprimere

depressed [di•PREST] adj
depresso; depressa

depressing [di•PRE•sing] adj
deprimente

depression [di•PRE•shn] n
depressione F

deprive [di•PRUYV] vt privare

depth [depth] n profonditá F

deputy [DE•pyu•tee] n
sostituto; sostituta

derail [di•RAIL] vi deragliare

deranged [di•RAINJD] adj
pazzo; pazza

deride [di•RUYD] vt deridere

derive [di•RUYV] vt derivare

descend [di•SEND] vt vi
discendere

descent [di•SENT] n discesa F

describe [di•SKRUYB] vt
descrivere

description [di•SKRIP•shn] n
descrizione F

desert [n. DE•zurt v. di•ZURT]
n deserto M; vt disertare

deserter [di•ZUR•tur] n
disertore M

deserve [di•ZURV] vt meritare

deserving [di•ZUR•ving] adj
meritevole

design [di•ZUYN] n disegno
M; vt progettare; destinare

designate [DE•zig•NAIT] vt
designare

designer [di•ZUY•nur] n
designer M

desirable [di•ZUY•ru•bl] adj
desiderabile

desire [di•ZUYUR] n
desiderio M

desist [di•SIST] vi desistere

desk [desk] n scrivania F

desolate [DE•su•lut] adj
desolato; desolata

despair [di•SPAIUR] n
disperazione F

desperate [DE•sprut] *adj*
disperato; disperata

desperation [DI•spu•RAI•shn]
n disperazione F

despicable [di•SPI•ku•bl] *adj*
spregevole

despise [di•SPUYZ] *vt*
disprezzare

despite [di•SPUYT] *prep*
malgrado

despondent [di•SPAHN•dunt]
adj abbattuto; abbattuta

despot [DE•sput] *n* despota

dessert [di•ZURT] *n* dolce M

destination [DE•sti•NAI•shn] *n*
destinazione F

destiny [DE•sti•nee] *n*
destino M

destitute [DE•sti•TOOT] *adj*
destituto, destituta

destroy [di•STROI] *vt*
distruggere

destruction [di•STRUHK•shn]
n distruzione F

destructive [di•STRUHK•tiv]
adj distruttivo; distruttiva

detach [di•TACH] *vt* staccare

detail [DEE•tail] *n* dettaglio M

detain [di•TAIN] *vt* trattenere

detect [di•TEKT] *vt* percepire

detection [di•TEK•shn] *n*
scoperta F

detention [di•TEN•shn] *n*
detenzione F

deter [di•TUR] *vt* dissuadere

detergent [di•TUR•junt] *n*
detersivo M

deteriorate
[di•TEER•ee•aur•AIT] *vi*
deteriorare

determination
[di•TUR•mi•NAI•shn] *n*
risolutezza F

determine [di•TUR•min] *vt*
determinare

detest [di•TEST] *vt* detestare

detonate [DE•tu•NAIT] *vt*
detonare

detour [DEE•toor] *n*
deviazione F

detract [di•TRAKT] *vt* detrarre

detrimental [DE•tri•MEN•tl]
adj dannoso; dannosa

devastate [DE•vu•STAIT] *vt*
devastare

devastating [DE•vu•STAI•ting]
adj devastante

develop [di•VE•lup] *vt*
sviluppare

development [di•VE•lup•munt]
n sviluppo M

deviate [DEE•vee•AIT] *vi*
deviare

device [di•VUYS] *n*
strattagemma M; (mechanical)
n dispositivo M

devil [DE•vl] *n* diavolo M

devious [DEE•vee•us] *adj*
tortuoso; tortuosa

devise [di•VUYZ] *vt* escogitare

devoid [di•VOID] *adj* privo;
priva

devote [di•VOT] *vt* dedicare

devoted [di•VO•tud] *adj*
devoto; devota

devotion [di•VO•shn] *n*
devozione

devour [di•VOUUR] *vt* divorare

devout [di•VOUT] *adj* devoto;
devota

dew [doo] *n* rugiada F

diabetes [DUY•u•BEE•teez] *n*
diabete M

diabetic [DUY•u•BE•tik] *adj n*
diabetico; diabetica

diagnose [DUY•ug•NOS] *vt*
diagnosticare

diagnosis [DUY•ug•NO•sis] *n*
diagnosi F

diagonal [duy•AG•nl] *adj*
diagonale

diagram [DUY•u•GRAM] *n*
diagramma M

dial [duyul] *n* quadrante M; *vt*
(number) compore

dialect [DUY•u•LEKT] *n*
dialetto M

dialog [DUY•u•LAHG] *n*
dialogo M

diameter [duy•A•mi•tur] *n*
diametro M

diamond [DUY•mund] *n*
brillante M

diamond-shaped [~ shaipt]
adj romboidale

diary [DUY•u•ree] *n* diario M

dice [duys] (sing: die) *npl*
dado M

dictate [DIK•tait] *vt* dettare
comando M

dictation [dik•TAI•shn] *n*
dettato M

dictator [DIK•TAI•tur] *n*
dittatore M

dictatorship
[dik•TAI•tur•SHIP] *n*
dittatura F

dictionary 1 [DIK•shu•NE•ree]
n vocabolario M

dictionary 2 (foreign language)
[DIK•shu•NE•ree] *n*
dizionario M

die [duy] *vi* morire

diet [DUY•ut] *n* dieta F

differ [DI•fur] *vi* differire

difference [DI•fruns] *n*
differenza F

different [DI•frunt] *adj*
differente

differentiate
[DI•fu•REN•shee•ait] *vt*
differenziare

difficult [DI•fi•kult] *adj* difficile

difficulty [DI•fi•kul•tee] *n*
difficoltá M

diffuse [di•FYOOZ] *vt*
diffondere

dig [dig] *vt* scavare

digest [n. DUY•jest v.
duy•JEST] *vt vi* digerire

digestion [duy•JES•chn] *n*
digestione F

digit [DI•jit] *n* cifra F

dignified [DIG•ni•FUYD] *adj*
dignitoso; dignitosa

dignify [DIG•ni•FUY] *vt*
nobilitare; *n* dignitá F

digress [duy•GRES] *vt* fare una
digressione

dilate [DUY•lait] *vt* dilatare

dilemma [di•LE•mu] *n*
dilemma M

diligence [DI•li•juns] *n*
diligenza F

diligent [DI•li•junt] *adj*
diligente

dilute [duy•LOOT] *vt* diluire

dim [dim] *adj* pallido; pallida; *vi*
attenuare

dimension [di•MEN•shn] *n*
dimensione F

diminish [di•MI•nish] *vt vi*
diminuire

dimple [DIM•pl] *n* fossetta F

din [din] *n* rumore M

dine [duyn] *vi* pranzare

diner 1 [DUY•nur] *n* commensale

diner 2 (restaurant) [DUY•nur] *n* ristorante M

dinghy [DING•gee] *n* dinghy M

dingy [din•jee] *adj* sporco; sporca

dining room [DUY•ning ~] *n* sala da pranzo F

dinner [DI•nur] *n* pranzo M

dinosaur [DUY•nu•SAUR] *n* dinosauro M

diocese [DUY•u•seez] *n* diocesi F

dip [dip] *n* tuffo M; *vi* abbassare; tuffare

diploma [di•PLO•mu] *n* diploma M

diplomacy [di•PLO•mu•see] *n* diplomazia F

diplomat [DI•plu•MAT] *n* diplomatico; diplomatica

diplomatic [DI•plu•MA•tik] *adj* diplomatico; diplomatica

dire [duyur] *adj* terribile

direct [di•REKT] *adj* diretto; diretta; *vt* dirigere

direction [di•REK•shn] *n* direzione F

directly [di•REKT•lee] *adv* drettamente

director [di•REK•tur] *n* direttore M

directory [di•REK•tu•ree] *n* elenco M

dirt [durt] *n* sporco M; (earth) *n* terra F

dirty [DUR•tee] *adj* sporco; sporca

disabled [di•SAI•bld] *adj* invalido; invalida

disadvantage [DI•sud•VAN•tij] *n* svantaggio M

disagree [DI•su•GREE] *vi* essere in disaccordo

disagreement [DI•su•GREE•munt] *n* disaccordo M

disappear [DI•su•PEEUR] *vi* sparire

disappoint [DI•su•POINT] *vt* deludere

disappointing [DI•su•POIN•ting] *adj* deludente

disappointment [DI•su•POINT•munt] *n* delusione F

disapproval [DI•su•PROO•vl] *n* disapprovazione F; *vi* disapprovare

disarm [di•SAHRM] *vt vi* disarmare

disarray [DI•su•RAI] *n* disordine M

disaster [di•ZA•stur] *n* disastro M

disastrous [di•ZA•strus] *adj* disastroso; disastrosa

disavow [DI•su•VOU] *vt* rinnegare

discard [di•SKAHRD] *vt* scartare

discern [di•SURN] *vt* discernere

discharge [n. DIS•charj v. dis•CHARJ] *n* perdita F; *vt*

scaricare; (shoot off) *vt*
sparare

disciple [di•SUY•pl] *n*
discepolo M

discipline [DI•si•plin] *n*
disciplina F

disclose [di•SKLOZ] *vt* svelare

disclosure [dis•KLO•zhur] *n*
rivelazione F

discomfort [di•SKUHM•furt] *n*
disagio M

disconnect [DI•sku•NEKT] *vt*
staccare

discord [DI•skaurd] *n* discordi F

discount [DI•skount] *n* sconto
M; *vi* (disregard) non badare

discourage [di•SKU•rij] *vt*
scoraggiare

discourse [di•SKAURS] *n*
discorso M

discover [di•SKUH•vur] *vt*
scoprire

discovery [di•SKUH•vu•ree] *n*
scoperta F

discredit [dis•KRE•dit] *n*
discredito M

discreet [di•SKREET] *adj*
disreto; discreta

discrepancy [di•SKRE•pun•see]
n contraddizione F

discretion [di•SKRE•shn] *n*
discrezione F

discriminate
[di•SKRI•mi•NAIT] *vi*
discriminare

discuss [di•SKUHS] *vt* discutere

discussion [di•SKUH•shn] *n*
discussione F

disdain [dis•DAIN] *n*
disprezzo M

disease [di•ZEEZ] *n* malattia F

disengage [DI•sin•GAIJ] *vt*
disimpegnare

disfigure [dis•FI•gyur] *vt*
sfregiare

disgrace [dis•GRAIS] *n*
vergogna F

disgraceful [dis•GRAIS•ful] *adj*
vergognoso; vergognosa

disgruntled [dis•GRUHN•tld]
adj malcontento; malcontenta

disguise [dis•GUYZ] *n*
travestimento M

disgust [dis•GUHST] *n* disgusto
M; *vi* disgustare; far schifo

disgusting [dis•GUH•sting] *adj*
disgustoso; disgustosa

dish [dish] *n* piatto M

dishearten [dis•HAHR•tn] *vt*
scoraggiare

dishevelled [di•SHE•vld] *adj*
arruffato; arruffata

dishonest [dis•AH•nist] *adj*
disonesto; disonesta

dishonor [dis•AH•nur] *n*
disonore M

dishwasher [DISH•WAH•shur]
n lavastoviglie F

disillusion [DIS•i•LOO•zhn] *n*
disinganno M

disinfect [DI•sin•FEKT] *vt*
disinfettare

disinfectant [DI•sin•FEK•tunt]
n disinfettante M

disintegrate
[di•SIN•tu•GRAIT] *vi*
disintegrare

disinterested [dis•IN•tru•stid]
adj disinteressato;
disinteressata

disk [disk] *n* disco M

dislike [di•SLUYK] *n*
avversione F

dislocate [DIS•lo•kait] *vt*
dislocare

disloyal [dis•LOI•ul] *adj* sleale

dismal [DI•zml] *adj* tetro; tetra

dismay [di•SMAI] *n*
costernazione F

dismiss [dis•MIS] *vt* congedare

dismissal [dis•MI•sl] *n*
congedo M

dismount [dis•MOUNT] *vi*
smontare

disobedient
[DI•so•BEE•dee•unt] *adj*
disobbediente

disobey [DI•so•BAI] *vt*
disobbedire

disorder [di•SAUR•dur] *n*
disordine M

disorganized
[di•SAUR•gu•NUYZD] *adj*
disorganizzato; disorganizzata

disoriented
[di•SAU•ree•EN•tud] *adj*
disorientato; disorientata.

disown [dis•ON] *vt* rinnegare

disparaging [di•SPA•ru•jing]
adj sprezzante

dispassionate [di•SPA•shu•nit]
adj spassionato; spassionata

dispel [di•SPEL] *vt* dissipare

dispense [di•SPENS] *vt*
dispensare

dispenser [di•SPEN•sur] *n*
distributore M

disperse [di•SPURS] *vt*
disperdere

displace [dis•PLAIS] *vt*
rimuovere

display [di•SPLAI] *n* mostra F

displease [dis•PLEEZ] *vt*
dispiacere

displeased [dis•PLEEZD] *adj*
dispiaciuto; dispiaciuta

disposal [di•SPO•zl] *n*
disposizione F

dispose 1 [di•SPOZ] *vt* disporre

dispose 2 (of something)
[di•SPOZ] *vi* disfarsi (di)

disposed [di•SPOZD] *adj*
disposto; disposta

disposition 1 [DI•spu•ZI•shn] *n*
disposizione F

disposition 2 (attitude)
[DI•spu•ZI•shn] *n* carattere M

disprove [dis•PROOV] *vt*
confutare M

dispute [di•SPYOOT] *n* disputa
F; *vt* contestare

disqualify [dis•KWAH•li•FUY]
vt squalificare

disregard [DIS•ree•GAHRD] *n*
noncuranza F

disreputable
[dis•RE•pyu•tu•bl] *adj*
sciupato; sciupata

disrespect [DIS•ru•SPEKT] *n*
irriverenza F

disrupt [dis•RUHPT] *vt*
disturbare

dissatisfy [di•SAT•is•FUY] *vt*
scontentare

dissect [duy•SEKT] *vt*
dissezionare

dissemble [di•SEM•bl] *vt vi*
simulare

disseminate [di•SE•mi•NAIT]
vt disseminare

dissent [di•SENT] *n* dissenso M

dissimulate [di•SI•myu•LAIT]
vt vi dissimulare

dissipate [DI•si•PAIT] *vt*
dissipare

dissociate [di•SO•shee•AIT] *vt*
dissociare

dissolute [DI•su•LOOT] *adj*
dissoluto; dissoluta

dissolve [di•ZAHLV] *vt*
dissolvere

dissuade [di•SWAID] *vt*
dissuadere

distance [DI•stuns] *n* distanza F

distant [DI•stunt] *adj* distante

distaste [dis•TAIST] *n*
ripugnanza F

distill [dis•TIL] *vt vi* distillare

distillery [dis•TI•lu•ree] *n*
distilleria F

distinct [dis•TINGKT] *adj*
distinto; distinta

distinguish [di•STING•gwish]
vt distinguere

distort [di•STAURT] *vt*
distorcere

distract [di•STRAKT] *vt*
distrarre

distraught [di•STRAUT] *adj*
turbato; turbata

distress [di•STRES] *n*
angoscia F

distribute [di•STRI•byoot] *vt*
distribuire

distribution
[DI•stri•BYOO•shn] *n*
distribuzione F

district [DI•strikt] *n* distretto M

distrust [dis•TRUST] *n*
diffidenza F

distrustful [dis•TRUST•ful] *adj*
diffidente

disturb [di•STURB] *vt*
disturbare

disturbance [di•STUR•buns] *n*
agitazione F

disturbing [di•STUR•bing] *adj*
inquietante

ditch [dich] *n* fosso M

ditto [DI•to] *adv* come sopra

dive [duyv] *n* tuffo M; *vt*
tuffarsi; fare un tuffo

diverge [di•VURJ] *vi* divergere

diverse [di•VURS] *adj* vario;
varia

diversify [di•VUR•si•FUY] *vt*
differenziare

diversity [di•VUR•si•tee] *n*
diversitá F

divert [di•VURT] *vt* deviare

divide [di•VUYD] *vt* dividere

divine [di•VUYN] *adj* divino;
divina

divinity [di•VI•ni•tee] *n*
divinitá F

division [di•VI•zhn] *n*
divisione F

divorce [di•VAURS] *n*
divorzio M

divulge [di•VUHLJ] *vt*
divulgare

dizzy [DI•zee] *adj* stordito;
stordita

do [doo] *vt* fare

docile [DAH•sul] *adj* docile

dock [dahk] *n* banchina F

doctor [DAHK•tur] *n* dottore M

doctorate [DAHK•tu•rut] *n*
laurea F

doctrine [DAHK•trin] *n*
dottrina F

document [DAH•kyu•munt] *n*
documento M

dodge [dahj] *vt* evitare

doe [do] *n* daina F

dog [daug] *n* cane M
dogma [DAUG•mu] *n*
dogma M
doings [DOO•ings] *npl* fatti M
doll [dahl] *n* bambola F
dollar [DAH•lur] *n* dollaro M
dolphin [DAHL•fin] *n*
delfino M
domain [do•MAIN] *n*
dominio M
dome [dom] *n* cupola F
domestic [du•ME•stik] *adj*
domestico; domestica
dominant [DAH•mi•nunt] *adj*
dominante
dominate [DAH•mi•NAIT] *vt*
dominare
domineering
[DAH•mi•NEEU•ring] *adj*
dispotico; dispotica
donate [do•NAIT] *vt* donare
donation [do•NAI•shn] *n*
donazione F
donkey [DAHNG•kee] *n*
asino M
donor [DO•nr] *n* donatore M
doodle [DOO•dl] *vi*
scarabocchiare
doom [doom] *n* destino M
doomed [doomd] *adj*
condannato; condannata
doomsday [DOOMZ•dai] *n*
Giudizio Universale M
door [daur] *n* porta F
doormat [DAUR•mat] *n*
stuoino M
doorstep [DAUR•step] *n*
soglia F
dope [dop] *n* narcotico M
dormitory
[DAUR•mi•TAU•ree] *n*
dormitorio M

dose [dos] *n* dose F; *vt* dosare
dot [daht] *n* puntino
double [DUH•bl] *adj* doppio;
doppia; *vi* raddoppiare
double vision [DUH•bl VI•shn]
n vedere doppio
double-breasted [~ bre•stid]
adj a doppio petto M
doubly [DUH•blee] *adv*
doppiamente
doubt [dout] *n* dubbio M
doubtful [DOUT•ful] *adj*
dubbio; dubbia
dough [do] *n* pasta F
douse [dous] *vt* bagnare
dove [duhv] *n* colomba F
down [doun] *adv* giú; di sotto;
per terro
down payment [DOUN
PAI•mint] *n* deposito M
downcast [DOUN•kast] *adj*
abbattuto; abbattuta
downpour [DOUN•paur] *n*
acquazzone M
downstairs [DOUN•STAIURZ]
adj dabasso
downward [DOUN•wurd] *adj*
in giú
dowry [DOUU•ree] *n* dote F
doze [doz] *vi* dormicchiare
dozen [DUH•zn] *n* dozzina F
draft [draft] *n* corrente F;
abbozzo M; (military) *n*
leva F
drag [drag] *vt vi* trascinare
dragon [DRA•gn] *n* drago M
dragonfly [DRA•gn•FLUY] *n*
libellula M
drain [drain] *n* scarico M
drama [DRAH•mu] *n*
dramma M

dramatic [dru•MA•tik] *adj* drammatico; drammatica

dramatist [DRAH•mu•tist] *n* drammaturgo M

dramatize [DRAH•mu•TUYZ] *vt* drammatizzare

drape [draip] *vt* drappeggiare

drapes [draips] *npl* tende F

drastic [DRA•stik] *adj* drastico; drastica

draw [drau] *n* pareggio M

drawer [draur] *n* cassetto M

drawing [DRAU•ing] *n* disegno M

dread [dred] *n* timore M; *v* aver paura di

dreadful [DRED•ful] *adj* spaventoso; spaventosa

dream [dreem] *n* sogno M

dreamy [DREE•mee] *adj* languido; languida

dreary [DREEU•ree] *adj* tetro; tetra

drench [drench] *vt* inzuppare

dress [dres] *n* abito M; vestire; (wounds) bendare

dresser [DRE•sur] *n* comó M

dressing [DRE•sing] *n* salsa F

dried [druyd] *adj* secco; secca

drift [drift] *n* significato M

drill [dril] *n* trapano M; esercitare

drink [dringk] *n* bevanda M; *vt* bere

drip [drip] *n* sgocciolio M; *vt* gocciolare

drive [druyv] *n* giro in macchina M

drivel [DRI•vl] *n* stupidaggine F

driver [DRUY•vur] *n* autista

drizzle [DRI•zl] *n* pioggerella F

droop [droop] *vi* abbattersi

drop [drahp] *n* goccia F; *vt* cadere; *vi* far cadere

drought [drout] *n* siccitá F

drove [drov] *n* gregge M

drown [droun] *vt* annegare

drowsy [DROU•zee] *adj* sonnolento; sonnolenta

drug [druhg] *n* droga F

drug addict [DRUG A•dikt] *n* tossicodipendente

druggist [DRUH•gist] *n* farmacista

drum [druhm] *n* tamburo M; *vt* suonare il tamburo

drummer [DRUH•mur] *n* tamburino M

drunk [druhngk] *adj* ubriaco; ubriaca

drunkenness [DRUHNG•kn•nis] *n* ubriachezza F

dry [druy] *adj* asciutto; asciutta; *vi* lavare a secco

dryer [DRUY•ur] *n* asciugatore M

dual [dooul] *adj* doppio; doppia

dubbed [duhbd] *adj* doppiato; doppiata

dubious [DOO•byus] *adj* dubbio; dubbia

Dublin [DUH•blin] *n* Dublino F

duchess [DUH•chis] *n* duchessa F

duck [duhk] *n* anatra F

duct [duhkt] *n* conduttura F

due [doo] *adj* da pagarsi

duel [dooul] *n* duello M

duet [doo•ET] *n* duetto M

duke [dook] *n* duc M

dull [duhl] *adj* monotono;
monotona

dumb [duhm] *adj* stupido;
stupida

dumbfound [DUHM•found] *vt*
confondere

dummy [DUH•mee] *n*
manichino M

dump [duhmp] *vt* scaricare

dunce [duns] *n* asino M

dune [doon] *n* duna F

dung [duhng] *n* sterco M

dungeon [DUHN•jun] *n* cella F

duplicate [adj; n. DOO•pli•kut
v. DOO•pli•KAIT] *adj* di
ricambio

duplicity [doo•PLI•si•tee] *n*
duplicitá F

durable [DOOU•ru•bl] *adj*
durevole

duration [du•RAI•shn] *n*
durata F

dusk [duhsk] *n* crepuscolo

dust [duhst] *n* polvere F

dustpan [DUHST•pan] *n*
paletta F

Dutch [duhch] *adj* olandese

duty [DOO•tee] *n* dovere M

duty-free [DOO-tee FREE] *adj*
duty-free

dwarf [dwaurf] *n* nano; nana

dwell [dwel] *vi* dimorare

dwelling [DWE•ling] *n*
abitazione F

dwindle [DWIN•dl] *vi*
diminuire

dye [duy] *n* tinta F; *vt* tingere

dying [DUY•ing] *adj* morente

dynamic 1 [duy•NA•mik] *adj*
dinamico

dynamic 2 [duy•NA•mik] *n*
dinamica F

dynamite [DUY•nu•MUYT] *n*
dinamite F

dynasty [DUY•nu•stee] *n*
dinastia F

E

each [eech] *adj* ognuno;
ognuna; l'uno; l'una

eager [EE•gur] *adj* avido; avida

eagle [EE•gl] *n* aquila F

ear [eeur] *n* orecchio M

early [UR•lee] *adj* mattiniero;
mattiniera

earn [urn] *vt* guadagnare

earnest [UR•nist] *adj* serio;
seria

earring [EEU•ring] *n*
orecchino M

earth [urth] *n* terra F

earthquake [URTH•kwaik] *n*
terremoto M

ease [eez] *n* agio M; *vi*
agevolare; alleggerire

easily [EE•zi•lee] *adv*
facilmente

east [eest] *n* est M

Easter [EE•stur] *n* Pasqua F

eastern [EE•sturn] *adj* orientale

eastward [EEST•wurd] *adv adj*
est

easy [EE•zee] *adj* facile

eat [eet] *vt vi* mangiare

ebb [eb] *n* riflusso M; *vi* rifluire

ebony [E•bu•nee] *adj* ebano M

eccentric [ek•SEN•trik] *adj n* eccentrico; eccentrica

ecclesiastic [ee•KLEE•zee•A•stik] *adj* ecclesistico; ecclesiastica

echo [E•ko] *n* eco M; *vi* echeggiare; far eco

eclipse [ee•KLIPS] *n* eclisse F; *vi* eclissare

ecology [ee•KAH•lu•jee] *n* ecologia F

economic [E•ku•NAH•mik] *adj* economico; economica

economical [E•ku•NAH•mi•kl] *adj* economico; economica

economics [E•ku•NAH•miks] *n* economia F

economy [ee•KAH•nu•mee] *n* economia F

ecstasy [EK•stu•see] *n* estasi F

ecstatic [ek•STA•tik] *adj* estatico; estatica

edge [ej] *n* orlo M

edible [E•di•bl] *adj* commestibile

edit [E•dit] *vt* curare

edition [e•DI•shn] *n* edizione F

editor [E•di•tur] *n* redattore M

editorial 1 [E•di•TAU•ree•ul] *n* editoriale M

editorial 2 [E•di•TAU•ree•ul] *adj* di redazione

educate [E•ju•KAIT] *vt* educare

education [E•ju•KAI•shn] *n* cultura F

educational [E•ju•KAI•shu•nl] *adj* educativo; educativa

eel [eeul] *n* anguilla F

effect [i•FEKT] *n* effetto M; *vi* effectuare; realizzare

effective [i•FEK•tiv] *adj* effettivo; effettiva

efficiency [i•FI•shun•see] *n* efficenza F

efficient [i•FI•shunt] *adj* efficente

effort [E•furt] *n* sforzo M

egg [eg] *n* uovo M

eggplant [EG•plant] *n* melanzana F

ego [EE•go] *n* io M

egotist [EE•go•tist] *n* egotista

Egypt [EE•jipt] *n* Egitto M

Egyptian [ee•JIP•shn] *adj* egiziano; egiziana

eight [ait] *num* otto

eighteen [ai•TEEN] *num* diciotto

eighteenth [ai•TEENTH] *num* diciottesimo; diciottesima

eighth [aith] *num* ottavo; ottava

eighty [AI•tee] *num* ottanta

either [EE•thur] *adj* l'uno e l'altro; l'una e l'altra

eject [ee•JEKT] *vt* espellere

elaborate [*adj* i•LA•brit v. i•LA•bu•RAIT] *adj* elaborare

elastic [i•LA•stik] *adj* elastico; elastica; *n* elastico M

elated [i•LAI•tid] *adj* esultante

elbow [EL•bo] *n* gomito M

elder [EL•dur] *adj* maggiore; *n* pastore M

elderly [EL•dur•lee] *adj* anziano; anziana

elect [e•LEKT] *vt* eleggere

election [i•LEK•shn] *n* elezione F

electric [i•LEK•trik] *adj*
elettrico; elettrica

electricity [i•LEK•TRI•si•tee] *n*
elettricitá F

electrocute
[i•LEK•tru•KYOOT] *vt*
fulminare

electronic [i•LEK•TRAH•nik]
adj elettronico; elettronica

elegance [E•li•guns] *n*
eleganza F

elegant [E•li•gunt] *adj* elegante

element [E•li•munt] *n*
elemento M

elementary [E•li•MEN•tu•ree]
adj elementare

elephant [E•lu•fint] *n*
elefante M

elevate [E•lu•VAIT] *vt* elevare

elevator [E•li•VAI•tur] *n*
ascensore M

eleven [i•LE•vn] *num* undici

eleventh [i•LE•vnth] *num*
undicesimo; undicesima

elicit [i•LI•sit] *vt* sollecitare

eligible [E•li•ju•bl] *adj* idoneo;
idonea

eliminate [i•LI•mi•NAIT] *vt*
eliminare

elite [i•LEET] *adj* il fior; fiore
M

elitist [i•LEE•tist] *adj n* elitista

elk [elk] *n* alce M

elm [elm] *n* olmo M

elope [i•LOP] *vi* fuggire

eloquence [E•lu•kwuns] *n*
eloquenza F

eloquent [E•lu•kwunt] *adj*
eloquente

else [els] *adv* altro

elsewhere [ELS•waiur] *adv*
altrove

elude [i•LOOD] *vt* eludere

emaciated [i•MAI•shee•AI•tid]
adj emaciato; emaciata

emanate [E•mu•NAIT] *vi*
emanare

emancipation
[i•MAN•si•PAI•shn] *n*
emancipazione F

embankment
[em•BANGK•munt] *n* argine

embargo [im•BAHR•go] *n*
fermo M

embarrass [im•BA•rus] *vt*
imbarazzare

embarrassed [im•BA•rust] *adj*
imbarazzato; imbarazzata

embarrassing [im•BA•ru•sing]
adj imbarazzante

embarrassment
[im•BA•rus•munt] *n*
imbarazzo M

embassy [EM•bu•see] *n*
ambasciata F

embellish [im•BE•lish] *vt*
abbellire

embers [EM•burz] *npl* braci F

embezzle [em•BE•zl] *vt*
appropriarsi indebitamente

emblem (badge) [EM•blum] *n*
emblema M

embody [im•BAH•dee] *vt*
rappresentare

embrace [im•BRAIS] *n*
abbracciare

embroidery [im•BROI•du•ree]
n ricamo M

embryo [EM•bree•O] *n*
embrione M

emerald [E•mu•ruld] *adj n*
smeraldo M

emerge [i•MURJ] *vi* emergere

emergency [i•MUR•jun•see] *n*
emergenza F

emergency exit
[i•MUR•jun•see EG•sit] *n*
uscita d'emergenza F

emigrant [E•mi•grunt] *n*
emigrante

emigrate [E•mi•GRAIT] *vi*
emigrare

eminence [E•mi•nuns] *n*
eminenza F

eminent [E•mi•nunt] *adj*
eminente

emissary [E•mi•SE•ree] *n*
emissario; emissaria

emission [i•MI•shn] *n*
emissione F

emit [i•MIT] *vt* emettere

emperor [EM•pu•rur] *n*
imperatore M

emphasis [EM•fu•sis] *n*
enfasi F

emphasize [EM•fu•SUYZ] *vt*
enfatizzare

empire [EM•puyur] *n* impero M

employ [em•PLOI] *vt* impiegare

employee [em•PLOI•YEE] *n*
impiegato; impiegata

employer [em•PLOI•yur] *n*
datore di lavoro M

employment [em•PLOI•munt]
n impiego M

empress [EM•pris] *n*
imperatrice F

empty [EMP•tee] *adj* vuoto;
vuota

emulate [E•myu•LAIT] *vt*
emulare

enable [e•NAI•bl] *vt* mettere in
grado di

enact [e•NAKT] *vt* emanare

enamel [i•NA•ml] *n* smalto M

enamored [i•NA•murd] *adj*
innamorato; innamorata

encampment [en•KAMP•munt]
n accampamento M

enchant [en•CHANT] *vt*
incantare

enclose [en•CLOZ] *vt*
circondare; *vt* accludere

encompass [en•KAHM•pus] *vt*
comprendere

encore [AHN•kaur] *n* bis M

encounter [en•KOUN•tur] *n*
incontro M

encourage [en•KU•rij] *vt*
incoraggiare

encouragement
[en•KU•rij•munt] *n*
incoraggiamento M

encroach [en•KROCH] *vi*
invadere

encyclopedia
[en•SUY•klo•PEE•dee•u] *n*
enciclopedia F

end [end] *n* fine F; *vi* finire;
concludere; terminare

endanger [en•DAIN•jur] *vt*
mettere in pericolo

endearing [en•DEEU•ring] *adj*
attraente

endeavor [en•DE•vur] *n*
sforzo M

ending [EN•ding] *n* fine M

endless [END•lis] *adj* infinito;
infinita

endorse [en•DAURS] *vt*
approvare; (a check) *vt* girare

endurance [en•DU•runs] *n*
resistenza F

enemy [E•nu•mee] *n* nemico;
nemica

energetic [E•nur•JE•tik] *adj*
energico; energica

energy [E•nur•jee] *n* energia F

enforce [en•FAURS] *vt* imporre

engage [en•GAIJ] *vt*
impegnare; assumere;
impiegare

engaged [en•GAIJD] *adj*
fidanzato; fidanzata

engagement [en•GAIJ•munt] *n*
fidanzamento M

engaging [en•GAI•jing] *adj*
attraente

engine [EN•jin] *n* motore M

engineer [EN•ji•NEEUR] *n*
ingegnere M

engineering
[EN•ji•NEEU•ring] *n*
ingegneria F

England [ING•glund] *n*
Inghilterra F

English [ING•glish] *adj* inglese

engrave [en•GRAIV] *vt*
incidere

engraving [en•GRAI•ving] *n*
incisione F

engulf [en•GUHLF] *vt*
sommergere

enhance [en•HANS] *vt*
intensificare

enigma [i•NIG•mu] *n*
enigma M

enjoy [en•JOI] *vt* provare
gusto a

enjoyable [en•JOI•u•bl] *adj*
gradevole

enlarge [en•LAHRJ] *vt*
ingrandire

enlighten [en•LUY•tn] *vt*
illuminare

Enlightenment
[en•LUY•tn•munt] *n*
Illuminismo M

enlist [en•LIST] *vt* arruolare

enormous [i•NAUR•mus] *adj*
enorme

enough [i•NUHF] *adv*
abbastanza

enrage [en•RAIJ] *vt*
imbestialire

enrich [en•RICH] *vt* arricchire

enroll [en•ROL] *vt* iscrivere

enslave [en•SLAIV] *vt* asservire

ensuing [en•SOO•ing] *adj*
risultante

ensure [en•SHOOUR] *vt*
assicurare

entail [en•TAIL] *vt* comportare

enter [EN•tur] *vt* entrare;
(record) notare

enterprise [EN•tur•PRUYZ] *n*
impresa F

enterprising
[EN•tur•PRUY•zing] *adj*
intraprendente

entertain [EN•tur•TAIN] *vt*
intrattenere

entertaining
[EN•tur•TAI•ning] *adj*
divertente

entertainment
[EN•tur•TAIN•munt] *n*
divertimento M

enthusiasm
[en•THOO•zee•A•zm] *n*
entusiasmo M

enthusiastic
[en•THOO•zee•A•stik] *adj*
entusiastico; entusiastica

enticing [en•TUY•sing] *adj*
seducente

entire [en•TUYUR] *adj* intero;
intera

entirely [en•TUYUR•lee] *adv*
interamente

entirety [en•TUYUR•tee] *n*
totalitá F

entitled (to be) [en•TUY•tld]
adj aver diritto

entity [EN•ti•tee] *n* entitá F

entrance 1 [EN•truns] *n*
entrata F

entrance 2 [en•TRANS] *vt*
incantare

entry [EN•tree] *n* ingresso M;
(record) parita F

enumerate [i•NOO•mu•RAIT]
vt enumerare

envelop [en•VE•luhp] *vt*
avviluppare

envelope [EN•vu•LOP] *n*
busta F

envious [EN•vee•us] *adj*
invidioso; invidiosa

environment
[en•VUY•run•munt] *n*
ambiente M

envoy [EN•voi] *n* inviato;
inviata

envy [EN•vee] *n* invidia F; *vi*
invidiare

epic [E•pik] *adj* epico; epica

epidemic [E•pi•DE•mik] *n*
epidemia F

episode [E•pi•SOD] *n*
episodio M

epistle [i•PI•sl] *n* epistola F

epitaph [E•pi•TAF] *n*
epitaffio M

epitome [e•PI•tu•mee] *n*
compendio M

epoch [E•puk] *n* epoca F

equal [EE•kwul] *adj* uguale; *vi*
uguagliare; fare

equality [ee•KWAH•li•tee] *n*
eguaglianza F

equally [EE•kwu•lee] *adv*
egualmente

equation [ee•KWAI•zhn] *n*
equazione F

equator [ee•KWAI•tur] *n*
equatore M

equip [i•KWIP] *vt* equipaggiare

equipment [i•KWIP•munt] *n*
attrezzatura F

equivalent [i•KWI•vu•lunt] *adj*
n equivalente

era [E•ru] *n* era F

eradicate [i•RA•di•KAIT] *vt*
estirpare

erase [i•RAIS] *vt* cancellare

eraser [i•RAI•sur] *n* gomma F

erect [i•REKT] *adj* eretto;
eretta; *vt* erigere; costruire

erection [i•REK•shn] *n*
erezione F

erode [i•ROD] *vt* erodere

erosion [i•RO•zhn] *n* erosione F

err [er] *vi* errare

errand [E•rund] *n*
commissione F

error [E•rur] *n* errore M

erudite [ER•yu•DUYT] *adj*
erudito; erudita

erupt [i•RUHPT] *vi* eruttare

eruption [i•RUHP•shn] *n*
eruzione F

escalate [E•sku•LAIT] *vt*
scalare

escalator [E•sku•LAI•tur] *n*
scala mobile F

escape [e•SKAIP] *n* fuga F

escort [n. E•skaurt v.
e•SKAURT] *n* scorta F

especially [e•SPE•shu•lee] *adv*
specialmente

espionage [E•spee•u•NAHZH]
n spionaggio M

essay [E•sai] *n* saggio M

essence [E•suns] *n* essenza F

essential [e•SEN•shl] *adj*
essenziale

essentially [e•SEN•shu•lee] *adv*
essenzialmente

establish [e•STA•blish] *vt*
stabilire

establishment
[e•STA•blish•munt] *n*
autoritá F

estate [e•STAIT] *n* proprietá F

esteem [e•STEEM] *n* stima F;
vi stimare; apprezzare

estimate [n. E•sti•mut v.
E•sti•MAIT] *n* stima F; *vi*
valutare; stimare

estranged [e•STRAINJD] *adj*
alienato; alienata

eternal [i•TUR•nl] *adj* eterno;
eterna

eternity [i•TUR•ni•tee] *n*
eternitá F

ethic [E•thik] *n* etica F

ethical [E•thi•kl] *adj* etico; etica

Ethiopia [EE•thee•O•pee•u] *n*
Etiopia F

ethnic [ETH•nik] *adj* etnico;
etnica

etiquette [E•ti•kut] *n*
etichetta F

eulogy [YOO•lu•jee] *n*
eulogia F

euphemism [YOO•fu•MI•zm] *n*
eufemismo M

Europe [YUH•rup] *n* Europa F

European [YUH•ru•PEE•un]
adj europeo; europea

European Community
[YUH•ru•PEE•un
kuh•MYU•ni•tee] *n* Comunitá
Europea F

euthanasia
[YOO•thu•NAI•zhu] *n*
eutanasia F

evacuate [i•VA•kyoo•AIT] *vt*
evacuare

evade [i•VAID] *vt* evadere

evaluate [i•VAL•yoo•AIT] *vt*
valutare

evaporate [i•VA•pu•RAIT] *vt*
evaporare

evasive [i•VAI•siv] *adj* evasivo;
evasiva

eve [eev] *n* vigilia F

even [EE•vn] *adj* anche

evening [EEV•ning] *n* sera F

evening gown [EEV•ning
GOWN] *n* abito da sera M

event [i•VENT] *n* caso M

eventual [i•VEN•chu•ul] *adj*
conclusivo; conclusiva

eventually [i•VEN•chuu•lee]
adv finalmente

ever [E•vur] *adv* mai

evergreen [E•vur•GREEN] *n*
sempreverde

every [E•vree] *adj* ogni

everybody [E•vree•BUH•dee]
pron ognuno M

everyday [E•vree•DAI] *adj*
quotidiano; quotidiana

everything [E•vree•THING]
pron tutto M

everywhere [E•vree•WAIUR]
adv dappertutto

evict [i•VIKT] *vt* sfrattare

evidence [E•vi•duns] *n*
evidenza F

evident [E•vi•dunt] *adj* evidente

evil [EE•vl] *adj* cattivo; cattiva

evoke [i•VOK] *vt* evocare

evolution [E•vu•LOO•shn] *n*
evoluzione F

evolve [i•VAHLV] *vi* evolvere

ewe [yoo] *n* pecora F

exact [eg•ZAKT] *adj* esatto;
esatta

exaggerate [eg•ZA•ju•RAIT]
vt vi esagerare

exaggeration
[eg•ZA•ju•RAI•shn] *n*
esagerazione F

exalt [eg•ZAULT] *vt* esaltare

exam [eg•ZAM] *n* esame M

examine [eg•ZA•min] *vt*
esaminare

example [eg•ZAM•pl] *n*
esempio M

exasperate [eg•ZA•spu•RAIT]
vt esasperare

excavate [EK•sku•VAIT] *vt*
fare scavi

exceed [ek•SEED] *vt* eccedere

excel [ek•SEL] *vi* eccellere

excellence [EK•su•luns] *n*
eccellenza F

excellent [EK•su•lunt] *adj*
eccellente

except [ek•SEPT] *prep conj*
eccetto

exception [ek•SEP•shn] *n*
eccezione F

exceptional [ek•SEP•shu•nl]
adj eccezionale

excerpt [EK•surpt] *n* brano M

excess [EK•ses] *adj* eccedente

exchange [eks•CHAINJ] *n*
scambio M

exchange (currency)
[eks•CHAINJ] *n* cambio M

excite [ek•SUYT] *vt* eccitare

excited [ek•SUY•tid] *adj*
eccitato; eccitata

exciting [ek•SUY•ting] *adj*
emozionante

exclaim [ek•SKLAIM] *vi*
esclamare

exclamation point
[ek•sklu•mai•shn ~] *n* punto
esclamativo M

exclude [ek•SKLOOD] *vt*
escludere

excrement [EK•skri•munt] *n*
escremento M

excursion [ek•SKUR•zhn] *n*
escursione F

excuse [n. ek•SKYOOS v.
ek•SKYOOZ] *n* scusa F

execute (a prisoner)
[EK•si•KYOOT] *vt* giustiziare

execute (sign) [EK•si•KYOOT]
vt firmare

execution [EK•si•KYOO•shn] *n*
esecuzione F

executioner
[EK•si•KYOO•shu•nur] *n*
boia M

executive [eg•ZE•kyu•tiv] *adj*
esecutivo; esecutiva

exemplary [eg•ZEM•plu•ree]
adj esemplare

exemplify [eg•ZEM•pli•FUY]
vt esemplificare

exempt [eg•ZEMPT] *adj* esente

exercise [EK•sur•SUYZ] *n*
esercizio M

exert [eg•ZURT] *vt* esercitare

exhale [eks•HAIL] *vt* esalare

exhaust [eg•ZAUST] *n*
scappamento M; *vi* stancare;
estenuare

exhausted [eg•ZAU•stid] *adj*
esausto; esausta

exhaustion [eg•ZAUS•chn] *n*
esaurimento M

exhibit [eg•ZI•bit] *n* mostra F;
vi esibire

exhilarating
[eg•ZI•lu•RAI•ting] *adj*
esilarante

exile [EG•zuyl] *n* esilio M; *vt*
esiliare

exist [EG•zist] *vi* esistere

existence [eg•ZI•stuns] *n*
esistenza F

exit [EG•zit] *n* uscita F; *vi*
uscire

exodus [EK•su•dus] *n* esodo M

exonerate [eg•ZAH•nu•RAIT]
vt esonerare

exotic [eg•ZAH•tik] *adj* esotico;
esotica

expand [ek•SPAND] *vt*
espandere

expansion [ek•SPAN•shn] *n*
espansione F

expect [ek•SPEKT] *vt* aspettare

expectation
[EK•SPEK•TAI•shn] *n*
aspettativa F

expecting [ek•SPEK•ting] *adj*
in attesa

expedition [EK•spu•DI•shn] *n*
spedizione F

expel [ek•SPEL] *vt* espellere

expend [ek•SPEND] *vt*
impiegare

expenditure [ek•SPEN•di•chur]
n spesa F

expense [ek•SPENS] *n* spesa F

expensive [ek•SPEN•siv] *adj*
costoso; costosa

experience
[ek•SPEEU•ree•uns] *n*
esperienza F

experienced
[ek•SPEEU•ree•unst] *adj*
esperto; esperta

experiment [ek•SPE•ri•munt] *n*
esperimento M

expert [EK•spurt] *adj n* esperto;
esperta

expire [ek•SPUYUR] *vi* scadere

explain [ek•SPLAIN] *vt*
spiegare

explanation
[EK•splu•NAI•shn] *n*
spiegazione F

explode [ek•SPLOD] *vt*
esplodere

exploit [n. EK•sploit v.
ek•SPLOIT] *n* impresa F; *vt*
sfruttare

exploration [EK•splu•RAI•shn]
n esplorazione F

explore [ek•SPLAUR] *vt vi*
esplorare

explorer [ek•SPLAU•rur] *n*
esploratore M

export [n. EK•spaurt v.
ek•SPAURT] *n* esportazione
F; *vt* esportare

expose [ek•SPOZ] *vt* svelare

exposure [ek•SPO•zhur] *n*
esposizione F; (cold) *n*
assideramento M

express [ek•SPRES] *adj*
espresso; *vt* esprimere

expression [ek•SPRE•shn] *n*
espressione F

expressive [ek•SPRE•siv] *adj*
espressivo; espressiva

exquisite [ek•SKWI•zit] *adj*
squisito; squisita

extend [ek•STEND] *vt* estendere

extension [ek•STEN•shn] *n*
estensione F

extensive [ek•STEN•siv] *adj*
estensivo; estensiva

extent [ek•STENT] *n* limite M

exterior [ek•STEEU•ree•ur] *adj*
esterno; esterna; *n* esterno M

exterminate
[ek•STUR•mi•NAIT] *vt*
sterminare

external [ek•STUR•nl] *adj*
esterno; esterna

extinct [ek•STINGKT] *adj*
estinto; estinta

extinguish [ek•STING•gwish]
vt estinguese

extort [ek•STAURT] *vt*
estorcere

extra [EK•stru] *adj* extra

extract [n. EK•strakt v.
ek•STRAKT] *n* estratto M; *vt*
estrarre

extradite [EK•stru•DUYT] *vt*
estradare

extraordinary
[ek•STRAU•di•NE•ree] *adj*
straordinario; straordinaria

extravagance
[ek•STRA•vu•guns] *n*
stravaganza F

extravagant [ek•STRA•vu•gunt]
adj stravagante

extreme [ek•STREEM] *adj n*
estremo; estrema

extremist [ek•STREE•mist] *adj*
n estremista

extrovert [EK•stru•VURT] *adj*
n estroverso; estroversa

exuberant [eg•ZOO•bu•runt]
adj esuberante

exult [eg•ZUHLT] *vi* esultare

eye [uy] *n* occhio M

eyewitness [uy•WIT•nis] *n*
testimone oculare

eyeball [UY•baul] *n* bulbo
oculare M

eyebrow [UY•brou] *n*
sopracciglio M

eyelash [UY•lash] *n* ciglia F

eyelid [UY•lid] *n* palpebra F

eyesight [UY•suyt] *n* vista F

F

fable [FAI•bl] *n* fiaba F

fabric [FA•brik] *n* stoffa F

fabricate [FA•bri•KAIT] *vt*
fabbricare

fabulous [FA•byu•lus] *adj*
favoloso; favolosa

facade [fu•SAHD] *n* facciata F

face [fais] *n* faccia F; volto;
viso; (look toward)
fronteggiare; (confront)
affrontare

facet [FA•sit] *n* faccetta F

facetious [fu•SEE•shus] *adj*
faceto; faceta

facilities [fu•SI•li•tees] *npl*
impianti M

facing [FAI•sing] *prep* di fronte

fact [fakt] *n* fatto M

factor [FAK•tur] *n* fattore M

factory [FAK•tu•ree] *n*
fabbrica F

faculty [FA•kul•tee] *n* facoltá F

fad [fad] *n* mania F

fade [faid] *vt* sbiadire

fail [fail] *vt* fallire

failure [FAIL•yur] *n*
fallimento M

faint [faint] *adj* debole

fair 1 [faiur] *adj* giusto; giusta

fair 2 [faiur] *n* mercato M

fairy [FAIU•ree] *n* fata F

fairy tale [FAIR•ee tail] *n*
fiaba F

faith [faith] *n* fede F

faithful [FAITH•ful] *adj* fedele

fake [faik] *adj* finto; finta

falcon [FAL•kn] *n* falcone M

fall [faul] *n* caduta F; *vt* cadere;
cascare; (season) autunno M

false [fauls] *adj* falso; falso

falsify [FAUL•si•FUY] *vt*
falsificare

falter [FAUL•tur] *vi* tremare

fame [faim] *n* fama F

famed [faimd] *adj* rinomato;
rinomata

familiar [fu•MI•lyur] *adj*
familiare

familiarize [fu•MI•lyu•RUYZ]
vt familiarizzarsi

family [FA•mu•lee] *n* famiglia F

famine [FA•min] *n* carestia F

famished [FA•misht] *adj*
famelico; famelica

famous [FAI•mus] *adj* famoso;
famosa

fan [fan] *n* ventola F; ventaglio;
soffiare su; sizzare; (oneself)
farsi vento

fancy [FAN•see] *adj* elaborato;
elaborata

fang [fang] *n* zanna F

fantastic [fan•TA•stik] *adj*
fantastico; fantastica

fantasy [FAN•tu•see] *n*
fantasia F

far [fahr] *adj* lontano; lontana

farce [fahrs] *n* farsa F

fare [faiur] *n* tariffa F; *vi* vivere;
trovarsi

farewell [faiur•WEL] *n*
addio M

farm [fahrm] *n* fattoria F

farmer [FAHR•mur] *n*
agricoltore M

farming [FAHR•ming] *n*
agricoltura F

farther [FAHR•thur] *adj* piú
lontano; piú lontana

farthest [FAHR•thist] *adj adv* il
piú lontano; la piú lontana

fascinate [FA•si•NAIT] *vt*
affascinare

fascinating [FA•si•NAI•ting]
adj affascinante

fascination [FA•si•NAI•shn] *n*
fascino M

fascism [FA•shi•zm] *n*
fascismo M

fashion [FA•shn] *n* moda F

fashionable [FA•shu•nu•bl] *adj*
alla moda

fast [fast] *adj* veloce

fasten [FA•sun] *vt* allacciare

fastidious [fa•STI•dee•us] *adj* schizzinoso; schizzinosa

fat [fat] *adj* grasso; grassa

fatal [FAI•tl] *adj* fatale

fate [fait] *n* fato M

fateful [FAIT•ful] *adj* decisivo; decisiva

father [FAH•thur] *n* padre M

father-in-law [FA•thur•in•LAU] *n* suocero M

fatherland [FAH•thur•LAND] *n* patria F

fatherly [FAH•thur•lee] *adj* paterno; paterna

fathom [FA•thum] *n* braccio M

fatigue [fu•TEEG] *n* stanchezza F

fatten [FA•tun] *vt* ingrassare

fatuous [FA•chu•us] *adj* fatuo; fatua

faucet [FAU•sit] *n* rubinetto M

fault [fault] *n* colpa F

faulty [FAUL•tee] *adj* difettoso; difettosa

fauna [FAU•nu] *n* fauna F

favor [FAI•vur] *n* favore M

favorable [FAI•vru•bl] *adj* favorevole

favorite [FAI•vrit] *adj* preferito; preferita; *n* favorito; favorita

fawn [faun] *n* cerbiatto M

fear [feeur] *n* paura F

fearful [FEEUR•ful] *adj* pauroso; paurosa

fearless [FEEUR•lis] *adj* impavido; impavida

feasible [FEE•zu•bl] *adj* fattibile

feast [feest] *n* banchetto M

feat [feet] *n* impresa F

feather [FE•thur] *n* piuma F

feature [FEE•chur] *n* caratteristica F

February [FE•broo•U•ree] *n* febbraio

federal [FE•du•rul] *adj n* federale

federation [FE•du•RAI•shn] *n* federazione F

fee [fee] *n* onorario M

feeble [FEE•bl] *adj* debole

feed [feed] *n* mangime M; *vi* nutrire; alimentare

feel [feeul] *vt* sentire; tasare; toccare; sentire

feeling [FEEU•ling] *n* sentimento M

feign [fain] *vt* fingere

fell 1 [fel] *vt* abbattere

fell 2 [fel] *v. form* (p. tense to fall) cadde

fellow [FE•lo] *n* persona F

fellowship [FE•lo•SHIP] *n* associazione F

felon [FE•lun] *n* criminale M

felt [felt] *n* feltro M

female [FEE•mail] *adj* femmina F

feminine [FE•mi•nin] *adj* femminile

fence [fens] *n* steccato M

fencing [FEN•sing] *n* scherma F

fend [fend] *vi* parare

fender [FEN•dur] *n* paraurti M

ferment [n. FUR•ment v. fur•MENT] *vi* fermentare; *n* fermento M

fern [furn] *n* felce F

ferocious [fu•RO•shus] *adj*
    feroce
ferret [FE•rit] *n* furetto M
ferry [FE•ree] *n* traghetto M
fertile [FUR•tl] *adj* fertile
fertility [fur•TI•li•tee] *n*
    fertilitá F
fertilize [FUR•ti•LUYZ] *vt*
    fertilizzare
fertilizer [FUR•ti•LUY•zur] *n*
    fertilizzante M
fervent [FUR•vunt] *adj* fervido;
    fervida
festival [FE•sti•vl] *n* festival
festive [FE•stiv] *adj* festoso;
    festosa
fetch [fech] *vt* andar a prendere
fetus [FEE•tus] *n* feto M
feud [fyood] *n* feud M
feudal [FYOO•dl] *adj* feudale
fever [FEE•vur] *n* febbre F
feverish [FEE•vu•rish] *adj*
    febbricitante
few [fyoo] *adj* pochi; poche
fiancé [fee•ahn•SAI] *n*
    fidanzato M
fiancée [fee•ahn•SAI] *n*
    fidanzata F
fib [fib] *n* bugia F; *vt* raccontar
    frottole
fiber [FUY•bur] *n* fibra F
fickle [FI•kl] *adj* incostante
fiction [FIK•shn] *n* letteratura
    d'immaginazione F
fiddle [FI•dl] *n* violino M
fidelity [fi•DE•li•tee] *n*
    fedeltá F
fidget [FI•jit] *vi* agitarsi
field [feeuld] *n* campo
fiend [feend] *n* demonio M

fiendish [FEEN•dish] *adj*
    diabolico; dibolica
fierce [feeurs] *adj* feroce
fiery [FUYU•ree] *adj*
    fiammeggiante
fifteen [fif•TEEN] *num* quindici
fifteenth [fif•TEENTH] *num*
    quindicesimo; quindicesima
fifth [fifth] *num* quinto; quinta
fiftieth [FIF•tee•ith] *num*
    cinquantesimo; cinquantesima
fifty [FIF•tee] *num* cinquanta
fig [fig] *n* fico M
fight [fuyt] *n* lotta;
    combatimento F; *vi* lottare;
    combattere
figurative [FI•gyu•ru•tiv] *adj*
    figurativo; figurativa
figure 1 [FI•gyur] *n* figura F
figure 2 (number) [FI•gyur] *n*
    cifra F
file [fuyul] *n* schedario M
fill [fil] *vt* riempire
fillet [fi•LAI] *n* filetto M
filling [FI•ling] *n* ripieno M
film [film] *n* pellicola F
filter [FIL•tur] *n* filtro M
filth [filth] *n* sudiciume M
filthy [FIL•thee] *adj* sudicio;
    sudicia
fin [fin] *n* pinna F
final [FUY•nl] *adj* finale
finally [FUY•nu•lee] *adv*
    finalmente
finance [fuy•NANS] *n*
    finanza F
financial [fuy•NAN•shl] *adj*
    finanziario; finanziaria
finch [finch] *n* fringuello M
find [fuynd] *n* scoperta F; *vt*
    trovare

fine 1 [fuyn] *adj* bello; bella; pregiato

fine 2 [fuyn] *n* multa F; *vi* multare

finger [FING•gur] *n* dito M

fingerprint [FING•gur•PRINT] *n* impronta digitale F

fingertip [FING•gur•TIP] *n* punta del dito F

finish [FI•nish] *n* finitura F; *vi* finire; concludere

finish line [FI•nish LUYN] *n* traguardo M

Finland [FIN•lund] *n* Finlandia F

Finn [fin] *n* finlandese

Finnish [FI•nish] *adj* finlandese

fir [fur] *n* abete M

fire [fuyur] *n* fuoco M; (shoot) sparare; (simiss) licenziare

fire station [FUYUR STAI•shn] *n* caserma dei pompieri F

fireman [FUYUR•man] *n* pompiere M

fireplace [FUYUR•plais] *n* camino M

firewood [FUYUR•wud] *n* legna da ardere F

fireworks [FUYUR•wurks] *npl* fuochi artificiali M

firm 1 [furm] *adj* compatto; compatta

firm 2 [furm] *n* ditta; azienda F

first [furst] *adj* primo; prima

first aid [FURST AID] *n* pronto soccorso M

first name [FURST NAIM] *n* nome M

first-class [FURST•KLAS] *adj* di prima classe

firsthand [FURST•HAND] *adj* *adv* direttamente

fiscal [FI•skl] *adj* fiscale

fish [fish] *n* pesce M; *vt* pescare

fisherman [FI•shur•mun] *n* pescatore M

fishing [FI•shing] *n* pescare

fission [FI•shn] *n* fissione F

fissure [FI•shur] *n* fessura F

fist [fist] *n* pugno M

fit 1 [fit] *adj* in forma; *vi* (clothes, etc) star bene; (suit) adeguare

fit 2 [fit] *m* accesso M; attacco M

fitting room [FI•ting ~] *n* camerino di prova M

five [fuyv] *num* cinque

fix [fiks] *vt* aggiustare

fixation [fik•SAI•shn] *n* fissazione F

fixed [fikst] *adj* fisso; fissa

fizz [fiz] *n* effervescenza F

flag 1 [flag] *n* bandiera F

flag 2 [flag] *v* indebolirsi; accasciarsi

flagpole [FLAG•pol] *n* asta di bandiera

flagrant [FLAI•grunt] *adj* flagrante

flair [flaiur] *n* estro M

flake [flaik] *n* fiocco M; *vi* sfaldare

flame [flaim] *n* fiamma F

flamingo [flu•MING•go] *n* fenicottero M

flammable [FLA•mu•bl] *adj* combustibile

flank [flangk] *n* fianco M

flannel [FLA•nl] *n* flanella F

flap [flap] *n* falda F; *vi* agitare;
battere (coll)

flare [flaiur] *n* razzo M

flash [flash] *n* baleno M; *vi*
balenare

flashback [FLASH•bak] *n*
retrospettiva F

flashlight [FLASH•luyt] *n*
pila F

flashy [FLA•shee] *adj* vistoso;
vistosa

flask [flask] *n* fiaschetta F

flat [flat] *adj* piatto; piatta

flatten [FLA•tn] *vt* appiattire

flatter [FLA•tur] *vt* lusingare

flattering [FLA•tu•ring] *adj*
lusinghiero; lusinghiera

flattery [FLA•tu•ree] *n*
adulazione F

flaunt [flaunt] *vt* ostentare

flavor [FLAI•vur] *n* sapore M

flaw [flau] *n* difetto M

flax [flaks] *n* lino M

flea [flee] *n* pulce F

fleck [flek] *n* chiazza F

flee [flee] *vt vi* fuggire

fleece [flees] *n* vello M

fleet [fleet] *n* flotta F

flesh [flesh] *n* carne F

fleshy [FLE•shee] *adj* carnoso;
carnosa

flex [fleks] *vt vi* flettere

flexible [FLEK•si•bl] *adj*
flessibile

flicker [FLI•kur] *vi* guizzare

flight [fluyt] *n* volo M

flimsy [FLIM•zee] *adj* leggero;
leggera

flinch [flinch] *vi* indietreggiare

fling [fling] *vt* gettare

flint [flint] *n* pietra focaia F

flip [flip] *vt* girare

flippant [FLI•punt] *adj* leggero;
leggera

flirt [flurt] *n* civetta F

float [flot] *vt* galleggiare

flock [flahk] *n* gregge M

flog [flahg] *vt* fustigare

flogging [FLAH•ging] *n*
flagellazione F

flood [fluhd] *n* inondazione F;
vi inondare; allagare

floodlight [FLUHD•luyt] *n*
riflettore M

floor [flaur] *n* pavimento M

flora [FLAU•ru] *n* flora F

florist [FLAU•rist] *n* fiorista M

floss [flaus] *n* filo M

flounder [FLOUN•dur] *n*
pianuzza F

flour [flouur] *n* farina F

flourish [FLU•rish] *vi*
prosperare

flout [flout] *vt* burlarsi

flow [flo] *n* flusso M

flower [flouur] *n* fiore M

flown [flon] *v form* (p.p. to fly)
volato

flu [floo] *n* influenza F

fluctuate [FLUHK•chu•AIT] *vi*
fluttuare

flue [floo] *n* canna fumaria F

fluency [FLOO•un•see] *n*
scioltezza F

fluent [FLOO•unt] *adj* spedito;
spedita

fluff [fluf] *n* lanugine F;
peluria F

fluid 1 [FLOO•id] *adj* fluido;
fluida

fluid 2 [FLOO•id] *n* fluido M

fluke [flook] *n* colpo
fortunato M

fluorescent [flau•RE•sunt] *adj*
fluorescente

fluoride [FLAU•ruyd] *n*
fluoro M

flurry [FLU•ree] *n* turbine M

flush [fluhsh] *vt* sciacquare; *n*
rossore M; flusso M; (blush)
vampa F; *vi* arrosire

fluster [FLUH•stur] *vt* stordire

flute [floot] *n* flauto M

flutter [FLUH•tur] *vi* eccitarsi

fly 1 [fluy] *n* mosca F

fly 2 [fluy] *vi* volare; (escape)
figgire; scappare

flying saucer [FLUY•ing
SAU•sur] *n* disco volante M

foam [fom] *n* schiuma F

focal [FO•kl] *adj* focale

focus [FO•kus] *n* fuoco M; *vi*
mettere a fuoco; concentrare

fodder [FAH•dur] *n* foraggio M

foe [fo] *n* nemico; nemica

fog [fahg] *n* nebbia F

foil 1 [foiul] *n* stagnola F

foil 2 [foiul] *vt* frustrare;
sventare

fold [fold] *n* piega F; *vt* piegare

foliage [FO•lee•ij] *n*
fogliame M

folk [fok] *adj* popolare

follow [FAH•lo] *vt vi* seguire

follower [FAH•lo•ur] *n* seguace

following [FAH•lo•ing] *adj*
seguito M

folly [FAH•lee] *n* follia F

foment [FO•ment] *vt* fomentare

fond [fahnd] *adj* amante (di)

fondle [FAHN•dl] *vt*
vezzeggiare

food [food] *n* cibo M

fool [fooul] *n* sciocco; sciocca

foolish [FOOU•lish] *adj*
sciocco; sciocca

foolproof [FOOUL•proof] *adj*
di uso semplicissimo

foot [fut] *n* piede M

football [FUT•baul] *n*
pallone M

footnote [FUT•not] *n* nota a
pié pagina F

footpath [FUT•oath] *n*
sentiero M

footprint [FUT•print] *n* orma F

footstep [FUT•step] *n* passo M

for [faur] *prep* per; di a; di; *conj*
poiché

forage [FAU•rij] *n* foraggio M

forbid [faur•BID] *vt* proibire

force [faurs] *n* forza F

forceful [FAURS•ful] *adj*
energico; energica

forceps [FAUR•seps] *npl*
forcipe M

ford [faurd] *n* guado M

forearm [FAUR•ahrm] *n*
avambraccio M

forecast [FAUR•kast] *n*
previsione F; *vt* pronosticare

forefather [FAUR•fah•thur] *n*
antenato M

forego [faur•GO] *vt*
rinunziare (a)

foreground [FAUR•ground] *n*
primo piano M

forehead [FAUR•hed] *n*
fronte F

foreign [FAU•run] *adj*
straniero; straniera

foreigner [FAU•ru•nur] *n*
straniero; straniera

foreman [FAUR•mun] *n* capo
operaio M

foremost [FAUR•most] *adj*
principale

forerunner [FAUU•ruh•nur] *n*
precursore

foresee [faur•SEE] *vt* prevedere

foreshadow [faur•SHA•do] *vt*
adombrare

foresight [FAUR•suyt] *n*
preveggenza F

forest [FAU•rist] *n* foresta F

foretell [faur•TEL] *vt* predire

forever [fu•RE•vur] *adv* per
sempre

foreword [FAUR•wurd] *n*
prefazione F

forfeit [FAUR•fit] *vt* perdere

forge [faurj] *n* fucina F

forget [faur•GET] *vt vi*
dimenticare

forgetful [faur•GET•fl] *adj*
immemor

forgive [faur•GIV] *vt* perdonare

forgo [faur•GO] *vt*
rinunziare (a)

fork [faurk] *n* forchetta F

forlorn [faur•LAURN] *adj*
trascurato; trascurata

form [faurm] *n* forma F; *vt*
formare

formal [FAUR•ml] *adj* formale

formality [faur•MA•li•tee] *n*
formalitá F

former [FAUR•mur] *adj*
precedente

formidable [FAUR•mi•du•bl]
adj formidabile

formula [FAUR•myu•lu] *n*
formula F

forsake [faur•SAIK] *vt*
abbandonare

forsaken [faur•SAI•kn] *adj*
abbandonato; abbandonata

fort [faurt] *n* forte M

forth [faurth] *adv* avanti

forthcoming
[faurth•CUH•ming] *adj*
prossimo; prossima

fortification
[FAUR•ti•fi•KAI•shn] *n*
fortificazione F

fortify [FAUR•ti•FUY] *vt*
fortificare

fortitude [FAUR•ti•TOOD] *n*
forza d'animo F

fortnight [FAURT•nuyt] *n* due
settimane F

fortress [FAUR•tris] *n*
fortezza F

fortuitous [faur•TOO•i•tus] *adj*
fortuito; fortuita

fortunate [FAUR•chu•nut] *adj*
fortunato; fortunata

fortunately
[FAUR•chu•nut•lee] *adv*
fortunatamente

fortune [FAUR•chun] *n*
fortuna F

forty [FAUR•tee] *num* quaranta

forward [FAUR•wurd] *adj*
sfrontato; sfrontata

fossil [FAH•sl] *n* fossile M

foul [foul] *adj* sporco; sporca

found [found] *v. form* (p.p to
find); (establish) trovato
trovata

foundation 1 [foun•DAI•shn] *n*
fondazione F

foundation 2 (building)
[foun•DAI•shn] *n*
fondamenta F

founder [FOUN•dur] *n*
fondatore M

fountain [FOUN•tuhn] *n*
fontana F

four [faur] *num* quattro

fourteen [faur•TEEN] *num*
quattordici

fourth [faurth] *num* quarto;
quarta

fowl [foul] *n* pollo M

fox [fahks] *n* volpe F

fraction [FRAK•shn] *n*
frazione F

fracture [FRAK•chur] *n* frattura
F; *vt* frattuare

fragile [FRA•jul] *adj* fragile

fragment [FRAG•munt] *n*
frammento M

fragrance [FRAI•gruns] *n*
fragranza F

fragrant [FRAI•grunt] *adj*
fragrante

frame [fraim] *n* cornice F; *vt*
(criminal) calunniare;
(compose) redigere

franc [frangk] *n* franco M

France [frans] *n* Francia F

franchise [FRAN•chuyz] *n*
franchigia F

frank [frangk] *adj* franco; franca

frantic [FRAN•tik] *adj*
frenetico; frenetica

fraternal [fru•TUR•nl] *adj*
fraterno; fraterna

fraternity [fru•TUR•ni•tee] *n*
confraternita F

fraud [fraud] *n* frode F

fraudulent [FRAU•dyu•lunt]
adj fraudolento; fraudolenta

frayed [fraid] *adj* logoro; logora

freak [freek] *adj* anomalo;
anomala

free [free] *adj* libero; libera

free speech [FREE SPEECH] *n*
libertá di parola F

free trade [FREE TRAID] *n*
libero scambio M

free will [FREE WILL] *n* libera
scelta F

freedom [FREE•dum] *n*
libertá F

freeze [freez] *vt* congelare

freezer [FREE•zur] *n*
congelatore M

freight [frait] *n* nolo M

French [french] *adj* francese

french fries [~ fruyz] *npl*
patatine fritte F

frenzy [FREN•zee] *n* frenesia F

frequency [FREE•kwun•see] *n*
frequenza F

frequent [adj. FREE•kwunt v.
free•KWENT] *adj* frequente;
vt frequentare

fresh [fresh] *adj* fresco; fresca

freshen [FRE•shn] *vt*
rinfrescare

freshman [FRESH•mun] *n*
matricola F

freshness [FRESH•nus] *n*
freschezza F

freshwater [FRESH•WAU•tur]
adj d'acqua dolce

fret [fret] *vi* crucciarsi

friar [fruyur] *n* frate M

friction [FRIK•shn] *n* frizione F

Friday [FRUY•dai] *n* venerdí M

friend [frend] *n* amico; amica

friendly [FREND•lee] *adj*
amichevole

friendship [FREND•ship] *n*
amicizia F

fright [fruyt] *n* spavento M

frighten [FRUY•tn] *vt*
spaventare

frightening [FRUY•tu•ning]
adj spaventoso; spaventosa

frigid [FRI•jid] *adj* frigido;
frigida

fringe [frinj] *n* frangia F

frisk [frisk] *vt* saltellare;
(search) *vt* perquisire

frisky [FRI•skee] *adj* vivace

frivolous [FRI•vu•lus] *adj*
frivolo; frivola

frog [frahg] *n* ranocchio M

frolic [FRAH•lik] *vi* trastullarsi

from [fruhm] *prep* da; per; da
parte di

front [fruhnt] *adj* di fronte

front door [FRUNT DOR] *n*
porta d'ingresso F

frontier [fruhn•TEER] *n*
frontiera F

frost [fraust] *n* gelo M; *vi*
brinare; (food) glasare

frostbite [FRAUST•buyt] *n*
congelamento M

froth [frauth] *n* schiuma F

frown [froun] *n* cipiglio M; *vt*
aggrottare le ciglia

frugal [FROO•gl] *adj* frugale

fruit [froot] *n* frutto M

fruitless [FROOT•lis] *adj*
infruttuoso; infruttuosa

frustrate [FRUH•strait] *vt*
frustrare

frustration [fruh•STRAI•shn] *n*
frustrazione F

fry [fruy] *vt vi* friggere

fudge [fuj] *n* cioccolata F

fuel [fyooul] *n* carburante M

fugitive [FYOO•ju•tiv] *n*
fuggitivo; fuggitiva

fulfill [ful•FIL] *vt* soddisfare

fulfillment [ful•FIL•munt] *n*
soddisfazione F

full [ful] *adj* pieno; piena

full moon [FUL MOON] *n* luna
piena F

full-time [ful•TUYM] *adj adv* a
tempo pieno

fumble [FUHM•bl] *vt* annaspare

fumes [fyoomz] *npl*
esalazione F

fumigate [FYOO•mi•GAIT] *vt*
fumigare

fun [fuhn] *adj* divertimento M;
n spaso M; scherzo M

function [FUNGK•shn] *n*
funzione F

fund [fuhnd] *n* fondo M

fundamental
[FUHN•du•MEN•tl] *adj*
fondamentale

funeral [FYOO•nu•rul] *n*
funerale M

fungus [FUNG•gus] *n* fungo M

funnel [FUH•nl] *n* imbuto M

funny [FUH•nee] *adj* buffo;
buffa; divertente; comico

fur [fur] *n* pelliccia F

furious [FYOOU•ree•us] *adj*
furioso; furiosa

furnace [FUR•nis] *n* fornace F

furnish [FUR•nish] *vt*
ammobiliare

furniture [FUR•ni•chur] *n*
mobili M

furry [FU•ree] *adj* peloso;
pelosa

further [FUR•thur] *adj* ulteriore

furthermore [FUR•thur•MAUR] *adv* inoltre
furthest [FUR•thist] *adj adv* il piú lontano
furtive [FUR•tiv] *adj* furtivo; furtiva
fury [FYUE•ree] *n* furia F
fuse [fyooz] *n* fusibile M; *vt* fondere

fusion [FYOO•zhn] *n* fusione F
fuss [fuhs] *n* trambusto M
futile [FYOO•tl] *adj* futile
future [FYOO•chur] *adj* futuro; futura
fuzzy [FUH•zee] *adj* lanuginoso; lanuginosa

G

gable [GAI•bl] *n* timpano M
gadget [GA•jit] *n* congegno M
Gaelic [GAIU•lik] *adj n* gaelico; gaelica
gag [gag] *n* bavaglio M
gage (gauge) [gaij] *n* misura F
gain [gain] *n* guadagno; *vi* guadagnare; ottenere
gait [gait] *n* passo M
gale [gaiul] *n* burrasca F
gall [gaul] *n* bile F
gallant [GA•lunt] *adj* valoroso; valorosa
gallery [GA•lu•ree] *n* galleria F
galley [GA•lee] *n* cambusa F
gallon [GA•ln] *n* gallone M
gallop [GA•lup] *n* galoppo M
gallows [GA•loz] *npl* forca F
gamble [GAM•bl] *n* azzardo M; *vt* rischiare; arrischiare; (game) giocare
game [gaim] *n* gioco M
gang [gang] *n* combriccola F
gangster [GANG•stur] *n* gangster M

gangway [GANG•wai] *n* passaggio M
gap [gap] *n* breccia F
gape [gaip] *vi* guardare a bocca aperta
gaping [GAI•ping] *adj* meravigliato; meravigliata
garage [gu•RAHZH] *n* garage M
garbage [GAHR•bij] *n* rifiuti F
garbage can [GAHR•bij KAN] *n* secchio dei rifiuti M
garden [GAHR•dn] *n* giardino M; *vt* fare del giardinaggio
gargle [GAHR•gl] *vi* gargarizzare
gargoyle [GAHR•goil] *n* doccione M
garland [GAHR•lund] *n* ghirlanda F
garlic [GAHR•lik] *n* aglio M
garment [GAHR•munt] *n* indumento M
garnish [GAHR•nish] *vt* guarnire

garrison [GA•ri•sn] *n*
presidio M

garter [GAHR•tr] *n*
giarrettiera F

gas [gas] *n* gas M

gaseous [GA•shs] *adj* gasoso;
gasosa

gasket [GA•skit] *n*
guarnizione F

gasoline [GA•su•LEEN] *n*
benzina F

gasp [gasp] *vi* boccheggiare

gate [gait] *n* cancello M

gather [GA•thur] *vi* raccogliere

gathering [GA•thu•ring] *n*
riunione F

gaudy [gau•dee] *adj* vistoso;
vistosa

gaunt [gaunt] *adj* emaciato;
emaciata•

gauntlet [GAUNT•lit] *n*
guanto M

gauze [gauz] *n* garza F

gay [gai] *adj* gaio; gaia; vivace;
allegro; omosessuale (coll)

gaze [gaiz] *vt* sguardo fisso M

gazette [gu•ZET] *n* gazzetta F

gear [geeur] *n* meccanismo M

gelatin [JE•lu•tin] *n* gelatina F

gem [jem] *n* gemma F

gender [JEN•dur] *n* genere M

gene [jeen] *n* gene M

general [JE•nu•rl] *adj n*
generale M

generalization
[JEN•ru•li•ZAI•shn] *n*
generalizzazione F

generalize [JE•nu•ru•LUYZ] *vt*
generalizzare

generally [JE•nu•ru•lee] *adv*
generalmente

generate [JE•nu•RAIT] *vt*
generare

generation [JE•nu•RAI•shn] *n*
generazione F

generator [JE•nu•RAI•tur] *n*
generatore M

generosity [JE•nu•RAH•si•tee]
n generositá F

generous [JE•nu•rus] *adj*
generoso; generosa

genetic [ji•NE•tik] *adj* genetico;
genetica

genial [JEE•nyul] *adj* gioviajle

genital [JE•ni•tl] *adj* genitale

genius [JEE•nyus] *n* genio M

gentle [JEN•tl] *adj* mite

gentleman [JEN•tl•mun] *n*
gentiluomo M

gently [JENT•lee] *adv*
gentilmente

gentry [JEN•tree] *n* nobiltá F

genuine [JE•nyoo•in] *adj*
genuino; genuina

geography [jee•AH•gru•fee] *n*
geografia F

geology [jee•AH•lu•jee] *n*
geologia F

geometric [JEE•u•ME•trik] *adj*
geometrico; geometrica

geometry [jee•AH•mu•tree] *n*
geometria F

germ [jerm] *n* germe M

German [JER•mun] *adj* tedesco;
tedesca

Germany [JER•mu•nee] *n*
Germania F

germinate [JER•mi•NAIT] *vi*
germinare

gesticulate [je•STI•kyu•LAIT]
vi gesticolare

gesture [JES•chur] *n* gesto M

get [get] *vt* ottenere; procurare;
(receive) ricevere;
(understand) capire; (reach)
arrivare

get away [GET•uh•WAI] *vi*
scappare

ghastly [GAST•lee] *adj*
orrendo; orrenda

ghost [gost] *n* fantasma M

giant [JUY•unt] *adj n*
gigante M

gibberish [JI•bu•rish] *n*
discorso inintelligibile M

giddy [GI•dee] *adj* vertiginoso;
vertiginosa

gift [gift] *n* regalo M

gifted [GIF•tid] *adj* dotato;
dotata

gigantic [juy•GAN•tik] *adj*
gigantesco; gigantesca

giggle [GI•gl] *vi* fare risatine

gilded [GIL•did] *adj* dorato;
dorata

ginger [JIN•jur] *n* zenzero M

gingerbread [JIN•jur•BRED] *n*
pan di zenzero M

gingerly [JIN•jur•lee] *adv* con
precauzione

gipsy [JIP•see] *n* zingaro;
zingara

giraffe [ji•RAF] *n* giraffa F

girder [GUR•dur] *n* trave
maestra F

girdle [GUR•dl] *n* ventriera F

girl [gurl] *n* ragazza F

girlfriend [GURL•frend] *n*
ragazza F

girth [gurth] *n* circonferenza F

gist [jist] *n* nocciolo M

give [giv] *vt* dare; (present)
regalare; (relinquish) cedere

given [GI•vn] *prep*
considerando

glacier [GLAI•shur] *n*
ghiacciaio M

glad [glad] *adj* contento;
contenta

gladly [GLAD•lee] *adv*
volentieri

glamor [GLA•mur] *n* n fascino
M; *adj* affascinante

glamorous [GLA•mu•rus] *adj*
attraente

glance [glans] *n* sguardo M; *vt*
dare unocchiata

gland [gland] *n* ghiandola F

glare [glaiur] *n* riverbero M; *vt*
~ at\ guardare con occhio
torvo

glaring [GLAIU•ring] *adj*
abbagliante

glass [glas] *n* vetro M

glasses [GLA•siz] *npl*
occhiali M

glassy [GLA•see] *adj* vitreo;
vitrea

glaze [glaiz] *n* vernice F; *vt*
smaltare; verniciare

gleam [gleem] *n* sprazzo M

glean [gleen] *vt* spigolare

glee [glee] *n* allegria F

glib [glib] *adj* loquace

glide [gluyd] *vi* scivolare

glimmer [GLI•mur] *n*
barlume M

glimpse [glimps] *n* visione F

glisten [GLI•sn] *vi* scintillare

glitter [GLI•tur] *v* rilucere

gloat [glot] *vi* esultare
silenziosamente

global [GLO•bl] *adj* globale

globe [glob] *n* globo M

gloom [gloom] *n* oscuritá F

gloomy [GLOO•mee] *adj* scuro; scura

glorify [GLAU•ri•FUY] *vt* glorificare

glorious [GLAU•ree•us] *adj* splendido; splendida

glory [GLAU•ree] *n* gloria F

gloss 1 [glaus] *n* lucentezza F

gloss 2 [glaus] *n* (explanation) chiosa F; *vt* chiosare; commentare

glossary [GLAU•su•ree] *n* glossario M

glossy [GLAU•see] *adj* lucido; lucida

glove [gluhv] *n* guanto M

glow [glo] *n* splendore M; *vi* risplendere

glowing [GLO•wing] *adj* splendente

glucose [GLOO•kos] *n* glucosio M

glue [gloo] *n* colla F

glum [gluhm] *adj* tetro; tetra

glut [gluht] *n* saturazione F

glutton [GLUH•tn] *n* ghiottone; ghiottona

gluttonous [GLUH•tu•nus] *adj* ghiotto; ghiotta

gluttony [GLUH•tu•nee] *n* ghiottoneria F

gnarled [nahrld] *adj* nodoso; nodosa

gnash [nash] *vt* digrignare

gnat [nat] *n* moscerino M

gnaw [nau] *vt* rodere

go [go] *vi* andare

go-between [GO•buh•TWEEN] *n* mezzano; mezzana

goal [goul] *n* scopo M

goat [got] *n* capra F

gobble [GAH•bl] *vt* trangugiare

goblin [GAH•blin] *n* demonietto M

God [gahd] *n* Dio M

goddaughter [GAHD•DAU•tur] *n* figlioccia F

goddess [GAH•dis] *n* dea F

godfather [GAHD•FAH•thur] *n* padrino M

godless [GAHD•lis] *adj* senza Dio

godmother [GAHD•MUH•thur] *n* madrina F

godsend [GAHD•send] *n* dono dal cielo M

goggles [GAH•glz] *npl* occhiali di protezione M

gold [gould] *n* oro M

gold-plated [GOLD•PLAI•tid] *adj* placcato; placcata (d'oro)

golden [GOL•dn] *adj* dorato; dorata

goldfish [GOLD•fish] *n* pesce rosso M

golf [gahlf] *n* golf M

gone [gahn] *v.* form *(p.p.)* andato; andata

gong [gahng] *n* gong M

good [gud] *adj* buono; buona; valido

good-looking [GUD•LU•king] *adj* bello; bella

goose [goos] *n* oca F

gore [gaur] *vt* sangue; *vt* trafiggere

gorge [gaurj] *n* gola F

gorgeous [GAUR•jus] *adj* magnifico; magnifica; splendido; splendida

gorilla [gu•RI•lu] *n* gorilla M

gory [GAU•ree] *adj* cruento; cruenta

gospel [GAH•spl] *n* vangelo M

gossip [GAH•sip] *n* pettegolezzo M; *vt* ciarlare; chiacchierare

gothic [GAH•thik] *adj* gotico; gotica

gourd [gaurd] *n* zucca F

gout [gout] *n* gotta F

govern [GUH•vurn] *vt vi* governare

governess [GUH•vur•nis] *n* governante F

government [GUH•vurn•munt] *n* governo M

governor [GUH•vur•nur] *n* governatore M

gown [goun] *n* abito M

grab [grab] *vt* afferrare

grace [grais] *n* grazia F

graceful [GRAIS•ful] *adj* leggiadro; leggiadra

gracious [GRAI•shus] *adj* cortese

grade [graid] *n* grado M; *vt* classificare

grade school [GRAID skool] *n* scuola elementare F

gradual [GRA•joo•ul] *adj* graduale

graduate [GRA•joo•AIT] *v* diplomarsi

graft [graft] *n* innesto M; (crime) *n* collusione F; *vt* innestarse

grain [grain] *n* grano M

gram [gram] *n* grammo M

grammar [GRA•mur] *n* grammatica F

grammatical [gru•MA•ti•kl] *adj* grammaticale

granary [GRAI•nu•ree] *n* granaio M

grand [grand] *adj* splendido; splendida

granddaughter [GRAN•DAU•tur] *n* nipote F

grandeur [GRAN•jur] *n* magnificenza F

grandfather [GRAND•FAH•thur] *n* nonno M

grandiose [GRAN•dee•OS] *adj* grandioso; grandiosa

grandma [GRAND•mah] *n* nonna F

grandmother [GRAND•MUH•thur] *n* nonna F

grandpa [GRAND•pah] *n* nonno M

grandparents [GRAND•PA•runts] *npl* nonni M

grandson [GRAND•suhn] *n* nipote M

granite [GRA•nit] *n* granito M

grant [grant] *n* concessione F; *vt* concedere; accordare; (give) dare

granule [GRA•nyoo•ul] *n* granello M

grape [graip] *n* chicco d'uva M

grapefruit [GRAIP•froot] *n* pompelmo M

graph [graf] *n* grafico M

graphic [GRA•fik] *adj* grafico;
grafica

grapple [GRA•pl] *vi* lottare

grasp [grasp] *vt* afferrare; *n*
presa F

grass [gras] *n* erba F

grasshopper [GRAS•HAH•pur]
n grillo M

grassy [GRA•see] *adj* erboso;
erbosa

grate [grait] *n* inferriata F; *vi*
grattugiare; stridere

grateful [GRAIT•ful] *adj* grato;
grata

grater [GRAI•tur] *n* grattugia F

gratification
[GRA•ti•fi•KAI•shn] *n*
ricompensa F

grating [GRAI•ting] *adj*
stridente

gratitude [GRA•ti•TOOD] *n*
gratitudine F

gratuity [gru•TOO•i•tee] *n*
mancia F

grave [graiv] *adj* grave

gravel [GRA•vl] *n* ghiaia F

gravity [GRA•vi•tee] *n*
gravitá F

gravy [GRAI•vee] *n* salsa F

gray [grai] *n* grigio M; *adj*
grigio; grigia

graze [graiz] *vt* passare rasente;
(livestock) *vi* pascolare

grease [grees] *n* unto M; *vt*
ungere; ingrassare

great [grait] *adj* grande

Great Britain [~ BRI•tn] *n*
Gran Bretagna F

great-granddaughter
[GRAIT•GRAN•DAW•tur] *n*
pronipote F

great-grandfather
[GRAIT•GRAND•FA•thur] *n*
bisnonno M

great-grandmother
[GRAIT•GRAND•MU•thur] *n*
bisnonna F

great-grandparents
[GRAIT•GRAND•PAI•rintz]
npl bisnonni M

great-grandson
[GRAIT•GRAND•son] *n*
pronipote M

greatness [GRAIT•nis] *n*
grandezza F

Greece [grees] *n* Grecia F

greed [greed] *n* aviditá F

greedy [GREE•dee] *adj* avid;
avida

Greek [greek] *adj* greco; greca

green [green] *adj n* verde

greenhouse [GREEN•hous] *n*
serra F

Greenland [GREEN•lund] *n*
Groenlandia F

greet [greet] *vt* salutare

greeting [GREE•ting] *n*
saluto M

grenade [gru•NAID] *n*
granata F

grid [grid] *n* griglia F

grief [greef] *n* dolore M

grievance [GREE•vuns] *n*
lagnanza F

grieve [greev] *vt* affliggere

grievous [GREE•vus] *adj*
doloroso; dolorosa

grill [gril] *n* griglia F; *vt*
cucinare ai ferri; (question)
sottoporre a un interrogatorio
severo

grille [gril] *n* griglia F

grim [grim] *adj* torvo; torva

grimace [GRI•mus] *n*
smorfia F

grime [gruym] *n* sudiciume M

grimy [GRUY•mee] *adj* sudicio;
sudicia

grin [grin] *n* sogghigno M; *vt*
fare un largo sorriso

grind [gruynd] *vt* macinare

grinder (coffee ~)
[GRUYN•dur] *n* macinino M

grip [grip] *n* presa F; *vt*
stingere; avvincere

gripe [gruyp] *n* lamentela F; *vt*
lagnarsi (coll)

grisly [GRIZ•lee] *adj* orribile

gristle [GRI•sl] *n* cartilagine F

grit [grit] *n* graniglia F; *vt*
(tteth) digrignare

groan [gron] *n* gemito M *vt*
gemere; lamentarsi

groceries [GROS•reez] *npl*
commestibili M

grocery (store) [GROS•ree] *n*
negozio d'alimentari M

groin [groin] *n* inguine M

groom [groom] *n* sposo M; *vt*
preparare; (horse) strigliare

groove [groov] *n* solco M

grope [grop] *vi* andare a tastoni

gross [gros] *n* grossa F; *adj*
volgare

grotesque [gro•TESK] *adj*
grottesco; grottesca

grouch [grouch] *n* brontolone;
brontolona

ground [ground] *n* terra F

ground floor [GROUND
FLOR] *n* piano terra M

groundless [GROUND•lis] *adj*
infondato; infondata

group [groop] *n* gruppo M

grove [grov] *n* boschetto M

grovel [GRAH•vl] *vi* strisciare

grow [gro] *vt* crescere

growl [grouul] *n* ringhiare

growth [groth] *n* crescita F

grub [gruhb] *n* larva F

grubby [GRUH•bee] *adj*
sporco; sporca

grudge [gruhj] *n* malanimo M

grueling [GROOU•ling] *adj*
estenuante

gruff [gruhf] *adj* burbero;
burbera

grumble [GRUHM•bl] *vi*
brontolare

grumpy [GRUHM•pee] *adj*
bisbetico; bisbetica

grunt [gruhnt] *n* grugnito M; *vt*
grugnier

guarantee [GA•run•TEE] *n*
garanzia F; *vt* garantire

guard [gahrd] *n* guardia F; *vt*
sorvegliare; custodire

guardian [GAHR•dee•un] *n*
guardiano; guardiana

guerrilla [gu•RI•lu] *n*
guerrilla M

guess [ges] *n* congettura F; *vt*
indovinare

guest [gest] *n* ospite

guestroom [GEST•ROOM] *n*
stanza degli ospiti F

guffaw [guh•FAU] *vi* risata F

guidance [GUY•duns] *n*
guida F

guide [guyd] *n* guida F; (of
tourists) ciceronne M; *vt*
guidare

guild [gild] *n* corporazione F

guile [guyul] *n* scaltrezza F

guillotine [GI•lu•TEEN] *n*
ghigliottina F

guilt [gilt] *n* colpa F

guilty [GIL•tee] *adj* colpevole

guinea pig [GI•nee ~] *n*
cavia F

guise [guyz] *n* aspetto M

guitar [gi•TAHR] *n* chitarra F

gulf [guhlf] *n* golfo M

gullet [GUH•lit] *n* gola F

gullible [GUH•li•bl] *adj*
credulone; credulona

gully [GUH•lee] *n* gola F

gulp [guhlp] *vt* trangugiare

gum [guhm] *n* gomma F

gun [guhn] *n* fucile M

gunfire [GUHN•fuyur] *n*
sparatoria F

gunpowder [GUHN•pow•dur]
n polvere da sparo F

gunshot [GUHN•shaht] *n*
sparo M

gurgle [GUR•gl] *vi* gorgogliare

gush [guhsh] *n* getto M; *vi*
scaturire; (speech) parlare con
effusione

gusset [GUH•sit] *n* gherone M

gust (of wind) [guhst] *n*
raffica F

gut [guht] *n* budella F

gutter [GUH•tur] *n* grondaia F

guy [guy] *n* tipo M

guzzle [GUH•zl] *vt* rimpinzarsi

gym [jim] *n* palestra F

gymnasium [jim•NAI•zee•um]
n palestra F

gymnast [JIM•nust] *n* ginnasta

gymnastics [jim•NA•stiks] *npl*
ginnastica F

Gypsy [JIP•see] *n adj* zingaro;
zingara

gyrate [JUY•rait] *vi* ruotare

H

habit 1 [HA•bit] *n* abitudine F

habit 2 [HA•bit] (monastic) *n*
abito M

habitual [hu•BI•choo•ul] *adj*
solito; solita

hack 1 [hak] *vt* fare a pezzi

hack 2 [hak] *n* ronzino M
(~ writer) scribacchino M

hackneyed [HAK•need] *adj*
trito; trita

hacksaw [HAK•sau] *n*
seghetta F

haggard [HA•gurd] *adj* sparuto;
sparuta

haggle [HA•gl] *vi* cavillare

hail1 [haiul] *n* grandine F

hail 2 [haiul] *vt* salutare;
chiamare

hailstone [HAIUL•ston] *n*
chicco di grandine M

hair [haiur] *n* capello M; *npl*
capelli M

hairbrush [HAIUR•bruhsh] *n*
spazzola F

haircut [HAIUR•kuht] *n* taglio
dei capelli M

hairdresser [HAIUR•DRE•sur]
n parrucchiere M

hairless [HAIUR•lis] *adj* calvo; calva

hairpin [HAIUR•pin] *n* forcina F

hairspray [HAIUR•sprai] *n* lacca F

hairstyle [HAIUR•stuyul] *n* pettinatura F

hairy [HAIUR•ee] *adj* peloso; pelosa

Haiti [HAI•tee] *n* Haiti M

half [haf] *adj* mezzo; mezza

half-hearted [~ HAR•tid] *adj* a malincuore

half hour [HAF OUR] *n* mezz'ora F

half-mast [HAF•MAST] *adj* abbrunato; abbrunata

half-price [HAF•PRUYS] *adj* a metá prezzo

halfway [HAF•WAI] *adj adv* a metá strada

halibut [HA•li•but] *n* passero di mare M

hall [haul] *n* sala F

hallowed [HA•lod] *adj* consacrato; consacrata

Halloween [HAH•lo•WEEN] *n* vigilia di Ognissanti F

hallucination [hu•LOO•si•NAI•shn] *n* allucinazione F

hallway [HAUL•wai] *n* vestibolo M

halo [HAI•lo] *n* aureola F

halt [hault] *n* sosta F; (stop) *vt* fermare

halter [HAUL•tur] *n* cavezza F

halve [hav] *vt* tagliare a metá

ham [ham] *n* prosciutto M

hamburger [HAM•BUR•gur] *n* hamburger M

hamlet [HAM•lit] *n* paesino M

hammer [HA•mur] *n* martello M; *vt* martellare

hammock [HA•muk] *n* amaca F

hamper [HAM•pur] *n* canestro M

hand [hand] *n* mano F

handbag [HAND•bag] *n* borsetta F

handcuff [HAND•kuhf] *n* manette F

handful [HAND•ful] *n* manciata F

handicap [HAN•dee•KAP] *n* handicap M

handicapped [HAN•dee•KAPT] *adj* andicappato; andicappata

handkerchief [HANG•kur•chif] *n* fazzoletto M

handle [HAN•dl] *n* manico M

handmade [HAND•MAID] *adj* fatto a mano; fatta a mano

handshake [HAND•shaik] *n* stretta di mano F

handwriting [HAND•WRUY•ting] *n* scrittura F

handy [HAN•dee] (near) *adj* sottomano; (skilled) *adj* abile

hang [hang] *vt* appendere

hangar [HANG•ur] *n* hangar M

hanger [HANG•ur] *n* attaccapanni M

hangover [HANG•O•vur] *npl* postumi di una sborina M

haphazard [hap•HA•zurd] *adj* casuale

hapless [HAP•lis] *adj*
sfortunato; sfortunata
happen [HA•pn] *vi* accadere
happening [HA•pu•ning] *n*
avvenimento M
happily [HA•pi•lee] *adv*
fortunatamente
happiness [HA•pee•nis] *n*
felicitá F
happy [HA•pee] *adj* felice
harass [hu•RAS] *vt* tormentare
harassment [hu•RAS•munt] *n*
vessazione F
harbor [HAHR•bur] *n* porto M
hard [hahrd] *adj* duro; dura
harden [HAHR•din] *vt* indurire
hardly [HAHRD•lee] *adv* a
malpena
hardship [HAHRD•ship] *n*
avveritá F
hardware [HAHRD•waiur] *n*
ferramenta F (computer)
meccanismo M
hardworking
[HAHRD•WUR•king] *adj*
lavoratore; lavoratrice
hardy [HAHR•dee] *adj* robusto;
robusta
hare [haiur] *n* lepre F
harm [hahrm] *n* torto M; *vt*
nuocere a; far male a
harmful [HAHRM•ful] *adj*
dannoso; dannosa
harmless [HAHRM•lis] *adj*
innocuo; innocua
harmonica [hahr•MAH•ni•ku] *n*
armonica a bocca F
harmonious [hahr•MO•nee•us]
adj armonioso; armoniosa
harmonize [HAHR•mu•NUYZ]
vt armonizzare

harmony [HAHR•mu•nee] *n*
armonia F
harness [HAHR•nis] *n*
finimenti M
harp [hahrp] *n* arpa F
harpoon [hahr•POON] *n*
arpione M
harpsichord
[HARP•si•KAURD] *n*
clavicembalo M
harsh [hahrsh] *adj* ruvido;
ruvida
harvest [HAHR•vist] *n* raccolto
M; *vt* raccogliere; mietere
haste [haist] *n* fretta F
hasten [HAI•sn] *vt* affrettare
hastily [HAI•sti•lee] *adv* in
fretta
hat [hat] *n* cappello M
hatch [hach] *vt* covare
hatchet [HA•chit] *n* accetta F
hate [hait] *n* odio M; *vt* odiare;
adj odioso; odiosa
hateful [HAIT•ful] *adj* odioso;
odiosa
hatred [HAI•trid] *n* odio M
haughty [HAU•tee] *adj*
altezzoso; altezzosa
haul [haul] *vt* trasportare
haunt [haunt] *vt* frequentare
have [hav] *aux verb* avere; ~ to\
avere de; dovere
haven [HAI•vn] *n* rifugio M
havoc [HA•vuk] *n* rovina F
hawk [hauk] *n* sparviero M
hay [hai] *n* fieno M
haystack [HAI•stak] *n*
covone M
hazard [HA•zurd] *n* pericolo M;
vt azzardare

hazardous [HA•zur•dus] *adj*
pericosa; pericolosa

haze [haiz] *n* foschia F

hazelnut [HAI•zl•NUHT] *n*
nocciola F

hazy [HAI•zee] *adj* nebbioso;
nebbiosa

he [hee] *pers pron* egli; lui M

head [hed] *n* capo M

headache [HE•daik] *n* mal di
testa M

heading [HE•ding] *n*
intestazione F

headlight [HED•luyt] *n* faro M

headline [HED•luyn] *n* titolo M

headphones [HED•fonz] *npl*
cuffia F

headquarters
[HED•KAUR•turz] *npl*
quartier generale M

headrest [HED•rest] *n*
poggiatesta M

headstrong [HED•straung] *adj*
ostinato; ostinata

headway [HED•wai] *n*
progresso M

heal [heeul] *vt* guarire

health [helth] *n* salute F

healthy [HEL•thee] *adj* sano;
sana

heap [heep] *n* mucchio M; *vt*
ammucchiare

hear [heeur] *vt* udire; sentire

hearing [HEEU•ring] *n* udito M

hearsay [HEEUR•sai] *n* sentito
dire M

hearse [hurs] *n* carro funebre M

heart [hahrt] *n* cuore M

heart attack [HART a•TAK] *n*
attacco cardiaco M

heartbeat [HAHRT•beet] *n*
pulsazione F

heartbroken
[HAHRT•BRO•kn] *adj*
desolato; desolata

hearth [hahrth] *n* focolare M

heartless [HAHRT•lis] *adj*
senza cuore

heartwarming
[HAHRT•WAR•ming] *adj*
confortante

hearty [HAHR•tee] *adj* cordiale

heat [heet] *n* calore M

heater [HEE•tur] *n* stufa F

heather [HE•thur] *n* erica F

heating [HEE•ting] *n*
riscaldamento M

heat wave [HEET WAIV] *n*
ondata di caldo F

heave [heev] *vt* sollevare

heaven [HE•vn] *n* cielo M

heavenly [HE•vn•lee] *adj*
celestiale

heavily [HE•vu•lee] *adv*
pesantemente

heavy [HE•vee] *adj* pesante

heckle [HE•kl] *vt* interrompere
con critiche

hectic [HEK•tik] *adj* febbrile

hedge [hej] *n* siepe F; *vt* (bet)
coprire dai rischi

hedgehog [HEJ•hahg] *n*
riccio M

heed [heed] *vt* seguire

height [huyt] *n* altezza F

heighten [HUY•tn] *vt*
accrescere

heir [aiur] *n* erede

heiress [AIU•ress] *n* erediteira

heirloom [AIUR•loom] *n*
cimelio di casa M

helicopter [HE•li•KAHP•tur] *n*
elicottero M

hell [hel] *n* inferno M

hellish [HE•lish] *adj* infernale

hello [hu•LO] *excl* ciao

helm [helm] *n* timone M

helmet [HEL•mit] *n* elmo M

help [help] *n* aiuto M;
assistenze F; *vt* aiutare;
assistere

helper [HEL•pur] *n* aiutante

helping [HEL•ping] *n*
porzione F

helpless [HELP•lis] *adj*
indifeso; indifesa

hem [hem] *n* orlo M

hemisphere [HE•mis•FEEUR]
n emisfero M

hemorrhage [HE•mu•rij] *n*
emoraggia F

hemorrhoids [HE•mu•roidz]
npl emorroidi F

hen [hen] *n* gallina F

henhouse [HEN•hous] *n*
pollaio M

hence [hens] *adv* perció

henceforth [HENS•faurth] *adv*
d'ora in avanti

her [hur] *pers pron* la; lei; *adj*
suo; sua; suoi; sue

herald [HE•ruld] *n* araldo M

heraldry [HE•rul•dree] *n*
araldica F

herb [urb] *n* erba F

herbal [UR•bl] *adj* alle erbe

herd [hurd] *n* mandria F

here [heeur] *adv* qui

hereby [heer•BY] *conj* con
questo mezzo

hereditary [he•RE•di•TE•ree]
adj ereditario; ereditaria

heredity [he•RE•di•tee] *n*
ereditarietá F

herein [heer•IN] *adv* nella
presente

heresy [HE•ru•see] *n* eresia F

herewith [heeur•WITH] *adv*
qui accluso; qui acclusa

heritage [HE•ri•tij] *n*
retaggio M

hermit [HUR•mit] *n* eremita M

hernia [HUR•nee•u] *n* ernia F

hero [HEEU•ro] *n* eroe M

heroic [hu•RO•ik] *adj* eroico;
eroica

heroin [HE•ro•in] *n* eroina F

heroine [HE•ro•in] *n* eroina F

heroism [HE•ro•I•zm] *n*
eroismo M

heron [HE•run] *n* airone M

herring [HE•ring] *n* aringa F

hers [hurz] *poss pron* il suo; la
sua

herself [hur•SELF] *pron* lei
stessa F

hesitant [HE•zi•tunt] *adj*
esitante

hesitate [HE•zi•TAIT] *vi*
esitare

hesitation [HE•zi•TAI•shn] *n*
esitazione F

heterosexual
[HE•tu•ro•SEK•shoo•ul] *adj n*
eterosessuale

hexagon [HEK•su•GAHN] *n*
esagono M

hey [hai] *excl* ehi

heyday [HAI•dai] *n* apice M

hibernate [HUY•bur•NAIT] *vi*
svernare

hibernation
[HUY•bur•NAI•shn] *n*
letargo M

hiccup [HI•kuhp] *n*
singhiozzo M

hidden [HI•dn] *adj* nascosto;
nascosta

hide [huyd] *vt* nascondere

hideous [HI•dee•us] *adj*
orrendo; orrenda

hiding [HUY•ding] *n*
bastonatura F

hiding place [HUY•ding
PLAIS] *n* nascondiglio M

hierarchy [HUYU•RAHR•kee]
n gerarchia F

high [huy] *adj* alt; alta

high school [HUY skool] *n*
liceo M

highlight [HUY•luyt] *n*
culmine M

highly [HUY•lee] *adj* altamente

highness [HUY•nis] *n* altezza F

highway [HUY•wai] *n*
autostrada F

hike [huyk] *vt* fare
un'escursione

hilarious [hi•LAU•ree•us] *adj*
buffo; buffa

hill [hil] *n* collina F

hillside [HIL•suyd] *n* pendio M

hilltop [HIL•tahp] *n* sommitá F

hilly [HI•lee] *adj* collinoso;
collinosa

hilt [hilt] *n* elsa F

him [him] *pers pron* lui; lo;
gli M

himself [him•SELF] *pron* lui
stesso M

hind [huynd] *adj* posteriore

hinder [HIN•dur] *vt* impedire

hindrance [HIN•druns] *n*
impaccio M

Hindu [HIN•doo] *adj* indú

hinge [hinj] *n* cardine M; *vi*
(depend) dipendere (da)

hint [hint] *n* suggerimento M; *vt*
suggerire M

hip [hip] *n* fianco M

hippopotamus
[HI•pu•PAH•tu•mus] *n*
ippopotamo M

hire [huyur] *vt* ingaggiare

his [huiz] *poss adj* suo; sua

Hispanic [hi•SPAN•ik] *adj*
ispanico; ispanica

hiss [his] *vi* sibilare

historian [hi•STAU•ree•un] *n*
storico M

historic [hi•STAU•rik] *adj*
storico; storica

history [HI•stu•ree] *n* storia F

hit [hit] *n* colpo M

hitch [hich] *vt* legare

hitchhike [HICH•huyk] *vi* fare
l'autostop

hitchhiker [HICH•HUY•kur] *n*
autostoppista

hitherto [HI•thur•TOO] *adv*
finora

hive [huyv] *n* alveare M

hoard [haurd] *n* tesoro M

hoarse [haurs] *adj* rauco; rauca

hoax [hoks] *n* burla F

hobble [HAH•bl] *vi* impastoiare

hobby [HAH•bee] *n* hobby M

hobo [HO•bo] *n* vagabondo;
vagabonda

hockey [HAH•kee] *n* hockey M

hocus-pocus [HO•kus•PO•kus]
n truffa F

hog [hahg] *n* maiale M

hoist [hoist] *vt* sollevare; *n*
montacarichi M

hold [hold] *n* presa F; stretta F;
vt afferrare; ottenere; tenere;
contenere

holder [HOL•dur] *n*
contenitore M

holding [HOL•ding] *n*
patrimonio M

holdup [HOLD•uhp] *n* rapina a
mano armata F

hole [hol] *n* buco M

holiday [HAH•li•DAI] *n* festa F

holiness [HO•lee•nis] *n*
santitá F

Holland [HAH•lund] *n*
Olanda F

hollow [HAH•lo] *adj* vuoto;
vuota; *n* cavo M

holly [HAH•lee] *n* pungitopo M

holocaust [HAH•lu•KAUST] *n*
olocausto M

holster [HOL•stur] *n* fondina F

holy [HO•lee] *adj* santo; santa

home [hom] *n* casa F; ~ land\
patria F; *adj* domestico;
casalingo

homeland [HOM•land] *n*
patria F

homeless [HOM•lis] *adj n*
senza tetto

homely [HOM•lee] *adj* scialbo;
scialba

homemade [HOM•MAID] *adj*
fatto in casa

homesick [HOM•sik] *n*
nostalgico; nostalgica

homeward [HOM•wurd] *adv*
verso casa

homework [HOM•wurk] *n*
compiti di casa M

homicide [HAH•mi•SUYD] *n*
omicidio M

homosexual
[HO•mo•SEK•shoo•ul] *adj n*
omosessuale

honest [AH•nist] *adj* onesto;
onesta

honesty [AH•ni•stee] *n*
onestá F

honey [HU•nee] *n* miele M

honeymoon
[HUH•nee•MOON] *n* luna di
miele F

honk [hahngk] *vi* ssuono del
clakson M

honor [AH•nur] *n* onore M

honorable [AH•nu•ru•bl] *adj*
onorevole

hood [hud] *n* cappuccio M

hoodlum [HUD•lum] *n* teppista

hoodwink [HUD•wingk] *vt*
imbrogliare

hoof [huf] *n* zoccolo M

hook [huk] *n* uncino M; *vt*
agganciare

hooky (to play) [HU•kee] *vt*
marinare (la scuola)

hoop [hoop] *n* cerchio M

hoot [hoot] *n* urlo M

hop [hahp] *vt* saltellare; *n*
salterello M

hope [hop] *n* speranza F

hopeful [HOP•ful] *adj*
fiducioso; fiduciosa

hopeless [HOP•lis] *adj*
sfiduciato; sfiduciata

horizon [hu•RUY•zn] *n*
orizzonte M

horizontal [HAU•ri•ZAHN•tl]
adj orizzontale

hormone [HAUR•mon] *n*
ormone M

horn [haurn] *n* corno M

hornet [HAUR•nit] *n* vespa F

horoscope [HAU•ru•SKOP] *n* oroscopo M

horrible [HAU•ri•bl] *adj* orribile

horrid [HAU•rid] *adj* orrido; orrida

horrify [HAU•ri•FUY] *vt* atterrire

horror [HAU•rur] *n* orrore M

horse [haurs] *n* cavallo M

horseback [HAURS•bak] *adj adv* a cavallo

horsepower [HAURS•POU•wur] *n* potenza cavalli F

horseradish [HAURS•RA•dish] *n* rafano M

horseshoe [HAURS•shoo] *n* ferro di cavallo M

hose [hoz] *n* manichetta F

hosiery [HO•zhu•ree] *n* calze F

hospitable [hah•SPI•tu•bl] *adj* ospitale

hospital [HAH•spi•tl] *n* ospedale M

hospitality [HAH•spi•TA•li•tee] *n* ospitalitá F

host [host] *n* ospite

hostage [HAH•stij] *n* ostaggio M

hostess [HO•stis] *n* ospite

hostile [HAH•stul] *adj* ostile

hostility [hah•STI•li•tee] *n* ostilitá F

hot [haht] *adj* caldo; calda

hot dog [HAHT daug] *n* salsiccia F

hot plate [HAHT plait] *n* fornello M

hot-tempered [HOT•TEM•purd] *adj* impetuoso; impetuosa

hotel [ho•TEL] *n* albergo M

hound [hound] *n* cane da caccia M

hour [ouur] *n* ora F

hourglass [OUUR•glas] *n* clessidra F

hourly [OUUR•lee] *adj adv* orario; oraria

house [n. hous v. houz] *n* casa F

housekeeper [HOUS•KEE•pur] *n* domestico; domestica

housekeeping [HOUS•KEE•ping] *n* andamento di casa M

housewife [HOUS•wuyf] *n* casalinga F

housework [HOUS•wurk] *n* lavori di casa M

housing [HOU•zing] *n* alloggio M

hovel [HUH•vl] *n* tugurio M

hover [HUH•vur] *vi* ronzare intorno

how [hou] *adv* come

however [hou•E•vur] *conj* comunque

howl [houul] *n* ululo M

hub [huhb] *n* centro M

huddle [HUH•dl] *vi* consultazione segreta F

hue [hyoo] *n* tinta F

huff [huhf] *n* stizza F

hug [huhg] *n* abbraccio M; *vt* abbracciare

huge [hyooj] *adj* enorme

hull 1 [huhl] *n* baccello M

hull 2 (of a ship) [huhl] *n* scafo
M

hum [huhm] *vt* cantare bocca
chiusa

human [HYOO•mun] *adj n*
umano; umana

human being [HYU•min
BEE•ing] *n* essere umano M

human rights [HYU•min
RUYTS] *npl* diritti umani M

humane [hyoo•MAIN] *adj*
umano; umana

humanitarian
[hyoo•MA•ni•TA•ree•un] *adj*
umanitario; umanitaria

humanity [hyoo•MA•ni•TEE] *n*
umanitá F

humble [HUHM•bl] *adj* umile

humid [HYOO•mid] *adj* umido;
umida

humidity [hyoo•MI•di•tee] *n*
umiditá F

humiliate [hyoo•MI•lee•AIT] v
umiliare

humiliation
[hyoo•MI•lee•AI•shn] *n*
umiliazione F

humility [hyoo•MI•li•tee] *n*
umiltá F

hummingbird
[HUH•ming•BURD] *n*
colibrí M

humor [HYOO•mur] *n*
umorismo M

humorous [HYOO•mu•rus] *adj*
comico; comica

hump [huhmp] *n* gobba F

hunch [huhnch] *n* impressione F

hunchback [HUHNCH•bak] *n*
gobbo; gobba

hunched [huhnchd] *adj* curvo;
curva

hundred [HUHN•drud] *num*
cento

hundredth [HUHN•druth] *num*
centesimo; centesima

Hungarian
[HUNG•GAU•ree•un] *adj*
ungherese

Hungary [HUNG•gu•ree] *n*
Ungheria F

hunger [HUNG•gur] *n* fame F

hungry [HUNG•gree] *adj*
affamato; affamata

hunt [huhnt] *n* caccia F; *vt*
andare a caccia di; inseguire;
cercare affanosamente

hunter [HUHN•tur] *n*
cacciatore M

hurdle [HUR•dl] *n* ostacolo M

hurl [hurl] *vt* lanciare

hurricane [HU•ri•KAIN] *n*
uragano M

hurried [HU•reed] *adj*
affrettato; affrettata

hurriedly [HU•red•lee] *adv*
frettolosamente

hurry [HU•ree] *n* fretta F

hurt [hurt] *vt* fare male; *n* male
M; dolore M

hurtful [HURT•ful] *adj* che fa
soffrire

husband [HUHZ•bund] *n*
marito M

hush [huhsh] *n* silenzio M; *vt*
far tacere

husk [huhsk] *n* cartoccio M

husky [HUH•skee] *adj* robusto;
robusta

hustle [HUH•sl] *n* fretta F; *vt*
spingere

hut [huht] *n* capanna F

hutch [huhch] *n* conigliera F

hyacinth [HUY•u•SINTH] *n*
giacinto M

hybrid [HUY•brid] *adj n* ibrido;
ibrida

hydrant [HUY•drunt] *n*
idrante F

hydraulic [huy•DRAU•lik] *adj*
idraulico; idraulica

hydrogen [HUY•dru•jun] *n*
idrogeno M

hyena [huy•EE•nu] *n* iena F

hygiene [HUY•jeen] *n* igiene F

hymn [him] *n* inno M

hyperactive [HUY•pur•AK•tiv]
adj iperattivo; iperattiva

hyphen [HUY•fn] *n* lineetta F

hypnosis [hip•NO•sis] *n*
ipnosi F

hypnotic [hip•NAH•tik] *adj*
ipnotico; ipnotica

hypnotize [HIP•nu•TUYZ] *vt*
ipnotizzare

hypocrisy [hi•PAH•kri•see] *n*
ipocrisia F

hypocrite [HI•pu•KRIT] *n*
ipocrita

hypocritical [HI•pu•KRI•ti•kl]
adj ipocrita

hypothesis [huy•PAH•thi•sis] *n*
ipotesi F

hypothetical
[HUY•pu•THE•ti•kl] *adj*
ipotetico; ipotetica

hysterical [hi•STE•ri•kl] *adj*
isterico; isterica

hysterics [hi•STE•riks] *npl*
attacco isterico M

I

I [uy] *pers pron* io

ice [uys] *n* ghiaccio M

ice cube [UYS KYUB] *n*
cubetto di ghiaccio M

ice skating [UYS SKAI•ting] *n*
pattinaggio sul ghiaccio M

ice-cream [uys•KREEM] *n*
gelato M

ice-skate [UY•skait] *vi* pattinare
sul ghiaccio

iceberg [UYS•burg] *n* iceberg

Iceland [UYS•lund] *n* Islanda F

icing [UY•sing] *n* glassa F

icy [UY•see] *adj* ghiacciato;
ghiacciata

idea [uy•DEE•u] *n* idea F

ideal [uy•DEEUL] *adj n* ideale

idealism [i•DEEUL•izm] *n*
idealismo M

idealistic [uy•DEEU•LI•stik]
adj idealistico; idealistica

identical [uy•DEN•ti•kl] *adj*
identico; identica

identification
[uy•DEN•ti•fi•KAI•shn] *n*
riconoscimento M

identify [uy•DEN•ti•FUY] *vt*
identificare

identity [uy•DEN•ti•tee] *n*
identitá F

ideology [UY•dee•AH•lu•jee] *n*
ideologia F

idiot [I•dee•ut] *n* idiota

idiotic [I•dee•AH•tik] *adj* idiota

idle [UY•dl] *adj* ozioso; oziosa;
vano; *vi* stare seza far nulla

idol [UY•dl] *n* idolo M

idolize [UY•du•LUYZ] *vt*
idolatrare

if [if] *conj* se; come se

ignite [ig•NUYT] *vt* accendere

ignition [ig•NI•shn] *n* messa in
moto F

ignorance [IG•nu•runs] *n*
ignoranza F

ignorant [IG•nu•runt] *adj*
ignorante

ignore [ig•NAUR] *vt* ignorare

ill [il] *adj* malato; malata

ill at ease [IL at EEZ] *adj* a
disagio

ill will [IL WIL] *n* malanimo M

illegal [i•LEE•gl] *adj* illegale

illegitimate [I•li•JI•ti•mut] *adj*
illegittimo; illegittima

illicit [i•LI•sit] *adj* illecito;
illecta

illiteracy [i•LI•tu•ru•see] *n*
analfabetismo M

illiterate [i•LI•tu•rut] *adj*
analfabeta

illness [IL•nis] *n* malattia F

illogical [i•LAH•ji•kl] *adj*
illogico; illogica

illuminate [i•LOO•mi•NAIT] *vt*
illuminare

illusion [i•LOO•zhn] *n*
illusione F

illustrate [I•lu•STRAIT] *vt*
illustrare

illustration [I•lu•STRAI•shn] *n*
illustrazione F

illustrious [i•LUH•stree•us] *adj*
illustre

image [I•mij] *n* immagine F

imagery [I•mu•jree] *n*
immagini F

imaginary [i•MA•ji•NE•ree] *adj*
immaginario; immaginaria

imagination [i•MA•ji•NAI•shn]
n immaginazione F

imaginative [i•MA•ji•nu•tiv]
adj fantasioso; fantasiosa

imagine [i•MA•jin] *vt*
immaginare

imbalance [im•BA•luns] *n*
squilibrio M

imbecile [IM•bu•sil] *n* imbecille

imitate [I•mi•TAIT] *vt* imitare

imitation [I•mi•TAI•shn] *n*
imitazione F

immaculate [i•MA•kyu•lut] *adj*
immacolato; immacolata

immaterial [I•mu•TEEU•ree•ul]
adj immateriale

immature [I•mu•CHOOUR] *adj*
immaturo; immatura

immediate [i•MEE•dee•ut] *adj*
immediato; immediata

immediately
[i•MEE•dee•ut•lee] *adv*
immediatamente

immense [i•MENS] *adj*
immenso; immensa

immerse [i•MURS] *vt*
immergere

immigrant [I•mi•grunt] *n*
immigrante

immigration [I•mi•GRAI•shn]
n immigrazione F

imminent [I•mi•nunt] *adj*
imminente

immobile [i•MO•bl] *adj*
immobile

immobilize [i•MO•bi•LUYZ] *vt*
immobilizzare

immoral [i•MAU•rl] *adj*
immorale

immorality [I•mau•RA•li•tee] *n*
immoralitá F

immortal [i•MAUR•tl] *adj*
immortale

immortality
[I•MAUR•TA•li•tee] *n*
immortalitá

immune [i•MYOON] *adj*
immune

immunity [i•MYOO•ni•tee] *n*
immunitá F

immunize [I•myu•NUYZ] *vt*
immunizzare

imp [imp] *n* diavoletto M

impact [IM•pakt] *n* impatto M

impair [im•PAIUR] *vt*
menomare

impart [im•PAHRT] *vt*
impartire

impartial [im•PAHR•shl] *adj*
imparziale

impassioned [im•PASH•und]
adj veemente

impatience [im•PAI•shns] *n*
impazienza F

impatient [im•PAI•shnt] *adj*
impaziente

impeach [im•PEECH] *vt*
accusare

impede [im•PEED] *n* impedire

impediment [im•PE•di•munt *n*
impedimento M

impel [im•PEL] *vt* incitare

imperative [im•PE•ru•tiv] *adj*
imperativo; imperativa

imperfect [im•PUR•fikt] *adj*
imperfetto; imperfetta

imperial [im•PEEU•ree•ul] *adj*
imperiale

imperious [im•PEEU•ree•us]
adj imperioso; imperiosa

impersonal [im•PUR•su•nl] *adj*
impersonale

impersonate
[im•PUR•so•NAIT]
impersonare

impertinent [im•PUR•ti•nunt]
adj impertinente

impervious [im•PUR•vee•us]
adj impervio; impervia

impetuous [im•PE•choo•us] *adj*
impetuoso; impetuosa

impetus [IM•pit•tus] *n*
impeto M

implant [im•PLANT] *vt* fissare

implement [n. IM•pli•munt v.
IM•pli•MENT] *n* apparecchio
M; *vt* adempiere

implicate [IM•pli•KAIT] *vt*
implicare

implicit [im•PLI•sit] *adj*
implicito; implicita

implore [im•PLAUR] *vt*
implorare

imply [im•PLUY] *vt* insinuare

impolite [IM•pu•LUYT] *adj*
scortese

import [n. IM•paurt v.
im•PAURT] *vt* importare; *n*
importazione M; importanza F

importance [im•PAUR•tuns] *n*
importanza F

important [im•PAUR•tunt] *adj*
importante

impose [im•POZ] *vt* imporre

imposition [IM•po•ZI•shn] *n*
imposizione F

impossible [im•PAH•si•bl] *adj*
impossibile

impostor [im•PAH•stur] *n*
impostore M

impotent [IM•pu•tunt] *adj*
impotente M

impress [im•PRES] *vt*
imprimere

impression [im•PRE•shn] *n*
impressione F

impressive [im•PRE•siv] *adj*
imponente

imprint [IM•print] *n* impronta F

imprison [im•PRI•zn] *vt*
imprigionare

improbable [im•PRAH•bu•bl]
adj improbabile

improper [im•PRAH•pur] *adj*
scorretto; scorretta

improve [im•PROOV] *vt*
migliorare

improvement
[im•PROOV•munt] *n*
miglioramento M

improvise [IM•pruh•VUYZ] *vt*
vi improvvisare

imprudent [im•PROO•dunt] *adj*
imprudente

impudent [IM•pyu•dunt] *adj*
impudente

impulsive [im•PUHL•siv] *adj*
impulsivo; impulsiva

impunity [im•PYOO•ni•tee] *n*
impunitá F

impure [im•PYUR] *adj* impuro;
impura

impurity [im•PYU•ri•tee] *n*
impuritá F

in [in] *prep* in; tra; entro; *adv*
dentro a (casa) in (sede)

in love (with) innamorato;
innamorata (di)

in-laws [IN•lauz] *npl* suoceri M

inability [I•nu•BI•li•tee] *n*
inabilitá F

inaccurate [in•A•kyu•rut] *adj*
inaccurato; inaccurata

inactive [in•AK•tiv] *adj*
inattivo; inattiva

inadequate [in•A•du•kwit] *adj*
inadeguato; indeguata

inadvertent [IN•ud•VER•tunt]
adj involontario; involontaria

inane [i•NAIN] *adj* inane

inanimate [in•AN•uh•muht] *adj*
inanimato; inanimata

inappropriate
[IN•u•PRO•pree•ut] *adj*
improprio; impropria

inauguration
[i•NAU•gyu•RAI•shn] *n*
inaugurazione F

incapable [in•KAI•pu•bl] *adj*
incapace

incense 1 [IN•sens] *n*
incenso M

incense 2 [in•SENS] *vi* irritare;
provocare

incentive [in•SEN•tiv] *n*
incentivo M

incessant [in•SE•sunt] *adj*
incessante

inch [inch] *n* pollice M; *vt* ~
forward\ avanzara poco alla
volta

incident [IN•si•dunt] *n*
incidente M

incidental [IN•si•DEN•tl] *adj*
fortuito; fortuita

incite [in•SUYT] *vt* incitare

incline [in•KLUYN] *n* pendio
M; *vt* inclinare; chinare; be ~d
to\ essere propenso

include [in•KLOOD] *vt*
includere

including [in•KLOO•ding] *adj*
compreso; compresa

income [IN•kuhm] *n* entrata F

income tax [IN•kum TAKS] *n*
imposta sui redditi F

incomparable
[in•KAHM•pra•bl] *adj*
incomparabile

incompatible
[IN•kum•PA•ti•bl] *adj*
incompatibile

incompetent
[in•KAHM•pu•tunt] *adj*
incompetente

incomplete [IN•kum•PLEET]
adj incompleto; incompleta

inconsiderate
[IN•kun•SI•du•rut] *adj*
sconsiderato; sconsiderata

inconsistent [IN•kun•SIS•tnt]
adj inconsistente

inconspicuous
[IN•kun•SPI•kyoo•us] *adj*
insignificante

inconvenient
[IN•kun•VEE•nyunt] *adj*
incomodo; incomoda

incorporate
[in•KAUR•pu•RAIT] *vt*
incorporare

incorrect [IN•ku•REKT] *adj*
scorretto; scorretta

increase [n. IN•krees v.
in•KREES] *n* aumento M; *vi*

aumentare; ingrandirsi;
crescere

increasingly
[in•KREE•sing•lee] *adv*
sempre piú

incredible [in•KRE•di•bl] *adj*
incredibile

incredulous [in•KRE•dyu•lus]
adj incredulo; incredula

incriminate [in•KRI•mi•NAIT]
vt incriminare

incur [in•KUR] *vt* incorrere

incurable [in•KYOOU•ru•bl]
adj incurabile

incursion [in•KUR•zjuhn] *n*
incursione

indebted [in•DE•tid] *adj*
indebitato; indebitata

indecent [in•DEE•sunt] *adj*
indecente

indeed [in•DEED] *adv* infatti

indefinite [in•DE•fi•nit] *adj*
indefinito; indefinita

indemnity [in•DEM•ni•tee] *n*
indennitá F

indent [in•DENT] *n* spazio a
capoverso M

independence
[IN•du•PEN•duns] *n*
indipendenza F

independent
[IN•du•PEN•dunt] *adj*
indipendente

indestructible
[IN•di•STRUHK•ti•bl] *adj*
indistruttibile

index [in•DEKS] *n* indice M

index finger [IN•dex FING•ur]
n indice M

India [IN•dee•u] *n* India F

Indian [IN•dee•un] *adj* indiano;
  indiana
indicate [IN•di•KAIT] *vt*
  indicare
indicator [IN•di•KAI•tur] *n*
  indicatore M
indict [in•DUYT] *vt* accusare
indifferent [in•DI•fu•runt] *adj*
  indifferente
indigenous [in•DI•ji•nus] *adj*
  indigeno; indigena
indigestion [in•di•JES•chn] *n*
  indigestione F
indignant [in•DIG•nunt] *adj*
  indignato; indignata
indigo [IN•di•GO] *adj n* indaco
indirect [IN•di•REKT] *adj*
  indiretto; indiretta
indiscreet [IN•di•SKREET] *adj*
  indiscreto; indiscreta
indispensable
  [IN•di•SPEN•su•bl] *adj*
  indispensabile
indisposed [IN•di•SPOSD] *adj*
  indisposto; indisposta
indistinct [IN•di•STINKT] *adj*
  indistinto; indistinta
individual [IN•di•VI•joo•ul] *adj*
  individuale
indoctrinate
  [in•DAHK•tri•NAIT] *vt*
  addottrinare
Indonesia [IN•do•NEE•zhu] *n*
  Indonesia F
indoor [IN•DAUR] *adj* al
  chiuso
induce [in•DOOS] *vt* indurre
induct [in•DUHKT] *vt* investire
indulge [in•DUHLJ] *vt*
  concedersi

industrial [in•DUH•stree•ul] *adj*
  industriale
industrious [in•DUH•stree•us]
  adj industrioso; industriosa
industry [IN•duh•stree] *n*
  industria F
inebriated [i•NEE•bree•AI•tid]
  adj inebriato; inebriata
ineffective [IN•u•FEK•tiv] *adj*
  inefficace
inequality
  [IN•ee•KWAH•li•tee] *n*
  ineguaglianza F
inevitable [i•NE•vi•tu•bl] *adj*
  inevitabile
inexpensive [IN•ek•SPEN•siv]
  adj poco costoso; poco
  costosa
inexperienced
  [IN•ek•SPEEU•ree•unst] *adj*
  inesperto; inesperta
infallible [in•FA•li•bl] *adj*
  infallibile
infamous [IN•fu•mus] *adj*
  malfamato; malfamata
infancy [IN•fun•see] *n*
  infanzia F
infant [IN•funt] *n* neonato;
  neonata
infantry [IN•fun•tree] *n*
  fanteria F
infect [in•FEKT] *vt* infettare
infection [in•FEK•shn] *n*
  infezione F
infectious [in•FEK•shus] *adj*
  infettivo; infettiva
infer [in•FUR] *vt* dedurre
inferior [in•FEEU•ree•ur] *adj n*
  inferiore
infidelity [IN•fi•DE•li•tee] *n*
  infedeltà F

infinite [IN•fi•nit] *adj* infinito; infinita

infinitive [in•FI•ni•tiv] *adj n* infinito; infinita

infinity [in•FI•ni•tee] *n* infinitá

infirmity [in•FUR•mi•tee] *n* acciacco M

inflame [in•FLAIM] *vt* infiammare

inflate [in•FLAIT] *vt* gonfiare

inflation [in•FLAI•shn] *n* svalutazione F

inflection [in•FLEK•shn] *n* inflessione F

inflict [in•FLIKT] *vt* infliggere

influence [IN•FLOO•uns] *n* influenza F

influenza [IN•floo•EN•zu] *n* influenza F

influx [IN•fluhks] *n* influsso M

inform [in•FAURM] *vt* informare

informal [in•FAUR•ml] *adj* non ufficiale

information [IN•fur•MAI•shn] *n* informazione F

infringe [in•FRINJ] *vt* violare

infuriate [in•FYU•ree•AIT] *vt* infuriare

ingenious [in•JEE•nyus] *adj* ingegnoso; ingegnosa

ingratitude [in•GRA•ti•TOOD] *n* ingratitudine F

ingredient [in•GREE•dee•unt *n* ingrediente M

inhabit [in•HA•bit] *vt* abitare

inhale [in•HAIUL] *vt* inalare

inherent [in•HE•runt] *adj* inerente

inherit [in•HE•rit] *vt* ereditare

inheritance [in•HE•ri•tuns] *n* ereditá F

inhibit [in•HI•bit] *vt* inibire

inhuman [in•HYOO•mun] *adj* inumano; inumana

initial [i•NI•shl] *adj n* iniziale

initiate [i•NI•shee•AIT] *vt* iniziare

inject [in•JEKT] *vt* iniettare

injure [IN•jur] *vt* ferire

injury [IN•ju•ree] *n* ferita F

injustice [in•JUH•stis] *n* ingiustiziia F

ink [ingk] *n* inchiostro M

inmate [IN•mait] *n* ricoverato; ricoverata

inmost [IN•most] *adj* intimo; intima

inn [in] *n* locanda F

innate [i•NAIT] *adj* innato; innata

inner [I•nur] *adj* interiore

innkeeper [IN•KEE•pur] *n* oste M; ostessa F

innocence [I•nu•suns] *n* innocenza F

innocent [I•nu•sunt] *adj* innocente

innovation [I•nu•VAI•shn] *n* innovazione F

innuendo [IN•yoo•EN•do] *n* insinuazione F

inoculate [i•NAH•kyu•LAIT] *vt* inoculare

inorganic [IN•aur•GA•nik] *adj* inorganico; inorganica

inquire [in•KWUY•ur] *vi* indagare

inquiry [in•KWU•ree] *n* indagine F

inquisition [IN•kwi•ZI•shn] *n*
  inquisizione F

inquisitive [in•KWI•zi•tiv] *adj*
  curioso; curiosa

insane [in•SAIN] *adj* pazzo;
  pazza

insanity [in•SA•ni•tee] *n*
  pazzia F

insatiable [in•SAI•shu•bl] *adj*
  insaziabile

inscription [in•SKRIP•shn] *n*
  iscrizione F

insect [IN•sekt] *n* insetto M

insecticide [in•SEK•ti•SUYD] *n*
  insetticida M

insecure [in•su•CYUR] *adj*
  malsicuro; malsicura

insensitive [in•SEN•si•tiv] *adj*
  insensibile

inseparable [in•SE•pru•bl] *adj*
  inseparabile

insert [in•SURT] *vt* inserire; *n*
  insertzione F

inside [in•SUYD] *adj* interno;
  interna

insight [IN•suyt] *n* intuito M

insignificant
  [IN•sig•NI•fi•kunt] *adj*
  insignificante

insipid [in•SI•pid] *adj* insipido;
  insipida

insist [in•SIST] *vi* insistere

insistent [in•SI•stunt] *adj*
  insistente

insolent [IN•su•lunt] *adj*
  insolente

insomnia [in•SAHM•nee•u] *n*
  insonnia F

inspect [in•SPEKT] *vt*
  ispezionare

inspection [in•SPEK•shn] *n*
  ispezione F

inspector [in•SPEK•tur] *n*
  ispettore M

inspiration [IN•spu•RAI•shn] *n*
  ispirazione F

inspire [in•SPUY•ur] *vt* ispirare

install [in•STAUL] *vt* installare

installation [IN•stu•LAI•shn] *n*
  installazione F

instance [IN•stuns] *n* caso M

instant [IN•stunt] *adj*
  istantaneo; istantanea

instead [in•STED] *adv* invece

instigate [IN•sti•GAIT] *vt*
  istigare

instill [in•STIL] *vt* instillare

instinct [IN•stingkt] *n* istinto M

institute [IN•sti•TOOT] *n*
  istituto M

instruct [in•STRUHKT] *vt*
  istruire

instruction [in•STRUHK•shn] *n*
  istruzione F

instructor [in•STRUHK•tor] *n*
  istruttore M

instrument [IN•stru•munt] *n*
  strumento M; (law) titolo M

insufficient [IN•su•FI•shunt]
  adj insufficiente

insulate [IN•su•LAIT] *vt* isolare

insulation [IN•su•LAI•shn] *n*
  isolamento M

insult [n. IN•suhlt v.
  in•SUHLT] *n* insulto M;
  offesa F; *vt* insultare;
  offendere

insurance [in•SHOOU•runs] *n*
  assicurazione F

insure [in•SHOOUR] *vt*
  assicurare

intact [in•TAKT] *adj* intatto; intatta

integral [IN•tu•grul] *adj* integrale

integration [IN•tu•GRAI•shn] *n* integrazione F

integrity [in•TE•gri•tee] *n* integritá F

intellectual [IN•tu•LEK•chu•ul] *adj n* intellettuale

intelligence [in•TE•li•juns] *n* intelligenza F

intelligent [in•TE•li•junt] *adj* intelligente

intend [in•TEND] *vt* avere l'intenzione di

intense [in•TENS] *adj* intenso; intensa

intensify [in•TEN•si•FUY] *vt* intensificare

intensity [in•TEN•si•tee] *n* intensitá F

intensive [in•TEN•siv] *adj* intensivo; intensiva

intent [in•TENT] *adj* intento; intenta

intention [in•TEN•shn] *n* intenzione F

intentional [in•TEN•shu•nl] *adj* premeditato; premeditata

intercept [IN•tur•SEPT] *vt* intercettare

interchange 1 [IN•tur•chainj] *n* scambio M

interchange 2 [in•tur•CHAINJ] *vt* scambiare

intercom [IN•tur•KAHM] *n* citofono M

intercourse [IN•tur•KAURS] *n* rapporto M

interest [IN•trust] *n* interesse M

interesting [IN•tru•sting] *adj* interessante

interfere [IN•tur•FEEUR] *vi* interferire

interference [IN•tur•FEEU•runs] *n* interferenza F

interim [IN•tu•rim] *adj* provvisorio; provvisoria

interior 1 [in•TEEU•ree•ur] *adj* interno; interna

interior 2 [in•TEEU•ree•ur] *n* interno M

interlock [IN•tur•LAHK] *vi* intrecciarsi

intermediate [IN•tur•MEE•dee•ut]] *adj* intermedio; intermedia

interminable [in•TUR•mi•nu•bl] *adj* interminabile

intermission [IN•tur•MI•shn] *n* intervallo M

intern [IN•turn] *n* interno M

internal [in•TUR•nl] *adj* interno; interna

international [IN•tur•NA•shu•nl] *adj* internazionale

interpret [in•TUR•prit] *vt* interpretare

interpretation [in•TUR•pru•TAI•shn] *n* interpretazione F

interpreter [in•TUR•pri•tur] *n* interprete

interrogate [in•TE•ru•GAIT] *vt* interrogare

interrogation [in•TE•ru•GAI•shn] *n* interrogazione F

interrupt [IN•tu•RUHPT] *vt vi*
interrompere

interruption [IN•tu•RUHP•shn]
n interruzione F

intersect [IN•tur•SEKT] *vt*
intersecare

intersection [IN•tur•SEK•shn]
n incrocio M

intertwine [IN•tur•TWUYN] *vt*
intrecciarsi

interval [IN•tur•vl] *n*
intervallo M

intervene [IN•tur•VEEN] *vt*
intervenire

intervention [IN•tur•VEN•shn]
n intervento M

interview [IN•tur•VYOO] *n*
intervista F

intestine [in•TE•stin] *n*
intestino M

intimacy [IN•ti•mu•see] *n*
intimitá F

intimate 1 [IN•ti•mit] *adj*
intimo; intima

intimate 2 [IN•ti•MAIT] *vi*
intimare; suggerire

into [IN•too] *prep* dentro

intolerable [in•TAH•lu•ru•bl]
adj intollerabile

intolerance [in•TAH•lu•runs] *n*
intolleranza F

intolerant [in•TAH•lu•runt] *adj*
intollerante

intoxicated
[in•TAHK•si•KAI•tid] *adj*
inebriato; inebriata

intravenous [IN•tru•VEE•nus]
adj indovenoso; indovenosa

intricate [IN•tri•kut] *adj*
intricato; intricata

intrigue [in•TREEG] *n*
intrigo M

introduce [IN•tru•DOOS] *vt*
introdurre

introduction
[IN•tru•DUHK•shn] *n*
introduzione F

introvert [IN•tru•VURT] *n*
introverso; introversa

introverted [IN•tru•VUR•tid]
adj introverso; introversa

intrude [in•TROOD] *vi* imporsi

intruder [in•TROO•dur] *n*
intruso; intrusa

intrusion [in•TROO•zhn] *n*
intrusione F

intuition [IN•too•I•shn] *n*
intuito M

inundate [I•nun•DAIT] *vt*
inondare

invade [in•VAID] *vt* invadere

invalid [adj. in•VA•lid n.
IN•vu•lid] *adj n* invalido;
invalida MF

invaluable [in•VA•lyu•bl] *adj*
inestimabile

invariably [in•VA•ryu•blee] *adv*
invariabilmente

invasion [in•VAI•zhn] *n*
invasione F

invent [in•VENT] *vt* inventare

invention [in•VEN•shn] *n*
invenzione F

inventive [in•VEN•tiv] *adj*
inventivo; inventiva

inventor [in•VEN•tur] *n*
inventore M

inventory [IN•vun•TAU•ree] *n*
inventario M

invest [in•VEST] *vt vi* investire

investigate [in•VE•sti•GAIT] *vt* investigare

investigation [in•VE•sti•GAI•shn] *n* investigazione F

investment [in•VEST•munt] *n* investimento M

investor [in•VE•stur] *n* investitore M

invigorating [in•VI•gu•RAI•ting] *adj* rinvigorente

invincible [in•VIN•si•bl] *adj* invincibile

invisible [in•VI•zi•bl] *adj* invisibile

invitation [IN•vi•TAI•shn] *n* invito M

invite [in•VUYT] *vt* invitare

inviting [in•VUY•ting] *adj* accogliente

invoice [IN•vois] *n* fattura F

invoke [in•VOK] *vt* invocare

involuntary [in•VAH•lun•TE•ree] *adj* involontario; involontaria

involve [in•VAHLV] *vt* coinvolgere

inward [IN•wurd] *adj* interno; interna; *adv* verso l'interno

iodine [UY•u•DUYN] *n* tintura d'iodio F

Iran [i•RAN] *n* Iran M

Iranian [i•RAI•nyun] *adj* iraniano; iraniana

Iraq [i•RAK] *n* Irak M

Iraqi [i•RA•kee] *adj* iracheno; irachena

Ireland [UYUR•lund] *n* Irlanda F

iris [UY•ris] *n* ireos M

Irish [UY•rish] *adj* irlandese

iron [UY•urn] *n* ferro M; (press) *vt* stirare

ironic [uy•RAH•nik] *adj* ironico; ironica

ironing [UY•ur•ning] *n* stiratura F

irony [UY•ru•nee] *n* ironia F

irrational [i•RA•shu•nl] *adj* irrazionale

irregular [i•RE•gyu•lur] *adj* irregolare

irregularity [i•RE•gyu•LA•ri•tee] *n* irregolaritá F

irrelevant [i•RE•lu•vunt] *adj* irrilevante

irreparable [i•RE•pru•bl] *adj* irreparabile

irreplaceable [i•ri•PLAI•su•bl] *adj* insostituibile

irresistible [I•ru•ZI•stu•bl] *adj* irresistibile

irresponsible [I•ri•SPAHN•su•bl] *adj* irresponsabile

irrigate [I•ri•GAIT] *vt* irrigare

irrigation [I•ri•GAI•shn] *n* irrigazione F

irritable [I•ri•tu•bl] *adj* irritabile

irritate [I•ri•TAIT] *vt* irritare

irritating [I•ri•TAI•ting] *adj* irritante

Islam [iz•LAHM] *n* Islamismo M

island [UY•lund] *n* isola F

isolate [UY•su•LAIT] *vt* isolare

isolation [UY•su•LAI•shn] *n* isolamento M

issue [I•shoo] *n* punto in discussione M; (publication) *vt* numero M

it *pron* esso; essa; *indir obj* gli; le

Italian [i•TAL•yun] *adj* italiano; italiana

italic [uy•TA•lik] *adj* corsivo; corsiva

itch [ich] *n* prurito M

itchy [I•chee] *adj* pruriginoso; pruriginosa

item [UY•tum] *n* articolo M

itemize [UY•tu•MUYZ] *vt* elencare

itinerary [uy•TI•nu•RE•ree] *n* itinerario M

its [its] *poss pron* i su; la sua

itself [it•SELF] *pron* sé stesso; sé stessa

ivory [UY•vree] *n* avorio M

ivy [UY•vee] *n* edera F

J

jab [jab] *n* stoccata F

jack [jak] *n* cricco M

jackal [JA•kl] *n* sciacallo M

jacket [JA•kit] *n* giacca F

jackpot [JAK•paht] *n* piatto M

jaded [JAI•did] *adj* stanco; stanca

jagged [JA•gid] *adj* frastagliato; frastagliata

jail [jaiul] *n* carcere M

jam 1 [jam] *n* marmellata F

jam 2 [jam] *vt* bloccare; intralaciare; traffic ~\ intasamento

janitor [JA•ni•tur] *n* portinaio M

January [JA•nyoo•E•ree] *n* gennaio M

Japan [ju•PAN] *n* Giappone M

Japanese [JA•pu•NEEZ] *adj* giapponese

jar 1 [jahr] *n* vasetto di vetro M

jar 2 [jahr] *vi* vibrare; produrre un suono aspro

jargon [JAHR•gun] *n* gergo M

jaundice [JAUN•dis] *n* itterizia F

javelin [JA•vu•lin] *n* giavellotto M

jaw [jau] *n* mascella F

jazz [jaz] *n* jazz M

jealous [JE•lus] *adj* geloso; gelosa

jealousy [JE•lu•see] *n* gelosia F

jeans [jeenz] *npl* jeans M

jeer [jeeur] *vt* schernire

jelly [JE•lee] *n* gelatina F

jellyfish [JE•lee•FISH] *n* medusa F

jeopardize [JE•pur•DUYZ] *vt* mettere a repentaglio

jerk [jurk] *n* cretino M; *n* (shock) scossa F; *vt* scuotere; dare uno strappoa

jersey [JUR•zee] *n* maglietta F

jest [jest] *n* scherzo M; *vt* scherzare

jet [jet] *n* getto M

jetty [JE•tee] *n* molo M

Jew [joo] *n* ebreo; ebrea

jewel [jooul] *n* gioiello M

jeweler [JOOU•lur] *n* gioielliere M

jewelry [JOOUL•ree] *n* gioielli M

Jewish [JOO•ish] *adj* ebreo; ebrea

jig 1 [jig] *n* giga F

jig 2 [jig] (tool) *n* crivello M

jiggle [JI•gl] *vt* ballonzolare

jigsaw (puzzle) [JIG•sau] *n* gioco di pazienza M

jilt [jilt] *vt* piantare in asso

jingle [JING•gl] *n* canzoncina F

job [jahb] *n* lavoro M

jockey [JAH•kee] *n* fantino M

jog [jahg] *vi* fare il footing

jogging [JAH•ging] *n* footing M

join [join] *vt* unire

joint [joint] *adj* unito; unita

joint account [JOYNT a•KOWNT] *n* conto di partecipazione M

joke [jok] *n* scherzo M; *vt* scherzare

joker [JO•kur] *n* burlone M

jolly [JAH•lee] *adj* allegro; allegra

jolt [jolt] *n* scossa F; *vt* scuotere; far sobbalazare

jot [jaht] *vt* prendere nota

journal [JUR•nl] *n* diario M

journalism [JUR•nu•LI•zm] *n* giornalismo M

journalist [JUR•nu•list] *n* giornalista

journey [JUR•nee] *n* viaggio M

jovial [JO•vyul] *adj* gioviale

joy [joi] *n* gioia F

joyful [JOI•ful] *adj* gioioso; gioiosa

jubilant [JOO•bi•lunt] *adj* giubilante

judge [juhj] *n* giudice M

judicial [joo•DI•shl] *adj* giudiziale

judicious [joo•DI•shus] *adj* giudizioso; giudiziosa

jug [juhg] *n* brocca F

juggle [JUH•gl] *vt* fare giochi di destrezza

juggler [JUH•glur] *n* giocoliere M

juice [joos] *n* succo M

juicy [JOO•see] *adj* sugoso; sugosa

jukebox [JOOK•bahks] *n* jukebox M

July [ju•LUY] *n* luglio M

jump [juhmp] *n* salto M

junction [JUHNGK•shn] *n* congiunzione F

June [joon] *n* giugno M

jungle [JUHNG•gl] *n* giungla F

junior [JOO•nyur] *adj* minore

junk [juhngk] *n* cianfrusaglie F

jurisdiction [JOOU•ris•DIK•shn] *n* giurisdizione F

juror [JOOU•rur] *n* giurato; giurata

jury [JOOU•ree] *n* giuria F

just [juhst] *adj* giusto; giusta; *adv* giusto per l'appunto; proprio; (barely) appena

justice [JUH•stis] *n* giustizia F

justify [JUH•sti•FUY] *vt* giustificare

juvenile [JOO•vu•NUYUL] *adj*
da ragazzo; da ragazza

juxtapose [JUHK•stu•POZ] *vt*
giustapporre

K

kaleidoscope
[ku•LUY•du•SKOP] *n*
caleidoscopio M

kangaroo [KANG•gu•ROO] *n*
canguro M

keen [keen] *adj* aguzzo; aguzza;
tagliente; (eager) appassionato

keep [keep] *vt* mantenere;
tenere; conservare; custodire

keeper [KEE•pur] *n* guardiano;
guardiana

keeping [KEE•ping] *n*
sorveglianza F

keepsake [KEEP•saik] *n*
oggetto ricordo M

keg [keg] *n* barile M

kennel [KE•nl] *n* canile M

Kenya [KE•nyu] *n* Kenya M

kernel [KUR•nl] *n* chicco M

kerosene [KE•ru•SEEN] *n*
cherosene M

ketchup [KE•chup] *n* salsa
Rubra F

kettle [KE•tl] *n* marmitta F

key [kee] *n* chiave F

keyboard [KEE•bord] *n*
tastiera F

key ring [KEE ring] *n*
portachiavi M

keyboard [KEE•baurd] *n*
tastiera F

khaki [KA•kee] *adj* cachi

kick [kik] *n* calcio M; *vt* dare un
calicio a; dare una pedata a;
protestare

kid 1 [kid] *n* ragazzino;
ragazzina

kid 2 [kid] *vt* prendere in giro
(coll)

kid 3 [kid] (young goat) *n*
capretto M

kidnap [KID•nap] *vt* rapire

kidnaping [KID•na•ping] *n*
rapimento M

kidnapper [KID•na•pur] *n*
rapitore M

kidney [KID•nee] *n* rene M

kill [kil] *vt* uccidere

killer [KI•lur] *n* assassino;
assassina

kiln [kiln] *n* fornace F

kilogram [KI•lu•GRAM] *n*
chilogrammo M

kilometer [ki•LAH•mi•tur] *n*
chilometro M

kilowatt [KI•lu•WAHT] *n*
chilowatt M

kilt [kilt] *n* kilt M

kin [kin] *n* parentel

kind 1 [kuynd] *adj* gentile;
cortese; buono

kind 2 [kuynd] *n* genere M;
specie F; raza F

kindergarten
[KIN•dur•GAHR•tn] *n* asilo
infantile M

kindle [KIN•dl] *vt* accendere

kindly [KUYND•lee] *adj* gentilmente

kindness [KUYND•nis] *n* gentilezza F

king [king] *n* re M

kingdom [KING•dum] *n* reame M

kinky [KING•kee] *adj* pervertito; pervertita

kiss [kis] *n* bacio M

kit [kit] *n* equipaggiamento M

kitchen [KI•chn] *n* cucina F

kitchen sink [KI•chin SINK] *n* lavandino di cucina M

kite [kuyt] *n* aquilone M

kitten [KI•tn] *n* gattino; gattina

knack [nak] *n* abilitá F

knapsack [NAP•sak] *n* zaino M

knead [need] *vt* impastare

knee [nee] *n* ginocchio M

kneecap [NEE•kap] *n* rotula F

kneel [neeul] *vi* inginocchiarsi

knife [nuyf] *n* coltello M

knight [nuyt] *n* cavaliere M

knit [nit] *vt vi* lavorare a maglia

knitting [NI•ting] *n* lavoro a maglia M

knob [nahb] *n* pomolo M

knock [nahk] *n vi* bussare M

knocker [NAH•kur] *n* battente M

knot [naht] *n* nodo M

know [no] *vt* sapere

know-how [NO•hou] *n* abilitá tecnica F

know-it-all [NO•it•ALL] *n* saccentone; saccentona

knowledge [NAH•lij] *n* consapevolezza F

knuckle [NUH•kl] *n* nocca F

Korea [ku•REE•u] *n* Corea F

kosher [KO•shur] *adj* lecita; lecita

Kuwait [ku•WAIT] *n* Kuwait M

L

lab [lab] *n* laboratorio M

label [LAI•bl] *n* etichetta F

labor [LAI•bur] *n* fatica F

Labor Party [LAI•bor PAR•tee] *n* partito laburista M

labor union [LAI•bor U•nyun] *n* sindacato M

laboratory [LA•bru•TAU•ree] *n* laboratorio M

laborer [LAI•bu•rur] *n* manovale M

lace [lais] *n* pizzo M

lack [lak] *n* mancanza F

lacquer [LA•kur] *n* lacca F

ladder [LA•dur] *n* scala a pioli F

ladle [LAI•dl] *n* mestolo M

lady [LAI•dee] *n* signora F

lag [lag] *vi* indugiare

lagoon [lu•GOON] *n* laguna F

lair [laiur] *n* tana F

lake [laik] *n* lago M

lamb [lam] *n* agnello M

lame [laim] *adj* zoppo; zoppa

lament [lu•MENT] *vt* lamentare

laminate [LA•mi•NAIT] *vt* laminare

lamp [lamp] *n* lampada F

lamp-post [LAMP•post] *n* palo del lampione M

lampoon [lam•POON] *n* satira F

lance [lans] *n* lancia F; *vt* incidere col bisturi

land [land] *n* terra F

landing [LAN•ding] *n* pianerottolo M

landlady [LAND•LAI•dee] *n* padrona di casa F

landlord [LAND•laurd] *n* padrone di casa M

landmark [LAND•mahrk] *n* punto di riferimento M

landowner [LAND•O•nur] *n* proprietario terriero M

landslide [LAND•sluyd] *n* frana F

lane [lain] *n* sentiero M

language [LANG•gwij] *n* lingua F

languid [LANG•gwid] *adj* languido; languida

lantern [LAN•turn] *n* lanterna F

lap 1 [lap] *n* grembo M

lap 2 [lap] *vt* lambire; accoltare (con avida)

lapel [lu•PEL] *n* bavero M

lapse [laps] *n* errore M; *vi* scadere

larceny [LAHR•su•nee] *n* furto M

lard [lahrd] *n* strutto M

large [lahrj] *n* ampio; ampia

largely [LAHRJ•lee] *adv* in gran misura

lark [lahrk] *n* allodola F

lash [lash] *n* guinzaglio F

last [last] *adj* ultimo; ultima

last name [LAST NAIM] *n* cognome M

lasting [LA•sting] *adj* durevole

latch [lach] *n* saliscendi M; *vt* chiudere con saliscendi

late [lait] *adj* tardo; tarda

latent [LAI•tunt] *adj* latente

lather [LA•thur] *n* schiuma F

Latin [LA•tin] *adj n* latino; latina

Latin America [LA•tin u•ME•ri•ku] *n* America Latina F

latitude [LA•ti•TOOD] *n* latitudine F

latter [LA•tur] *adj* il secondo; la seconda

lattice [LA•tis] *n* traliccio M

Latvia [LAHT•vee•u] *n* Latvia F

laugh [laf] *vi* ridere; *n* risata F

laughter [LAF•tur] *n* risata F

launch [launch] *vt* lanciare; varare; (naut, space) *n* lancia F

launder [LAUN•dur] *vt* lavare

laundry [LAUN•dree] *n* bucato M

laurel [LAU•rl] *n* alloro M

lava [LAH•vu] *n* lava F

lavatory [LA•vu•TAU•ree] *n* gabinetto M

lavish [LA•vish] *adj* abbondante

law [lau] *n* legge F

law school [LAW skool] *n* facoltà di giurisprudenza F

law-abiding [LAW•a•BUY•ding] *adj* probo; proba

lawful [LAU•ful] *adj* legittimo; legittima

lawn [laun] *n* prato M

lawn mower [LAWN MO•wur] *n* taglia erba M

lawsuit [LAU•soot] *n* causa F

lawyer [LAU•yur] *n* avvocato M

lax [laks] *adj* negligente

laxative [LAK•su•tiv] *n* lassativo M

lay 1 [lai] *vt* stendere; poare; mettere

lay 2 [lai] *adj* laico; non professionale

layer [LAI•ur] *n* strato M

layout [LAI•out] *n* tracciato M

lazy [LAI•zee] *adj* pigro; pigra

lead 1 [leed] *n* piombo M

lead 2 [led] *n* comando M; *vt* condurre; influenzare; portare; (theat) primo attore; prima attrice MF

leader [LEE•dur] *n* capo M

leadership [LEE•dur•SHIP] *n* comando M

leading [LEE•ding] *adj* principale

leaf [leef] *n* (tree) foglia F; (paper) foglio M; *vt* sfogliare

league [leeg] *n* lega F

leak [leek] *n* perdita F; *vi* perdere; trapelare

lean 1 [leen] *adj* magro; magra

lean 2 [leen] *vi* appoggiare; inclinare; pendere

leap [leep] *n* balzo M

leap year [LEEP YEER] *n* anno bisestile M

learn [lurn] *vt vi* imparare

learning [LUR•ning] *n* cultura F

lease [lees] *n* contratto d'affitt M; *vt* affittare

leash [leesh] *n* guinzaglio M

least [leest] *adj* minimo; minima

leather [LE•thur] *n* cuoio M

leave 1 [leev] *n* permesso M

leave 2 [leev] *vt* lasciare; abbandonare; uscire da

Lebanon [LE•bu•nahn] *n* Libano M

lecherous [LE•chu•rus] *adj* lascivo; lasciva

lecture [LEK•chur] *n* conferenza F; *vt* tenere una conferenza; dare un corso di lezioni; fare una lezioni

ledge [lej] *n* sporgenza F

ledger [LE•jur] *n* libro mastro M

leech [leech] *n* sanguisuga F

leek [leek] *n* porro M

leer [leeur] *n* occhiata maliziosa F; *vt* guardare di sbieco

left 1 [left] *pt pp* a leave lasciato; lasciata

left 2 [left] *adj* sinistro; *n* sinistra F; *adv* a/verso/sulla sinistra

left-handed [~ HAN•did] *adj* mancino; mancina

left-overs [LEFT•O•vurz] *npl* avanzi M

left-wing [LEFT•WING] *adj* di sinistra

leftist [LEF•tist] *adj n* membro della sinistra; membra della sinistra

leg [leg] *n* gamba F

legacy [LE•gu•see] *n*
retaggio M

legal [LEE•gl] *adj* legale

legalize [LEE•gu•LUYZ] *vt*
legalizzare

legend [LE•jund] *n* leggenda F

legendary [LE•jun•DE•ree] *adj*
leggendario; leggendaria

legible [LE•ji•bl] *adj* leggibile

legislation [LE•jis•LAI•shn] *n*
legislazione F

legislature [LE•jis•LAI•chur] *n*
corpo legislativo M

legitimate [lu•JI•tu•mit] *adj*
legittimo; legittima

leisure [LEE•zhur] *n* agio M

lemon [LE•mun] *m* limone M

lemonade [LE•mu•NAID] *n*
limonata F

lend [lend] *vt* prestare

length [length] *n* lunghezza F

lengthen [LENG•thun] *vt*
allungare

lens [lenz] *n* lente F

Lent [lent] *n* Quaresima F

leopard [LE•purd] *n*
leopardo M

leper [LE•pur] *n* lebbroso;
lebbrosa

leprosy [LE•pru•see] *n* lebbra F

lesbian [LEZ•bee•un] *n*
lesbica F

less [les] *adj* meno; minore

lessen [LE•sn] *vt* diminuire

lesser [LE•sur] *adj* minore

lesson [LE•sn] *n* lezione F

let [let] *vt* lasciare; permettere;
(rent) affitare

lethal [LEE•thl] *adj* letale

lethargy [LE•thur•jee] *n*
letargo M

letter [LE•tur] *n* lettera F

lettuce [LE•tus] *n* lattuga F

level [LE•vl] *adj* piano; piana;
vt livellare; spianare

lever [LE•vur] *n* leva F

levy [LE•vee] *n* imposta F; *vt*
imporre; esigere

lewd [lood] *adj* indecente

liability [LUY•u•BI•li•tee] *n*
responsabilitá F

liable [LUY•u•bl] *adj*
responsabile

liaison [LEE•ai•ZAUN] *n*
collegamento M

liar [LUY•ur] *n* bugiardo;
bugiarda

libel [LUY•bl] *n* diffamazione F

liberal [LI•brul] *adj n* liberale

liberate [LI•bu•RAIT] *vt*
liberare

liberation [LI•bu•RAI•shn] *n*
liberazione F

liberty [LI•bur•tee] *n* libertá F

librarian [luy•BRE•ree•un] *n*
bibliotecario; bibliotecaria

library [LUY•BRE•ree] *n*
biblioteca F

Libya [LI•bee•u] *n* Libia F

license [LUY•sns] *n* licenza F

lick [lik] *vt* leccare

lid [lid] *n* coperchio F

lie [luy] *n* bugia F

lieutenant [loo•TE•nunt] *n*
tenente M

life [luyf] *n* vita F

life expectancy [LUYF
ek•SPEK•ten•cee] *n* vita
presunta F

life jacket [LUYF JA•ket] *n*
cintura di salvataggio F

life sentence [LUYF SEN•tinz]
n ergastolo M

lifeboat [LUYF•bot] *n*
scialuppa di salvataggio F

lifeless [LUYF•lis] *adj*
inanimato; inanimata

lifelike [LUYF•luyk] *adj*
realistico; realistica

lifelong [LUYF•laung] *adj* da
sempre

lifespan [LUYF•span] *n*
durata F

lifestyle [LUYF•stuyul] *n* modo
di vivere M

lift [lift] *n* passaggio M;
(elevator) ascensore M; *vi*
sollevare; alzare

ligament [LI•gi•mint] *n*
legamento M

light [luyt] *adj* leggero; leggera

lighten [LUY•tn] *vt* alleggerire

lighter [LUY•tur] *n*
accendino M

lighthouse [LUYT•haus] *n*
faro M

lighting [LUY•ting] *n*
illuminazione F

lightly [LUYT•lee] *adv*
leggermente

lightness [LUYT•nis] *n*
leggerezza F

lightning [LUYT•ning] *n*
lampo M

like 1 [luyk] *adj* simile; uguale;
pre come

like 2 [luyk] *vi* gradier; (want)
volere; I ~\ mi piace

likeable [LUY•ku•bl] *adj*
simpatico; simpatica

likely [LUYK•lee] *adj* probabile

likeness [LUYK•nis] *n*
somiglianza F

likewise [LUYK•wuyz] *adv*
altrettanto

liking [LUY•king] *n* simpatia F

limb [lim] *n* arto M; *n* ramo M

lime [luym] *n* limone verde M;
limetta F

limelight [LUYM•luyt] *n* luce
della ribalta F

limit [LI•mit] *n* limite M; *vi*
limitare

limitation [LI•mi•TAI•shn] *n*
restrizione F

limousine [LI•mu•ZEEN] *n*
limousine F

limp [limp] *adj* molle

line [luyn] *n* linea F; *vt* rigare;
(clothes, etc) foderare

linen [LI•nun] *n* lino M

linger [LING•gur] *vi* indugiare

lingerie [LAHN•zhu•RAI] *n*
intimi M

lingo [LING•go] *n* gergo M

linguistics [ling•GWI•stiks] *n*
linguistica F

lining [LUY•ning] *n* fodera F

link [lingk] *n* anello M

lint [lint] *n* pelucco M

lion [LUY•un] *n* leone M

lioness [LUY•u•nes] *n*
leonessa F

lip [lip] *n* labbro M

lip-read [LIP•reed] *vt* leggere le
labbra

lipstick [LIP•stik] *n* rossetto M

liquid [LI•kwid] *n* liquido M;
adj liquido; liquida

liquidate [LI•kwi•DAIT] *vt*
liquidare

liquor [LI•kur] *n* bevanda
alcoolica F

list 1 [list] *n* lista F; *vt* elencare;
registrare

list 2 [list] (natu) *vi* sbandare; *n*
sbandamento M

listen [LI•sn] *vi* ascoltare

listener [LI•su•nur] *n*
ascoltatore; ascoltatrice

literal [LI•tu•rl] *adj* letterale

literary [LI•tu•RE•ree] *adj*
letterario; letteraria

literature [LI•tu•RU•chur] *n*
letteratura F

litigation [LI•ti•GAI•shn] *n*
causa F

litter [LI•tur] *n* rifiuti M; *vt*
scarpagliare; lasciare in
disordine

little [LI•tl] *adj* piccolo; piccola;
(not much) un po' di; pocco
(short) breve

live [adj. luyv v. liv] *adj* vivo;
viva; *vi* vivere; (reside)
abitare; stare

lively [LUYV•lee] *adj* vivace

liven [LUY•vn] *vt* ravvivare

liver [LI•vur] *n* fegato M

livery [LI•vu•ree] *n* veicolo
pubblico M

livestock [LUYV•stahk] *n*
bestiame M

livid [LI•vid] *adj* livido; livida

living [LI•ving] *adj* vivente

lizard [LI•zurd] *n* lucertola F

load [lod] *n* carico M; *vt*
caricare

loaf 1 [lof] *n* pagnotta F

loaf 2 [lof] *vt* oziare; girellare;
stare con le mani in mano

loafer 1 [LO•fur] *n* poltrone;
poltrona

loafer 2 [LO•fur] *n* bighellone;
bighellona MF

loan [lon] *n* prestito M; *vt*
prestare; dare in prestito

loathe [loth] *vt* detestare

loathsome [LOTH•sum] *adj*
odioso; odiosa

lobby [LAH•bee] *n*
anticamera F

lobe [lob] *n* lobo M

lobster [LAHB•stur] *n*
aragosta F

local [LO•kl] *adj* locale

locality [lo•KA•li•tee] *n*
localitá F

locate [LO•kait] *vt* individuare

location [lo•KAI•shn] *n*
posizione F

lock [lahk] *n* serratura F; *vt*
serrare; chiudere a chiave

locomotive [LO•ku•MO•tiv] *n*
locomotiva F

locust [LO•kust] *n* cavalletta F

lodge [lahj] *n* loggia F; *vt*
alloggiare

lodger [LAH•jur] *n* inquilino;
inquilina

lodgings [LAH•jingz] *n*
alloggio M

loft [lauft] *n* soppalco M

log [lahg] *n* ceppo M

logic [LAH•jik] *n* logica F

logical [LAH•ji•kl] *adj* logico;
logica

logo [LO•go] *n* logotipo M

loin [loin] *n* lonza F

loiter [LOI•tur] *vi* bighellonare

lollipop [LAH•lee•PAHP] *n*
lecca lecca F

London [LUHN•dn] *n* Londra F

lone [lon] *adj* solitario; solitaria

loneliness [LON•lee•nis] *n* solitudine F

lonely [LON•lee] *adj* isolato; isolata

long 1 [laung] *adj* lungo; lunga

long 2 [laung] *vi* bramare; aver gran desiderio (di)

longitude [LAUN•ji•TOOD] *n* longitudine F

look [luk] *n* sguardo M

look at (view) *vi* guardare

loom [loom] *n* telaio M

loony [LOO•nee] *adj* pazzo; pazza

loop [loop] *n* cappio M; *vt* fare un cappio

loophole [LOOP•houl] *n* scappatoia F

loose [loos] *adj* sciolto; sciolta

loosely [LOOS•lee] *adv* scioltamente

loosen [LOO•sn] *vt* sciogliere

loot [loot] *n* bottino M; *vt* far man bassa; saccheggiare

lord [laurd] *n* signore M

lore [laur] *n* insieme di fatti e tradizione M

lose [looz] *vt* perdere

loss [laus] *n* perdita F

lost [laust] *adj* perduto; perduta

lot [laht] *n* appezzamento M

lotion [LO•shn] *n* lozione F

loud [loud] *adj* fragoroso; fragorosa

loudspeaker [LOUD•SPEE•kur] *n* altoparlante M

lounge [lounj] *n* sala d'aspetto F; *vt* oziare; dondolarsi

louse [lous] *n* pidocchio M

lout [lout] *n* zoticone M

lovable [LUH•vu•bl] *adj* amabile

love [luhv] *n* amore M; *vi* amare; voler bene a

love affair [LUV a•FAIR] *n* relazione amorosa F

lovely [LUHV•lee] *adj* grazioso; graziosa

lover [LUH•vur] *n* amante

low [lo] *adj* basso; bassa; depresso (coll)

lower [LO•ur] *adj* piú basso; piú bassa

lowly [LO•lee] *adj* umile

loyal [LOI•ul] *adj* leale

loyalty [LOI•ul•tee] *n* lealtà F

lubricant [LOO•bri•kunt] *n* lubrificante

lubricate [LOO•bri•KAIT] *vt* lubrificare

lucid [LOO•sid] *adj* lucido; lucida

luck [luhk] *n* fortuna F

luckily [LUH•ku•lee] *adv* fortunatamente

lucky [LUH•kee] *adj* fortunato; fortunata

ludicrous [LOO•di•krus] *adj* ridicolo; ridicola

lug [luhg] *vt* trascinare

luggage [LUH•gij] *n* bagaglio M

lukewarm [look•waurm] *adj* tiepido; tiepida

lull [luhl] *n* calma F; *vt* (put to sleep) far adormentare; calmare

lullaby [LUH•lu•BUY] *n* ninna nanna F

lumber [LUHM•bur] *n*
legname M

lumberjack [LUHM•bur•JAK]
n boscaiolo M

luminous [LOO•mi•nus] *adj*
luminoso; luminosa

lump [luhmp] *n* massa F; (anat)
gonfiore M

lunar [LOO•nur] *adj* lunare

lunatic [LOO•nu•TIK] *n* pazzo;
pazza

lunch [luhnch] *n* seconda
colazione F

lunch hour [LUHNCH ouur] *n*
ora di pranzo F

lung [luhng] *n* polmone M

lunge [luhnj] *vi* dare una
stoccata

lurch [lurch] *n* barcollare;
sbandare; *vt* barcollare;
sbandare

lure [loour] *n* esca F; *vt*
adescare; attirare

lurid [LU•rid] *adj* sensazionale;
raccapricciante

lurk [lurk] *vi* nascondersi

luscious [LUH•shs] *adj*
succulento; succulenta

lust [luhst] *n* lussuria F; *vi* aver
brama

luster [LUH•stur] *n*
lucentezza F

luxurious [luhg•ZHU•ree•us]
adj lussuoso; lussuosa

luxury [LUHK•shu•ree] *adj*
lusso M

lying [LUY•ing] *adj* bugiardo;
bugiarda

lynch [linch] *vt* linciare

lyric [LEEU•rik] *adj* lirico;
lirica

lyrical [LEEU•ri•kl] *adj* lirico;
lirica

lyrics [LEEU•riks] *npl* parole di
canzone F

M

macaroni [MA•ku•RO•nee] *n*
pasta F; *npl* maccheroni M

machine [mu•SHEEN] *n*
macchina F

machine gun [ma•SHEEN
GUN] *n* mitragliatrice F

machinery [mu•SHEE•nu•ree]
n macchinario M

mackerel [MA•krul] *n*
sgombro M

mad [mad] *adj* matto; matta

madam [MU•dam] *n*
signora F

madden [MA•dn] *vt* far
disperare

madly [MAD•lee] *adv* alla follia

madman [MAD•man] *n*
pazzo M

madness [MAD•nis] *n* pazzia F

magazine [MA•gu•ZEEN] *n*
rivista F

magic [MA•jik] *adj* magico;
magica

magical [MA•ji•kl] *adj* magico;
magica

magician [ma•JI•shn] *n* mago M

magistrate [MA•ji•STRAIT] *n*
magistrato M

magnet [MAG•nit] *n*
calamita F

magnetic [mag•NE•tik] *adj*
magnetico; magnetica

magnificence [mag•NI•fi•suns]
n magnificenza F

magnificent [mag•NI•fi•sunt]
adj magnifico; magnifica

magnify [MAG•ni•FUY] *vt*
ingrandire

magnifying glass
[MAG•ni•FUY•ing GLAS] *n*
lente d'ingrandimento F

magnitude [MAG•ni•TOOD] *n*
importanza F

mahogany [mu•HAH•gu•nee] *n*
mogano M

maid [maid] *n* donna di
servizio F

maiden name [MAI•dn NAIM]
n cognome da nubile M

mail [maiul] *n* posta F; *vt*
imbucare; mandare per posta

mailbox [MAIUL•bahks] *n*
buca delle lettere F

mailman [MAIUL•man] *n*
postino M

maim [maim] *vt* mutilare

main [main] *adj* principale

main course [MAIN KORS] *n*
piatto forte M

mainland [MAIN•land] *n*
continente M

maintain [main•TAIN] *vt*
mantenere

maintenance [MAIN•tu•nuns]
n manutenzione F

majestic [mu•JE•stik] *adj*
maestoso; maestosa

majesty [MA•ji•stee] *n*
maestá F

major [MAI•jur] *adj* maggiore

majority [mu•JAU•ri•tee] *n*
maggioranza F

make [maik] *vt* fare; produre; *n.*
truco M; composizione F

make-up [MAI•kuhp] *n*
trucco M

male [maiul] *adj* maschio M

malice [MA•lis] *n* malizia F

malicious [mu•LI•shus] *adj*
maligno; maligna

malign [mu•LUYN] *vt*
malignare

malignant [mu•LIG•nunt] *adj*
maligno; maligna

mallet [MA•lit] *n* mazzuolo M

malpractice [MAL•PRAK•tis] *n*
prevaricazione F

mammal [MA•ml] *n*
mammifero; mammifera

mammoth [MA•muth] *adj*
mastodontico; mastodontica

man [man] *n* uomo M; *vi*
equipaggiare; presidare

manly [MAN•lee] *adj* virile

manage [MA•nij] *vt* dirigere

management [MA•nij•munt] *n*
direzione F

manager [MA•ni•jur] *n*
direttore M

mandate [MAN•dait] *n*
mandato M

mandatory
[MAN•du•TAU•ree] *adj*
obbligatorio; obbligatoria

mane [main] *n* criniera F

maneuver [mu•NOO•vur] *n*
manovra F; *vt* monovrare

manhood [MAN•hud] *n* virilitá F

mania [MAI•nee•u] *n* mania F

manicure [MA•ni•KYUR] *n* manicure M

manifest [MA•ni•FEST] *adj* chiaro; chiara

manipulate [mu•NI•pyu•LAIT] *vt* manipolare

mankind [MAN•KUYND] *n* umanitá F

manner [MA•nur] *n* maniera F; *npl* maniere F

manor [MA•nur] *n* proprietá terriera F

manpower [MAN•pouur] *n* manodopera F

mansion [MAN•shn] *n* palazzo M

manslaughter [MAN•SLAU•tur] *n* omicidio colposo M

mantelpiece [MAN•tl•PEES] *n* cappa del caminetto F

manual [MA•nyoo•ul] *adj n* manuale M; *adj* a mano

manufacture [MA•nyu•FAK•chur] *n* manifattura F

manufacturer [MA•nyu•FAK•chu•rur] *n* fabbricante M

manure [mu•NOOUR] *n* letame M

manuscript [MA•nyu•SKRIPT] *n* manoscritto M

many [ME•nee] *adj* molti; molte; too ~\ troppi

map [map] *n* carta geografica F

maple [MAI•pl] *n* acero M

mar [mahr] *vt* guastare

marathon [MA•ru•THAHN] *n* maratona F

marble [MAHR•bl] *n* marmo M

march 1 [mahrch] *n* marcia F; *vt* marciare

March 2 [mahrch] *n* marzo M

mare [maiur] *n* cavalla F

margarine [MAHR•ju•rin] *n* margarina F

margin [MAHR•jin] *n* margine M

marginal [MAHR•ji•nl] *adj* marginale

marigold [MA•ri•GOLD] *n* calendula F

marijuana [MA•ri•WAH•nu] *n* marijuana F

marinate [MA•ri•NAIT] *vt* marinare

marine 1 [mu•REEN] *adj* marino; marina

marine 2 [mu•REEN] *n* marine M

mark [mahrk] *n* segno M; *n* marchio M; *vt* delimitare

marker [MAHR•kur] *n* lapide F

market [MAHR•kit] *n* mercato M

market value [MAR•kit va•lyu] *n* valore corrente M

marmalade [MAHR•mu•LAID] *n* marmellata d'arance F

maroon 1 [mu•ROON] *adj* marrone rossastro

maroon 2 [mu•ROON] *vt* abbandonare

marriage [MA•rij] *n* matrimonio M

married [MA•reed] *adj* sposato; sposata

marry [MA•ree] *vt* sposare

Mars [mahrz] *n* Marte M

marsh [mahrsh] *n* palude F

marshal [MAHR•shl] *n* maresciallo M; *vt* desporre; (mil) schierare

marshy [MAHR•shee] *adj* paludoso; paludosa

martial [MAHR•shl] *adj* marziale

martyr [MAHR•tur] *n* martire; *vi* martirizare

marvel [MAHR•vl] *n* meraviglia F

marvelous [MAHR•vu•lus] *adj* meraviglioso; meravigliosa

mascara [ma•SKA•ru] *n* cosmetico per ciglia M

masculine [MA•skyu•lin] *adj* maschio M

mash [mash] *vt* schiacciare

mask [mask] *n* maschera F

mason [MAI•sn] *n* muratore M

masquerade [MA•sku•RAID] *n* mascherata F

mass 1 [mass] *n* massa F

mass 2 [mass] *n* (church) messa F

massacre [MA•su•kr] *n* massacro M

massage [mu•SAHZJ] *n* massaggio M

massive [MA•siv] *adj* massiccio; massiccia

mast [mast] *n* albero maestro M

master [MA•stur] *adj* generale; *n* padrone M; *vi* dominare; conocere a perfezione

masterpiece [MA•stur•PEES] *n* capolavoro M

mat [mat] *n* stoino M

match1 [mach] *n* fiammifero M

match 2 [mach] *vi* andare bene; corrispondere; *n* uguale MF; pari MF

mate [mait] *n* compagno; compagna

material [mu•TEEU•ree•ul] *àdj* materiale

materialist [mu•TEEU•ree•u•list] *n* materialista

materialistic [mu•TEEU•ree•u•LI•stik] *adj* materialistico; materialistica

maternal [mu•TUR•nl] *adj* materno; materna

mathematics [MA•thu•MA•tiks] *n* matematica F

matriculation [mu•TRI•kyu•LAI•shn] *n* immatricolazione F

matrimony [MA•tri•MO•nee] *n* matrimonio M

matrix [MAI•triks] *n* matrice F

matter [MA•tur] *n* faccenda F; *n* materia F; what's the ~ ?\ cosa c'è?

mattress [MA•tris] *n* materasso M

mature [mu•CHOOUR] *adj* maturo; matura; *vi* maturare; (bill) scadere

maturity [mu•CHOOU•ri•tee] *n* maturitá F

maximum [MAK•si•mum] *adj* massimo; massima; *n* massimo M

may [mai] *modal v* potere

May [mai] *n* maggio M

mayonnaise [MAI•u•NAIZ] *n* maionese F

mayor [MAI•yur] *n* sindaco M

maze [maiz] *n* labirinto M

me [mee] *pers pron* me

meadow [ME•do] *n* prato M

meager [MEE•gr] *adj* scarso;
scarsa

meal [meeul] *n* pasto M

mean 1 [meen] *adj* senza
scrupoli; *vi* significare

mean 2 [meen] *adj* gretto; avaro

meaning [MEE•ning] *n*
significato M

means [meenz] *npl* mezzi M

meantime [MEEN•tuym] *adv*
nel frattempo

meanwhile [MEEN•wuyul] *adv*
intanto

measles [MEE•zlz] *n*
morbillo M

measure [ME•zhur] *n* misura F;
vt misurare; valutare

measurement [ME•zhur•munt]
n misura F

meat [meet] *n* carne F

meatball [MEET•baul] *n*
polpetta F

mechanic [mu•KA•nik] *n*
meccanico M

mechanical [mu•KA•ni•kl] *adj*
meccanico; meccanica

mechanism [ME•ku•NI•zm] *n*
meccanismo M

medal [ME•dl] *n* medaglia F

medallion [mu•DAHL•yun] *n*
medaglione M

meddle [ME•dl] *vi* intromettersi

media [MEE•dee•u] *npl* mezzi
di comunicazione M

mediate [MEE•dee•AIT] *vt* fare
da intermediario

mediator [MEE•dee•AI•tur] *n*
intermediario M

medical [ME•di•kl] *adj* medico;
medica

medicate [ME•di•KAIT] *vt*
medicare

medicine [ME•di•sin] *n*
medicina F

medieval [mi•DEE•vl] *adj*
medievale

mediocre [MEE•dee•O•kr] *adj*
mediocre

meditate [ME•di•TAIT] *vi*
meditare

medium [MEE•dee•um] *adj*
medio; media

meek [meek] *adj* mansueto;
mansueta

meet [meet] *vt* incontrare

meeting [MEE•ting] *n*
incontro M

megaphone [ME•gu•FON] *n*
megafono M

melancholy [ME•lun•KAH•lee]
adj melanconico; melanconica

mellow [ME•lo] *adj* caldo;
calda

melody [ME•lu•dee] *n*
melodia F

melon [ME•lun] *n* melone M

melt [melt] *vt* sciogliere

member [MEM•bur] *n* membro;
membra

membership [MEM•bur•SHIP]
n appartenenza F

memo [ME•mo] *n* appunto M

memoirs [MEM•wahrz] *npl*
autobiografia F

memorial [me•MAU•ree•ul] *adj*
commemorativo;
commemorativa

memorize [ME•mu•RUYZ] *vt*
imparare a memoria

memory [ME•mu•ree] *n*
memoria F

menace [ME•nus] *n* minaccia F

menacing [ME•nu•sing] *adj*
minaccioso; minacciosa

mend [mend] *vt* aggiustare

menial [MEEN•yul] *adj* servile

menopause [ME•nu•PAUZ] *n*
menopausa F

menstruation
[MEN•stroo•AI•shn] *n*
mestruazioni F

mental [MEN•tl] *adj* mentale

mentality [men•TA•li•tee] *n*
mentalitá F

mention [MEN•chn] *vt*
menzionare

menu [ME•nyoo] *n* menú M

mercenary [MUR•su•NE•ree]
adj n mercenario; mercenaria

merchandise
[MUR•chun•DUYS] *n*
merce F

merchant [MUR•chunt] *n*
commerciante M

merciful [MUR•si•ful] *adj*
misericordioso; misericordiosa

merciless [MUR•si•lis] *adj*
spietato; spietata

mercury [MUR•kyu•ree] *n*
mercurio M

mercy [MUR•see] *n*
misericordia F

mere [meeur] *adj* mero; mera

merely [MEEUR•lee] *adv*
puramente

merge [murj] *vt* assorbire

merger [MUR•jur] *n*
incorporamento M

merit [ME•rit] *n* merito M'; *vi*
meritare

mermaid [MUR•maid] *n*
sirena F

merry [ME•ree] *adj* gaio; gaia

merry-go-round
[MAI•ree•go•ROUND] *n*
giostra F

mesh [mesh] *n* rete F

mesmerize [MEZ•mu•RUYZ]
vt ipnotizzare

mess [mes] *n* pasticcio M; *vt*
rovinare

message [ME•sij] *n*
messaggio M

messenger [ME•sin•jur] *n*
messaggero M

messy [ME•see] *adj* disordinato;
disordinata; confuso; confusa

metal [ME•tl] *n* metallo M

metallic [mu•TA•lik] *adj*
metallico; metallica

metaphor [ME•tu•FAUR] *n*
metafora F

meteor [MEE•tee•ur] *n*
meteora F

meteorology
[MEE•tee•u•RAH•lu•jee] *n*
meteorologia F

meter [MEE•tur] *n* metro M

method [ME•thud] *n* metodo M

meticulous [mu•TI•kyu•lus] *adj*
meticoloso; meticolosa

metric [ME•trik] *adj* metrico;
metrica

metropolitan
[ME•tru•PAH•li•tun] *adj*
metropolitano; metropolitana

Mexican [MEK•si•kun] *adj*
messicano; messicana

Mexico [MEK•si•KO] *n*
Messico M

mice [muys] *npl* topi M

microchip [MUY•cro•CHIP] *n*
microchip F

microphone [MUY•kru•FON]
n microfono M

microscope [MUY•kru•SKOP]
n microscopio M

microscopic
[MUY•kru•SKO•pik] *adj*
microscopico; microscopica

microwave [MUY•kru•WAIV]
n micro onde M

mid [mid] *adj* metá

middle [MI•dl] *n* mezzo M

Middle Ages [MI•dl A•jis] *npl*
Medioevo M

middle class [MI•dl KLASS] *n*
ceto medio M

Middle East [MI•dl EEST] *n*
Medio Oriente M

midnight [MID•nuyt] *n*
mezzanotte F

midst [midst] *n* mezzo M

midwife [MID•wuyf] *n*
levatrice F

might 1 [muyt] *modal v* may

might 2 [muyt] *n* forza F;
potenza

mighty [MUY•tee] *adj* potente

migraine [MUY•grain] *n*
emicrania F

migrant [MUY•grunt] *n*
migratore M

migrate [MUY•grait] *vi*
emigrare

mild [muyuld] *adj* mite

mildew [MIL•doo] *n* muffa F

mile [muyul] *n* miglio M

militant [MI•li•tunt] *adj n*
militante

military [MI•li•TE•ree] *adj*
militare

militia [mi•LI•shu] *n* milizia F

milk [milk] *n* latte M

mill [mil] *n* fabbrica F; *vt*
fabbricare

millenium [mi•LE•nee•um] *n*
millennio M

million [MIL•yun] *num*
milione M

millionaire [MIL•yu•NAIUR] *n*
milionario; milionaria

mimic [MI•mik] *n* mimo; mima

mince [mins] *vt* tritare

mind [muynd] *n* mente F;
spirito M; never ~\ non
importa

mindful [MUYND•ful] *adj*
memore

mine 1 [muyn] il mio; la mio

mine 2 [muyn] *n* miniera F

mineral [MI•nu•rul] *adj n*
minerale

mingle [MING•gl] *vi* mescolare

miniature [MI•nu•CHUR] *adj*
in miniatura; *n* miniatura F

minimize [MI•ni•MUYZ] *vt*
ridurre ai minimi termini

minimum [MI•ni•mum] *n*
minimo; *adj* minimo; minima

mining [MUY•ning] *n* scavo M

minister [MI•ni•stur] *n* ministro
M; *vt* soccorrere

ministry [MI•ni•stree] *n*
ministero M

mink [mingk] *n* visone M

minor [MUY•nur] *adj n* minore

minority [muy•NAU•ri•tee] *n*
minoranza F

mint [mint] *n* menta F

minus [MUY•nus] *prep* meno

minute [adj. muy•NYOOT n. MI•nit] *adj* minuto; minuta; *n* minuto; M momento

miracle [MI•ru•kl] *n* miracolo M

miraculous [mi•RA•kyu•lus] *adj* miracoloso; miracolosa

mirage [mi•RAHZJ] *n* miraggio M

mirror [MI•rur] *n* specchio M

misanthrope [mi•SAN•throp] *n* misantropo M

misappropriation [mis•U•PRO•pree•AI•shn] *n* appropriazione indebita F

misbehave [MIS•bee•HAIV] *vi* comportarsi male

miscarriage [MIS•KA•rij] *n* aborto M

miscellaneous [MI•su•LAI•nee•us] *adj* miscellaneo; miscellanea

mischief [MIS•chif] *n* birichinata F

mischievous [MIS•chi•vus] *adj* malizioso; maliziosa

misconception [MIS•kun•SEP•shn] *n* concetto errato M

misconduct [mis•KAHN•duhkt] *n* cattiva condotta F

misconstrue [mis•KUN•stroo] *vt* interpretare male

miscount [mis•KOUNT] *vt vi* sbagliare un conto

misdeed [mis•DEED] *n* misfatto M

misdemeanor [MIS•du•MEE•nur] *n* atto contrario alla legge M

miser [MUY•zur] *n* avaro; avara

miserable [MIZ•ru•bl] *adj* triste

miserly [MUY•zur•lee] *adj* avaro; avara

misery [MI•zu•ree] *n* sofferenza F

misfire [mis•FUYUR] *vi* fare cilecca

misfit [MIS•fit] *n* spostato; spostata

misfortune [MIS•FAUR•chun] *n* sfortuna F

misgivings [MIS•GI•vingz] *npl* apprensione F

mishap [MIS•hap] *n* infortunio M

misinform [MIS•in•FAURM] *vt* informare male

misjudge [mis•JUHJ] *vt* giudicare male

misleading [MIS•LEE•ding] *adj* ingannevole

misplace [mis•PLAIS] *vt* riporre male

misprint [MIS•print] *n* sbaglio di stampa M

Miss [mis] *n* signorina F

miss [mis] *vt* mancare

missile [MI•sul] *n* missile M

missing [MI•sing] *adj* mancante

mission [MI•shn] *n* missione F

missionary [MI•shu•NE•ree] *n* missionario; missionaria

misspell [mis•SPEL] *vt* sbagliare l'ortografia

mist [mist] *n* nebbia F

mistake [mi•STAIK] *n* errore M

mistaken [mi•STAI•kn] *adj* in errore

mister [MI•stur] *n* signore M

mistreat [mis•TREET] *vt*
maltrattare

mistress 1 [MI•strus] *n*
mantenuta

mistress 2 [MI•strus] (owner) *n*
padrona; *n* diffidenza F

misty [MI•stee] *adj* nebbioso;
nebbiosa

misunderstand
[mis•UHN•dur•STAND] *vt*
capire male

misunderstanding
[mis•UHN•dur•STAN•ding] *n*
malinteso M

misuse 1 [mis•YOOS] *n* cattivo
uso M

misuse 2 [mis•YOOZ] *vt*
abusare

mitigating [MI•ti•GAI•ting] *adj*
mitigante

mitten [MI•tn] *n* manopola F

mix [miks] *vt* mescolare

mixture [MIKS•chur] *n*
miscuglio M

moan [mon] *n* gemito M

moat [mot] *n* fossato M

mob [mahb] *n* folla F

mobile [MO•bl] *adj* mobile

mobilize [MO•bu•LUYZ] *vt*
mobilizzare

mock [mahk] *vt* deridere

mockery [MAH•ku•ree] *n*
beffa F

mode [mod] *n* modo M

model [MAH•dl] *adj* modello;
vt modellare

moderate 1 [MAH•du•rit] *adj n*
moderato; moderata

moderate 2 [MAH•du•RAIT]
vt moderare

moderation
[MAH•du•RAI•shn] *n*
moderazione F

modern [MAH•durn] *adj*
moderno; moderna

modernize [MAH•dur•NUYZ]
vt modernizzare

modest [MAH•dist] *adj*
modesto; modesta

modesty [MAH•di•stee] *n*
modestia F

modify [MAH•di•FUY] *vt*
modificare

moist [moist] *adj* umido; umida

moisten [MOI•sn] *vt* inumidire

moisture [MOIS•chur] *n*
umiditá F

molar [MO•lur] *n* molare M

molasses [mu•LA•sis] *n*
melassa F

mold 1 [mold] *n* muffa F

mold 2 [mold] (shape) *n*
stampo M

mole [mol] *n* talpa F

molest [mu•LEST] *vt* molestare

mollusk [MAH•lusk] *n*
mollusco M

molten [MOL•tn] *adj* liquefatto;
liquefatta

moment [MO•munt] *n*
momento M

momentary [MO•mun•TE•ree]
adj transitorio; transitoria

momentous [mo•MEN•tus] *adj*
importante

monarch [MAH•nahrk] *n*
monarca M

monarchy [MAH•nahr•kee] *n*
monarchia F

monastery [MAH•nu•STE•ree]
n monastero M

Monday [MUHN•dai] *n*
lunedí M

monetary [MAH•nu•TE•ree]
adj monetario; monetaria

money [MUH•nee] *n* denaro M

mongrel [MAHN•grul] *n* cane
bastardo M

monk [muhngk] *n* monaco M

monkey [MUHNG•kee] *n*
scimmi F

monologue [MAH•nu•LAHG]
n monologo M

monopolize
[mu•NAH•pu•LUYZ] *vt*
monopolizzare

monopoly [mu•NAH•pu•lee] *n*
monopolio M

monotone [MAH•nu•TON] *n*
monotonia F

monotonous [mu•NAH•tu•nus]
adj monotono; monotona

monotony [mu•NAH•tu•nee] *n*
monotonia F

monsoon [mahn•SOON] *n*
monsone M

monster [MAHN•stur] *n*
mostro M

monstrosity
[mahn•STRAH•si•tee] *n*
mostruositá F

monstrous [MAHN•strus] *adj*
mostruoso; mostruosa

month [muhnth] *n* mese M

monthly [MUHNTH•lee] *adj n*
mensile

monument [MAH•nyu•munt] *n*
monumento M

monumental
[MAH•nyu•MEN•tl] *adj*
monumentale

moo [moo] *n* muggito M

mood [mood] *n* umore M

moody [MOO•dee] *adj*
lunatico; lunatica

moon [moon] *n* luna F

moonlight [MOON•luyt] *n*
chiaro di luna M

moor [moour] *n* brughiera F

Moor [moour] *n* Moro M

mop [mahp] *n* moccio per
pavimenti M; *vt* asciugare

mope [mop] *vi* avvilirsi

moral [MAU•rul] *adj* morale

morale [mau•RAL] *n* morale M

morality [mu•RA•li•tee] *n*
moralitá F

morbid [MAUR•bid] *adj*
morboso; morbosa

more [maur] *adj* piú

moreover [mau•RO•vur] *adv* in
piú

morgue [maurg] *n* obitorio M

morning [MAUR•ning] *n*
mattino M

Morocco [mu•RAH•ko] *n*
Marocco M

moron [MAU•rahn] *n* idiota

morsel [MAUR•sl] *n*
bocconcino M

mortal [MAUR•tl] *adj n*
mortale

mortality [maur•TA•li•tee] *n*
mortalitá F

mortar [MAUR•tur] *n*
mortaio M

mortgage [MAUR•gij] *n*
ipoteca F

mortify [MAUR•ti•FUY] *vt*
mortificare

mosaic [mo•ZAI•ik] *n*
mosaico M

Moscow [MAH•skou] *n*
Mosca F

mosque [mahsk] *n* moschea F

mosquito [mu•SKEE•to] *n*
zanzara F

moss [maus] *n* muscio M

most [most] *adj* il massimo

mostly [MOST•lee] *adv* per lo
piú

moth [mauth] *n* falena F

mother [MUH•thur] *n* madre F

mother-in-law
[MUH•thur•in•LAU] *n*
suocera F

motherhood [MUH•thur•HUD]
n maternitá F

motherly [MUH•thur•lee] *adj*
materno; materna

motif [mo•TEEF] *n* motivo M

motion [MO•shn] *n* moto M;
(legal) *n* mozione F; *vt*
accennare a; far ceno a

motivate [MO•ti•VAIT] *vt*
motivare

motivation [MO•ti•VAI•shn] *n*
stimolo M

motive [MO•tiv] *n* motivo M

motor [MO•tur] *n* motore M

motorboat [MO•tur•BOT] *n*
motoscafo M

motorcycle [MO•tur•SUY•kl] *n*
ciclomotore M

motto [MAH•to] *n* motto M

mound [mound] *n* tumulo M

mount [mount] *n* cavalcatura F;
vi montare

mountaineer
[MOUN•tu•NEEUR] *n*
montanaro; montanara

mountainous [MOUN•tu•nus]
adj montuoso; montuosa

mourn [maurn] *vt* piangere

mourning [MAUR•ning] *n*
lutto M

mouse [mous] *n* topo M

moustache [MUH•stash] *n*
baffi M

mouth [mouth] *n* bocca F

mouthful [MOUTH•ful] *n*
boccone M

mouthwash [MOUTH•wahsh]
n colluttorio M

movable [MOO•vu•bl] *adj*
mobile

move [moov] *n* mossa F; *vt*
muovare; spostare; (feelings)
commuovere

movement [MOOV•munt] *n*
movimento M

movie [MOO•vee] *n* film M

moving [MOO•ving] *adj*
commovente

mow [mo] *vt* falciare

much [muhch] *adj* molto; molta

mucous (membrane)
[MYOO•kus] *n* mucosa F

mud [muhd] *n* fango M

muddle [MUH•dl] *n*
confusione F

muddy [MUH•dee] *adj* fangoso;
fangosa

muffin [MUH•fin] *n* muffin M

muffle [MUH•fl] *vt* smorzare

mug [muhg] *n* boccale M

mule [myooul] *n* mulo M

multiple [MUHL•ti•pl] *adj*
multiplo; multipla; *n*
multiplo M

multiplication
[MUHL•ti•pli•KAI•shn] *n*
moltiplicazione F

multiply [MUHL•ti•PLUY] *vt*
moltiplicare

multitude [MUHL•ti•TOOD] *n*
moltitudine F

mumble [MUHM•bl] *vt vi*
borbottare

mummy [MUH•mee] *n*
mummia F

mumps [muhmps] *n*
orecchioni M

munch [muhnch] *vt vi*
sgranocchiare

mundane [muhn•DAIN] *adj*
mondano; mondana

municipal [myoo•NI•si•pl] *adj*
municipale

municipality
[myoo•NI•si•PA•li•tee] *n*
municipalitá F

mural [MYOOU•rul] *n*
affresco M

murder [MUR•dur] *n* omicidio
M; assassinio M; *vt*
asassinare; ammazzare

murderer [MUR•du•rur] *n*
assassino M

murderous [MUR•du•rus] *adj*
omicida

murky [MUR•kee] *adj* torbido;
torbida

murmur [MUR•mur] *n*
mormorio M

muscle [MUH•sl] *n* muscolo M

muscular [MUH•skyu•lur] *adj*
muscoloso; muscolosa

muse [myooz] *n* musa F

museum [myoo•ZEE•um] *n*
museo M

mushroom [MUHSH•rum] *n*
fungo M

music [MYOO•zik] *n* musica F

musical [MYOO•zi•kl] *adj*
musicale

musician [myoo•ZI•shn] *n*
musicista

Muslim [MUHZ•lim] *adj*
mussulmano; mussulmana

mussel [MUH•sl] *n* muscolo M

must [muhst] *modal v* dovere

mustache [MUH•stash] baffi M

mustard [MUH•sturd] *n*
senape F

muster [MUH•stur] *vt* radunare

musty [MUH•stee] *adj*
ammuffito; ammuffita

mute [myoot] *adj n* muto; muta

mutilate [MYOO•ti•LAIT] *vt*
mutilare

mutiny [MYOO•ti•nee] *n*
ammutinamento M

mutter [MUH•tur] *vt vi*
borbottare

mutton [MUH•tn] *n*
montone M

mutual [MYOO•choo•ul] *adj*
reciproco; reciproca

muzzle [MUH•zl] *n*
museruola F

my [muy] *poss adj* mio; mia

myself [muy•SELF] *pron* io
stesso; io stessa

mysterious [mi•STEEU•ree•us]
adj misterioso; misteriosa

mystery [MI•stu•ree] *n*
mistero M

mystic [MI•stik] *n* mistico;
mistica

mystical [MI•sti•kl] *adj* mistico;
mistica

myth [mith] *n* mito M

mythical [MI•thi•kl] *adj* mitico; mitica

mythology [mi•THAH•lu•jee] *n* mitologia F

N

nab [nab] *vt* catturare

nag [nag] *vt* assillare

nail [naiul] *n* chiodo M; (finger) *n* unghia F

naive [nuy•EEV] *adj* ingenuo; ingenua

naked [NAI•kid] *adj* nudo; nuda

nakedness [NAI•kid•nis] *n* nudità F

name [naim] *n* nome M; *vt* chiamare

namely [NAIM•lee] *adv* vale a dire

nap [nap] *n* sonnellino M; *vt* fare un pisolino

napkin [NAP•kin] *n* tovagliolo M

narcotic [nahr•KAH•tik] *adj* narcotico; narcotica; *n* narcotico M

narrate [NA•rait] *vt* narrare

narration [na•RAI•shn] *n* narrazione F

narrative [NA•ru•tiv] *adj* narrativo; narrativa

narrator [na•RAI•tur] *n* narratore M

narrow [NA•ro] *adj* stretto; stretta

narrow-minded [NAI•row•MUYN•did] *adj* prevenuto; prevenuta

nasal [NAI•zl] *adj* nasale

nasturtium [nu•STUR•shum] *n* nasturzio M

nasty [NA•stee] *adj* sgradevole

nation [NAI•shn] *n* nazione F

national [NA•shu•nl] *adj* nazionale

nationality [NA•shu•NA•li•tee] *n* nazionalità F

nationalize [NA•shu•nu•LUYZ] *vt* nazionalizzare

native [NAI•tiv] *adj* innato; innata; *n* indigeno; indigena

Nativity [nu•TI•vi•tee] *n* Natività F

natural [NA•chrul] *adj* naturale

naturalize [NA•chru•LUYZ] *vt* naturalizzare

naturally [NA•chru•lee] *adv* naturalmente

nature [NA•chur] *n* natura F

naughty [NAU•tee] *adj* impertinente

nausea [NAU•zee•u] *n* nausea F

nauseate [NAU•zee•AIT] *vt* nauseare

nauseous [NAU•shus] *adj* nauseabondo; nauseabonda

naval [NAI•vl] *adj* navale

navel [NAI•vl] *n* ombelico M

navigate [NA•vi•GAIT] *vt*
navigare

navigation [NA•vi•GAI•shn] *n*
navigazione F

navigator [NA•vi•GAI•tur] *n*
navigatore M

navy [NAI•vee] *adj* marina F

near [neeur] *adj* vicino; vicina;
prep viciono a; *adv* vicino; *vt*
avvicinare

near-sighted [NEEUR•suy•tid]
adj miope

nearby [neeur•BUY] *adj* vicino;
vicina

nearly [NEEUR•lee] *adv* quasi

neat [neet] *adj* ordinato;
ordinata

necessary [NE•su•SE•ree] *adj*
necessario; necessaria

necessity [nu•SE•si•tee] *n*
necessitá F

neck [nek] *n* collo M

need [need] *n* bisogno M; *vi*
aver bisogno di; richiedere

needle [NEE•dl] *n* ago M; *vt*
punzecchiare (coll)

needless [NEED•lis] *adj* inutile

needy [NEE•dee] *adj*
bisognoso; bisognosa

negative [NE•gu•tiv] *adj*
negativo; negativa

neglect [ni•GLEKT] *n*
trascuratezza F

negligence [NE•gli•juns] *n*
negligenza

negligent [NE•gli•junt] *adj*
negligente

negotiate [ni•GO•shee•AIT] *vt*
vi trattare

negotiation
[ni•GO•shee•AI•shn] *n*
trattativa F

Negro [NEE•gro] *adj n* negro;
negra

neigh [nai] *vi* nitrire

neighbor [NAI•bur] *n* vicino;
vicina

neighborhood [NAI•bur•HUD]
n vicinato M

neither [NEE•thur] *adj* nessuno
dei due; nessuna delle due

nephew [NE•fyoo] *n* nipote

Neptune [NEP•toon] *n*
Nettuno M

nerve [nurv] *n* nervo M

nervous [NUR•vus] *adj*
nervoso; nervosa

nest [nest] *n* nido M; *vt*
annidarsi

net [net] *adj* rete F; *adj* netto

Netherlands [NE•thur•lundz]
npl Paesi Bassi M

nettle [NE•tl] *n* ortica F

network [NET•wurk] *n* rete F

neurosis [nu•RO•sis] *n*
nevrosi F

neurotic [nu•RAH•tik] *adj n*
nevrotico; nevrotica

neuter [NOO•tur] *adj* neutro;
neutra

neutral [NOO•trul] *adj* neutrale

neutrality [noo•TRA•li•tee] *n*
neutralitá F

neutralize [NOO•tru•LUYZ] *vt*
neutralizzare

never [NE•vr] *adv* mai;
(negative) no . . .

nevertheless [NE•vur•thu•LES]
adv tuttavia

new [noo] *adj* nuovo; nuova

New Year [NOO yeer] *n* anno
nuovo M

newly [NOO•lee] *adv* di fresco

news [nooz] *n* notizia F

newscast [NOOZ•kast] *n* notiziario M

newspaper [NOOZ•pai•pur] *n* giornale M

next [nekst] *adj* prossimo; prossima

next-door [NEXT•DOR] *adj* della porta accanto

nibble [NI•bl] *vt* mordicchiare

nice [nuys] *adj* simpatico; simpattica

nicely [NUYS•lee] *adv* bene

niche [nich] *n* nicchia F

nick [nik] *n* tacca F; *vt* intaccare

nickname [NIK•naim] *n* nomignolo M

nicotine [NI•ku•TEEN] *n* nicotina F

niece [nees] *n* nipote F

night [nuyt] *n* notte F

nightclub [NUYT•kluhb] *n* nightclub M

nightfall [NUYT•faul] *n* crepuscolo M

nightingale [NUY•ting•GAIUL] *n* usgnolo M

nightly [NUYT•lee] *adj* notturno; notturna

nightmare [NUYT•maiur] *n* incubo M

nimble [NIM•bl] *adj* agile

nine [nuyn] *num* nove

nineteen [nuyn•TEEN] *num* diciannove

ninety [NUYN•tee] *num* novanta

ninth [nuynth] *num* nono; nona

nipple [NI•pl] *n* capezzolo M

nitrogen [NUY•tru•jun] *n* azoto M

no [no] *adv* no; *adj* nessuno; neppure uno; (with compar) non

nobility [no•BI•li•tee] *n* nobiltá F

noble [NO•bl] *adj* nobile

nobody [NO•bu•dee] *pron* nessuno

nocturnal [nahk•TUR•nl] *adj* notturno; notturna

nod [nahd] *n* cenno del capo M; *vt* fare un cenno del capo; salutare

noise [noiz] *n* rumore M

noisy [NOY•zee] *adj* rumoroso; rumorosa

nominal [NAH•mi•nul] *adj* nominale

nominate [NAH•mi•NAIT] *vt* nominare

nomination [NAH•mi•NAI•shn] *n* nomina F

nonchalant [NAHN•shu•LAHNT] *adj* noncurante

nonconformist [NAHN•kun•FAUR•mist] *adj* *n* nonconformista

none [nuhn] *pron adj* nessuno; nessuna; nulla; niente; *adv* affatto; punto

nonentity [NAHN•EN•ti•tee] *n* persona insignificante F

nonetheless [NUHN•thu•LES] *adv* nondimeno

nonfiction [nahn•FIK•shn] *n* saggistica F

nonsense [NAHN•sens] *n*
frottole; assurdita F

nonsmoker [NAHN•SMO•kur]
n non fumatore M

nonstop [NAHN•STAHP] *adj*
continuo; continua

noodles [NOO•dlz] *npl*
tagliatelle F

noon [noon] *n* mezzogiorno M

noose [noos] *n* cappio M

nor [naur] *conj* né; neppure;
nemmeno

norm [naurm] *n* norma F

normal [NAUR•ml] *adj*
normale

normally [NAUR•mu•lee] *adv*
normalmente

north [naurth] *adj* a nord; *n*
nord M

North America [NORTH
u•ME•ri•ku] *n* nord america M

North Pole [NORTH POL] *n*
polo nord M

northern [NAUR•thurn] *adj*
settentrionale

Northern Ireland [NOR•thurn
UYUR•luhnd] *n* Irlanda del
Nord F

northward
[NAURTH•wurd(z)] *adv*
versonord

Norway [NAUR•wai] *n*
Norvegia F

Norwegian [naur•WEE•jun] *adj*
norvegese

nose [noz] *n* naso M

nostalgia [nah•STAL•ju] *n*
nostalgia F

nostril [NAH•stril] *n* narice F

nosy [NO•zee] *adj* curioso;
curiosa

not [naht] *adv* non

notable [NO•tu•bl] *adj* notabile

notably [NO•tu•blee] *adv*
notevolmente

notary [NO•tu•ree] *n* notaio M

notch [nahch] *n* tacca F

note [not] *n* nota F

notebook [NOT•buk] *n*
quaderno M.

noteworthy [NOT•wur•thee]
adj notevole

nothing [NUH•thing] *pron*
nulla F

notice [NO•tis] *n* avviso M;
vi notare; rilevare; far
attenzione a

noticeable [NO•ti•su•bl] *adj*
rilevante; apparente

notify [NO•ti•FUY] *vt* notificare

notion [NO•shn] *n* nozione F

notoriety [NO•tu•RUY•u•tee] *n*
notorietá F

notorious [no•TAU•ree•us] *adj*
famigerato; famigerta

notwithstanding
[NAHT•with•STAN•ding] *adv*
nonostante

noun [noun] *n* nome M

nourish [NU•rish] *vt* nutrire

nourishing [NU•ri•shing] *adj*
nutriente

nourishment [NU•rish•munt] *n*
nutrimento M

novel [NAH•vl] *n* romanzo M

novelist [NAH•vu•list] *n*
romanziere M

novelty [NAH•vul•tee] *n*
novitá F

November [no•VEM•bur] *n*
novembre M

novice [NAH•vis] *n* novizio; novizia

now [nau] *adv* ora; adesso

nowhere [NO•waiur] *adv* in nessun luogo

noxious [NAHK•shus] *adj* nocivo; nociva

nozzle [NAH•zl] *n* beccuccio M

nuance [NOO•ahns] *n* sfumatura F

nuclear [NOO•klee•ur] *adj* nucleare

nucleus [NOO•klee•us] *n* nucleo M

nude [nood] *adj n* nudo; nuda

nudge [nuhj] *n* gomitata F

nudist [NOO•dist] *n* nudista

nudity [NOO•di•tee] *n* nuditá F

nuisance [NOO•suns] *n* seccatura F

null [nuhl] *adj* nullo; nulla

nullify [NUH•li•FUY] *vt* annullare

numb [nuhm] *adj* insensibile

number [NUHM•bur] *n* numero M; *vi* numerare; contare

numeral [NOO•mu•rul] *n* numerale

numerous [NOO•mu•rus] *adj* numeroso; numerosa

nuptial [NUHP•shl] *adj* nuziale

nurse [nurs] *n* infermiera F

nursery [NUR•su•ree] *n* camera dei bambini F

nursery rhyme [NUR•su•ree RYM] *n* filastrocca F

nurture [NUR•chur] *vt* allevare

nut [nuht] *n* noce F

nutcracker [NUHT•kra•kurz] *n* schiaccianoci M

nutrition [noo•TRI•shn] *n* nutrizione F

nutritious [noo•TRI•shus] *adj* nutriente

nylon [NUY•lahn] *n* nylon M

nymph [nimf] *n* ninfa F

O

o'clock [u•KLAHK] *adv* ora

oak [ok] *n* quercia F

oar [aur] *n* remo M

oasis [o•AI•sis] *n* oasi F

oath [oth] *n* giuramento M

oatmeal [OT•meeul] *n* fiocchi d'avena M

oats [ots] *npl* avena F

obedience [o•BEE•dee•uns] *n* obbedienza F

obedient [o•BEE•dee•unt] *adj* obbediente

obese [o•BEES] *adj* obeso; obesa

obey [o•BAI] *vt* obbedir

obituary [o•BI•choo•E•ree] *n* necrologia F

object [n. AHB•jekt v. ub•JEKT] *n* oggetto M; *vi* obiettare; protestare

objection [ub•JEK•shn] *n* obiezione F

objective 1 [ub•JEK•tiv] *adj* oggettivo; oggettiva

objective 2 [ub•JEK•tiv] *n*
obbiettivo M

obligation [AH•bli•GAI•shn] *n*
obbligo M

obligatory [u•BLI•gu•TAU•ree]
adj obbligatorio; obbligatoria

oblige [u•BLUYJ] *vt* fare un
favore

obliging [u•BLUY•jing] *adj*
compiacente

oblique [o•BLEEK] *adj*
obliquo; obliqua

obliterate [u•BLI•tu•RAIT] *vt*
cancellare

oblivion [u•BLI•vee•un] *n*
oblio M

oblivious [u•BLI•vee•us] *adj*
dimentico; dimentica

obnoxious [ub•NAHK•shus]
adj oioso; odiosa

obscene [ub•SEEN] *adj* osceno;
oscena

obscenity [ub•SE•ni•tee] *n*
oscenitá F

obscure [ub•SKYOOUR] *adj*
oscuro; oscura; *vi* offuscare;
velare

obscurity [ub•SKYU•ri•tee] *n*
oscuritá F

observance [ub•ZUR•vuns] *n*
osservanza F

observant [ub•ZUR•vunt] *adj*
osservante

observation
[AHB•sur•VAI•shn] *n*
osservazione F

observatory
[ob•SUR•vuh•TOR•ee]
osservatorio M

observe [ub•ZURV] *vt*
osservare

observer [ub•ZUR•vur] *adj*
osservatore M

obsess [ub•SES] *vt* ossessionare

obsession [ub•SE•shn] *n*
ossessione F

obsessive [ub•SE•siv] *adj*
ossessivo; ossessiva

obsolete [AHB•su•LEET] *adj*
antiquato; antiquata

obstacle [AHB•stu•kl] *n*
ostacolo M

obstinacy [AHB•sti•ni•cee] *n*
ostinatezza F

obstinate [AHB•sti•nit] *adj*
ostinato; ostinata

obstruct [ub•STRUHKT] *vt*
ostruire

obstruction [ub•STRUHK•shn]
n ostruzione F

obtain [ub•TAIN] *vt* ottenere

obtuse [ub•TOOS] *adj* ottuso;
ottusa

obvious [AHB•vee•us] *adj*
ovvio; ovvia

obviously [AHB•vee•us•lee] *adj*
ovviamente

occasion [u•KAI•zhn] *n*
occasione F

occasional [u•KAI•zhu•nl] *adj*
occasionale

occasionally
[u•KAI•zhu•nu•lee] *adv*
occasionalmente

occult [u•KUHLT] *adj* occulto;
occulta

occupant [AH•kyu•punt] *n*
occupante

occupation [AH•kyu•PAI•shn]
occupazione F

occupy [AH•kyu•PUY] *vt*
occupare

occur [u•KUR], *vi* accadere

occurence [u•KU•runs] *n* avvenimento M

ocean [O•shn] *n* oceano M

octagon [AHK•tu•GAHN] *n* ottagono M

October [ahk•TO•bur] *n* ottobre M

octupus [AHK•tu•pus] *n* polipo M

odd [ahd] *adj* strano; strana

oddity [AH•di•tee] *n* stranezza F

odious [O•dee•us] *adj* odioso; odiosa

odor [O•dur] *n* odore M

of [uhv] *prep* di

off [auf] *adj* esterno; esterna; *adv* vi; distante; *prep* lontano da; fuori (di)

offend [u•FEND] *vt* offendere

offense [u•FENS] *n* offesa F

offensive [u•FEN•siv] *adj* offensivo; offensiva

offer [AU•fur] *n* offrire

offering [AU•fu•ring] *n* offerta F

offhand [AUF•HAND] *adj* disinvolto; disinvolta

office [AU•fis] *n* ufficio M

officer [AU•fi•sur] *n* ufficiale M

official [u•FI•shl] *adj* ufficiale

offspring [AUF•spring] *n* prole F

offstage [AUF•STAIJ] *adj adv* tra le quinte

often [AU•fn] *adv* spesso; sovento; molte volte

oil [oiul] *n* olio M; petrolio M; *vt* ungere; lubrificare

oily [OIU•lee] *adj* oleoso; oleosa

ointment [OINT•munt] *n* unguento M

old [old] *adj* vecchio; vecchia

old age [OLD AIG] *n* vecchiaia F

old-fashioned [OLD•FA•shund] *adj* antiquato; antiquata

olive 1 [AH•liv] *n* oliva F

olive 2 [AH•liv] *adj* olivastro; olivastra

omelet [AHM•lit] *n* frittata F

omen [O•mn] *n* auspicio M

ominous [AH•mi•nus] *adj* sinistro; sinistra

omission [o•MI•shn] *n* omissione F

omit [o•MIT] *vt* omettere

omnipotent [ahm•NI•pu•tunt] *adj* onnipotente

omniscience [ahm•NI•shents] *adj* onnisciente

on [ahn] *prep* su; sopra; *adv* su; *adj* accesso

once [wuhns] *adv* una volta

one [wuhn] *num* uno; una

one-sided [WUHN•SUY•did] *adj* unilaterale

one-way [WUHN•WAI] *adj* a senso unico

oneself [wuhn•SELF] *pron* sé stesso; sé stessa

onion [UH•nyun] *n* cipolla F

onlooker [AHN•lu•kur] *n* astante

only [ON•lee] *adj* unico; unica

onslaught [AHN•slaut] *n* assalto M

onward [AHN•wurd] *adv* avanti

ooze [ooz] *vi* colare lentamente

opal [O•pl] *n* opale M

opaque [o•PAIK] *adj* opaco; opaca

open [O•pn] *adj* aperto; aperta

open-minded [O•pn•MUYN•did] *adj* senza preconcetti

opening [O•pu•ning] *n* apertura F; *adj* iniziale

openly [O•pn•lee] *adv* apertamente

opera [AH•pru] *n* opera F

operate [AH•pu•RAIT] *vt* operare

operation [AH•pu•RAI•shn] *n* operazione F

operator (machine) [AH•pu•RAI•tur] *n* operatore M; (telephone) [ah•pu•rai•tur] *n* centralinista

opinion [u•PI•nyun] *n* opinone F

opinionated [u•PI•nyu•NAI•tid] *adj* dogmatico; dogmatica

opponent [u•PO•nunt] *n* avversario; avversaria

opportune [AH•pur•TOON] *adj* opportuno; opportuna

opportunist [AH•pur•TOO•nist] *n* opportunista

opportunity [AH•pur•TOON•ah•tee] *n* opportunitá F

oppose [u•POZ] *vt* opporre

opposed [u•POZD] *adj* opposto; opposta

opposing [u•PO•zing] *adj* opposto; opposta

opposite [AH•pu•sit] *adj* di fronte

opposition [AH•pu•ZI•shn] *n* opposizione F

oppress [u•PRES] *vt* opprimere

oppression [u•PRE•shn] *n* oppressione F

oppressive [u•PRE•siv] *adj* oppressivo; oppressiva

opt [ahpt] *vi* optare

optical [AHP•ti•kl] *adj* ottico; ottica

optician [ahp•TI•shn] *n* ottico M

optimism [AHP•ti•MI•zm] *n* ottimismo M

optimist [AHP•ti•mist] *n* ottimista

optimistic [AHP•ti•MI•stik] *adj* ottimistico; ottimistica

option [AHP•shn] *n* opzione F

optional [AHP•shu•nl] *adj* facoltativo; facoltativa

opulence [AH•pyu•luns] *n* opulenza F

opulent [AH•pyu•lunt] *adj* opulento; opulenta

or [aur] *conj* o

oracle [AU•ru•kl] *n* oracolo M

orange [AU•runj] *adj* arancio; *n* arancia F

orator [AU•rai•tur] *n* oratore M

oratory [AU•ru•TAU•ree] *n* eloquenza F

orbit [AUR•bit] *n* orbita F

orchard [AUR•churd] *n* frutteto M

orchestra [AUR•ku•stru] *n* orchestra F

orchestral [aur•KE•strul] *adj* orchestrale

orchid [AUR•kid] *n* orchidea F

order [AUR•dur] *n* odine M

orderly [AUR•dur•lee] *adj*
disciplinato; disciplinata

ordinarily 1
[AUR•di•NE•ri•lee] *adv*
normalmente

ordinarily 2
[AUR•di•NE•ri•lee] *adv* di
solito

ordinary [AUR•di•NE•ree] *adj*
ordinario; ordinaria

ore [aur] *n* metallo grezzo M

oregano [au•RE•gu•NO] *n*
origano M

organ [AUR•gn] *n* organo M

organic [aur•GA•nik] *adj*
organico; organica

organism [AUR•gu•NI•zm] *n*
organismo M

organization
[AUR•gu•ni•ZAI•shn] *n*
organizzazione F

organize [AUR•gu•NUYZ] *vt*
organizzare

orgasm [AUR•ga•zm] *n*
orgasmo M

orgy [AUR•gee] *n* orgia F

oriental [AU•ree•EN•tl] *adj*
orientale

orientate [AU•ree•un•TAIT] *vt*
orientare

orientation
[AU•ree•un•TAI•shn] *n*
orientamento M

orifice [AU•ri•fis] *n* orificio M

origin [AU•ri•jin] *n* origine F

original [u•RI•ji•nl] *adj n*
originale

originality [u•RI•ji•NA•li•tee] *n*
originalitá F

originally [u•RI•ji•nu•lee] *adv*
originariamente

originate [or•RI•ji•NAIT] *vt*
originare

ornament [AUR•nu•munt] *n*
ornamento M

ornamental [AUR•nu•MEN•tl]
adj ornamentale

ornate [aur•NAIT] *adj* ornato;
ornata

orphan [AUR•fn] *n* orfano;
orfana

orphanage [AUR•fu•nij] *n*
orfanotrofio M

orthodox [AUR•thu•DAHKS]
adj ortodosso; ortodossa

oscillate [AH•si•LAIT] *vi*
oscillare

ostensible [ah•STEN•si•bl] *adj*
apparente

ostentatious
[AH•stun•TAI•shus] *adj*
ostentato; ostentata

ostrich [AHS•trich] *n* struzzo M

other [UH•thur] *adj* altro; altra

otherwise [UH•thur•WUYZ]
adv altrimenti

otter [AH•tur] *n* lontra F

ought [aut] *aux v* dovere

ounce [ouns] *n* oncia F

our [ouur] *poss adj* nostro;
nostra

ours [ouurz] *poss pron* nostro;
nostra

ourselves [ouur•SELVZ] *pron*
pl noi stessi; noi stesse

oust [oust] *vt* espellere

out [out] *adv* fuori

outbreak [OUT•braik] *n*
scoppio M

outburst [OUT•burst] *n*
eruzione F

outcast [OUT•kast] *n* reietto;
reietta

outcome [OUT•kuhm] *n*
risultato M

outcry [OUT•cruy] *n* grido M

outdated [out•DAI•tid] *adj*
fuori moda

outdoor [OUT•dauur] *adj*
all'aperto

outdoors [out•DAUURZ] *adv*
all'aperto

outer [OU•tur] *adj* esterno;
esterna

outfit [OUT•fit] *n* compagnia F

outgoing [OUT•go•ing] *adj*
espansivo; espansiva

outhouse [OUT•hous] *n*
latrina F

outing [OU•ting] *n* gita F

outlaw [n. OUT•lau v.
OUT•lau] *n* fuori legge; *vt*
bandire

outlet [OUT•let] *n* sbocco M

outline [OUT•luyn] *n*
contorno M

outlive [out•LIV] *vt*
sopravvivere

outlook [OUT•luk] *n*
prospettiva F

outmoded [out•MO•did] *adj*
fuori moda

outnumber [out•NUHM•bur] *vt*
superare in numero

output [OUT•put] *n*
produzione F

outrage [OUT•raij] *n*
oltraggio M

outrageous [out•RAI•jus] *adj*
eccessivo; eccessiva

outright [out•RUYT] *adj*
diretto; diretta

outset [OUT•set] *n* principio M

outside [out•SUYD] *prep adv*
fuori

outsider [out•SUY•dur] *n*
estraneo; estranea

outskirts [OUT•skurts] *npl*
periferia F

outspoken [out•SPO•kn] *adj*
franco; franca

outstanding [out•STAN•ding]
adj rilevante

outward [OUT•wurd] *adj*
esteriore

outwardly [OUT•wurd•lee] *adv*
esternamente

outweigh [out•WAI] *vt*
superare in importanza

oval [O•vl] *adj n* ovale

ovary [O•vu•ree] *n* ovaia F

ovation [o•VAI•shn] *n*
ovazione F

oven [UH•vn] *n* forno M

over [O•vr] *adj* di sopra

overall [O•vur•AUL] *adj*
globale; *adv*
complessivamente

overalls [O•vur•aulz] *npl* tuta F

overbearing [O•vur•BAIU•ring]
adj arrogante

overboard [O•vur•baurd] *adv*
fuori bordo

overcast [O•vur•kast] *adj*
coperto; coperta (di nubi)

overcharge [O•vur•CHAHRJ]
vt far pagare in piú

overcoat [O•vur•KOT] *n*
cappotto `M

overcome [O•vur•KUHM] *vt*
sopraffare

overdo [O•vur•DOO] *vt* strafare
overdraw [O•vur•DRAU] *vt* scoprire (an account)
overdrawn [O•vur•DRAUN] *adj* scoperto; scoperta
overflow [O•vur•FLO] *n* scarico M; *vt* inondare
overgrown [O•vur•GRON] *adj* cresciuto troppo
overhaul [O•vur•HAUL] *vt* revisionare
overhear [O•vur•HEEUR] *vt* udire per caso
overjoyed [O•vur•JOID] *adj* felicissimo; felicissima
overlap [O•vur•LAP] *vt* sovrapporre
overlook [O•vur•LUK] *vt* trascurare
overnight [O•vur•NUYT] *adj* dall'oggi al domani
overpower [O•vur•POU•ur] *vt* sopraffare
overrun [O•vur•RUHN] *adj* infestato; infestata
overseas [O•vur•SEEZ] *adj* d'oltremare; *adv* oltremare
oversee [O•vur•SEE] *vt* soprintendere
overseer [O•vur•SEE•ur] *n* soprintendente

overshadow [O•vur•SHA•do] *vt* adombrare
overstep [O•vur•STEP] *vt* oltrepassare
overtake [O•vur•TAIK] *vt* sorpassare
overthrow [O•vur•THRO] *vt* rovesciare
overtime [O•vur•tuym] *n* straordinario M
overture [O•vur•chur] *n* approccio M
overweight [O•vur•WAIT] *adj* che pesa troppo
overwhelm [O•vur•WELM] *vt* sopraffare
overwhelming [O•vur•WEL•ming] *adj* sfrenato; sfrenata
overwork [O•vur•WURK] *vt* lavorare eccessivamente
owe [o] *vt* dovere
owl [ouul] *n* gufo M
own [on] *adj* proprio; propria
owner [O•nur] *n* proprietario; proprietaria
ownership [O•nur•SHIP] *n* possesso M
ox [ahks] *n* bue M
oxygen [AHK•si•jun] *n* ossigeno M
oyster [OI•stur] *n* ostrica F

P

pace [pais] *n* passo M
Pacific [pu•SI•fik] *adj n* Pacifico
pacify [PA•si•FUY] *vt* placare

pack [pak] *n* pacchetto M; *vt* imballare
package [PA•kij] *n* pacco M

packet [PA•kit] *n* pacchetto M

packing [PA•king] *n* imballaggio M

pact [pakt] *n* patto M

pad [pad] *n* assorbente M

padding [PA•ding] *n* imbottitura F

paddle [PA•dl] *n* pagaia F

padlock [PAD•lahk] *n* lucchetto M

pagan [PAI•gn] *adj n* pagano; pagana

page [paij] *n* pagina F

pail [paiul] *n* secchio M

pain [pain] *n* dolore M

painful [PAIN•ful] *adj* doloroso; dolorosa

painless [PAIN•lis] *adj* indolore

painstaking [PAIN•STAI•king] *adj* meticoloso; meticolosa

paint [paint] *n* colore M

paintbrush [PAINT•bruhsh] *n* pennello M

painter [PAIN•tur] *n* pittore M

painting [PAIN•ting] *n* dipinto M

pair [paiur] *n* paio M

pajamas [pu•JA•muz] *npl* pigiama M

Pakistan [PA•ki•STAN] *n* Pakistan M

pal [pal] *n* amico M

palace [PA•lis] *n* palazzo M

palatable [PA•li•tu•bl] *adj* gustoso; gustosa

palate [PA•lit] *n* palato M

pale [paiul] *adj* pallido; pallida

Palestine [PA•li•STUYN] *n* Palestina F

palette [PA•lit] *n* tavolozza F

palm [pahm] *n* palmo M

Palm Sunday [PALM SUN•dai] *n* Domenica delle palme F

palpable [PAL•pu•bl] *adj* palpabile

paltry [PAUL•tree] *adj* irrisorio; irrisoria

pamper [PAM•pur] *vt* coccolare

pamphlet [PAM•flit] *n* opuscolo M

pan [pan] *n* tegame M

panacea [PA•nu•SEE•uh] *n* panacea F

Panama [PA•nu•MAH] *n* Panama F

pancake [PAN•kaik] *n* frittella F

panda [PAN•du] *n* panda M

pane [pain] *n* vetro M

panel [PA•nl] *n* pannello M

pang [pang] *n* fitta F

panic [PA•nik] *n* panico M; *vi* essere in preda al panico

pansy [PAN•zee] *n* viola del pensiero F

pant [pant] *vi* ansare

panther [PAN•thur] *n* pantera F

panties [PAN•teez] *npl* mutandine F

pantyhose [PAN•tee•HOZ] *n* collant M

pantry [PAN•tree] *n* dispensa F

pants [pants] *npl* pantaloni M

papa [PAH•pu] *n* papá M

papal [PAI•pl] *adj* papale

paper [PAI•pur] *n* carta F; documento M; giornale M; *vt* tappezzare

paperback [PAI•pur•BAK] *n* edizione economica F

par [pahr] *n* pari F

parable [PA•ru•bl] *n* parabola F

parachute [PA•ru•SHOOT] *n*
paracadute M

parade [pu•RAID] *n* parata F;
vt ostentare; sfoggiare

paradise [PA•ru•DUYS] *n*
paradiso M

paradox [PA•ru•DAHKS] *n*
paradosso M

paragraph (break; pause)
[PA•ru•GRAF] *n* paragrafo M

Paraguay [PA•ru•GWAI] *n*
Paraguay M

parakeet [PA•ru•KEET] *n*
cocorita F

parallel [PA•ru•LEL] *adj*
parallelo; parallela

paralysis [pu•RA•lu•sis] *n*
paralisi F

paralyze [PA•ru•LUYZ] *vt*
paralizzare

paranoid [PA•ru•NOID] *adj*
paranoico; paranoica

paraphernalia
[PA•ru•fu•NAIU•lyu] *n*
armamentario M

parasite [PA•ru•SUYT] *n*
parassita M

parasol [PA•ru•SAUL] *n*
parasole M

parcel [PAHR•sl] *n* pacchetto M

parched [pahrchd] *adj* inaridito;
inaridita

parchment [PAHRCH•munt] *n*
pergamena F

pardon [PAHR•dn] *n*
perdono M

parent [PA•runt] *n* genitore M

parenthesis [pu•REN•thu•sis] *n*
parentesi F

parish [PA•rish] *n* parrocchia F

park [pahrk] *n* parco M; *vt*
parcheggiare; posteggiare

parking [PAHR•king] *n*
parcheggio M

parking lot [~ LAHT] *n*
parcheggio M

parlance [PAHR•luns] *n*
linguaggio M

parliament [PAHR•lu•munt] *n*
parlamento M

parliamentary
[PAHR•lu•MEN•tu•ree] *adj*
parlamentare

parlor [PAHR•lur] *n* salotto M

parochial [pu•RO•kee•ul] *adj*
parrocchiale

parody [PA•ru•dee] *n* parodia
F; *vt* parodiare

parole [pu•ROUL] *n* parola
d'onore F

parrot [PA•rut] *n* pappagallo M

parsley [PAHR•slee] *n*
prezzemolo M

parsnip [PAR•snip] *n*
pastinaca F

parson [PAHR•sn] *n* pastore M

part [pahrt] *n* parte F; (theat)
ruolo; (district) quartiere F;
adv adj a mezzo tempo; *vi*
separare; spatire

part-time [PAHRT•TUYM] *adj*
adv a mezza giornata

partial [PAHR•shl] *adj* parziale

partiality [PAHR•shee•A•li•tee]
n parzialitá F

partially [PAHR•shu•lee] *adv*
parzialmente

participant [pahr•TI•si•punt] *n*
partecipante

participate [pahr•TI•si•PAIT] *vi*
partecipare

participation
[pahr•TI•si•PAI•shn] *n*
partecipazione F

particle [PAHR•ti•kl] *n*
particella F

particular [pur•TI•kyu•lur] *adj*
particolare

particularly
[pur•TI•kyu•lur•lee] *adv*
particolarmente

parting [PAHR•ting] *n*
separazione F

partisan [PAHR•ti•sun] *adj n*
partigiano; partigiana

partition [pahr•TI•shn] *n*
divisione F

partly [PAHRT•lee] *adv* in
parte

partner [PAHRT•nur] *n* socio;
socia

partnership
[PAHRT•nur•SHIP] *n*
societá F

partridge [PAHR•trij] *n*
pernice F

party [PAHR•tee] *n* festa F

pass [pas] *n* lasciapassare M

passage [PA•sij] *n* passaggio M

passenger [PA•sin•jur] *n*
passeggero; passeggera

passerby [PA•sur•BUY] *n*
passante

passion [PA•shn] *n* passione F

passionate [PA•shu•nit] *adj*
appassionato; appassionata

passive [PA•siv] *adj* passivo;
passiva

passport [PAS•paurt] *n*
passaporto M

password [PAS•wurd] *n* parola
d'ordine F

past [past] *adj* passato; passata;
prep al do là di; oltre; *n*
passato M

pasta [PAH•stu] *n* pasta F

paste [paist] *n* pasta F

pastel [pa•STEL] *adj n*
pastello M

pasteurize [PAS•chu•RUYZ] *vt*
pastorizzare

pastime [PAS•tuym] *n*
passatempo

pastor [PA•stur] *n* pastore M

pastry [PAI•stree] *n*
pasticceria F

pastry shop [PAI•stree SHOP]
n pasticceria F

pasture [PAS•chur] *n* pascolo M

pat [pat] *n* buffetto M; *vt* dare
un buffeto a

patch [pach] *n* pezza F; *vi*
rattoppare

pâté [pa•TAI] *n* pâté M

patent [PA•tunt] *adj* chiaro;
chiara

patent leather [PA•tunt
LE•thur] *n* pellucida F

paternal [pu•TUR•nl] *adj*
paterno; paterna

paternity [pu•TUR•ni•tee] *n*
paternitá F

path [path] *n* sentiero M

pathetic [pu•THE•tik] *adj*
patetico; patetica

pathology [pa•THAH•lu•jee] *n*
patologia F

pathway [PATH•wai] *n*
sentiero M

patience [PAI•shns] *n*
pazienza F

patient [PAI•shnt] *adj n*
paziente

patriot [PAI•tree•ut] *n* patriota

patriotic [PAI•tree•AH•tik] *adj*
patriottico; patriottica

patriotism [PAI•tree•u•TI•zm]
n patriottismo M

patrol [pu•TROUL] *n*
pattuglia F

patron [PAI•trun] *n* cliente

patronize [PAI•tru•NUYZ] *vt*
patrocinare

patronizing
[PAI•tru•NUY•zing] *adj*
condiscendente

patter [PA•tur] *n* discorso M

pattern [PA•turn] *n* modello M

pause [pauz] *n* pausa F

pave [paiv] *vt* lastricare

pavement [PAIV•munt] *n*
lastrico M

pavilion [pu•VIL•yun] *n*
padiglione M

paw [pau] *n* zampa F; *vt*
palpeggiare

pawn [paun] *n* pedina F

pawnshop [PAUN•shahp] *n*
monte dei pegni M

pay [pai] *n* paga F

pay off (dismiss) [PAI AHF] *vt*
liquidare

pay phone [PAI fon] *n* telefono
pubblico M

payable [PAI•yu•bl] *adj*
pagabile

paycheck [PAI•chek] *n* busta
paga F

payment [PAI•munt] *n*
pagamento M

payroll [PAI•roul] *n* libro
paga M

pea [pee] *n* pisello M

peace [pees] *n* pace F;
tranquillità F

peaceful [PEES•ful] *adj*
pacifico; pacifica

peach [peech] *n* pesca F

peacock [PEE•cahk] *n*
pavone M

peak [peek] *n* picco M

peal [peeul] *vt* scampanare

peanut [PEE•nuht] *n* arachide F

peanut butter [PEE•nut
BUH•tur] *n* burro di
arachidi M

pear [paiur] *n* pera F

pearl [purl] *n* perla F

peasant [PE•znt] *n* contadino;
contadina

peat [peet] *n* torba F

pebble [PE•bl] *n* sassolino M

peck [pek] *n* beccata F; *vt*
beccare; (food)
mangiucchiare; (kiss) dare un
bacetto a

peculiar [pi•KYOOU•lyur] *adj*
particolare

pedal [PE•dl] *n* pedale M; *vt*
pedalare

pedant [PE•dunt] *n* pedante

pedantic [pi•DAN•tik] *adj*
pedantesco; pedantesca

peddle [PE•dl] *vt* vendere al
minuto

pedestal [PE•du•stl] *n*
pedestallo M

pedestrian [pi•DE•stree•un] *n*
pedone M

pedigree [PE•di•GREE] *adj* di
razza

peek [peek] *vi* sbirciare

peel [peeul] *n* buccia F; *vt*
sbucciare; (paint; skin)
staccarsi

peep [peep] *vi* guardare
furtivamente

peephole [PEEP•houl] *n* spioncino M

peer 1 [peeùr] *n* pari M

peer 2 [peeur] *vt* scrutare; guardare da presso

peg [peg] *n* piuolo M

pellet [PE•lit] *n* pallottolina F

pelt [pelt] *n* pelle F

pen 1 [pen] *n* penna F; *vt* scrivere

pen 2 [pen] *n* recinto M; *vt* ~ in\ rinchiudere

penal [PEE•nl] *adj* penale

penalty [PE•nl•tee] *n* penalitá F

penance [PE•nuns] *n* penitenza F

penchant [PEN•chnt] *n* inclinazione F

pencil [PEN•sl] *n* matita F

pencil sharpener [pen•sil shar•pin•ur] *n* temperamatite M

pendant [PEN•dnt] *n* pendente M

pending [PEN•ding] *adj* in sospeso

pendulum [PEN•dyu•lum] *n* pendolo M

penetrate [PE•nu•TRAIT] *vt* penetrare

penguin [PENG•gwin] *n* pinguino M

penicillin [PE•ni•SI•lin] *n* penicillina F

peninsula [pu•NIN•su•lu] *n* penisola F

penis [PEE•nis] *n* pene M

pennant [PE•nunt] *n* gagliardetto M

penniless [PE•nee•lis] *adj* senza un soldo

penny [PE•nee] *n* centesimo M

pension [PEN•shn] *n* pensione F

pensive [PEN•siv] *adj* pensoso; pensosa

penthouse [PENT•haus] *n* attico M

people [PEE•pl] *npl* gente F

pepper [PE•pur] *n* pepe M

peppermint [PE•pur•mint] *n* menta peperita F

per [pur] *prep* per

perceive [pur•SEEV] *vt* percepire

percent [pur•SENT] *adv* per cento

percentage [pur•SEN•tij] *n* percentuale F

perception [pur•SEP•shn] *n* percezione F

perch [purch] *n* gruccia F

perennial [pu•RE•nee•ul] *adj* perenne

perfect [adj. PUR•fikt v. pur•FEKT] *adj* perfetto; perfetta; *vi* perfezionare

perfection [pur•FEK•shn] *n* perfezione F

perfectionist [pur•FEK•shu•nist] *n* perfezionista

perfectly [PUR•fikt•lee] *adv* perfettamente

perforate [PUR•fu•RAIT] *vt* perforare

perform [pur•FAURM] *vi* eseguire; (mus/theat) recitare

performance [pur•FAUR•mns] *n* rappresentazione F

perfume [PUR•fyoom] *n* profumo M; *vt* profumare

perhaps [pur•HAPS] *adv* forse; magari

peril [PE•ril] *n* pericolo M

perimeter [pu•RI•mi•tur] *n* perimetro M

period [PEEU•ree•ud] *n* periodo M; punto fermo; *adj* antico; storico

periodic [PI•ree•AH•dik] *adj* periodico; periodica

periodical [PI•ree•AH•di•kl] *n* periodico M

perish [PE•rish] *vi* perire

perjury [PUR•ju•ree] *n* spergiuro M

perm [purm] *n* permanente F

permanent [PUR•mi•nunt] *adj* permanente

permeate [PUR•mee•AIT] *vt* permeare

permission [pur•MI•shn] *n* permess M

permit [n. PUR•mit v. pur•MIT] *n* permesso M; *vt* permettere

perpendicular [PUR•pn•DI•kyu•lur] *adj n* perpendicolare

perpetrate [PUR•pu•TRAIT] *vt* perpetrare

perpetual [pur•PE•choo•ul] *adj* perpetuo; perpetua

perplex [pur•PLEKS] *vt* rendere perplesso

perplexed [pur•PLEKST] *adj* perplesso; perplessa

persecute [PUR•si•KYOOT] *vt* perseguitare

perseverance [PUR•si•VEEU•rns] *n* perseveranza F

persevere [PUR•si•VEEUR] *vi* perseverare

Persian Gulf [PUR•zhn ~] *n* Golfo Persico M

persist [pur•SIST] *vi* persistere

persistence [pur•SI•stns] *n* persistenza F

persistent [pur•SI•stnt] *adj* persistente

person [PUR•sn] *n* persona F

personal [PUR•su•nl] *adj* personale

personality [PUR•su•NA•li•tee] *n* personalitá F

personnel [PUR•su•NEL] *n* personale M

perspective [pur•SPEK•tiv] *n* prospettiva F

perspiration [PUR•spu•RAI•shn] *n* traspirazione F

perspire [pur•SPUYUR] *vi* sudare

persuade [pur•SWAID] *vt* persuadere

persuasion [pur•SWAI•zhn] *n* persuasione F

persuasive [pur•SWAI•siv] *adj* persuasivo; persuasiva

pertain [pur•TAIN] *vi* appartenere

pertinent [PUR•ti•nunt] *adj* pertinente

perturb [pur•TURB] *vt* sconvolgere

perverse [pur•VURS] *adj* perverso; perversa

pervert [n. PUR•vurt v. pur•VURT] *n* pervertito; pervertita; *vt* pervertire

pessimism [PE•si•MI•zm] *n*
pessimismo M

pessimist [PE•si•mist] *n*
pessimista

pessimistic [PE•si•MI•stik] *adj*
pessimistico; pessimistica

pest [pest] *n* flagello M

pester [PE•stur] *vt* importunare

pet [pet] *n* animale di casa M;
npl carezze amorose; F *vt*
coccolare

petal [PE•tl] *n* petalo M

petition [pu•TI•shn] *n* petizione
F; *vi* presentare un petizione

petrified [PE•tri•FUYD] *adj*
petrificato; petrificata

petroleum [pu•TRO•lee•um] *n*
petrolio M

petty [PE•tee] *adj* insignificante

pew [pyoo] *n* banco M

phantom [FAN•tum]-*n*
fantasma M

pharmacist [FAHR•mu•sist] *n*
farmacista

pharmacy [FAHR•mu•see] *n*
farmacia F

phase [faiz] *n* fase F

phenomenon
[fu•NAH•mu•NAHN] *n*
fenomeno M

philosopher [fi•LAH•su•fur] *n*
filosofo M

philosophical [FI•lu•SAH•fi•kl]
adj filosofico; filosofica

philosophy [fi•LAH•su•fee] *n*
filosofia F

phone [fon] *n* telefono M

phone booth [fon booth] *n*
cabina telefonica F

phone call [fon kal] *n*
telefonata F

phonetics [fu•NE•tiks] *n*
fonetica F

phony [FO•nee] *adj* falso; falsa

photo [FO•to] *n* foto F

photograph [FO•tu•graf] *n*
fotografia F; *vt* fotografare

photographer
[fu•TAH•gru•fur] *n* fotografo;
fotografa

photography [fu•TAH•gru•fee]
n fotografia F

phrase [fraiz] *n* frase F; *vi*
esprimere; formulare

physical [FI•zi•kl] *adj* fisico;
fisica F

physician [fi•ZI•shn] *n*
medico M

physicist [FI•zi•sist] *n* fisico;
fisica

physics [FI•ziks] *n* fisica F

physique [fi•ZEEK] *n* fisico M

pianist [pee•U•nist] *n* pianista

piano [pee•A•no] *n* piano M

pick [pik] *n* strumento appuntito
M; *vt* scegliere; cogliere

picket [PI•kit] *n* picchetto M

pickle [PI•kl] *n* sottaceto M

pickpocket [PIK•PAH•kit] *n*
borsaiolo M

picnic [PIK•nik] *n*
scampagnata F

picture [PIK•chur] *n* quadro M;
vi immaginare; figurare

picturesque [PIK•chu•RESK]
adj pittoresco; pittoresca

pie [puy] *n* torta F

piece [pees] *n* pezzo M

pier [peeur] *n* banchina F

pierce [peeurs] *vt* bucare

pig [pig] *n* maiale M

pig-headed [PIG•HE•did] *adj*
ostinato; ostinata

pigeon [PI•jn] *n* piccione M

pigment [PIG•munt] *n*
pigmento M

pigsty [PIG•stuy] *n* porcle M

pile [puyul] *n* mucchio M; *vi*
accummulare

pilgrim [PIL•grim] *n* pellegrino;
pellegrina

pilgrimage [PIL•gri•mij] *n*
pellegrinaggio M

pill [pil] *n* pillola F

pillar [PI•lur] *n* pilastro M

pillow [PI•lo] *n* cuscino M

pillowcase [PI•lo•KAIS] *n*
federa F

pilot [PUY•lut] *n* pilota; *vt*
pilotare

pimp [pimp] *n* mezzano M

pimple [PIM•pl] *n* foruncolo M

pin [pin] *n* spillo M

pinch [pinch] *n* pizzico M

pine [puyn] *n* pino M

pineapple [PUY•NA•pul] *n*
ananas M

pink [pingk] *adj n* rosa

pinnacle [PI•nu•kl] *n*
pinnacolo M

pint [puynt] *n* pinta F

pioneer [PUY•u•NEEUR] *n*
pioniere; pioniera

pious [PUY•us] *adj* pio; pia

pipe [puyp] *n* tubatura F

pique [peek] *n* ripicco M

pirate [PUY•rit] *adj* pirata

pistol [PI•stl] *n* pistola F

piston [PI•stn] *n* pistone M

pitch [pich] *n* bitume M

pitcher [PI•chur] *n* brocca F

pitchfork [PICH•faurk] *n*
forcone M

piteous [PI•tee•us] *adj* pietoso;
pietosa

pitiful [PI•ti•ful] *adj* pietoso;
pietosa

pitiless [PI•tee•lis] *adj* spietato;
spietata

pity [PI•tee] *n* pietá F

pivot [PI•vut] *n* perno M

placard [PLA•kurd] *n* targa F

placate [PLAI•kait] *vt* placare

place [plais] *n* posto M

placid [PLA•sid] *adj* placido;
placida

plague [plaig] *n* peste F

plaid [plad] *n* stoffa scozzese F

plain [plain] *adj* semplice

plainly [PLAIN•lee] *adv*
chiaramente

plaintiff [PLAIN•tif] *n*
querelante

plan [plan] *n* progetto M; *vt*
progettare; intendere; (econ)
pianificare

plane [plain] *n* piano M

planet [PLA•nit] *n* pianeta M

plank [plangk] *n* asse F

planning [PLA•ning] *n*
progettazione F

plant [plant] *n* pianta F

plantation [plan•TAI•shn] *n*
pintagione F

plaque [plak] *n* placca F

plaster [PLA•stur] *n* gesso M;
vt intonacare

plastic [PLA•stik] *adj* di
plastica; *n* plastica F

plate [plait] *n* piatto M

plateau [pla•TO] *n* altipiano M

plated [PLAI•tid] *adj* placcato;
placcata

platform [PLAT•faurm] *n*
piattaforma F

platinum [PLAT•num] *n*
platino M

platter [PLA•tur] *n* piatto
grande M

play [plai] *n* gioco M

playboy [PLAI•boi] *n*
playboy M

player [PLAI•ur] *n* giocatore M

playful [PLAI•ful] *adj* giocoso;
giocosa

playground [PLAI•ground] *n*
campo giochi M

plaything [PLAI•thing] *n*
giocattolo M

playwright [PLAI•rùyt] *n*
drammaturgo M

plea [plee] *n* scusa F

plead [pleed] *vt* supplicare

pleasant [PLE•znt] *adj*
piacevole

please [pleez] *vt* far piacere

pleased [pleezd] *adj*
compiaciuto; compiaciuta

pleasing [PLEE•zing] *adj*
gradevole

pleasure [PLE•zhur] *n*
piacere M

pleat [pleet] *n* piega F

pledge [plej] *n* pegno M

plentiful [PLEN•ti•ful] *adj*
abbondante

plenty [PLEN•tee] *n*
abbondanza F

pliable [PLUY•u•bl] *adj*
flessibile

pliers [PLUY•urz] *npl* pinza F

plight [pluyt] *n* condizione F; *n*
stato M

plod [plahd] *vi* sfacchinare

plot 1 [plaht] *n* trama F;
intreccio M

plot 2 [plaht] *n* lotto; pezzo di
tereno

plow [plou] *n* aratro M

pluck [pluhk] *vt* strappare;
cogliere

plug [pluhg] *n* tappo M; *vt*
tappare

plum [pluhm] *n* prugna F

plumber [PLUH•mur] *n*
idraulico M

plumbing [PLUH•ming] *n*
impianto idraulico M

plume [ploom] *n* piuma F

plump [pluhmp] *adj*
grassottello; grassottella

plunder [PLUHN•dur] *vt*
saccheggiare

plunge [pluhnj] *n* tuffo M

plunger [PLUHN•jur] *n*
stantuffo M

plural [PLOOU•rl] *adj n*
plurale M

plus [pluhs] *n* addizionale

plush [pluhsh] *n* peluche M

ply [pluy] *vt* applicarsi

plywood [PLUY•wud] *n* legno
compensato M

pneumonia [noo•MO•nyu] *n*
polmonite F

poach [poch] *vt* cuocere in
acqua

pocket [PAH•kit] *n* tasca F

pocketbook [PAH•kit•BUK] *n*
borsetta F

pocketknife [PAH•kit•NUYF]
n temperino M

pod [pahd] *n* baccello M
poem [pom] *n* poesia F
poet [PO•it] *n* poeta M
poetic [po•E•tik] *adj* poetico;
poetica
poetry [PO•e•tree] *n* poesia F
point [point] *n* punto M; *vt*
indicare; additatre; (aim)
puntare
point of view [POYNT uv
VYU] *n* ottica F
pointed [POIN•tid] *adj*
appuntito; appuntita
pointer [POIN•tur] *n* indice M
pointless [POINT•lis] *adj*
inutile
poise [poiz] *n* equilibrio M
poison [POI•zn] *n* veleno M
poisoning [POI•zu•ning] *n*
avvelenamento M
poisonous [POI•zu•nus] *adj*
velenoso; velenosa
poke [pok] *vt* spingere
poker 1 [PO•kur] *n* attizzatoio M
poker 2 [PO•kur] *n* poker M
(game)
Poland [PO•lund] *n* Polonia F
polar [PO•lur] *adj* polare
pole [poul] *n* polo M
Pole [poul] *n* polacco; polacca
police [pu•LEES] *npl* polizia F
police officer [po•LEES
AW•fi•sir] *n* poliziotto M
police station [po•LEES
STAI•shn] *n* caserma di
polizia F
policeman [pu•LEES•man] *n*
poliziotto M
policewoman
[pu•LEES•WU•mun] *n*
poliziotta F

policy [PAH•li•see] *n* linea di
condotta F
Polish [PO•lish] *adj* polacco;
polacca
polish [PAH•lish] *n* lucido M;
vt lucidare; lustrare
polite [pu•LUYT] *adj* ben
educato; ben educata
politeness [pu•LUYT•nis] *n*
buona educazione F
political [pu•LI•ti•kl] *adj*
politico; politica
politician [PAH•li•TI•shn] *n*
uomo politico M
politics [PAH•li•TIKS] *n*
politica F
poll [poul] *n* inchiesta F; (vote)
votazione; *vt* ottenere voti
pollen [PAH•ln] *n* polline M
pollute [pu•LOOT] *vt* inquinare
pollution [pu•LOO•shn] *n*
inquinamento M
polo [PO•lo] *n* polo M
Polynesia [PAH•li•NEE•zhu] *n*
Polinesia F
pomp [pahmp] *n* pompa F
pompous [PAHM•pus] *adj*
pomposo; pomposa
pond [pahnd] *n* stagno M
ponder [PAHN•dur] *vt* riflettere
pony [PO•nee] *n* pony M
ponytail [PO•nee•TAIUL] *n*
coda di cavallo F
poodle [POO•dl] *n*
barboncino M
pool [pooul] *n* piscina F
poor [poour] *adj* povero; povera
pop 1 [pahp] *n* botto M; *vi*
schioccare; saltare
pop 2 [pahp] *adj* poplolare
pope [pop] *n* papa M

poplar [PAHP•lur] *n* pioppo M

poppy [PAH•pee] *n* papavero M

populace [PAH•pyu•lus] *n* plebaglia F

popular [PAH•pyu•lur] *adj* popolare

popularity [PAH•pyu•LA•ri•tee] *n* popolaritá F

popularize [PAH•pyu•lu•RUYZ] *vt* divulgare

populate [PAH•pyu•LAIT] *vt* popolare

population [PAH•pyu•LAI•shn] *n* popolazione F

porcelain [PAURS•lun] *n* porcellana F

porch [paurch] *n* veranda F

porcupine [PAUR•kyu•PUYN] *n* porcospino M

pore [paur] *n* poro M

pork [paurk] *n* maiale M

pornography [paur•NAH•gru•fee] *n* pornografia F

porous [PAU•rus] *adj* poroso; porosa

porpoise [PAUR•pus] *n* focena F

porridge [PAU•rij] *n* pappa d'avena F

port [paurt] *n* porto M

portable [PAUR•tu•bl] *adj* portatile

porter [PAUR•tur] *n* inserviente M

portfolio [paurt•FO•lee•O] *n* cartella F

porthole [PAURT•houl] *n* obló M

portion [PAUR•shn] *n* porzione F

portly [PAURT•lee] *adj* corpulento; corpulenta

portrait [PAUR•trit] *n* ritratto M

portray [paur•TRAI] *vt* dipingere

portrayal [paur•TRAI•ul] *n* descrizone F

Portugal [PAUR•chu•gl] *n* Portogallo M

Portuguese [PAUR•chu•geez] *adj* portoghese

pose [poz] *vi* posare

position [pu•ZI•shn] *n* posizione F

positive [PAH•zi•tiv] *adj* positivo; positiva

possess [pu•ZES] *vt* possedere

possession [pu•ZE•shn] *n* possesso M

possibility [PAH•si•BI•li•tee] *n* possibilitá F

possible [PAH•si•bl] *adj* possibile

possibly [PAH•si•blee] *adv* possibilmente

post 1 [post] *n* (pole) palo M

post 2 [post] *n* (job) posto; *vt* collocare

post 3 [post] *n* (mail) posta; *vt* imbucare; (record) registrare

postcard [POST•kard] *n* cartolina postale F

postdate [post•DAIT] *vt* posdatare

post office [POST AW•fis] *n* ufficio postale M

postage [PO•stij] *n*
affrancatura F

postal [PO•stl] *adj* postale

poster [PO•stur] *n* manifesto M

posterior [pah•STEEU•ree•ur]
adj n posteriore

posthumous [PAH•styu•mus]
adj postumo; postuma

postman [POST•man] *n*
postino M

postpone [post•PON] *vt*
posporre

posture [PAHS•chur] *vt* posare

pot [paht] *n* pentola F

potassium [pu•TA•see•um] *n*
potassio M

potato [pu•TAI•to] *n* patata F

potent [PO•tunt] *adj* potent

potential 1 [pu•TEN•shl] *adj*
latente

potential 2 [pu•TEN•shl] *n*
potenziale M

potentially [pu•TEN•shu•lee]
adv potenzialmente

pothole [PAHT•houl] *n* buca F

potion [PO•shn] *n* pozione F

pottery [PAH•tu•ree] *n*
ceramica F

pouch [pouch] *n* borsa F

poultry [POUL•tree] *n*
pollame M

pounce [pouns] *vi* avventarsi

pound [pound] *n* libbra F

pour [paur] *vt* versare

pout [pout] *vi* fare il broncio

poverty [PAH•vur•tee] *n*
povertá F

powder [POU•dur] *n* polvere F

powdered [POU•durd] *adj* in
polvere

power [POU•ur] *n* potere M

powerful [POU•ur•ful] *adj*
potente

powerless [POU•ur•lis] *adj*
impotente

practical [PRAK•ti•kl] *adj*
pratico; pratica

practical joke [PRAK•ti•kul
JOK] *n* scherzo M

practice [PRAK•tis] *n* pratica F;
vt practicare

practicing [PRAK•ti•sing] *adj*
che esercita la professione

prairie [PRAIU•ree] *n* prateria F

praise [praiz] *n* elogio M

prance [prans] *vi* impennarsi

prank [prangk] *n* tiro M

pray [prai] *vi* pregare

prayer [praiur] *n* preghiera F

preach [preech] *vt vi* predicare

preacher [PREE•chur] *n*
predicatore M

precarious [pri•KA•ree•us] *adj*
precario; precaria

precaution [pree•KAU•shn] *n*
precauzione F

precede [pri•SEED] *vt*
precedere

precedence [PRE•si•duns] *n*
precedenza F

precedent [PRE•si•dunt] *n*
precedente M

precious [PRE•shus] *adj*
prezioso; preziosa

precipitate [pri•SI•pi•TAIT] *vi*
precipitare

precipitation
[pri•SI•pi•TAI•shn] *n*
precipitazione F

precise [pri•SUYS] *adj* preciso;
precisa

precisely [pri•SUYS•lee] *adv*
precisamente

precision [pri•SI•zhn] *n*
precisione F

preclude [pri•KLOOD] *vt*
precludere

precocious [pri•KO•shus] *adj*
precoce

predator [PRE•du•tur] *n*
predatore M

predecessor [PRE•di•SE•sur] *n*
predecessore M

predestined [pree•DES•tind]
adj predestinato; predestinata

predicament [pri•DI•ku•munt]
n situazione difficile F

predicate [PRE•di•kit] *n*
predicato M

predict [pri•DIKT] *vt*
profetizzare

predictable [pri•DIK•tu•bl] *adj*
prevedibile

prediction [pri•DIK•shn] *n*
predizione F

predisposed [PREE•dis•POZD]
adj predisposto; predisposta

predominant
[pri•DAH•mi•nunt] *adj*
predominante

preface [PRE•fus] *n*
prefazione F

prefer [pri•FUR] *vt* preferire

preferable [PRE•fru•bl] *adj*
preferibile

preferably [PRE•fru•blee] *adv*
preferibilmente

preference [PRE•fruns] *n*
preferenza F

preferential [PRE•fu•REN•shl]
adj preferenziale

prefix [PREE•fiks] *n* prefisso M

pregnancy [PREG•nun•see] *n*
gravidanza F

pregnant [PREG•nunt] *adj*
incinta F

prejudice [PRE•ju•dis] *n*
pregiudizio M

prejudiced [PRE•ju•dist] *adj*
prevenuto; prevenuta

preliminary [pri•LI•mi•NE•ree]
adj preliminare

prelude [PRAI•lood] *n*
preludio M

premarital [pree•MA•ri•tl] *adj*
prematrimoniale

premature
[PREE•mu•CHOOUR] *adj*
prematuro; prematura

premier [pre•MEEUR] *adj*
primo; prima

premiere [pri•MEEUR] *n*
primo M

premise [PRE•mis] *n*
premessa F

premium [PREE•mee•um] *n*
ricompensa F

premonition [PRE•mu•NI•shn]
n premonizione F

preoccupied
[pree•AH•kyu•PUYD] *adj*
preoccupato; preoccupata

prepaid [pree•PAID] *adj*
prepagato; prepagata

preparation [PRE•pu•RAI•shn]
n preparazione F

prepare [pri•PAIUR] *vt*
preparare

preposition [PRE•pu•ZI•shn] *n*
preposizione F

preposterous [pri•PAH•stu•rus]
adj assurdo; assurda

prerequisite [pri•RE•kwi•zit] *n*
requisito primo M

prerogative [pru•RAH•gu•tuv]
n prerogativa F

prescribe [pri•SKRUYB] *vt*
prescrivere

prescription [pri•SKRIP•shn] *n*
ricetta F

presence [PRE•zns] *n*
presenza F

present 1 [PRE•znt] *adj*
presente

present 2 [PRE•znt] *n* regalo M

present 3 [pri•ZENT] *vt*
presentare

presentable [pri•ZEN•tu•bl]
adj presentabile

presentation
[PRE•zn•TAI•shn] *n*
presentazione F

presently [PRE•znt•lee] *adv*
tra poco

preserve [pri•ZURV] *vt*
conservare

preserve (keep; maintain)
[pree•ZURV] presavare

president [PRE•zi•dunt] *n*
presidente

press [pres] *n* stampa F; *vt*
premere; schiacciare; (iron)
sitrare

pressing [PRE•sing] *adj* urgente

pressure [PRE•shur] *n*
pressione F

prestige [pre•STEEZH] *n*
prestigio M

presumably [pri•ZOO•mu•blee]
adj presumabilmente

presume [pri•ZOOM] *vt*
presumere

presumption [pri•ZUMP•shn]
n presunzione F

pretend [pri•TEND] *vi* fingere

pretension [pri•TEN•shn] *n*
presunzione F

pretentious [pri•TEN•shus] *adj*
pretenzioso; pretenziosa

pretext [PREE•tekst] *n*
pretesto M

pretty [PRI•tee] *adj* carino;
carina

prevail [pri•VAIUL] *vi*
prevalere

prevailing [pree•VAIU•ling]
adj prevalente

prevalent [PRE•vu•lunt] *adj*
prevalente

prevent [pri•VENT] *vt*
prevenire

preventive [pri•VEN•tiv] *adj*
preventivo; preventiva

preview [PREE•vyoo] *n*
anteprima F

previous [PREE•vee•us] *adj*
precedente

prey [prai] *n* preda F

price [pruys] *n* prezzo M

priceless [PRUYS•lis] *adj*
inestimabile

prick [prik] *vt* pungere

pride [pruyd] *n* orgoglio M

priest [preest] *n* prete M

priesthood [PREEST•hud] *n*
sacerdozio M

prim [prim] *adj* compito;
compita

primarily [pruy•ME•ri•lee] *adv*
in primo luogo

primary [PRUY•me•ree] *adj*
primario; primaria

primate [PRUY•mait] *n*
primate M

prime [pruym] *adj* di prima
qualitá

primer [PRUY•mur] *n*
sillabario M

primitive [PRI•mi•tiv] *adj*
primitivo; primitiva

primrose [PRIM•roz] *n*
primula F

prince [prins] *n* principe M

princess [PRIN•ses] *n*
principessa F

principal [PRIN•si•pl] *adj*
principale

principle [PRIN•si•pl] *n*
principio M

print [print] *n* stampa;
impressione F; *vt* stampare;
imprimere;

printer [PRIN•tur] *n*
tipografo M

printing [PRIN•ting] *n*
tiratura F

prior [PRUY•ur] *adj* precedente

priority [pruy•AU•ri•tee] *n*
prioritá F

prism [PRI•zm] *n* prisma M

prison [PRI•zn] *n* prigione F

prisoner [PRI•zu•nur] *n*
prigioniero; prigioniera

privacy [PRUY•vu•see] *n*
intimitá F

private [PRUY•vit] *adj* privato;
privata

privation [pruy•VAI•shn] *n*
privazione F

privilege [PRIV•lij] *n*
privilegio M

prize [pruyz] *adj* premio M

pro [pro] *n* professionista

probability
[PRAH•bu•BI•li•tee] *n*
probabilitá F

probable [PRAH•bu•bl] *adj*
probabile

probably [PRAH•bu•blee] *adv*
probabilmente

probation [pro•BAI•shn] *n*
probazione F

probe [prob] *n* sonda F

problem [PRAH•blum] *n*
problema M

procedure [pru•SEE•jur] *n*
procedura F

proceed [pru•SEED] *vi*
procedere

proceeding [pru•SEE•ding] *adj*
azione legale F

proceeds [PRO•seedz] *npl*
profitto M

process [PRAH•ses] *n*
processo M

procession [pru•SE•shn] *n*
processione F

proclaim [pru•CLAIM] *vt*
proclamare

procrastinate
[pru•KRA•sti•NAIT] *vi*
procrastinare

procure [pru•KYOOUR] *vt*
procurare

prod [prahd] *vt* pungolare;
spingere

prodigal [PRAH•di•gl] *adj*
prodigo; prodiga

prodigy [PRAH•di•jee] *n*
prodigio M

produce 1 [PRO•doos] *n*
verdure F

produce 2 [pru•DOOS] *vt*
produrre

producer [pru•DOO•sur] *n*
produttore M

product [PRAH•duhkt] *n*
prodotto M

production [pru•DUHK•shn] *n*
produzione F

productive [pru•DUHK•tiv] *adj*
produttivo; produttiva

profane [pru•FAIN] *adj*
profano; profana

profession [pru•FE•shn] *n*
professione F

professional [pru•FE•shu•nl]
adj professionale; *n*
professionista

professor [pru•FE•sur] *n*
professore; professoressa

proficiency [pru•FI•shn•see] *n*
abilitá F

profile [PRO•fuyul] *n* profilo M

profit [PRAH•fit] *n* profitto M

profitable [PRAH•fi•tu•bl] *adj*
vantaggioso; vantaggiosa

profound [pru•FOUND] *adj*
profondo; profonda

profuse [pru•FYOOS] *adj*
abbondante

program [PRO•gram] *n*
programma M

progress 1 [PRAH•gres] *n*
progresso M

progress 2 [pru•GRES] *vi*
progredire

progressive [pru•GRE•siv] *adj*
progressivo; progressiva

prohibit [pru•HI•bit] *vt* proibire

prohibition [PRO•hi•BI•shn] *n*
proibizione

project 1 [PRAH•jekt] *n*
progetto M

project 2 [pru•JEKT] *vt*
proiettare

projection [pru•JEK•shn] *n*
proiezione F

proletariat [PRO•lu•TA•ree•ut]
n proletariato M

prolong [pro•LAUNG] *vt*
prolungare

promenade
[PRAH•mu•NAHD] *n*
passeggiata F; *vt* fare
passeggiata

prominent [PRAH•mi•nunt] *adj*
prominente

promiscuous
[pru•MI•skyoo•us] *adj*
promiscuo; promiscua

promise [PRAH•mis] *n*
promessa F; *vt* prometter;
assicurare

promising [PRAH•mi•sing] *adj*
promettente

promote [pru•MOT] *vt*
promuovere

promoter [pru•MO•tur] *n*
promotore M

promotion [pru•MO•shn] *n*
promozione F

prompt [prahmpt] *adj* sollecito;
sollecita

promptly [PRAHMPT•lee] *adv*
prontamente

prone [pron] *adj* prono; prona

prong [prahng] *n* forca F

pronoun [PRO•noun] *n*
pronome M

pronounce [pru•NOUNS] *vt*
pronunciare

pronounced [pru•NOUNST]
adj pronunciato; pronunciata

pronunciation
[pru•NUHN•see•AI•shn] *n*
pronuncia F

proof [proof] *n* prova F

prop [prahp] *n* puntello M; *vt*
sorreggere; appoggiare

propaganda
[PRAH•pu•GAN•du]
propaganda F

propel [pru•PEL] *vt* spingere
avanti

propeller [pru•PE•lur] *n* elica F

proper [PRAH•pur] *adj*
decoroso; decorosa

properly [PRAH•pur•lee] *adv*
ammodo

property [PRAH•pur•tee] *n*
proprietá F

prophecy [PRAH•fi•see] *n*
profezia F

prophesy [PRAH•fi•SUY] *vt*
profetizzare

prophet [PRAH•fit] *n*
profeta M

proportion [pru•PAUR•shn] *n*
proporzione F

proposal [pru•PO•zl] *n*
proposta F

propose [pru•POZ] *vt* proporre

proposition [PRAH•pu•ZI•shn]
n proposta F

proprietor [pru•PRUY•u•tur] *n*
proprietario M

prose [proz] *n* prosa F

prosecute [PRAH•si•KYOOT]
vt intentare

prosecution
[PRAH•si•KYOO•shn] *n*
accusa F

prosecutor
[PRAH•si•KYOO•tur] *n*
pubblico ministero M

prospect [PRAH•spekt] *n*
prospettiva F; *vt* esplorare

prospective [prah•SPEK•tiv]
adj prospettivo; prospettiva

prosper [PRAH•spur] *vi*
prosperare

prosperity [prah•SPE•ri•tee] *n*
prosperitá F

prosperous [PRAH•spu•rus]
adj prosperoso; prosperosa

prostitute [PRAH•sti•TOOT] *n*
prostituta F

prostrate [PRAH•strait] *adj*
prostrato; prostrata

protect [pru•TEKT] *vt*
proteggere

protection [pru•TEK•shn] *n*
protezione F

protective [pru•TEK•tiv] *adj*
protettivo; protettiva

protector [pru•TEK•tur] *n*
protettore M

protein [PRO•teen] *n* proteina F

protest [PRO•test] *n* protesta F

Protestant [PRAH•ti•stunt] *adj*
protestante

protoplasm [PRO•tu•PLA•zm]
n protoplasma M

protract [pro•TRAKT] *vt*
protrarre

protrude [pru•TROOD] *vi*
protrudere

protuberance
[pru•TOO•bur•uns] *n*
protuberanza F

proud [proud] *adj* orgoglioso;
orgogliosa

prove [proov] *vt* provare

proverb [PRAH•vurb] *n*
proverbio M

provide [pru•VUYD] *vt*
provvedere

providence [PRAH•vuh•dens] *n*
provvidenza F

provider [pru•VUYD•ur] *n*
fornitore M

province [PRAH•vins] *n*
provincia F

provincial [pru•VIN•shl] *adj*
provincial

provision [pru•VI•zhun] *n*
provvedimento M

proviso [pru•VEE•zo] *n*
clausola condizionale M

provoke [pru•VOK] *vt*
provocare

provost [PRO•vost] *n*
prevosto M

prow [prou] *n* prua F

prowess [PROU•es] *n*
prodezza F

prowl [proul] *vi* vagare in cerca
di bottino

proximity [prahk•SI•mu•tee] *n*
prossimitá F

proxy [PRAHK•see] *n*
procura F

prude [prood] *n* pudibondo;
pudibonda

prudence [PROO•dens] *n*
prudenza F

prudent [PROO•dunt] *adj*
prudente

prune [proon] *n* prugna secca F

pry [pruy] *vi* scrutare

psalm [salm] *n* salmo M

pseudonym [SOO•do•NIM] *n*
pseudonimo M

psychiatrist [sy•KUY•a•trist] *n*
psichiatra

psychiatry [sy•KUY•a•tree]
psichiatria F

psychological
[SUY•ko•LA•ji•kl] *n*
psicologico; psicologica

psychologist [suy•KA•lo•jist] *n*
psicologo; psicologa

psychology [suy•KA•lo•jee] *n*
psicologia F

public [PUH•blik] *adj* pubblico;
pubblica

publication [PUH•bli•KAI•shn]
n pubblicazione F

publicize [PUH•bli•SUYZ] *vt*
fare la pubblicitá

publisher [PUH•bli•shur] *n*
editore M

pucker [PUH•kur] *vt* corrugare

pudding [PU•ding] *n* budino M

puddle [PUH•dl] *n*
pozzanghera F

puff [puhf] *vi* sbuffare

pug [puhg] *n* carlino M

pull [puhl] *vt* tirare; *n* tirare F;
(influence) ascendente M

pulley [PUHL•ee] *n* carrucola F

pulp [puhlp] *n* polpa F

pulpit [PUHL•pit] *n* pulpito M

pulsate [PUHL•sait] *vi* pulsare

pulsation [puhl•SAI•shn] *n*
pulsazione F

pulse [puhlz] *n* polso M

pulverize [PUHL•vur•UYZ] *vt*
polverizzare

pumice [PUH•mis] *n* pomice F

pump [puhmp] *n* pompa F; *vt*
pompare

pumpkin [PUHMP•kin] *n*
zucca F

pun [puhn] *n* gioco di parole M

punch 1 [puhnch] *vt* dare un pugno; picchiare

punch 2 [puhnch] *n* (drink) ponce

punch 3 [puhnch] *n* (tool) punzone; *vt* forare

punctual [PUHNK•tyu•ul] *adj* puntuale

punctuation [PUHNK•tyu•AI•shn] *n* punteggiatura F

puncture [PUHNK•tyur] *n* puntura F; *vi* forare; bucare

punish [PUH•nish] *vt* punire

punishment [PUH•nish•mint] *n* punizione F

pup [puhp] *n* cucciolo M

pupil [PYOO•pil] *n* pupilla F

puppet [PUH•pit] *n* burattino M

purchase [PUR•chis] *n* acquisto M; acquisitare

pure [pyur] *adj* puro; pura

purgatory [PUR•gi•TOR•ee] *n* purgatorio M

purge [purj] *vt* purgare

purify [PYUR•i•FUY] *vt* purificare

purity [PYUR•i•tee] *n* purezza F

purple [PUR•pl] *n adj* viola

purport [pur•PORT] *vt* implicar

purpose [PUR•pus] *n* scopo M

purr [pur] *vi* fare le fusa

purse [purs] *n* borsa F

pursue [pur•SOO] *vt* inseguire

pursuit [pur•SOOT] *n* inseguimento M

push [push] *vt* spingere; *n* spinta; (effort) sforze

put [put] *vt* mettere; porre; (idea) esprimere

putrefy [PYU•tri•FUY] *vt* putrefare

putrid [PYU•trid] *adj* putrido; putrida

putter [PUH•tir] *vi* sfaccendare

putty [PUH•tee] *n* stucco M

puzzle [PUH•zl] *n* gioco di pazienza M

pylon [PY•lon] *n* pilone M

pyramid [PEER•uh•MID] *n* piramide F

Q

quack [kwak] *n* ciarlatano; ciarlatana

quadrant [KWA•drant] *n* quadrante M

quadrilateral [KWAH•dri•LA•tu•rl] *adj* quadrilatero; qudrilatera

quagmire [KWAG•myr] *n* pantano M

quail [kwail] *n* quaglia F

quaint [kwaint] *adj* bizzarro; bizzarra

quake [kwaik] *vi* tremare; *n* terremoto M

qualification
[KWA•li•fi•KAI•shn] *n*
qualificazione F

qualify [KWA•li•FUY] *vt*
qualificare

qualitative [kwa•li•TAI•tiv] *adj*
qualitativo; qualitativa

quality [KWA•li•tee] *n*
qualitá F

qualm [kwalm] *n* rimorso M

quantitative
[KWAHN•ti•TAI•tiv] *adj*
quantotativo; quantitativa

quantity [KWAHN•ti•tee] *n*
quantitá F

quarantine
[KWAHR•in•TEEN] *n*
quarantina F

quarrel [KWAH•rl] *vi* litigare;
n lite F; bisticcio M

quarry 1 [KWAH•ree] *n*
preda F

quarry 2 (stone) [KWAH•ree] *n*
cava F

quart [kwart] *n* quarto di
gallone M

quarter [KWAH•tur] *n* quarto
M; *vt* dividere in quattro

quarterly [KWAHR•tur•lee] *adj*
trimestrale

quartet [kwar•TET] *n*
quartetto M

quartz [kwartz] *n* quarzo M

quaver [KWAI•vur] *vi* tremare

quay [kway] *n* banchina F

queen [kween] *n* regina F

queer [kweer] *adj* strano; strana

quell [kwell] *vt* reprimere

quench [kwench] *vt* spegnere

query [KWEER•ee] *n*
domanda F

quest [kwest] *n* ricerca F

question [KWEST•shn] *n*
domanda F; questione F; *vt*
interrogare; *vi* mettere in
dubbio

question mark [KWEST•shn
MARK] *n* punto di
domanda M

questionable
[KWEST•shn•uh•bl] *adj*
discutibile

questionnaire
[KWEST•shn•AIR] *n*
questionario M

quibble [KWIH•bl] *vi* cavillare

quick [kwik] *adj* svelto; svelta

quicken [KWIK•in] *vt* affrettare

quickly [KWIK•lee] *adv*
rapidamente

quickness [KWIK•nis] *n*
rapiditá F

quicksand [KWIK•sand] *n*
sabbie mobili F

quicksilver [KWIK•SIL•vur] *n*
mercurio M

quid [kwid] *n* sterlina F

quiescence [kwee•EH•sinz] *n*
quiescenza F

quiet [KWUY•it] *adj* tranquillo;
tranquilla

quietly [KWUY•it•lee] *adv*
tranquillamente

quietness [KWUY•it•nis] *n*
quiete F

quill [kwill] *n* penna F

quilt [kwilt] *n* trapunta F

quince [kwinz] *n* cotogna F

quinine [KWUY•nuyn] *n*
chinino M

quintet [kwin•TET] *n*
quintetto M

quintuplet [kwin•TUH•plit] *n*
gruppo di cinque gemelli M

quip [kwip] *n* frizzo M; *vt*
scherzare

quit [kwit] *vt* abbandonare

quite [kwuyt] *adv* proprio

quitter [KWIH•tur] *n* chi
rinunzia facilmente M

quiver [KWIH•vur] *vi* tremare

quixotic [kwihk•ZAH•tik] *adj*
donchisciottesco;
donchisciottesca

quiz [kwiz] *n* quiz M

quorum [KWOR•uhm] *n*
quorum M

quota (part; portion) [KWO•ta]
n quota F

quotation [kwo•TAI•shn] *n*
citazione F

quote [kwot] *vt* citare

quotient [KWO•shnt] *n*
quoziente M

R

rabbi [RA•buy] *n* rabbino M

rabbit [RA•bit] *n* coniglio M

rabble [RA•bl] *n* plebaglia F

rabid [RA•bid] *adj* rabbioso;
rabbiosa

raccoon [ra•KOON] *n*
procione M

race 1 [rais] *n* razza F

race 2 [rais] *n* corsa F; gara F;
vt correre

racer [RAI•sur] *n* corridore M

rack [rak] *n* rastrelliera F

racket [RA•kit] *n* racchetta F

racketeer [RA•ki•TEER] *n*
gangster M

radiance [RAI•dee•enz] *n*
radiositá F

radiant [RAI•dee•ent] *adj*
raggiante

radiation [RAI•dee•AI•shn] *n*
radiazione F

radiator [RAI•dee•AI•tur] *n*
radiatore M

radical [RA•di•kul] *adj* radicale

radio [RAI•dee•O] *n* radio F

radish [RA•dish] *n* ravanello M

radius [RAI•dee•is] *n* raggio M

raffle [RA•fl] *n* lotteria F

raft [raft] *n* zattera F

rafter [RAF•tur] *n* trave M

rag [rag] *n* straccio M

rage [raij] *n* rabbia F; *vi*
infuriarsi; montare; su tutte le
furie

ragged [RA•gid] *adj* stracciato,
stracciata

raid [rayd] *n* scorreria F;
ringhiera F; *vt* fare
un'iccursione in; razziare

railroad [RAIL•rod] *n*
ferrovia F

railroad station [RAIL•rod
STAI•shn] *n* stazione F

railway [RAIL•wai] *n*
ferrovia F

rain [rain] *n* pioggia F; *vi*
   piovere
rainbow [RAIN•bo] *n*
   arcobaleno M
raindrop [RAIN•drahp] *n*
   goccia di pioggia F
rainfall [RAIN•fahl] *n*
   precipitazione F
rainy [RAI•nee] *adj* piovoso;
   piovosa
raise [raiz] *vt* alzare; (increase)
   aumentare
raisin [RAIZ•in] *n* uvetta F
rally [RA•lee] *vi* riprendersi; *n*
   raduno M
ram [ram] *n* ariete M
ramble [RAM•bl] *vi* gironzolare
rancid [RAN•sid] *adj* rancido;
   rancida
rancor [RAN•kor] *n* rancore M
random [RAN•dom] *adj* a caso
rang [rang] *pp* ring
range [rainj] *n* serie F
rank [rank] *n* fila F
ransack [RAN•sak] *vt* frugare
ransom [RAN•som] *n* riscatto F
rant [rant] *vi* sbraitare
rap [rap] *vi* bussare; *n*
   colpetto M
rape [raip] *vt* violentare; *n*
   violenza sessuale F
rapid [RAP•id] *adj* rapido;
   rapida
rapt [rapt] *adj* estatico; estatica
rapture [RAP•chur] *n* estasi F
rare [rair] *adj* raro
rarity [RAIR•i•tee] *n* raritá F
rascal [RA•skul] *n* buona lana
rash [rash] *n* eruzione F; *n*
   raspa F

raspberry [RAZ•bur•ee] *n*
   lampone M
rat [rat] *n* ratto M
rate [rait] *n* tasso M
rather [RA•thur] *adv* piuttosto
ratify [RA•ti•FUY] *vt*
   sanzionare
rating [RAI•ting] *n*
   valutazione F
ratio [RAI•she•O] *n* rapporto M
rational [RA•sha•nl] *adj*
   razionale
rattle [RAT•tl] *vt* scuotere; *n*
   sbatacchio M; (toy)
   raganella F
rattlesnake [RAT•tl•SNAIK] *n*
   serpente a sonagli M
raucous [RAW•kus] *adj*
   sguaiato; sguaiata
ravage [RA•vij] *vt* devastare
rave [raiv] *vi* delirare
raven [RAI•vin] *n* corvo M
ravenous [RA•vi•nis] *adj*
   famelico; famelica
ravine [ruh•VEEN] *n*
   burrone M
ravish [RA•vish] *vt* rapire
raw [raw] *adj* crudo; cruda
raw material [RAW
   muh•TEE•ree•ul] *n* materia
   prima F
ray [rai] *n* raggio M
rayon [RAI•on] *n* raion M
raze [raiz] *vt* radere al suolo
razor [RAI•zor] *n* rasoio M
re-enter [REE•EN•tur] *vt*
   rientrare
re-establish [REE•a•STA•blish]
   vt ristabilire
reach [reech] *n* portata F
react [ree•AKT] *vi* reagire

reaction [ree•AK•shn] *n*
reazione F

reactionary
[ree•AK•shn•AIR•ee] *adj n*
reazionario; reazionaria

read [reed] *vt* leggere

reader [REE•dur] *n* lettore;
lettrice

readily [RED•i•lee] *adv*
prontamente

readiness [RED•i•nis] *n*
prontezza F

reading [REE•ding] *n* lettura F

readjust [REE•uh•JUST] *vt*
riassestare

ready [REH•dee] *adj* pronto;
pronta

real [reel] *adj* vero; vera

realism [REEL•izm] *n*
realismo M

realist [REEL•ist] *n* realista

realistic [reel•IS•tik] *adj*
realistico; realistica

reality [ree•A•li•tee] *n* realtá F

realization [REEL•i•ZAI•shn] *n*
percezione F

realize [REE•LUYZ] *vt* capire

really [REEL•lee] *adv*
veramente

realm [relm] *n* regno M

reap [reep] *vt* raccogliere

reappear [REE•uh•PEER] *vi*
riapparire

rear [reer] *adj* posteriore; *n*
dietro M

reason [REE•zun] *n* ragione F;
vi ragionare

reasonable [REE•zun•uh•bl]
adj ragionevole

reasonably [REE•zun•uh•blee]
adv ragionevolmente

reasoning [REE•zun•ing] *n*
ragionamento M

reassure [REE•uh•SHUR] *vt*
riassicurare

rebate [REE•bait] *n* sconto M

rebel [REH•bl] *n adj* ribelle

rebellion [ree•BEL•yin] *n*
ribellione F

rebellious [re•BEL•yis] *adj*
ribelle

rebirth [REE•burth] *n*
rinascita F

rebound [REE•bound] *n*
ripercussione F

rebuild [ree•BILD] *vt* ricostruire

rebuke [ree•BYOOK] *vt*
rimproverare; *n* rimprovero M

recall [ree•KAUL] *vt* richiamare

recede [re•SEED] *vi* recedere

receipt [re•SEET] *n* ricevuta F

receive [re•SEEV] *vt* ricevere

receiver 1 [re•SEE•vur] *n*
destinatario; desinataria MF

receiver 2 (telephone)
[re•SEE•vur] *n* ricevitore M

recent [REE•sent] *adj* recente

receptacle [re•SEP•ti•kl] *n*
ricettacolo M

reception [re•SEP•shn] *n*
ricevimento M

recess [REE•ses] *n* intervallo M

recipe [RE•si•pee] *n* ricetta F

recipient [re•SI•pee•int] *n*
destinatario; destinataria

reciprocal [re•SI•pri•kl] *adj*
reciproco; reciproca

reciprocate [re•SI•pri•KAIT] *vt*
reciprocare

recital [ree•SUY•tl] *n*
racconto M

recite [ri•SUYT] *vt* recitare

reckless [REK•lis] *adj*
avventato; avventata

recklessness [REK•lis•nis] *n*
avventatezza F

reckon [REK•kon] *vt* calcolare

reckoning [REK•kon•ning] *n*
calcolo M

reclaim [ree•KLAIM] *vt*
redimere

recline [ree•KLUYN] *vi* giacere

recluse [REH•klooz] *adj*
recluso; reclusa

recognition [RE•kuh•NI•shn] *n*
riconoscimento M

recognize [RE•kug•NUYZ] *vt*
riconoscere

recoil [ree•KOYL] *vi*
indietreggiare

recollect [RE•ku•LEKT] *vt*
ricordare

recollection [RE•ku•LEK•shn]
n memoria F

recommend [RE•ku•MEND] *vt*
raccomandare

recommendation
[RE•ku•men•DAI•shn] *n*
raccomandazione F

recompense [RE•kom•PENZ] *n*
ricompensa F

reconcile [RE•kun•SUYL] *vt*
riconciiare

reconciliation
[RE•kun•SI•lee•AI•shn] *n*
riconciliazione F

reconnaissance
[re•KAHN•ni•zanz] *n*
ricognizione F

reconsider [REE•kun•SI•dur] *vt*
riconsiderare

reconstruct
[REE•kun•STRUKT] *vt*
ricostruire

record [n. RE•kord v. ri•KORD]
n documento M; *vt* registrare

recount [ree•KOUNT] *vt*
ricontare

recoup [ri•KOOP] *vt* risarcire

recourse [REE•korz] *n*
ricorso M

recover [ree•KUH•vur] *vt*
riprendere

recovery [ree•KUH•vree] *n*
guarigione F

recreation [RE•kree•AI•shn] *n*
svago M

recruit [re•KROOT] *vt* reclutare

rectangle [REK•TAN•gl] *n*
rettangolo M

rectify [REK•ti•FUY] *vt*
rettificare

rector [REK•tur] *n* rettore M

recuperate [ree•KOO•pur•AIT]
vi ristabilirsi

recur [ri•KUR] *vi* ricorrere

red [red] *adj* rosso; rossa

redden [RED•din] *vi* arrossare

redeem [ri•DEEM] *vt* redimere

redeemer [ri•DEE•mur] *n*
redentore M

redemption [ree•DEM•shn] *n*
redenzione F

redness [RED•nis] *n*
arrossamento M

redress [ree•DRES] *vt* riparare;
n riparazione

reduce [ree•DOOS] *vt* ridurre

reed [reed] *n* canna F

reef [reef] *n* scogliera F

reek [reek] *vi* puzzare

reel [reel] *vi* girare
vorticosamente

refer [ri•FUR] *vt* attribuire

referee [RE•fur•EE] *n* arbitro M

reference [RE•fur•enz] *n*
referenza F

refill [REE•fil] *n* ricambio M

refine [ree•FUYN] *vt* raffinare

refined [ree•FUYND] *adj*
raffinato; raffinata

refinement [ree•FUYN•mint] *n*
raffinatezza F

refinery [ree•FUY•nur•ee] *n*
raffineria F

reflect [ree•FLEKT] *vt* riflettere

reflection [ree•FLEK•shn] *n*
riflessione F

reflexive [ree•FLEK•ziv] *adj*
riflessivo; riflessiva

reform [ree•FORM] *n* riforma F

refraction [re•FRAK•shn] *n*
rifrazione F

refrain [ree•FRAIN] *n* ritornello
M; *vi* trattenersi

refresh [ree•FRESH] *vt*
rinfrescare

refreshing [ree•FRESH•ing] *adj*
rinfrescante

refreshment [ree•FRESH•mint]
n rinfresco M

refrigeration
[re•FRI•jur•AI•shn] *n*
refrigeramento M

refuge [RE•fyudj] *n* rifugio M

refund [REE•fund] *n* rimborso
M; *vt* rimborsare

refusal [ree•FYOO•sl] *n*
rifiuto M

refuse [ree•FYOOZ] *vt* rifiutare

refute [ree•FYOOT] *vt* refutare

regain [ree•GAIN] *vt* recuperare

regal [REE•gul] *adj* regale

regalia [ree•GAI•lee•uh] *n*
insegne regali F

regard [ree•GARD] *n*
considerazione F

regarding [ree•GAR•ding] *adv*
a proposito di

regime [re•JEEM] *n* regime M

regiment [RE•ji•mint] *n*
reggimento M

region [REE•jin] *n* regione F

register [RE•jis•tur] *n* registro
M; *vt* iscrivere

registration [RE•jis•TRAI•shn]
n iscrizione F

regret [ree•GRET] *n* rimpianto
M; *vt* rimpiangere

regular [RE•gyu•lur] *adj*
regolare

regularly [RE•gyu•lur•lee] *adv*
regolarmente

regulate [RE•gyu•LAIT] *vt*
regolare

regulation [RE•gyu•LAI•shn] *n*
regolamento M

rehearsal [ree•HUR•sul] *n*
prova F

rehearse [ree•HURS] *vt* provare

reign [rain] *n* regno M

reimburse [REE•im•BURS] *vt*
rimborsare

rein [rain] *vt* controllare

reindeer [RAIN•deer] *n* renna F

reinforce [REE•in•FAURS] *vt*
rinforzare

reiterate [ree•I•tur•AIT] *vt*
reiterare

reject [ri•JEKT] *vt* rifiutare

rejoice [ree•JOIS] *vi* rallegrarsi

rejoicing [ree•JOI•sing] *n*
esultanza F

rejoin [ree•JOIN] *vt*
ricongiungere

rejuvenate [ree•JOO•vi•NAIT]
 vt ringiovanire

relapse [ree•LAPS] *n*
 riacaduta F

relate [ree•LAIT] *vt* riferire

related [ree•LAI•tid] *adj*
 imparentato; imparentata

relation [ree•LAI•shn] *n*
 relazione F

relationship
 [ree•LAI•shn•SHIP] *n*
 rapporto M

relative [RE•luh•tiv] *n* parente

relax [ree•LAKS] *vt* rilassare

relaxation [ree•LAK•SAI•shn]
 n rilassamento M

relay [REE•lai] *n* staffetta F

release [ree•LEES] *n*
 liberarazione F; *vt* rilasciare

relent [ri•LENT] *vi* intenerirsi

relentless [ri•LENT•les] *adj*
 inflessibile

relevant [RE•li•vint] *adj*
 rilevante

reliability
 [ree•LUY•uh•BI•li•tee] *n*
 attendibilitá F

reliable [ree•LUY•uh•bl] *adj*
 attendibile

reliance [ree•LUY•enz] *n*
 fiducia F

relief [ree•LEEF] *n* sollievo M

relieve [ree•LEEV] *vt* alleviare

religion [re•LI•jin] *n* religione F

religious [re•LI•jis] *adj*
 religioso; religiosa

relinquish [re•LIN•kwish] *vt*
 abbandonare

relish [RE•lish] *vt* gustare; *n*
 piacere M

reluctant [ree•LUK•tant] *adj*
 riluttante

reluctantly [ree•LUK•tant•lee]
 adv con riluttanza

rely [ree•LUY] *vi* fidarsi

remain [ree•MAIN] *vi* rimanere

remainder [ree•MAIN•dur] *n*
 resto M

remains [ree•MAINZ] *n* resti M

remark [ree•MAHRK] *n*
 osservazione F

remarkable
 [ree•MAHR•kuh•bl] *adj*
 notevole

remedy [RE•mi•dee] *n*
 rimedio M

remember [re•MEM•bur] *vt*
 ricordare

remind [ree•MUYND] *vi*
 ricordare

reminder [ree•MUYN•der] *n*
 promemoria M

reminiscence [RE•mi•NI•senz]
 n reminiscenza F

remiss [re•MIS] *adj* negligente

remission [re•MI•shn] *n*
 remisssione F

remit [ree•MIT] *vt* rimettere

remnant [REM•nent] *n*
 scampolo M

remodel [ree•MO•dl] *vt*
 ripristinare

remorse [ree•MAURS]
 rimorso M

remote [ree•MOT] *adj* remoto;
 remota

removal [ree•MOO•vl] *n*
 rimozione F

remove [ree•MOOV] *vt*
 rimuovere

removed [ree•MOOVD] *adj*
rimosso; rimossa

renaissance [RE•nai•SAHNZ]
n rinascimento M

render [REN•dur] *vt* rendere

renew [re•NOO] *vt* rinnovare

renewal [re•NOO•wl] *n*
rinnovamento M

renovate [RE•no•VAIT] *vt*
rinnovare

renown [ree•NOUN] *n*
rinomanza F

rent [rent] *n* affitto M; *vt*
affittare

rental [REN•tl] *adj* in affitto

reopen [ree•O•pin] *vt* riaprire

repair [ree•PAIR] *vt* riparare

reparation [RE•pur•AI•shn] *n*
riparazione F

repay [ree•PAI] *vt* ripagare

repeal [ree•PEEL] *vt* abrogare

repeat [ree•PEET] *vt* ripetere

repel [re•PEL] *vt* respingere

repent [re•PENT] *vi* pentirsi

repetition [RE•pi•TI•shn] *n*
ripetizione F

replace [re•PLAIS] *vt* sostituire

replenish [ree•PLE•nish] *vt*
rifornire

replica [RE•pli•kuh] *n* replica F

reply [re•PLUY] *n* risposta F; *vi*
rispondere

report [re•PAURT] *n* verbale
M; *vi* reportare

reporter [re•PAUR•tur] *n*
giornalista

repose [ree•POZ] *n* riposo M;
vt riposari

represent [RE•pree•ZENT] *vt*
rappresentare

representation
[RE•pree•ZEN•TAI•shn] *n*
rappresentazione F

representative
[RE•pree•ZEN•te•tiv] *n*
delegato; delegata

repress [re•PRES] *vt* reprimere

reprimand [RE•pri•MAND] *vt*
rimproverare

reproach [re•PROCH] *n*
biasimo M

reproduce [REE•pro•DOOS] *vt*
riprodurre

reproduction
[REE•pro•DUK•shn] *n*
riproduzione F

reproof [re•PROOF] *n*
rimprovero M

reprove [re•PROOV] *vt*
biasimare

reptile [REP•tuyl] *n adj* rettile

republic [ree•PUH•blik] *n*
repubblica F

republican [ree•PUH•bli•ken]
adj repubblicano; repubblicana

repudiate [re•PYOO•di•AIT] *vt*
ripudiare

repugnant [ree•PUG•nent] *adj*
ripugnante

repulse [ree•PULS] *n* ripulsa F

repulsive [ree•PUL•siv] *adj*
ripulsivo; ripulsiva

reputable [RE•PYOO•tuh•bl]
adj rispettabile

reputation [RE•pyoo•TAI•shn]
n reputazione F

repute [re•PYOOT] *n*
reputazione F

request [re•KWEST] *n*
richiesta F

require [re•KWUYR] *vt*
richiedere

requirement
[re•KWUYR•mint] *n*
necessitá F

rescue [RES•kyoo] *n*
salvataggio M; *vt* liberare

research [REE•surch] *n*
ricerca F

resemblance [re•ZEM•blins] *n*
somiglianza F

resemble [re•ZEM•bl] *vt*
assomigliare

resent [re•ZENT] *vt* risentirsi

resentful [re•ZENT•ful] *adj*
permaloso; permalosa

reservation [RE•zur•VAI•shn]
n prenotazione F

reserve [re•ZURV] *n* riserva F

reside [re•ZUYD] *vi* risiedere

residence [RE•zi•denz] *n*
residenza F

residue [RE•zi•DOO] *n*
residuo M

resign [ree•ZUYN] *vi* dimettersi

resignation [RE•zig•NAI•shn]
n rassegnazione F

resist [re•ZIST] *vt* resistere

resistance [re•ZI•stenz] *n*
resistenza F

resolute [RE•zo•LOOT] *adj*
risoluto; risoluta

resolution [RE•zo•LOO•shn] *n*
risoluzione F

resolve [re•ZOLV] *vi* decidere

resonance [RE•zo•nenz] *n*
risonanza F

resonant [RE•zo•nent] *adj*
risonante

resort [ree•ZAURT] *vi* ricorrere

resource [REE•saurs] *n*
risorsa F

respect [re•SPEKT] *n*
rispetto M

respectable [re•SPEK•tuh•bl]
adj rispettabile

respectful [re•SPEKT•fl] *adj*
rispettoso; rispettosa

respective [re•SPEK•tiv] *adj*
rispettivo; rispettiva

respite [RE•spit] *n* dilazione F

respond [re•SPAHND] *vi*
rispondere

response [re•SPAHNS] *n*
risposta F

responsibility
[re•SPAHN•si•BI•li•tee] *n*
responsabilitá F

responsible [re•SPAHN•si•bl]
adj responsabile

rest [rest] *vi* riposarsi; *n* resto M

restaurant [RES•trahnt] *n*
ristorante M

restful [REST•fl] *adj* riposante

restitution [RE•sti•TOO•shn] *n*
restituzione F

restless [REST•les] *adj*
inquieto; inquieta

restlessness [REST•les•nes] *n*
inquietudine F

restoration [RES•tau•RAI•shn]
n restauro M

restore [re•STAUR] *vt*
restaurare

restrain [re•STRAIN] *vt* frenare

restrict [re•STRIKT] *vt* limitare

restriction [re•STRIK•shn] *n*
restrizione F

result [re•ZUHLT] *n* risultato M

resume [ree•ZOOM] *vt*
riprendere

résumé [REH•zoo•MAI] *n*
riassunto M

resuscitate [re•SUS•si•TAIT] *vt*
risuscitare

retail [REE•tail] *n adj* dettaglio
M; *vi* (sell) vendere

retailer [REE•tai•lur] *n*
dettagliante

retaliate [ree•TA•lee•AIT] *vi*
fare rappresaglie

retaliation [ree•TA•lee•AI•shn]
n rappresaglia F

retard [ree•TARD] *vt* ritardare

retinue [RE•ti•NOO] *n*
seguito M

retire [ree•TUYR] *vt* ritirare

retirement [ree•TUYR•mint] *n*
pensione F

retort [ree•TORT] *n* risposta F

retract [ree•TRAKT] *vt* ritrarre

retreat [ree•TREET] *vt* ritirarsi
F; *n* ritire M; rifugio M;
ritirata F

retrieve [ree•TREEV] *vt*
rintracciare

retroactive [RE•tro•AK•tiv] *adj*
retroattivo; retroattiva

return [ree•TURN] *n* ritorno M

return address [ree•TURN
a•DRES] *n* indirizzo del
mittente M

returns (election)
[ree•TURNZ] *n* risultati
(elettorali) M

reunion [ree•YOO•nyun] *n*
riunione F

reunite [REE•yoo•NUYT] *vt*
riunire

reveal [ree•VEEL] *vt* rivelare

revelation [RE•vi•LAI•shn] *n*
rivelazione F

revelry [RE•vil•ree] *n* baldoria F

revenge [ree•VENJ] *n*
vendetta F

revenue [RE•vi•NOO] *n*
entrata F

revere [re•VEER] *vt* riverire

reverence [RE•vur•enz] *n*
rispetto M

reverend [RE•vur•end] *adj*
reverendo; reverenda

reverent [RE•vur•ent] *adj*
rispettoso; rispettosa

reverse [re•VERS] *vi* rovesciare

revert [re•VERT] *vi* ritornare

review [re•VYOO] *n*
recensione F

revile [re•VUYL] *vt* ingiuriare

revise [re•VUYZ] *vt* riesaminare

revision [re•VI•shn] *n*
revisione F

revival [re•VUY•vul] *n*
ripristino M

revoke [re•VOK] *vt* revocare

revolt [re•VOLT] *vt* rivoltare

revolution [RE•vo•LOO•shn] *n*
rivoluzione F

revolutionary
[RE•vo•LOO•shn•AI•ree] *adj*
rivoluzionario; rivoluzionaria

revolve [re•VOLV] *vi* rotare

reward [re•WAURD] *n*
ricompensa F; *vi*
ricompensarse

rewrite [ree•RUYT] *vt*
riscrivere

rhetoric [RE•tau•rik] *n*
retorica F

rheumatism [ROO•muh•TIZM]
n reumatismo M

rhinoceros [ruy•NOS•rus] *n*
rinoceronte M

rhubarb [ROO•barb] *n*
rabarbaro M

rhyme [ruym] *n* rima F

rhythm [RI•thim] *n* ritmo M; *vi*
rimare

rib [rib] *n* costola F

ribbon [RI•bin] *n* nastro M

rice [ruyz] *n* riso M

rich [rich] *adj* ricco; ricca

richness [RICH•nes] *n*
abbondanza F

rid [rid] *vt* sbarazzare

riddle [RI•dl] *n* indovinello M

ride [ruyd] *n* giro M; (bicycle)
vt andare in bicicletta;
(horseback) *vt* cavalcare

rider [RUY•dur] *n* cavallerizzo;
cavallerizza

ridge [rij] *n* spigolo M

ridicule [RI•di•KYOOL] *n*
ridicolo M

ridiculous [ri•DI•kyu•lus] *adj*
ridicolo; ridicola

rifle [RUY•fl] *n* fucile M

rig [rig] *n* attrezzatura F; *vt*
attrezzare

right [ruyt] *adj* giusto; giusta;
correto; guisto; *n adj*
(direction) destro; destra M

right away [RUYT a•WAI] *adv*
immediatamente

right-hand [RUYT•hand] *adj*
braccio destro

righteous [RUY•chus] *adj*
retto; retta

righteousness [RUY•chus•nes]
n rettitudine F

rigid [RI•jid] *adj* rigido; rigida

rigidity [ri•JI•di•tee] *n* rigiditá F

rigor [RI•gor] *n* rigore M

rim [rim] *n* orlo M

rind [ruynd] *n* buccia F

ring 1 [ring] *n* anello M

ring 2 [ring] *n* (sound) suono;
squillo M; *vi* suonare

rink [rink] *n* pista per
pattinaggio F

rinse [rins] *vt* sciacquare

riot [RUY•ut] *n* tumulto M;
insorgere

ripe [ruyp] *adj* maturo; matura

ripple [RI•pul] *n* increspatura F

rise [ruys] *vi* sorgere; *n* salita F;
aumento M

risk [risk] *n* rischio M

rite [ruyt] *n* rito M

ritual [RI•chu•ul] *adj* rituale

rival [RUY•vl] *n* rivale

rivalry [RUY•vl•ree] *n* rivalitá F

river [RI•vur] *n* fiume M

road [rod] *n* strada F

roam [rom] *vi* vagabondare

roar [ror] *vi* ruggire

roast [rost] *vt* arrostire; *n*
arrosto M

rob [rahb] *vt* derubare

robber [RAH•bur] *n* ladro;
ladra

robbery [RAH•bree] *n* furto M

robe [rob] *n* tunica F

robin [RAH•bin] *n* pettirosso M

robust [ro•BUST] *adj* robusto;
robusta

rock 1 [rahk] *n* roccia F

rock 2 [rahk] *vt* dondolare;
oscillare

rocket [RAH•kit] *n* razzo M

rocking chair [RAH•king
CHAIR] *n* sedia a dondolo F

rocky [RAH•kee] *adj* roccioso;
rocciosa

rod [rahd] *n* bastone M

role [rol] *n* ruolo M

roll [rol] *n* rotolo M

Roman [RO•man] *adj* romano; romana

romance [ro•MANS] *n* avventura romantica F

romantic [ro•MAN•tik] *adj* romantico; romantica

romanticism [ro•MAN•ti•SIZM] *n* romanticismo M

romanticist [ro•MAN•ti•sist] *n* romantico; romantica

room [room] *n* stanza F

roommate [ROOM•mait] *n* compagno di camera; compagna di camera

roomy [ROO•mee] *adj* spazioso; spaziosa

roost [roost] *vi* appollaiarsi

root [root] *n* radice F

rope [rop] *n* corda F

rosary [RO•zuh•ree] *n* rosario M

rose [roz] *n* rosa F

rosy [RO•zee] *adj* roseo; rosea

rot [raht] *vi* marcire

rotary [RO•tuh•ree] *adj* rotante

rotation [ro•TAI•shn] *n* rotazione F

rote [rot] *n* memoria F

rotten [RAH•tin] *adj* marcio; marcia

rough [ruhf] *adj* ruvido; ruvida

rough estimate [RUHF E•sti•MAIT] *n* valutazione approssimativa F

roughen [RUHF•in] *vt* irruvidire

roughly [RUHF•lee] *adv* approssimativamente

round [rond] *adj* rotondo; rotonda

rouse [rowz] *vt* svegliare

route [root] *n* strada F

routine [roo•TEEN] *n* abitudine F

row 1 [ro] *n* fila F;

row 2 [ro] *vt* remare; *n* remata F

rub-down [RUHB•doun] *n* fregagione F

rubber [RUH•bur] *n* gomma F

rubbish (waste) [RUH•bish] *n* rifiuti M

rubble [RUH•bl] *n* pietrisco M

ruby [ROO•bee] *n* rubino M

rudder [RUH•dur] *n* timone M

rude [rood] *adj* maleducato; maleducata

rueful [ROO•ful] *adj* contrito; contrita

ruffian [RUH•fee•in] *n* scellerato; scellerata

ruffle [RUH•fl] *vt* arruffare

rug [ruhg] *n* tappeto M

rugged [RUH•gid] *adj* ruvido; ruvida

ruin [ROO•in] *n* rovina F; *vt* rovinare

rule [rool] *vt* governare

rum [ruhm] *n* rum M

rumble [RUHM•bl] *n* rombo M

ruminate [ROO•mi•NAIT] *vi* ruminare

rumor [ROO•mur] *n* pettegolezzo M

rump [ruhmp] *n* groppa F

rumple [RUHM•pl] *vt* spiegazzare

run [ruhn] *n* corsa; serie F; *vi* correre

run-down [RUHN•DOUN] *vi*
scaricarsi

runaway 1 [RUHN•uh•WAI] *n*
adj fuggiasco; fuggiasca

runaway 2 [RUHN•uh•WAI] *n*
disertore M

runner [RUH•nur] *n* corridore M

running [RUH•ning] *adj*
corrente

runt [ruhnt] *n* mezza cartuccia

rupture [RUHP•chur] *vt*
rompere

rural [RUR•uhl] *adj* rurale

ruse [rooz] *n* trucco M

rush [ruhsh] *n* fretta F; *vt*
precipitarsi; avventarsi

rush hour [RUHSH OUR] *n*
ora di punta F

russet [RUH•sit] *adj* color
ruggine

Russia [RUH•sha] *n* Russia F

Russian [RUH•shin] *adj* russo;
russa

rust [ruhst] *n* ruggine F

rustic [RUH•stik] *adj* rustico;
rustica

rusty [RUH•stee] *adj* rugginoso;
rugginosa

rut [ruht] *n* carreggiata F

ruthless [ROOTH•les] *adj*
spietato; spietata

rye [ruy] *n* segala F

S

Sabbath [SA•beth] *n*
sabato M

saber [SAI•bur] *n* sciabola F

sabotage [SA•bo•TAHJZ] *n*
sabotaggio M; *vi* sabotare

sack [sak] *n* sacco M; *vt*
mandare a spasso (coll)

sacrament [SA•kra•mint] *n*
sacramento M

sacred [SAI•krid] *adj* sacro;
sacra

sacrifice [SA•kri•FUYS] *n*
sacrificio M

sad [sad] *adj* triste

sadden [SA•din] *vt* rattristare

saddle [SAD•dl] *n* sella F

sadistic [sa•DIS•tik] *adj* sadico;
sadica

sadness [SAD•nes] *n* tristezza F

safe [saif] *adj* sicuro; sicura; *n*
savlacondotto M

safely [SAIF•lee] *adv* senza
pericolo

safety [SAIF•tee] *n* sicurezza F

safety pin [SAIF•tee PIN] *n*
ago di sicurezza M

saffron [SA•frahn] *n*
zafferano M

sag [sag] *vi* pendere

sagacious [sa•GAI•shus] *adj*
sagace

sagacity [sa•GA•si•tee] *n*
sagacia F

sage 1 [saij] *n adj* saggio;
saggia MF;

sage 2 [saij] *n* (bot.) salvia F

sail [sail] *n* vela F; *vt*
veleggiare; navigare

sailboat [SAIL•bot] *n* barca a vela F

sailing [SAI•ling] *n* navigazione F

sailor [SAI•lur] *n* marinaio M

saint [saint] *n* santo; santa

saintly [SAINT•lee] *adj* santo; santa

sake [saik] *n* amore M

salad [SA•lid] *n* insalata F

salad bowl [SA•lid BOL] *n* insalatiera

salad dressing [SA•lid DRE•sing] *n* condimento per l'insalata F

salary [SA•lu•ree] *n* stipendio M

sale [saiul] *n* (of articles) vendita F; for ~\ vendisi, vendonsi; be on ~\ essere en vendita

salesman [SAIULZ•man] *n* comesso, raprasentante M

saleswoman [SAIULZ•WU•man] *n* comessa F

saliva [su•LUY•vu]

salmon [SA•mun] *n* saliva F

salon [suh•LAHN] *n* salone M

salt [sault] *n* sale M; *vt* salare

saltwater [SAULT•WAU•tur] *adj* (of fish, etc) di mare

salty [SAHL•tee] *adj* salato

salute [su•LOOT] *n* salva M; *vt* salutare

salvage [SAL•vij] *n* salvaggio M; *vt* ricuperare; ~ vessel\ di salvataggio

salvation [sal•VAI•shn] *n* salvezza M

same [saim] *adj* stesso; on the ~ day\ lo stesso giorno; it's all the same\ è la stessa coda; the ~\ lo stesso; just the ~\ lo stesso; and the ~ to you!\ alrettanto a te!; feel the ~ about\ non la vedo allo stesso modo

sample [SAM•pls] *n* campione M; *vt* assagiare

sanction [SANGK•shn] *n* sanzione F; *vt* sancire; sanziionare

sanctity [SANG•ti•tee] *n* (of people) santità; (of place) carrettere sacro sanctuary [SANG•choo•E•ree] *n* santuario M (for animals) riserva F; (political) asilo M

sand [sand] *n* sabbia M; *vt* cartavetrare

sandal [SAN•dl] *n* sanalo M

sandpaper [SAND•PAI•pur] *n* carta vetrata

sandwich [SAND•wich] *n* tramezzino, sandwich M

sandy [SAN•dee] *adj* sabbioso -a

sane [sain] *adj* sano; di mento

sanitary [SA•ni•TE•ree] *adj* igencio -a

sanitary napkin [SA•ni•TE•ree NAP•kin] *n* assorbente M

sanity [SA•ni•tee] *n* sanità mentale

Santa Claus [SAN•tu KLAUZ] *n* Babbo Natale

sap 1 (of trees) [sap] *n* infa F

sap 1 (of strength) [sap] *vt* ficcare

sapling [SAP•ling] *n* albrello M

sapphire [SA•fuyur] *n* zaffiro

sarcastic [sahr•KA•stik] *adj* sarcasticova

sardine [sahr•DEEN] *n* sardina F

Sardinia [sahr•DEE•nyu] *n* Sardegna

sash 1 [sash] *n* (of dress) *n* fusciacca F; fascia F

sash 2 [sash] *n* (of window) telaio M

Satan [SAI•tn] *n* Santana M

satellite [SA•tu•LUYT] *n* satellite M

satin [SA•tin] *n* raso M; *adj* di raso

satire [SA•tuyur] *n* satira F

satisfaction [SA•tis•FAK•shn] *n* soddisfazione F

satisfactory [SA•tis•FAK•tu•ree] *adj* soddisfacente

satisfy [SA•tis•FUY] *vt* sodisfare; contentare

saturate [SA•chu•RAIT] *vt* inzuppare de

Saturday [SA•tur•dai] *n* Sabato

sauce [saus] *n* salsa F

saucer [SAU•sur] *n* piattino F

Saudi Arabia [SAU•dee u•RAI•bee•u] *n* Arabia Saudita

sauna [SAU•nu] *n* sauna F

sausage [SAU•sij] *n* salsiccia F

savage [SA•vij] *adj* feroce; *vt* sbranare

save [saiv] *vt* (rescue) salvare; ~ up\ risparmare; mettere da parte

savings [SA•vingz] *n* risparmio M

savings account [SA•vings u•KOUNT] *n* libretto di risparmio

savior [SAI•vyur] *n* MF salvatore; salvatrice

savor [SAI•vur] *n* sapore, gusto M; *vt* assaporare, gustare

saw [sau] *n* sega M; *vt* segare;

sawdust [SAU•duhst] *n* segatura M

saxaphone [SAK•su•FON] *n* sassofono M

say [sai] *vt* dire; ~ mass\ dire messa; that is to ~\ vale a dire; I'll ~!\ è come!; ~ no more!\ basta cosi!

scab [skab] *n* crosta F

scaffolding [SKA•ful•ding] *n* implacatura; ponteggio

scale 1 [skail] *n* (of fish) scaglia F; *vt* (fish) squamare

scale 2 [skail] *n* (of ruler) scala graudta; *vt* (mountain etc) scalare; ~ drawing\ segno en scala

scallop [SKA•lup] *n* ettine M; (sewing) smerlo M

scalp [skalp] *n* culo capelluto; *vt* scontennare

scalpel [SKAL•pl] *n* bisturi M

scan [skan] *vt* scruatre; *vi* (poetr) scandire

scandal [SKAN•dl] *n* scandalo M

scandalize [SCAN•du•LUYZ] *vt* scandalizzare

Scandinavia [SKAN•di•NAI•vee•u] *n* Scandinavia

Scandinavian [SKAN•di•NAI•vee•un] *adj n* scanidavo -a MF

scapegoat [SKAIP•got] *n* cpro
expitorio

scar [skahr] *n* stregio; cicatrice
F; *vt* lasicare delle cicatrici su

scarab [SKA•rub] *n* scarabeo M

scarce [skairs] *adj* scarso

scare [skair] *vt* spaventare

scarf [skahrf] *n* sciarpa F

scarlet [SKAHR•let] *adj*
scarlatto; scarlatta

scary [SKAIR•ee] *adj*
allarmante

scathe [skaith] *vt* stroncare

scatter [SKA•tur] *vt* spargere

scavenger [SKA•ven•jur] *n*
saprofago; saprofaga

scenario [suh•NAI•ree•O] *n*
sceneggiatura F

scene [seen] *n* scena F

scenery [SEE•nur•ee] *n*
scenario M

scepter [SEP•tur] *n* scettro M

schedule [SKE•dyool] *n* orario
M; *vt* programmare; *vi* (list)
elencare

scheme [skeem] *n* schema M

schism [SKI•zim] *n* scisma M

schist [shist] *n* schisto M

scholar [SKAH•lur]' *n* studioso;
studiosa

scholarly [SKAH•lur•lee] *adj*
dotto; dotta

scholarship [SKAH•lur•ship] *n*
borsa di studio F

scholastic [sku•LAS•tik] *adj*
scolastico; scolastica

school [skool] *n* scuola F;
(boarding) *n* collegio M

schoolboy [SKOOL•boi] *n*
scolaro M

schoolmaster
[SKOOL•MA•stur] *n*
preside M

schoolteacher
[SKOOL•TEE•chur] *n* maestro
di scuola M

schooner [SKOO•nur] *n*
goletta F

science [SUY•enz] *n* scienza F

scientific [SUY•yen•TI•fik] *adj*
scientifico; scientifica

scientist [SUY•yen•tist] *n*
scienziato M

scissors [SI•surz] *n* forbici F

scoff [skof] *vi* deridere

scold [skold] *vt* rimproverare

scolding [SKOL•ding] *n*
ramanzina F

sconce [skahnz] *n* candeliere M

scone [skon] *n* focaccia F

scoop [skoop] *n* mestolata F

scope [skop] *n* portata F

scorch [skaurch] *n* scottatura F;
vt bruciacchiare

score [skaur] *n* punteggio M

scorn [skaurn] *vt* disprezzare

scorpion [SKAUR•pee•in] *n*
scorpione M

Scot [skot] *n* scozzese

Scotland [SKOT•lind] *n*
Scozia F

scoundrel [SKOUN•drul] *n*
farabutto M

scour [skour] *vt* strofinare

scourge [skurj] *n* flagello M

scout [skout] *vt* esplorare

scouting [SKOUT•ting] *n*
scoutismo M

scowl [skoul] *n* cipiglio M; *vt*
accigliarsi

scramble [SKRAM•bl] *vi*
arrampicarsi

scrap [skrap] *n* avanzo M; *vt*
scartare; mettere fuori

scrape [skraip] *vt* raschiare

scraper [SKRAI•pur] *n*
raschietto M

scratch [skrach] *vt* graffiare

scrawl [skrahl] *vt*
scarabocchiare

scream [skreem] *vi* urlare; *n*
strillo M

screech [skreech] *n* strillo M; *vi*
strillare

screen 1 [skreen] *vt* selezionare

screen 2 (movies) [skreen] *n*
schermo M

screw [skrew] *n* vite F

screwdriver
[SKROO•DRUY•vur] *n*
cacciavite M

scribble [SKRIB•bl] *vt*
scribacchiare

scribe [skruyb] *n* scrivano M

script [skript] *n* corsivo M

scripture [SKRIP•chur] *n*
Scrittura F

scroll [skroll] *n* rotolo di
pergamena M

scrub [skrub] *vt* pulire

scruff [skruff] *n* collottola F

scruple [SKROO•pl] *n*
scrupolo M

scrupulous [SKROO•pyu•lus]
adj scrupoloso; scrupolosa

scrutinize [SKROO•ti•NUYZ]
vt scrutare

scrutiny [SKROO•ti•nee] *n*
scrutinio M

sculptor [SKULP•tur] *n*
scultore M

sculpture [SKULP•chur] *n*
scultura F

scum [skuhm] *n* feccia F

scurrilous [SKUR•ri•les] *adj*
scurrile

scurry [SKUR•ree] *vi* affrettarsi

scythe [suyth] *n* falce F

sea [see] *n* mare M

seal [seel] *n* foca F

seam [seem] *n* cucitura F

seamstress [SEEM•stres] *n*
sarta F

sear [seer] *vt* bruciare

search [surch] *vi* cercare

search warrant [SURCH
WAHR•rent] *n* mandato di
perquisizione M

seasick [SEE•sik] *adj* nauseato;
nauseata

season [SEE•zun] *n* stagione F

season ticket [SEE•zun
TIK•ket] *n* biglietto in
abbonamento M

seasonable [SEE•zun•uh•bl]
adj di stagione

seasoning [SEE•zun•ning] *n*
condimento M

seat [seet] *n* posto M; *vi*
accommodarsi

secede [se•SEED] *vi* secedere

secession [se•SES•shn] *n*
secessione F

seclude [se•KLOOD] *vi*
secludere

seclusion [se•KLOO•shn] *n*
seclusione F

second 1 [SE•kond] *adj*
secondo; seconda

second 2 [SE•kond] *vt*
assecondare

second-hand [SE•kond•HAND]
adj di seconda mano

second-rate [SE•kond•RAIT]
adj di qualitá inferiore

secondary [SE•kun•DE•ree] *adj*
secondario; secondaria

secondly [SE•kund•lee] *adv*
secondariamente

secrecy [SEE•kruh•see] *n*
segretezza F

secret [SEE•kret] *n* segreto M

secretary [SE•kre•TE•ree] *n*
segretario segretaria

secrete [se•KREET] *vt*
secernere; (hide) *vt*
nascondere

secretion [se•KREE•shn] *n*
secrezione F

secretive [SE•kreh•tiv] *adj*
reticente

sect [sekt] *n* setta F

sectarian [sek•TAI•ree•in] *adj*
settario; settaria

section [SEK•shun] *n* sezione F

sector [SEK•tor] *n* settore M

secular [SE•kyu•lur] *adj*
secolare

secularize [SE•kyu•la•RUYZ]
vt secolarizzare

secure [se•KYOOR] *adj* sicuro;
sicura

security [se•KYOO•ri•tee] *n*
sicurezza F

sedan [se•DAN] *n* berlina F

sedate [se•DAIT] *adj* posato;
posata

sedative [SE•duh•tiv] *n*
sedativo M

sedentary [SE•din•TAI•ree] *adj*
sedentario; sedentaria

sediment [SE•di•mint] *n*
sedimento M

sedition [se•DI•shn] *n*
sedizione F

seditious [se•DI•shus] *adj*
sedizioso; sediziosa

seduce [se•DOOS] *vt* sedurre

seducer [se•DOO•sur] *n*
seduttore M

seduction [se•DUK•shn] *n*
seduzione F

seductive [se•DUK•tiv] *adj*
seducente

see [see] *vt* vedere

seed [seed] *n* seme M; *vi*
seminare

seek [seek] *vt* cercare

seem [seem] *vi* sembrare

seep [seep] *vi* colare

seer [SEE•ur] *n* veggente

seesaw [SEE•sau] *n* altalena F

seethe [seeth] *vi* ribollire

segment [SEG•mint] *n*
segmento M

segregate [SE•gruh•GAIT] *vt*
segregare

seize [seez] *vt* impadronirsi

seizure [SEE•zhur] *n*
sequestro M

seldom [SEL•dum] *adv*
raramente

select [se•LEKT] *vt* scegliere

selection [se•LEK•shn] *n*
selezione F

selective [se•LEK•tiv] *adj*
selettivo; selettiva

self [self] *n* io M

self-centered [SELF•SEN•turd]
adj egoista

self-confident
[SELF•KAHN•fi•dint] *adj*
sicuro di sé; sicura di sé

self-conscious
[SELF•KAHN•shus] *adj*
impacciato; impacciata
self-control
[SELF•kahn•TROL] *n*
autocontrollo M
self-defense [SELF•dee•FENS]
n legittima difesa F
self-respect [SELF•ree•SPEKT]
n amor proprio M
self-taught [SELF•TAUT] *adj*
autodidatta
selfish [SEL•fish] *adj* egoista
selfishness [SEL•fish•nis] *n*
egoismo M
sell [sel] *vt* vendere
semblance [SEM•blens] *n*
sembianza F
semiannual [SE•mee•AN•yul]
adj semestrale
semicolon [SE•mee•KO•lun] *n*
punto e virgola M
seminary [SE•mi•NAI•ree] *n*
seminario M
senate [SE•nit] *n* senato M
senator [SE•ni•tur] *n* senatore M
send [send] *vt* mandare
sender [SEN•dur] *n* mittente
senile [SEE•nuyl] *adj* senile
senility [se•NI•li•tee] *n*
senilitá F
senior [SE•nyur] *adj* piú
vecchio; piú vecchia
seniority [se•NYAU•ri•tee] *n*
anzianitá F
sensation [sen•SAI•shn] *n*
sensazione F
sense [sens] *n* senso M; *vi*
intuire; capire; (common ~)
n buon senso M

senseless [SENS•les] *adj*
inanimato; inanimata
sensibility [SEN•si•BI•li•tee] *n*
sensibilitá F
sensible [SEN•si•bl] *adj*
sensato; sensata
sensitive [SEN•si•tiv] *adj*
sensibile
sensitivity [SEN•si•ti•vi•tee] *n*
sensibilitá F
sensual [SEN•shoo•ul] *adj*
sensuale
sentence [SEN•tuns] *n* frase F;
[sen•tinz] (jur) *n* sentenza F;
vi condonnare
sentiment [SEN•ti•mint] *n*
sentimento M
sentimentality
[SEN•ti•men•TA•li•tee] *n*
sentimentalismo M
sentinel [SEN•ti•nel] *n*
sentinella F
separable [SE•pruh•bl] *adj*
separabile
separate [SE•pa•RAIT] *vt*
separare
separately [SE•prit•lee] *adv*
separatamente
separation [SE•puh•RAI•shn] *n*
separazione F
separatism [SE•pruh•TI•zim] *n*
separatismo M
September [sep•TEM•bur] *n*
settembre M
septic [SEP•tik] *adj* settico;
settica
sepulcher [SE•pul•kur] *n*
sepolcro M
sequel [SEE•kwel] *n* sequela F
sequence [SEE•kwens] *n*
sequenza F

sequester [se•KWES•tur] *vt*
isolare

sequestration
[SEE•kwes•TRAI•shn] *n*
confisca F

serenade [SAIR•uh•NAID] *n*
serenata F; *vt* fare una
serenata

serene [suh•REEN] *adj* sereno;
serena

serenity [suh•RE•ni•tee] *n*
serenitá F

sergeant [SAHR•jint] *n*
sergente M

serial [SEE•ree•ul] *adj* a puntate

series [SEE•reez] *n* seri F

serious [SEE•ree•us] *adj* serio;
seria

seriously [SEE•ree•us•lee] *adv*
seriamente

seriousness [SEE•ree•us•nes] *n*
serietá F

sermon [SUR•min] *n*
sermone M

serpent [SUR•pint] *n*
serpente M

serum [SEER•uhm] *n* siero M

servant [SUR•vint] *n* servo;
serva; (civil) *n* impiegato
statale M

serve [surv] *vt* servire

serviceable [SUR•vi•suh•bl]
adj pratico; pratica

servile [SUR•vuyl] *adj* servile

servitude [SUR•vi•TOOD] *n*
servitú F

session [SE•shun] *n* sessione F

set 1 [set] *adj* fermo; ferma;
fisso fissa (ready) pronto; *vt*
mettere; posare

set 2 [set] *n* serie completa F

setting [SET•ting] *n*
ambiente M

settle [SET•tl] *vt* sistemare

settlement [SET•tl•mint] *n*
risoluzione F

seven [SE•vin] *num* sette

seventeen [SE•vin•TEEN] *num*
diciassette

seventeenth
[SE•vin•TEENTH] *adj*
diciassettesimo;
diciassettesima

seventh [SE•vinth] *adj* settimo;
settima

seventieth [SE•vin•tee•eth] *adj*
settentesimo; settantesima

seventy [SE•vin•tee] *num*
settanta

sever [SE•vur] *vt* recidere

several [SE•vur•uhl] *adj*
parecchi; parecchie

severe [se•VEER] *adj* severo;
severa

sew [so] *vt* cucire

sewer [SOO•ur] *n* fogna F

sewing [SO•ing] *n* cucito M

sewing machine [SO•ing
muh•SHEEN] *n* macchina da
cucire F

sewn [son] *p. part.* cucito;
cucita

sex [seks] *n* sesso M

sexton [SEKS•tin] *n*
sacrestano M

sexual [SEK•shoo•uhl] *adj*
sessuale

shabby [SHA•bee] *adj* male in
arnese

shack [shak] *n* capanna F

shackle [SHA•kl] *vt* incatenare

shad [shad] *n* alosa F

shade [shaid] *n* ombra F; *vi* sfumatura F

shiver [SHI•vur] *vi* rabbrividire

shake [shaik] *n* scossa; *vt* scuotere; agitare

shallow [SHA•lo] *ad* poco profundo

shame [shaim] *vt* svergognare; *n* vergogna F

shape [shaip] *n* forma; condiaione; *vt* formare

share [shair] *n* porzione; *vt* dividere

shark [shark] *n* pescecane

sharp [sharp] *ad* tagliente; aguzzo

sharpen [SHAR•pin] *vt* affilare

shave [shaiv] *n* rastura; *vi* farsi la barba

shawl [shaul] *n* scialle M

she [shee] *pron* ella lei

shear [sheer] *vt* tosare; *npl* cesoie F

shed [shed] 1 *n* capannone M

shed [shed] *v* verare; perdere

sheep [sheep] *n* pecora F

sheer 1 [sheer] *adj* mero; assoluto

sheer 2 [sheer] *vt* cambiar rotta

sheet [sheet] *n* lenzuolo M

shelf [shelf] *n* mensola F; ripiano M

shell [shel] *n* guscio M; *vt* (mil) bomardere; eggs, etc) sgusciare

shelter [SHEL•tur] *n* riparo *vi* proteggere

shield [sheeld] *n* schermo M; *vi* proteggere

shift [shift] *vt* spostarse; *n* turno M

shine [shuyn] *n* splendore m; vtibrillare

ship [ship] *n* armatore; *vt* spedire

shirt [shirt] *n* camica F

shit [shit] *n* merda F; *vt* cacare (coll)

shock [shok] *n* coplo M; *vi* colpire; collisione F

shoddy [SHAH•dee] *adj* scadente

shoe [shoo] *n* scarpa F

shoelace [SHOO•lais] *n* stringa F

shoemaker [SHOO•MAI•kur] *n* calzolaio M

shoot [shoot] *vi* sparare

shooter [SHOO•tur] *n* tiratore M

shooting [SHOO•ting] *adj* da caccia

shop [shahp] *n* negozio M; *vt* fare la spesa

shopkeeper [SHAHP•KEE•pur] *n* negoziante M

shopper [SHAH•pur] *n* compratore M

shopping 1 [SHAH•ping] *n* compere F

shopping 2 (to go) [SHAH•ping] *vi* fare acquisti; fare la spesa

shore [shaur] *n* spiaggia F

short [shaurt] *adj* corto; corta

short story [SHAURT STAUR•ee] *n* novella F

shortage [SHAUR•tij] *n* deficienza F

shortcoming [SHAURT•KUH•ming] *n* difetto M

shortcut [SHAURT•kut] *n* scorciatoia F

shorten [SHAUR•tin] *vt* accorciare

shortening [SHAURT•ning] *n* grasso M

shorthand [SHAURT•hand] *n* stenografia F

shortly [SHAURT•lee] *adv* fra poco

shot [shaht] *n* sparo M

shotgun [SHAHT•gun] *n* fucile M

shoulder [SHOL•dur] *n* spalla F

shout [shout] *n* grido M; *vt* gridare

shove [shuhv] *n* spinta F *vt* spingere

shovel [SHUH•vl] *n* vanga F

show [sho] *n* spettacolo M; *vt* mostrare

shower [SHOU•ur] *n* doccia F

showy [SHO•ee] *adj* vistoso; vistosa

shred [shred] *n* brandello M

shrew [shroo] *n* bisbetica F

shrewd [shrood] *adj* sagace

shrewish [SHROO•ish] *adj* petulante

shriek [shreek] *n* strillo M

shrike [shruyk] *n* averla F

shrill [shril] *adj* stridente

shrimp [shrimp] *n* gambero M

shrine [shruyn] *n* reliquiario M

shrink [shrink] *vt* restringere

shrinkage [SHRINK•kij] *n* restringimento M

shrivel [SHRI•vil] *vt* aggrinzare

shroud 1 [shroud] *n* sudario M

shroud 2 [shroud] *vt* nascondere

Shrove Tuesday [SHROV TOOZ•dai] *n* martedí grasso M

shrub [shruhb] *n* cespuglio M

shrubbery [SHRUHB•bree] *n* macchia F

shrunk [shrunk] *adj* raggrinzito; raggrinzita

shudder [SHUH•dur] *n* brivido M

shuffle 1 [SHUH•fl] *vt* trascinare i piedi

shuffle 2 (cards) [SHUH•fl] *vt* mischiare (le carte)

shun [shun] *vt* sfuggire

shunt [shunt] *n* derivazione F

shut [shut] *vt* chiudere

shutter [SHUH•dur] *n* imposta F

shuttle [SHUH•tl] *n* spola F

shy [shuy] *adj* timido; timida

shyness [SHUY•nis] *n* timidezza F

sibyl [SI•bil] *n* sibilla F

sick [sik] *adj* malato; malata

sicken [SI•kin] *vi* ammalarsi

sickening [SIK•ning] *adj* nausebondo; nauseabonda

sickle [SI•kil] *n* falce F

sickly [SIK•lee] *adj* malaticcio; malaticcia

sickness [SIK•nis] *n* malattia F

side [suyd] *n* parte F; *vi* (~ with) essere dalla aparte di

sideboard [SUYD•bord] *n* credenza F

sidetrack [SUYD•trak] *vt* distrarre

sidewalk [SUYD•walk] *n* marciapiede M

sideways [SUYD•waiz] *adj*
laterale

siding [SUY•ding] *n*
rivestitura F

siege [seej] *n* assedio M

sieve [siv] *n* setaccio M

sift [sift] *vt* setacciare

sigh [suy] *n* sospiro M

sight [suyt] *n* vista F; *vi*
intravedere

sightseeing [SUYT•SEE•ing] *n*
visita turistica F

sign [suyn] *vt* firmare; *n* segno
M; (street) *n* cartello M

signal [SIG•nuhl] *n* segnale M

signalize [SIG•nuh•LUYZ] *vi*
segnalare

signature [SIG•nuh•CHUR] *n*
firma F

signet [SIG•nit] *n* sigillo M

significance [sig•NI•fi•kenz] *n*
significato M

significant [sig•NI•fi•kent] *adj*
significativo; significativa

signify [SIG•ni•FUY] *vi*
significare

silence [SUY•lenz] *n* silenzio M

silencer [SUY•len•sur] *n*
silenziatore M

silently [SUY•lent•lee] *adv*
silenziosamente

silhouette [SIL•o•WET] *n*
siluetta F

silk [silk] *n* seta F

silken [SILK•in] *adj* di seta

sill [sil] *n* davanzale M

silly [SIL•lee] *adj* sciocco;
sciocca

silt [silt] *n* melma F

silver [SIL•vur] *n* argento M

silversmith [SIL•vur•smith]' *n*
argentiere M

silverware [SIL•vur•WAIR] *n*
argenteria F

similar [SI•mi•lur] *adj* simile

similarly [SI•mi•lur•lee] *adv*
similmente

similitude [si•MI•li•TOOD] *n*
somiglianza F

simmer [SIM•mur] *vt* sobbollire

simple [SIM•pl] *adj* semplice

simpleton [SIM•pl•tin] *n*
sempliciotto; sempliciotta

simplicity [sim•PLI•ci•tee] *n*
semplicitá F

simplification
[SIM•pli•fi•KAI•shn] *n*
semplificazione F

simplify [SIM•pli•FUY] *vt*
semplificare

simulate [SIM•yoo•LAIT] *vt*
simulare

simultaneous
[SUY•muhl•TAI•nee•us] *adj*
simultaneo; simultanea

sin [sin] *n* peccato M; *vi* peccare

since [sins] *adv* da

sincere [sin•SEER] *adj* sincero;
sincera

sincerity [sin•SAIR•i•tee] *n*
sinceritá F

sinew [SI•noo] *n* tendine M

sing [sing] *vt* cantare

singe [sinj] *vt* bruciare

single [SIN•gl] *adj* singolo;
singola

single-handed
[SIN•gl•HAN•did] *adj* da
solo; da sola

singular [SIN•gyu•lur] *adj*
singolare

sinister [SI•ni•stur] *adj* sinistro; sinistra

sink [singk] *vi* sprofondare; *n* lavandino M

sinker [SINK•kur] *n* piombino M

sinless [SIN•les] *adj* senza peccato

sinner [SIN•nur] *n* peccatore; peccatrice

sinus [SUY•nis] *n* cavitá F

sinusitis [SUY•nyu•SUY•tis] *n* sinusite F

sip [sip] *n* sorso M

siphon [SUY•fuhn] *n* sifone M

sir [sur] *n* signore M

sire [suyr] *vt* generare

siren [SUY•rin] *n* sirena F

sirloin [SUR•loin] *n* filetto M

sister [SIS•tur] *n* sorella F

sister-in-law [SIS•tur•in•LAU] *n* cognata F

sit [sit] *vi* sedere

site [suyt] *n* terreno M

sitter [SI•tur] *n* bambinaia F

sitting [SIT•ting] *n* posa F

sitting-room [SIT•ting ROOM] *n* salotto M

situate [SI•choo•WAIT] *vt* situare

situation [SI•choo•WAI•shn] *n* situazione F

six [siks] *num* sei

sixteen [siks•TEEN] *num* sedici

sixteenth [siks•TEENTH] *adj* sedicesimo; sedicesima

sixth [siksth] *adj* sesto; sesta

sixtieth [SIKS•tee•ith] *adj* sessantesimo; sessantesima

sixty [SIKS•tee] *num* sessanta

size [suyz] *n* taglia F; *vi* valutare

sizzle [SI•zul] *vi* sfrigolare

skate [skait] *vi* pattinare; *n* (ice) pattino M; (roller) pattino a rotelle M

skein [skain] *n* matassa F

skeleton [SKEL•i•tin] *n* scheletro M

skeptic [SKEP•tik] *adj n* scettico; scettica

sketch [skech] *vt* abbozzare M; *n* schizzo M

skewer [SKYOO•ur] *n* spiedo M

ski [skee] *vi* sciare

skid [skid] *vi* scivolare

skill [skil] *n* abilitá F

skilled [skild] *adj* esperto; esperta

skillet [SKI•lit] *n* padella F

skillful [SKIL•ful] *adj* abile

skim [skim] *vt* schiumare

skin [skin] *n* pelle F

skin-deep [SKIN•DEEP] *adj* superficiale

skinflint [SKIN•flint] *n* taccagno; taccagna

skinny [SKI•nee] *adj* magro; magra

skip [skip] *vt* saltare

skipper [SKIP•pur] *n* capitano M

skirt [skurt] *n* gonna F

skit [skit] *n* sketch M

skittish [SKI•tish] *adj* ombroso; ombrosa

skulk [skuhlk] *vi* imboscarsi

skull [skuhl] *n* teschio M

skunk [skuhnk] *n* puzzola F

sky [skuy] *n* cielo M

skylight [SKUY•luyt] *n*
lucernario M

skyscraper [SKUY•SKRAI•pur]
n grattacielo M

slab [slab] *n* lastra F

slack [slak] *adj* lento; lenta

slacken [SLAK•kin] *vt* allentare

slacker [SLAK•kur] *n*
fannullone; fannullona

slag [slag] *n* scoria F

slam [slam] *vt* sbattere

slander [SLAN•dur] *n*
calunnia F

slang [slang] *n* gergo M

slant [slant] *n* inclinazione F; *vi*
inclinare

slap [slap] *vt* schiaffeggiare

slash [slash] *n* taglia F; *vt*
tagliare

slat [slat] *n* assicella F

slate [slait] *n* ardesia F

slattern [SLA•turn] *n*
sciattona F

slaughter [SLAU•tur] *vt*
macellare

slave [slaiv] *n* schiavo; schiava

slavish [SLAI•vish] *adj* servile

slaw [slau] *n* insalata di
cavolo F

slay [slai] *vt* ammazzare

sled [sled] *vi* andare in slitta

sledge [slej] *n* slitta F

sleek [sleek] *adj* lustro; lustra

sleep [sleep] *n* sonno M; *vi*
dormire; addomentarsi

sleeper [SLEE•pur] *n* vagone
letto M

sleepiness [SLEE•pee•nis] *n*
sopore M

sleeping [SLEE•ping] *adj*
dormiente

sleepless [SLEEP•les] *adj*
insonne

sleepy [SLEE•pee] *adj*
sonnolento; sonnolenta

sleet [sleet] *n* nevischio M

sleeve [sleev] *n* manica F

sleigh [slai] *n* slitta F

sleight [sluyt] *n* destrezza F

sleuth [slooth] *n*
investigatore M

slice [sluys] *n* fetta F

slick [slik] *adj* liscio; liscia

slicker [SLI•kur] *n*
impemeabile M

slide [sluyd] *n* scivolata F; *vi*
scivolare

slight [sluyt] *adj* esile; *vi*
mancare di rispetto; ignorare

slightly [SLUYT•lee] *adv*
leggermente

slim [slim] *adj* smilzo; smilza

slime [sluym] *n* fanghiglia F

sling [sling] *n* imbracatura F

slink [slingk] *vi* sgattaiolare

slip [slip] *vi* scivolare

slipper [SLIP•pur] *n* pantofola F

slippery [SLIP•pree] *adj*
scivoloso; scivolosa

slit [slit] *vt* fendere

slither [SLI•thur] *vi* strisciare

sliver [SLI•vur] *n* scheggia F

slobber [SLAH•bur] *vi* sbavare

slogan [SLO•gun] *n* slogan M

sloop [sloop] *n* sloop M

slop [slahp] *n* brodaglia F

slope [slop] *n* pendenza F

small [smaul] *adj* piccolo

smart [smart] *adj* acuto;
intelligente; elegante; *vi*
bruciare

smell [smehl] *vi* sentire; lodore di; *n* odore M; profumo M

smile [smuyl] *n* sorriso M; *vi* sorridere

smiling [SMUYL•ing] *adj* souriant; agréable

smoke [smohk] *n* n fumo M; *vt vi* fumare

smooth [smooth] *adj* lisco; calmo; *vt* lisciare; spinare

smother [SMUH•ther] *vt* soffocare

smuggle [SMUH•gl] *vt* entrare/uscire di contrabbando

snack [snak] *n* spuntino M

snake [snaik] *n* serpente M

snap [snap] *vi* schioccare; spezzarsi; *n* schiocco M

snatch [snach] *vt* ghermire

sneak [sneek] *vt* muoversi furitvamente

sneakers [SNEE•kurs] *npl* scare da tennis/ginnastica F

sneeze [sneez] *vt* starnutire; starnuto M

snooze [snooz] *vt* sonnecchiare; *n* pissolino M

snore [snaur] *vt* sbuffare; *n* sbuffata F

snort [snaurt] *vt* fiutare

snout [snout] *n* grugno M

snow [sno] *n* neve F; *vi* nevicare

snowball [SNO•baul] *n* palla di neve F

snowdrift [SNO•drift] *n* cumulo di neve M

snowfall [SNO•fahl] *n* nevicata F

snowflake [SNO•flaik] *n* fiocco di neve M

snowplow [SNO•plou] *n* spazzaneve M

snub [snuhb] *vt* rabbuffare

snuff [snuhf] *n* tabacco da fiuto

snuffle [SNUHF•fl] *vt* avere il raffreddore

snug [snuhg] *adj* stretto; stretta

so [so] *adv* cosí; tanto

soak [sok] *vt* ammollare

soap [sop] *n* sapone M

soar [saur] *vi* librarsi in volo

sob [sahb] *vi* singhiozzare

sober [SO•bur] *adj* sobrio; sobria

soberly [SO•bur•lee] *adv* sobriamente

sobriety [so•BRUY•i•tee] *n* sobrietá F

sociable [SO•shuh•bl] *adv* socievole

social [SO•shuhl] *adj* sociale

socialism [SO•shuh•LIZM] *n* socialismo M

socialist [SO•shuh•list] *n adj* socialista

society [so•SUY•i•tee] *n* societá F

sociology [SO•see•YAH•lo•gee] *n* sociologia F

sock [sahk] *n* calzino M

socket [SAH•kit] *n* presa F

sod [sahd] *n* zolla F

soda [SO•duh] *n* bibita F

sodium [SO•dee•um] *n* sodio M

sofa [SO•fuh] *n* sofá M

soft [sauft] *adj* morbido; morbida

soften [SAU•fin] *vt* ammorbidire

softness [SAUFT•nis] *n* morbidezza F

soil [soil] *n* suolo M

sojourn [SO•jurn] *n* soggiorno M

solace [SAH•les] *n* sollievo M

solar [SO•lur] *adj* solare

solder [SAH•dur] *vt* saldare

soldier [SOL•jur] *n* soldato M

sole [sol] *n* suola F

solecism [SAH•lu•SI•zm] *n* solecismo M

solemn [SAH•lim] *adj* solenne

solemnity [suh•LEM•ni•tee] *n* solennitá F

solemnize [SAH•lem•NUYZ] *vt* solennizzare

solicit [suh•LI•sit] *vt* sollecitare

solicitation [suh•LI•si•TAI•shn] *n* sollecitazione F

solicitor lawyer [so•LI•si•tur] *n* avvocato M

solicitous [so•LI•si•tus] *adj* sollecito; sollecita

solid [SAH•lid] *adj* solido; solida

solidarity [SAH•li•DAIR•i•tee] *n* solidarietá F

solidify [suh•LI•di•FUY] *vt* solidificare

solidity [suh•LI•di•tee] *n* soliditá F

soliloquy [suh•LIL•uh•kwee] *n* soliloquio M

solitary [SAH•li•TAI•ree] *adj* solitario; solitaria

solitude [SAH•li•TOOD] *n* solitudine F

solo [SO•lo] *adj* a solo

solstice [SOL•stis] *n* solstizio M

solution [so•LOO•shn] *n* soluzione F

solve [sahlv] *vt* risolvere

solvent [SAHL•vint] *adj* solvente

somber [SAHM•bur] *adj* fosco; fosca

some [suhm] *adj* del; della; qualche

somebody [SUHM•buh•dee] *pron* qualcuno M

somehow [SUHM•hou] *adv* in qualche modo

someone [SUHM•wuhn] *pron* qualcuno M

somersault [SUHM•ur•SAULT] *n* capriola F

something [SUHM•thing] *pron* qualcosa F

sometime [SUHM•tuym] *adv* a volte

sometimes [SUHM•tuymz] *adv* qualche volta

somewhat [SUHM•wuht] *pron* piuttosto

somewhere [SUHM•wair] *adv* in qualche luogo

somnolent [SAHM•nuh•lint] *adj* sonnolento; sonnolenta

son [suhn] *n* figlio M

son-in-law [SUHN•in•LAU] *n* genero M

sonata [so•NAH•tuh] *n* sonata F

song [saung] *n* canzone F

song-bird [SAUNG•burd] *n* uccello canterino M

sonnet [SAH•nit] *n* sonetto M

sonorous [sah•NU•ruhs] *adj* sonoro; sonora

soon [soon] *adv* presto; tra poco

soot [sut] *n* fuliggine F

soothe [sooth] *vt* calmare

soothsayer [SOOTH•SAI•ur] *n*
indovino; indovina

sooty [SUT•tee] *adj*
fuligginoso; fuliggiosa

sop [sahp] *vt* inzuppare

sophisticated
[so•FI•sti•KAI•tid] *adj*
sofisticato; sofisticata

sophistication
[so•FI•sti•KAI•shn] *n*
sofisticazione

sophomore [SAUF•maur] *n*
fagiolo M

soporific [SAH•po•RI•fik] *adj*
soporifico; soporifica

soprano [suh•PRA•no] *n*
soprano F

sorcerer [SAUR•sir•ur] *n*
mago M

sordid [SAUR•did] *adj* sordido;
sordida

sore [saur] *adj* indolenzito;
indolenzita

sorrow [SAH•ro] *n* dolore M

sorrowful [SAH•ro•ful] *adj*
infelice

sorry [SAH•ree] *adj* spiacente;
dolente

sort [saurt] *vt* classificare; *n*
sorta; specie F

soul [sol] *n* anima F

sound [sound] *n* suono M

soundless [SOUND•les] *adj*
silenzioso; silenziosa

soundproof [SOUND•pruhf]
adj isolato acusticamente;
isolata acusticamente

soup [soop] *n* minestra F

sour [SOU•ur] *adj* agro; agra

source [sors] *n* fonte F

south [south] *n* sud M

South America [SOUTH
u•ME•ri•ku] *n* Sud
America M

southeast [south•EEST] *n* sud
est M

southerner [SUHTH•thur•nur]
adj meridionale

southward [SOUTH•wurd] *adv*
verso sud

southwest [south•WEST] *n* sud
ovest M

souvenir [SOO•ven•NEER] *n*
ricordo M

sovereign [SAHV•rin] *adj*
sovrano; sovrana

Soviet [SO•vee•it] *n* Soviet M

sow 1 [sou] *n* scrofa F

sow 2 [so] *vt* seminare;
disseminare

space [spais] *n* spazio M

spacious [SPAI•shus] *adj*
spazioso; spaziosa

spade [spaid] *n* vanga F

span [span] *n* campata F

spangle [SPANG•gl] *n*
lustrino M

Spaniard [SPAN•yurd] *n*
spagnolo; spagnola

spaniel [SPAN•yuhl] *n*
spaniel M

Spanish [SPA•nish] *adj*
spagnolo; spagnola

spank [spangk] *vt* sculacciare

spanking [SPANG•king] *n*
sculacciata F

spar [spahr] *vi* combattere

spare [spair] *vt* risparmiare

spark [spahrk] *n* scintilla F

spark plug [SPAHRK PLUHG]
n candela F

sparkle [SPAHR•kl] *vi*
scintillare

sparkling [SPAHRK•kling] *adj*
scintillante

sparrow [SPAIR•ro] *n*
passero M

sparse [spahrs] *adj* rado; rada

spasm [SPA•zim] *n* spasimo M

spatter [SPA•tur] *vt* schizzare

spawn [spahn] *vt* generare; *n*
uova F

speak [speek] *vi* parlare

speaker [SPEE•kur] *n*
altoparlante M

spear [speer] *n* lancia F; *vt*
trafiggere

special [SPE•shul] *adj* speciale

specialist [SPE•shuh•list] *n*
specialista

specialize [SPE•shuh•LUYZ] *vi*
specializzarsi

species [SPEE•sheez] *n*
specie F

specific [spuh•SI•fik] *adj*
specifico; specifica

specify [SPEH•si•FUY] *vi*
specificare

specimen [SPE•si•min] *n*
esemplare M

specious [SPEE•shus] *adj*
specioso; speciosa

speckle [SPE•kl] *vt*
macchiettare

spectacle [SPEK•ti•kl] *n*
spettacolo M

spectacular
[spek•TAK•kyu•lur] *adj*
spettacolare F

spectator [SPEK•TAI•tur] *n*
spettatore; spettatrice

specter [SPEK•tur] *n* spettro M

spectrum [SPEK•trum] *n*
spettro M

speculate [SPEK•kyu•LAIT] *vi*
speculare

speculation
[SPEK•kyu•LAI•shn] *n*
speculazione F

speculative [SPEK•kyu•luh•tiv]
adj speculativo; speculativa

speculator [SPEK•kyu•LAI•tur]
n speculatore; speculatrice

speech [speech] *n* discorso M

speed [speed] *n* velocitá F; *vt*
andare in fretta

speed limit [SPEED LI•mit] *n*
limite di velocitá M

speedily [SPEED•di•lee] *adv*
rapidamente

speedway [SPEED•wai] *n* pista
da corsa F

speedy [SPEED•dee] *adj*
rapido; rapida

spell [spel] *n* incantesimo M

spellbound [SPEL•bound] *adj*
incantato; incantata

spelling [SPEL•ling] *n*
ortografia F

spend [spend] *vt* spendere

spendthrift [SPEND•thrift] *n*
spendaccione; spendacciona

spew [spyoo] *vt* scaturire

sphere [sfeer] *n* sfera F

spherical [SFEER•i•kl] *adj*
sferico; sferica

spice [spuys] *n* spezeia F

spider [SPUY•dur] *n* ragno M

spigot [SPI•git] *n* rubinetto M

spike [spuyk] *n* aculeo M

spill [spil] *vt* versare

spin [spin] *vt* roteare

spinach [SPI•nich] *n* spinaci M

spinal [SPUY•nl] *adj* spinale

spinal column [SPUY•nl KAH•lim] *n* colonna vertebrale F

spinal cord [SPUY•nl KORD] *n* filo spinale M

spinner [SPI•nur] *n* filatrice F

spinning wheel [SPIN•ning WEEL] *n* filatoio M

spinster [SPIN•stur]

spiral 1 [SPUY•rl] *n* spirale F

spiral 2 [SPUY•rl] *adj* spirale F

spire [spuyr] *n* guglia F

spirit [SPEER•it] *n* spirito M

spirited [SPEER•i•tid] *adj* vivace

spiritual [SPEER•i•chul] *adj* spirituale

spiritualism [SPEER•i•chuh•LI•zm] *n* spiritualismo M

spirituality [SPEER•i•choo•AL•i•tee] *n* spiritualitá F

spit [spit] *vt* sputare

spite [spuyt] *n* dispetto M

splash [splash] *vt* schizzare

spleen [spleen] *n* milza F

splendid [SPLEN•did] *adj* splendido; splendida

splendor [SPLEN•dor] *n* splendore M

splice [spluys] *vt* congiungere

splint [splint] *n* stecca F

splinter [SPLIN•tur] *n* scheggia F

split [split] *vt* dividere

spoil 1 [spoil] *vt* rovinare

spoil 2 (a child) [spoil] *vt* viziare

spoke [spok] *n* raggio M

spokesperson [SPOKS•PUR•sin] *n* portavoce

sponge [spuhnj] *n* spugna F

sponge cake [SPUHNJ caik] *n* pan di Spagna M

sponger [SPUHN•jur] *n* scroccone; scroccona

sponsor [SPAHN•sur] *n* garante

spontaneity [SPAHN•tuh•NAI•i•tee] *n* spontaneitá F

spontaneous [spahn•TAI•nee•us] *adj* spontaneo; spontanea

spook [spook] *n* spettro M

spool [spool] *n* spola F

spoon [spoon] *n* cucchiaio M

spoonful [SPOON•ful] *n* cucchiaiata F

sport [spaurt] *n* sport M

sportsman [SPAURTS•mun] *n* sportivo; sportiva

spot [spaht] *n* macchia F; *vt* macchiare; riconoscere

spotted [spah•tid] *adj* macchiato; macchiata

spouse [spous] *n* coniuge

spout [spout] *n* beccuccio M

sprain [sprain] *n* slogatura F

sprawl [sprahl] *vi* estendersi

spray [sprai] *vt* spruzzare

sprayer [SPRAI•ur] *n* spruzzatore M

spread 1 [spred] *vt* stendere

spread 2 [spred] *n* pasta da spalmare F

spree [spree] *n* bisboccia F

sprightly [SPRUYT•lee] *adj* allegro; allegra

spring [spring] *n* molla F; *vt* saltare

sprinkle [SPRING•kl] *vt* spargere

sprint [sprint] *n* scatto finale M; *vt* correre

sprout [sprout] *vi* germogliare

spruce [sproos] *n* abete M

spun [spuhn] *pp* spin

spur [spuhr] *n* sperone M

spurn [spuhrn] *vt* respingere

spurt [spuhrt] *vt* zampillare

spy [spuy] *n* spia F; *vi* spiare

squabble 1 [SKWAH•bl] *n* battibecco M

squabble 2 [SKWAH•bl] *vi* altercare

squadron [SKWAH•druhn] *n* squadriglia F

squalid [SKWAH•lid] *adj* squallido; squallida

squall [skwahl] *n* burrasca F

squander [SKWAHN•dur] *vt* scialacquare

square [skwair] *n* piazza F; *n* quadrato M; *vt* quadrare; saldare

squash [skwahsh] *vt* schiacciare

squat [skwaht] *adj* tozzo; tozza

squawk [skwahk] *n* grido rauco M

squeak [skweek] *vi* cigolare

squeal [skweel] *vi* strillare

squeamish [SKWEE•mish] *adj* schizzinoso; schizzinosa

squeeze [skweez] *vt* strizzare

squelch [skwelch] *vt* soffocare

squint [skwint] *vi* socchiudere gli occhi

squire [skwuyr] *n* scudiero M

squirm [skwirm] *vi* dimenarsi

squirrel [skwirl] *n* scoiattolo M

squirt [skwirt] *vt* schizzare

stab [stab] *vt* pugnalare

stability [stuh•BI•li•tee] *n* stabilitá F

stabilize [STAI•bi•LUYZ] *vt* stabilizzare

stable 1 [STAI•bl] *n* stalla F

stable 2 [STAI•bl] *adj* stabile

stack [stak] *vt* accatastare

stadium [STAI•dee•um] *n* stadio M

staff [staf] *n* personale M

stag [stag] *n* cervo M

stage [staij] *n* palcoscenico M

stage door [STAIJ DAUR] *n* entrata di servizio F

stage fright [STAIJ FRUYT] *n* panico M

stage-struck [STAIJ•struk] *adj* affascinato dal teatro; affascinata dal teatro

stagger [STAG•gur] *vi* barcollare

stagnant [STAG•nint] *adj* stagnante

staid [staid] *adj* sobrio; sobria

stain [stain] *n* macchia F; *vt* macchiare; colorire

stainless [STAIN•lis] *adj* inossidabile

stair [stair] *n* scala F

stake [staik] *vt* mettere in gioco

stale [stail] *adj* stantio; stantia

stalk [stauk] *n* gambo M; *vt* inseguire furtivamente

stall 1 [stal] *n* chiosco M

stall 2 [stal] *vt* stallare

stallion [STAL•yun] *n* stallone

stalwart [STAL•wurt] *adj* robusto; robusta

stamina [STA•mi•nuh] *n*
vigore M

stammer [STAM•mur] *vi*
balbettare

stamp [stamp] *n* bollo M; *vt*
marcare; imprimere

stampede [stam•PEED] *n* fuggi
fuggi M

stand [stand] *n* posizione F
tribuna F *vi* stare in piedi

standard [STAN•dird] *n*
livello M

standardization
[STAN•dir•di•ZAI•shn] *n*
standardizzazione F

standardize [STAN•dir•DUYZ]
vt standardizzare

standing [STAN•ding] *n*
posizione F

stanza [STAN•zuh] *n* stanza F

staple 1 [STAI•pl] *vt* cucire con
graffette

staple 2 [STAI•pl] *n* prodotto
principale M

star [stahr] *n* stella F

starboard [STAHR•baurd] *n*
tribordo M

starch [stahrch] *n* amido M

starchy [STAHR•chee] *adj*
farinaceo; farinacea

stark [stahrk] *adv*
completamente

start [stahrt] *vt* cominciare

starting [STAHR•ting] *adj* di
partenza

starting point [STAHR•ting
POINT] *n* punto di
partenza M

startle [STAHR•tl] *vt*
sorprendere

starvation [stahr•VAI•shn] *n*
inedia F

starve [stahrv] *vt* affamare

state [stait] *n* stato M

stately [STAIT•lee] *adj*
maestoso; maestosa

statement [STAIT•mint] *n*
rapporto M

stateroom [STAIT•room] *n*
cabina F

statesman [STAITZ•min] *n*
• statista M

static [STA•tik] *adj* statico;
statica

station [STAI•shin] *n*
stazione F

stationary [STAI•shi•NAI•ree]
adj stazionario; stazionaria

stationery
[STAI•shun•NAI•ree] *n*
cancelleria F

statistics [stuh•TI•stiks] *n*
statistica F

statue [STA•choo] *n* statua F

status [STA•tus] *n* stato M

statute [STA•choot] *n*
statuto M

staunch [staunch] *vt* arrestare;
adj fedele

stay [stai] *vi* rimanere

stead [sted] *n* vece F

steadfast [STED•fast] *adj*
incrollabile

steadily [STED•i•lee] *adv*
saldamente

steadiness [STEH•dee•nes] *n*
fermezza F

steady [STEH•dee] *adj* saldo;
salda

steak [staik] *n* bistecca F

steal [steel] *vt* rubare

stealth [stelth] *n* procedimento furtivo M

steam [steem] *n* vapore M

steam engine [STEEM EN•jin] *n* vaporiera F

steamboat [STEEM•bot] *n* vapore M

steamer [STEE•mur] *n* piroscafo M

steamship [STEEM•ship] *n* piroscafo M

steed [steed] *n* destriero M

steel [steel] *n* acciaio M

steep 1 [steep] *adj* ripido; ripida

steep 2 [steep] *vt* macerare

steeple [STEE•pl] *n* campanile M

steer 1 [steer] *vt* sterzare

steer 2 [steer] *n* bue M

stem 1 [stem] *n* stelo M

stem 2 [stem] *vt* arrestare

stem 3 [stem] *n* gambo M

stench [stench] *n* puzzo M

stencil [STEN•sul] *n* stampino M

stenographer [ste•NAH•gruh•fur] *n* stenografo; stenografa

step [step] *n* passo M

stepchild [STEP•chuyld] *n* figliastro; figliastra

stepdaughter [STEP•DAU•tur] *n* figliastra F

stepfather [STEP•FA•thur] *n* padrigno M

stepladder [STEP•LA•dur] *n* scala a pioli F

stepmother [STEP•MUH•thur] *n* matrigna F

stepson [STEP•suhn] *n* figliastro M

stereo [STAIR•ree•O] *n* stereo M

stereotype [STAIR•ree•o•TUYP] *n* stereotipo M

sterile [STAIR•ruyl] *adj* sterile

sterility [stair•RI•li•tee] *n* sterilitá F

sterilize [STAIR•ri•LUYZ] *vt* sterilizzare

sterling [STUR•ling] *adj* di buona lega

stern [sturn] *adj* severo; severa

stethoscope [STETH•uh•SKOP] *n* stetoscopio M

stevedore [STEEV•dor] *n* stivatore M

stew [stoo] *n* stufato M; *vt* stufare

steward [STOO•wurd] *n* intendente M

stewardess [STOO•wur•des] *n* hostess F

stick 1 [stik] *n* bastone M

stick 2 [stik] *vi* appiccicarsi

stiff [stif] *adj* rigido; rigida

stiffen [STIF•fin] *vt* irrigidire

stiffness [STIF•nes] *n* rigidezza F

stifle [STUY•fl] *vt* soffocare

stigma [STIG•muh] *n* stigma M

still 1 [stil] *adj* immobile

still 2 [stil] *adv* tuttora

stillness [STIL•nis] *n* quiete F

stilt [stilt] *n* trampolo M

stimulant [STIM•yoo•lint] *adj* eccitante

stimulate [STIM•yoo•LAIT] *vt* stimolare

stimulation [STIM•yoo•LAI•shn] *n* eccitamento M

stimulus [STIM•yoo•lus] *n* stimolo M

sting [sting] *vt* pungere

stinginess [STIN•jee•nes] *n* avarizia F

stingy [STIN•jee] *adj* avaro; avara

stink [stingk] *vi* puzzare; *n* puzzo

stint [stint] *vt* limitare

stipend [STUY•pend] *n* stipendio M

stipulate [STIP•yoo•LAIT] *vt* stipolare

stir [stur] *vt* mescolare

stirring [STUR•ring] *adj* commovente

stirrup [STUR•rip] *n* staffa F

stitch [stich] *n* punto M

stock [stahk] *vt* approvvigionare

Stock Exchange [STAHK eks•CHAINJ] *n* borsa F

stock market [STAHK MAHR•kit] *n* borsa valori

stockade [stah•KAID] *n* stecconata F

stockbroker [STAHK•BRO•kur] *n* agente di cambio M

stockholder [STAHK•HOL•dur] *n* azionista

stocking [STAHK•king] *n* calza F

stockroom [STAHK•room] *n* magazzino M

stocky [STAHK•kee] *adj* tarchiato; tarchiata

stockyards [STAHK•yardz] *n* recinto per animali da macello M

stoic [STO•ik] *n adj* stoico; stoica

stoicism [STO•i•SIZM] *n* stoicismo M

stoke [stok] *vt* attizzare

stole [stol] *n* stola F

stolid [STAH•lid] *adj* flemmatico; flemmatica

stomach [STUH•mik] *n* stomaco M

stomachache [STUH•mik•AIK] *n* mal di stomaco M

stone [ston] *n* pietra F

stonework [STON•wurk] *n* muratura F

stony [STO•nee] *adj* di pietra

stool [stool] *n* sgabello M

stool pigeon [STOOL PI•jin] *n* informatore; informatrice

stoop [stoop] *vi* incurvarsi

stop [stahp] *vt* fermare

stoppage [STAH•pij] *n* ostruzione F

stopper [STAH•pur] *n* tappo M

stopwatch [STAHP•wahch] *n* cronometro M

storage [STAUR•aij] *n* immagazinamento M

store [staur] *vt* riporre

storekeeper [STAUR•KEE•pur] *n* bottegaio; bottegaia

stork [staurk] *n* cicogna F

storm [staurm] *n* tempesta F

stormy [STAUR•mee] *adj* tempestoso; tempestosa

story 1 [STAU•ree] *n* storia F

story 2 (of house) |STAU•ree|
 n piano M

stout |stout| *adj* forte

stove |stov| *n* stufa F

stow |sto| *vt* stipare

straddle |STRAD•dl| *vt* stare a
 cavalcioni

straggle |STRAG•gl| *vi*
 sparpagliarsi

straight |strait| *adj* dritto; dritta

straighten |STRAI•tin| *vt*
 drizzare

straightforward
 |STRAIT•FOR•wurd| *adj*
 schietto; schietta

strain |strain| *n* sforzo M

strainer |STRAI•nur| *n* colino

strait |strait| *n* stretto M

strand 1 |strand| *n* filo M

strand 2 |strand| *vi* arenarsi

strange |strainj| *adj* strano;
 strana

strangeness |STRAINJ•nes| *n*
 singolaritá F

stranger |STRAIN•jur| *n*
 straniero; straniera

strangle |STRAN•gl| *vt*
 strangolare

strangulate
 |STRAN•gyu•LAIT| *vt*
 strozzare

strangulation
 |STRAN•gyu•LAI•shn| *n*
 strangolamento M

strap *n* bretella F

strategic |struh•TEE•jik| *adj*
 strategico; strategica

strategy |stra•TI•jee| *n*
 strategia F

stratosphere
 |STRA•to•SFEER| *n*
 stratosfera F

straw |strau| *n* paglia F;
 (drinking) cannuccia F

strawberry |STRAU•bair•ree| *n*
 fragola F

stray |strai| *vi* vagare

streak |streek| *n* stria F

stream |streem| *n* corrente F

streamer |STREE•mur| *n* stella
 filante F

streamlined
 |STREEM•LUYND| *adj*
 aerodinamico; aerodinamica

street |street| *n* strada F

streetcar |STREET•kahr| *n*
 tram M

strength |strength| *n* forza F

strengthen |STRENGTH•en| *vt*
 rinforzare

strenuous |STREN•yoo•us| *adj*
 strenuo; strenua

stress 1 |stres| *n* sforzo M

stress 2 |stres| *vt* sottolineare

stretch |strech| *vt* tirare

stretcher |STRECH•ur| *n*
 barella F

strew |stroo| *vt* sparpagliare

strict |strikt| *adj* severo; severa

stride |struyd| *n* progresso M

strident |STRUY•dint| *n*
 stridente

strife |struyf| *n* conflitto M

strike |struyk| *n* sciopero M

striker |STRUY•kur| *n*
 scioperante

striking |STRUY•king| *adj* che
 fa colpo

string |string| *n* spago M

strip |strip| *n* striscia F; *vt*
 (clothes) spogliare

stripe 1 |struyp| *vt* striare

stripe 2 |struyp| *n* striscia F

strive [struyv] *vi* sforzarsi

stroke 1 [strok] *n* colpo M

stroke 2 (medical) [strok] *n* colpo apoplettico M

stroll [strol] *n* passeggiata F

strong [straung] *adj* forte

stronghold [STRAUNG•hold] *n* roccaforte F

strongly [STRAUNG•lee] *adv* fortemente

structural [STRUK•chur•ul] *adj* strutturale

structure [STRUK•chur] *n* struttura F

struggle [STRUH•gl] *n* lotta F

strut 1 [struht] *n* puntone M

strut 2 [struht] *vi* andare con sussiego

stub [stuhb] *n* mozzicone M

stubble [STUHB•bl] *n* stoppia F

stubborn [STUHB•born] *adj* testardo; testarda

stubbornness [STUHB•born•nes] *n* testardaggine F

stucco [STUH•ko] *n* intonaco M

stuck-up [STUH•KUHP] *adj* presuntuoso; presuntuosa

stud 1 [stuhd] *n* borchia F

stud 2 (animal) [stuhd] *n* stallone M

student [STOO•dint] *n* studente

studio [STOO•dee•o] *n* studio M

study [STUH•dee] *n* studio M

stuff [stuhf] *vt* imbottire

stuffing [STUHF•fing] *n* ripieno M

stuffy [STUH•fee] *adj* noioso; noiosa

stumble [STUHMB•bl] *v* inciamparsi

stump [stuhmp] *n* moncherino M; [stuhmp] *n* (tree) tronco M

stun [stuhn] *vt* stordire

stunt [stuhnt] *n* bravata F: *vt* stentare la crescita

stupefy [STOO•pi•FUY] *vt* instupidire

stupendous [stoo•PEN•dus] *adj* stupendo; stupenda

stupid [STOO•pid] *adj* stupido; stupida

stupidity [stoo•PI•di•tee] *n* stupiditá F

stupor [STOO•pur] *n* stupore M

sturdy [STUR•dee] *adj* robusto; robusta

sturgeon [STUR•jun] *n* storione M

stutter [STUH•tur] *n* balbuzie F

sty 1 [stuy] *n* stia F

sty 2 (eye) [stuy] *n* orzaiolo F

style [stuyl] *n* stile M

stylish [STUY•lish] *adj* elegante

subcommittee [SUHB•ko•MI•tee] *n* sottocomitato M

subconscious 1 [suhb•KON•shus] *adj* subcosciente

subconscious 2 [suhb•KON•shus] *n* subcosciente M

subdivision [SUHB•di•VI•shn] *n* suddivisione F

subdue [suhb•DOO] *vt* reprimere

subject [SUHB•jekt] *n* soggetto M

subjection [suhb•JEK•shn] *n*
assoggettamento M

subjective [suhb•JEK•tiv] *adj*
soggettivo; soggettiva

subjugate [SUHB•juh•GAIT] *vt*
soggiogare

subjunctive [suhb•JUNK•tiv] *n*
congiuntivo M

sublet [SUHB•LET] *vt*
subaffittare

sublime [suhb•LUYM] *adj*
sublime

submarine [SUHB•muh•REEN]
n sottomarino M

submerge [suhb•MURJ] *vt*
sommergere

submission [suhb•MI•shn] *n*
sottomissione F

submit [suhb•MIT] *vt*
sottomettere

subordinate [suhb•BOR•di•nit]
n adj subordinato; subodinata

subpoena [suh•PEE•nuh] *n*
mandato di comparizione M

subscribe [suhb•SKRUYB] *vi*
abbonare

subscriber [suhb•SKRUY•bur]
n abbonato; abbonata

subscription [suhb•SKRIP•shn]
n abbonamento M

subsequent [SUHB•se•kwent]
adj susseguente

subservient [sub•SUR•vee•ent]
adj ossequente

subside [suhb•SUYD] *vi*
decrescere

subsidize [SUHB•si•DUYZ] *vt*
sovvenzionare

subsist [suhb•SIST] *vi* sussistere

substance [SUHB•stenz] *n*
sostanza F

substantial [suhb•STAN•shul]
n notevole

substantive [SUHB•stan•tiv] *n*
sostantivo M

subterranean
[SUHB•tur•RAI•nee•yen] *adj*
sotterraneo; sotterranea

subtle [SUH•tl] *adj* sottile

subtract (deduct)
[suhb•TRAKT] *vt* sottrarre

subtraction [suhb•TRAK•shn]
n sottrazione F

suburb [SUH•burb] *n*
suburbo M

suburban [suh•BUR•ban] *adj*
suburbano; suburbana

subversive [suhb•VUR•siv] *adj*
sovversivo; sovversiva

subway [SUHB•wai] *n*
sotterranea F

succeed [suhk•SEED] *vi*
riuscire

success [suhk•SES] *n*
successo M

successful [suhk•SES•fl] *adj*
che ha successo

succession [suhk•SES•shn] *n*
successione F

succor [SUHK•or] *n* soccorso M

succulent [SUHK•yoo•lint] *adj*
succolento; succolenta

succumb [suh•KUM] *vi*
soccombere

such [suhch] *adj* tale

suck [suhk] *vt* succhiare

suction [SUHK•shn] *n*
risucchio M

sudden [SUH•din] *adj*
improvviso; improvvisa

suddenly [SUH•din•lee] *adv*
improvvisamente

suddenness [SUH•din•nes] *n*
subitaneitá F

suds [suhdz] *n* schiuma F

sue [soo] *vt* fare causa

suet [SOO•it] *n* grasso di bue M

suffer [SUH•fur] *vi* soffrire

suffering [SUHF•fring] *n*
sofferenza F

suffice [suh•FUYS] *vi* bastare

sufficiency [suh•FI•shen•see] *n*
sufficienza F

sufficient [suh•FI•shent] *adj*
sufficiente

suffocate [SUH•fo•KAIT] *vt*
soffocare

suffocation [SUH•fo•KAI•shn]
n soffocamento M

suffrage [SUH•frij] *n*
suffragio M

suffuse [suh•FYOOZ] *vt*
soffondere

sugar [SHUH•gur] *n*
zucchero M

sugar bowl [SHUH•gur BOL]
n zuccheriera F

suggest [sug•JEST] *vt* suggerire

suggestion [sug•JES•shn] *n*
suggerimento M

suggestive [sug•JES•tiv] *adj*
suggestivo; suggestiva

suicide [SOO•i•SUYD] *n*
suicidio M

suit [soot] *n* costume (man's);
completo

suitcase [soot•KAIS] *n* valgia F

suite [sweet] *n* suite F;
apartamento M

sulk [suhlk] *vt* tenere il broncio;
tenere il muso

sullen [suh•LEN] *adj* brusco;
brusca

sultan [suhl•TIN] *n* sultanto M

sum [suhm] *n* somma addozione
F

summarize
[SUHM•muh•RUYZ] *vi*
riassumere

summary [SUH•muh•ree] *n*
sommario M

summer [SUHM•mur] *n*
estate F

summit [SUHM•mit] *n* cima;
vetta F

summon [SUH•mun] *vt*
(meeting) convocare; (help)
chiamare

summons [SUH•munz] *n*
citazione; mandato di
comparizione F (law)

sun [suhn] *n* sole M; *vt* goderse
il sole

sunbathe [SUHN•bayth] *vi*
prendere il sole

sunbeam [SUHN•beem] *n*
raggio di sole M

sunburn [SUHN•birn] *n* (tan)
abbronzatura; (painfully)
scottatura

Sunday [SUHN•dai] *n*
domenica F

sunflower [SUHN•flouur] *n*
girasole M

sunglasses [SUHN•glah•sez]
npl occhiali da sole M

sunlight [SUHN•luyt] *n* sole M

sunny [SUHN•nee] *adj*
soleggiato -a

sunshine [SUHN•shuyn] *n*
sole M

super [SOO•pur] *adj*
fantastico -a

superficial [SOO•pur•FI•shul] *adj* superficiale

superintendent [SOO•pur•in•TEN•dunt] *n* soprintendente MF (police) comissario di Pubblica Sicurezza

superior [soo•PEE•ree•ur] *adj* superiore; di prim'ordine

superlative [soo•PUR•la•tiv] *adj* eccellente; superlativo

supermarket [SOO•pur•MAHR•ket] *n* supermercato M

supernatural [SOO•pur•NA•chur•el] *adj* soprannaturale

supersede [SOO•pur•SEED] *vt* sostituire; soppiantare

superstition [SOO•pur•STI•shun] *n* superstizione F

supervise [SOO•pur•VUYZ] *vt* (person) sorvegliare; (work) soprintendere a

supervision [SOO•pur•VI•zhun] *n* supervisione; sorveglianza F

supper [SUH•pur] *n* cena F to have ~\ cenare

supplement [SUH•pluh•munt] *n* supplemento M; *vt* integrare; arrotondare; completare

supply [SUH•pluy] *n* fornitura F; *vt* soddisfare; fornire

supplies [SUH•pluyz] *npl* materiele M

support 1 [suh•PAURT] *n* appoggio M; *vt* sopprtare

support 2 [suh•PAURT] *n* sotegno; *vt* sotegnere; sorreggere

suppose [suh•POZ] *vi* supporre; ritenere

suppress [suh•PRES] *vt* (emotion) reprimere; (information) soffocare; (yawn) tratenere

supreme [suh•PREEM] *adj* supremo -a

sure [shoor] *adj* sicuro - a certo - a; be ~ of something\ essere sicuro di; *adv* certo!

surely [SHAUR•lee] *adv* certamente; sicuramente

surf [surf] *npl* cavallone M; (foam) spuma

surface [SUR•fas] *n* superficie F; on the ~\ superficialmente; *vt* (road) asfaltare; *vi* person farsi vivo -a

surge [surj] *n* (sea) impeto M; (crowd) ondata F; *vi* riversarsi

surgeon [SUR•jun] *n* chirugo M

surgery [SUR•jur•ee] *n* chirigia F

surgical [SUR•ji•kul] *adj* chiurgico -a

surly [SUR•lee] *adj* burbero -a

surmount [sur•MOUNT] *vt* sormontare

surname [SUR•naim] *n* cognome M

surpass [sur•PAS] *vt* superare

surplus [SUR•plus] *n* surplus M; *adj* che avanza; (finance) di sovrappiù

surprise [sur•PRUYZ] *n* sopresa F; *adj* soprendente; *vt* soprendere; stupire

surrealism [sur•REE•uh•LIZM] *n* surrealismo M

surrealistic
[sur•REE•uh•LIS•tic] *adj*
surreale

surrender [sur•REN•dur] *vt* to
~ to\ consegnare; (lease)
cedere; (claim) ruinciare a
(hope) abbandonare; *n* resa F;
no ~!\ non ci arrendiamo!

surreptitious [SU•rep•TI•shus]
adj furtivo -a

surround [su•ROUND] *vt*
circondare; ~ed by\ circóndata
da

surrounding [su•ROUN•ding]
adj circostante

surroundings
[su•ROUN•dingz] *npl*
dintorni; (environment)
ambiente M

survey 1 [SIR•veh] *n* qudro
generale M; (study) indagine
F; *vt* (look at) guardare

survey 2 [sir•VEH] *vi*
(examine) studiare; esaminare;
(land) fare il rilevamento
topografico di

survival [sur•VUY•vul] *n*
sopravvivenza F

survive [sur•VUYV] *vi*
sopravvivere

survivor [sur•VUY•vur] *n*
superstite

susceptibility
[suh•SEP•ti•BI•li•tee] *n*
suscettibilitá F

susceptible [suh•SEP•ti•bl] *adj*
suscettibile

suspect [sus•PEKT] *vt*
sospettare

suspend [sus•SPEND] *vt*
sospendere

suspenders [sus•SPEN•durz] *n*
bretelle F

suspense [suhs•SPENS] *n*
suspense M

suspicion [suhs•SPI•shn] *n*
sospetto M

sustain [suh•STAIN] *vt*
sostenere

sustenance [SUH•ste•nens] *n*
sostentamento M

suture [SOO•chur] *n* sutura F

swab [swaub] *n* tampone M

swagger [SWAG•gur] *vi*
vantarsi

swain [swain] *n* corteggiatore M

swallow 1 [SWAH•lo] *n*
rondine F

swallow 2 [SWAH•lo] *vt*
ingoiare

swamp [swaump] *n* palude F

swan [swahn] *n* cigno M

swap [swahp] *vt* scambiare

swarm [swaurm] *n* (bees)
sciame M; (crowd) folla F *vi*
sciamare

swarthy [SWAUR•thee] *adj*
olivastro; olivastra

swat [swaut] *vt* schiacciare

swathe [swath] *vt* fasciare

sway [swai] *vi* ondulare

swear [swair] *vi* giurare

sweat [swet] *n* sudore M

sweater [SWET•tur] *n*
maglione M

Swede [sweed] *n* svedese

Sweden [SWEED•din] *n*
Svezia F

Swedish [SWEED•dish] *adj*
svedese

sweep [sweep] *vt* scopare

sweeper [SWEEP•pur] *n*
spazzino M

sweeping [SWEEP•ping] *adj*
vasto; vasta

sweet [sweet] *adj* dolce

sweet potato [SWEET
pu•TAI•to] *n* patata dolce F

sweetbread [SWEET•bred] *n*
animella F

sweeten [SWEET•tin] *vt*
addolcire

sweetness [SWEET•nis] *n*
dolcezza F

swell [swel] *vi* gonfiarsi

swelling [SWEL•ing] *n*
gonfiore M

swelter [SWEL•tur] *vi*
soffocare per il caldo

swerve [swurv] *vi* deviare

swift [swift] *adj* rapido; rapida

swiftness [SWIFT•nes] *n*
rapiditá F

swim [swim] *vi* nuotare

swimmer [SWIM•mur] *n*
nuotatore; nuotatrice

swimming [SWIM•ming] *n*
nuoto M

swimming pool [SWIM•ming
POOL] *n* piscina F

swimsuit [SWIM•soot] *n*
costume da bagno M

swindle [SWIN•dl] *vt* truffare;
n truffa F

swing [swing] *vt* dondolare; *n*
oscillazione F

swipe [swuyp] *vt* rubacchiare

swirl [swirl] *vi* girare
vorticosamente

Swiss [swis] *n adj* svizzero;
svizzera

switch [swich] *vt* scambiare; *n*
interruttore M

switchboard [SWICH•bord] *n*
centralino M

Switzerland [SWIT•zur•land] *n*
Svizzera F

swivel [SWI•vul] *vi* ruotare

swivel chair [SWI•vul CHAIR]
n sedia girevole F

swoon [swoon] *vi* svenire

swoop [swoop] *vi* abbattersi

sword [sord] *n* spada F

sycamore [SI•ki•MOR] *n*
platano M

syllable [SI•li•bl] *n* sillaba F

syllogism [SI•lo•JIZM] *n*
sillogismo M

symbol [SIM•buhl] *n* simbolo M

symbolic [sim•BAH•lik] *adj*
simbolico; simbolica

symmetrical [sim•ME•tri•kuhl]
adj simmetrico; simmetrica

sympathetic
[SIM•puh•THE•tik] *adj*
comprensivo; comprensiva

sympathy [SIM•puh•thee] *n*
comprensione F

symphony [SIM•fo•nee] *n*
sinfonia F

symptom [SIMP•tum] *n*
sintomo M

symptomatic
[SIMP•to•MA•tik] *adj*
sintomatico; sintomatica

synagogue [SI•no•GAHG] *n*
sinagoga F

synchronize [SIN•kro•NUYZ]
vt sincronizzare

syndicate 1 [SIN•di•kit] *n*
sindacato M

syndicate 2 [SIN•di•KAIT] *vt*
pubblicare su diversi giornali

synonym [SI•ni•NIM] *n*
snonimo M

synonymous
[si•NAHN•ni•mus] *adj*
sinonimo; sinonima

syntax [SIN•taks] *n* sintassi F

synthesis [SIN•thuh•sis] *n*
sintesi F

Syria [SEE•ree•uh] *n* Siria F

Syrian [SEE•ree•yen] *adj*
siriano; siriana

syringe [sir•RINJ] *n* siringa F

syrup [SEER•rup] *n*
sciroppo M

system [SIS•tim] *n*
sistema M

systematic [SIS•te•MA•tik] *adj*
sistematico; sistematica

T

tab [tab] *n* liguetta F; cartellino

table [TAI•bl] *n* tabella F;
(card) *n* tavolo M

tablet [TAB•lit] *n* tavoletta F

tableware [TAI•bl•WAIR] *n*
stoviglie F

tabloid [TAB•bloid] *n* rivista
scandalistica F

tabular [TAB•yoo•lar] *adj*
piano; piana

tabulate [TAB•yoo•LAIT] *vt*
disporre in tabella

tachometer [ta•KO•muh•tur] *n*
tacometro M

tacit [TA•sit] *adj* tacito; tacita

taciturn [TA•si•TURN] *adj*
taciturno; taciturna

tack [tak] *n* puntina F; *vt*
(sewing) imbastire; (sailing)
bordeggiare

tackle 1 [TAK•kl] *n* paranco M;
vt venire alle prese con;
affrontare

tackle 2 (fishing) [TAK•kl] *n*
arnesi da pesca M

tact [takt] *n* tatto M

tactical [TAK•ti•kul] *adj* tattico;
tattica

tactics [TAK•tiks] *n* tattica F

tactile [TAK•tul] *adj* tattile

tadpole [TAD•pol] *n* girino M

taffeta [TA•fit•tuh] *n* taffetá M

tag [tag] *n* cartellino M; *vi*
agguingere; ~ along\ *vi*
seguire

tail [tail] *n* coda F

tailor [TAI•lur] *n* sarto M

taint [taint] *vt* contaminare

take [taik] *vt* prendere: ~ off\ *vi*
andare via; (detach) *vt*
staccare

talcum [TAL•kum] *n* talco M

tale [tail] *n* storia F

talent [TAL•int] *n* talento M

talk [tauk] *vi* parlare

talkative [TAUK•uh•tiv] *adj*
loquace

talker [TAU•kur] *n*
chiaccherone; chiaccherona

talking [TAU•king] *adj* parlante

tall [taul] *adj* alto; alta

tallow [TA•lo] *n* sego M

tally [TA•lee] *vt* riscontrare

tam o' shanter [TAM o' SHAN•tur] *n* berretto scozzese M

tame [taim] *adj* addomesticato; addomesticata; *vt* addomesticare

tamper [TAM•pur] *vi* manomettere

tan [tan] *n* abbronzatura F; (color) costano M

tandem [TAN•dim] *n* tandem M

tangent [TAN•jent] *n* tangente F

tangerine [TAN•juh•REEN] *n* mandarino M

tangible [TAN•juh•bl] *adj* tangibile

Tangiers [tan•JEERZ] *n* Tangeri F

tangle [TANG•gl] *n* groviglio M

tank [tank] *n* vasca F; (gasoline) *n* serbatoio M

tanker [TANK•kur] *n* petroliera F

tannery [TAN•nur•ree] *n* conceria F

tantalize [TAN•tuh•LUYZ] *vt* tantalizzare

tantrum [TAN•trum] *n* capriccio M

tap [tap] *n* rubinetto M; *vt* spillare

tape [taip] *n* nastro M; (tie) *vt* allacciare; (record) registrare

taper [TAI•pur] *n* candela F

tapestry [TA•pe•stree] *n* arazzo M

tar [tar] *n* pece F

tardy [TAR•dee] *adj* tardivo; tardiva

tare [tair] *n* tara F

target [TAR•git] *n* bersaglio M

tariff [TAIR•rif] *n* tariffa F

tarnish [TAR•nish] *vt* annerire

tarpaulin [tar•PO•lin] *n* telone M

tarry [TAIR•ree] *vi* indugiare

tart 1 [tart] *adj* agro; agra

tart 2 [tart] *n* crostata F

tartar [TAR•tur] *n* tartaro M

task [task] *n* compito M

tassel [TA•suhl] *n* fiocco M

taste [taist] *n* sapore M; assaggiare

tasteless [TAIST•les] *adj* insipido; insipida

tasty [TAI•stee] *n* gustoso; gustosa

tattered [TAT•turd] *adj* sbrindellato; sbrindellata

tattle [TAT•tl] *vi* spettegolare

tattletale [TAT•tl•TAIL] *n* chiacchierone; chiacchierona

tattoo [tat•TOO] *n* tatuaggio M; *vt* tatuare

taunt [taunt] *vt* schernire

tavern [TA•vurn] *n* taverna F

tax [taks] *n* imposta F *vt* tassare; (income) *n* imposta su redditi F; (state tax) *n* imposta su stato

taxi [TAK•see] *n* tassí M

taxpayer [TAKS•PAI•ur] *n* contribuente

tea [tee] *n* the M

tea party [TEE PAHR•tee] *n* ricevimento da the M

teach [teech] *vt* insegnare

teacher [TEE•chur] *n*
insegnante

teaching [TEE•ching] *n*
insegnamento M

teacup [TEE•kup] *n* tazza da
the F

teakettle [TEE•KET•tl] *n*
bollitore M

teal [teel] *adj* verde blu

team [teem] *n* squadra F

teamwork [TEEM•wurk] *n*
lavoro di gruppo M

teapot [TEE•pot] *n* teiera F

tear 1 [tair] *n* strappo M; *vt*
strappare

tear 2 [teer] *n* lacrima F

tease [teez] *vt* stuzzicare

teaspoon [TEE•spoon] *n*
cucchiaino M

technical [TEK•ni•kul] *adj*
tecnico; tecnica

technician [tek•NI•shn] *n*
tecnico; tecnica

tedious [TEE•dee•is] *adj*
tedioso; tediosa

teem [teem] *vi* formicolare

teens [teenz] *n* anni
dell'adolescenza M

teethe [teeth] *vi* mettere i denti

telegram [TEL•le•GRAM] *n*
telegramma M

telegraph [TEL•le•GRAF] *n*
telegrafo M

telephone [TEL•le•FON] *n*
telefono M

telephone number
[TEL•le•FON NUHM•bur] *n*
numero di telefono M

telephone operator
[TEL•le•FON AH•pu•RAI•tur]
n centralinista

telescope [TEL•le•SKOP] *n*
telescopio M

televise [TEL•le•VUYZ] *vt*
teletrasmettere

television [TEL•le•VI•shn] *n*
televisione F

television set [TE•li•VI•shn
SET] *n* televisore M

tell [tel] *vt* dire; raccontare;
distinguere

teller [TEL•lur] *n* commesso di
banca; commessa di banca

telling [TEL•ling] *adj*
espressivo; espressiva

telltale [TEL•tail] *adj*
rivelatore; rivelatrice

temerity [te•MAIR•ri•tee] *n*
temerarietà F

temper [TEM•pur] *n* carattere
M; *vi* moderare; temperare

temperament [TEM•pur•ment]
n temperamento M

temperance [TEM•prens] *n*
temperanza F

temperate [TEM•pret] *adj*
temperato; temperata

temperature
[TEM•pruh•CHUR] *n*
temperatura F

tempest [TEM•pest] *n*
tempesta F

tempestuous [tem•PES•chus]
adj tempestoso; tempestosa

temple 1 [TEM•pl] *n* tempio M

temple 2 [TEM•pl] *n* tempia F

temporal [TEM•pruhl] *adj*
temporale M

temporary [TEM•po•RAI•ree]
adj temporaneo; temporanea

temporize [TEM•po•RUYZ] *vi*
temporeggiare

tempt [tempt] *vt* tentare

temptation [tem•TAI•shn] *n* tentazione F

tempting [TEMP•ting] *adj* allettante

ten [ten] *num* dieci

tenable [TEN•uh•bl] *adj* sostenibile

tenacious [ten•AI•shus] *adj* tenace

tenacity [ten•A•si•tee] *n* tenacia F

tenant [TEN•nant] *n* inquilino; inquilina

tend [tend] *vi* tendere; (a machine, etc.) *vt* badare

tendency [TEN•den•cee] *n* tendenza F

tender 1 [TEN•dur] *n* offerta F; *vt* presentare

tender 2 [TEN•dur] *adj* tenero; tenera

tenderloin [TEN•dur•LOIN] *n* filetto M

tenderness [TEN•dur•nes] *n* tenerezza F

tendon [TEN•din] *n* tendine M

tendril [TEN•dril] *n* viticcio M

tenement [TEN•ne•mint] *n* casamento M

tennis [TEN•nis] *n* tennis M

tenor [TEN•nor] *n* tenore M

tense 1 [tens] *adj* teso; tesa

tense 2 [tens] *n* tempo M

tensile [TEN•sil] *adj* tensile

tension [TEN•shun] *n* tensione F

tent [tent] *n* tenda F

tentative [TEN•tuh•tiv] *adj* provvisorio; provvisoria

tenth [tenth] *adj* decimo; decima

tenuous [TEN•yoo•us] *adj* tenue

tepid [TE•pid] *adj* tiepido; tiepida

term [turm] *n* termine M

terminal 1 [TUR•min•nl] *adj* estremo; estrema

terminal 2 [TUR•min•nl] *n* stazione F

terminate [TUR•min•NAIT] *vt* licenziare

terrace [TAIR•res] *n* terrazzo M

terrain [tuh•RAIN] *n* terreno M

terrestrial [tuh•RES•stree•ul] *adj* terrestre

terrible [TAIR•uh•bl] *adj* terribile

terrific [tuhr•RIF•fik *adj* straordinario; straordinaria

terrify [TAIR•ri•FUY] *vt* atterrire

territory [TAIR•ri•TO•ree] *n* territorio M

terror [TAIR•ror] *n* terrore M

terrorize [TAIR•ro•RUYZ] *vt* terrorizzare

terse [turs] *adj* terso; tersa

test [test] *n* esame M; (blood) *n* esame del sangue; *vi* provare

test tube [TEST TOOB] *n* provetta F

testament [TES•tuh•mint] *n* testamento M

testify [TES•ti•FUY] *vi* attestare

testimony [TES•ti•MO•nee] *n* testimonianza F

tetanus [TE•tuh•nes] *n* tetano M

tether [TE•thur] *n* pastoia F

text [tekst] *n* testo M

textbook [TEKST•buk] *n* libro
di testo M

textile [TEKS•tuyl] *adj* tessile

texture [TEKS•chur] *n* grana F

than [than] *conj* di

thank [thangk] *vt* ringraziare

thankful [THANGK•fuhl] *adj*
grato; grata

thankfully [THANGK•fuh•lee]
adv con gratitudine

thankless [THANGK•les] *adj*
ingrato; ingrata

thanklessness
[THANGK•les•nes] *n*
ingratitudine F

thanksgiving [thangks•GI•ving]
n ringraziamento M

that [that] *adj* quello; quella

thatch [thach] *n* copertura di
paglia F

thaw [thau] *vt* sgelare

the [thuh] *art* il; la; lo

theater [THEE•i•tir] *n* teatro M

theatrical [thee•A•trik•kl] *adj*
teatrale

theft [theft] *n* furto M

their [thair] *adj pos* loro

theirs [thairz] *pron pos* loro

them [them] *per pron* loro

theme [theem] *n* tema M

themselves [them•SELVZ] *per
pron* loro stessi; loro stesse

then [then] *adv* allora

theology [thee•AH•lo•gee] *n*
teologia F

theorem [THEE•or•em] *n*
teorema M

theoretical [THEE•o•RE•tik•kl]
adj teoretico; teoretica

theory [THEE•or•ree] *n* teoria F

therapeutic
[THAIR•uh•PYU•tik] *adj*
terapeutico; terapeutica

there [thair] *adv* lá

thereabouts
[THAIR•uh•BOUTZ] *adv* nei
dintorni

thereafter [thair•AF•tur] *adv*
poscia

thereby [thair•BUY] *adv* per
mezzo

therefore [thair•FOR] *adv*
quindi

therein [thair•IN] *adv* in ció

thereof [thair•UHV] *adv* di ció

thereon [thair•AHN] *adv* al che

thereupon [THAIR•uh•PAHN]
adv al che

thermal [THUR•muhl] *adj*
termico; termica

thermometer
[thur•MAH•me•tur] *n*
termometro M

thermostat [THUR•mo•STAT]
n termostato M

these [theez] *adj pl* questi;
queste

thesis [THEE•sis] *n* tesi F

they [thai] *per pron* essi; esse

thick [thik] *adj* spesso; spessa

thicken [THIK•kin] *vt* ispessire

thickness [THIK•nes] *n*
spessore M

thief [theef] *n* ladro; ladr

thigh [thuy] *n* coscia F

thimble [THIM•bl] *n* ditale M

thin [thin] *adj* sottile

thing [thing] *n* cosa F

think [thingk] *vi* pensare

thinker [THINGK•kur] *n*
pensatore M

thinking [THINGK•king] *adj* ragionevole

thinly [THIN•lee] *adv* scarsamente

thinness [THIN•nes] *n* magrezza F

third [thurd] *adj* terzo; terza

thirdly [THURD•lee] *adv* in terzo luogo

thirst [thurst] *n* sete F

thirteen [thur•TEEN] *num* tredici

thirteenth [thur•TEENTH] *adj* tredicesimo; tredicesima

thirtieth [THUR•tee•eth] *adj* trentesimo; trentesima

thirty [THUR•tee] *num* trenta

thirty-first [THUR•tee•FURST] *adj* trentunesimo; trentunesima

this [this] *adj* questo; questa

thistle [THIS•tl] *n* cardo M

thong [thahng] *n* correggia F

thorn [thaurn] *n* spina F

thorough [THUR•ro] *adj* compiuto; compiuta

thoroughbred [THUR•ro•BRED] *n adj* purosangue

thoroughfare [THUR•ro•FAIR] *n* arteria di grande traffico F

thoroughly [THUR•ro•lee] *adv* completamente

those [thoz] *adj* pl quelli; quelle

thou [thou] *per pron* tu

though [tho] *adv* benché

thought [thaut] *n* pensier M

thoughtful [THAUT•fl] *adj* pensoso; pensosa

thoughtfulness [THAUT•fl•nes] *n* premura F; *adj* sventato; sventata

thoughtlessness [THAUT•les•nes] *n* sventatezza F

thousand [THOU•zund] *num* mille

thousandth [THOU•zundth] *adj* millesimo; millesima

thrash [thrash] *vt* battere

thread [thred] *n* filo M

threadbare [THRED•bair] *adj* consunto; consunta

threat [thret] *n* minaccia F

threaten [THRET•tin] *vt* minacciare

threatening [THRET•ning] *adj* minaccioso; minacciosa

three [three] *num* tre

thresh [thresh] *vt* trebbiare

threshing [THRESH•ing] *n* trebbiatura F

threshold [THRESH•hold] *n* soglia F

thrice [thruys] *adv* tre volte

thrift [thrift] *n* risparmio M

thrill [thril] *vi* fremere

thrive [thruyv] *vi* prosperare

throat [throt] *n* gola F

throb [thrahb] *vi* pulsare

throne [thron] *n* trono M

throng [thraung] *n* folla F

throttle [THRAH•tl] *vt* strozzare

through [throo] *adv* attraverso

throw [thro] *vt* lanciare

throw out [THRO OUT] *vt* gettare via

throw up [THRO UHP] *vt* vomitare

thrush [thruhsh] *n* tordo M

thrust [thruhst] *n* spinta F

thug [thuhg] *n* energumeno; energumena

thumb [thuhmb] *n* pollice M

thump [thuhmp] *vt* battere

thunder [THUHN•dur] *n* tuono M

thunderbolt [THUHN•dur•BOLT] *n* fulmine M

thunderclap [THUHN•dur•KLAP] *n* scoppio di tuono M

thundering [THUHN•dring] *adj* tonante

thunderous [THUHN•drus] *adj* fragoroso; fragorosa

thunderstorm [THUHN•dur•STAURM] *n* temporale M

Thursday [THURZ•dai] *n* giovedí M

thus [thuhs] *adv* cosí

thus far [THUHS FAHR] *adv* finora

thwart [thwaurt] *vt* ostacolare

thyme [tuym] *n* timo M

tiara [tee•AHR•uh] *n* tiara

tibia [TI•bee•uh] *n* tibia F

tick 1 [tik] *vi* ticchettare

tick 2 [tik] *n* (insect) zecca F

ticket [TIK•kit] *n* biglietto F

ticket office [TIK•kit AW•fis] *n* biglietteria F

tickle [TIK•kl] *n* solletico M; *vt* solleticare

tidal [TUY•dl] *adj* della marea

tide [tuyd] *n* marea F

tidiness [TUY•dee•nes] *n* ordine M

tidings [TUY•dings] *n* notizie F

tidy [TUY•dee] *adj* ordinato; ordinata

tie [tuy] *n* cravatta F; *vt* legare

tie-up [TUY•uhp] *n* blocco M

tier [teer] *n* ordine M

tiger [TUY•gur] *n* tigre

tight [tuyt] *adj* stretto; stretta

tighten [TUY•tin] *vt* tirare

tightness [TUYT•nes] *n* tenuta F

tightwad [TUYT•wahd] *n* spilorcio; spilorcia

tigress [TUY•gris] *n* tigre F

tile [tuyl] *vt* piastrellare

till 1 [til] *n* cassa F

till 2 [til] *vt* arare

tilt 1 [tilt] *vt* inclinare

tilt 2 [tilt] *n* giostra F

timber [TIM•bur] *n* legname M

time [tuym] *n* tempo M

timekeeper [TUYM•KEE•pur] *n* cronometrista

timely [TUYM•lee] *adj* tempestivo; tempestiva

timepiece [TUYM•pees] *n* orologio M

timer [TUY•mur] *n* cronometro M

timetable [TUYM•TAI•bl] *n* orario M

timid [TI•mid] *adj* timido; timida

tin [tin] *n* latta F

tin can [TIN KAN] *n* lattina F

tincture [TINK•chur] *n* tintura F

tinder [TIN•dur] *n* esca F

tinfoil [TIN•foil] *n* stagnola F

tinge [tinj] *n* sfumatura F

tingle [TING•gl] *vi* vibrare

tinkle [TINK•kl] *vi* tintinnare

tinned [tind] *adj* in scatola

tint [tint] *vt* colorire

tiny [TUY•nee] *adj* piccolo; piccola

tip 1 [tip] *n* mancia F

tip 2 [tip] *vt* rovesciare

tipsy [TIP•see] *adj* brillo; brilla

tiptoe [TIP•to] *vi* andare in punta di piedi

tirade [TUY•raid] *n* diatriba F

tire 1 [tuyr] *vi* stancaresi

tire 2 [tuyr] (flat) *n* gomma a terra F; (spare) di scorta F

tired [tuyrd] *adj* stanco; stanca

tiredness [TUYRD•nes] *n* stanchezza F

tireless [TUYR•les] *adj* instancabile

tiresome [TUYR•suhm] *adj* noioso; noiosa

tissue [TI•shyoo] *n* tessuto M

tissue-paper [TI•shyoo•PAI•pur] *n* velina F

tithe [tuyth] *n* decima F

title [TUY•tl] *n* titolo M

titular [TI•choo•lur] *adj* titolare

to [too] *prep* a

toad [tod] *n* rospo M

toast [tost] *n* brindisi M; (bread) *n* pan tostato M; *vt* tostare

tobacco [tuh•BAK•ko] *n* tabacco M

tobacconist [tuh•BAK•ko•nist] *n* tabaccaio; tabaccaia

toboggan [tuh•BAUG•gin] *n* toboga M

today [too•DAI] *n* oggi M

toe [to] *n* dito del piede M

toenail [TO•nail] *n* unghia del piede F

together [too•GE•thur] *adv* insieme

toil [toil] *n* fatica F

toilet [TOI•let] *n* gabinetto M

toilet paper [TOI•let PAI•pur] *n* carta igienica F

toilet water [TOI•let WAH•tur] *n* colonia F

token [TO•kin] *n* gettone M

tolerable [TAH•lur•uh•bl] *adj* sopportabile

tolerance [TAH•luh•renz] *n* tolleranza F

tolerant [TAH•luh•rent] *adj* tollerante

tolerate [TAH•luh•RAIT] *vt* tollerare

toll [tol] *n* pedaggio M; *vi* rintoccare

toll-bridge [TOL•brij] *n* ponte a pedaggio M

tomato [to•MAI•to] *n* pomodoro M

tomb [toomb] *n* tomba F

tombstone [TOOMB•stòn] *n* lapide F

tomcat [TAHM•kat] *n* gatto M

tomorrow [too•MAH•ro] *n* domani M

ton [tuhn] *n* tonnellata F

tone [ton] *n* tono M

tongs [taungz] *n* pinza F

tongue [tuhng] *n* lingua F

tongue-tied [TUHNG•tuyd] *adj* bleso; blesa

tonic [TAH•nik] *n* tonico M

tonight [too•NUYT] *n* stanotte F

tonnage [TUH•nij] *n* tonnellaggio M

tonsil [TAHN•sil] *n* tonsilla F

tonsillitis [TAHN•si•LUY•tis] *n* tonsillite F

tonsure [TAHN•shur] *n* tonsura F

too [too] *adv* anche; pure; inoltre; troppo

tool [tool] *n* arnese M

tooth [tooth] *n* dente M

toothache [TOOTH•aik] *n* mal di denti M

toothpaste [TOOTH•paist] *n* dentifricio M

toothpick [TOOTH•pik] *n* stecchino M

top [tahp] *n* coperchio M

topaz [TO•paz] *n* topazio M

topcoat [TAHP•kot] *n* soprabito M

topic [TAH•pik] *n* argomento M

topmost [TAHP•most] *adj* il piú alto; la piú alta

topography [tah•PAH•grah•fee] *n* topografia F

topple [TAH•pl] *vi* traballare

topsy-turvy [TAHP•zee TUHR•vee] *adj* sottosopra

torch [taurch] *n* torcia F

torment [TAUR•ment] *n* tormento M

tormentor [taur•MEN•taur] *n* tormentatore; tormentatrice

tornado [taur•NAI•do] *n* tornado M

torpedo [taur•PEE•do] *n* torpedine F

torpid [TAUR•pid] *adj* intorpidito; intorpidita

torrent [TAUR•rint] *n* torrente M

torrid [TAUR•rid] *adj* torrido; torrida

tortoise [TAUR•tus] *n* tartaruga M

tortuous [TAUR•choo•us] *adj* tortuoso; tortuosa

torture [TAUR•chur] *n* tortura F

torturer [TAUR•chur•rur] *n* carnefice M

toss [taus] *vt* lanciare

tot [taht] *n* bimbetto; bimbetta

total [TO•tl] *n* totale M

totalitarian [to•TA•li•TAI•ree•yen] *adj* totalitario totalitaria

totality [to•TA•li•tee] *n* totalitá F

totally [TO•tuh•lee] *adv* totalmente

totter [TAH•tur] *vi* barcollare

touch [tuhch] *n* tocco M

touching [TUHCH•ching] *adj* commovente

touchy [TUH•chee] *adj* suscettibile

tough [tuhf] *adj* duro; dura

toughen [TUH•fin] *vt* indurire

toughness [TUHF•nis] *n* durezza F

tour [taur] *n* giro M; *vt* viaggere; fare un giro

tourist [TAUR•rist] *n* turista

tournament [TAUR•nuh•mint] *n* torneo M

tow [to] *vt* trainare

towards [TOO•wahrdz] *prep* verso

towel [TOW•wuhl] *n* asciugamano M

tower [TOW•wur] *n* torre F; *vi* torreggiare

towing [TOW•wing] *n* rimorchio M

town [toun] *n* città F

township [TOUN•ship] *n* comune M

toxic [TAHK•sik] *adj* tossico; tossica

toxin [TAHK•sin] *n* tossina F

toy [toi] *n* giocattolo M

trace [trais] *n* traccia F; *vt* tracciare; rintracciare

tracer [TRAI•sur] *n* modulo per rintracciare

trachea [TRAI•kee•uh] *n* trachea F

track [trak] *n* pista F

tract [trakt] *n* trattato M

tractable [TRAK•tuh•bl] *adj* trattabile

traction [TRAK•shn] *n* trazione F

tractor [TRAK•tur] *n* trattore M

trade [traid] *n* commercio M; affari M; *vt* fare affari; commerciare

trade school [TRAID SKOOL] *n* scuola industriale F

trade-union [TRAID YOON•yun] *n* sindacato M

trademark [TRAID•mahrk] *n* marchio di fabbrica M

trader [TRAI•dur] *n* commerciante

tradesman [TRAIDZ•man] *n* negoziante

tradewind [TRAID•wind] *n* venti alisei M

trading [TRAI•ding] *adj* commerciale

tradition [truh•DI•shn] *n* tradizione F

traffic [TRAF•fik] *n* traffico M

tragedy [TRA•ji•dee] *n* tragedia F

tragic [TRA•jik] *adj* tragico; tragica

trail [trail] *n* pista F; *vt* trascinare

trailer [TRAI•lur] *n* rimorchio M

train [train] *n* treno M; *vt* allenare; (express) *n* treno espresso M

trainer [TRAI•nur] *n* allenatore M

training [TRAI•ning] *n* allenamento M

trainman [TRAIN•man] *n* ferroviere M

trait [trait] *n* tratto M

traitor [TRAI•tor] *n* traditore M

trajectory [truh•JEK•to•ree] *n* traiettoria F

tram [tram] *n* tram M

tramp [tramp] *n* vagabondo; vagabonda

trample [TRAM•pl] *vt* calpestare

trance [trans] *n* trance F

tranquil [TRAN•kwil] *adj* tranquillo; tranquilla

tranquillity [tran•KWIL•li•tee] *n* tranquillità F

transact [tranz•AKT] *vt* negoziare

transaction [tranz•AK•shn] *n* transazione F

transcend [tran•SEND] *vt* trascendere

transcribe [tran•SCRUYB] *vt*
trascrivere

transept [TRAN•sept] *n*
transetto M

transfer [TRANS•fur] *vt*
trasferire

transform [tranz•FAURM] *vt*
trasformare

transformation
[TRANZ•faur•MAI•shn] *n*
trasformazione F

transformer [tranz•FAUR•mur]
n trasformatore M

transfusion [tranz•FYU•shn] *n*
trasfusione F

transgress [tranz•GRES] *vt*
trasgredire

transgression [tranz•GRE•shn]
n trasgressione F

transient [TRAN•zee•int] *adj*
transitorio; transitoria

transit [TRANS•zit] *n*
transito M

transition [trans•ZI•shn] *n*
transizione F

transitive [TRAN•zi•tiv] *adj*
transitivo; transitiva

translate [tranz•LAIT] *vt*
tradurre

translation [tranz•LAI•shn] *n*
traduzione F

translator [tranz•LAI•tur] *n*
traduttore; traduttrice

translucent [tranz•LOO•sent]
adj traslucido; traslucida

transmission [tranz•MI•shn] *n*
trasmissione F

transmit [trans•MIT] *vt*
trasmettere

transmitter [tranz•MI•tur] *n*
trasmettitore M

transom [TRAN•sum] *n*
traversa F

transparent [tranz•PAIR•rent]
adj trasparente

transpiration
[TRANZ•pi•RAI•shn] *n*
traspirazione F

transpire [tran•SPUYR] *vi*
accadere

transplant [tranz•PLANT] *vt*
trapiantare

transport [TRANZ•port] *n*
trasporto M

transpose [tranz•POZ] *vt*
trasporre

transverse [tranz•VURS] *adj*
trasversale

trap [trap] *n* trappola F

trap-door [TRAP•DOR] *n*
botola F

trapeze [tra•PEEZ] *n*
trapezio M

trappings [TRAP•pings] *n*
bardatura F

trash [trash] *n* rifiuti M

travel [TRA•vul] *vi* viggiare

travel agency [TRA•vul
AI•jin•cee] *n* agenzia di
viaggi F

traveler [TRA•vuh•lur] *n*
viaggiatore; vaggiatrice

traveling [TRA•vuh•ling] *adj*
da viaggio

traverse [tra•VURS] *adv*
trasversale

travesty [TRA•ve•stee] *n*
parodia F

tray [trai] *n* vassoio M

treacherous [TRE•chur•us] *adj*
traditore; traditrice

treachery [TRE•chur•ree] *n*
tradimento M

tread [tred] *n* filo M

treason [TREE•zun] *n*
tradimento M

treasure [TRE•shur] *n* tesoro M

treasurer [TRE•shuh•ur] *n*
tesoriere; tesoriera

treasury [TRE•shuh•ree] *n*
tesoreria F

treat [treet] *vt* trattare; *n*
piacere M

treatise [TREE•tis] dissertation
essay [tree•tis] *n* trattato M

treatment [TREET•mint] *n*
trattamento M

treaty [TREE•tee] *n* trattato M

treble [TRE•bl] *vt* triplicare

treble clef [TREB•bl KLEF] *n*
chiave di violino F

treble voice [TRE•bl VOIS] *n*
soprano M

tree 1 [tree] *n* albero M

tree 2 (family) [tree] *n* albero
genealogico M

trefoil [TREE•foil] *n* trifoglio M

trellis [TRE•lis] *n* graticcio M

tremble [TREM•bl] *vi* tremare

tremendous [tre•MEN•dus]
tremendo

tremor [TRE•mur] *n* tremito M

tremulous [TRE•myu•lus] *adj*
tremulo; tremula

trench [trench] *n* trincea F

trench coat [TRENCH KOT] *n*
trench coat M

trend [trend] *n* tendenza F

trespass [TRES•pas] *vt*
oltrepassare i confini

trespasser [TRES•pa•sur] *n*
trasgressore M

tress [tres] *n* ciocca F

trestle [TRE•sl] *n* cavalletto M

trial [truyl] *n* processo M

triangle [TRUY•an•gl] *n*
triangolo M

tribe [truyb] *n* tribú F

tribulation [TRI•byoo•LAI•shn]
n tribolazione F

tribunal [truy•BYOO•nl] *n*
tribunale M

tribune [TRI•byoon] *n*
tribuna F

tributary [TRI•byoo•TAI•ree]
adj tributario; tributaria

trick [trik] *vt* ingannare; *n*
espediente M; (prank) tiro M

trickery [TRIK•ree] *n*
inganno M

trickle [TRIK•kl] *n* gocciolio

tricky [TRIK•kee] *adj*
complicato; complicata

trifle [TRUY•fl] *n* sciocchezza F

trigger [TRI•gur] *n* grilletto M

trill [tril] *n* trillo M

trim [trim] *vt* spuntare

trinket [TRINK•kit] *n*
gingillo M

trio [TREE•o] *n* trio M

trip [trip] *n* viaggio M

triple [TRIP•pl] *adj* triplo; tripla

tripod [TRUY•pod] *n*
treppiedi M

trite [truyt] *adj* trito; trita

triumph [TRUY•uhmf] *n*
trionfo M

triumphant [truy•UHM•fint]
adj trionfante

triumphantly
[truy•UHM•fint•lee] *adv*
trionfalmente

trivial [TRI•vee•ul] *adj* banale

trolley [TRAH•lee] *n* tram M

trombone [trahm•BON] *n* trombone M

troop [troop] *n* truppa F

trooper [TROOP•pur] *n* soldato M

trophy [TRO•fee] *n* trofeo M

tropic [TRAH•pik] *n* tropico M

tropical [TRAH•pi•kl] *adj* tropicale

trot 1 [traht] *n* trotto M

trot 2 [traht] *vi* trottare

trouble [TRUH•bl] *n* guaio M

trouble maker [TRUH•bl MAI•kur] *n* fomentatore M

trouble shooter [TRUH•bl SHOO•tur] *n* localizzatore di guasti M

troublesome [TRUH•bl•suhm] *adj* importuno; importuna

trough [trahf] *n* truogolo M

trousers [TROU•zurz] *n* calzoni M

trousseau [troo•SO] *n* corredo M

trowel [TROU•wl] *n* cazzuola F

truant [TROO•int] *n* poltrone; poltrona

truce [troos] *n* tregua F

truck [truhk] *n* camion M

trudge [truhj] *vi* camminare faticosamente

true [troo] *adj* vero; vera

truly [TROO•lee] *adv* veramente

trump [truhmp] *n* briscola F

trumpet [TRUHM•pit] *n* tromba F

trunk 1 [truhnk] *n* baule M

trunk 2 [truhnk] *n* proboscide F

truss [truhs] *vt* legare come un salame

trust [truhst] *n* fiduccia F; (hope) fede F; *vi* fidarsi

trustee [truhs•STEE] *n* fiduciario M

trustworthy [TRUHST•wur•thee] *adj* affidabile

trusty [TRUH•stee] *adj* fidato; fidata

truth [trooth] *n* veritá F

truthful [TROOTH•fl] *adj* veritiero; veritiera

truthfulness [TROOTH•fl•nes] *n* sinceritá F

try [truy] *vt* provare

trying [TRUY•ying] *adj* dificile

tub [tuhb] *n* vasca F

tube [toob] *n* tubetto M

tubercular [too•BUR•kyoo•lur] *adj* tubercolare

tuberculosis [too•BUR•kyoo•LO•sis] *n* tubercolosi F

tubing [TOO•bing] *n* tubazione F

tuck [tuk] *vt* ripiegare

Tuesday [TOOZ•dai] *n* martedí M

tuft [tuhft] *n* ciuffo M

tug [tuhg] *vt* tirare

tuition [TOO•i•shn] *n* retta F

tulip [TOO•lip] *n* tulipano M

tulle [tool] *n* tulle M

tumble [TUHM•bl] *vt* agitarsi

tumbler [TUHM•blur] *n* saltimbanco M

tumor [TOO•mur] *n* tumore M

tumult [TUH•muhlt] *n* tumulto M

tumultuous [too•MUHL•choo•us] *adj* tumultuoso; tumultuosa

tun [tuhn] *n* botte F

tuna [TOO•nuh] *n* tonno M

tune [toon] *n* aria F; accordare (radio, etc) sintonizzare

tunic [TOO•nik] *n* tunica F

tuning [TOO•ning] *n* accordatura F

tunnel [TUH•nuhl] *n* tunnel M

turbid [TUR•bid] *adj* torbido; torbida

turbine [TUR•buyn] *n* turbina F

turbulent [tur•BYOO•lint] *adj* turbolento; turbolenta

turf [turf] *n* zolla erbosa F

turgid [TUR•jid] *adj* turgido; turgida

Turk [turk] *n* turco; turca

turkey [TUR•kee] *n* tacchino M

Turkey [TUR•kee] *n* Turchia F

Turkish [TUR•kish] *adj* turco; turca

turmoil [TUR•moil] *n* agitazione F

turn [turn] *n* turno M

turn off [TURN AHF] *vt* spegnere

turnip [TURN•ip] *n* rapa F

turnover [TUR•NO•vur] *n* riordinamento M

turntable [TURN•TAI•bl] *n* giradischi M

turpentine [TUR•pin•TUYN] *n* trementina F

turpitude [TUR•pi•TOOD] *n* turpitudine F

turquoise [TUR•koiz] *adj* turchese

turret [TUR•rit] *n* torretta F

turtle [TUR•tl] *n* tartaruga F

tusk [tuhsk] *n* zanna F

tutor [TOO•tur] *n* tutore M

tuxedo [tuk•SEE•do] *n* frac M

twang [twang] *vi* vibrare

tweed [tweed] *n* tweed M

tweezers [TWEE•zurz] *n* pinzetta F

twelfth [twelfth] *adj* dodicesimo; dodicesima

twelve [twelv] *num* dodici

twentieth [TWEN•tee•ith] *adj* ventesimo; ventesima

twenty [TWEN•tee] *num* venti

twice [twuys] *adv* due volte

twig [twig] *n* stecco M

twilight [TWUY•luyt] *n* crepuscolo M

twin [twin] *n adj* gemello; gemella

twine [twuyn] *n* cordicella F

twinge [twinj] *n* fitta F

twinkle [TWINK•kl] *vi* scintillare

twinkling [TWINK•kling] *adj* ammiccante

twirl [twirl] *vt* far girare

twist [twist] *vt* ritorcere

twitch [twich] *vt* contrarre

twitter [TWI•tur] *n* cinguettio M

two [too] *num* due

tympani [TIM•puh•nee] *n* timpani M

type [tuyp] *n* tipo M

typewriter [TUYP•RUY•tur] *n* macchina da scrivere F

typhoid [TUY•foyd] *adj* tifoideo; tifoidea

typhoon [tuy•FOON] *n* tifone M

typhus [TUY•fus] *n* tifo M

typical [TI•pi•kl] *adj* tipico; tipica

typist [TUY•pist] *n* dattilografo; dattilografa

typography [tuy•PAH•gruh•fee] *n* tipografia F

tyrannical [teer•RA•ni•kl] *adj* tirannico; tirannica

tyranny [TEER•ri•nee] *n* tirannia F

tyrant [TUY•rent] *n* tiranno; tiranna

U

udder [UH•dur] *n* mammella F

ugliness [UH•glee•nes] *n* bruttezza F

ugly [UH•glee] *adj* brutto; brutta

ulcer [UHL•sur] *n* ulcera F

ulceration [UHL•sur•RAI•shn] *n* ulcerazione F

ulterior [uhl•TEE•ree•ur] *adj* ulteriore

ultimate [UHL•ti•mit] *adj* estremo; estrema

ultimately [UHL•ti•mit•lee] *adv* in definitiva

umbilicus [uhm•BI•li•kus] *n* ombellico M

umbrage [UHM•brij] *n* offesa F

umbrella [uhm•BREL•luh] *n* ombrello M

umpire [UHM•puyr] *n* arbitro M

un- [uhn] *pref* non-

unable [uhn•AI•bl] *adj* incapace

unaccountable [UHN•a•koun•tuh•bl] *adj* irresponsabile

unaccustomed [UHN•uh•KUH•stumd] *adj* non avvezzo; non avvezza

unacknowledged [UHN•ak•NAH•lejd] *adj* non riconosciuto; non riconosciuta

unaffected [UHN•uh•FEK•ted] *adj* semplice

unanimity [YOO•nuh•NI•mi•tee] *n* unanimitá F

unanimous [yoo•NA•ni•mus] *adj* unanime

unapproachable [UHN•uh•PRO•chuh•bl] *adj* inaccessbile

unarmed [uhn•ARMD] *adj* inerme

unassailable [UHN•uh•SAIL•luh•bl] *adj* inattaccabile

unassuming [UHN•uh•SOO•ming] *adj* modesto; modesta

unattractive [UHN•uh•TRAK•tiv] *adj* poco attraente

unavailable [UHN•uh•VAI•luh•bl] *adj* non disponbile

unavoidable [UHN•uh•VOI•duh•bl] *adj* inevitabile

unaware [UHN•uh•WAIR] *adj*
ignaro; ignara

unawares [UHN•uh•WAIRZ]
adv inaspettatamente

unbalanced [uhn•BAL•enzd]
adj sbilanciato; sbilanciata

unbearable [uhn•BAI•ruh•bl]
adj insopportabile

unbecoming
[UHN•bee•KUH•ming] *adj*
disdicevole

unbelievable
[UHN•bee•LEE•vuh•bl] *adj*
incredibile

unbeliever [UHN•bee•LEE•vur]
n miscredente

unbelieving
[UHN•bee•LEE•ving] *adj*
incredulo; incredula

unbending [uhn•BEN•ding] *adj*
inflessibile

unbiased [uhn•BUY•esd] *adj*
imparziale

unbounded [uhn•BOUN•ded]
adj sconfinato; sconfinata

unbreakable
[uhn•BRAI•kuh•bl] *adj*
infrangibile

unbroken [uhn•BRO•ken] *adj*
intatto; intatta

unburden [uhn•BUR•den] *vt*
scaricare

unbutton [uhn•BUH•ten] *vt*
sbottonare

uncanny [uhn•KA•nee] *adj*
misterioso; misteriosa

unceasing [uhn•SEE•sing] *adj*
incessante

uncertain [uhn•SUR•ten] *adj*
incerto; incerta

unchangeable
[uhn•CHAIN•juh•bl] *adj*
immutabile

unchanged [uhn•CHAINJD]
adj immutato; immutata

uncharted [uhn•CHAHR•ted]
adj inesplorato; inesplorata

uncivil [uhn•SI•vil] *adj* incivile

unclaimed [uhn•KLAI•med] *adj*
non reclamato; non reclamata

uncle [UHN•kl] *n* zio M

unclean [uhn•KLEEN] *adj*
sporco; sporca

uncomfortable
[uhn•KOM•faur•tuh•bl] *adj*
scomodo; scomoda

uncommon [uhn•KAH•men]
adj fuori dal comune

uncompromising
[uhn•KAHM•pro•MUY•zing]
adj intransigente

unconcerned
[uhn•KUHN•surnd] *adj*
noncurante

unconditional
[UHN•kun•DI•shuh•nl] *adj*
incondizionato; incondizionata

unconquered
[uhn•KAHN•kurd] *adj* invitto;
invitta

unconscious [uhn•KAHN•shus]
adj inconscio; inconscia

unconsciousness
[uhn•KAHN•shus•nes] *n*
incoscienza F

uncontrollable
[UHN•kuhn•TRO•luh•bl] *adj*
incontrollabile

uncontrolled
[UHN•kuhn•TROLD] *adj*
sfrenato; sfrenata

unconventional
[UHN•kuhn•VEN•shuh•nl] *adj*
anticonvenzionale

uncork [uhn•KAURK] *vt*
stappare

uncouth [uhn•KOOTH] *adj*
rozzo; rozza

uncover [uhn•KUH•vur] *vt*
scoprire

unction [UHNK•shun] *n*
unzione F

unctuous [UHNK•shus] *adj*
untuoso; untuosa

uncultured [uhn•KUL•churd]
adj incolto; incolta

undeceive [UHN•dee•SEEV] *vt*
disingannare

undecided
[UHN•dee•SUY•ded] *adj*
indeciso; indecisa

undeniable
[UHN•dee•NUY•uh•bl] *adj*
innegabile

under [UHN•dur] *prep* sotto

underbrush
[UHN•dur•BRUSH] *n*
sottobosco M

undercarriage
[UHN•dur•KAI•rij] *n* telaio M

underclothes
[UHN•dur•KLOTHZ] *n*
biancheria F

underestimate
[UHN•dur•ES•ti•MAIT] *vt*
sottovalutare

undergo [UHN•dur•GO] *vt*
subire

undergraduate
[UHN•dur•GRA•joo•wait] *n*
studente d'università

underground
[UHN•dur•GROUND] *adj*
sotterraneo; sotterranea

underhanded
[UHN•dur•HAN•ded] *adj*
clandestino; clandestina

underline [UHN•dur•LUYN] *vt*
sottolineare

underlying
[UHN•dur•LUY•ing] *adj*
sottostante

undermine [UHN•dur•MUYN]
vt minare

underneath [uhn•dur•NEETH]
adv di sotto

underpay [UHN•dur•PAI] *vt*
pagare inadeguatamete

undersell [UHN•dur•SEL] *vt*
svendere

undershirt [UHN•dur•SHURT]
n maglietta F

undersigned
[UHN•dur•SUYND] *adj*
sottoscritto; sottoscritta

undersized [UHN•dur•SUYZD]
adj sotto la media

understand
[UHN•dur•STAND] *vt* capire

understandable
[UHN•dur•STAN•duh•bl] *adj*
comprensibile

understanding
[UHN•dur•STAN•ding] *n*
comprensione F

understate [UHN•dur•STAIT]
vt attenuare

understudy
[UHN•dur•STUH•dee] *n*
sostituto; sostituta

undertake [uhn•dur•TAIK] *vt*
intraprendere

undertaker [UHN•dur•TAI•kur] *n* imprenditore di pompe funebri M

undertaking [UHN•dur•TAI•king] *n* impresa F

undertow [UHN•dur•TO] *n* risucchio M

underwear [UHN•dur•WAIR] *n* biancheria F

underworld [UHN•dur•WURLD] *n* oltretomba M

underwrite [UHN•dur•WRUYT] *vt* sottoscrivere

undeviating [UHN•DEE•vee•AI•ting] *adj* costante

undiscriminating [UHN•di•SKRI•mi•NAI•ting] *adj* che non fa distinzioni

undistinguished [UHN•di•STIN•gwish•ed] *adj* mediocre

undisturbed [UHN•di•STUR•bed] *adj* indisturbato; indisturbata

undo [uhn•DO] *vt* disfare

undress [uhn•DRES] *vt* svestire

undue [uhn•DOO] *adj* sproporzionato; sproporzionata

undulate [UHN•joo•LAIT] *vt* ondulare

undying [uhn•DUY•ing] *adj* imperituro; imperitura

unearned [uhn•URN•ed] *adj* immeritato; immeritata

unearth [uhn•URTH] *vt* scoprire

uneasy [uhn•EE•zee] *adj* a disagio

uneducated [uhn•ED•joo•KAI•ted] *adj* rozzo; rozza

unemployed [UHN•em•PLOID] *adj n* disoccupato; disoccupata

unemployment [UHN•em•PLOI•ment] *n* disoccupazione F

unending [uhn•EN•ding] *adj* infinito; infinita

unequal [uhn•EE•kwell] *adj* disuguale

uneven [uhn•EE•ven] *adj* ineguale (ground) disguale; (heartbeat) irregolare

unexpected [UHN•ek•SPEK•tid] *adj* inatteso -a

unfair [uhn•FAIR] *adj* inguisto -a; (tactics) sleale

unfaithful [uhn•FAITH•ful] *adj* infedele

unfasten [uhn•FAS•sin] *vt* slacciare; sciogliere; (gate) aprire

unfinished [uhn•FIN•ishd] *adj* (letter) non finito; (business) in sospeso

unfit [uhn•FIT] *adj* inadatto -a; (for service, etc.) inabile

unfold [uhn•FAULD] *vt* (item) spiegare; aprire; (arms) distendere; (secret) svelare; (story) snodarsi

unfortunate [uhn•FAUR•tchoo•net] *adj* povero -a; (unlucky) sfortunato -a

unfortunately
[uhn•FAUR•tchoo•net•lee] *adv*
purtroppo; sfortunamente

unfriendly [uhn•FREND•lee]
adj scostante; antipatico

ungrateful [uhn•GRAIT•ful]
adj ingrato -a

unhappy [uhn•HA•pee] *adj*
infelice; (not pleased)
scotento -a

unhappiness [uhn•HA•pee•nes]
n infelicità F

unhealthy [uhn•HEL•thee] *adj*
(person) malaticcio; a poco
sano -a; (place) malsano -a

unicorn [YOO•nee•KAURN] *n*
unicorno M

unidentified
[UHN•uh•DEN•ti•FUYD] *adj*
non indentificato

uniform [YOO•ni•FAURM] *adj*
uniforme; *n* uniforme F

unimportant
[UHN•im•PAUR•tant] *adj*
senza importanza

uninterested
[uhn•IN•ter•ehs•tid] *adj*
indifferente; to be ~\ non
interessarsi de

union [YOO•nyuhn] *n* unione
F; (movement) sindacale

unique [yoo•NEEK] *adj*
unico -a

unison [YOO•ni•suhn] *n*
all'unisono

unit [YOO•nit] *n* unità F

unite [yoo•NUYT] *vt* unoire; *vi*
unirsi

united [yoo•NUY•td] *adj*
unto -a

United Kingdom [yoo•NUY•td
KING•dum] *n* Regno Unito M

United Nations [yoo•NUY•td
NAI•shuns] *n* Organizzazione
delle Nazioni Unite FPL

United States [yoo•NUY•td
STAITS] *n* Stati Uniti
d'America MPL

universe [YOO•ni•VERS] *n*
universo M

universal [YOO•nee•VER•sal]
adj universel

university
[YOO•nee•VER•si•tee] *n*
università F

unjust [uhn•JUHST] *adj*
injgusto -a

unkind [uhn•KUYND] *adj*
(person, remark) poco gentile;
scortese; villano -a

unkindess [uhn•KUYND•nes] *n*
sgarbatezza; cattiveria F

unknown [uhn•NOHN] *adj*
incsconsciuto - a; ignoto -a

unless [uhn•LES] *conj* a meno
che non

unlike [uhn•LUYK] *adj* diverso
-a; dissimile; *prep* a differenza
di; contrariamente

unlikely [uhn•LUYK•lee] *adj*
improbabile; (story)
inverosimile

unlimited [uhn•LIM•i•tud] *ad*
illimitato -a

unload [uhn•LOD] *vt vi*
scaricare

unlock [uhn•LAHK] *vt* aprire

unlucky [uhn•LUH•kee] *adj*
sfortunato

unmarried [uhn•MA•reed] *adj*
scapolo -a; non sposato -a

unnatural [uhn•NA•chur•el] *adj*
innaturale; contro natura

unnecessary
[uhn•NE•si•SAI•ree] *adj* non
necessario -a; (useless) inutile

unnoticed [uhn•NO•tisd] *ad*
passare inosservanto -a

unoccupied
[uhn•AH•kyoo•PUYD] *adj*
(place) vuoto -a; non
occupato -a

unofficial [uhn•o•FI•shul] *adj*
privato -a non ufficiale

unpack [uhn•PAK] *vt* (suitcase)
disfare; (contents) sballare

unpaid [uhn•PAID] *adj* da
pagare; (work) non
retribuito -a

unpleasant [uhn•PLEH•zunt]
adj sgrandavole; spiacavole

unpopular [uhn•PAH•pyoo•lur]
adj impopulare

unpredictable
[uhn•pree•DIC•tuh•bul] *adj*
imprevedibile

unqualified
[uhn•KWAH•li•FUYD] *adj*
non qualificato -a; non
abilitato -a

unravel [uhn•RA•vul] *vt*
disfare; (mystery) sbrogliare

unreal [uhn•REEL] *adj* irreale

unrealistic
[uhn•REE•uh•LIS•tik] *adj*
illusorio -a; non realistico -a

unreasonable
[urhn•REE•sohn•uh•bl] *adj*
(behavior) irrazionale;
(person) irragionevole; (idea)
assurdo -a

unsuccessful
[UHN•suhk•SES•fl] *adj*
fallito; fallita

unsuitable [uhn•SOO•tuh•bl]
adj inadatto; inadatta

unsuspected
[UHN•suh•SPEK•ted] *adj*
insospettato; insospettata

unsuspecting
[UHN•suh•SPEK•ting] *adj*
non sospettoso; non sospettosa

unthinkable
[uhn•THING•kuh•bl] *adj*
impensabile

unthinking [uhn•THING•king]
adj sventato; sventata

untidiness [uhn•TUY•dee•nes]
n disordine M

untie [uhn•TUY] *vt* slegare

until [uhn•TIL] *adv* finché

untimely [uhn•TUYM•lee] *adj*
prematuro; prematura

untiring [uhn•TUYR•ring] *adj*
instancabile

unto [UHN•too] *prep* sopra

untold [uhn•TOLD] *adj*
innumerevole

untouched [uhn•TUCHD] *adj*
intatto; intatta

untrained [uhn•TRAIND] *adj*
inesperto; inesperta

untried [uhn•TRUYD] *adj*
intentato; intentata

untroubled [uhn•TRUH•bld]
adj calmo; calma

untrue [uhn•TROO] *adj* falso;
falsa

unused [uhn•YOOSD] *adj* non
usato; no usata

unveil [uhn•VAIYL] *vt* scoprite

unwarranted
[uhn•WAH•ren•ted] *adj*
ingiustificato; ingiustificata

unwary [uhn•WAI•ree] *adj*
incauto; incauta

unwashed [uhn•WASHD] *adj*
non lavato; non lavata

unwelcome [uhn•WEL•kom]
adj sgradito; sgradita

unwholesome [uhn•HOL•sum]
adj malsano; malsana

unwieldy [uhn•WEEL•dee] *adj*
pesante

unwilling [uhn•WIL•ling] *adj*
riluttante

unwillingness
[uhn•WIL•ling•nes] *n*
riluttanza F

unwind [uhn•WUYND] *vt*
scaricare

unwise [uhn•WUYZ] *adj*
imprudente

unworthy [uhn•WUR•thee] *adj*
indegno; indegna

unwrap [uhn•RAP] *vt* svolgere

unyielding [uhn•YEEL•ding]
adj inflessibile

up [uhp] *prep* su

up-to-date [UHP•too•DAIT]
adj al corrente

upbraid [uhp•BRAIYD] *vt*
rimproverare

upgrade 1 [UHP•graid] *vt*
migliorare

upgrade 2 [UHP•graid] *n*
salita F

upheaval [uhp•HEE•vul] *n*
sconvolgimento M

uphill [UHP•hil] *adj* scosceso;
scoscesa

uphold [uhp•HOLD] *vt*
sostenere

upholster [uh•POL•stur] *vt*
tappezzare

upholstery [uh•POL•stree] *n*
imbottitura F

upkeep [UHP•keep] *n*
manutenzione F

uplift [uhp•LIFT] *vt* sollevare

upon [uh•PAHN] *prep* sopra

upper [UH•pur] *adj* superiore

upright [UHP•ruyt] *adj* ritto;
ritta

uprising [UHP•ruy•zing] *n*
rivolta F

uproar [UHP•ror] *n* tumulto M

upset [uhp•SET] *adj* sconvolto;
sconvolta; *vi* sconvolgere; *n*
disturbo M

upshot [UHP•shot] *n* esito M

upside [UHP•suyd] *n* lato
superiore M

upstairs [uhp•STAIRZ] *adv* al
piano superiore

upstart [UHP•start] *n* nuovo
ricco; nuova ricca

upward [UHP•wurd] *adv* in su

uranium [yur•AI•nee•um] *n*
uranio M

urban [UR•bin] *adj* urbano;
urbana

urchin [UR•chin] *n* monello;
monella

urge [urj] *n* impulso M

urgency [UR•jen•see] *n*
urgenza F

urgent [UR•jent] *adj* urgente

urgently [UR•jent•lee] *adv*
urgentemente

urinate [YUR•in•NAIT] *vi*
orinare

urine [YUR•rin] *n* orina F

urn [urn] *n* urna F

us [uhs] *pers pron* noi

usage [YOO•sej] *n* uso M

use [yooz] *vt* usare

used (second-hand) [yoozd] *adj* di seconda mano

used up [YOOZD UHP] *adj* esaurito; esaurita

useful [YOOS•ful] *adj* utile

usefulness [YOOS•ful•ness] *n* vantaggio M

useless [YOOS•les] *adj* inutile

uselessness [YOOS•les•nes] *n* inutilitá F

usher [UH•shur] *n* usciere M

usual [YOO•zjuh•wul] *adj* solito; solita

usually [YOO•zjwuh•lee] *adv* normalmente

usurer [YOO•zoo•rur] *n* usuraio; usuraia

usurp [yoo•SURP] *vt* usurpare

usury [YOO•zur•ee] *n* usura F

utensil [yoo•TEN•sul] *n* utensile M

utility [yoo•TI•li•tee] *n* servizio pubblico M

utilize [YOO•ti•LUYZ] *vt* utilizzare

utmost [UHT•most] *adj* estremo; estrema

utter [UHT•tur] *vt* emettere

utterance [UHT•tur•anz] *n* espressione F

uvula [YOO•vyu•luh] *n* ugola F

V

vacancy [VAI•ken•see] *n* posto vacante M

vacant [VAI•kint] *adj* vacante

vacate [VAI•kait] *vt* sgomberare

vacation [vai•KAI•shn] *n* vacanza F

vaccinate [VAK•zin•NAIT] *vt* vaccinare

vaccine [vak•SEEN] *n* vaccino M

vacillate [VA•sil•LAIT] *vi* vacillare

vacuum [VA•kyum] *vt* passare l'aspirapolvere

vagabond [VA•guh•BAUND] *n* *adj* vagabondo; vagabonda

vague [vaig] *adj* vago; vaga

vain [vain] *adj* vanitoso; vanitosa

valentine [VA•len•TUYN] *n* biglietto di San Valentino M

valet [va•LAIT] *n* valletto M

valiant [VA•lee•ent] *adj* valoroso; valorosa

valid [VA•lid] *adj* valido; valida

validity [va•LI•di•tee] *n* validitá F

valise [va•LEES] *n* valigia F

valley [VAL•lee] *n* vallata F

valor [VA•lor] *n* valore M

valorous [VA•lo•rus] *adj* valoroso; valorosa

valuable [VAL•yoo•bl] *adj* di gran valore

value 1 [VAL•yoo] *n* valore M

value 2 (market) [val•yoo] *n* valore commerciale M

valve [valv] *n* valvola F

van [van] *n* pulmino M

vane [vain] *n* banderuola F

vanilla [vuh•NIL•luh] *n* vaniglia F

vanish [VA•nish] *vt* svanire

vanity [VA•ni•tee] *n* vanitá F

vanquish [VAN•kwish] *vt* vincere

vantage [VAN•tij] *n* vantaggio M

vapid [VA•pid] *adj* insulso; insulsa

vapor [VAI•por] *n* vapore M

vaporize [VAI•po•RUYZ] *vt* vaporizzare

variable [VAIR•ree•uh•bl] *adj* variabile

variance [VAIR•ree•éns] *n* variazione F

variation [VAIR•ree•AI•shn] *n* variazione F

varied [VAIR•reed] *adj* variato; variato

variegated [VAI•re•uh•GAI•ted] *adj* variegato; variegata

variety [vuh•RUY•i•tee] *n* varietá F

various [VAIR•ee•us] *adj* vario; varia

varnish [VAR•nish] *vt* verniciare

vary [VAIR•ree] *vi* variare

vase [vaiz] *n* vaso M

vast [vast] *adj* vasto; vasta

vastness [VAST•nis] *n* vastitá F

vat [vat] *n* tino M

vaudeville [VAUD•vil] *n* varietá M

vault [vault] *n* volta F

vaunt [vaunt] *vt* vantare

veal [veel] *n* vitello M

veer [veer] *vi* cambiare direzione

vegetable [VE•je•tuh•bl] *n* verdura F

vegetarian [VE•je•TAI•ree•en] *n adj* vegetariano; vegetariana

vegetate [VE•je•TAIT] *vi* vegetare

vegetation [VE•je•TAI•shn] *n* vegetazione F

vehemence [VEE•him•menz] *n* veemenza F

vehicle [VEE•hi•kl] *n* veicolo M

veil [vail] *n* velo M

vein [vain] *n* vena F

velocity [ve•LAH•si•tee] *n* velocitá F

velvet [VEL•vit] *n* velluto M

vendor [VEN•dur] *n* venditore venditrice M

veneer [vuh•NEER] *n* impiallacciatura F

venerable [VE•nur•uh•bl] *adj* venerabile

venerate [VE•nur•RAIT] *vi* venerare

veneration [VE•nur•RAI•shn] *n* venerazione F

vengeance [VEN•jenz] *n* vendetta F

venison [VE•ni•sun] *n* carne di cervo F

venom [VE•nuhm] *n* veleno M

venomous [VE•nuh•mus] *n*
velenoso; velenosa

vent [vent] *n* sfogo M

ventilate [VEN•ti•LAIT] *vt*
ventilare

ventilation [VEN•ti•LAI•shn] *n*
ventilazione F

ventilator [VEN•ti•LAI•tur] *n*.
ventilatore M

venture [VEN•chur] *vi*
avventurarsi; (business) *n*
investimento M

venue [VEN•yoo] *n* sede F

verandah [vur•AN•duh] *n*
veranda F

verb [vurb] *n* verbo M

verbal [VER•bul] *adj* verbale

verbose [vur•BOS] *adj* verboso;
verbosa

verdict [VUR•dikt] *n*
verdetto M

verge [vurj] *n* margine M

verification
[VAI•ri•fi•KAI•shn] *n*
verifica F

verify [VAI•ri•FUY] *vt*
verificare

veritable [VAI•rih•ti•bl] *adj*
genuino; genuina

vermin [VUR•min] *n* animaletti
nocivi M

vernacular [vur•NAK•kyu•lur]
n vernacolo M

verse [vurs] *n* verso M

versed [vursd] *adj* versato;
versata

version [VUR•zhin] *n*
versione F

vertebra [VUR•ti•bruh] *n*
vertebra F

vertical [VUR•ti•kl] *adj*
verticale

vertigo [VUR•ti•GO] *n*
vertigine F

very [VAIR•ree] *adv* molto

vespers [VE•spurz] *n* vespro M

vessel [VE•sul] *n* vascello M

vest [vest] *n* gilé

vestibule [VE•sti•BYOOL] *n*
vestibolo M

vestige [VE•stij] *n* vestigio M

vestigial [ve•STI•jul] *adj*
vestigiale

vestment official attire
[VEST•mint] *n* pianeta F

vestry [VES•stree] *n* sagrestia F

veteran [VE•tur•rin] *adj n*
veterano; veterana

veterinarian
[VE•truh•NAI•ree•en] *n*
veterinario M

veterinary [VE•truh•NAI•ree]
adj veterinario; veterinaria

veto [VEE•to] *n* veto M

vex [veks] *vt* vessare

via [VEE•yuh] *adv* via

viaduct [VUY•uh•DUKT] *n*
viadotto M

vial [vuyl] *n* fiala F

viands [VEE•endz] *n* vivanda F

viaticum [vee•A•ti•kum] *n*
viatico M

vibrate [VUY•brait] *vi* vibrare

vibration [vuy•BRAI•shn] *n*
vibrazione F

vice 1 [vuys] *n* vizio M

vice 2 (tool) [vuys] *n* morsa F

vicinity [ve•SIN•i•tee] *n*
vicinanza F

vicious [VI•shus] *adj* rabbioso;
rabbiosa

victim [VIK•tim] *n* vittima M

victor [VIK•tor] *n* vincitore M

victorious [vik•TAU•ree•us] *adj*
vittorioso; vittoriosa

victory [VIK•tree] *n* vittoria F

victuals [VIK•chulz] *n*
vettovaglie F

vie [vùy] *vi* gareggiare

view 1 [vyoo] *n* vista F

view 2 (bird's eye) [vyoo] *n*
vista aerea F

vigil [VI•jil] *n* veglia F

vigilant [VI•ji•lint] *adj* vigile

vigor [VI•gur] *n* vigore M

vigorous [VI•gur•us] *adj*
vigoroso; vigorosa

vile [vuyl] *adj* spregevole

villa [VI•luh] *n* villa F

village [VI•lij] *n* villaggio M

villager [VI•li•jur] *n* abitante di
villaggio

villain [VI•lin] *n* furfante

villainous [VI•lin•nis] *adj*
scellerato; scellerata

villainy [VI•lin•nee] *n*
scelleratezza F

vim [vim] *n* forza F

vindicate [VIN•di•KAIT] *vt*
rivendicare

vindictive [vin•DIK•tiv] *adj*
vendicativo; vendicativa

vine [vuyn] *n* rampicante M

vinegar [VI•ni•gur] *n* aceto M

vineyard [VIN•yurd] *n*
vigneto M

vintage [VIN•tij] *n*
vendemmia F

violate [VUY•uh•LAIT] *vt*
violare

violation [VUY•uh•LAI•shn] *n*
violazione F

violence [VUY•uh•lenz] *n*
violenza F

violent [VUY•uh•lent] *adj*
violento; violenta

violet [VUY•uh•let] *n*
violetta M

violin [VUY•uh•lin] *n* violino M

violinist [VUY•uh•LI•nist] *n*
violinista

viper [VUY•pur] *n* vipera F

virgin [VUR•jin] *adj n* vergine

virginity [vur•JI•ni•tee] *n*
verginitá F

virile [VEER•rl] *adj* virile

virility [vur•RI•li•tee] *n*
virilitá F

virtual [VUR•choo•ul] *adj*
virtuale

virtually [VUR•chuh•lee] *adj*
virtualmente

virulence [VEER•yoo•lenz] *n*
virulenza F

virus [VUY•rus] *n* virus M

visa [VEE•zuh] *n* visto M

visage [VI•sej] *n* viso M

viscera [VI•suh•ruh] *n* viscere F

viscosity [vi•SKAH•si•tee] *n*
viscositah F

visibility [VI•si•BI•li•tee] *n*
visibiltá

visible [VI•si•bl] *adj* visibile

vision [VI•shin] *n* visione F

visionary [VI•shin•NAI•ree] *adj*
n visionario; visionaria

visit [VI•zit] *n* visita F

visitation [VI•zi•TAI•shn] *n*
visita ufficiale F

visitor [VI•zi•tur] *n* visitatore;
visitatrice

visor [VUY•zur] *n* visiera F

vista [VIS•tuh] *n* prospettiva F

visual [VI•zjhoo•ul] *adj* visivo; visiva

visualize [VI•zjhoo•LUYZ] *vt* raffiguraree

vital [VUY•tl] *adj* vitale

vitality [vuy•TA•li•tee] *n* vitalitá F

vitamin [VUY•tuh•min] *n* vitamina F

vitreous [VI•tree•us] *adj* vitreo; vitrea

vitriol [VI•tree•ol] *n* vetriolo M

vivacious [vuy•VAI•shus] *adj* vivace

vivacity [vuy•VA•si•tee] *n* vivacitá F

vivid [VI•vid] *adj* vivido; vivida

vocabulary [vo•KA•byoo•LAI•ree] *n* vocabolario M

vocal [VO•kul] *adj* vocale

vocation [vo•KAI•shn] *n* vocazione F

vogue [vog] *n* voga F

voice [vois] *n* voce F

void [void] *n* vuoto M

volatile [VAH•li•tl] *adj* volatile

volcanic [vol•KA•nik] *adj* vulcanico; vulcanica

volcano [vol•KAI•no] *n* vulcano M

volley [VAH•lee] *n* scarica F

volt [volt] *n* volt M

voltage [VOL•tej] *n* voltaggio M

volume [VAHL•yoom] *n* volume M

voluntary [VAH•lun•TAI•ree] *adj* volontario; volontaria

volunteer [VAH•lun•TEER] *n* volontario; volontaria

voluptuous [vuh•LUP•shus] *adj* voluttuoso; voluttuosa

vomit [VAH•mit] *vt* vomitare

voracious [vor•RAI•shus] *adj* vorace

vote [vot] *vi* votare

voter [VO•tur] *n* votante

voting [VO•ting] *adj* votante

vouch [vouch] *vi* attestare

voucher [VOU•chur] *n* buono M

vow [vou] *n* voto M

vowel [VOU•wul] *n* vocale F

voyage [VOI•ij] *n* viaggio M

vulgar [VUL•gur] *adj* volgare

vulgarity [vul•GAI•ri•tee] *n* volgaritá F

vulnerable [VUHL•nur•uh•bl] *adj* vulnerabile

vulture [VUHL•chur] *n* avvoltoio M

W

wad [wahd] *n* tampone M

waddle [WAH•dl] *vi* camminare ondeggiando

wade [waid] *vi* guadare

wafer [WAI•fur] *n* ostia F

waffle [WAH•fl] *n* cialda F

waft [wahft] *vi* diffondersi

wag [wag] *vt* dimenare

wage [waij] *n* paga F

wager [WAI•jur] *n*
scommessa F

wagon [WAG•gin] *n* vagone M

waif [waif] *n* trovatello;
trovatella

wail [wail] *n* gemito M

waist [waist] *n* vita F

wait [wait] *vi* aspettare

waiter [WAI•tur] *n*
cameriere M

waiting [WAI•ting] *n* attesa F

waiting room [WAI•ting
ROOM] *n* sala d'attesa F

waitress [WAI•tres] *n*
cameriera F

waive [waiv] *vt* rinunciare (a)

wake 1 [waik] *vi* svegliarsi

wake 2 [waik] *n* veglia
funebre F

waken [wai•kin] *vt* svegliare

walk [wauk] *vi* camminare

wall [waul] *n* muro M

walled [wauld] *adj* circdato da
mura; circondata da mura

wallet [WAU•lit] *n*
portafoglio M

wallflower
[WAUL•FLOU•wur] *n*
ragazza che fa tappezzeria F

wallop [WHAH•lop] *vt*
percuotere

wallow [WHAH•lo] *vi* rotolarsi

wallpaper [WAUL•PAI•pur] *n*
carta da parati F

walnut [WAHL•nut] *n* noce F

waltz [wahlz] *n* valzer M

wan [wan] *adj* pallido; pallida

wand [wand] *n* bacchetta F

wander [WAN•dur] *vi*
vagabondare

wanderer [WAHN•dur•rur] *n*
vagbondo; vagabonda

wane (decrease; lessen) [wain]
vi calare

want [wahnt] *vt* volere

wanton [WAHN•tin] *adj*
licenzioso; licenziosa

war [waur] *n* guerra F

warble [WAUR•bl] *vi*
gorgheggiare

ward [waurd] *vt* parare

warden [waurd] *n* guardia F

wardrobe [WAUR•drob] *n*
guardaroba M

ware [wair] *n* merce F

warehouse [WAIR•houz] *n*
magazzino M

warlike [WAUR•luyk] *adj*
guerriero; guerriera

warm [waurm] *adj* caldo; calda

warmth [waurmth] *n* calore M

warn [waurn] *vt* avvertire

warning [WAUR•ning] *n*
avvertimento M

warp [waurp] *vt* deformare

warped [waurpt] *adj* deformato;
deformata

warrant [WAUR•rint] *n*
autorizzazione F

warrior [WAUR•yur] *n*
guerriero M

wart [waurt] *n* porro M

wary [wair•ree] *adj* cauto; cauta

wash [wahsh] *vt* lavare

washer [WAHSH•ur] *n*
guarnizione F

washing [WAH•shing] *n*
lavaggio M

washing-machine
[WAH•shing muh•SHEEN] *n*
lavatrice F

wasp [wahsp] *n* vespa F

waste [waist] *vt* sprecare

wastepaper basket
[WAIST•PAI•pur BA•skit] *n*
cestino M

wasteful [waist•fl] *adj*
rovinoso; rovinosa

watch [wahch] *n* orologio M

watchdog [WAHCH•daug] *n*
cane da guardia M

watchman [WAHCH•man] *n*
guardiano M

water [WAH•tur] *n* acqua F

water sports [WAH•tur
SPAURTS] *n* sport
acquatici M

watercolor [WAH•tur
KUH•lur] *n* acquarello M

waterfall [WAH•tur•FAL] *n*
cascata F

waterproof
[WAH•tur•PROOF] *adj*
impermeabile

watertight [WAH•tur•TUYT]
adj stagno; stagna

waterway [WAH•tur•WAI] *n*
trincarino M

watery [WAH•tur•ree] *adj*
acquoso; acquosa

wave [waiv] *n* onda F

wavelength [WAIV•length] *n*
lunghezza d'onda F

wavy [WAIV•vee] *adj* ondulato;
ondulata

wax [waks] *n* cera F; *vt* dar la
cera a

way [wai] *n* modo M

waylay [WAI•lai] *vt* attendere
al varco

wayward [WAI•wurd] *adj*
ribelle

we [wee] *per pron* noi

weak [week] *adj* debole

weaken [WEE•kin] *vt*
indebolire

weakly [WEEK•lee] *adv*
debolmente

wealth [welth] *n* ricchezza F

wealthy [WEL•thee] *adj* ricco;
ricca

wean [ween] *vt* slattare

weapon [WE•pun] *n* arma F

wear [wair] *vt* indossare

weariness [WEE•ree•ness] *n*
stanchezza F

wearisome [WEE•ree•suhm]
adj faticoso; faticosa

weary [WEE•ree] *adj* stanco;
stanca

weasel [WEE•zul] *n* donnola F

weather [WE•thur] *n* tempo M

weather conditions [WE•thur
kun•DI•shns] *n* condizioni
metereologiche F

weave [weev] *n* trama F

web [web] *n* ragnatela F

webbing [WEB•bing] *n*
cinghia F

wed [wed] *vt* sposare

wedded [WED•ded] *adj*
sposato; sposata

wedding [WED•ding] *n*
matrimonio M

wedge [wej] *n* cuneo M

Wednesday [WENS•dai] *n*
mercoledí M

weed [weed] *n* erbaccia F

weedy [WEE•dee] *adj* coperto
d'erbacce; coperta d'erbacce

week [week] *n* settimana F

weekday [WEEK•dai] *n* giorno
feriale M

weekly [WEEK•lee] *adj*
settimanale

weep [weep] *vi* piangere

weeping [WEE•ping] *adj*
piangente

weevil [WEE•vul] *n*
curcolionide M

weigh [wai] *vt* pesare

weight [wait] *n* peso M

weighty [WAI•tee] *adj* pesante

welcome [WEL•kum] *adj*
benvenuto; benvenuta

weld [weld] *vt* saldare

welfare [WEL•fair] *n*
benessere M

well 1 [wel] *adv* bene

well 2 [wel] *n* pozzo M

well 3 (oil) [wel] *n* pozzo di
petrolio M

well-being [WEL•BEE•ing] *n*
benessere M

well-bred [WEL•BRED] *adj*
beneducato; beneducata

well-to-do [WEL•too•DOO]
adj benestante

werewolf [WAIR•wolf] *n* lupo
manarro M

west [west] *n* ovest M

western [WES•turn] *adj*
occidentale

westerner [WES•tur•nur] *n*
occidentale

westward [WEST•wurd] *adv*
verso ovest

wet [wet] *adj* bagnato; bagnata

whack [wak] *vt* bastonare

whale [wail] *n* balena F

wharf [warf] *n* pontile M

what [waht] *pron* che cosa

whatever [waht•EV•vur] *adj*
qualsiasi

wheat [weet] *n* grano M

wheel [weel] *n* ruota F

wheelbarrow
[WEEL•BAIR•ro] *n* carriola F

wheelchair [WEEL•chair] *n*
sedia a rotelle F

wheezy [WHEE•zee] *adj*
affannoso; affannosa

when [wen] *adv* quando

whenever [wen•EV•vur] *adv*
ogniqualvolta

where [wair] *adv* dove

whereabouts
[WAIR•uh•BOUTZ] *n*
ubicazione F

whereas [wair•AS] *conj* poiché

whereby [wair•BUY] *pron*
tramite cui

wherefore [WAIR•for] *conj*
perció

wherever [wair•EV•vur] *adv*
dovunque

wherewithal [WAIR•with•AL]
n mezzi M

whet [wet] *vt* affilare

whether [WE•thur] *conj* se

which [wich] *pron* che

whichever [wich•EV•vur] *adj*
qualunque

whiff [wif] *n* buffo M

while [wuyl] *conj* mentre

whim [wim] *n* capriccio M

whimper [WIM•pur] *vi* gemere

whimsical [WIM•si•kl] *adj*
capriccioso; capricciosa

whine [wuyn] *n* uggiolio M

whip [wip] *n* frusta F

whipping [WIP•ping] *n*
flagellazione F

whir [wur] *vi* rombare

whirl [wurl] *vi* turbinare

whirlpool [WURL•pool] *n*
vortice M

whirlwind [WURL•wind] *n*
turbine M

whisk [wisk] *n* frullino M

whisker [WIS•kur] *n* baffi M

whiskey [WIS•kee] *n*
whiskey M

whisper [WIS•pur] *vt*
mormorare

whistle [WIS•sl] *vt* fischiare

whit [wit] *n* particella F

white [wuyt] *adj* bianco; bianca

whiten [WUY•tin] *vt* sbiancare

whiteness [WUYT•nis] *n*
biancore M

whitewash [WUYT•wahsh] *vt*
imbiancare

Whitsuntide [WIT•zun•tuyd] *n*
settimana di Pentecoste F

whittle [WIT•tl] *vt* scolpire nel
legno

whiz [wiz] *n* ronzio M

who [hoo] *pron* chi

whole [hol] *adj* intero; intera

wholesale [HOL•sail] *adj*
all'ingrosso

wholesome [HOL•sum] *adj*
salutare

wholly [HOL•lee] *adv*
completamente

whom [hoom] *pron* chi

whomever [hoom•EV•vur]
pron chiunque

whoop [woop] *vi* urlare

whore [hor] *n* prostituta F

whose [hooz] *pron* di chi

why [wuy] *conj* perché

wick [wik] *n* stoppino M

wicked [WIK•kid] *adj*
malizioso; maliziosa

wickedness [WIK•kid•nes] *n*
malvagitá F

wicker [WIK•kur] *n* vimine M

wicket [WIK•kit] *n*
cancelletto M

wide [wuyd] *adj* largo; larga

wide awake [WUYD
uh•WAIK] *adj* sveglio;
sveglia

widely [WUYD•lee] *adj*
largamente

widespread [WUYD•SPRED]
adj esteso; estesa

widow [WI•do] *n* vedova F

widower [WI•do•wur] *n*
vedovo M

width [width] *n* larghezza F

wield [weeld] *vt* brandire

wife [wuyf] *n* moglie F

wig [wig] *n* parrucca F

wild [wuyld] *adj* selvaggio;
selvaggia

wile [wuyl] *n* astuzia F

will [wil] *n* volontá F

willful [WIL•ful] *adj* caparbio;
caparbia

willing [WIL•ling] *adj*
volonteroso; volonterosa

willingly [WIL•ling•lee] *adv*
volentieri

willingness [WIL•ling•nis] *n*
buona volontá F

willow [WIL•lo] *n* salice M

wilt [wilt] *vi* appassire

wily [WUY•lee] *adj* scaltro;
scaltra

win [win] *vt* vincere

wince [winz] *vi* trasalire

winch [winch] *n* argano M

wind 1 [wind] *n* vento M

wind 2 [wuynd] *vt* caricare

windfall [WIND•fal] *n* fortuna inaspettata F

winding [WUYN•ding] *adj* tortuoso; tortuosa

windmill [WIND•mil] *n* mulino a vento M

window [WIN•do] *n* finestra F

window shade [WIN•do SHAID] *n* persiana F

windowsill [WIN•do•SIL] *n* davanzale M

windshield [WIND•sheeld] *n* parabrezza M

windy [WIN•dee] *adj* ventoso; ventosa

wine [wuyn] *n* vino M

wine cellar [WUYN SEL•lur] *n* cantina F

wineglass [WUYN•glas] *n* bicchiere da vino M

wing [wing] *n* ala F

winged [WING•gid] *adj* alato; alata

wink [wingk] *vt* ammiccare

winner [WIN•nur] *n* vincitore; vincitrice

winning [WIN•ning] *adj* vincente

winter [WIN•tur] *n* inverno M

wintry [WIN•tree] *adj* invernale

wipe [wuyp] *vt* asciugare

wiper [WUY•pur] *n* strofinaccio M

wire [wuyr] *n* fil di ferro M

wireless [WUYR•les] *adj* senza fili

wiry [WUYR•ree] *adj* forte e magro; forte e magra

wisdom [WIZ•dom] *n* saggezza F

wise [wuyz] *adj* saggio; saggia

wiseacre [WUYZ•AI•kur] *n* saccentone; saccentona

wisecrack [WUYZ•krak] *n* spiritosaggine F

wish [wish] *vt* desiderare

wish [wish] *n* desiderio M

wistful [WIST•ful] *adj* pensoso; pensosa

wit [wit] *n* acutezza d'ingegno F

witch [which] *n* strega F

with [with] *conj* con

withdraw [with•DRAU] *vt* ritirare

withdrawal [with•DRAU•wul] *n* ritirata F; *n* prelievo M

withdrawn [with•DRAUN] *adj* chiuso; chiusa

wither [WITH•thur] *vi* appassire

withhold [with•HOLD] *vt* trattenere

within [with•THIN] *prep* entro

without [with•THOUT] *prep* senza

withstand [with•STAND] *vt* resistere

witness [WIT•nes] *n* testimone

witticism [WIT•ti•CIZM] *n* frizzo M

witty [WIT•tee] *adj* arguto; arguta

wizard [WIZ•zurd] *n* mago M

woe [wo] *n* dolore M

wolf [wolf] *n* lupo M

woman [WUH•man] *n* donna F

womanhood [WUH•min•HUD] *n* femminilitá F

womanly [WUH•min•lee] *adj* femminile

womb [woom] *n* utero M

wonder [WUN•dur] *n*
meraviglia F; *n* meraviglia F

wonderful [WUN•dur•fl] *adj*
meraviglioso; meravigliosa

wonderfully
[WUN•dur•ful•lee] *adv* in
modo stupendo

wont [wahnt] *adj* abitudine F

woo [woo] *vt* corteggiare

wood [wud] *n* legno M

woodland [WUD•land] *n*
terreno boscoso M

woodpecker [WUD•PEK•kur]
n picchio M

woodworker
[WUD•WUR•kur] *n*
falegname M

woof [wuf] *n* trama M

wool [wul] *n* lana F

woolen [WUH•lin] *adj* di lana

woolly [WUH•lee] *adj* lanoso;
lanosa

word [wurd] *n* parola F

work [wurk] *n* lavoro M

workday [WURK•dai] *n* giorno
lavorativo M

worker [WURK•ur] *n*
lavoratore M

working [WUR•king] *adj* che
lavora

workman [WURK•man] *n*
operaio M

workmanship
[WURK•man•SHIP] *n*
lavorazione F

workshop [WURK•shop] *n*
officina F

world [wurld] *n* mondo M

worldly [WURLD•lee] *adj*
mondano; mondana

worm [wurm] *n* verme M

worry 1 [WUR•ree] *n*
preoccupazione F

worry 2 (bother) [WUR•ree]
vt preoccuparsi

worse [wurs] *adj* peggiore

worship [WUR•ship] *vt*
venerare

worshipper [WUR•ship•pur] *n*
fedele

worst [wurst] *adj* il peggiore; la
peggiore

worth [wurth] *n* valore M

worthless [WURTH•les] *adj*
immeritevole

worthy [WUR•thee] *adj* degno;
degna

would-be [WUD•BEE] *adj*
sedicente

wound [woond] *n* ferita F

wrangle [RAN•gl] *vi* azzuffarsi

wrap [rap] *vt* avvolgere

wrapper [RAP•pur] *n*
copertina F

wrapping paper [RAP•ping
PAI•pur] *n* carta da
imballaggio F

wrath [rath] *n* ira F

wreath [reeth] *n* ghirlanda F

wreck [rek] *n* relitto M

wrench [rench] *n* chiave
inglese F

wrest [rest] *vt* strappare

wrestle [RES•tl] *vt* lottare

wretch [retch] *n* infelice

wretched [RETCH•chid] *adj*
disgraziato; disgraziata

wring [ring] *vt* strizzare

wrinkle [RINK•kl] *n* ruga F

wrist [rist] *n* polso M

writ [rit] *n* mandato M

write [ruyt] *vt* scrivere

writer [RUY•tur] *n* scrittore;
scrittrice
writhe [ruyth] *vi* contorcersi
writing [RUY•ting] *n*
scritto M

wrong [rong] *adj* sbagliato;
sbagliat
wrought iron [RAUT I•urn] *n*
ferro battuto M
wry [ruy] *adj* obliquo; obliqua

X

X-ray [EKS•rai] *n* raggi
x M
xenophobe [ZEE•no•fob] *n*
xenofobo; xenofoba

xylography [zuy•LOG•gruh•fee]
n xilografia F
xylophone [ZUY•luh•FON] *n*
xilofono M

Y

yacht [yaht] *n* yacht M
yank [yank] *n* strattone M
yard 1 [yahrd] *n* iarda F
yard 2 [yahrd] *n* cortile M
yardstick [YAHRD•stik] *n*
metro M
yawn [yaun] *n* sbadiglio M
yea [yai] *n* si M
year [yeer] *n* anno M
yearn [yurn] *vt* desiderare
yearning [YUR•ning] *n*
desiderio M
yeast [yeest] *n* lievito di
birra M
yell [yel] *vi* gridare
yellow [YEL•lo] *adj* giallo;
gialla
yeoman [YO•min] *n* coltivatore
diretto M
yes [yes] *n* si M

yesterday [YES•tur•dai] *n*
ieri M
yet [yet] *conj* tuttavia
yield [yeeld] *vt* fruttare
yielding [YEEL•ding] *adj*
docile
yoke [yok] *n* giogo M
yolk [yok] *n* rosso d'uovo M
yonder [YON•dur] *adj* quello
lá; quella lá
yore [yor] *n* tempo antico M
you [yoo] *pers pron* tu
young [yuhng] *adj* giovane
youngster [yuhng•stur] *n*
giovincello; giovincella
your [yor] *adj* tuo; tua
yours [yorz] *pron* tuo; tua
yourself [yor•SELF] *pers pron*
tu stesso; tu stessa
youth [yooth] *n* giovinezza F

youthful [YOOTH•fl] *adj*
giovanile

Yuletide [YOOL•tuyd] *n*
feste F

Z

Zaire [zuy•EER] *n* Zaire M
zeal [zeel] *n* zelo M
zealot [ZE•lot] *n* fanatico;
fanatica
zealous [ZE•lus] *adj* zelante
zebra [ZEE•bruh] *n* zebra F
zenith [ZEE•nith] *n* zenith
zephyr [ZE•fur] *n* zefiro M
zeppelin [ZE•pi•lin] *n* zeppelin
zero [ZEE•ro] *n* zero M
zest [zest] *n* gusto M
zigzag [ZIG•zag] *vi* andare zig
zag
zinc [zink] *n* zinco M

zip [zip] *vi* correre
zipper [ZIP•pur] *n* cerniera F
zither [ZITH•thur] *n* cetra F
zodiac [ZO•dee•ak] *n* zodiaco M
zodiacal zo•DUY•i•kl] *adj*
zodiacale
zone [zon] *n* zona F
zoo [zoo] *n* zoo M
zoological
[ZOO•uh•LAH•jik•kl] *adj*
zoologico; zoologica
zoology [zoo•AH•lo•gee] *n*
zoologia F
zoom [zoom] *vi* sfrecciare